Frommer's®

New Mexico
8th Edition

by Lesley S. King

Here's what the critics say about Frommer's:

"Amazingly easy to use. Very portable, very complete."
—*Booklist*

"Detailed, accurate, and easy-to-read information for all price ranges."
—*Glamour Magazine*

"Hotel information is close to encyclopedic."
—*Des Moines Sunday Register*

"Frommer's Guides have a way of giving you a real feel for a place."
—*Knight Ridder Newspapers*

WILEY

Wiley Publishing, Inc.

About the Author

Lesley S. King grew up on a ranch in northern New Mexico, where she still returns on weekends to help work cattle. She's a freelance writer and photographer, and she's a columnist for *New Mexico* magazine—as well as an avid kayaker and skier. Formerly the managing editor for *The Santa Fean,* she has written about food and restaurants for *The New York Times;* the Anasazi culture for United Airline's *Hemispheres* magazine; and the environment for *Audubon.* She is also the author of *Frommer's Santa Fe, Taos & Albuquerque, Frommer's Great Outdoor Guide to Arizona & New Mexico,* and *New Mexico For Dummies,* and she's the co-author of *Frommer's American Southwest.*

Published by:

Wiley Publishing, Inc.

111 River St.
Hoboken, NJ 07030-5774

ISBN 0-7645-7307-1

Editor: Kitty Wilson Jarrett
Production Editor: Blair J. Pottenger
Cartographer: Nicholas Trotter
Photo Editor: Richard Fox
Production by Wiley Indianapolis Composition Services

For information on our other products and services or to obtain technical support, please contact our Customer Care Department within the U.S. at 800/762-2974, outside the U.S. at 317/572-3993 or fax 317/572-4002.

Wiley also publishes its books in a variety of electronic formats. Some content that appears in print may not be available in electronic formats.

Manufactured in the United States of America

5   4   3   2

Contents

8   Northeastern New Mexico   245

9   Northwestern New Mexico   266

10   Southwestern New Mexico   304

11   Southeastern New Mexico   341

Appendix: New Mexico in Depth   377

Index   393

List of Maps

Acknowledgments

My sincere thanks to all the tourism agencies, restaurant and hotel owners and managers, and attraction public relations people who helped me get the facts straight. Also, thanks to my family and friends for cheering me on and reporting back to me about their travel experiences. Finally, thanks to my assistant on the project, Kathleen Raphael.

An Invitation to the Reader

In researching this book, we discovered many wonderful places—hotels, restaurants, shops, and more. We're sure you'll find others. Please tell us about them, so we can share the information with your fellow travelers in upcoming editions. If you were disappointed with a recommendation, we'd love to know that, too. Please write to:

Frommer's New Mexico, 8th Edition
Wiley Publishing, Inc. • 111 River St. • Hoboken, NJ 07030-5774

An Additional Note

Please be advised that travel information is subject to change at any time—and this is especially true of prices. We therefore suggest that you write or call ahead for confirmation when making your travel plans. The authors, editors, and publisher cannot be held responsible for the experiences of readers while traveling. Your safety is important to us, however, so we encourage you to stay alert and be aware of your surroundings. Keep a close eye on cameras, purses, and wallets, all favorite targets of thieves and pickpockets.

Other Great Guides for Your Trip:

Frommer's National Parks of the American West
Frommer's Santa Fe, Taos & Albuquerque
New Mexico For Dummies

Frommer's Star Ratings, Icons & Abbreviations

Every hotel, restaurant, and attraction listing in this guide has been ranked for quality, value, service, amenities, and special features using a **star-rating system.** In country, state, and regional guides, we also rate towns and regions to help you narrow down your choices and budget your time accordingly. Hotels and restaurants are rated on a scale of zero (recommended) to three stars (exceptional). Attractions, shopping, nightlife, towns, and regions are rated according to the following scale: zero stars (recommended), one star (highly recommended), two stars (very highly recommended), and three stars (must-see).

In addition to the star-rating system, we also use **eight feature icons** that point you to the great deals, in-the-know advice, and unique experiences that separate travelers from tourists. Throughout the book, look for:

Finds	Special finds—those places only insiders know about
Fun Fact	Fun facts—details that make travelers more informed and their trips more fun
Kids	Best bets for kids and advice for the whole family
Moments	Special moments—those experiences that memories are made of
Overrated	Places or experiences not worth your time or money
Tips	Insider tips—great ways to save time and money
Value	Great values—where to get the best deals
Warning	Warning—traveler's advisories are usually in effect

The following **abbreviations** are used for credit cards:

AE	American Express	DISC	Discover	V	Visa
DC	Diners Club	MC	MasterCard		

Frommers.com

Now that you have the guidebook to a great trip, visit our website at **www.frommers.com** for travel information on more than 3,000 destinations. With features updated regularly, we give you instant access to the most current trip-planning information available. At Frommers.com, you'll also find the best prices on airfares, accommodations, and car rentals—and you can even book travel online through our travel booking partners. At Frommers.com, you'll also find the following:

- Online updates to our most popular guidebooks
- Vacation sweepstakes and contest giveaways
- Newsletter highlighting the hottest travel trends
- Online travel message boards with featured travel discussions

What's New in New Mexico

New Mexico has come by its "mañana" reputation honestly. Usually change happens . . . tomorrow. But some lively additions have occurred in the region that are well worth exploring.

WHERE TO DINE IN ALBU-QUERQUE Albuquerque's most happening new dining spot, **Zinc Wine Bar and Bistro,** 3009 Central Ave. NE (© **505/254-ZINC**), offers inventive meals such as blackened sliced flank steak over a Greek salad, with interesting deals, such as wine flights, which allow diners to sample a variety of wines from a particular region, all within a moody, urban atmosphere. Almost across the street from Zinc, noted chef Jennifer James has opened a more reasonably priced sister restaurant to her namesake one. **Graze,** 3128 Central Ave. SE (© **505/268-4729**), offers small plates of new American cuisine, with such interesting flavor spins that you'll reel delightfully. The penne with goat cheese and chorizo is delectable. See chapter 5 for details.

WHAT TO SEE & DO IN ALBU-QUERQUE Head through a tunnel with turquoise embedded in the walls, and you'll find yourself in one of Albuquerque's most colorful museums, the **Turquoise Museum,** 2107 Central Ave. NW (© **505/247-8650**), west of Old Town. It lays claim to the world's largest collection of the blue stone. Within the same district has moved **¡Explora! Science Center and Children's Museum,** 1701 Mountain Rd. (© **505/224-8300**). The museum features hands-on scientific exhibits for kids of all ages, even 40-something ones like me. See chapter 5.

EXPLORING NEARBY PUEBLOS & MONUMENTS If you make your way north on the Jemez Mountain Trail, make reservations at the **Cañon del Rio–Riverside Inn,** 16445 Scenic Hwy. 4, Jemez Springs (© **505/829-4377;** www.canondelrio.com). Formerly the Riverdancer, this inn near the Jemez River has been refurbished by new owners. See p. 110.

GETTING TO KNOW SANTA FE Visitors now have their own health service, just blocks from the plaza. **Ultimed,** 707 Paseo de Peralta (© **505/989-8707**), a new urgent-care facility, offers comprehensive health care. See chapter 6 for details.

WHERE TO STAY IN SANTA FE Along historic Barrio de Analco in the center of downtown, **The Inn of the Five Graces,** 150 E. de Vargas St. (© **505/992-0957;** www.fivegraces. com), Santa Fe's newest and best-kept secret, offers a lovely melding of Asia and the Old West, with elaborately decorated suites with kilim rugs, ornately carved beds, and mosaic tile work in the bathrooms. The notable spa **Ten Thousand Waves,** 3451 Hyde Park Rd. (© **505/982-9304** or 505/992-5025; www.tenthousand waves.com), nestled in piñon trees just outside town, now offers accommodations. There are minimalist Japanese-adobe rooms and casitas for those seeking silence and solitude. New to this book is the **Don Gaspar Inn,** 623 Don Gaspar (© **888/986-8664** or

505/986-8664; www.dongaspar.com), a quiet and elegant place nestled in a historic neighborhood, for those who want to feel like they live in Santa Fe. See chapter 6 for details.

WHERE TO DINE IN SANTA FE Santa Fe's most happening moderately priced new restaurant, **Santa Fe Railyard Restaurant & Bar,** 530 S. Guadalupe (© **505/989-8363**), offers imaginative new American food in a historic rail-yard building. Rated by local media as the best new inexpensive restaurant in town, **Bumble Bee's Baja Grill,** 301 Jefferson St. (© **505/820-2862**), offers fast and healthy Old Mexico tacos and other spicy delights. See chapter 6 for details.

WHAT TO SEE & DO IN SANTA FE The newest news in the "City Different" is a **performance gazebo** erected on the plaza in 2004. Summer evenings and during festivals and markets, bands play under the copper-roofed stage. See p. 115.

EXCURSIONS FROM SANTA FE Tesuque Pueblo (9 miles north of Santa Fe on US 84/285) has a new church. The **San Diego Church,** a three-story structure, replaces an older church that burned in 1988. The **Castillo Gallery** (a mile into the village of Cordova on the High Road to Taos; © **505/351-4067**) has moved next door, into a brighter and more expansive space, still operated by a fine husband-and-wife artist team. See chapter 6 for details.

WHERE TO STAY IN TAOS The biggest news in the region is the opening of **El Monte Sagrado,** 317 Kit Carson Rd. (© **800/828-TAOS** or 505/758-3502; www.elmontsagrado. com). This eco-resort offers impeccable, imaginative accommodations surrounding a "Sacred Circle," an open grassy area. The resort also offers fine food and spa treatments. Taos is also celebrating finally having a good hotel on its plaza. **Hotel La Fonda de Taos,** 108 South Plaza (© **800/833-2211** or 505/758-2211;www.hotellafonda. com), provides com-fortable, smartly decorated rooms with a dash of history. **The Bavarian Lodge,** above Taos Ski Valley (© **888/205-8020** or 505/776-8020. www.thebavarian. com), offers its guests first access to the back bowls as well as Bavarian-style rooms in an authentic log cabin. Also at Taos Ski Valley, **Edelweiss Lodge & Spa,** 106 Sutton Place (© **800/I-LUV-SKI** or 505/776-2301; www.edelweisslodgeandspa. com), has been rebuilt into an upscale condo-hotel, with luxury rooms and a complete spa. The owners are especially intent on attracting summer spa guests. For more details, see chapter 7.

WHERE TO DINE IN TAOS Located at El Monte Sagrado, the new **De La Tierra,** 317 Kit Carson Rd. (© **800/828-TAOS** or 505/758-3502), offers regional American food in a refined atmosphere. Diners feast on food ranging from venison medallions to rosemary-skewered shrimp. For a while, Taos was without **Joseph's Table;** this fine restaurant had closed. But it has reopened in an even larger space, in the Hotel La Fonda on the plaza, and it still serves some of the most imaginative food in the Southwest. It's located at 108A South Taos Plaza (© **505/751-4512;** www.josephs table.com). Worth the trip to Taos Ski Valley even if you're not going to strap on the boards, **The Bavarian Restaurant,** above Taos Ski Valley (© **888/205-8020** or 505/776-8020), serves up delicious Bavarian-style fare such as goulash and sauerbraten in an old-world log cabin nestled in high alpine forest. Take the shuttle from the ski area up. In the quaint Arroyo Seco village, en route to the ski area, **Gypsy 360°,** 480 NM 150, Seco Plaza (© **505/776-3166**), could just be the region's best new casual spot. Serving Asian and American dishes ranging from pad Thai to Angus burgers, the place serves recipes as fresh as the ingredients in them. See chapter 7 for details.

WHAT TO SEE & DO IN TAOS

A sad change has come to the **Taos Historic Museums** (© 505/758-0505): The Kit Carson Home has passed out of their hands. Exhibits from the museum will be moved to the **Martinez Hacienda** (Lower Ranchitos Road, Hwy. 240; © 505/758-1000). The Kit Carson Home owners plan to open their own museum. Another big change in the Taos museum scene is the shifting of the **Taos Art Museum** (© 505/758-2690) collection from the Van Vechten Lineberry Museum (now closed) to the **Fechin House,** 227 Paseo del Pueblo Norte. Though the museum lost some space, it gained a lovely venue. A new hot spot for those who like to browse little villages is **Arroyo Seco,** on NM 150, about 5 miles north of town en route to Taos Ski Valley. Arroyo Seco has Gypsy 360° (see above) and fun shops and amazing mountain views. See chapter 7 for details.

TAOS AFTER DARK

Nights will never be the same in Taos, now that the **Anaconda Bar,** 317 Kit Carson Rd. (© 505/758-3502), has opened at El Monte Sagrado resort. A contemporary feel, accented by a giant anaconda snake sculpture, as well as tasty tapas and live music, draws the hippest Taoseños and visitors to the spot. See p. 240.

NORTHEASTERN NEW MEXICO

The **Pastime Café,** 113 Bridge St. (© 505/454-1755), brings a bit of sophistication and health to the Las Vegas Plaza area. Diners feast on grilled chicken over fresh greens or meatloaf sandwiches in a friendly, earthy atmosphere.

While on the Las Vegas Plaza, stop in at **Tapetes de Lana,** 1814 Plaza (© 505/426-8638), to watch weavers

make scarves, ponchos, and Rio Grande–style rugs. You can buy the creations, too.

For those getting their kicks on Route 66, also known as I-40, a newish **La Quinta,** 1701 Will Rogers Dr. (© 800/531-5900 or 505/472-4800; www.laquinta.com), on a hill above Santa Rosa offers a good place to cool your heels. Lots of amenities, including a hot tub in a lovely grotto, add character to the predictability of this chain hotel.

A fun historic stay in Raton, **Heart's Desire Bed & Breakfast,** 301 S. Third St. (© 866/488-1028 or 505/445-1000; www.heartsdesireraton.com), offers Victorian-decorated rooms in an 1885-era boarding house. The proprietor will regale you with stories of the region, where she grew up out on the plains. See chapter 8 for details.

NORTHWESTERN NEW MEXICO

In a search to find a Gallup accommodation where mythic but loud train sounds don't keep me up at night, I landed at **Holiday Inn Express,** 1500 W. Maloney Ave. (© 800/HOLIDAY or 505/726-1000; www.hiexpress.com), a chain option—sitting on a hill above town—with lots of amenities.

All the Mediterranean standards such as hummus and falafel spill from the kitchen of Gallup's new **Oasis Mediterranean Restaurant & Hookah Lounge,** 100 E. 66 Ave. (© 505/722-9572), but the real treats are chicken and meat dishes bravely spiced. The setting is a gallery, where diners can look at art.

Cherrywood floors and flowing fountains create an oasis feel at the completely renovated **Casa Blanca,** 505 E. La Plata St. (© 800/550-6503 or 505/327-6503; www.4cornersbandb.com), in Farmington. Just blocks from Main Street, the inn has large rooms, well stocked with amenities; it's a great home base to explore area ruins.

Finally, Farmington has a fine-dining spot. **The Bluffs,** 3450 E. Main St. (© **505/325-8155**), serves quality steaks and seafood in a comfortable wood-accented ambience. Any of the angus beef steaks will please.

With bagels baked in-house, **Bagel Conspiracy,** 3554 E. Main St., Suite H (© **505/564-8888**), is a good stop in east Farmington for those on the go. Feast on bagel sandwiches for breakfast or lunch.

In Chama, the **Village Bean,** 425 Terrace Ave. (© **505/756-1663**), pours steamy brews such as cappuccino and espresso and stacks up sandwiches with fresh ingredients on home-baked bread. See chapter 9 for details.

SOUTHWESTERN NEW MEX-ICO In **Truth or Consequences,** the restoration a few years back of a 1920s hot springs resort, now the **Sierra Grande Lodge & Spa,** 501 McAdoo St. (© **505/894-6976;** www. sierragrandelodge.com), brought luxury to this odd outpost town. Now, the lodge's restaurant is serving year-round. When it opened, it made *Condé Nast Traveler's* top 50 new restaurants in the world list. The bistro warrants a stop, even if you're just cruising by T or C on I-25. The olive-crusted salmon is delectable.

Though not new to New Mexico, **Chope's Bar and Cafe,** on NM 28 (© **505/233-3420**), is new to this book. The legendary spot 15 minutes south of Mesilla (near Las Cruces) serves up big plates of enchiladas and chile rellenos with lots of chile and southern New Mexican attitude—olé!

Shevek & Mi, 602 N. Bullard St. (© **505/534-9168**), in Silver City offers a whirlwind taste tour of the world, with cuisine ranging from New York deli to Moroccan, all well prepared by a chef who has immersed himself in many cultures. Try the *zarzuela,* a Spanish bouillabaisse. See chapter 10 for details.

SOUTHEASTERN NEW MEXICO Set outside the tiny hamlet of Tularosa, **Casa de Sueños,** 35 St. Francis Dr. (© **505/585-3494**), offers tasty New Mexican fare in a whimsical Mexican setting. Start with the guacamole and move on to anything smothered in chile.

The village of Capitan has woken up from a long, small-town sleep and is suddenly a culinary center in southern New Mexico. Two excellent restaurants have opened there. **Greenhouse Café,** 103 S. Lincoln St. (© **505/354-0373**), serves chicken, meat, and fish dishes with veggies grown in their own greenhouse. Try the chicken stroganoff, served in a puff pastry. Nearby, **Rodney's Copa Cabana,** 321 Smokey Bear Blvd. (© **505/354-7637**), creates a festive Caribbean mood while delighting diners with New American flavors. The steak and shrimp kabob is outstanding.

Big portions of pasta, lasagna, and more refined fare, such as veal picatta, flow from the kitchen of **Pasta Café Italian Bistro,** 710 Canal St. (© **505/ 887-7211**), in Carlsbad. The wraparound patio is a favorite hangout spot on cool summer evenings. See chapter 11 for details.

1

The Best of New Mexico

I will never forget when I was in second grade, standing on the dusty playground at Alvarado Elementary School in Albuquerque, pointing west toward the volcanoes. "We went beyond those volcanoes," I bragged to my friend about what my family had done over the weekend. "No way," my friend replied. Actually, a number of times I'd been much farther than the 10 miles between us and the volcanoes, and I now know that the strong impact of the journey's distance had to do with culture rather than miles. In a half-day drive we had traveled to the Intertribal Indian Ceremonial in Gallup, where I had eaten blue, crepe-paper-thin *piki* bread and gazed up at people dressed in dreamy rich velvet, their limbs draped in turquoise. I had seen painted warriors twirl in the dust and felt drum rhythm pulse in my heart. In short, we had traveled to another world, and that otherworldliness is characteristic of New Mexico.

Never have I taken my strangely exotic home state for granted, nor has more traditional culture let me. When I was a kid, we used to travel to Illinois to visit my grandfather, and when people there heard we were from New Mexico, they would often cock their heads and say things like, "Do you have sidewalks there?" and, "This bubble gum must be a real treat for you," as though such inventions hadn't yet arrived in my home state.

Our state magazine even dedicates a full page each month to the variety of ways in which New Mexico is forgotten. The most notable was when a New Mexico resident called the Atlanta Olympic committee to reserve tickets and the salesperson insisted that the person contact their international sales office. So, it seems people either don't know the state exists at all, or they believe it's a foreign country south of the border.

Ironically, those naive impressions hold some truth. New Mexico is definitely lost in some kind of time warp. Its history dates back far before Columbus set foot on the continent. The whole attitude here is often slower than that of the rest of the world. Like our neighbors down in Mexico, we use the word *mañana*—which doesn't so much mean "tomorrow" as it does "not today."

When you set foot here, you may find yourself a bit lost within the otherworldliness. You may be shocked at the way people so readily stop and converse with you, or you may find yourself in a landscape where there isn't a single landmark from which to negotiate.

In the chapters that follow, I give you some signposts to help you discover for yourself the many mysteries of this otherworldly state. But first, here are my most cherished New Mexico experiences.

1 The Best of Natural New Mexico

- **Rio Grande Gorge:** A hike into this dramatic gorge is unforgettable. You'll first see it as you come over a rise heading toward Taos. It's a colossal slice in the earth, formed during the late Cretaceous

New Mexico

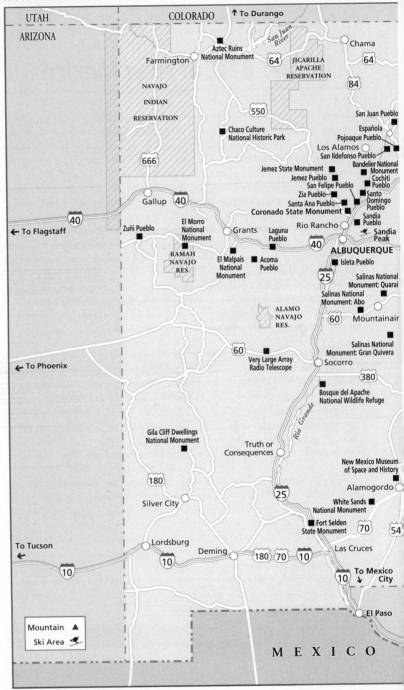

UTAH

ARIZONA

COLORADO

↑ To Durango

San Juan River

Aztec Ruins National Monument

Farmington

Chama

64

64

JICARILLA APACHE RESERVATION

84

NAVAJO INDIAN RESERVATION

550

San Juan Pueblo

Española

Pojoaque Pueblo

Los Alamos

San Ildefonso Pueblo

Chaco Culture National Historic Park

Bandelier National Monument

666

Jemez State Monument

Jemez Pueblo

Cochiti Pueblo

San Felipe Pueblo

Santo Domingo Pueblo

Zia Pueblo

Gallup

40

Santa Ana Pueblo

Coronado State Monument

Sandia Pueblo

El Morro National Monument

Zuñi Pueblo

Grants

Laguna Pueblo

Rio Rancho

40

Sandia Peak

ALBUQUERQUE

← To Flagstaff

40

RAMAH NAVAJO RES.

El Malpais National Monument

Acoma Pueblo

Isleta Pueblo

25

Salinas National Monument: Quarai

ALAMO NAVAJO RES.

Salinas National Monument: Abo

60

Mountainair

Salinas National Monument: Gran Quivera

60

Very Large Array Radio Telescope

Socorro

← To Phoenix

380

Bosque del Apache National Wildlife Refuge

Rio Grande

Gila Cliff Dwellings National Monument

Truth or Consequences

New Mexico Museum of Space and History

180

Alamogordo

Silver City

25

White Sands National Monument

Fort Selden State Monument

70

54

To Tucson ←

Lordsburg

Deming

180 70

10

Las Cruces

10

10

To Mexico City ↓

El Paso

Mountain ▲

Ski Area

MEXICO

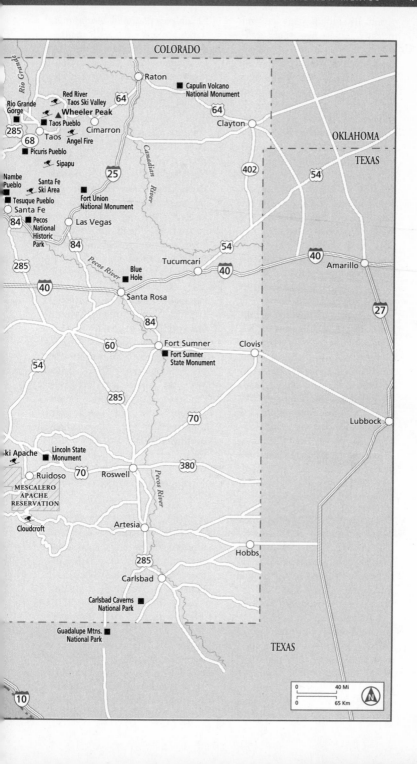

COLORADO

Rio Grande

Raton

Capulin Volcano
National Monument

Red River
Rio Grande   Taos Ski Valley
Gorge   **Wheeler Peak**
              64
285   Taos Pueblo
              Cimarron   Clayton
68   Taos   OKLAHOMA
              Angel Fire
Picuris Pueblo
       Sipapu   TEXAS

Nambe   402
Pueblo   Santa Fe
          Ski Area   54
Tesuque Pueblo   Fort Union
Santa Fe   National Monument
84   Pecos
      National   Las Vegas
      Historic
      Park   84   54

285   Tucumcari
40   40
              Blue   Amarillo
              Hole
              Santa Rosa

              84   27

       60   Fort Sumner   Clovis
                  Fort Sumner
54   State Monument

       285

                    70
                                             Lubbock

ki Apache   Lincoln State
             Monument
    Ruidoso   70   Roswell   380
MESCALERO
APACHE
RESERVATION

Cloudcroft   Artesia

                                 Hobbs
              285

              Carlsbad

       Carlsbad Caverns
       National Park

Guadalupe Mtns.
National Park   TEXAS

Canadian River

25

Pecos River

Pecos River

0   40 Mi
0   65 Km

10

period, 130 million years ago, and the early Tertiary period, about 70 million years ago. Drive about 35 miles north of Taos, near the village of Cerro, to the Wild Rivers Recreation Area. From the lip of the canyon, you descend through millions of years of geologic history and land inhabited by Native Americans since 16,000 B.C. If you're visiting during spring and early summer and like an adrenaline rush, be sure to hook up with a professional guide and raft the Taos Box, a 17-mile stretch of class IV white water. See chapter 7.

- **Blue Hole** (Santa Rosa): You'll find this odd natural wonder in Santa Rosa, "city of natural lakes." An 81-foot-deep artesian well, its waters are cool and completely clear. Often it appears like a fishbowl, full of scuba divers. See "The I-40 Corridor" in chapter 8.

- **Capulin Volcano National Monument:** Last active 60,000 years ago, the volcano is located about 27 miles east of Raton. A hike around its rim offers views into neighboring Oklahoma and Colorado, and another walk down into its lush mouth allows you to see the point from which the lava spewed. See "Capulin Volcano National Monument" in chapter 8.

- **El Malpais National Monument** (Grants): Near Grants, the incredible volcanic landscape known as El Malpais (The Badlands) features vast lava flows, lava tubes, ice caves, sandstone cliffs, and natural bridges. You'll also find Anasazi ruins and ancient Native American trails. See "El Malpais & El Morro National Monuments" in chapter 9.

- **Carlsbad Caverns National Park:** One of the world's largest and most complex cave systems is located in the southeastern region of the state. The 80 known caves have spectacular stalagmite and stalactite formations. Explore the Big Room in a 1-mile, self-guided tour and then catch the massive bat flight from the cave entrance at sunset. See "Carlsbad Caverns National Park" in chapter 11.

- **White Sands National Monument:** Located 15 miles southwest of Alamogordo, White Sands National Monument preserves the best part of the world's largest gypsum dune field. For a truly unforgettable experience, camp overnight so that you can watch the sun rise on the smooth, endless dunes. See "White Sands National Monument" in chapter 11.

2 The Best Native American Sights

- **Coronado State Monument** (Bernalillo): Excavated ruins reveal hundreds of rooms and unique murals, examples of which are displayed in the monument's small archaeological museum. See p. 109.

- **Indian Pueblo Cultural Center** (Albuquerque): Owned and operated as a nonprofit organization by the 19 pueblos of New Mexico, this is a fine place to begin an exploration of Native American culture. The museum is modeled after Pueblo Bonito, a spectacular 9th-century ruin in Chaco Culture National Historic Park, and contains art and artifacts old and new. See p. 88.

- **Petroglyph National Monument** (Albuquerque): In the past few years, this monument has made national news due to conflict over whether to allow a road through these lava flows that were once a hunting and gathering area for prehistoric Native Americans. History in the making aside, the site has 25,000 petroglyphs (prehistoric rock carvings) and provides a variety of hiking trails in differing levels of difficulty, right on the outskirts of Albuquerque. See p. 90.

- **Bandelier National Monument** (Los Alamos): These ruins provide a spectacular peek into the lives of the Anasazi Pueblo culture, which flourished in the area between A.D. 1100 and 1550, a period later than the time when Chaco Canyon was a cultural center. (Recent findings suggest that some Chaco residents ended up at Bandelier.) Less than 15 miles south of Los Alamos, the ruins spread across a peaceful canyon. The most dramatic site is a dwelling and *kiva* (a room used for religious activities) in a cave 140 feet above the canyon floor— reached by a climb up long pueblo-style ladders. A visitor center and museum offer self-guided and ranger-led tours. See p. 188.
- **Pecos National Historical Park:** It's hard to rank New Mexico's many ruins, but this one, sprawled on a plain about 25 miles east of Santa Fe, is one of the most impressive, resonating with the history of the Pueblo Revolt of 1680. You'll see evidence of where the Pecos people burned the mission church before joining in the attack on Santa Fe. You'll also see where the Spanish conquistadors later compromised, allowing sacred kivas to be built next to the reconstructed mission. See p. 185.
- **Taos Pueblo** (Taos): This is a rich place to stroll and eat *fry bread* while glimpsing the lifestyles of some 200 Taos Pueblo residents who still live much as their ancestors did 1,000 years ago, in

sculpted mud homes without electricity and running water. The remaining 2,000 residents of Taos Pueblo live in conventional homes on the Pueblo's 95,000 acres. See p. 223.

- **Acoma Pueblo** (Acoma): This spectacular adobe village sits high atop a sheer rock mesa. Known as "Sky City," it is home to 65 or so inhabitants who still live without electricity and running water. The sculpted mission church and the cemetery seem to be perched on the very edge of the world. Visitors can hike down through a rock cut, once the main entrance to the pueblo. See "Acoma & Laguna Pueblos" in chapter 9.
- **Aztec Ruins National Monument** (Aztec): These ruins of a 500-room Native American pueblo abandoned by the ancestral Puebloans more than 200 years ago feature a completely reconstructed kiva that is 50 feet in diameter. See "Farmington: Gateway to the Four Corners Region" in chapter 9.
- **Chaco Culture National Historical Park** (Nageezi): A combination of a stunning setting and well-preserved ruins makes the long drive to Chaco Canyon an incredible adventure into ancestral Puebloan culture. Many good hikes and bike rides are in the area, and there's also a campground. See "Chaco Culture National Historical Park" in chapter 9.
- **Gila Cliff Dwellings:** Perched in deep caves within a narrow canyon outside Silver City, these ruins tell the mysterious tale of the Mogollon people who lived in the area from the late 1200s through the early 1300s. See "Gila Cliff Dwellings National Monument" in chapter 10.

3 The Best Outdoor Activities

- **Ballooning:** Back in the 1960s, my parents were part owners of the first hot-air balloon in New Mexico. We'd spend weekends riding the air over Albuquerque. Today, with the Albuquerque International Balloon Fiesta bringing more than 800 balloons to the area, it's become the sport's world capital. Fortunately, visitors can let loose the tethers and float free, too. Most of the operators are located in Albuquerque; see "Outdoor Activities" in chapter 5 for recommendations.

- **Horseback riding:** New Mexico's history is stamped with the hoof, originating when the Spanish Conquistadors brought horses to the New World. Riding in New Mexico still has that Old West feel, with trails that wind through wilderness, traversing passes and broad meadows. Some of the best rides are in the Pecos Wilderness and on Taos Pueblo land. See "Outdoor Activities" in chapter 6 and "Other Outdoor Pursuits" in chapter 7.

- **Biking:** New Mexico's varied terrain offers a broad range of biking options, from long stretches of empty asphalt to steep mountain descents. Almost anywhere you go within the state you'll find trails. I've hooked onto some fun old mining roads in the Black Range down south and explored sage forest on the rim of the Taos Gorge in the north. See the "Biking" sections found in the city and regional chapters, especially Taos (chapter 7).

- **Llama trekking:** Careful, they may spit at you, but that's the only drawback of these docile creatures, who gladly carry all your gear while you dance freely along the trail. Most outfitters are into gourmet food, so whether you choose a half-day trek or a weeklong one, you'll eat well. Some of the best llama trekking is in the Taos area, which has two excellent operators. See "Other Outdoor Pursuits" in chapter 7.

- **River rafting and kayaking:** I spend April to October in my kayak, so I can vouch for both the adrenaline rush and the pristine scenery you'll encounter rafting or kayaking in New Mexico. Half- or full-day white-water rafting trips down the Rio Grande and Rio Chama originate in Taos and can be booked through a variety of outfitters in the area. The wild **Taos Box,** a steep-sided canyon south of the Wild Rivers Recreation Area, offers a series of class IV rapids that rarely lets up for some 17 miles, providing one of the most exciting 1-day white-water tours in the West. See "Other Outdoor Pursuits" in chapter 7.

- **Fishing:** Ask any avid fisher in the nation if he's fished the San Juan (see "The Great Outdoors in Northwestern New Mexico" in chapter 9), and if he hasn't been there, he'll still know what you're talking about. A world-class, catch-and-release fishing spot in northwestern New Mexico, it's ideal for the competent caster because many of the fish have been caught so many times they'll swim around your ankles and dare you to figure out exactly what they want to eat. Other rivers in New Mexico provide a less frustrating but equally beautiful challenge, and the lakes offer plenty of angling, too. Bass, trout, cutthroat, walleye, and perch are among the varieties of fish that may nibble at your hook.

- **Hiking:** What's unique about hiking in New Mexico is the variety of terrain, from the pure desert of White Sands in the south to the alpine forest of Valle Vidal in the north. In between, there's everything from the lava flow badlands of El Malpais to the hauntingly sculpted rock formations at Abiquiu that artist Georgia O'Keeffe made famous in her paintings. For details about White Sands hikes, see chapter 11; for northern New Mexico hikes, see especially chapters 6 and 7; and for El Malpais and Georgia O'Keeffe country, see chapter 9.

- **Skiing:** Many, such as me, who have skied in the East and widely in Colorado, Utah, and Wyoming, still find Taos Ski Valley (see "Skiing" in chapter 7) to be one of the most fun mountain romps there is. With its rustic Bavarian feel and its steep mogul runs, it's an awesome playland. Santa Fe (see "Outdoor Activities" in chapter 6) and Ski Apache (see "The Great Outdoors in Southeastern New Mexico" in chapter 11) also provide some challenge, plus plenty of terrain for beginners and intermediates, as do some of the smaller areas in the state. If you're into cross-country or backcountry adventure, you'll find plenty of that here, too, especially in the Taos, Red River (see "Other Outdoor Pursuits" in chapter 7), and Chama (see "The Great Outdoors in Northwestern New Mexico" in chapter 9) areas.

4 The Best Museums

- **Albuquerque Museum of Art and History** (Albuquerque): Take a journey down into the caverns of New Mexico's past in this museum, which owns the largest U.S. collection of Spanish colonial artifacts. Displays include Don Quixote–style helmets, swords, and even horse armor. You can wander through an 18th-century house compound with adobe floors and walls, and see gear used by *vaqueros,* the original cowboys who came to the area in the 16th century. See p. 88.

- **Museum of Fine Arts** (Santa Fe): This museum's permanent collection of more than 8,000 works emphasizes regional art and includes landscapes and portraits by all the Taos masters as well as contemporary artists, including R. C. Gorman, Amado Peña, Jr., and Georgia O'Keeffe. The museum also has a collection of photographic works by such masters as Ansel Adams, Edward Weston, and Elliot Porter. See p. 150.

- **Museum of International Folk Art** (Santa Fe): Whenever I want to escape the routine of everyday life, I stroll through this museum and witness the magic created by cultures all over the planet. Its perpetually expanding collection of folk art is the largest in the world, with 130,000 objects from more than 100 countries. You'll find an amazing array of imaginative works, ranging from Hispanic folk art *santos* (painted and carved saints) to Indonesian textiles and African sculptures. See p. 155.

- **Taos Historic Museums** (Taos): What's nice about Taos is that you can see historic homes inside and out. You can wander through Taos Society artist **Ernest Blumenschein's home,** which is a museum. Built in 1797 and restored by Blumenschein in 1919, it represents another New Mexico architectural phenomenon: homes that were added on to year after year. Doorways are typically low, and floors rise and fall at the whim of the earth beneath them. The **Martinez Hacienda** is an example of a hacienda stronghold. Built without windows facing outward, it originally had 20 small rooms, many with doors opening out to the courtyard. The hacienda has been developed into a living museum featuring weavers, blacksmiths, and woodcarvers. See p. 222.

• **Millicent Rogers Museum of Northern New Mexico** (Taos): This museum is small enough to offer a glimpse of some of the finest Southwestern arts and crafts you'll see, without being overwhelming. It was founded in 1953 by family members after the death of Millicent Rogers, a wealthy Taos émigré who in 1947 began acquiring a magnificent collection of beautiful Native American arts and crafts. Included are jewelry, textiles, pottery, kachina dolls, paintings, and basketry from a wide variety of Southwestern tribes. See p. 220.

• **The Hubbard Museum of the American West** (Ruidoso): This museum holds a collection of more than 10,000 horse-related items, including saddles, sleighs, a horse-drawn fire engine, a stagecoach, and paintings by artists such as Frederic Remington, Charles Russell, and Frank Tenney Johnson. See p. 352.

5 The Best Places to Discover New Mexico's History

• **Old Town** (Albuquerque): Once the center of Albuquerque commerce, Old Town thrived until the early 1880s, when businesses relocated nearer to the railroad tracks. It has been a center of tourism since being rediscovered in the 1930s. Today you can visit shops, galleries, and restaurants in Old Town, as well as the Church of San Felipe de Neri, the first structure built when colonists established Albuquerque in 1706. See chapter 5.

• **Georgia O'Keeffe's Home** (Abiquiu): Hand-smoothed adobe walls, elk antlers, and a blue door—you'll encounter these images and many more that inspired the famous artist's work. When you view the landscape surrounding her residence in Abiquiu, you'll understand why she was so inspired. Be sure to make a reservation months in advance. See p. 303.

• **Palace of the Governors** (Santa Fe): In order to fully appreciate this structure at the heart of Santa Fe, it's important to know that this is where, in 1680, the only successful Native American uprising took place. Before the uprising, this was the seat of power in the area, and after de Vargas reconquered the American Indians, it resumed that position. Built in 1610 as the original capitol of New Mexico, the palace has been in continuous public use longer than any other structure in the United States. A watchful eye can find remnants of the history this building has seen through the years, such as a fireplace and chimney chiseled into the adobe wall, and storage pits where the Pueblo Indians kept corn, wheat, barley, and other goods during their reign at the palace. After the reconquest, the pits were used to dispose of trash. Most notable is the front of the palace, where Native Americans sell jewelry, pottery, and some weavings under the protection of the portal. See p. 152.

• **St. Francis Cathedral** (Santa Fe): Santa Fe's grandest religious structure is an architectural anomaly here because its design is French. Just a block east of the plaza, it was built between 1869 and 1886 by Archbishop Jean Baptiste Lamy, in the style of the great cathedrals of Europe. Inside the small adobe, Our Lady of the Rosary chapel is full of the romance of Spanish Catholicism. The chapel was built in 1807 and is the only portion that remains from Our Lady of the Assumption Church, founded along with Santa Fe in 1610. See p. 153.

• **San Francisco de Asis church** (Taos): To me this is the most beautiful church in the world. Though some might not see how it could compete with elaborate structures such as Chartres or Notre Dame de Paris, I see it like a Picasso sculpture: Simple and direct, it has massive, hand-smoothed adobe walls and a rising sense that nearly lifts the heavy structure off the ground. Maybe that's why such notables as Ansel Adams and Georgia O'Keeffe have recorded its presence in art. See p. 225.

• **Cimarron:** Nestled against the eastern slope of the Sangre de Cristo mountain range, this town was a "wild and woolly" outpost on the Santa Fe Trail between the 1850s and 1880s and a gathering place for area ranchers, traders, gamblers, gunslingers, and other characters. See "Cimarron & Raton: Historic Towns on the Santa Fe Trail" in chapter 8.

• **El Morro National Monument:** In the Grants area, this sandstone monolith is known as "Inscription Rock," because travelers and explorers documented their journeys for centuries on its smooth face. See "El Malpais & El Morro National Monuments," in chapter 9.

• **New Mexico Museum of Space History** (Alamogordo): Tracing the story of space travel, this five-story museum recalls the accomplishments of America's Mercury, Gemini, and Apollo programs, including New Mexico's participation in space exploration, from ancient American Indians to rocketry pioneer Robert Goddard to astronauts. See p. 344.

6 The Best Family Experiences

• **Albuquerque Aquarium:** For those of us born and raised in the desert, this attraction quenches years of soul thirst. Exhibits focus on sea areas fed by the Rio Grande. You'll pass by many large tanks and within an eels' den; the star attraction is a 285,000-gallon shark tank, where many species of fish and 15 to 20 sand tiger, brown, and nurse sharks swim around, looking ominous. The aquarium is one of three destinations inside the Albuquerque Biological Park (the other two are the botanic garden and zoo, discussed in the following two entries). See p. 93.

• **Rio Grande Botanic Garden** (Albuquerque): Within a state-of-the-art, 10,000-square-foot conservatory, a desert collection features plants from the lower Chihuahuan and Sonoran deserts, and a Mediterranean collection includes many exotic species native to the Mediterranean climates of Southern California, South Africa, Australia, and the Mediterranean Basin. See p. 93.

• **Rio Grande Zoo** (Albuquerque): More than 1,200 animals of 300 species live on 60 acres of riverside bosque among ancient cottonwoods. Open-moat exhibits with animals in naturalized habitats are a treat for zoo-goers. Major exhibits include the polar bears, the giraffes, the sea lions (with underwater viewing), the cat walk, the bird show, and ape country, with its gorilla and orangutans. The zoo has an especially fine collection of elephants, mountain lions, koalas, reptiles, and native Southwestern species. During summer, a children's petting zoo is open, and the New Mexico Symphony Orchestra performs. You'll find numerous snack bars on the zoo grounds, and La Ventana Gift Shop carries film and souvenirs. See p. 94.

- **Sandia Peak Tramway** (Albuquerque): The world's longest tramway ferries passengers about 3 miles from Albuquerque's city limits to the summit of the 10,378-foot Sandia Peak. On the way, you'll likely see birds of prey and rare Rocky Mountain bighorn sheep. In the summer, you may see hang gliders taking off from the giant precipice to soar in the drafts that sweep up the mountain. Go in the evening to watch the sun burn its way out of the western sky; then enjoy the glimmering city lights on your way down. See p. 90.
- **El Rancho de las Golondrinas** (Santa Fe): This living museum re-creates an 18th- and 19th-century Spanish village. Kids like to visit the working molasses mill, the blacksmith shop, the shearing and weaving rooms, and the water mills, as well as the resident animals. See p. 158.
- **Santa Fe Children's Museum** (Santa Fe): Designed for the whole family to experience, this museum offers interactive exhibits and hands-on activities in the arts, humanities, science, and technology. Most notable is a 16-foot climbing wall that kids can scale, outfitted with helmets and harnesses. A 1-acre Southwestern horticulture garden features animals, wetlands, and a greenhouse. Special performances and hands-on sessions with artists and scientists are regularly scheduled. Recently, *Family Life* magazine named this one of the 10 hottest children's museums in the nation. See p. 161.
- **New Mexico Mining Museum** (Grants): This museum takes you down into a spooky, low-lit replica mine. You begin in the station where uranium was loaded and unloaded, and travel back into the earth through places defined on wall plaques with such interesting names as "track drift" (where ore comes up in cars from the mine) and "stope" (a room stripped of all ore and off-limits in an actual mine). See p. 273.
- **Carlsbad Caverns National Park:** Truly one of the world's natural wonders, these caverns swallow visitors into what feels like a journey to the center of the earth, where nocturnal creatures thrive and water drips onto your body. Stalactites and stalagmites create another universe of seemingly alien life forms. Kids won't like the fact that they can't go climbing on the formations, but they'll be too fascinated to complain much. See "Carlsbad Caverns National Park" in chapter 11.
- **Living Desert Zoo & Gardens State Park** (Carlsbad): Spread across a vast plateau, this park offers visitors an hour-long trek through desert lands full of odd plants that survive on who knows what to zoo exhibits of hawks, cats, and bears. What's best about this zoo is that the animals aren't just captive, they're rehabilitating. See p. 369.

- **White Sands National Monument:** Like a bizarre, lost land of white, this place is a dream for kids. They can roll around in the fine sand or sled across it, all the while discovering the mysterious creatures that inhabit this truest of deserts. Bring extra clothing and lots of sunscreen (the reflection off the sand can cause some pretty nasty sunburns). See "White Sands National Monument" in chapter 11.

7 The Best Bed & Breakfast Inns

- **Hacienda Antigua** (Albuquerque): This 200-year-old adobe inn was once the first stagecoach stop out of Old Town in Albuquerque and now offers a glimpse of those old days with refreshing modern touches. The guest rooms surround a quiet courtyard, and a pool and hot tub nestle near towering cottonwoods. The place sings of old New Mexico, with history evident in places such as La Capilla, the home's former chapel, which is now a guest room. See p. 78.
- **Dos Casas Viejas** (Santa Fe): These two old houses *(dos casas viejas)* offer the kind of luxury accommodations you'd expect from a fine hotel. The rooms, each with a patio and private entrance, are finely renovated and richly decorated, all with Mexican-tile floors and kiva fireplaces. Enjoy your breakfast alongside the elegant lap pool or on your private patio. See p. 134.
- **Casa de las Chimeneas** (Taos): This 80-year-old adobe home has been a model of Southwestern elegance since its opening in 1988.

  As well as lovely gardens and comfortable rooms, the inn offers a spa with a small fitness room and sauna, as well as complete massage and facial treatments. The newest rooms have heated Saltillo tile floors, gas kiva fireplaces, and jetted tubs. The older section is delightful as well, with more of an antique feel. See p. 207.
- **Casa Blanca** (Farmington): Recent renovation to a 1940s home has brought verdant gardens, flowing fountains, hand-carved portal posts, and Southwest-chic decor to this inn overlooking Farmington. Breakfasts are always gourmet. See p. 294.
- **Kokopelli's Cave** (Farmington): This is an actual cave, but it's like none you've ever seen. Carved deep into the side of a cliff, it's a three-room luxury apartment, complete with carpet, VCR, kitchen, and space enough for a family. Best of all is the bathroom, where water pours off rocks, creating a waterfall. Golden eagles nest in the area, and ringtail cats tend to wander across the balcony. See p. 294.

8 The Best Historic Hotels

- **La Posada de Albuquerque** (Albuquerque): Built in 1939 by Conrad Hilton as the famed hotelier's first inn in his home state of New Mexico, this hostelry on the National Register of Historic Places feels like old Spain. Though it was remodeled in 1996, the owners have kept the finer qualities. An elaborate, Moorish, brass-and-mosaic fountain stands in the center of the tiled lobby floor, and old-fashioned tin chandeliers hang from the two-story ceiling. All guest room furniture is hand-crafted and covered with cushions of Southwestern design. Spacious rooms with big windows look out across the city and toward the mountains. See p. 94.

- **The Bishop's Lodge** (Santa Fe): More than a century ago, when Bishop Jean Baptiste Lamy was the spiritual leader of northern New Mexico's Roman Catholic population, he often escaped clerical politics by hiking into this valley called Little Tesuque. He built a retreat and the humble chapel (now on the National Register of Historic Places) with high-vaulted ceilings and a hand-built altar. Today, Lamy's 1,000-acre getaway has become The Bishop's Lodge. The guest rooms, spread through many buildings, all feature handcrafted furniture and regional artwork. The Lodge is an active resort with activities such as horseback riding, hiking, tennis, and swimming filling guests' time. See p. 130.

- **The Historic Taos Inn** (Taos): Dr. Thomas Paul Martin, Taos's first (and for many years only) physician, purchased this complex in 1895. Now this inn at the center of Taos provides unique and comfortable rooms, decorated with Spanish colonial art, Taos-style furniture, and interesting touches such as hand-woven Oaxacan bedspreads and little *nichos* often adorned with Mexican pottery. See p 202.

- **St. James Hotel** (Cimarron): This landmark hotel offers travelers a romantically historic stay in the Old West town of Cimarron. It looks much the same today as it did in 1873, when it was built by Henri Lambert, previously a chef for Napoleon, Abraham Lincoln, and General Ulysses S. Grant. In its early years, as a rare luxury on the Santa Fe Trail, it had a dining

room, a saloon, gambling rooms, and lavish guest rooms outfitted with Victorian furniture. Today, the rooms maintain the frontier elegance of those days. See p. 256.

- **Bear Mountain Lodge** (Silver City): After the death of longtime innkeeper and naturalist Myra McCormick, this lodge came under the care of the Nature Conservancy, which has, with a complete renovation, turned it into a nature lovers' paradise. The inn itself was built in 1928, but the grounds show evidence of hunter and gatherer visitors dating from 6000 B.C. Nature Conservancy staff members are on hand to guide visitors in their bird-, wildlife-, and plant-viewing pursuits. Rooms are large, with maple floors, high ceilings, and French windows. See p. 335.

- **Casa de Patrón Bed and Breakfast** (Lincoln): The main building of Casa de Patrón, an adobe, was built around 1860 and housed Juan Patrón's old store (the home is on the National Register of Historic Places). In addition, Billy the Kid used part of the house as a hideout at some point during his time in the Lincoln area. Jeremy and Cleis Jordan have capitalized on the presence of that notorious punk by collecting portraits and photographs and hanging them throughout the cozy sitting and dining areas of this inn, which has a variety of comfortable rooms. See p. 355.

- **Ellis Store and Co. Country Inn** (Lincoln): With part of this house dating from 1850, this is believed to be the oldest existing residence in Lincoln County. Billy the Kid spent several weeks here, although somewhat unwillingly, according to court records that show payment of $64 for 2 weeks' food and lodging for the Kid and a companion held under house arrest. The guest rooms offer a step back into the 1800s, with wood-burning fireplaces or stoves providing heat, antique furnishings, and handmade quilts. With prior notice, the innkeepers will prepare a six-course meal; specialties include exotic game, such as African antelope or venison. See p. 356.

- **The Lodge at Cloudcroft** (Cloudcroft): This lodge is an antique jewel, a well-preserved survivor of another era. From the grand fireplace in the lobby to the homey Victorian decor in the guest rooms, it exudes gentility and class. Its nine-hole golf course, one of the nation's highest, challenges golfers across rolling hills between 8,600 and 9,200 feet elevation and is the site of numerous regional tournaments. Rooms in the lodge are filled with antiques, from sideboards and lamps to mirrors and steam radiators. See p. 348.

9 The Best Resorts

- **La Posada de Santa Fe Resort and Spa** (Santa Fe): With the feel of a meandering adobe village but the service of a fine hotel, this has become one of New Mexico's premier resorts. A recent $23-million face-lift added a Zen-Southwestern-style spa and pool and spacious spa rooms. Most rooms don't have views but have outdoor patios, and most are tucked back into the quiet compound. See p. 126.

- **Hyatt Regency Tamaya Resort and Spa** (Santa Ana Pueblo): Situated on Santa Ana Pueblo land, this grand resort has all a human might need to get away from the world. Three swimming pools, a 16,000-square-foot full-service spa and fitness center, an 18-hole Twin Warriors Championship Golf Course designed by Gary Panks, and views of the Sandia Mountains make for plenty to do. Meanwhile, spacious rooms offer plenty of quiet for those who'd rather do nothing. Though the resort is surrounded by acres of countryside, it's only 15 minutes from Albuquerque and 45 minutes from Santa Fe. See p. 79.

- **El Monte Sagrado** (Taos): With guest rooms and casitas set around a grassy "Sacred Circle," this new eco-resort is the quintessence of refinement. Every detail, from the waterfalls and chemical-free pool and hot tubs to the authentic theme decor in the rooms, has been created with conscious care. See p. 201.

10 The Best Restaurants

- **Jennifer James** (Albuquerque) This French bistro-style restaurant serves contemporary American cuisine with plenty of panache. You might feast on pan-seared pork with apple bread pudding or grilled quail over endive and radicchio. See p. 83.

- **The Compound** (Santa Fe) This reincarnation of one of Santa Fe's classic restaurants serves daring contemporary American food in a soulful setting. Such delicacies as monkfish chorizo with watercress or grilled beef tenderloin with Italian potatoes will please sophisticated palates, and probably simpler ones, too. See p. 138.

- **Coyote Café** (Santa Fe): World-renowned chef, cookbook author, and owner Mark Miller has been "charged with single-handedly elevating the chile to haute status." That statement from the *New York Times Magazine* sums up the experience of eating at this trendy nouveau–Southwestern restaurant a block from the plaza. Feast on delicacies such as braised ancho lamb shank or horseradish-crusted Maine haddock. See p. 138.

- **Santacafé** (Santa Fe): The food here is daring, drawing from an International palate. Diners feast while surrounded by a minimalist decor that accentuates the beautiful architecture of the 18th-century Padre Gallegos House. The dishes change according to the seasons. One of my favorites is the Alaskan halibut with English peas and saffron couscous. See p. 143.

- **The Shed** (Santa Fe): A Santa Fe luncheon institution since 1954, The Shed occupies several rooms in part of a rambling hacienda that was built in 1692. The sauces here have been refined over the years, creating amazing flavors in basic dishes such as enchiladas, burritos, and stuffed sopaipillas. The mocha cake is renowned. See p. 147. (Sister restaurant **La Choza** is just as good, with a similar menu; see p. 149.)

- **De La Tierra** (Taos): Located at the new eco-resort El Monte Sagrado, this elegant restaurant serves imaginative regional American food and other delights such as wild game. The venison medallions with garlic mashed potatoes is excellent, as is the rosemary skewered shrimp with corn polenta. An expansive wine list completes the experience. See p. 213.

- **Joseph's Table** (Taos): Now in new digs on Taos Plaza, this font of creativity serves delightful dishes with plenty of flair. Try the steak au poivre over mashed potatoes with a wild mushroom salad. Delectable. See p. 214.

- **Blackjack's Grill** (Las Vegas): Las Vegas has needed a sophisticated restaurant, and now it finally has one. The atmosphere is festive, especially on the patio, where diners sit under elm trees. My favorite dish is sautéed beef medallions with garlic mashed potatoes. See p. 254.

- **The Bluffs** (Farmington): Wooden partitions topped with glazed glass shaped like towering bluffs surround diners at this new restaurant serving sandwiches and salads at lunch and steaks and seafood at dinner. The turkey bacon club is amazing, as are any of the angus beef steaks. See p. 295.

- **Double Eagle** (Las Cruces): Continental cuisine is alive and well behind the walls of this historic hacienda (it's more than 150 years old) located in Las Cruces. The decor is lush and dramatic—chandeliers hung with Baccarat crystals—and the food is richly traditional. Steaks are the way to go. See p. 325.

- **Diane's Bakery & Café** (Silver City): Diane Barrett, who was once a pastry chef at La Traviata and Eldorado in Santa Fe, has brought refined flavors to the little mining town of Silver City. You'll feast on sumptuous baked goods and sophisticated meals such as rack of lamb. See p. 337.

- **La Lorraine** (Ruidoso): This little slice of France offers specialties such as duck à l'orange and chateaubriand in an elegant French provincial decor, with lace curtains and candlelight. See p. 357.

2

Planning Your Trip
to New Mexico

As with any trip, a little preparation is essential before you start your journey to New Mexico. This chapter provides you with a variety of planning tools, including information on when to go, how to get there, how to get around once you're there, and some suggested itineraries.

1 The Regions in Brief

North-Central New Mexico The most highly populated and well-traveled area of the state, north-central New Mexico roughly includes the cities of Albuquerque, Santa Fe, and Taos. It is also the economic center of New Mexico. In this portion of the state, lush mountains seem to rise directly out of the parched plateaus that have made New Mexico's landscape famous. Temperatures are generally lower in this area than they are in the rest of the state, and skiing is one of the most popular winter activities in both Santa Fe and Taos.

Northeastern New Mexico Covering the area north of I-40 and east of the Sangre de Cristo Mountains, northeastern New Mexico is prairie land once inhabited or visited by some of the West's most legendary gunslingers. Towns to visit for a bit of Wild West history are Cimarron and Las Vegas. The northeastern portion of the state also includes attractions such as Fort Union National Monument, a portion of the Santa Fe Trail, Kiowa and Rita National Grasslands, and Capulin Volcano National Monument. Due to its abundance of state parks and wildlife reserves, as well as the fact that it borders the ski resort towns of Angel Fire, Taos, Red River,

and Santa Fe, this region is an excellent area for sports enthusiasts.

Northwestern New Mexico Head to this region if you're interested in Native American culture. Sandstone bluffs here mark the homes of Pueblo, Navajo, and Apache Indians, in an area once inhabited by the ancestral Puebloans (also known as Anasazi) of the past. My favorite places to visit in this section of the state are Acoma Pueblo, Chaco Culture National Historical Park, and Aztec Ruins National Monument. A major portion of the northwestern region is part of a Navajo reservation, the largest in the country. This is also the gateway to the famous Four Corners region. The town of Grants, near Acoma, offers a glimpse into uranium mining. Railroad fanatics, hikers, hunters, and fishers should make a trip to Chama, home of the Cumbres & Toltec Railroad and a popular starting point for outdoor adventures.

Southwestern New Mexico This region, like northeastern New Mexico, is another great place to visit if you're interested in the history of the Wild West and Native American culture, for it was once home to Billy the Kid and Geronimo. The Rio Grande, lifeline to this part of the state, acts as a border between the southwestern and southeastern portions of the state. Attractions west of the river include Gila National Forest, once home to the Mogollon Indians, whose past is preserved in the Gila Cliff Dwellings National Monument. The Chiricahua Apaches, a tribe once led by Geronimo, also lived in this area. The town of Silver City, which survives as an economic center of this area, was once a booming mining town. Surrounding ghost towns weren't as lucky. Las Cruces, at the foot of the Organ Mountains, is the state's second largest city, and Truth or Consequences, named for a television and radio game show, is north of Las Cruces off I-25.

Southeastern New Mexico   Bounded on the west by the Rio Grande, to the north by I-40, and to the east by Texas, southeastern New Mexico is home to two of the most interesting natural wonders in this part of the country: Carlsbad Caverns and White Sands National Monument. The underground caverns, filled with stalactites and stalagmites, are infinitely interesting and hauntingly beautiful. Snow-white dunes at White Sands National Monument, which rise out of the desert landscape, are an extraordinary sight as you make the drive to Alamogordo. White Sands is a great place to camp out and watch the sunrise. This portion of the state is yet another former home of Billy the Kid. It is also where he died. Southeastern New Mexico has something of a dubious past as well: The world's first atomic bomb was detonated here.

2 Visitor Information

Numerous agencies can assist you with planning your trip. The Visitors Information Center for the **New Mexico Department of Tourism** is located at 491 Old Santa Fe Trail, Santa Fe, NM 87501 (© **800/545-2070** or 505/827-7336). You can also find general New Mexico information on the Department of Tourism's website at **www.newmexico.org**. Santa Fe, Taos, and Albuquerque each have their own information service for visitors (see the "Orientation" sections in chapters 5, 6, and 7, respectively).

A valuable resource for information on outdoor recreation is the **Public Lands Information Center,** located on the south side of town at 1474 Rodeo Rd., Santa Fe, NM 87505

(© **877/276-9404** or 505/438-7542). Here, adventurers can find out what's available on lands administered by the National Forest Service, the Bureau of Land Management, the Fish and Wildlife Service, the National Park Service, the New Mexico Department of Game and Fish (which sells hunting and fishing licenses), and the New Mexico State Parks Division. The Information Center collaborates with the New Mexico Department of Tourism. Visit **www.publiclands.org** and you'll also be able to access links to 261 separate sites, which can be found by looking up either a particular activity or agency.

For Internet addresses of cities' visitor centers, see chapters 5, 6, and 7.

3 Money

If you come from a major city such as New York or London, you might find New Mexico fairly inexpensive. In Taos and Albuquerque, you can get good accommodations and meals without even wincing. Santa Fe, however, may hurt a bit, especially if you hit the hottest spots in town, which cater to sophisticated tastes.

What Things Cost in Santa Fe	US$	Euro €	UK£
Double room in high season at La Posada de Santa Fe Resort & Spa	279	243	151
Double room in high season at Santa Fe Motel and Inn	114	99	62
Dinner for two at Geronimo, without drinks, tax, or tip	105	91	57
Dinner for two at La Choza, without drinks, tax, or tip	25	22	14
An imported Mexican beer at the Dragon Room	3.50	3	2
One-hour massage at Ten Thousand Waves Japanese Health Spa	80	70	43
Adult admission to the Museum of International Folk Art	7	6	4

ATMs

As in most U.S. destinations, ATMs are ubiquitous in the cities of New Mexico.

TRAVELER'S CHECKS

Traveler's checks are something of an anachronism from the days before the ATM made cash accessible at any time. However, if you decide to use them, you can still purchase traveler's checks at any bank.

CREDIT CARDS

Credit cards are invaluable when you're traveling. They are a safe way to carry money and provide a record of your expenses. You can also withdraw cash advances from your credit cards at any bank (though you'll start paying hefty interest on the advance the moment you receive the cash). At most banks, you don't need to go to a teller; you can get a cash advance at the ATM if you know your PIN.

The most commonly accepted credit cards are American Express, Diners Club, Discover, MasterCard, and Visa.

What Things Cost in Las Cruces	US$	Euro €	UK£
Double room in high season at the Las Cruces Hilton	105	86	58
Double room in high season at La Quinta	80	66	45
Dinner for two at the Double Eagle, without drinks, tax, or tip	66	54	36
Dinner for two at Nellie's, without drinks, tax, or tip	18	15	10
An imported Mexican beer at La Posta de Mesilla	3.50	2	1.25
Hiking in the Organ Mountains	Free		
Adult admission to the New Mexico Farm and Ranch Heritage Museum	3	2.50	1.50

4 When to Go

Summers are hot throughout most of the state, though distinctly cooler at higher elevations. Winters are relatively mild in the south, harsher in the north and in the mountains. Spring and fall have pleasant temperatures, though in spring the wind blows throughout the state. Rainfall is sparse except in the higher mountains; summer afternoon thunderstorms and winter snows account for most precipitation.

Santa Fe and Taos, at 7,000 feet, have midsummer highs in the low 90s (about 32°C), overnight midwinter lows in the teens (between –12° and –7°C). Temperatures in Albuquerque, at 5,300 feet, often run about 10°F warmer than elsewhere in the northern region. Snowfall is common November through March, and sometimes as late as May, though it seldom lasts long. Santa Fe averages 32 inches total annual snowfall. At the high-mountain ski resorts, as much as 300 inches may fall in a season—and stay. The plains and deserts of the southeast and south commonly have summer temperatures in excess of 100°F (38°C).

New Mexico Temperatures (in °F) & Precipitation

	Jan	Apr	July	Oct	Annual Precipitation
	High–Low	High–Low	High–Low	High–Low	(in Inches)
Alamogordo	57–28	78–40	95–65	79–42	7.5
Albuquerque	47–28	70–41	91–66	72–45	8.9
Carlsbad	60–28	81–46	96–67	79–47	13.5
Chama	33–3	54–22	73–37	52–18	9.3
Cloudcroft	41–19	56–33	73–48	59–36	25.8
Farmington	44–16	70–36	92–58	70–37	7.5
Las Cruces	56–29	79–48	96–68	78–50	8.6
Roswell	56–24	78–42	91–65	75–45	12.7
Ruidoso	50–17	65–28	82–48	67–31	21.4
Santa Fe	40–18	59–35	80–57	62–38	14.0
Taos	40–10	62–30	87–50	64–32	12.1
Truth or Consequences	54–27	75–44	92–66	75–47	8.5

NEW MEXICO CALENDAR OF EVENTS

January

New Year's Day. There is a transfer of canes to new officials and various dances at most pueblos. Check out the Turtle Dance at Taos Pueblo (no photography allowed). Call ⓒ **800/793-4955** for more information. January 1.

Winter Wine Festival, Taos Ski Valley. This festival features a variety of wine offerings and food tastings prepared by local chefs. Call ⓒ **505/776-2291** for details. Mid-January.

¡Magnifico! Albuquerque Festival of the Arts. This celebration features various visual and performing arts events held throughout the year. For a schedule of all events, call ⓒ **505/242-8244** or visit **www.magnifico.org**.

February

Candelaria Day Celebration, Picuris Pueblo. This celebration features many traditional dances. Call ⓒ **505/587-2519** for more information. February 2.

Mt. Taylor Winter Quadrathlon, Grants. Hundreds of athletes come from all over the West to bicycle, run, cross-country ski, and snow-shoe up and down this mountain. For information, call © **800/748-2142.** Mid-February.

Edible Art Tour, Santa Fe. Santa Fe's top chefs and galleries team up to create a gastro-aesthetic feast. For information, call © **505/982-1648.** Late February.

Just Desserts Eat and Ski, near Red River. Cross-country skiers glide from point to point on the Enchanted Forest course, tasting decadent desserts supplied by area restaurants. Call © **505/754-2374.** Late February.

March

National Fiery Foods/Barbecue Show, Albuquerque. Here's your chance to taste the hottest of the hot and plenty of milder flavors, too. Some 10,000 general public attendees show up to taste sauces, salsas, candies, and more, and to see cooking demonstrations at the Albuquerque Convention Center. For information call © **505/873-8680** or go to **www.fiery-foods.com.** Early March.

Rio Grande Arts and Crafts Festival, Albuquerque. A juried show featuring 200 artists and craftspeople from around the country takes place at the State Fairgrounds in Albuquerque. Call © **505/292-7457** for more information, or visit **www.rio grandefestivals.com.** Second week of March.

Rockhound Roundup, Deming. Gems, jewelry, tools, and crafted items are displayed and sold at the Southwest New Mexico State Fairgrounds. Call © **505/544-8643.** Mid-March.

April

Easter Weekend Celebration. There are dances at most pueblos. Celebrations include Masses, parades, corn dances, and other dances, such as the bow and arrow dance at Nambe. Call © **800/793-4955** for information. Easter Weekend.

American Indian Week, Indian Pueblo Cultural Center, Albuquerque. A celebration of Native American traditions and culture. For dates and information, call © **505/843-7270.**

Gathering of Nations Powwow, University Arena, Albuquerque. At this event, you can see dance competitions, arts-and-crafts exhibitions, and the Miss Indian World contest. Call © **505/836-2810,** or visit **www.gatheringofnations.com** for more information. Late April.

May

Cinco de Mayo Fiestas, statewide. The restoration of the Mexican republic (from French occupation during 1863–67) is celebrated in, among other places, Las Cruces at Old Mesilla Plaza (© **505/524-3262**); and Truth or Consequences (© **800/831-9487** or 505/894-3536). First weekend in May.

Taos Spring Arts Festival. Contemporary visual, performing, and literary arts are highlighted during a month of gallery openings, studio tours, performances by visiting theatrical and dance troupes, live musical events, traditional ethnic entertainment, literary readings, and more.

Events are held at venues throughout Taos and Taos County. For dates and ticket info contact the Taos County Chamber of Commerce, P.O. Drawer I, Taos, NM 87571 (© **800/732-TAOS** or 505/758-3873; www.taoschamber.com). All month.

Taste of Santa Fe. Sample Santa Fe's best chefs' recipes, including appetizers, entrees, and desserts. At Santa Fe's Sweeney Center. For information, call ✆ **505/983-4823.** First Tuesday in May.

June

Aztec Fiesta Days, Aztec. Celebrate the arrival of summer with three parades, games, food, arts and crafts, and a carnival. Call ✆ **505/334-9551.** First full weekend in June.

St. Anthony Feast Day. Enjoy corn dances at many of the pueblos. For information, call ✆ **505/843-7270.** June 13.

Rodeo de Santa Fe. This 4-day event features a Western parade, a rodeo dance, and five rodeo performances. It attracts hundreds of cowboys and cowgirls from all over the Southwest who compete in such events as Brahma bull and bronco riding, calf roping, steer wrestling, barrel racing, trick riding, and clown and animal acts. The rodeo grounds are at 3237 Rodeo Rd., off Cerrillos Road, 5½ miles south of the plaza. Performances are in the evening Wednesday to Saturday; and on Saturday afternoon. For tickets, actual dates, and other information, call ✆ **505/471-4300** or visit **www.rodeodesantafe.org.**

Taos Solar Music Festival, Kit Carson Municipal Park, Taos. Sit out on the grass, under the sun, and listen to music at this event celebrating the summer solstice. A tribute to solar energy, the event has a stage powered by a solar generator and educational displays within a "Solar Village." For information, call ✆ **505/758-9191.** Late June.

Rodeo de Taos, County Fairgrounds, Taos. A fun event featuring local and regional participants. For information, call ✆ **505/758-5700** or, in mid- to late June call ✆ **505/758-3974.** Third or fourth weekend in June.

New Mexico Arts and Crafts Fair. A tradition for 41 years, this juried show offers work from more than 200 New Mexico artisans, accompanied by nonstop entertainment for the whole family. This can be a good place to find Hispanic arts and crafts. The fair is held at the State Fairgrounds in Albuquerque. Admission varies. For information, call ✆ **505/884-9043** or visit **www.nmartsandcraftsfair.org.** Last full weekend in June

July

Santa Fe Opera. The world-class Santa Fe Opera season runs from the beginning of July to the end of August. Call ✆ **505/986-5955** for more information. July through August.

Fourth of July celebrations (including fireworks displays) are held all over New Mexico. Call the chambers of commerce in specific towns and cities for information.

Santa Fe Wine Festival at Rancho de las Golondrinas. This event boasts live entertainment and wine tastings, presided over by hosts dressed in period clothing. Call ✆ **505/892-4178.** Early July.

Apache Maidens' Puberty Rites, Mescalero. This 4-day ceremony concludes with a rodeo and the dance of the mountain spirits. Call ✆ **505/671-4494** for more information. July 1–4.

Taos Pueblo Powwow, Taos Pueblo. Intertribal competitions in traditional and contemporary dances are held. For more information, call ✆ **505/758-1028.** Second weekend in July.

Eight Northern Pueblos Artist and Craftsman Show. More than 600 Native American artists exhibit their work at the eight northern pueblos. Traditional dances and food booths; location varies. Call ✆ **505/747-1593** for location and exact dates. Third weekend in July.

Fiestas de Santiago y Santa Ana, Taos area. The celebration begins with a Friday-night Mass at one of the three Taos-area parishes, where the fiesta queen is crowned. During the weekend there are candlelight processions, special Masses, music, dancing, parades, crafts, and food booths. Taos Plaza hosts many events, and most are free. For information, contact the Taos Fiesta Council, P.O. Box 3300, Taos, NM 87571 (© **800/732-8267;** www.fiestasdetaos.com). Third weekend in July.

Spanish Markets. More than 300 Hispanic artists from New Mexico and southern Colorado exhibit and sell their work in this lively community event. Artists are featured in special demonstrations, while an entertaining mix of traditional Hispanic music, dance, foods, and pageantry creates the ambience of a village celebration. Artwork for sale includes *santos* (painted and carved saints), textiles, tinwork, furniture, straw appliqué, and metalwork. The markets are found at Santa Fe Plaza in Santa Fe. For information, contact the Spanish Colonial Arts Society, P.O. Box 5378, Santa Fe, NM 87502 (© **505/982-2226;** www.spanishcolonial.org). Last full weekend in July.

August

Connie Mack World Series Baseball Tournament, Ricketts Park, Farmington. The very best high school players from throughout the United States, Puerto Rico, and Canada compete in a 7-day, 17-game series, which is closely watched by scouts from college and professional teams. Call © **505/327-9673** for details. Early August.

Old Lincoln Days and Billy the Kid Pageant, Lincoln. The main attraction is a reenactment of Billy the Kid's escape from the Lincoln jail. There are also a fiddling contest and living-history demonstrations (such as weaving and blacksmithing). Call © **505/653-4025** for more information. First weekend in August.

Bat Flight Breakfast, Carlsbad Caverns National Park. An early-morning buffet breakfast is served while participants watch the bats return to the cave. Call © **505/785-3012** for details and exact date. Second Thursday of August.

Intertribal Indian Ceremonial, near Gallup. Thirty tribes from the United States and Mexico participate in rodeos, parades, dances, athletic competitions, and an arts and crafts show at Red Rock State Park, east of Gallup. Call © **800/242-4282.** Second week in August.

Zuni Arts & Cultural Expo, Zuni. This 3-day event features arts and craft sales and traditional food and dances. Call © **505/782-2869.** Second week in August.

Chama Days, Chama. A rodeo, parade, and arts and crafts fair highlight this mountain-town event. Call © **800/477-0149.** Second weekend of August.

The Indian Market. This is the largest all–Native American market in the country. About 1,000 artisans display their baskets and blankets, jewelry, pottery, woodcarvings, rugs, sand paintings, and sculptures at rows of booths around Santa Fe Plaza, surrounding streets, and de Vargas Mall. Sales are brisk. Costumed tribal dancing and crafts demonstrations are scheduled in the afternoon. The market is free, but hotels are booked months in advance. For information, contact the **Southwestern Association for Indian Arts,** P.O. Box 969, Santa Fe, NM 87504-0969 (© **505/983-5220;** www.swaia.org). Third weekend in August.

Music from Angel Fire. World-class musicians gather in Angel Fire to perform classical and chamber music. For information and schedules, call ☎ **505/377-3233** or go to **www.angelfirenm.com.** Mid-August to the first week in September.

Great American Duck Race, Deming. Devised in a bar in 1979, this event has grown to include a parade, a tortilla toss, an outhouse race, ballooning, dances, and, of course, the duck race. It takes place on the courthouse lawn ("Duck Downs"). For details, call ☎ **888/ 345-1125** or visit **www.deming duckrace.com.** Fourth weekend in August.

September

The All American Futurity, Ruidoso Downs, Ruidoso. With a purse of $2 million, this is the world's richest quarter-horse race. Call ☎ **505/378-4431.** Labor Day.

Chile Festival, Hatch. New Mexicans celebrate their favorite fiery food item with a festival in the "Chile Capital of the World." Call ☎ **505/294-6722.** Labor Day weekend.

New Mexico Wine Festival at Bernalillo, near Albuquerque. New Mexico wines are showcased at this annual event, which includes wine tastings, an art show, and live entertainment. For a schedule of events, call ☎ **505/867-3311.** Labor Day weekend.

La Fiesta de Santa Fe. An exuberant combination of spirit, history, and general merrymaking, La Fiesta is the oldest community celebration in the United States. The first fiesta was celebrated in 1712, 20 years after the peaceful resettlement of New Mexico by Spanish conquistadors in 1692. La Conquistadora, a carved Madonna credited with the victory, is the focus of the celebration, which includes Masses, a parade for children and their pets, a historical/hysterical parade, mariachi concerts, dances, food, and arts, as well as local entertainment on the plaza. Zozobra, "Old Man Gloom," a 40-foot-tall effigy made of wood, canvas, and paper, is burned at dusk on Thursday to revitalize the community. Zozobra kicks off La Fiesta. For information call ☎ **505/988-7575.** Weekend following Labor Day.

Enchanted Circle Century Bike Tour. About 500 cyclists turn out to ride 100 miles of scenic mountain roads, starting and ending in Red River. All levels of riders are welcome, though not everyone completes this test of endurance. Call ☎ **505/754-2366.** Weekend following Labor Day.

New Mexico State Fair and Rodeo, Albuquerque. This is one of America's top state fairs; it features parimutuel horse racing, a nationally acclaimed rodeo, entertainment by top country artists, Native American and Spanish villages, the requisite midway, livestock shows, and arts and crafts. The fair and rodeo, which last 17 days, are held at the State Fairgrounds in Albuquerque. Advance tickets can be ordered by calling ☎ **505/265-1791** or visiting www.nmstatefair. com. Early September.

Stone Lake Fiesta, Jicarilla Reservation, 19 miles south of Dulce. This is an Apache festival with a rodeo, ceremonial dances, and a foot race. Call ☎ **505/759-3242,** ext. 275 or 277, for more information. September 15.

Mexican Independence Day. A parade and dances take place in Las Cruces at Old Mesilla Plaza (☎ **505/ 543-3262**) and Carlsbad at San Jose Plaza (☎ **800/221-1224** or 505/887-6516), with a rodeo as well in Carlsbad. Weekend closest to September 16.

Taos Fall Arts Festival. Highlights include arts-and-crafts exhibitions and competitions, studio tours, gallery openings, lectures, concerts, dances, and stage plays. Simultaneous events include the **Old Taos Trade Fair,** the **Wool Festival,** and **San Geronimo Day** at Taos Pueblo. The festival is held throughout Taos and Taos County Events, schedules, and tickets (where required) can be obtained from the **Taos County Chamber of Commerce,** P.O. Drawer I, Taos, NM 87571 (© **800/732-8267** or 505/758-3873; www.taoschamber. com). Mid-September (or the third weekend) to the first week in October.

Taos Trade Fair, La Hacienda de los Martinez, Lower Ranchitos Road, Taos. This 2-day affair reenacts Spanish colonial life of the mid-1820s and features Hispanic and Native American music, weaving and crafts demonstrations, traditional foods, dancing, and visits by mountain men. Call © **505/ 758-0505.** Last full weekend in September.

San Geronimo Vespers Sundown Dance and Trade Fair, Taos Pueblo. This event features a Mass and procession; traditional corn, buffalo, and Comanche dances; an arts-and-crafts fair; foot races; and pole climbs by clowns. Call © **505/ 758-1028** for details. Last weekend in September.

Santa Fe Wine & Chile Fiesta. This lively celebration boasts 5 days of wine and food events, including seminars, guest chef demonstrations and luncheons, tours, a grand tasting and reserve tasting, an auction, and a golf tournament. It takes place at many venues in downtown Santa Fe, with the big event on the last Saturday. Tickets go on sale in early July and sell out quickly. For information call © **505/ 438-8060** or visit **www.santafe wineandchile.org**. Last Wednesday through Sunday in September.

The Whole Enchilada Fiesta, Las Cruces. The world's biggest enchilada (sometimes over 7 ft. wide) is created and eaten. Call © **505/ 524-1968.** Late September or early October.

October

Shiprock Navajo Fair, Shiprock. The oldest and most traditional Navajo fair, it features a rodeo, dancing and singing, a parade, and arts-and-crafts exhibits. Call © **800/ 448-1240** for details. Early October.

Rio Grande Arts and Crafts Festival, Albuquerque. This event features artists and craftspeople from around the country. For more information, call © **505/292-7457.** First and second weekends in October.

Albuquerque International Balloon Fiesta. The world's largest balloon rally, this 9-day festival brings together more than 750 colorful balloons and includes races and contests. There are mass ascensions at sunrise, "balloon glows" in the evening, and balloon rides for those desiring a little lift. Special events are staged all week. Balloons lift off at Balloon Fiesta Park (at I-25 and Alameda NE) on Albuquerque's northern city limits. For information, call © **800/733-9918** or visit **www.balloonfiesta.com**. Second week in October.

Taos Mountain Balloon Rally. The Albuquerque fiesta's "little brother" offers mass dawn ascensions, tethered balloon rides for the public, and a Saturday parade of balloon baskets (in pickup trucks) from Kit Carson Park around the plaza. Call © **800/732-8267** for more information. Last weekend of October.

November

Dixon Art Studio Tour. Northern New Mexico's most notable village studio tour. Walk Dixon's main street, which winds through hills planted with fruit trees, and wander into artists' homes and studios, where you're likely to see some excellent arts-and-crafts finds. For more details, call © **505/579-4363.** You can find information about this and other area art studio tours at **www.artnewmexico.com**. First weekend in November.

Weems Artfest, State Fairgrounds in Albuquerque. Approximately 260 artisans, who work in a variety of media, come from throughout the world to attend this 3-day fair. It's one of the top 100 arts-and-crafts fairs in the country. For details, call © **505/293-6133.** Early November.

Festival of the Cranes, Socorro. People come from all over the world to attend this bird-watching event just an hour and a half south of Albuquerque at Bosque del Apache National Wildlife Refuge, near Socorro. Call © **505/835-1828.** Weekend before Thanksgiving.

Yuletide in Taos. This holiday event emphasizes northern New Mexican traditions, cultures, and arts, with carols, festive classical music, Hispanic and Native American songs and dances, historic walking tours, art exhibitions, dance performances, candlelight dinners, and more. Events are staged by the **Taos County Chamber of Commerce,** P.O. Drawer I, Taos, NM 87571 (© **800/732-8267;** www. taoschamber.com). Thanksgiving through New Year's Day.

December

Christmas on the Pecos, Carlsbad. Pontoon-boat rides take place each evening, past a fascinating display of Christmas lights on riverside homes and businesses. Call © **800/221-1224** or 505/887-6516. Thanksgiving to New Year's Eve (except Christmas Eve).

Winter Spanish Market, Sweeney Convention Center, Santa Fe. Approximately 150 artists show their wares at this little sister to July's event. See "Spanish Markets" in July (above) for more information. Call © **505/982-2226.** First weekend in December.

Christmas in Madrid Open House. Even if you never get out of your car, it's worth going to see the spectacular lights display in this village between Albuquerque and Santa Fe on the Turquoise Trail. You'll also find entertainment, refreshments in shops, and Santa Claus. For additional information call © **505/471-1054.** First two weekends in December.

Our Lady of Guadalupe Fiesta, Tortugas, near Las Cruces. This pilgrimage to Tortugas Mountain and torchlight descent is followed by a Mass and traditional Native American and Hispanic dances. Call © **505/526-8171** for more information. December 10 to 12.

Sundown Torchlight Procession of the Virgin. Vespers at San Juan, Picuris, Tesuque, Nambe, and Taos Pueblos; Matachine dances at Taos Pueblo; and buffalo dances at Nambe Pueblo. For more information, call © **800/793-4955** or 505/852-4265. December 24.

Canyon Road Farolito Walk, Santa Fe. Locals and visitors bundle up and stroll Canyon Road, where streets and rooftops are lined with *farolitos* (candle lamps). Musicians play and carolers sing around *luminarias.* Though it's not responsible for the event, **Santa Fe Convention and Visitors Bureau** (© **505/955-6200**) can help direct you there; or ask your hotel concierge. Christmas Eve at dusk.

Dance of the Matachines and Other Dances. Many pueblos celebrate the Christmas holiday with dances. The Dance of the Matachines takes place at Picuris and San Juan pueblos on Christmas day. Contact ☎ **505/852-5265** for dance schedules for these and other pueblos. Christmas Eve through Christmas Day.

Torchlight Procession, Taos Ski Valley. Bold skiers carve down a steep run named Snakedance in the dark while carrying golden fire. For information call ☎ **800/992-7669** or 505/776-2291 or visit **www.ski taos.org**. December 31.

5 Insurance, Health & Safety

TRAVEL INSURANCE AT A GLANCE

Check your existing insurance policies before you buy travel insurance to cover trip cancellation, lost luggage, medical expenses, or car-rental insurance. You're likely to have partial or complete coverage. But if you need some, ask your travel agent about a comprehensive package. The cost of travel insurance varies widely, depending on the cost and length of your trip, your age and overall health, and the type of trip you're taking, but expect to pay between 5% and 8% of the vacation itself.

TRIP-CANCELLATION INSURANCE (TCI)

TCI helps you get your money back if you have to back out of a trip, if you have to go home early, or if your travel supplier goes bankrupt. Allowed reasons for cancellation can range from sickness to natural disasters to the State Department declaring your destination unsafe for travel. (Insurers usually won't cover vague fears, though, as many travelers discovered when they tried to cancel their trips in Oct 2001 because they were wary of flying.) In this unstable world, TCI is a good buy if you're getting tickets well in advance. Insurance policy details vary, so read the fine print—and make sure your airline is on the list of carriers covered in case of bankruptcy.

For more information, contact one of the following recommended insurers:

Access America (☎ 866/807-3982; www.accessamerica.com); **Travel Guard International** (☎ 800/826-4919; www.travelguard.com); **Travel Insured International** (☎ 800/243-3174; www.travelinsured.com); or **Travelex Insurance Services** (☎ 888/457-4602; www.travelex-insurance.com).

MEDICAL INSURANCE

Most health insurance policies cover you if you get sick away from home—but check, particularly if you're insured by an HMO. Members of **Blue Cross/Blue Shield** can now use their cards at select hospitals in most major cities worldwide (☎ **800/810-BLUE** or www.bluecares.com).

Some credit card companies (American Express and certain Visa and MasterCards, for example) offer automatic flight insurance against death or dismemberment in case of an airplane crash if you paid for your ticket with their card.

If you require additional medical insurance, try **MEDEX Assistance** (☎ **410/453-6300;** www.medexassist. com) or **Travel Assistance International** (☎ 800/821-2828; www.travel assistance.com; for general information on services, call the company's Worldwide Assistance Services, Inc., at ☎ 800/777-8710).

The cost of medical travel insurance varies widely. Check your existing policies before you buy additional coverage.

LOST-LUGGAGE INSURANCE

On domestic flights, checked baggage is covered up to $2,500 per ticketed passenger. If you plan to check items more valuable than the standard liability, see if your valuables are covered by your homeowner's policy, get baggage insurance as part of your comprehensive travel-insurance package, or buy Travel Guard's "BagTrak" product. Don't buy insurance at the airport, as it's usually overpriced. Be sure to take any valuables or irreplaceable items with you in your carry-on luggage, as many valuables (including books, money, and electronics) aren't covered by airline policies.

If your luggage is lost, immediately file a lost-luggage claim at the airport, detailing the luggage contents. For most airlines, you must report delayed, damaged, or lost baggage within 4 hours of arrival. The airlines are required to deliver luggage, once found, directly to your house or destination free of charge.

CAR-RENTAL INSURANCE

If you hold a private auto insurance policy, you are probably covered in the U.S. for loss or damage to the car, and for liability in case a passenger is injured. The credit card you used to rent the car may also provide some coverage.

Car-rental insurance probably does not cover liability if you caused the accident. Check your own auto insurance policy, the rental company policy, and your credit card coverage for the extent of coverage: Is your destination covered? Are other drivers covered? How much liability is covered if a passenger is injured?

Car-rental insurance costs about $20 a day.

THE HEALTHY TRAVELER

One thing that sets New Mexico apart from most other states is its elevation. Santa Fe and Taos are about 7,000 feet above sea level; Albuquerque is more than 5,000 feet above sea level. The reduced oxygen and humidity can precipitate some unique problems, not the least of which is acute mountain sickness. In its early stages, you might experience headaches, shortness of breath, loss of appetite and/or nausea, tingling in the fingers or toes, lethargy, and insomnia. The condition can usually be treated by taking aspirin as well as getting plenty of rest, avoiding large meals, and drinking lots of nonalcoholic fluids (especially water). If it persists or worsens, you must return to a lower altitude. Other dangers of higher elevations include hypothermia and sun exposure, and these should be taken seriously. To avoid dehydration, drink water as often as possible.

Limit your exposure to the sun, especially during the first few days of your trip and, thereafter, between 11am and 2pm. Liberally apply sunscreen with a high protection factor. Remember that children need more protection than adults do.

It is important to monitor your children's health while in New Mexico. They are just as susceptible to mountain sickness, hypothermia, sunburn, and dehydration as you are.

Also, in arroyos—creek beds in the desert—flash floods can occur without warning. If water is flowing across a road, *do not* try to drive through it because chances are good the water is deeper and flowing faster than you think. Just wait it out. Arroyo floods don't last long.

Finally, if you're an outdoorsperson, be on the lookout for snakes—particularly rattlers. Avoid them. Don't even get close enough to take a picture (unless you have a very good zoom lens).

The most reliable hospitals in the area are **St. Vincent's Hospital,** 455

St. Michaels Dr. in Santa Fe (© **505/ 820-5250**), and **Presbyterian Hospital,** 1100 Central Ave. SE in Albuquerque (© **505/841-1234,** or 505/ 841-1111 for emergency service).

WHAT TO DO IF YOU GET SICK AWAY FROM HOME

If you worry about getting sick away from home, consider purchasing **medical travel insurance.** In most cases, your existing health plan will provide the coverage you need. See "Medical Insurance," above, for more information.

If you suffer from a chronic illness, consult your doctor before your departure. For conditions such as epilepsy, diabetes, or heart problems, wear a **MedicAlert identification tag** (© **800/825-3785;** www.medicalert. org), which will immediately alert doctors to your condition and give them access to your records through MedicAlert's 24-hour hot line.

Pack **prescription medications** in your carry-on luggage, and carry them in their original containers. Also bring along copies of your prescriptions in case you lose your pills or run out. And don't forget **sunglasses** and an extra pair of **contact lenses** or **prescription glasses.**

THE SAFE TRAVELER

Tourist areas as a rule are safe, but, despite recent reports of decreases in violent crime in Santa Fe, it would be wise to check with the tourist offices in Santa Fe, Taos, and Albuquerque if you are in doubt about which neighborhoods are safe. (See the "Orientation" sections in chapters 5, 6, and 7 for the names and addresses of the specific tourist bureaus.)

Remember that hotels are open to the public, and in a large hotel, security may not be able to screen everyone who enters. Always lock your room door; don't assume that once inside your hotel you are automatically safe and no longer need to be aware of your surroundings.

New Mexico has a higher-than-average reported incidence of rape. Women should not walk alone in isolated places, particularly at night.

6 Tips for Travelers with Special Needs

TRAVELERS WITH DISABILITIES

Most disabilities shouldn't stop anyone from traveling. There are more options and resources out there than ever before. Throughout New Mexico, measures have been taken to provide access for travelers with disabilities. Several bed-and-breakfasts have made one or more of their rooms completely wheelchair accessible. The **Information Center for New Mexicans with Disabilities** (© **800/552-8195** in New Mexico, or 505/272-8549 outside the state) accesses a database with lists of services ranging from restaurants and hotels to wheelchair rentals. It's a service of the **Developmental Disabilities Planning Council** (© **505/827-7590**). The *Access New Mexico* guide lists accessible hotels, attractions, and restaurants throughout the state. For more information, contact the **Governor's Committee on Concerns of the Handicapped,** 491 Old Santa Fe Trail, Lamy Building, Room 117, Santa Fe, NM 87503 (© **505/827-6465;** www.state.nm.us/ gcch/accessnm.htm). The chambers of commerce in Santa Fe and Taos will answer questions regarding accessibility in their areas. It is advisable to call hotels, restaurants, and attractions in advance to be sure that they are fully accessible.

ORGANIZATIONS

- **The MossRehab Hospital** (© **215/456-9603;** www.moss resourcenet.org) provides friendly, helpful phone assistance through its **Travel Information Service.**

- **The Society for Accessible Travel & Hospitality** (© 212/447-7284; fax 212/725-8253; www.sath.org) offers a wealth of travel resources for all types of disabilities, and informed recommendations on destinations, access guides, travel agents, tour operators, vehicle rentals, and companion services. Annual membership costs $45 for adults, $30 for seniors and students.
- **The American Foundation for the Blind** (© 800/232-5463; www.afb.org) provides information on traveling with Seeing Eye dogs.

PUBLICATIONS

- **Mobility International USA** (© 541/343-1284; www.miusa. org) publishes *A World of Options*, a 658-page book of resources, covering everything from biking trips to scuba outfitters, and a biannual newsletter, *MIUSA'S Global Impact.* Minimum donation $35.
- **Twin Peaks Press** (© 360/694-2462) publishes travel-related books for travelers with special needs.
- *Open World for Disability and Mature Travel* magazine, published by the Society for Accessible Travel & Hospitality (see above), is full of good resources and information. A year's subscription is $13 ($21 outside the U.S.).

GAY & LESBIAN TRAVELERS
Common Bond (© 505/891-3647) provides information and outreach services for Albuquerque's gay and lesbian community as well as referrals for other New Mexico cities. A recorded message on this phone line provides lists of bars and clubs, businesses, and publications, as well as health and crisis information and a calendar of events. Volunteers are on hand (generally in the evenings) to answer questions.

The **International Gay and Lesbian Travel Association** (**IGLTA;** © 800/448-8550 or 954/776-2626; fax 954/776-3303; www.iglta.org) links travelers up with gay-friendly hoteliers, tour operators, and airline and cruise-line representatives. It offers monthly newsletters, marketing mailings, and a membership directory that's updated once a year. Membership is $200 yearly, plus a $100 administration fee for new members.

PUBLICATIONS

- *Out & About* (© 800/929-2268 or 415/644-8044; www.outand about.com) offers guidebooks and a newsletter 10 times a year that is packed with solid information on the global gay and lesbian scene.
- *Spartacus International Gay Guide* and *Odysseus* are good, annual guidebooks focused on gay men, with some information for lesbians. You can get them from most gay and lesbian bookstores, or order them from **Giovanni's Room,** 1145 Pine St., Philadelphia, PA 19107 (© 215/923-2960; www.giovannisroom.com).
- *Gay Travel A to Z: The World of Gay & Lesbian Travel Options at Your Fingertips,* by Marianne Ferrari (Ferrari Publications), is a very good gay and lesbian guidebook series.

SENIOR TRAVEL
Mention the fact that you're a senior when you make your travel reservations. Although all of the major U.S. airlines except America West have canceled their senior discount and coupon book programs, many hotels still offer discounts for seniors. In most cities, people over the age of 60 qualify for reduced admission to theaters, museums, and other attractions, as well as discounted fares on public transportation.

Warning: Senior travelers are often more susceptible than others to changes in elevation and may experience heart or respiratory problems. Consult your physician before your trip.

Members of **AARP,** 601 E St., NW, Washington, DC 20049 (© **888/ 687-2277;** www.aarp.org), get discounts on hotels, airfares, and car rentals. AARP offers members a wide range of benefits, including *AARP: The Magazine* and a monthly newsletter. Anyone over 50 can join.

Alliance for Retired Americans, 888 16th St. NW, Suite 520, Washington, DC 20006 (© **800/333-7212;** www.retiredamericans.org), offers a newsletter six times a year and discounts on hotel and auto rentals.

Many reliable agencies and organizations target the 50-plus market. **Elderhostel** (© **877/426-8056;** www.elderhostel.org) arranges study programs for adults 55 and over (and a spouse or companion of any age) in the U.S. and in more than 80 countries around the world, with 13 sites within New Mexico. Most courses last 5 to 7 days in the U.S. (2–4 weeks abroad), and many include airfare, accommodations in university dormitories or modest inns, meals, and tuition. **ElderTreks** (© **800/741-7956;** www.eldertreks.com) offers small-group tours to off-the-beaten-path or adventure-travel locations, restricted to travelers 50 and older.

PUBLICATIONS

- The Albuquerque-based monthly tabloid *Prime Time* (© 505/880-0470) publishes a variety of articles aimed at New Mexicans 50 years and older.
- *101 Tips for Mature Travelers,* available from Grand Circle Travel (© **800/221-2610** or 617/350-7500; www.gct.com).
- *The 50+ Traveler's Guidebook* (St. Martin's Press).

- *Travel Unlimited: Uncommon Adventures for the Mature Traveler* (Avalon).
- *Unbelievably Good Deals and Great Adventures That You Absolutely Can't Get Unless You're Over 50* (McGraw-Hill), by Joann Rattner Heilman.

FAMILY TRAVEL

If you have enough trouble getting your kids out of the house in the morning, dragging them thousands of miles away may seem like an insurmountable challenge. But family travel can be immensely rewarding, giving you new ways of seeing the world through smaller pairs of eyes.

Be aware that family travel in northern New Mexico may be a little different from what you're accustomed to. You'll find few huge Disneylike attractions here. Instead, the draws are culture and the outdoors. Rather than spending time in theme parks, you may go white-water rafting down the Rio Grande, skiing at one of the many family-friendly areas, climbing a wooden ladder up to a cliff dwelling, or trekking through the wilderness with a llama.

If your brood is not very adventurous, don't worry. Some of the hotels and resorts listed in this book have inviting pools to laze around. Whatever your choice, northern New Mexico will offer your children a new perspective on the United States by exposing them to ancient ruins, Southwestern cuisine, and Hispanic and Native American cultures that they may not experience elsewhere.

To locate those accommodations, restaurants, and attractions that are particularly kid friendly, refer to the "Kids" icon throughout this guide.

Familyhostel (© **800/733-9753;** www.learn.unh.edu/familyhostel) takes the whole family, including kids ages 8 to 15, on moderately priced domestic and international learning vacations. Lectures, field trips, and sightseeing are guided by a team of academics.

PUBLICATIONS

- The Santa Fe quarterly *Tumble-weeds* (☎ **505/984-3171**) offers useful articles on family-oriented subjects in the Santa Fe area and a quarterly day-by-day calendar of family events. Free in locations all over Santa Fe or by mail for $15.
- Lynnell Diamond's *New Mexico for Kids* (Otter Be Reading Books), a learning activity guidebook for young people, is available at **Amazon.com**.
- *How to Take Great Trips with Your Kids* (The Harvard Common Press) is full of good advice that applies to travel anywhere.

WEBSITES

- **Family Travel Files** (www.the familytravelfiles.com) offers an online magazine and a directory of tours and tour operators for families.
- **Family Travel Forum** (www.family travelforum.com) is a comprehensive site that offers customized trip planning.
- **Family Travel Network** (www. familytravelnetwork.com) offers travel tips and reviews of family-friendly destinations, vacation deals, and other features.
- **Traveling Internationally with Your Kids** (www.travelwithyour kids.com) offers sound advice for traveling with children.

STUDENT TRAVEL

Always carry your student identification with you. Tourist attractions, transportation systems, and other services may offer discounts if you have appropriate proof of your student status. Don't be afraid to ask. A high school or college ID card or International Student Card will suffice.

Student-oriented activities abound on and around college campuses, especially at the University of New Mexico in Albuquerque. In Santa Fe, there are two small 4-year colleges: the College of Santa Fe and the liberal arts school St. John's College. Santa Fe Community College is a 2-year college that offers associate degrees.

STA Travel (☎ **800/781-4040;** www.sta.com or www.statravel.com) is the biggest student-travel agency in the world, although its bargain-basement prices are available to people of all ages. (*Note:* In 2002, STA Travel bought competitors **Council Travel** and **USIT Campus** after they went bankrupt. It's still operating some offices under the Council name, but they are owned by STA.) **Travel CUTS** (☎ **800/667-2887** or 416/614-2887; www.travelcuts.com) offers similar services for both Canadians and U.S. residents.

7 Getting There

BY PLANE

The **Albuquerque International Sunport** (☎ **505/842-4366** for the administrative offices; www.cabq.gov/airport; call the individual airlines for flight information) is the hub for travel to most parts of New Mexico. A secondary hub for southern New Mexico is **El Paso International Airport** (☎ **915/780-4700;** www.elpaso internationalairport.com) in western Texas. Both airports are served by **American** (☎ 800/433-7300), **America West** (☎ 800/235-9292), **Continental** (☎ 800/523-3273), **Delta** (☎ 800/221-1212), **Frontier** (☎ 800/432-1359), **Mesa** (☎ 800/637-2247), and **Southwest** (☎ 800/435-9792). Additional airlines serving Albuquerque include **Northwest** (☎ 800/225-2525), **United** (☎ 800/241-6522), and **US Airways** (☎ 800/428-4322).

In conjunction with United Airlines, commuter flights are offered to and from Santa Fe via Denver by **United Express,** which is operated by Great Lakes Aviation ℅ **800/241-6522.**

GETTING THROUGH THE AIRPORT

With the federalization of airport security, security procedures at U.S. airports are more stable and consistent than ever before. Generally, you'll be fine if you arrive at the airport **1 hour** before a domestic flight; if you show up late, tell an airline employee, and she'll probably whisk you to the front of the line.

Bring a **current, government-issued photo ID** such as a driver's license or passport. Keep your ID at the ready to show at check-in, the security checkpoint, and sometimes even the gate. (Children under 18 do not need government-issued photo IDs for domestic flights.)

In 2003, the TSA phased out **gate check-in** at all U.S. airports. And **e-tickets** have made paper tickets nearly obsolete. Passengers with e-tickets can beat the ticket-counter lines by using airport **electronic kiosks** or even **online check-in** from any computer with a printer. Online check-in involves logging on to your airline's website, accessing your reservation, and printing your boarding pass. If you're using a kiosk at the airport, bring the credit card you used to book the ticket or your frequent-flier card. Print your boarding pass from the kiosk and proceed to the security checkpoint with your pass and a photo ID. If you're checking bags or looking to snag an exit-row seat, you will be able to do so using most airline kiosks. **Curbside check-in** is also a good way to avoid lines, although a few airlines still ban curbside check-in; call before you go.

Security checkpoint lines are getting shorter than they were during 2001 and 2002, but some doozies remain. If you have trouble standing for long periods of time, tell an airline employee; the airline will provide a wheelchair. Speed up security by **not wearing metal objects** such as big belt buckles. If you've got metallic body parts, a note from your doctor can prevent a long chat with the security screeners. Keep in mind that only **ticketed passengers** are allowed past security, except for folks escorting children or travelers with disabilities.

Federalization has stabilized **what you can carry on** and **what you can't.** The general rule is that sharp things are out, nail clippers are okay, and food and beverages must be passed through the X-ray machine—but that security screeners can't make you drink from your coffee cup. Bring food in your carry-on rather than checking it, as explosive-detection machines used on checked luggage have been known to mistake food (especially chocolate, for some reason) for bombs. Travelers in the U.S. are allowed one carry-on bag, plus a "personal item" such as a purse, briefcase, or laptop bag. Carry-on hoarders can stuff all sorts of things into a laptop bag; as long as it has a laptop in it, it's still considered a personal item. The **Transportation Security Administration (TSA)** has issued a list of restricted items; check its website (www.tsa.gov) for details.

Airport screeners may decide that your checked luggage needs to be searched by hand. You can now purchase luggage locks that allow screeners to open and relock a checked bag if hand-searching is necessary. Look for Travel Sentry certified locks at luggage or travel shops and Brookstone stores (you can buy them online at www.brookstone.com). These locks, approved by the TSA, can be opened by luggage inspectors with a special code or key. For more information on the locks, visit www.travelsentry.org. If you use something other than TSA-approved locks, your lock will be cut off your suitcase if a TSA agent needs to hand-search your luggage.

FLYING FOR LESS: TIPS FOR GETTING THE BEST AIRFARE

Passengers sharing the same airplane cabin rarely pay the same fare. Travelers who need to purchase tickets at the last minute, change their itinerary at a moment's notice, or fly one-way often get stuck paying the premium rate. Here are some ways to keep your airfare costs down:

- Passengers who can book their ticket **far in advance,** who can **stay over Saturday night,** or who **fly midweek** or **at less-trafficked hours** may pay a fraction of the full fare. If your schedule is flexible, say so, and ask if you can secure a cheaper fare by changing your flight plans.
- You can also save on airfares by keeping an eye out for **promotional specials** or **fare wars,** when airlines lower prices on their most popular routes. You rarely see fare wars offered for peak travel times, but if you can travel in the off-months, you may snag a bargain.
- Search **the Internet** for cheap fares (see "Planning Your Trip Online," below).
- Join **frequent-flier clubs.** Accrue enough miles, and you'll be rewarded with free flights and elite status. It's free, and you'll get the best choice of seats, faster response to phone inquiries, and prompter service if your luggage is stolen, if your flight is canceled or delayed, or if you want to change your seat. You don't need to fly to build frequent-flier miles—**frequent-flier**

credit cards can provide thousands of miles for doing your everyday shopping.

- For many more tips about air travel, including a rundown of the major frequent-flier credit cards, pick up a copy of ***Frommer's Fly Safe, Fly Smart*** (Wiley Publishing, Inc.).

GETTING INTO TOWN FROM THE AIRPORT

Most hotels have courtesy vans to meet their guests and take them to their respective destinations. In addition, **Checker Airport Express** (© 505/765-1234) in Albuquerque runs vans to and from city hotels. Find their booth near the baggage claim area. In Santa Fe, **Roadrunner Shuttle** (© 505/424-3367) meets every flight and takes visitors anywhere in Santa Fe. **Las Cruces Shuttle Service** (© 800/288-1784) travels between the El Paso International Airport and Las Cruces.

BY CAR

Three interstate highways cross New Mexico. The north–south I-25 bisects the state, passing through Albuquerque and Las Cruces. The east–west I-40 follows the path of the old Route 66 through Gallup, Albuquerque, and Tucumcari in the north; while I-10 from San Diego crosses southwestern New Mexico until intersecting I-25 at Las Cruces.

See "Getting Around New Mexico," below, for information about driving in New Mexico.

BY BUS

The **public bus depot** in Albuquerque is located on 2nd Street at Lead (300 2nd St. SW). Contact **Texas, New Mexico, and Oklahoma** (TNM&O; © 505/242-4998) for information and schedules. Fares run about $11 to Santa Fe and $22 to Taos. However, the **bus stations** in

Santa Fe (858 St. Michael's Dr.; ✆ 505/471-0008) and Taos (5 miles south of the plaza at 1386 Paseo del Pueblo Sur; ✆ 505/758-1144) are several miles south of each city center. Because additional taxi or shuttle service is needed to reach most accommodations, travelers usually find it more convenient to pay a few extra dollars for an airport-to-hotel shuttle.

BY TRAIN

Amtrak has two routes through the state. Greyhound/Trailways bus lines provide through-ticketing for Amtrak between Albuquerque and El Paso.

You can get a copy of Amtrak's National Timetable from any Amtrak station, from travel agents, or by contacting Amtrak (✆ **800/USA-RAIL;** www.amtrak.com).

8 Escorted Tours, Package Deals & Special-Interest Vacations

Before you start searching for the lowest airfare, you may want to consider booking your flight as part of a travel package such as an escorted tour or a package tour. What you lose in adventure, you'll gain in time and money saved when you book accommodations, and maybe even food and entertainment, along with your flight.

PACKAGE TOURS FOR INDEPENDENT TRAVELERS

Package tours are not the same thing as escorted tours. With a package tour, you travel independently but pay a group rate. Packages usually include airfare, a choice of hotels, and car rentals, and packagers often offer several options at different prices. In many cases, a package that includes airfare, hotel, and transportation to and from the airport will cost you less than just the hotel alone would have, had you booked it yourself. That's because packages are sold in bulk to tour operators—who resell them to the public at a cost that drastically undercuts standard rates.

RECOMMENDED PACKAGE TOUR OPERATORS

One good source of package deals is the airlines and train companies themselves. Try **Southwest Airlines Vacations** (✆ **800/243-8372;** www.swavacations.com) and **Amtrak Vacations** (✆ **800/654-5748;** www.amtrakvacations.com).

Vacation Together (✆ **800/839-9851;** www.vacationtogether.com) enables you to search for and book packages offered by a number of tour operators and airlines. The **United States Tour Operators Association**'s website (www.ustoa.com) has a search engine that enables you to look for operators that offer packages to a specific destination. Travel packages are also listed in the travel section of your local Sunday newspaper. **Liberty Travel** (✆ **888/271-1584;** www.libertytravel.com), one of the biggest packagers in the Northeast, often runs full-page ads in Sunday papers. Or check ads in the national travel magazines, such as *Arthur Frommer's Budget Travel Magazine, Travel & Leisure, National Geographic Traveler,* and *Condé Nast Traveler.*

PROS & CONS OF PACKAGE TOURS

Packages can save you money because they are sold in bulk to tour operators, who sell them to the public. They offer group prices but allow for independent travel. The disadvantages are that you're usually required to make a large payment up front, you may end up on a charter flight, and you have to deal with your own luggage and with transfers between your hotel and the airport, if transfers are not included in the package price. Packages often don't allow for complete flexibility or a wide range of choices. For instance, you may prefer a quiet inn but have to settle for a popular chain hotel instead. Your choice of travel days may be limited as well.

ESCORTED TOURS (TRIPS WITH GUIDES)

Escorted tours are structured group tours, with a group leader. The price usually includes everything from airfare to hotels, meals, tours, admission costs, and local transportation.

RECOMMENDED ESCORTED TOUR OPERATORS

Not many escorted tours are offered in New Mexico. The tour companies I spoke to said most visitors to New Mexico have such disparate interests it's difficult to create packages to

please them. Still, a few tour companies can help you arrange a variety of day trips during your visit and can also secure lodging. **Tauck World Discovery** (© 800/788-7885; www.tauck.com), 10 Norden Place, Norwalk, CT 06855, offers weeklong cultural trips to northern New Mexico. **Destination Southwest, Inc.,** 20 First Plaza Galeria, Suite 212, Albuquerque, NM 87102 (© 800/ 999-3109 or 505/766-9068; www. destinationsouthwest.com), offers an escorted tour to the Albuquerque International Balloon Fiesta. **Rojotours & Services,** P.O. Box 15744, Santa Fe, NM 87506-5744 (© 505/ 474-8333), can help with a variety of day trips during your visit.

9 Planning Your Trip Online

SURFING FOR AIRFARES

The "big three" online travel agencies, **Expedia.com, Travelocity,** and **Orbitz,** sell most of the air tickets bought on the Internet. (Canadian travelers should try www.expedia.ca and www. travelocity.ca; U.K. residents can go to www.expedia.co.uk and www.opodo. co.uk.) Each has different business deals with the airlines and may offer different fares on the same flights, so it's wise to shop around. Expedia and Travelocity will also send you **e-mail notification** when a cheap fare becomes available to your favorite destination.

Also remember to check **airline websites,** especially those for low-fare carriers such as Southwest, JetBlue, AirTran, WestJet, or Ryanair, whose fares are often misreported or simply missing from travel agency websites. Even with major airlines, you can often shave a few bucks from a fare by booking directly through the airline and avoiding a travel agency's transaction fee. But you'll get these discounts only by **booking online:** Most airlines now offer online-only fares that even their phone agents know nothing about.

Great **last-minute deals** are available through free weekly e-mail services provided directly by the airlines. Most of these are announced on Tuesday or Wednesday and must be purchased online. Most are only valid for travel that weekend, but some (such as Southwest's) can be booked weeks or months in advance. Sign up for weekly e-mail alerts at airline websites or check mega-sites that compile comprehensive lists of last-minute specials, such as **Smarter Living** (www. smarterliving.com). For last-minute trips, **site59.com** and **lastminute travel.com** in the U.S. and **last minute.com** in Europe often have better air-and-hotel package deals than the major-label sites. A website listing numerous bargain sites and airlines around the world is **iTravelnet** (www.itravelnet.com).

If you're willing to give up some control over your flight details, use what is called an **"opaque" fare service** such as **Priceline** (www.priceline. com; www.priceline.co.uk for Europeans) or its competitor **Hotwire** (www.hotwire.com). Both offer rock-bottom prices in exchange for travel on a "mystery airline" at a mysterious time of day, often with a mysterious change of planes en route. The mystery airlines are all major, well-known carriers—and the possibility of being sent from Philadelphia to Chicago via Tampa is remote; the airlines' routing computers have gotten a lot better than they used to be. But your chances of getting a 6am or 11pm flight are pretty high. Hotwire tells you flight prices before you buy; Priceline usually has better deals than Hotwire, but you have to play their "name our price" game. The helpful folks at **BiddingForTravel** (www.biddingfor travel.com) do a good job of demystifying Priceline's prices and strategies. Priceline and Hotwire are great for flights within North America and between the U.S. and Europe. But for flights to other parts of the world, consolidators will almost always beat their fares. *Note:* In 2004 Priceline added non-opaque service to its roster. You now have the option to pick exact flights, times, and airlines from a list of offers—or opt to bid on opaque fares.

For much more about airfares and savvy air-travel tips and advice, pick up a copy of *Frommer's Fly Safe, Fly Smart* (Wiley Publishing, Inc.).

SURFING FOR HOTELS

Shopping online for hotels is generally done one of two ways: by booking through the hotel's own website or through an independent booking agency (or a fare-service agency like Priceline; see below). These Internet hotel agencies have multiplied in mind-boggling numbers of late, competing for the business of millions of consumers surfing for accommodations around the world. This competitiveness can be a boon to consumers who have the patience and time to shop and compare the online sites for good deals—but shop you must, for prices can vary considerably from site to site. And keep in mind that hotels

at the top of a site's listing may be there for no other reason than that they paid money to get the placement.

Of the "big three" sites, **Expedia. com** offers a long list of special deals and "virtual tours" or photos of available rooms so you can see what you're paying for (a feature that helps counter the claims that the best rooms are often held back from bargain-booking websites). **Travelocity** posts unvarnished customer reviews and ranks its properties according to the AAA rating system. Also reliable are **Hotels.com** and **Quikbook.com**. An excellent free program, **TravelAxe** (www.travelaxe.net), can help you search multiple hotel sites at once, even ones you may never have heard of—and conveniently lists the total price of a room, including the taxes and service charges. Another booking site, **Travelweb** (www.travelweb.com), is partly owned by the hotels it represents (including the Hilton, Hyatt, and Starwood chains) and is therefore plugged directly into the hotels' reservations systems—unlike independent online agencies, which have to fax or e-mail reservation requests to the hotel, a good portion of which get misplaced in the shuffle. More than once, travelers have arrived at the hotel, only to be told that they have no reservation. To be fair, many of the major sites are undergoing improvements in service and ease of use, and Expedia will soon be able to plug directly into the reservations systems of many hotel chains—none of which can be bad news for consumers. In the meantime, it's a good idea to **get a confirmation number** and **make a printout** of any online booking transaction.

In the opaque website category, **Priceline** and **Hotwire** are even better for hotels than for airfares; with both, you're allowed to pick the neighborhood and quality level of your hotel before offering up your money. Priceline's hotel product is much better at

Frommers.com: The Complete Travel Resource

For an excellent travel-planning resource, we highly recommend **Frommers.com** (www.frommers.com), voted Best Travel Site by *PC Magazine*. We're a little biased, of course, but we guarantee that you'll find the travel tips, reviews, monthly vacation giveaways, bookstore, and online-booking capabilities thoroughly indispensable. Among the special features are our popular **Destinations** section, where you'll get expert travel tips, hotel and dining recommendations, and advice on the sights to see for more than 3,500 destinations around the globe; the **Frommers.com Newsletter,** with the latest deals, travel trends, and money-saving secrets; our **Community** area featuring **Message Boards,** where Frommer's readers post queries and share advice (sometimes even our authors show up to answer questions); and our **Photo Center,** where you can post and share vacation tips. When your research is done, the **Online Reservations System** (www.frommers.com/book_a_trip) takes you to Frommer's preferred online partners for booking your vacation at affordable prices.

getting five-star lodging for three-star prices than at finding anything at the bottom of the scale. On the down side, many hotels stick Priceline guests in their least desirable rooms. Be sure to go to the BiddingForTravel website (see above) before bidding on a hotel room on Priceline; it features a fairly up-to-date list of hotels that Priceline uses in major cities. For both Priceline and Hotwire, you pay up front, and the fee is nonrefundable. *Note:* Some hotels do not provide loyalty program credits or points or other frequent-stay amenities when you book a room through an opaque online service.

SURFING FOR RENTAL CARS

For booking rental cars online, the best deals are usually found at **rental-car company websites,** although all the major online travel agencies also offer rental-car reservations services. **Priceline** and **Hotwire** work well for rental cars, too; the only "mystery" is which major rental company you get.

10 Getting Around New Mexico

BY CAR

If you plan to drive your own vehicle to and around New Mexico, give it a thorough road check before starting out. The state offers plenty of wide-open desert and wilderness spaces, and it's not fun to be stranded in the heat or cold with a vehicle that doesn't run. Check with your auto insurance company to make sure you're covered when out of state or when driving a rental car.

Gasoline is readily available at service stations throughout the state. Prices are cheapest in Albuquerque and 10% to 15% more expensive in more isolated communities. All prices are subject to the same fluctuations as elsewhere in the United States.

CAR RENTALS Car rentals are available in every sizable town and city in the state, always at the local airport, and usually also downtown. Widely represented agencies include **Alamo** (© 800/327-9633), **Avis** (© 800/831-2847), **Budget** (© 800/527-0700), **Dollar** (© 800/369-4226), **Enterprise** (© 800/325-8007), **Hertz**

(© 800/654-3131), and **Thrifty** (© 800/367-2277).

Drivers who need wheelchair-accessible transportation should call **Wheelchair Getaways of New Mexico** in Albuquerque (© **800/408-2626** or 505/247-2626; www.wheelchairgetaways.com); the company rents vans by the day, week, or month.

DRIVING RULES Unless otherwise posted, the **speed limits** on open roads are 75 miles (120km) per hour on interstate highways, 65 miles (105km) per hour on U.S. highways, and 55 miles (90km) per hour on state highways. The minimum age for drivers is 16. Safety belts are required for drivers and all passengers age 5 and over; children under age 5 riding in the front must be in an approved child seat secured by the seat belt; and children age 1 year or younger must ride in a child restraint seat in the back seat of the vehicle. Motorcyclists must wear helmets.

Indian reservations are considered sovereign nations, and they enforce their own laws. For instance, on the Navajo reservation (New Mexico's largest), it is prohibited to transport alcoholic beverages, to leave established roadways, or to travel without a seat belt.

EMERGENCIES The State Highway and Transportation Department has a toll-free hot line (© **800/432-4269**) that provides up-to-the-hour information on road closures and conditions.

Members of the **American Automobile Association** can get free emergency road service by calling AAA's emergency number (© **800/AAA-HELP**).

MAPS An excellent state highway map can be obtained from the **New Mexico Department of Tourism** (see "Visitor Information," earlier in this chapter). The American Automobile Association (AAA) supplies detailed state and city maps free to members (see "Emergencies," above).

BY PLANE

If you don't have a car and don't want to rent one, your options for getting around New Mexico are very limited. Two airlines fly between a selected number of cities and towns: **Rio Grande Air** (© 877/435-9742; www.riograndeair.com) flies between Albuquerque, Santa Fe, Farmington, Ruidoso, and Taos; and **Mesa Airlines** (© 800/637-2247; www.mesa-air.com) flies between Albuquerque, Farmington, Carlsbad, Clovis, Roswell, and Hobbs.

BY TRAIN

Amtrak's northern New Mexico line, the *Southwest Chief,* runs west–east and east–west once daily, with stops in Gallup, Grants, Albuquerque, Lamy (for Santa Fe), Las Vegas, and Raton. The *Sunset Unlimited* connects Lordsburg and Deming with El Paso, Texas, three times weekly each direction. Greyhound/Trailways bus lines provide through-ticketing for Amtrak passengers between Albuquerque and El Paso. For information, call © **800/USA-RAIL;** www.amtrak.com.

(*Warning*   **Drive Carefully**

US 491, formerly US 666, between Gallup and Shiprock, was at one time labeled America's "most dangerous highway" by *USA Today*. Though in recent years it has become safer, it still merits cautious driving. In addition, New Mexico has a high per capita rate of traffic deaths. Drive carefully!

11 Tips on Accommodations

No two travelers are alike; fortunately, New Mexico has a broad enough range of accommodations to satisfy even the most eccentric adventurer. If you long to be pampered, you'll find a few swanky resorts within the region, with a variety of luxury options such as pool and exercise facilities, golf, tennis, horseback riding, and spa treatments. Of course, none of it comes cheap. If you're looking to really savor the flavor of New Mexico, you may want to opt for one of its historic hotels. This may include a hacienda-style inn—an adobe one- or two-story structure often built around a courtyard. You'll also find some Victorian inns that have a frontier flavor. Within this variety of architecture, the amenities vary, from places with antique but workable plumbing and no television, to those with hot tubs and dataports in rooms.

In recent years, bed-and-breakfast inns (B&Bs) have proliferated in New Mexico. Though you can find traditional Victorian-style B&Bs here (and some lovely ones at that), complete with lacy bedding and elaborately carved accents, you can also choose from old hacienda–style homes or tiered adobe structures. All are comfortable and a few luxurious, with prices in the moderate to expensive range.

We all have those nights when only predictability will do. That's when a chain hotel comes in handy. You'll find all the major ones in New Mexico, though not quite everywhere. The small villages still shun such cookie-cutter establishments, but most everywhere else you can find them along the highways or in the town centers.

12 Suggested Itineraries

You may already have an idea of how you want to spend your time in New Mexico—power shopping, maybe, or time-traveling through ancient culture. But if you're not sure what to do, here are some suggestions, outlined in 1-week and 2-week segments. For each itinerary, I assume that you're flying into the Albuquerque International Sunport, the air transportation hub of the state.

CULTURE CRUISING: NORTHERN NEW MEXICO IN 1 WEEK

Most visitors to New Mexico keep their compass pointed to the north because that's where the greatest concentration of culture and beauty resides. With elevations upwards of 7,000 feet, the region can be cold in winter, but its beauty resonates through all four seasons (although spring is . . . well, bring your windbreaker). And usually, winter days are warm enough to convince you that you're still on a Southwestern vacation. However, if you just can't stand the idea of cold, consider the next itinerary, "Family Time: New Mexico for Kids and the Young at Heart in One Week," which takes you south, into the warmer lands.

If you arrive in Albuquerque on **day one** and have some energy after traveling, head to **Old Town,** where you can wander the **plaza,** peruse some shops, and, if you have time, head over to the **Albuquerque Museum of Art and History** and the **New Mexico Museum of Natural History and Science.** Finish the day with one of New Mexico's premier treats—an enchilada—at **Sadie's.** (See chapter 5 for information on the activities listed in this paragraph).

For **day two,** start out at the **Indian Pueblo Cultural Center,** and then head to the **Albuquerque Biological**

Park, both in the vicinity of **Old Town Plaza.** Next, head out to **Petroglyph National Monument,** west of town. In the late afternoon, find your way to Central Avenue, just south of Old Town, and drive east on **Route 66.** This takes you right through downtown, to the Nob Hill district and the Sandia Mountains foothills, respectively. Finish your day with a ride up the **Sandia Peak Tramway.** After you reach the top, you may want to hike along the crest. Ideally, you should ride up during daylight and ride down at night for a view of the city lights. You may even want to dine at **High Finance Restaurant and Tavern** at the top (see chapter 5).

On **day three,** strike out for the ghost towns and other sights along the **Turquoise Trail** to Santa Fe. This will put you in Santa Fe in time to do some sightseeing. Head straight to the **plaza,** the **Palace of the Governors,** and **St. Francis Cathedral.** Next, make your way over to the **Georgia O'Keeffe Museum.** Finish your day with an enchilada at **The Shed.** In the evening, depending on the season, you may want to take in some of Santa Fe's excellent arts, such as the **Santa Fe Opera,** the **Santa Fe Chamber Music Festival,** or **Shakespeare in Santa Fe.**

On **day four,** head up to Museum Hill, where you can take your pick from four very unique museums: the **Museum of International Folk Art,** the **Museum of Indian Arts & Culture,** the **Wheelwright Museum of the American Indian,** and the **Museum of Spanish Colonial Art.** You can have lunch at the Museum Hill Café. En route back to the plaza, take a stroll and do some shopping on Canyon Road. If you have any energy left, you may want to take a peek in the **Loretto Chapel Museum.** At sunset during the warmer months, you can enjoy a cocktail from atop the bell tower of the historic **La Fonda Hotel.**

Eat dinner at **Coyote Café** or **Santacafé,** or if you lingered over your shopping, stop in at **Geronimo** or **The Compound** on Canyon Road. If you like live music and dancing, head to the **Paramount Lounge.** (See chapter 6 for information on Santa Fe attractions, hotels, and restaurants.)

On **day five,** head out of town to **Bandelier National Monument,** and then continue north to Taos. On the way into Taos, stop at the **San Francisco de Asis church.** If you like music, head out to the **Sagebrush Inn** for some country-and-western music or to **Momentitos de la Vida** to hear some jazz. (See chapter 7 for information.)

For **day six,** spend your morning at **Taos Pueblo,** the **Millicent Rogers Museum,** and the **Rio Grande Gorge Bridge.** You can then ditch your car for the afternoon and step out on foot. Do some shopping around **Taos Plaza.** At cocktail hour, head to the **Adobe Bar** at The Historic Taos Inn or the **Anaconda Bar** at the new El Monte Sagrado. (Check out chapter 7.)

On your last day, **day seven,** after a leisurely morning, head south on the **High Road to Taos** (see chapter 6). You may want to spend the night at a bed-and-breakfast in **Chimayo** along the way, or, depending on your flight time the next morning, stay the night in Santa Fe or Albuquerque.

FAMILY TIME: NEW MEXICO FOR KIDS AND THE YOUNG AT HEART IN 1 WEEK

Although wonderful, northern New Mexico is not the most suitable vacationland for kids—unless they already have a credit card and a precocious interest in history and architecture. Some hearts are better suited to Wild West action and natural wonders than gourmet food and history. If you prefer a more active vacation, this 1-week trip is for you, whatever your age.

The climate in this region is fairly mild, but summers in the south can be quite hot.

After you arrive in Albuquerque on **day one,** devote some time to wandering around **Old Town Plaza.** Head to the **New Mexico Museum of Natural History and Science** and, if you have time, visit the **Albuquerque Biological Park.** Finish the day with an enchilada at Sadie's. Or, if you have time and energy, ride the **Sandia Peak Tramway.** (See chapter 5 for information on these attractions.)

On **day two,** head west about 70 miles to **Acoma Pueblo** (see chapter 9). Stop for lunch in Grants and visit the **New Mexico Mining Museum** (p. 273), where you can go underground in a simulated mine. Next, head south on NM 117 to **El Malpais** and **El Morro National Monuments** (see chapter 9), where you can stretch your legs on a short or long hike. Continue south through Quemado, and then turn east and drive to Socorro, where you can spend the night, or continue south to San Antonio, which has the nice B&B **Casa Blanca** (see chapter 10).

On **day three,** if it's wintertime, wake before dawn and head out to **Bosque del Apache National Wildlife Refuge** (see chapter 10), where you can watch thousands of cranes and snow geese take flight. (Even if it's not winter, you can still tour the refuge to see birds and wildlife and stretch your legs on a hike.) From the refuge, head east on US 380 to the **Valley of Fires Recreation Area** (see chapter 11), an amazing lava field. Your next stop is Carrizozo, where you can have New Mexico's best green chile cheeseburger at the **Outpost.** Continue east to **Capitan** and **Smokey Bear Historical State Park.** (See chapter 11 for more on these attractions.) Farther east, along the **Lincoln Loop,** you come to the **Lincoln historic district.** You

may want to spend the night there. Both of the excellent B&Bs rent casitas for families. You may need to get dinner in one of the cafes in Capitan, about 10 miles away. If you'd rather stay the night in Ruidoso, you can start the day four itinerary.

On **day four,** drive the rest of the Lincoln Loop, stopping at the **Hurd–La Rinconada Gallery** and then cruising into the mountains of **Ruidoso.** If you like to hike, stop at the Lincoln National Forest Ranger Station for directions to the many trails in the area. Otherwise, you may want to shop a little. If it's winter, you can ski at **Ski Apache.** Or, if you or your kids have any interest in horses, head over to **The Hubbard Museum of the American West.** In the evening, check out the **Flying J Ranch** for a chuck-wagon dinner and an Old-West show. Spend the night in Ruidoso. (See chapter 11 for information on the attractions in this paragraph.)

Day five takes you south out of Ruidoso, through the **Mescalero Apache Indian Reservation** on US 70 and NM 244. Just outside the reservation, you arrive in **Cloudcroft,** a darling mountain town with some good hiking and mountain biking. Next, head down the spectacularly scenic pass on NM 244 into **Alamogordo** to visit the **New Mexico Museum of Space History** and, one of the stars of this trip, **White Sands National Monument.** Spend the night in Alamogordo. (Chapter 11 gives you more information on these attractions.)

On **day six,** head east to **Carlsbad** to visit the **Living Desert Zoo & Gardens State Park.** Have lunch in Carlsbad, and then head out to the most spectacular sight in New Mexico, **Carlsbad Caverns National Park,** where you want to *walk* down into the cave rather than ride the elevator (trust me). Or, you may want to call ahead and schedule one of the guided tours. If it's summer when you visit, you may want to end a hot day at your hotel pool or, alternatively, at the **Riverwalk,** where the kids can swim and peddle paddleboats. (See chapter 11 for details.)

Spend your last day, **day seven,** taking a long cruise north to Albuquerque. Take US 285 to Roswell, where your kids can stock up on little-green-men stickers and see the **International UFO Museum and Research Center.** (The drive takes you across fairly barren plains.) History buffs may want to detour to Fort Sumner to see **Billy the Kid's grave,** but more importantly to see the tragedy commemorated at **Fort Sumner State Monument.** If you take this option, stop for a bite afterward at **Joseph's Restaurant & Cantina ("Joe's")** in Santa Rosa. (See chapter 11 for information on all these attractions except Joe's, which is included in chapter 8.)

Tip: Parents who are first-time visitors to New Mexico may want to trade the day one and day two schedules for a trip north to **Santa Fe** (see chapter 6) to take in the cultural sights there. You can then skim down I-25 and resume the itinerary in Socorro on the evening of day two.

THE WHOLE ENCHILADA: THE BEST OF NEW MEXICO IN 2 WEEKS

If you're fortunate enough to spend 2 weeks in New Mexico, you're in for a treat. The itinerary that I suggest is a counterclockwise loop that incorporates most of the two preceding itineraries.

But because you don't have to return to Albuquerque between the two, you have an added bonus.

For **days one through four,** follow the itinerary "Culture Cruising: Northern New Mexico in One Week," earlier in this chapter.

On **day five,** travel the High Road to Taos, following the directions in chapter 6. On the way into Taos, stop at the **San Francisco de Asis church.** If you like music, head out to the **Sagebrush Inn** for some country-and-western music or to **Momentitos de la Vida** to hear some jazz (see chapter 7).

Spend the morning of **day six** at **Taos Pueblo,** the **Millicent Rogers Museum,** and the **Rio Grande Gorge Bridge.** During the afternoon, do some shopping around the **Taos Plaza,** and then visit the **Kit Carson Home and Museum.** At cocktail hour, head to the **Adobe Bar** at The Historic Taos Inn. (See chapter 7 for information on these attractions.)

On **day seven,** get up very early and head west on a scenic drive to Chama, where you can spend the day riding the **Cumbres & Toltec Scenic Railroad** (see chapter 9). Be sure to check departure times for the train. Spend the night in Chama. On **day eight,** head to the **Chaco Culture National Historical Park** (see chapter 9), and spend the night in Grants.

On **days 9 through 14,** follow days two through seven in the "Family Time: New Mexico for Kids and the Young at Heart in 1 Week" itinerary, above, which concludes in Albuquerque.

13 The 21st-Century Traveler

INTERNET ACCESS AWAY FROM HOME

Travelers have a number of ways to check their e-mail and access the Internet on the road. Of course, using your own laptop or PDA gives you the most flexibility. But even if you don't have a computer, you can still access your e-mail and even your office computer from cybercafes.

WITHOUT YOUR OWN COMPUTER

It's hard nowadays to find a city that *doesn't* have a few cybercafes. Although there's no definitive directory for cyber-cafes—these are independent businesses, after all—two places to start looking are at **www.cybercaptive.com** and **www.cybercafe.com**.

Aside from formal cybercafes, most **youth hostels** nowadays have at least one computer you can get to the Internet on. And most **public libraries** across the world offer Internet access free or for a small charge. Avoid **hotel business centers** unless you're willing to pay exorbitant rates.

Most major airports now have **Internet kiosks** scattered throughout their gates. These kiosks, which you'll also see in shopping malls, hotel lobbies, and tourist information offices around the world, give you basic Web access for a per-minute fee that's usually higher than cybercafe prices. The kiosks' clunkiness and high price mean they should be avoided whenever possible.

To retrieve your e-mail, ask your **Internet service provider (ISP)** if it has a Web-based interface tied to your existing e-mail account. If your ISP doesn't have such an interface, you can use the free **mail2web** service (www.mail2web.com) to view and reply to your home e-mail. For more flexibility, you may want to open a free, Web-based e-mail account with **Yahoo! Mail** (www.mail.yahoo.com). (Microsoft's Hotmail is another popular option.) Your home ISP may be able to forward your e-mail to the Web-based account automatically.

If you need to access files on your office computer, look into a service called **GoToMyPC** (www.gotomypc.com). The service provides a Web-based interface for you to access and manipulate a distant PC from any-where—even a cybercafe—provided that your "target" PC is on and has an always-on connection to the Internet (such as with a cable modem or DSL). The service offers top-quality security, but if you're worried about hackers, use your own laptop rather than a cybercafe computer to access the GoToMyPC system.

WITH YOUR OWN COMPUTER

Wi-fi (wireless fidelity) is the buzz-word in computer access, and more and more hotels, cafes, and retailers are signing on as wireless "hotspots" from which you can get a high-speed connection without cable wires, net-working hardware, or a phone line (see below).

Most business-class hotels through-out the world offer dataports for lap-top modems, and a few thousand hotels in the U.S. and Europe now offer free high-speed Internet access using an Ethernet network cable.

In addition, major ISPs have **local access numbers** around the world, enabling you to go online by simply placing a local call. Check your ISP's website or call its toll-free number and ask how you can use your current account away from home and how much it will cost.

If you're traveling outside the reach of your ISP, you may be able to use the **iPass** network, which has dial-up numbers in most countries. You'll have to sign up with an iPass provider, which will then tell you how to set up your computer for your destination(s). For a list of iPass providers, go to www.ipass.com and click on "Individuals Buy Now." One solid provider is **i2roam** (www.i2roam.com; © **866/811-6209** or 920/235-0475).

Wherever you go, bring a **connection kit** of the right power and phone adapters, a spare phone cord, and a spare Ethernet network cable—or find out whether your hotel supplies them to guests.

USING A CELLPHONE

Just because your cellphone works at home doesn't mean it'll work elsewhere in the country (thanks to the fragmented U.S. cellphone system). It's a good bet that your phone will work in major cities. But take a look at your wireless company's coverage map on its website before heading out—T-Mobile, Sprint, and Nextel are particularly weak in rural areas. If you need to stay in touch at a destination where you know your phone won't work, **rent** a phone that does from **InTouch Global** (✆ 800/872-7626; www.intouchglobal.com) or a rental-car location, but be aware that you'll pay $1 a minute or more for airtime.

If you're venturing deep into national parks, you may want to consider renting a **satellite phone ("satphone"),** which is different from a cellphone in that it connects to satellites rather than ground-based towers. A satphone is more costly than a cellphone but works where there are no cellular signals and no towers. You can rent satphones from **Roadpost** (✆ 888/290-1606; www.roadpost.com) or **InTouch Global** (see above).

If you're not from the U.S., you'll be appalled at the poor reach of our **GSM (Global System for Mobiles) wireless network,** which is used by much of the rest of the world (see below). Your phone will probably work in most major U.S. cities; it definitely won't work in many rural areas. (To see where GSM phones work in the U.S., check out www.t-mobile.com/coverage/national_popup.asp.) And you may or may not be able to send SMS (text messaging) home—something Americans tend not to do anyway. Assume nothing—call your wireless provider and get the full scoop. In a worst-case scenario, you can always rent a phone; InTouch Global delivers to hotels.

14 Recommended Reading

Many well-known writers made their homes in northern New Mexico in the 20th century. In the 1920s, the most celebrated were **D. H. Lawrence** and **Willa Cather,** both short-term Taos residents. Lawrence, the romantic and controversial English novelist, spent time here between 1922 and 1925; he reflected on his sojourn in *Mornings in Mexico* and *Etruscan Places.* Lawrence's Taos period is described in *Lorenzo in Taos,* which his patron, Mabel Dodge Luhan, wrote. Cather, a Pulitzer-prizewinner famous for her depictions of the pioneer spirit, penned *Death Comes for the Archbishop,* among other works. This fictionalized account of the 19th-century Santa Fe bishop Jean-Baptiste Lamy was inspired by her stay in the region.

Many contemporary authors also live in and write about New Mexico. John Nichols, of Taos, whose *Milagro Beanfield War* was made into a Robert Redford movie in 1987, writes insightfully about the problems of poor Hispanic farming communities. Albuquerque's Tony Hillerman has for 2 decades woven mysteries around Navajo tribal police in books such as *Listening Woman* and *A Thief of Time.* (Robert Redford, this time as director, is making a movie version for PBS of each of Hillerman's novels, featuring the character Jim Chee.) In recent years, Sarah Lovett has joined his ranks with a series of gripping mysteries, most notably *Dangerous Attachments.* The Hispanic novelist Rudolfo Anaya's *Bless Me, Ultima* and Pueblo writer Leslie Marmon Silko's *Ceremony* capture the lifestyles of their respective peoples. A coming-of-age story, Richard Bradford's *Red Sky at Morning* juxtaposes the various cultures of New Mexico. Edward Abbey wrote of the desert environment and politics; *Fire on the Mountain,* set in New Mexico, is one of his most powerful works.

Excellent works about Native Americans of New Mexico include *The Pueblo Indians of North America* (Holt, Rinehart & Winston, 1970) by Edward P. Dozier and *Living the Sky: The Cosmos of the American Indian* (University of Oklahoma Press, 1987) by Ray A. Williamson. Also look for *American Indian Literature 1979–1994* (Ballantine, 1996), an anthology edited by Paula Gunn Allen.

For general histories of the state, try Myra Ellen Jenkins and Albert H. Schroeder's *A Brief History of New Mexico* (University of New Mexico Press, 1974) and Marc Simmons's *New Mexico: An Interpretive History* (University of New Mexico Press, 1988). In addition, Claire Morrill's *A Taos Mosaic: Portrait of a New Mexico Village* (University of New Mexico Press, 1973) does an excellent job of portraying the history of that small New Mexican town. I have also enjoyed Tony Hillerman's (ed.) *The Spell of New Mexico* (University of New Mexico Press, 1976) and John Nichols and William Davis's *If Mountains Die: A New Mexico Memoir* (Alfred A. Knopf, 1979). *Talking Ground* (University of New Mexico Press, 1996), by Santa Fe author Douglas Preston, tells of a contemporary horseback trip through Navajoland, exploring the native mythology. One of my favorite texts is *Enchantment and Exploitation* (University of New Mexico Press, 1985) by William deBuys. A new, very extensive book that attempts to capture the multiplicity of the region is *Legends of the American Southwest* (Alfred A. Knopf, 1997) by Alex Shoumatoff.

Enduring Visions: 1,000 Years of Southwestern Indian Art, by the Aspen Center for the Visual Arts (Publishing Center for Cultural Resources, 1969), and Roland F. Dickey's *New Mexico Village Arts* (University of New Mexico Press, 1990) are both excellent resources for those interested in Native American art. If you become intrigued with Spanish art during your visit to New Mexico, you'll find E. Boyd's *Popular Arts of Spanish New Mexico* (Museum of New Mexico Press, 1974) to be quite informative.

FAST FACTS: New Mexico

Area Code The telephone area code for all of New Mexico is **505,** though at press time plans were rumbling to add new ones in the state. No matter where you are in the state, if you're placing a call outside city limits, it's usually considered long distance, and you must use the 505 area code.

ATMs ATMs are ubiquitous in the cities of New Mexico. However, in the small mountain towns, they're scarce. **Cirrus** (© 800/424-7787; www.mastercard.com) and **PLUS** (© 800/843-7587; www.visa.com) are the two most popular ATM networks in the U.S. and in this region. Major statewide banks are **Bank of America** and **Wells Fargo.** They have ATMs, as do most other banks in the state. You can also find ATMs at some supermarkets and drive-throughs.

Business Hours **Offices** and **stores** are generally open Monday to Friday, 9am to 5pm, with many stores also open Friday night, Saturday, and Sunday in the summer season. Most **banks** are open Monday to Thursday, 9am to 5pm, and Friday, 9am to 6pm. Some may also be open Saturday morning. Most branches have ATMs available 24 hours. Call establishments for specific hours.

Car Rentals See "Getting Around New Mexico," earlier in this chapter.

Climate See "When to Go," earlier in this chapter.

Currency Exchange Foreign currency can be exchanged at any of the branches of **Bank of America.**

Driving Rules See "Getting Around New Mexico," earlier in this chapter.

Embassies and Consulates See "Fast Facts: For the International Traveler," in chapter 3.

Emergencies For emergency medical help or information, call the **New Mexico Medical Crisis Center** at © **505/277-3013.** The center is open 24 hours a day. In most cities, for **police, sheriff, fire department, or ambulance,** dial © **911** at any time; otherwise, dial © **0** and ask the operator to connect you.

Information See "Visitor Information," earlier in this chapter.

Internet Access See "The 21st-Century Traveler," earlier in this chapter.

Language Spanish is spoken often, particularly in the small villages. You'll also hear Native American languages—Navajo (the most widely spoken surviving North American Indian dialect), Apache, Tewa, Tiwa, Zuni, Tanoan, and Keresan.

Liquor Laws The legal drinking age is 21 throughout New Mexico. Bars may remain open until 2am Monday to Saturday and until midnight on Sunday. Wine, beer, and spirits are sold at licensed supermarkets and liquor stores, but there are no package sales on election days until after 7pm, and on Sundays before noon. It is illegal to transport liquor through most Native American reservations.

Newspapers & Magazines The ***Albuquerque Journal,*** published mornings, and the ***Albuquerque Tribune,*** published evenings, are widely available around the state. The ***El Paso Times*** is favored in southern New Mexico. National newspapers such as ***USA Today*** and the ***Wall Street Journal*** can be purchased in cities and major hotels. The state's favorite magazine is ***New Mexico*** (www.nmmagazine.com), a high-quality monthly published by the State Tourism and Travel Division since 1923. Check out my monthly "King of the Road" column in the magazine.

Pets Dogs, cats, and other small pets are accepted at some motels in most parts of the state. Some properties require owners to pay a deposit in advance. In this book, when a hotel or motel accepts pets, I've noted that.

Police In **any emergency,** dial © **911.** The number for the **New Mexico State Police** district office in Albuquerque is © **505/841-9256.**

Post Offices To find the nearest U.S. Post Office, dial © **800/275-8777.** The service will ask for your zip code and give you the closest post office address and hours.

Safety See "Insurance, Health & Safety," earlier in this chapter.

Taxes The amount of gross receipts tax varies from town to town, currently ranging from 5.13% to 6.94%, and is applied to purchases, including hotel bills. On top of this amount, local governments add their own lodging tax, which also varies throughout the state.

Time Zone New Mexico is on Mountain Standard Time, 1 hour ahead of the West Coast and 2 hours behind the East Coast. Daylight saving time is in effect from early April to late October.

Useful Telephone Numbers For **road information,** call ✆ **800/432-4269;** and for **emergency road service (AAA),** call ✆ **505/291-6600.**

Weather For **time** and **temperature,** call ✆ **505/247-1611.** To get **weather forecasts** on the Internet, go to **www.accuweather.com** and enter the local zip code.

3

For International Visitors

Howling coyotes and parched cow skulls, dusty cowboys and noble Native Americans—you've seen them in the movies, along with dreamy sunsets. Though the denizens and landscapes of the southwestern U.S. may seem familiar, for most the reality is quite different. This chapter will help you prepare for some of the uniquely American situations you are likely to encounter.

1 Preparing for Your Trip

ENTRY REQUIREMENTS

Check at any U.S. embassy or consulate for current information and requirements. You can also obtain a visa application and other information at the **U.S. State Department**'s website, at **www.travel.state.gov**.

VISAS The U.S. State Department has a **Visa Waiver Program** that allows citizens of certain countries to enter the United States without visas for stays of up to 90 days. At press time these included Andorra, Australia, Austria, Belgium, Brunei, Denmark, Finland, France, Germany, Iceland, Ireland, Italy, Japan, Liechtenstein, Luxembourg, Monaco, the Netherlands, New Zealand, Norway, Portugal, San Marino, Singapore, Slovenia, Spain, Sweden, Switzerland, and the United Kingdom. Citizens of these countries need only a valid passport and a round-trip air or cruise ticket in their possession upon arrival. Information is available from any U.S. embassy or consulate. Canadian citizens may enter the United States without visas; they need only proof of residence.

Citizens of all other countries must have a valid passport that expires at least 6 months later than the scheduled end of their visit to the United States, and a tourist visa, which may be obtained from any U.S. consulate.

To obtain a visa, the traveler must submit a completed application form (either in person or by mail) with a 1½-inch-square photo, and must demonstrate binding ties to a residence abroad. Usually you can obtain a visa at once or within 24 hours, but it may take longer from June through August. If you cannot go in person, contact the nearest U.S. embassy or consulate for directions on applying by mail. Your travel agent or airline office may also be able to provide you with visa applications and instructions. The U.S. consulate or embassy that issues your visa will determine whether you will be issued a multiple- or single-entry visa and any restrictions regarding the length of your stay.

British subjects can obtain up-to-date passport and visa information by calling the **U.S. Embassy Visa Information Line** (© 0891/200-290) or the **London Passport Office** (© 0990/210-410 for recorded information), or they can find the visa information on the **U.S. Embassy Great Britain** website (www.passport.gov.uk).

Irish citizens can obtain up-to-date passport and visa information through the **Embassy of USA Dublin,** 42 Elgin Rd., Dublin 4, Ireland (© 353/1-668-8777; http://dublin.usembassy.gov).

Australian citizens can obtain up-to-date passport and visa information by contacting the **U.S. Embassy Canberra,** Moonah Place, Yarralumla, ACT 2600 (© **02/6214-5600;** http://canberra.usembassy.gov) or by checking the **U.S. Diplomatic Mission** website, **http://usembassy-australia.state.gov/consular**.

Citizens of **New Zealand** can obtain up-to-date passport and visa information by calling the **U.S. Embassy New Zealand,** 29 Fitzherbert Terrace, Thorndon, Wellington, New Zealand (© **644/462-6000**), or get the information directly from the "Services to New Zealanders" section of the website **http://usembassy.org.nz**.

Canadians need only show proof of residence to enter the United States, but showing a passport is often the easiest and most convenient way to do this. You can pick up a passport application at any of the 28 regional passport offices or at most travel agencies. Applications, which must be accompanied by two identical passport-size photographs and proof of Canadian citizenship, are available at travel agencies throughout Canada or from the central **Passport Office,** Department of Foreign Affairs and International Trade, Ottawa, ON K1A 0G3 (© **800/567-6868;** www.dfait-maeci.gc.ca/passport). Processing takes 5 to 10 days if you apply in person and about 3 weeks by mail.

MEDICAL REQUIREMENTS
Unless you're arriving from an area known to be suffering from an epidemic (particularly cholera or yellow fever), inoculations or vaccinations are not required for entry into the United States. If you have a medical condition that requires **syringe-administered medications,** carry a valid signed prescription from your physician; the Federal Aviation Administration (FAA) no longer allows airline passengers to pack syringes in their carry-on baggage without documented proof of

medical need. If you have a disease that requires treatment with **narcotics,** you should also carry documented proof with you—smuggling narcotics aboard a plane is a serious offense that carries severe penalties in the U.S.

For **HIV-positive visitors,** requirements for entering the U.S. are somewhat vague and change frequently. According to the latest publication of *HIV and Immigrants: A Manual for AIDS Service Providers,* the Immigration and Naturalization Service (INS) doesn't require a medical exam for entry into the U.S., but INS officials may stop individuals because they look sick or because they are carrying AIDS/HIV medicine.

For up-to-the-minute information, contact **AIDSinfo** (© **800/448-0440,** or 301/519-6616 outside the U.S.; www.aidsinfo.nih.gov) or the **Gay Men's Health Crisis** (© **212/367-1000;** www.gmhc.org).

DRIVER'S LICENSES Foreign driver's licenses are mostly recognized in the U.S., although you may want to get an international driver's license if your home license is not in English.

CUSTOMS
WHAT YOU CAN BRING IN
Every visitor over 21 years of age may bring in, free of duty, the following: (1) 1 liter of wine or hard liquor; (2) 200 cigarettes, 100 cigars (but not from Cuba), or 3 pounds of smoking tobacco; and (3) $100 worth of gifts. These exemptions are offered to travelers who spend at least 72 hours in the United States and who have not claimed them within the preceding 6 months. It is altogether forbidden to bring into the country foodstuffs (particularly fruit, cooked meats, and canned goods) and plants (vegetables, seeds, tropical plants, and the like). Foreign tourists may bring in or take out up to $10,000 in U.S. or foreign currency with no formalities; larger

sums must be declared to U.S. Customs on entering or leaving, which includes filing form CM 4790. For more specific information regarding U.S. Customs and Border Protection, contact your nearest U.S. embassy or consulate, or the **U.S. Customs** office (✆ **202/927-1770**; www.customs.us treas.gov).

WHAT YOU CAN TAKE HOME

U.K. citizens returning from a non-E.U. country have a Customs allowance of: 200 cigarettes; 50 cigars; 250 grams of smoking tobacco; 2 liters of still table wine; 1 liter of spirits or strong liqueurs (over 22% volume); 2 liters of fortified wine, sparkling wine, or other liqueurs; 60cc (ml) of perfume; 250cc (ml) of toilet water; and £145 worth of all other goods, including gifts and souvenirs. People under 17 cannot have the tobacco or alcohol allowance. For more information, contact **HM Customs & Excise** at ✆ **0845/010-9000** (020/8929-0152 from outside the U.K.), or visit www.hmce.gov.uk.

For a clear summary of **Canadian** rules, request the booklet *I Declare,* issued by the **Canada Revenue Agency** (✆ **800/461-9999** in Canada, or 204/983-3500; www.ccra-adrc.gc.ca). Canada allows its citizens a C$750 exemption, and you're allowed to bring back duty-free 1 carton of cigarettes, 1 can of tobacco, 40 imperial ounces of liquor, and 50 cigars. In addition, you're allowed to mail to Canada gifts valued at less than C$60 a day, provided they're unsolicited and don't contain alcohol or tobacco (write on the package, "Unsolicited gift, under $60 value"). All valuables should be declared on the Y-38 form before departure from Canada, including serial numbers of valuables you already own, such as expensive foreign cameras. *Note:* The C$750 exemption can be used only once a year and only after an absence of 7 days.

The duty-free allowance in **Australia** is A$400 or, for those under 18, A$200. Citizens ages 18 and over can bring in 250 cigarettes or 250 grams of loose tobacco, and 1,125 milliliters of alcohol. If you're returning with valuables you already own, such as foreign-made cameras, you should file form B263. A helpful brochure available from Australian consulates or Customs offices is *Know Before You Go.* For more information, call the **Australian Customs Service** at ✆ **1300/363-263** or visit www.customs.gov.au.

The duty-free allowance for **New Zealand** is NZ$700. Citizens over 17 can bring in 200 cigarettes, 50 cigars, or 250 grams of tobacco (or a mixture of all three if their combined weight doesn't exceed 250g), plus 4.5 liters of wine and beer or 1.125 liters of liquor. New Zealand currency does not carry import or export restrictions. Fill out a certificate of export, listing the valuables you are taking out of the country; that way, you can bring them back without paying duty. Most questions are answered in a free pamphlet available at New Zealand consulates and Customs offices: *New Zealand Customs Guide for Travellers, Notice no. 4.* For more information, contact **New Zealand Customs Service,** The Customhouse, 17–21 Whitmore St., Box 2218, Wellington (✆ **0800/428-786** or 04/473-6099; www.customs.govt. nz).

HEALTH INSURANCE

Although it's not required of travelers, health insurance is highly recommended. Unlike many European countries, the U.S. does not usually offer free or low-cost medical care to its citizens or visitors. Doctors and hospitals are expensive, and in most cases they require advance payment or proof of coverage before they render their services. See "Insurance, Health & Safety," in chapter 2 for more information. Packages such as **Europ**

Assistance's "Worldwide Healthcare Plan" are sold by European automobile clubs and travel agencies at attractive rates. **Worldwide Assistance Services, Inc.** (© 800/821-2828; www.worldwideassistance.com) is the agent for Europ Assistance in the U.S.

Although lack of health insurance may prevent you from being admitted to a hospital in non-emergencies, don't worry about being left on a street corner to die: The American way is to fix you now and bill the living daylights out of you later.

INSURANCE FOR BRITISH TRAVELERS Most big travel agents offer their own insurance and will probably try to sell you their package when you book a holiday. Think before you sign. **Britain's Consumers' Association** recommends that you insist on seeing the policy and reading the fine print before buying travel insurance. **The Association of British Insurers** (© 020/7600-3333; www.abi.org.uk) gives advice by phone and publishes *Holiday Insurance,* a free guide to policy provisions and prices. You might also shop around for better deals: Try **Columbus Direct** (© 0845/330-8518; www.columbusdirect.net).

INSURANCE FOR CANADIAN TRAVELERS Canadians should check with their provincial health plan offices or call **Health Canada** (© 613/957-2991; www.hc-sc.gc.ca) to find out the extent of their coverage and what documentation and receipts they must take home in case they are treated in the United States.

MONEY

CURRENCY The U.S. monetary system is very simple: The most common **bills** are the $1 (colloquially, a "buck"), $5, $10, and $20 denominations. There are also $2 bills (seldom encountered), $50 bills, and $100 bills (the last two are usually not welcome as payment for small purchases).

The paper money was recently redesigned, making the famous faces adorning them disproportionately large. The old-style bills are still legal tender.

There are seven denominations of coins: 1¢ (1 cent, or a penny); 5¢ (5 cents, or a nickel); 10¢ (10 cents, or a dime); 25¢ (25 cents, or a quarter); 50¢ (50 cents, or a half dollar); the gold-colored "Sacagawea" coin worth $1; and, prized by collectors, the rare, older silver dollar.

Note: The "foreign-exchange bureaus" so common in Europe are rare even at airports in the United States and nonexistent outside major cities. It's best not to change foreign money (or traveler's checks denominated in a currency other than U.S. dollars) at a small-town bank or even a branch in a big city; in fact, leave any currency other than U.S. dollars at home—it may prove a greater nuisance to you than it's worth.

TRAVELER'S CHECKS Traveler's checks are widely accepted, but make sure they're denominated in U.S. dollars, as foreign-currency checks are often difficult to exchange. The three traveler's checks that are most widely recognized are **Visa, American Express,** and **Thomas Cook.** Be sure to record the numbers of the checks, and keep that information in a separate place in case they get lost or stolen. Most businesses are pretty good about taking traveler's checks, but you're better off cashing them in at a bank (in small amounts, of course) and paying in cash. Remember: You'll need identification, such as a driver's license or passport, to change a traveler's check.

CREDIT CARDS & ATMs Credit cards are the most widely used form of payment in the United States: **Visa** (Barclaycard in Britain), **MasterCard** (Eurocard in Europe, Access in Britain, Chargex in Canada), **American Express, Diners Club,** and **Discover.**

However, a handful of stores and restaurants do not take credit cards, so be sure to ask in advance. Most businesses display a sticker near their entrance to let you know which cards they accept. *Note:* Businesses may require a minimum purchase, usually around $10, to use a credit card.

It is strongly recommended that you bring at least one major credit card. You must have a credit or charge card to rent a car. Hotels usually require a credit-card imprint as a deposit against expenses, and in an emergency, a credit card can be priceless.

You'll find **automated teller machines (ATMs)** on just about every block—at least in almost every town—across the country. Some ATMs will allow you to draw U.S. currency against your bank and credit cards. Check with your bank before leaving home, and remember that you will need your personal identification number (PIN) to do so. Most ATMs accept American Express, MasterCard, and Visa, as well as ATM cards from other U.S. banks. Expect to be charged up to $3 per transaction if you're not using your own bank's ATM.

ATM cards with major credit card backing, known as **"debit cards,"** are now a commonly acceptable form of payment in most U.S. stores and restaurants. Debit cards draw money directly from your checking account. Some stores enable you to receive "cash back" on your debit-card purchases. This is one way around ATM fees.

SAFETY
GENERAL SUGGESTIONS Tourist areas as a rule are safe, but, despite recent reports of decreases in violent crime in many cities, it would be wise to check with the tourist offices in Santa Fe, Taos, and Albuquerque if you are in doubt about which neighborhoods are safe. (See the "Orientation" sections in chapters 5, 6, and 7 for the names and addresses of the specific tourist bureaus.)

Remember that hotels are open to the public, and in a large hotel, security may not be able to screen everyone who enters. Always lock your room door; don't assume that once inside your hotel you are automatically safe and no longer need to be aware of your surroundings.

Be aware that New Mexico has a fairly high reported incidence of rape. Women should not walk alone in isolated places, particularly at night.

DRIVING SAFETY Question your rental agency about personal safety, or ask for a brochure of traveler safety tips when you pick up your car. Obtain written directions, or a map with the route clearly marked, from the agency to show you how to get to your destination. (Many agencies now offer the option of renting a cellphone for the duration of your car rental; check with the rental agent when you pick up the car. Otherwise, contact **InTouch USA** at © 800/872-7626 or www.intouchusa.com for short-term cellphone rental.) And, if possible, arrive and depart during daylight.

In recent years, carjacking, a crime that targets both cars and drivers, has been on the rise in all U.S. cities. If you exit a highway into a questionable neighborhood, leave the area as quickly as possible. If you have an accident, even on the highway, stay in your car with the doors locked until you are able to assess the situation or until the police arrive. If you are involved in a minor accident with no injuries and the situation appears to be suspicious, motion to the other driver to follow you to the nearest police precinct or well-lit service station.

If you see someone on the road who indicates a need for help, do not stop.

Take note of the location, drive to a well-lighted area, and telephone the police by dialing © **911.**

Also, make sure that you have enough fuel in your tank to reach your intended destination, so that you're not forced to look for a service station in an unfamiliar and possibly unsafe neighborhood—especially at night.

2 Getting to the U.S.

AIRLINE DISCOUNTS   The smart traveler can find numerable ways to reduce the price of a plane ticket simply by taking time to shop around. For example, travelers from overseas can take advantage of the **APEX (Advance-Purchase Excursion)** fares offered by all the major international carriers. British travelers should check out **British Airways** (© 0845/77-333-77 in the U.K., or 800/247-9297 in the U.S.; www.britishairways.com), which offers direct flights from London to New York and to Los Angeles, as does **Virgin Atlantic Airways** (© 0870/380-2007 in the U.K., or 800/862-8621 in the U.S.; www.virgin-atlantic.com). Canadian readers might book flights on **Air Canada** (© 888/247-2262; www.aircanada.ca), which offers service from Toronto, Montreal, and Calgary to New York and Los Angeles. In addition, many other international carriers serve the New

York and Los Angeles airports, including **Air France** (© 800/237-2747; www.airfrance.com), **Alitalia** (© 800/223-5730; www.alitalia.com), **Japan Airlines** (© 800/525-3663; www.jal.co.jp/en), **Lufthansa** (© 800/645-3880; www.lufthansa.com), and **Qantas** (© 300/650-729 in Australia, and 800/227-4500 in the U.S.; www.qantas.com). **SAS** (© 800/221-2350; www.scandinavian.net) serves New York, Chicago, and Seattle, but not Los Angeles. Connecting flights to New Mexico can be obtained at the major U.S. airports mentioned above. For more money-saving airline advice, see "Getting There," in chapter 2.

IMMIGRATION AND CUSTOMS CLEARANCE   Visitors arriving by air, no matter what the port of entry, should cultivate patience and resignation before setting foot on U.S. soil. Getting through immigration control can take as long as 2 hours, especially

Tips Prepare to Be Fingerprinted

Starting in January 2004, many international visitors traveling on visas to the United States will be photographed and fingerprinted at Customs in a new program created by the Department of Homeland Security called **US-VISIT.** Non–U.S. citizens arriving at airports and on cruise ships must undergo an instant background check as part of the government's ongoing efforts to deter terrorism by verifying the identity of incoming and outgoing visitors. Exempt from the extra scrutiny are visitors entering by land or those from 28 countries (mostly in Europe) that don't require visas for short-term visits. For more information, go to the **Department of Homeland Security** website, at **www.dhs.gov/dhspublic.**

on summer weekends, so be sure to carry this guidebook or something else to read. This is especially true in the aftermath of the September 11, 2001, terrorist attacks.

People traveling by air from Canada, Bermuda, and certain countries in the Caribbean can sometimes clear Customs and Immigration at the point of departure, which is much quicker.

Travelers arriving by car or by rail from Canada will find that the border-crossing formalities are more streamlined.

For further information about transportation to Albuquerque, Santa Fe, and Taos, see "Orientation" in chapters 5, 6, and 7, respectively.

3 Getting Around the U.S.

BY PLANE Some large airlines (for example, Northwest and Delta) offer travelers on their transatlantic or transpacific flights special discount tickets under the name **Visit USA,** allowing mostly one-way travel from one U.S. destination to another at very low prices. These discount tickets are not on sale in the United States and must be purchased abroad in conjunction with your international ticket. This system is the best, easiest, and fastest way to see the United States at low cost. You should obtain information well in advance from your travel agent or the office of the airline concerned because the conditions attached to these discount tickets can be changed without advance notice.

BY TRAIN International visitors (excluding those from Canada) can also buy a **USA Rail Pass,** good for 15 or 30 days of unlimited travel on **Amtrak** (© **800/USA-RAIL;** www. amtrak.com). The pass is available through many overseas travel agents. Prices in 2004 for a 15-day pass were $295 off-peak, $440 peak; a 30-day pass costs $385 off-peak, $550 peak. With a foreign passport, you can also buy passes at some Amtrak offices in the United States, including locations in San Francisco, Los Angeles, Chicago, New York, Miami, Boston, and Washington, D.C. Reservations are generally required and should be made for each part of your trip as early

as possible. Regional rail passes are also available.

BY BUS Although bus travel can be an economical form of public transit for short hops between U.S. cities, it can also be slow and uncomfortable—certainly not an option for everyone (particularly when Amtrak, which is far more luxurious, offers similar rates). **Greyhound/Trailways** (© **800/ 231-2222;** www.greyhound.com), the sole nationwide bus line, offers an **International Ameripass** that must be purchased before coming to the United States, or by phone through the Greyhound International Office at the Port Authority Bus Terminal in New York City (© **212/971-0492**). The pass can be obtained from foreign travel agents or through Greyhound's website (order at least 21 days before your departure to the U.S.) and costs less than the domestic version. You can get more info about the pass from the website or by calling © **402/330-8552.** In addition, special rates are available for seniors and students.

BY CAR Unless you plan to spend the bulk of your vacation time in a city where walking is the best and easiest way to get around (such as New York City or New Orleans), the most cost-effective, convenient, and comfortable way to travel around the United States is by car. The interstate highway system connects cities and towns all over the country; in addition to these high-speed, limited-access roadways, there's an extensive network of federal, state, and local highways and roads. Some of the national car-rental companies include **Alamo** (✆ 800/462-5266; www.alamo.com), **Avis** (✆ 800/230-4898; www.avis.com), **Budget** (✆ 800/527-0700; www.budget.com), **Dollar** (✆ 800/800-3665; www.dollar.com), **Hertz** (✆ 800/654-3131; www.hertz.com), **National** (✆ 800/227-7368; www.nationalcar.com), and **Thrifty** (✆ 800/847-4389; www.thrifty.com).

If you plan to rent a car in the United States, you probably won't need the services of an additional automobile organization. If you're planning to buy or borrow a car, automobile-association membership is recommended. **AAA, the American Automobile Association** (✆ 800/222-4357), is the country's largest auto club and supplies its members with maps, insurance, and, most importantly, emergency road service. The cost of joining runs from $63 for singles to $87 for two members, but if you're a member of a foreign auto club with reciprocal arrangements, you can enjoy free AAA service in America.

For information on renting cars in the United States, see "Automobile Organizations" and "Automobile Rentals" in "Fast Facts: For the International Traveler," below; "By Car" in "Getting There," in chapter 2; and "By Car" in "Getting Around," in chapters 5, 6, and 7.

FAST FACTS: For the International Traveler

Automobile Organizations Auto clubs supply maps, suggested routes, guidebooks, accident and bail-bond insurance, and emergency road service. The **American Automobile Association (AAA)** is the major auto club in the United States. If you belong to an auto club in your home country, inquire about AAA reciprocity before you leave. You may be able to join AAA even if you're not a member of a reciprocal club; to inquire, call AAA (✆ **800/222-4357**). AAA is actually an organization of regional auto clubs; so look under "AAA Automobile Club" in the White Pages of the telephone directory. AAA has a nationwide emergency road service telephone number: ✆ **800/AAA-HELP.**

In addition, some automobile-rental agencies now provide many of these same services. Inquire about their availability when you rent a car.

Automobile Rentals To rent a car you need a major credit card and a valid driver's license. In addition, you usually need to be at least 25 years old (some companies do rent to younger people but add a daily surcharge). Be sure to return your car with the same amount of gas you started with; rental companies charge excessive prices for gasoline. See "By Car" in "Getting Around," in chapters 5, 6, and 7, for the phone numbers of car-rental companies in Albuquerque, Santa Fe, and Taos, respectively.

Business Hours See "Fast Facts," in chapters 5, 6, and 7.

Climate See "When to Go," in chapter 2.

Currency Exchange You'll find currency-exchange services at major airports with international service. Elsewhere, they may be quite difficult to come by. In the United States, a very reliable choice is **Thomas Cook Currency Services, Inc.** It sells commission-free foreign and U.S. traveler's checks, drafts, and wire transfers. Its rates are competitive, and the service is excellent. Thomas Cook maintains several offices in New York City, including one at 511 Madison Ave. For the locations and hours of offices nationwide, call ℂ 800/287-7362.

For Albuquerque, Santa Fe, and Taos banks that handle foreign-currency exchange, see the "Fast Facts" sections in chapters 5, 6, and 7, respectively.

Drinking Laws The legal age for purchase and consumption of alcoholic beverages is 21; proof of age is required and often requested at bars, nightclubs, and restaurants, so it's always a good idea to bring ID when you go out. Beer and wine often can be purchased in supermarkets, but liquor laws vary from state to state. In New Mexico, major supermarkets and liquor stores sell beer, wine, and liquor.

Do not carry open containers of alcohol in your car or any public area that isn't zoned for alcohol consumption. The police can fine you on the spot. And nothing will ruin your trip faster than getting a citation for DUI ("driving under the influence"), so don't even think about driving while intoxicated.

Electricity Like Canada, the United States uses 110–120 volts AC (60 cycles), compared to 220–240 volts AC (50 cycles) in most of Europe, Australia, and New Zealand. If your small appliances use 220–240 volts, you'll need a 110-volt transformer and a plug adapter with two flat parallel pins to operate them here. Downward converters that change 220–240 volts to 110–120 volts are difficult to find in the United States, so bring one with you.

Embassies & Consulates All embassies are located in the nation's capital, Washington, D.C. Some consulates are located in major U.S. cities, and most nations have missions to the United Nations in New York City. If your country isn't listed below, call for directory information in Washington, D.C. (ℂ 202/555-1212) or visit **www.embassy.org/embassies**.

The embassy of **Australia** is at 1601 Massachusetts Ave. NW, Washington, DC 20036 (ℂ **202/797-3000**; www.austemb.org). There are consulates in New York, Honolulu, Houston, Los Angeles, and San Francisco.

The embassy of **Canada** is at 501 Pennsylvania Ave. NW, Washington, DC 20001 (ℂ **202/682-1740**; www.canadianembassy.org). Other Canadian consulates are in Buffalo, Detroit, Los Angeles, New York, and Seattle.

The embassy of **Ireland** is at 2234 Massachusetts Ave. NW, Washington, DC 20008 (ℂ **202/462-3939**; www.irelandemb.org). Irish consulates are in Boston, Chicago, New York, and San Francisco.

The embassy of **Japan** is at 2520 Massachusetts Ave. NW, Washington, DC 20008 (ℂ **202/238-6700**; www.embjapan.org). Japanese consulates are located in many cities, including Atlanta, Boston, Detroit, New York, San Francisco, and Seattle.

The embassy of **New Zealand** is at 37 Observatory Circle NW, Washington, DC 20008 (ℂ **202/328-4800**; www.nzemb.org). New Zealand consulates are in Los Angeles, Salt Lake City, San Francisco, and Seattle.

The embassy of the **United Kingdom** is at 3100 Massachusetts Ave. NW, Washington, DC 20008 (ℂ **202/462-1340**; www.britainusa.com). Other British consulates are in Atlanta, Boston, Chicago, Cleveland, Houston, Los Angeles, New York, San Francisco, and Seattle.

Emergencies Call ℂ **911** to report a fire, call the police, or get an ambulance anywhere in the United States. This is a toll-free call. (No coins are required at public telephones.)

If you encounter serious problems, contact **Travelers Aid International** (℡ **202/546-1127;** www.travelersaid.org) to help direct you to a local branch. This nationwide, nonprofit, social-service organization geared to helping travelers in difficult straits offers services that might include reuniting families separated while traveling, providing food and/or shelter to people stranded without cash, or even emotional counseling. If you're in trouble, seek out Travelers Aid.

Gasoline (Petrol) Petrol is known as gasoline (or simply "gas") in the United States, and petrol stations are known as both gas stations and service stations. Taxes are already included in the printed price of gas. One U.S. gallon equals 3.8 liters or 0.83 imperial gallons. There are usually several grades (and price levels) of gasoline available at most gas stations, and their names change from company to company. Unleaded gas with the highest octane ratings is the most expensive; however, most rental cars take the least expensive—"regular" unleaded gas.

Most gas stations are essentially self-service, although some offer higher-priced full service as well. Late- or all-night stations are usually self-service only.

Holidays Banks, government offices, post offices, and many stores, restaurants, and museums are closed on the following legal national holidays: January 1 (New Year's Day), the third Monday in January (Martin Luther King, Jr., Day), the third Monday in February (Presidents' Day, Washington's Birthday), the last Monday in May (Memorial Day), July 4 (Independence Day), the first Monday in September (Labor Day), the second Monday in October (Columbus Day), November 11 (Veterans' Day/Armistice Day), the fourth Thursday in November (Thanksgiving Day), and December 25 (Christmas). Also, the Tuesday following the first Monday in November is Election Day and is a federal government holiday in presidential-election years (held every 4 years, and next in 2008).

Internet Access Most city libraries in New Mexico have computers on which visitors can access the Internet for a small fee. In a few cities you'll find cybercafes and other businesses that offer service for a fee. See the "Fast Facts" sections in chapters 5, 6, and 7.

Legal Aid If you are "pulled over" for a minor infraction (such as speeding), never attempt to pay the fine directly to a police officer; this could be construed as attempted bribery, which is a serious crime. Pay fines by mail or directly into the hands of the clerk of the court. If you're accused of a serious offense, say and do nothing before consulting a lawyer. In the U.S. the burden is on the state to prove a person's guilt beyond a reasonable doubt, and everyone has the right to remain silent, whether he or she is suspected of a crime or actually arrested. Once arrested, a person can make one telephone call to a party of his or her choice. Call your embassy or consulate.

Mail If you aren't sure what your address will be in the United States, mail can be sent to you, in your name, **c/o General Delivery** at the main post office of the city or region where you expect to be. (Call ℡ **800/275-8777** in the U.S. for information on the nearest post office.) The addressee must pick up mail in person and must produce proof of identity (such as driver's license or passport). Most post offices will hold your mail for up to 1 month and are open Monday to Friday from 8am to 6pm and Saturday from 9am to 3pm.

Generally found at intersections, **mailboxes** are blue with a red-and-white stripe and carry the inscription "U.S. Mail." If your mail is addressed to a U.S. destination, don't forget to include the five-digit **postal code** (or zip code) after the two-letter abbreviation of the state to which the mail is addressed. This is essential for prompt delivery.

At press time, domestic **postage rates** were 23¢ for a postcard and 37¢ for a letter. For international mail, a first-class letter of up to ½ ounce costs 80¢ (60¢ to Canada and Mexico); a first-class postcard costs 70¢ (50¢ to Canada and Mexico); and a preprinted postal aerogramme costs 70¢.

Measurements See the chart on the inside front cover of this book for details on converting metric measurements to U.S. equivalents.

Newspapers & Magazines National newspapers include the *New York Times, USA Today,* and the *Wall Street Journal.* National news weeklies include *Newsweek, Time,* and *U.S. News and World Report.* In large cities, most newsstands offer a small selection of the most popular foreign periodicals and newspapers, such as the *Economist* and *Le Monde.* For information on local publications, see the "Fast Facts" sections in chapters 5, 6, and 7.

Radio & Television Audiovisual media, with six coast-to-coast networks—ABC, CBS, NBC, Fox, the Public Broadcasting System (PBS), and the cable network CNN—play a major part in American life. In big cities, viewers have a choice of several dozen channels (including basic cable), most of them transmitting 24 hours a day, not counting the pay-TV channels that show recent movies or sports events. All options are usually indicated on your hotel TV set. You'll also find a wide choice of local radio stations, both AM and FM, each broadcasting particular kinds of talk shows and/or music—classical, country, jazz, pop, gospel—punctuated by news broadcasts and frequent commercials. For information on local stations, see the "Fast Facts" sections in chapters 5, 6, and 7.

Safety See "Safety" in "Preparing for Your Trip," earlier in this chapter.

Taxes The United States has no value-added tax (VAT) or other indirect tax at the national level. Every state, county, and city has the right to levy its own local tax on all purchases, including hotel and restaurant checks, airline tickets, and so on. For information on taxes in Santa Fe, Taos, and Albuquerque, see the "Fast Facts" sections in chapters 5, 6, and 7.

Telephone, Telegraph, Telex & Fax The telephone system in the United States is run by private corporations, so rates, especially for long-distance service and operator-assisted calls, can vary widely. Generally, hotel surcharges on long-distance and local calls are astronomical, so you're usually better off using a **public pay telephone,** which you'll find clearly marked in most public buildings and private establishments as well as on the street. Convenience grocery stores and gas stations always have them. Many convenience groceries and packaging services sell **prepaid calling cards** in denominations up to $50; using these can be the least expensive way to call home. Many public phones at airports and other locations now accept American Express, MasterCard, and Visa credit cards. **Local**

calls made from public pay phones in most locales cost either 25¢ or 35¢. Pay phones do not accept pennies, and few will take anything larger than a quarter.

You may want to look into leasing a cellphone for the duration of your trip. For information, see "Using a Cellphone" under "The 21st-Century Traveler," in chapter 2.

Most long-distance and international calls can be dialed directly from any phone. **For calls within the United States and to Canada,** dial 1 followed by the area code and the seven-digit number. **For other international calls,** dial 011 followed by the country code, city code, and the telephone number of the person you are calling.

Calls to area codes **800, 888, 877,** and **866** are toll-free. However, calls to numbers in area codes **700** and **900** (chat lines, bulletin boards, "dating" services, and so on) can be very expensive—usually a charge of 95¢ to $3 or more per minute, and they sometimes have minimum charges that can run as high as $15 or more.

For **reversed-charge or collect calls,** and for person-to-person calls, dial 0 (zero, not the letter O) followed by the area code and number you want; an operator will then come on the line, and you should specify that you are calling collect, or person-to-person, or both. If your operator-assisted call is international, ask for the overseas operator.

For **local directory assistance** ("information"), dial ✆ 411; for **long-distance information,** dial 1, then the appropriate area code and 555-1212.

Telegraph and telex services are provided primarily by Western Union. You can bring your telegram into the nearest Western Union office (there are hundreds across the country) or dictate it over the phone (✆ 800/325-6000). You can also telegraph money, or have it telegraphed to you, very quickly over the Western Union system, but this service can cost as much as 15% to 20% of the amount sent.

Most hotels have **fax machines** available for guest use (be sure to ask about the charge to use it). Many hotel rooms are even wired for guests' fax machines. A less expensive way to send and receive faxes may be at stores such as **The UPS Store** (formerly Mail Boxes Etc.), a national chain of retail packing service shops. (Look in the Yellow Pages directory under "Packing Services.")

There are two kinds of telephone directories in the United States. The so-called **White Pages** list private households and business subscribers in alphabetical order. The inside front cover lists emergency numbers for police, fire, ambulance, the Coast Guard, poison-control center, crime-victims hot line, and so on. The first few pages tell you how to make long-distance and international calls, complete with country codes and area codes. Government numbers are usually printed on blue paper within the White Pages. Printed on yellow paper, the so-called **Yellow Pages** list all local services, businesses, industries, and houses of worship, according to activity, with an index at the front or back. (Drugstores/pharmacies and restaurants are also generally listed by geographic location.) The Yellow Pages also include city plans or detailed area maps, postal zip codes, public transportation routes, and local coupons.

Time The continental United States is divided into **four time zones:** Eastern Standard Time (EST), Central Standard Time (CST), Mountain Standard Time (MST), and Pacific Standard Time (PST). Alaska and Hawaii have their own zones. For example, noon in New York City (EST) is 11am in Chicago (CST), 10am in Santa Fe (MST), 9am in Los Angeles (PST), 8am in Anchorage (AST), and 7am in Honolulu (HST).

New Mexico is on MST, 7 hours behind Greenwich Mean Time. **Daylight saving time** is in effect from the first Sunday in April through the last Saturday in October (actually, the change is made at 2am on Sun), except in parts of Arizona (the Navajo reservation *does* observe daylight saving time; the rest of the state does not), Hawaii, part of Indiana, and Puerto Rico. Daylight saving time moves the clock 1 hour ahead of standard time. (Americans use the adage "Spring forward, fall back" to remember which way to change their clocks and watches.)

Tipping Tips are a very important part of certain workers' income, and gratuities are the standard way of showing appreciation for services provided. Tipping is so ingrained in the American way of life that the annual income tax of tip-earning service personnel is based on how much they should have received in light of their employers' gross revenues. Accordingly, they may have to pay tax on a tip you didn't actually give them. (Tipping is certainly not compulsory if the service is poor!)

Here are some rules of thumb: In hotels, tip **bellhops** at least $1 per bag ($2–$3 if you have a lot of luggage) and tip the **chamber staff** $1 to $2 per day (more if you've left a disaster area for him or her to clean up). Tip the **doorman** or **concierge** only if he or she has provided you with some specific service (for example, calling a cab for you or obtaining difficult-to-get theater tickets). Tip the **valet-parking attendant** $1 every time you get your car.

In restaurants, bars, and nightclubs, tip **service staff** 15% to 20% of the check, tip **bartenders** 10% to 15%, tip **checkroom attendants** $1 per garment, and tip **valet-parking attendants** $1 per vehicle.

For other service personnel, tip **cab drivers** 15% of the fare; tip **skycaps** at airports at least $1 per bag ($2–$3 if you have a lot of luggage); and tip **hairdressers** and **barbers** 15% to 20%.

Tipping ushers at movies and theaters, and gas-station attendants, is not expected.

Toilets You won't find public toilets, or "restrooms," on the streets in most U.S. cities, but they can be found in hotel lobbies, bars, restaurants, museums, department stores, railway and bus stations, and service stations. Large hotels and fast-food restaurants are probably the best bet for good, clean facilities. If possible, avoid the toilets at parks and beaches, which tend to be dirty; some may be unsafe. Restaurants and bars in resorts or heavily visited areas may reserve their restrooms for patrons. Some establishments display a notice indicating this. You can ignore this sign or, better yet, avoid arguments by paying for a cup of coffee or a soft drink, which will qualify you as a patron. Along major highways are "rest stops," many with restroom facilities.

4

The Active Vacation Planner

You may be pleasantly surprised at the range of outdoor fun available in this state. From the dry flatlands of the southern regions to the mountains and forests of the north-central part of the state, diversity reigns here. Whether you're interested in a short day hike or an overnight horse trip, groomed ski trails or backcountry adventures, you won't be disappointed.

For more in-depth coverage of the activities that follow, contact some of the local outfitters or organizations that are listed in the "Outdoor Activities" and "Getting Outside" sections later in this book.

For tips on staying healthy outdoors, see "Insurance, Health & Safety," in chapter 2.

1 Ballooning

New Mexico and **hot-air ballooning** go hand in hand. In fact, one of the state's greatest attractions is the annual Albuquerque International Balloon Fiesta in early October (see "New Mexico Calendar of Events," in chapter 2), which draws thousands of people from all over the world. It is possible to charter hot-air balloon rides in all regions of the state. Most companies offer a variety of packages, from a standard flight to a more elaborate all-day affair that includes meals. For more information, contact individual chambers of commerce.

2 Bird-Watching

New Mexico is located directly on the Central Flyway, which makes it a great spot for bird-watching all year long. Each region of the state offers refuge to a wide variety of birds, including everything from doves, finches, bluebirds, and roadrunners (the state bird), to the rare and wonderful whooping crane. The bald eagle is also frequently spotted during winter and spring migrations. A good place to pull out your binoculars is the **Gila National Forest** (© 505/388-8201) near Silver City. Also check out the wildlife refuge centers in New Mexico, most notably the **Bosque del Apache National Wildlife Refuge,** 93 miles south of Albuquerque (© 505/835-1828). Others include the **Rio Grande Nature Center,** Albuquerque (© 505/344-7240), the **Las Vegas National Wildlife Refuge,** 5 miles southeast of Las Vegas (© 505/425-3581), and **Bitter Lake National Wildlife Refuge,** 13 miles northeast of Roswell (© 505/622-6755). Some common sightings at these areas might include sandhill cranes, snow geese, a wide variety of ducks, and falcons. New Mexico is also home to an amazing variety of hummingbirds. In fact, in early 1996, New Mexico was able to add the Cinnamon Hummingbird to its list of birds. Its sighting in Santa Teresa marked only its second sighting in the United States. The number of verified species in New Mexico is now 478. New Mexico ranks fourth (behind Texas, California, and Arizona) in the number of birds that live in or have passed through the state.

To find out about bird-watching activities in New Mexico, contact the state office of the **National Audubon Society,** 1800 Upper Canyon Rd., Santa Fe (© **505/983-4609;** www.nm.audubon.org).

3 Hiking

Everywhere you go in New Mexico you'll find opportunities for hiking adventures. The terrain and climate vary from the heat and flatness of the desert plains to the cold, forested alpine areas of the northern region of the state. You can visit both (going from 3,000–13,000 ft. in elevation) and anything in between in the same day without much trouble. As you can read in this book's Appendix, the plant and animal life you'll see along the way is as varied and interesting as the terrain. You can go hiking virtually anywhere you please (except on private land or Native American land without permission); however, it's wise to stick to designated trails.

I mention some of the best hiking trails in each region of the state below. See later chapters for details about outfitters, guides, llama trekking services, and who to contact for maps and other information.

BEST HIKES

If you're around **Santa Fe,** I recommend hiking Santa Fe Baldy. It's a hike you can do in a day if you start out early; if you'd like a less strenuous walk, plan to spend a night camping. This is a good first hike for those who come from lower altitudes but are in good shape. Once you get to the top, you'll have panoramic views of the Sangre de Cristo and Jemez mountains, as well as the Rio Grande Valley. See chapter 6 for details.

If you're looking for something more challenging in the **north-central region** of the state, head to Taos and give Wheeler Peak your best shot. The hike up New Mexico's highest peak is about 15 miles round-trip. If you're incredibly well conditioned, you may be able to do the hike in a day. Otherwise, plan to hike and camp for several days. The pain of getting to the top is worth it—at the top you'll find some of New Mexico's most spectacular views. See chapter 7 for details.

For a much easier hike in the Taos area, try hiking down into Rio Grande Gorge. It's beautiful and can be hiked year-round. See chapter 7 for details.

In the **northeastern region** of New Mexico, I recommend taking the 1-mile loop around Capulin Volcano. The crater rim offers stunning views, and you can look down into the dormant caldera. It's a nice, easy walk for those who'd rather not overexert themselves. Any time except winter is good for this hike. See chapter 8 for details.

If you're heading to the **northwestern region** of the state, try hiking the Bisti/De-Na-Zin Wilderness, 37 miles south of Farmington. Though there are no marked trails, the hiking is easy in this area of low, eroded hills and fanciful rock formations. You may see petrified wood or fossils from the dinosaurs that lived here millions of years ago. A walk to one of the more interesting areas is about 4 miles round-trip and is best taken in spring or fall. See chapter 9 for details.

The northwestern region is also home to El Malpais National Monument, where you can hike into great lava tubes. The hiking is easy, but it's also easy to get lost in this area, so be sure to carry a compass and a topographical map. Also in El Malpais National Monument is the Zuni–Acoma Trail, which used to connect the Pueblo villages of Zuni and Acoma. If you're up for this moderate-to-difficult 15-mile (round-trip) hike, you'll be trekking across three lava flows, and you won't have to fight for trail space with other hikers. This hike is an especially good one to take in spring or fall. See chapter 9 for details.

In the **southwestern region** is the Gila National Forest, which has approxi-mately 1,500 miles of trails, with varying ranges of length and difficulty. Your best bet is to purchase a guidebook devoted entirely to hiking the Gila Forest, but popular areas include the Crest Trail, the West Fork Trail, and the Aldo Leopold Wilderness. One favorite day hike in the forest is The Catwalk, a mod-erately strenuous hike along a series of steel bridges and walkways suspended over Whitewater Canyon. See chapter 10 for details.

In the **southeastern region,** you'll find one of my favorite places in all of New Mexico: White Sands National Monument. Hiking the white-sand dunes is easy, if sometimes awkward, and the magnificence of the views is unsurpassed. Be sure to take sunscreen, plenty of water, and a compass on this hike; there's no shade, and it's difficult to tell one dune from another here. See chapter 11 for more information.

Of course, you can choose from hundreds of other hikes. You can purchase a hiking book or contact the National Park Service, National Forest Service, Bureau of Land Management, or other appropriate agency directly. The best guides for the region are *The Hiker's Guide to New Mexico* (Falcon Press Pub-lishing Co.), by Laurence Parent, which outlines 70 hikes throughout the state, and *75 Hikes in New Mexico,* by Craig Martin (The Mountaineers). My book *Frommer's Great Outdoor Guide to Arizona & New Mexico* (Wiley Publishing, Inc.) details many of my favorite hikes. A popular guide with Santa Feans is *Day Hikes in the Santa Fe Area,* published by the local branch of the Sierra Club and available in most local bookstores.

4 Fishing

You'll find scores of **fishing** opportunities in New Mexico. Warm-water lakes and streams are home to large- and small-mouth bass, walleye, stripers, catfish, crappie, and bluegill. In cold-water lakes and streams, look for the state fish, the Rio Grande cutthroat, as well as kokanee salmon and rainbow, brown, lake, and brook trout.

Two of the best places for fishing are the San Juan River near Farmington (see chapter 9) and **Elephant Butte Lake** (see chapter 10), not far from Truth or Consequences. The **San Juan River** offers excellent trout fishing and is extremely popular with fly fishers. Elephant Butte Lake is great for bass fishing; in fact, it is considered one of the top 10 bass fishing locations in the United States.

All sorts of other possibilities are available, such as the Rio Grande, the Chama, Jemez, and Gila watershed areas, and the Pecos River. I recommend Ti Piper's *Fishing in New Mexico* (University of New Mexico Press). This excellent and wonderfully comprehensive book describes every waterway in New Mexico in great detail. It includes information about regulations and descriptions of the types and varieties of fish you're likely to catch in New Mexico.

For information on obtaining fishing licensing, call the **New Mexico Game and Fish Department,** 1 Wildlife St., Santa Fe (© **505/476-8000;** www.wildlife. state.nm.us).

Although it is not necessary to have a fishing license in order to fish on Native American reservation land, you must still receive written permission and an offi-cial tribal document before setting out on any fishing trips there. Phone num-bers for tribes and pueblos are listed separately in the regional and city chapters in this book.

5 Mountain Biking

It's awesome to pedal out into the dry New Mexico air and see not only incredible terrain but also ancient history. Just about the entire state is conducive to the sport, making it one of the most popular places in the United States for avid mountain bikers.

Albuquerque has some excellent and very challenging trails in the Sandia Mountains, as well as less strenuous routes west of town, through Petroglyph National Monument (see chapter 5). In **Santa Fe,** you'll find some very rugged and steep mountain trails, most accessed off the road to Ski Santa Fe (see chapter 6). **Taos** is a rider's paradise, with lots of extreme mountain trails, as well as some that are purely scenic, such as the west rim of the Rio Grande Gorge (see chapter 7).

In northwestern New Mexico, you can ride around El Malpais National Monument in the **Grants** area. You can also take your bike with you to Chaco Culture National Historical Park and ride from Anasazi ruin to ruin. The **Farmington** area has its renowned Road Apple Trail within Lions Wilderness Park, which you can ride even through the winter. See chapter 9.

In the southwestern region, bikes are not allowed in the Gila Wilderness, but they are permitted in other parts of Gila National Forest; you'll find terrific trails that originate in **Silver City,** particularly the Continental Divide Trail (see chapter 10). In the southeastern region, the **Cloudcroft** area has some excellent trails; there are a few that explore history as well as natural terrain, most notably the 17-mile Rim Trail (see chapter 11).

Some books to check out are my book *Frommer's Great Outdoor Guide to Arizona & New Mexico* (Wiley Publishing, Inc.) and Sarah Bennett's *Mountain Biker's Guide to New Mexico* (Falcon Press).

Known World Guides, in Velarde (no street address; © 800/983-7756 or 505/983-7756; www.knownworldguides.com), offers single-day and multiday trips all over New Mexico, with options such as 3 days in the Jemez Mountains west of Santa Fe or 5 days in the Gila National Forest in Silver City. **Sun Mountain Bike Company,** 102 E. Water St., Santa Fe (© 505/982-8986; www.sunmountainbikeco.com) runs bike tours to some of the most spectacular spots in northern New Mexico. Trips range from the easy Train Tour south of Santa Fe, in which you ride the scenic Santa Fe Southern Railroad back, to a challenging Borrego Bust ride in the Santa Fe National Forest.

6 Rockhounding

New Mexico abounds in rockhounding opportunities. Of course, you can't just go around picking up and taking rocks whenever it strikes your fancy—in many places it's illegal to take rocks—but a few places not only allow rockhounding but even encourage it. **Rockhound State Park** (© 505/546-6182; www.emnrd.state.nm.us/nmparks), located about 14 miles from Deming, is one such place (see chapter 10 for information). Rockhounds from all over the country descend on this part of the state to find great rocks, such as agate, jasper, and opal. At Rockhound State Park, you're allowed to camp and take a handful or two of rocks home with you. For information on other popular rockhounding sites, contact the **New Mexico Bureau of Geology & Mineral Resources** (© 505/835-5410; www.geoinfo.nmt.edu).

7 Skiing & Snowboarding

New Mexico has some of the best **downhill skiing** in the United States. With most alpine areas above 10,000 feet and many above 12,000 feet, several ski areas offer vertical drops of over 2,000 feet. Average annual snowfall at the nine major areas ranges from 100 to 300 inches. Many areas, aided by vigorous snow-making efforts, are able to open around Thanksgiving, and most open by mid-December, making New Mexico a popular vacation spot around the holidays. As a result, you'll see a definite rise in hotel room rates in or around ski areas during the holiday season. The ski season runs through March and often into the first week in April.

Some of the best skiing in the state is at Taos and the nearby resort towns of Angel Fire and Red River (see chapter 7). In addition, Taos Ski Valley is home to one of the best ski schools in the country. Ski areas in New Mexico offer runs for a variety of skill levels, and all-day adult lift tickets range from about $35 to $51.

Snowboarding is permitted at all New Mexico ski areas with the exception of Taos Ski Valley, and some of the best **cross-country skiing** in the region can be found at the Enchanted Forest near Taos Ski Valley and in Chama.

Equipment for alpine, telemark, and cross-country skiing, as well as for snowboarding, can be rented at ski areas and nearby towns. Lessons are widely available.

For more information about individual ski areas, see regional and city chapters later in this book.

8 Watersports

Watersports in New Mexico? Absolutely! Here you'll find a variety of watersports activities, ranging from pleasure boating to white-water rafting and windsurfing.

New Mexico offers fantastic opportunities for **white-water rafting** and **kayaking.** The waters in the Chama River and the Rio Grande are generally at their best during the spring and summer (May–July); however, some areas of the Rio Grande are negotiable year-round, especially those that fall at lower elevations, where temperatures are warmer. If you opt not to schlep your own rafting gear with you to New Mexico, you can work with one of the many companies that will supply you with everything you need. *Note:* I recommend contacting some of the outfitters listed in later chapters no matter what you've brought with you or what your level of experience because white-water rafting and kayaking in certain areas of New Mexico (such as the Taos Box) can be quite dangerous. You should get tips from the professionals before you set out on your own. In addition to calling outfitters, you can also contact the **Bureau of Land Management,** 226 Cruz Alta Rd., Taos, NM 87571 (© **505/758-8851;** www.nm.blm.gov), for information.

Opportunities for **pleasure boating** are available on many of New Mexico's lakes and reservoirs, with boat ramps at more than 45 state parks, dams, and lakes. Elephant Butte Lake is one of the best and most beautiful spots for boating (see chapter 10). Unfortunately, the rules and regulations vary greatly from one body of water to another, so you'll have to contact the governing agencies for each place in which you intend to go boating.

The **U.S. Army Corps of Engineers,** 4101 Jefferson Plaza NE, Albuquerque (© **505/342-3100;** www.usace.army.mil), oversees the following lakes: Abiquiu, Cochiti, Conchas, Galisteo, Jemez, Santa Rosa, and Two Rivers. Most other boating areas are regulated by the **State Parks Division,** 1220 S. St. Francis, Santa Fe (© **888/NM-PARKS** or 505/476-3355; www.emnrd.state.nm.us/nmparks), or by the **New Mexico Game and Fish Department,** 1 Wildlife St., Santa Fe (© **505/476-8000;** www.wildlife.state.nm.us). Some are, of course, overseen by tribes and pueblos, and in those cases, you'll have to contact them directly.

Another popular pastime, particularly at Cochiti and Storrie lakes in summer, is **windsurfing.** Elephant Butte is good for windsurfing all year.

9 Other Outdoor Activities

In addition to the activities listed so far in this chapter, many other recreational opportunities are available in New Mexico. **Hot springs,** for example, are quite popular with locals and visitors. They take many different forms and offer a wide variety of facilities and amenities; some, which aren't owned and operated by anyone but Mother Nature, offer no amenities. You'll find hot springs in the Taos and Las Vegas areas as well as in the southwestern region of New Mexico. Many of them are listed later in this book. You may also try calling local chambers of commerce to find out whether they have any information on area hot springs.

GOLF

New Mexico provides the clear air and oft-cool climates that draw many golfers. The most challenging course in the state is the **University of New Mexico Championship Golf Course,** 3601 University Blvd. SE, Albuquerque (© **505/277-4546**), and one of the most scenic is the **Cochiti Lake Golf Course,** 5200 Cochiti Highway, Cochiti Lake, NM (© **505/465-2239**). If you're in the Farmington area, check out **Piñon Hills Golf Course,** 2101 Sunrise Parkway (© **505/326-6066**), a few years ago rated by *Golf Digest* as the "best public golf course" in New Mexico. In the south, you can enjoy views, a challenging course, and cool climes even in summer at **The Links at Sierra Blanca,** in Ruidoso, 105 Sierra Blanca Dr. (© **800/854-6571** or 505/258-5330; www.trekwest.com/linksgolf). See individual chapters for more suggestions.

HORSEBACK RIDING

What's unique about much of New Mexico's horseback riding is its variety. You'll find a broad range of riding terrain, from open plains to high mountain wilderness. In the Santa Fe area, you can ride across the plains of the spectacular Galisteo basin with **Santa Fe Detours,** 54½ East San Francisco St. (© **800/338-6877** or 505/983-6565; www.sfdetours.com). In Taos, you can explore secluded Taos Pueblo land with the **Taos Indian Horse Ranch,** on Pueblo land off Ski Valley Road, just before Arroyo Seco (© **800/659-3210** or 505/758-3212; www.taoshorseranch.fws1.com). In the northwest, in the village of Chama, try **5M Outfitters** (no street address; © **505/588-7003;** www.5moutfitters.com). In the southeast, try **Inn of the Mountain Gods,** Carrizo Canyon Rd. (© **800/545-9011** or 505/464-5141; www.innofthemountaingods.com). If you're looking for a resort horseback riding experience, contact **Bishop's Lodge,** Bishop's Lodge Rd., Santa Fe (© **800/732-2240** or 505/983-6377; www.bishopslodge.com). If you want an authentic cowpoke experience, I recommend the **Double E Guest Ranch,** 67 Double E Ranch Road, Gila (© **866/242-3500** or 505/535-2048; www.doubleeranch.com), in the Silver City area.

TENNIS

Although New Mexico's high and dry climate is ideal for tennis much of the year, the sport is somewhat underdeveloped in the state. Certainly each of the major cities has municipal courts, information about which you'll find in the city and regional chapters of this book. If you're looking for a tennis resort experience, try **Bishop's Lodge,** Bishop's Lodge Rd., Santa Fe (© **800/732-2240** or 505/983-6377; www.bishopslodge.com), or **Salsa del Salto** in Taos, 543 NM 150 (© **800/530-3097** or 505/776-2422; www.bandbtaos.com).

5

Albuquerque

From the rocky crest of Sandia Peak at sunset, one can see the lights of this city spread out across 16 miles of high desert grassland. As the sun drops beyond the western horizon, it reflects off the Rio Grande, flowing through Albuquerque more than a mile below.

This waterway is the bloodline for the area, what allowed a city to spring up in this vast desert, and it continues to be at the center of the area's growth. Farming villages that line its banks are being stampeded by expansion. As the west side of the city sprawls, more means for transporting traffic across the river have had to be built, breaking up the pastoral valley area.

The railroad, which set up a major stop here in 1880, prompted much of Albuquerque's initial growth, but that economic explosion was nothing compared with what has happened since World War II. Designated a major national center for military research and production, Albuquerque became a trading center for New Mexico, whose populace is spread widely across the land. That's why the city may strike visitors as nothing more than one big strip mall. Look closely, and you'll see ranchers, Native Americans, and Hispanic villagers stocking up on goods to take home.

Climbing out of the valley is **Route 66,** well worth a drive, if only to see

the rust that time has left. Old court motels still line the street, many with their funky '50s signage. One enclave on this route is the **University of New Mexico district,** with a number of hippie-ish cafes and shops.

Farther downhill, you'll come to **downtown Albuquerque.** During the day, this area is all suits and heels, but at night it boasts a hip nightlife scene. People from all over the state come to Albuquerque to check out the live music and dance clubs, most within walking distance from each other.

The section called **Old Town** is worth a visit. Though it's the most touristy part of town, it's also a unique Southwestern village with a beautiful and intact plaza. Also in this area are Albuquerque's aquarium and botanical gardens, as well as its zoo.

Indian pueblos in the area welcome tourists, and, along with other pueblos throughout New Mexico, have worked to create the Pueblo Cultural Center, a showplace of Indian crafts of both past and present. The country's longest aerial tramway takes visitors to the top of Sandia Peak, which protects the city's eastern flank. To the west run a series of volcanoes; the Petroglyph National Monument there is an amazing tribute to the area's ancient Native American past.

1 Orientation

ARRIVING

Albuquerque is the transportation hub for New Mexico, so getting in and out of town is easy. For more detailed information, see "Getting There," in chapter 2.

Greater Albuquerque

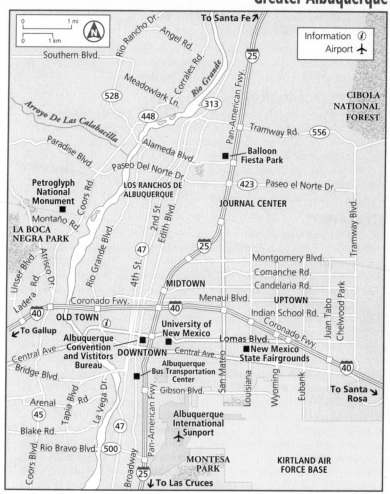

BY PLANE The **Albuquerque International Sunport** (© 505/842-4366) is in the south-central part of the city, between I-25 on the west and Kirtland Air Force Base on the east, just south of Gibson Boulevard. Sleek and efficient, the airport is served by most national airlines and two local ones.

Most hotels have courtesy vans to meet their guests and take them to their respective destinations. In addition, **Checker Airport Express** (© 505/765-1234) runs services to and from city hotels. **ABQ Ride** (© 505/243-7433), Albuquerque's public bus system, also makes airport stops. There is efficient taxi service to and from the airport, and you can find numerous car-rental agencies.

BY TRAIN **Amtrak**'s "Southwest Chief" arrives and departs daily to and from Los Angeles and Chicago. The station is at 214 First St. SW, 2 blocks south of Central Avenue (© 800/USA-RAIL or 505/842-9650).

BY BUS **Greyhound/Trailways** (© 800/231-2222 for schedules, fares, and information) and **TNM&O** (© 505/243-4435) arrive and depart from the

Albuquerque Bus Transportation Center, 300 Second St. SW (at the corner of Lead and Second, near the train station).

BY CAR   If you're driving, you'll probably arrive via either the east–west I-40 or the north–south I-25. Exits are well marked. For information and advice on driving in New Mexico, see "Getting There," in chapter 2.

VISITOR INFORMATION

The main office of the **Albuquerque Convention and Visitors Bureau** is at 20 First Plaza NW (© **800/284-2282** or 505/842-9918). It's open Monday to Friday 8am to 5pm. There are information centers at the airport, on the lower level at the bottom of the escalator, open daily 9:30am to 8pm; and in Old Town, at 303 Romero St. NW, Suite 107, open daily 9am to 5pm. Tape-recorded information about current local events is available from the bureau after 5pm weekdays and all day Saturday and Sunday. Call © **800/284-2282.**

CITY LAYOUT

The city's sprawl takes awhile to get used to. A visitor's first impression is of a grid of arteries lined with shopping malls and fast-food eateries, with residences tucked behind on side streets.

If you look at a map of Albuquerque, you'll notice that it lies at the crossroads of I-25 north–south and I-40 east–west. Focus your attention on the southwest quadrant: Here, you'll find both downtown Albuquerque and Old Town, site of many tourist attractions. Lomas Boulevard and Central Avenue, the old Route 66 (US 66), flank downtown on the north and south. They come together 2 miles west of downtown, near Old Town Plaza, the historical and spiritual heart of the city. Lomas and Central continue east across I-25, staying about half a mile apart as they pass by the University of New Mexico and the New Mexico State Fairgrounds. The airport is directly south of the UNM campus, about 3 miles via Yale Boulevard. Kirtland Air Force Base—site of Sandia National Laboratories—is an equal distance south of the fairgrounds, on Louisiana Boulevard.

Roughly paralleling I-40 to the north is Menaul Boulevard, the focus of midtown and uptown shopping, as well as the hotel districts. As Albuquerque expands northward, the Journal Center business park area, about 4½ miles north of the freeway interchange, is getting more attention. East of Eubank Boulevard lie the Sandia Foothills, where the alluvial plain slants a bit more steeply toward the mountains.

When looking for an address, it is helpful to know that Central Avenue divides the city into north and south, and the railroad tracks—which run just east of First Street downtown—comprise the dividing line between east and west. Street names are followed by a directional: NE, NW, SE, or SW.

MAPS   The most comprehensive Albuquerque street map is distributed by the **Convention and Visitors Bureau,** 20 First Plaza NW (© **800/284-2282** or 505/842-9918).

2 Getting Around

Albuquerque is easy to get around, thanks to its wide thoroughfares and grid layout, combined with its efficient transportation systems.

BY PUBLIC TRANSPORTATION   ABQ Ride (© **505/243-7433**) cloaks the city with its bus network. Call for information on routes and fares.

BY TAXI   Yellow Cab (© **505/247-8888**) serves the city and surrounding area 24 hours a day.

BY CAR   The Yellow Pages list more than 30 car-rental agencies in Albuquerque. Among them are the following well-known national firms: **Alamo,** 3400 University Blvd. SE (© **505/842-4057**); **Avis,** at the airport (© **505/842-4080**); **Budget,** at the airport (© **505/247-3443**); **Dollar,** at the airport (© **505/842-4224**); **Hertz,** at the airport (© **505/842-4235**); **Rent-A-Wreck,** 500 Yale Blvd. SE (© **505/232-7552**); and **Thrifty,** 2039 Yale Blvd. SE (© **505/842-8733**). Those not located at the airport itself are close by and can provide rapid airport pickup and delivery service.

Parking is generally not difficult in Albuquerque. Meters operate weekdays 8am to 6pm and are not monitored at other times. Only the large downtown hotels charge for parking. Traffic is a problem only at certain hours. Avoid I-25 and I-40 at the center of town around 5pm.

FAST FACTS: Albuquerque

Airport See "Orientation," above.

Area Code The telephone area code for all of New Mexico is **505**, though at press time plans were rumbling to add new ones in the state.

ATMs You can find ATMs (also known as *cash pueblos*) all over town, at supermarkets, banks, and drive-throughs.

Business Hours **Offices** and **stores** are generally open Monday to Friday, 9am to 5pm, with many stores also open Friday night, Saturday, and Sunday in the summer season. Most **banks** are also open Monday to Friday, 9am to 5pm. Some may be open Saturday morning. Most branches have ATMs available 24 hours. Call establishments for specific hours.

Car Rentals See "Getting Around New Mexico," in chapter 2, or "Getting Around," above.

Climate See "When to Go," in chapter 2.

Currency Exchange Foreign currency can be exchanged at any of the branches of **Bank of America** (its main office is at 303 Roma NW; © **505/282-2450**).

Dentists Call the **Albuquerque District Dental Society,** at © **505/237-1412,** for emergency service.

Doctors Call the **Greater Albuquerque Medical Association,** at © **505/821-4583,** for information.

Embassies and Consulates See "Fast Facts: For the International Traveler," in chapter 3.

Emergencies For police, fire, or ambulance, dial © **911.**

Hospitals The major hospital facilities are **Presbyterian Hospital,** 1100 Central Ave. SE (© **505/841-1234,** or 505/841-1111 for emergency services); and **University of New Mexico Hospital,** 2211 Lomas Blvd. NE (© **505/272-2111,** or 505/272-2411 for emergency services).

Hot Lines The following hot lines are available in Albuquerque: rape crises (© **505/266-7711**), poison control (© **800/432-6866**), suicide (© **505/247-1121**), and UNM Children's Hospital emergency crisis (© **505/272-2920**).

Information See "Visitor Information," under "Orientation," above.

Internet Access **FedEx Kinko's** provides high-speed Internet access at five locations throughout the city. Two convenient ones are 6220 San Mateo Blvd. NE at Academy Boulevard (© **505/821-2222**) and 2706 Central Ave. SE at Princeton Boulevard (© **505/255-9673**).

Library The Albuquerque/Bernalillo County Public Library's **main branch** is at 501 Copper Ave. NW, between Fifth and Sixth streets (© **505/768-5140**). You can find the locations of the 17 other library facilities in the area by checking **www.cabq.gov/library**.

Liquor Laws The legal drinking age is 21 throughout New Mexico. Bars may remain open until 2am Monday to Saturday and until midnight on Sunday. Wine, beer, and spirits are sold at licensed supermarkets and liquor stores. It is illegal to transport liquor through most Native American reservations.

Lost Property Contact the city police at © **505/242-COPS.**

Newspapers & Magazines The two daily newspapers are the *Albu-querque Tribune* (© 505/823-7777; www.abqtrib.com) and the *Albu-querque Journal* (© 505/823-7777; www.abqjournal.com). You can pick up the *Alibi* (© 505/346-0660; www.alibi.com), Albuquerque's free alter-native weekly, at newsstands all over town, especially around the Univer-sity of New Mexico. It offers entertainment listings and alternative views on a variety of subjects.

Pharmacies **Walgreens** has many locations throughout Albuquerque. To find one near you, call © **800-WALGREENS.** Two centrally located ones that are open 24 hours are 8011 Harper Dr. NE at Wyoming (© **505/858-3134**) and 5001 Montgomery Blvd. NE at San Mateo (© **505/881-5210**).

Police For emergencies, call © **911.** For other business, contact the **Albu-querque City Police** (© 505/242-COPS) or the **New Mexico State Police** (© **505/841-9256**).

Post Offices To find the nearest U.S. Post Office, dial © **800/275-8777.** The service will ask for your zip code and give you the closest post office address and hours.

Radio The local AM station **KKOB** (770) broadcasts news and events. FM band stations include **KUNM** (89.9), the University of New Mexico station, which broadcasts Public Radio programming and a variety of music; **KPEK** (100.3), which plays alternative rock music; and **KHFM** (95.5), which broad-casts classical music.

Taxes In Albuquerque, the sales tax is 5.8125%. An additional hotel tax of 5% will be added to your bill.

Taxis See "Getting Around," above.

Television There are five Albuquerque network affiliates: **KOB-TV** (Chan-nel 4, NBC), **KOAT-TV** (Channel 7, ABC), **KQRE-TV** (Channel 13, CBS), **KASA TV** (Channel 2, FOX), and **KNME-TV** (Channel 5, PBS).

Time As is true throughout New Mexico, Albuquerque is on **Mountain Standard Time.** It's 2 hours earlier than New York, 1 hour earlier than Chicago, and 1 hour later than Los Angeles. Daylight saving time is in effect from early April to late October.

Transit Information **ABQ Ride** is the public bus system. Call © **505/243-7433** for schedules and information.

Useful Telephone Numbers For **road information,** call 🕿 **800/432-4269;** and for **emergency road service** (AAA), call 🕿 **505/291-6600.**

Weather For **time** and **temperature,** call 🕿 **505/247-1611.** To get **weather forecasts** on the Internet, check **www.accuweather.com** and use the Albuquerque zip code 87104.

3 Where to Stay

Albuquerque's hotel glut is good news for travelers looking for quality rooms at a reasonable cost. Except during peak periods—specifically, the New Mexico Arts and Crafts Fair (late June), the New Mexico State Fair (Sept), and the Balloon Fiesta (early Oct)—most of the city's hotels have vacant rooms, so guests can frequently request and get lower room rates than the ones posted.

A tax of nearly 11% is added to every hotel bill. All hotels and bed-and-breakfasts listed offer rooms for nonsmokers and travelers with disabilities.

HOTELS/MOTELS
EXPENSIVE

Albuquerque Marriott Pyramid North 🍃   About a 15-minute drive from Old Town and downtown, this Aztec pyramid–shaped structure provides decent rooms in an interesting environment. The 10 guest floors are grouped around a hollow skylit atrium. Vines drape from planter boxes on the balconies, and water falls five stories to a pool between the two glass elevators. The rooms, remodeled in 2003, are spacious, though not extraordinary, all with picture windows and ample views. With lots of convention space at the hotel, you're likely to encounter name-tagged conventioneers here. Overall, the service seems to be good enough to handle the crowds, but there are only two elevators, so guests often must wait.

5151 San Francisco Rd. NE, Albuquerque, NM 87109. 🕿 **800/228-9290** or 505/821-3333. Fax 505/822-8115. www.marriott.com. 310 units. $139–$184 double; $140–$275 suite. Ask about special weekend and package rates. AE, DC, DISC, MC, V. Free parking. **Amenities:** Restaurant; lounge; indoor/outdoor pool; medium-size health club; Jacuzzi; sauna; concierge; business center; room service; valet laundry. *In room:* A/C, TV, dataport, coffeemaker, hair dryer, iron.

Hyatt Regency Albuquerque 🍃🍃   If you're looking for luxury and want to be right downtown, this is the place to stay. This $60-million hotel, which opened in 1990, is pure shiny gloss and Art Deco. The lobby features a palm-shaded fountain beneath a pyramidal skylight, and throughout the hotel's public areas is an extensive art collection, including original Frederic Remington sculptures. The spacious guest rooms enhance the feeling of richness with mahogany furnishings, full-length mirrors, and views of the mountains. The hotel is located right next door to the Galeria, a shopping area, and has a number of shops itself. McGrath's serves three meals daily in a setting of forest-green upholstery and black-cherry furniture. Bolo Saloon is noted for its whimsical oil paintings depicting "where the deer and the antelope play."

330 Tijeras Ave. NW, Albuquerque, NM 87102. 🕿 **800/233-1234** or 505/842-1234. Fax 505/766-6710. www.hyatt.com. 395 units. Weekdays $225 double; weekends $105 double; $335–$435 suite. AE, DC, DISC, MC, V. Self-parking $8, valet $11. **Amenities:** Restaurant; bar; outdoor pool; health club; sauna; concierge; car-rental desk; business center and secretarial services; salon; room service; babysitting; laundry service; dry cleaning. *In room:* A/C, TV, dataport, coffeemaker, hair dryer.

Sheraton Old Town ⭐ No Albuquerque hotel is closer to top tourist attractions than the Sheraton. It's only a 5-minute walk from Old Town Plaza and two important museums. Constructed in 1975, it has undergone an estimated $4-million renovation. The building has mezzanine-level windows lighting the adobe-toned lobby, creating an airiness that carries into the rooms. Request a south-side room, and you'll get a balcony overlooking Old Town and the pool. The medium-size rooms have handcrafted Southwestern furniture.

800 Rio Grande Blvd. NW, Albuquerque, NM 87104. ℂ **800/237-2133** reservations only, or 505/843-6300. Fax 505/842-9863. www.sheraton.com. 188 units. $119–$169 double; $189 suite. Children stay free in parent's room. AE, DC, DISC, MC, V. Free parking. **Amenities:** 2 restaurants; outdoor pool; Jacuzzi; concierge; business center; limited room service; babysitting; valet laundry; same-day dry cleaning; executive-level rooms. *In room:* A/C, TV, pay movies, dataport, minibar, coffeemaker, hair dryer, iron.

MODERATE
Courtyard by Marriott ⭐ If you don't like high-rises such as the Wyndham Albuquerque Hotel, this is the best selection for airport-area hotels. Opened in 1990, this four-story member of the Marriott family is built around an attractively landscaped courtyard. Families appreciate the security system—access is only by key card between 11pm and 6am—though most of the hotel's clients are business travelers. The units are roomy and comfortable, with walnut furniture and firm beds. Ask for a balcony room on the courtyard.

1920 Yale Blvd. SE, Albuquerque, NM 87106. ℂ **800/321-2211** or 505/843-6600. Fax 505/843-8740. www.marriott.com. 150 units. $71–$107 double. Weekend rates available. AE, DC, DISC, MC, V. Free parking. **Amenities:** Restaurant; lounge; indoor pool; exercise room; Jacuzzi; valet and coin-op laundry. *In room:* A/C, TV, dataport, hair dryer, iron.

La Posada de Albuquerque ⭐ Built in 1939 by Conrad Hilton as the famed hotelier's first inn in his home state of New Mexico, this hostelry on the National Register of Historic Places feels like old Spain. Though remodeled in 1996, it still maintains its historic atmosphere. An elaborate Moorish brass-and-mosaic fountain stands in the center of the tiled lobby, which is surrounded on all sides by high archways, creating the feel of a 19th-century hacienda courtyard. As in the lobby, all guest-room furniture is handcrafted, but here it's covered with Southwestern-style cushions. The more spacious rooms have big windows looking out across the city and toward the mountains. Though the rooms here are fine, they have some of the quirks of an older hotel. But if you want a feel for downtown Albuquerque as well as easy access to the Civic Plaza, nightclubs, and Old Town, this hotel will suit you well. Conrad's Downtown, La Posada's elegantly redesigned restaurant, features Southwestern cuisine from Jane Butel, who has a cooking school on the premises. The Lobby Bar is a favorite gathering place and has entertainment Wednesday through Saturday evenings.

125 Second St. NW (at Copper Ave.), Albuquerque, NM 87102. ℂ **800/777-5732** or 505/242-9090. Fax 505/242-8664. www.laposada-abq.com. 114 units. $89–$115 double; $195–$275 suite. AE, DISC, MC, V. Free parking. **Amenities:** Restaurant; bar; access to nearby health club; room service; dry cleaning/laundry. *In room:* A/C, TV, dataport, coffeemaker, hair dryer, iron.

Wyndham Albuquerque Hotel ⭐⭐ This 15-story hotel right at the airport provides spacious rooms with a touch of elegance. The lobby, grill, and lounge areas employ a lot of sandstone, wood, copper, and tile to lend an Anasazi feel, which carries into the rooms, each with a broad view from a balcony. Air travelers enjoy this hotel's location, but because it has good access to freeways and excellent views, it could also be a wise choice for a few days of browsing around Albuquerque. Of course, you will hear some jet noise. The Rojo Grill serves a variety of American and Southwestern dishes.

Where to Stay in Central Albuquerque

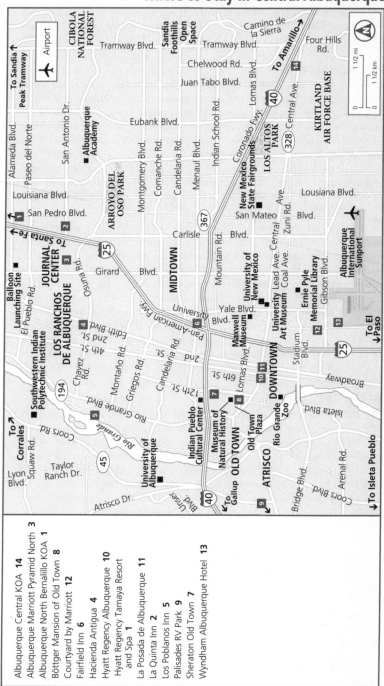

Albuquerque Central KOA **14**
Albuquerque Marriott Pyramid North **3**
Albuquerque North Bernalillo KOA **1**
Böttger Mansion of Old Town **8**
Courtyard by Marriott **12**
Fairfield Inn **6**
Hacienda Antigua **4**
Hyatt Regency Albuquerque **10**
Hyatt Regency Tamaya Resort
and Spa **1**
La Posada de Albuquerque **11**
La Quinta Inn **2**
Los Poblanos Inn **5**
Palisades RV Park **9**
Sheraton Old Town **7**
Wyndham Albuquerque Hotel **13**

2910 Yale Blvd. SE, Albuquerque, NM 87106. ℂ **800/227-1117** or 505/843-7000. Fax 505/843-6307. www.
wyndham.com. 276 units. $99–$179 double. AE, DC, DISC, MC, V. Free parking. Small pets welcome with prior
approval. **Amenities:** Restaurant; outdoor pool; access to golf club; 2 tennis courts; concierge; business center; coin-op laundry. *In room:* A/C, TV, dataport, coffeemaker, hair dryer, iron.

INEXPENSIVE

Fairfield Inn *(Value* Owned by Marriott, this hotel has exceptionally clean
rooms and a location with easy access to freeways that can quickly get you to
Old Town, downtown, or the heights. Ask for an east-facing room to avoid the
noise and a view of the highway. Rooms are medium-size and have medium-size
bathrooms. Each has a balcony or terrace. You probably couldn't get more for
your money in a chain hotel anywhere else.

1760 Menaul Blvd. NE, Albuquerque, NM 87102. ℂ **800/228-2800** or 505/889-4000. Fax 505/872-3094.
www.fairfieldinn.com. 188 units. $69 double. Additional person $10. Children 18 and under stay free in parent's room. Rates include continental breakfast. AE, DC, DISC, MC, V. Free parking. **Amenities:** Indoor/out-
door pool; health club; Jacuzzi; sauna; laundry service. *In room:* A/C, TV, dataport.

La Quinta Inn La Quinta offers reliable, clean rooms at a decent price.
Rooms are tastefully decorated, fairly spacious, and comfortable, each with a
table and chairs and a shower-only bathroom big enough to move around in.
Each king room has a recliner, and two-room suites are available. If you're
headed to the Balloon Fiesta, this is a good choice because it's not far from the
launch site, though you'll have to reserve as much as a year in advance.

There's another La Quinta near the airport (La Quinta Airport Inn, 2116 Yale
Blvd. SE); you can make reservations for either branch at the toll-free number.

5241 San Antonio Dr. NE, Albuquerque, NM 87109. ℂ **800/531-5900** or 505/821-9000. Fax 505/821-2399.
www.lq.com. 130 units. $70–$76 double (higher during Balloon Fiesta). Children stay free in parent's room.
AE, DC, DISC, MC, V. Free parking. Pets welcome. **Amenities:** Heated outdoor pool open May–Oct. *In room:*
A/C, TV, dataport, coffeemaker, hair dryer, iron.

BED & BREAKFASTS

The Böttger Mansion of Old Town 𝓡𝓡 This Victorian inn in Old Town
offers a sweet taste of a past era. Decorated with antiques but not overdone with
chintz, it's an excellent choice. My favorite room is the Carole Rose, with a
canopy bed and lots of sun; also lovely is the Rebecca Leah, with pink marble
tile and a Jacuzzi tub. All rooms are medium-size and have excellent beds; most
have small bathrooms. The rooms facing south let in the most sun but pick up
a bit of street noise from nearby Central Avenue and a nearby elementary school
(both quiet down at night). Breakfast (such as green-chile quiche) is elaborate
enough to keep you going through the day, at the end of which you can enjoy
treats from the guest snack bar (try the chocolate cookies with a little chile in
them). During warm months the patio is lovely.

110 San Felipe NW, Albuquerque, NM 87104. ℂ **800/758-3639** or 505/243-3639. www.bottger.com.
8 units. $109–$179 double. Rates include full breakfast and snack bar. AE, MC, V. Free parking. **Amenities:**
In-room massage. *In room:* A/C, TV/VCR, hair dryer.

Hacienda Antigua 𝓡𝓡 *(Finds* This 200-year-old adobe home was once the
first stagecoach stop out of Old Town in Albuquerque. Now, it's one of Albuquerque's most elegant inns. The artistically landscaped courtyard, with its large
cottonwood tree and abundance of greenery, offers a welcome respite for tired
travelers. The rooms are gracefully and comfortably furnished with antiques. La
Capilla, the home's former chapel, is furnished with a queen-size bed, a fireplace,
and a carving of St. Francis (the patron saint of the garden). La Sala has a king-
size bed and a large Jacuzzi, with a view of the Sandia Mountains. All the rooms

are equipped with fireplaces and signature soaps. A gourmet breakfast is served in the garden during warm weather and by the fire in winter. The inn is a 20-minute drive from the airport. Light sleepers beware—the Santa Fe Railroad runs by this inn, with one to three trains passing by each night.

6708 Tierra Dr. NW, Albuquerque, NM 87107. © 800/201-2986 or 505/345-5399. Fax 505/345-3855. www. haciendantigua.com. 8 units. $129–$209 double. Additional person $25. Rates include gourmet breakfast. AE, MC, V. Free parking. Pets welcome with $30 fee. **Amenities:** Outdoor pool; Jacuzzi. *In room:* A/C, TV/VCR, coffeemaker, hair dryer.

Los Poblanos Inn ⊕ Lushness in the desert city of Albuquerque? It's no mirage. Nestled among century-old cottonwoods, this bed-and-breakfast sits on 25 acres of European-style gardens and peasantlike vegetable and lavender fields. Notable architect John Gaw Meem built the structure in the 1930s. Each of the six guest rooms, most arranged around a poetically planted courtyard, has unique touches such as hand-carved doors, traditional tin fixtures, fireplaces, and views across the lushly landscaped grounds. At breakfast, you might feast on walnut-topped French toast and bacon while watching peacocks preen outside the windows of the very Mexican-feeling, boldly decorated cantina. Light sleepers should be aware that the peacocks can be noisy at night.

4803 Rio Grande Blvd. NW, Albuquerque, NM 87107 © **866/344-9297** or 505/344-9297. Fax 505/342-1302. www.lospoblanos.com. 6 units. $135–$250 double. Rates include full breakfast. AE, MC, V. Free parking. *In room:* A/C, dataport, hair dryer, iron.

NEAR ALBUQUERQUE

Hyatt Regency Tamaya Resort and Spa ⊕⊕⊕ This is the spot for a getaway-from-it-all luxury vacation. Set in the hills above the lush Rio Grande Valley on Santa Ana Pueblo, this Pueblo-style resort offers a 16,000-square-foot full-service spa and fitness center, an 18-hole Twin Warriors Championship Golf Course designed by Gary Panks, and views of the Sandia Mountains. Rooms are

---

Finds **Cruising Corrales**

If you'd like to travel along meadows and apple orchards into a place where life is a little slower and sweeter, head 15 minutes north of Albuquerque to the village of Corrales. Home to farmers, artists, and affluent landowners, this is a fun place to roam through shops and galleries, and, in the fall, sample vegetables from roadside vendors. Two excellent restaurants, both serving imaginative new American cuisine, sit on the main street. **Indigo Crow** ⊕⊕, 4515 Corrales Rd. (© **505/898-7000**), serves lunch and dinner Tuesday to Saturday and brunch on Sunday, and Jim White's **Casa Vieja** ⊕⊕, 4541 Corrales Rd. (© **505/898-7489**), serves dinner nightly.

The town also has a nature preserve and a historic church. In September, the Harvest Festival is well worth the trip. For more information about Corrales, contact **Corrales Village** (© **505/897-0502;** www. corralesnm.org).

To get to the village, head north on either I-25 or Rio Grande Boulevard, turn west on Alameda Boulevard, cross the Rio Grande, and turn north on Corrales Road (NM 448). The village is just a few minutes up the road.

spacious, with large tile bathrooms. Request one that faces the mountains for one of the state's most spectacular vistas. Other rooms look out across a large courtyard, where the pools and hot tub are. Though the resort is surrounded by acres of quiet countryside, it's only 15 minutes from Albuquerque and 45 minutes from Santa Fe. The concierge offers trips to attractions, as well as on-site activities such as hot air balloon rides, horseback rides, and nature/cultural walks or carriage rides by the river. Plan at least one dinner at the innovative Corn Maiden.

1300 Tuyuna Trail, Santa Ana Pueblo, NM 87004. © **800/55-HYATT** or 505/867-1234. www.hyatt.com. 350 units. May–Oct $200–$350; Nov–Apr $135–$250, depending on the type of room. Suite rates available upon request. Inquire about spa, horseback riding, golf, and family packages. AE, DC, DISC, MC, V. Free parking. From I-25 take exit 242, following US 550 west to Tamaya Blvd.; drive 1½ miles to the resort. **Amenities:** 2 restaurants; 2 snack bars; lounge; 3 pools (heated year-round); golf course; 2 tennis courts; health club & spa; children's programs; concierge; tour desk; elaborate business center; room service; laundry; basketball court. *In room:* A/C, TV, dataport, fridge, coffeemaker, hair dryer, iron, safe.

RV PARKS

Albuquerque Central KOA   This RV park in the foothills east of Albuquerque is a good choice for those who want to be close to town. It offers lots of amenities and convenient freeway access. Cabins are available.

12400 Skyline Rd. NE, Albuquerque, NM 87123. © **800/562-7781** or 505/296-2729. www.koa.com. $19–$36 tent site; $33–$51 RV site, depending on hook-up; $38–$55 1-room cabin; $48–$65 2-room cabin. All prices valid for up to 2 people. Additional adult $5, child $3. AE, DISC, MC, V. Free parking. Pets welcome. **Amenities:** Outdoor pool (summer only); Jacuzzi; bike rentals; store; coin-op laundry; bathhouse; miniature golf; playground; wheelchair-accessible restroom.

Albuquerque North Bernalillo KOA ⍟   More than 1,000 cottonwood and pine trees shade this park, and in the warm months there are many flowers. Located at the foot of the mountains, 14 miles from Albuquerque, this campground has plenty of amenities. Guests enjoy a free pancake breakfast daily. Reservations are recommended. Six camping cabins are also available.

555 Hill Rd., Bernalillo, NM 87004. © **800/562-3616** or 505/867-5227. www.koa.com. $20–$22 tent site; $30–$36 RV site, depending on hook-up; $35 1-bedroom cabin; $45 2-bedroom cabin. Rates include pancake breakfast and are valid for up to 2 people. Additional person $4. Children 5 and under free with parent. AE, DISC, MC, V. Free parking. Pets welcome. **Amenities:** Restaurant; outdoor pool (summer only); store; coin-op laundry; playground; free outdoor movies.

Palisades RV Park   Sitting out on the barren west mesa, this RV park has nice views of the Sandia Mountains and is the closest RV park to Old Town and the Biological Park (10-min. drive; see "Especially for Kids," later in this chapter); however, it is also in a fairly desolate setting, with only a few trees about. In midsummer it is hot.

9201 Central Ave. NW, Albuquerque, NM 87121. © **888/922-9595** or 505/831-5000. Fax 505/352-9599. www.palisadesrvpark.com. 110 sites. $27 per day; $110 per week; $250 per month plus electricity. MC, V. Free parking. Pets welcome. **Amenities:** Store; coin-op laundry; reception room; bathhouse; propane.

4 Where to Dine

IN OR NEAR OLD TOWN
MODERATE
La Crêpe Michel ⍟⍟ FRENCH   For years my father raved about the crepes at this small cafe tucked away in a secluded walkway not far from the plaza. Finally, he took me there, and now I understand what all the fuss was about. Run by chef Claudie Zamet-Wilcox from France, it has a cozy, informal European feel, with checked table coverings and simple furnishings. Service is

Where to Dine in Central Albuquerque

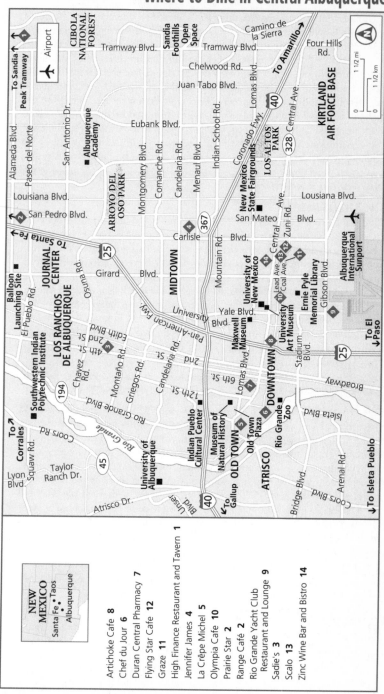

Artichoke Cafe **8**
Chef du Jour **6**
Duran Central Pharmacy **7**
Flying Star Cafe **12**
Graze **11**
High Finance Restaurant and Tavern **1**
Jennifer James **4**
La Crêpe Michel **5**
Olympia Cafe **10**
Prairie Star **2**
Range Café **2**
Rio Grande Yacht Club Restaurant and Lounge **9**
Sadie's **3**
Scalo **13**
Zinc Wine Bar and Bistro **14**

friendly and calm, which makes this a good place for a romantic meal. You can't miss with any of the crepes. The *crêpe aux fruits de mer* (blend of sea scallops, bay scallops, and shrimp in a velouté sauce with mushrooms) is especially nice, as is the *crêpe à la volaille* (chunks of chicken in a cream sauce with mushrooms and Madeira wine). For a heartier meal, try one of the specials listed on the board on the wall, such as the beef filet (tenderloin finished with either black peppercorn-brandy cream sauce or Roquefort-brandy cream sauce) or the *saumon au poivre vert* (filet of salmon with green peppercorn brandy sauce). Both are served with vegetables cooked just enough to leave them crisp and tasty. For dessert, don't leave without having a *crêpe aux fraises* (strawberry crepe). To accompany your meal, choose from a carefully planned beer and wine menu.

400 San Felipe St. NW. ☎ **505/242-1251.** Reservations recommended on weekends. Main courses $6–$24. MC, V. Tues–Sun 11:30am–2pm; Thurs–Sat 6–9pm.

INEXPENSIVE

Chef du Jour ⟨★⟩ ECLECTIC This small, quiet, and informal one-room cafe (with a few outdoor tables) serves elegantly prepared food at very reasonable prices. There's an open kitchen along one side and oddly matched tables. Once you get a taste of what's on the menu (which changes every week), you'll be coming back for more. Take special note of the condiments, all of which—from the ketchup to the salsa—are homemade. Recent menu offerings included a smoked chicken quesadilla with barbecue drizzle and a garden burger with smoked gouda cheese. There is also a salad du jour. If you call in advance, the restaurant will fax you a copy of its current menu. Microbrewed beers and hard ciders are available. The restaurant is a little difficult to find; travel south from the plaza, cross Lomas, and find San Pasquale.

119 San Pasquale SW. ☎ **505/247-8998.** Reservations recommended. Lunch $3–$9, dinner $6–$20. AE, DISC, MC, V. Mon–Fri 11am–2pm; Fri–Sat 5:30–10pm. Closed Christmas Eve–New Year's Day.

Duran Central Pharmacy ⟨★⟩ *(Finds)* NEW MEXICAN Sounds like an odd place to eat, I know. Although you could go to one of the touristy New Mexican restaurants in the middle of Old Town and have lots of atmosphere and mediocre food, you could instead come here, where locals eat, and feast on better, more authentic fare. It's a few blocks up Central, east of Old Town. On your way through the pharmacy, you may want to stock up on specialty soaps; there's a pretty good variety here. The restaurant itself is plain, with a red tile floor and small tables, as well as a counter. For years, I used to come here for a bowl of green chile stew and a homemade tortilla, which is still an excellent choice. Now I go for the full meals, such as the blue-corn enchilada plate or the *huevos rancheros* (eggs over corn tortillas, smothered with chile). The menu is short, but you can count on authentic northern New Mexican food. No smoking is permitted.

1815 Central Ave. NW. ☎ **505/247-4141.** Menu items $4.20–$8.10. No credit cards. Mon–Fri 9am–6:30pm; Sat 9am–2pm.

Sadie's ⟨★⟩ *(Kids)* NEW MEXICAN Many New Mexicans lament the lost days when this restaurant was in a bowling alley. In fact, much of my family has refused to go to its new, larger location, fearing that it has lost its good food. Well, it hasn't. Sure, you can no longer hear the pins fall, and the main dining room is a little too big and the atmosphere a little too bright, but something is still drawing crowds: It's the food—simply some of the best in New Mexico, with tasty sauces and large portions. I recommend the enchilada, either chicken or beef. The stuffed *sopaipilla* dinner is also delicious and is one of the signature dishes. All meals come with chips and salsa, beans, and *sopaipillas*. There's a full bar, with excellent margaritas (and TV screens for you sports lovers). A casual atmosphere where kids can be themselves makes this a nice spot for families.

6230 4th St. NW. ✆ 505/345-5339. Main courses $7–$14. AE, DC, DISC, MC, V. Mon–Sat 11am–10pm; Sun 11am–9pm.

DOWNTOWN
MODERATE

Artichoke Cafe ★★ CONTINENTAL   An art gallery as well as a restaurant, this popular spot has modern paintings and sculptures set against azure walls, a hint at the innovative dining experience offered here. Set in three rooms, with dim lighting, this is a nice romantic place. The staff is friendly and efficient, though a little slow on busy nights. I was impressed by the list of special drinks available: a variety of interesting waters that included my favorite, Ame, as well as ginger beer, Jamaican iced coffee, microbrews, and an excellent list of California and French wines. You might start with an artichoke, steamed with three dipping sauces, or have roasted garlic with Montrachet goat cheese. For lunch, there are a number of salads and gourmet sandwiches, as well as dishes such as garlic and lime prawns with orzo. Check out the fresh fish specials; my favorite is wahoo on glass noodles with miso broth. From the menu, try the pumpkin ravioli with butternut squash, spinach, and ricotta filling with hazelnut-sage butter sauce.

424 Central Ave. SE. ✆ 505/243-0200. Reservations recommended. Main courses $7–$12 lunch, $13–$24 dinner. AE, DC, DISC, MC, V. Mon–Fri 11am–2:30pm; Mon 5:30–9pm; Tues–Sat 5:30–10pm; Sun 5–9pm.

THE NORTHEAST HEIGHTS
EXPENSIVE

High Finance Restaurant and Tavern ★ CONTINENTAL   People don't rave about the food at this restaurant, but they do rave about the experience of eating here. Set high above Albuquerque, at the top of the Sandia Peak Tramway, it offers a fun and romantic adventure. The decor includes lots of shiny brass and comfortable furniture, and the service is decent. You might start with the sesame-fried calamari, served with greens and Thai dipping sauce. There are a number of pasta dishes, or you can try skillet-roasted ahi tuna served with spicy curry glaze. For meat lovers, there's prime rib or a filet. High Finance has a full bar. The restaurant recommends that you arrive at the Tramway base 45 minutes before your reservation.

40 Tramway Rd. NE (atop Sandia Peak). ✆ 505/243-9742. www.highfinancerestaurant.com. Reservations requested. Main courses $8–$13 lunch, $15–$45 dinner. Tramway $10 with dinner reservations ($15 without). AE, DC, DISC, MC, V. Summer daily 11am–9pm; winter daily 11am–8pm.

Jennifer James ★★★ CONTEMPORARY AMERICAN   Between pale yellow walls accented with bright strokes of red, creating a French bistro feel, this restaurant's namesake serves excellent contemporary American cuisine, with even more panache than she once did in her little Chef du Jour near Old Town (now under new ownership, p. 82). Service is friendly, though not especially efficient, but the food makes up for that lack. Start with roasted butternut squash soup with chipotle chiles and cilantro. For an entree, I recommend the pan-seared pork with apple bread pudding and herbed Brussels sprouts. The grilled quail over endive and radicchio with pomegranate date chutney is also delicious. A carefully selected wine list complements the menu.

2813 San Mateo NE. ✆ 505/884-3665. Reservations recommended. Main courses $16–$26. AE, DISC, MC, V. Tues–Sat 5–9pm.

Kids **Family-Friendly Restaurants**

Range Café (p. 86)   The fun and funky decor and Taos Cow Ice Cream make this a good spot for kids.

Sadie's (p. 82)   Kids like the quesadillas, tacos, and *sopaipillas* drizzled with honey; parents like the casual atmosphere where kid noise isn't scorned.

UNIVERSITY & NOB HILL

EXPENSIVE

Zinc Wine Bar and Bistro ★★ NEW AMERICAN   In a moody, urban atmosphere with wood floors and a high ceiling, this newest "in" place serves imaginative food meticulously prepared. The bi-level dining room with well-spaced tables can get crowded and noisy at peak hours (especially under the balcony, so avoid sitting there then). Service is congenial but inconsistent. Businesspeople and others fill the seats here, dining on such treats as blackened flank steak, Greek salad at lunch (my favorite), or portobello-crusted Alaskan halibut with chorizo sausage polenta at dinner. The restaurant offers other inventive elements, such as "wine flights," in which diners may sample a variety of wines from a particular region for a set and fairly reasonable price. Or, you may simply opt for an excellent martini from the full bar. In the lower level, a lounge serves less formally in a wine cellar atmosphere with live music playing 2 to 3 nights a week (open Mon–Sat 4pm–1am; food served to midnight).

3009 Central Ave. NE. © 505/254-ZINC. Reservations recommended. Main courses $7.50–$12 lunch, $14–$25 dinner. AE, DC, DISC, MC, V. Sun–Fri 11am–2:30pm; Mon–Thurs 5–10pm; Fri–Sat 5–11pm.

MODERATE

Graze ★★ *Finds* NEW AMERICAN   My first trip to this new restaurant not far from the university was with a relative from a small Texas town. The place offers a chance to sample the divine creations of chef Jennifer James without the higher costs at her namesake restaurant (p. 83). My relative looked at the menu and then looked at me with consternation. Be aware that this isn't a chicken-fried steak kind of place, though I wouldn't be surprised to see some refined version of that on this inventive menu. Set in a minimalist room, with hardwood floors and sunny colored walls, it's a fun spot for a culinary adventure, even for a small-town Texas girl, it turned out. Service is excellent. The portion sizes here are intentionally small, with the notion that diners will order many and share, though they're larger than tapas, so will suffice for a meal for a medium-size appetite. You might try the "piccolo frito," flash-fried calamari, with baby tomatoes, garbanzo beans, and basil, or the grilled tuna, with nori, daikon salad, and nicely sweet ponzu sauce. My relative loved the penne tossed with sun-dried tomatoes, New Mexico goat cheese, and chorizo sausage. A nice selection of beers and wines accompanies the menu, and inventive desserts appear daily.

3128 Central Ave. SE. © 505/268-4729. Reservations recommended on weekend nights. Individual plates $6–$20. AE, DISC, MC, V. Tues–Sat 11am–11pm.

Scalo ★ INTERNATIONAL/ITALIAN   This Italian restaurant is a local favorite, but over the years frequent chef turnover has made it less reliable than it once was, and the service varies greatly as well. The place has a simple, bistro-style elegance, with white-linen-clothed tables indoors, plus outdoor tables in a covered, temperature-controlled patio. The kitchen, which makes its own pasta and breads, has recently moved to a more international menu and offers meals in small, medium, and large portions. Seasonal menus focus on New Mexico–grown produce. One signature dish is a risotto-fried calamari with a spicy marinara sauce. A hearty main dish is the double-cut pork chop with champagne-roasted peaches, kale, and fried shallots. The daily specials are big hits. Dessert selections change daily. There's a good wine list, from which you can sample 30 wines by the glass; or you may order from the full bar.

3500 Central Ave. SE. ℭ 505/255-8781. Reservations recommended. Lunch $6–$12, dinner $8–$26. AE, DC, DISC, MC, V. Tues–Thurs 11:30am–10pm; Fri 11:30am–11pm; Sat 5–11pm; Sun 5–10pm.

INEXPENSIVE

Flying Star Cafe CAFE/BAKERY   The new Flying Star Cafe makes good on its promise of uptown food with down-home ingredients. This restaurant, with four locations, has actually been around Albuquerque awhile, under the moniker Double Rainbow, but it's been renamed and revamped into a more hip and urban restaurant with excellent contemporary international food. ***Beware:*** During mealtime the university location gets packed and rowdy. The selections range broadly, from 16 different breakfast options to homemade soups and salads to sandwiches and pasta (and pizza at the Juan Tabo and Rio Grande locations). Try the Rancher's melt (New Zealand sirloin sautéed with green chile, provolone, and horseradish on sourdough), or the Buddha's bowl (sautéed vegetables in ginger sauce with tofu over jasmine rice). Flying Star also has locations at 4501 Juan Tabo Blvd. NE (ℭ 505/275-8311); 8001 Menaul Blvd. NE (ℭ 505/293-6911); and 4026 Rio Grande Blvd. NW (ℭ 505/344-6714). They don't serve alcohol, but they do brew up plenty of espresso and cappuccino. Though hours vary for each location, they are all open daily for breakfast, lunch, and dinner.

3416 Central Ave. SE. ℭ 505/255-6633. Reservations not accepted. All menu items under $10. AE, DISC, MC, V. Daily 6am–11pm.

Olympia Cafe GREEK   Ask any northern New Mexico resident where they go for Greek food, and the hands-down favorite is Olympia. It's very informal (you order at a counter), it's right across from the university, and diners eat there at all times of day. It has a lively atmosphere, with bursts of enthusiastic Greek chatter emanating from the kitchen. With a full carryout menu, it's also a great place to grab a meal on the run. I like to get the Greek salad, served with fresh pita bread, and white-bean soup. A standard is the falafel sandwich with tahini. The restaurant is well known for its gyros, and I hear the moussaka is excellent. For dessert try the baklava.

2210 Central Ave. SE. ℭ 505/266-5222. Menu items $2–$12. DISC, MC, V. Mon–Fri 11am–10pm.

SOUTHEAST, NEAR THE AIRPORT

Rio Grande Yacht Club Restaurant and Lounge ✸ SEAFOOD   This festive restaurant serves decent seafood and steaks. Red, white, and blue sails hang beneath the skylight of a large room dominated by a tropical garden. The lunch menu features burgers, sandwiches, salads, and a few New Mexican specialties. At dinner, however, fresh fish is the main attraction. Snapper, sea scallops, ahi tuna, fresh oysters, and other denizens of the deep are prepared broiled, poached, blackened, teriyaki, Vera Cruz, au gratin, mornay, stuffed, and more. You select how you want your fish prepared; however, I suggest asking the chef for the best cooking style to suit your fish. If you'd rather have something else, the chef also prepares certified Angus beef, shrimp, Alaskan king crab, several chicken dishes, and even barbecued baby back pork ribs. The bar here is a good place for evening drinks. You'll hobnob with flight crews and sample such delicacies as smoked trout and *lahvosh* (Armenian cracker bread covered with havarti and Parmesan, baked until bubbly). Don't leave without sharing an Aspen snowball (vanilla ice cream rolled in walnuts and covered in hot fudge).

2500 Yale Blvd. SE. ✆ **505/243-6111.** Reservations recommended at dinner. Main courses $6–$12 lunch, $13–$41 dinner. AE, DC, DISC, MC, V. Mon–Fri 11am–2pm; Fri–Sat 5–11pm; Sun–Thurs 5–10pm.

OUTSIDE ALBUQUERQUE

Prairie Star ✦✦ NEW AMERICAN Located on the Santa Ana Pueblo, about 30 minutes north of Albuquerque, and set in a sprawling adobe home with a marvelous view across the high plains and a golf course, this restaurant offers an interesting blend of old and new, both in terms of atmosphere and flavor. It was built in the 1940s in Mission architectural style. Exposed vigas and full *latilla* ceilings, as well as hand-carved fireplaces and *bancos,* complement the thick adobe walls. There is a lounge at the top of the circular stairway. Diners can start with wild mushroom bruschetta, with kalamata olive tapenade and goat chevre. Signature dishes include Chama Valley lamb chops with caramelized apple torte and white asparagus (delicious), and soy-grilled quail with wasabi potatoes and Asian shrimp mousse. An extensive wine list with more than 30 varieties by the glass tops out the menu, as do special desserts, which vary nightly.

288 Prairie Star Rd., Santa Ana Pueblo. ✆ **505/867-3327.** Reservations recommended. Main courses $17–$33. AE, DC, DISC, MC, V. Tues–Sun 5:30–9pm (lounge opens at 4:30pm).

Range Café ✦ (Kids) NEW MEXICAN/AMERICAN This cafe on the main drag of Bernalillo, about 15 minutes north of Albuquerque, is a perfect place to stop on your way out of town. Housed in what was once an old drugstore, the restaurant has a pressed tin ceiling and is decorated with Western touches, such as cowboy boots and whimsical art. The food ranges from enchiladas and burritos to chicken-fried steak to more elegantly prepared meals. The proprietors and chef here have come from such notable restaurants as Scalo in Albuquerque (p. 84) and Prairie Star at Santa Ana Pueblo (above), so you can count on great food. For breakfast, try the pancakes or the breakfast burrito. For lunch or dinner, I recommend Tom's meatloaf, served with roasted-garlic mashed potatoes, mushroom gravy, and sautéed vegetables. For dinner, you might try pan-seared trout with sun-dried tomato and caper butter sauce. Taos Cow ice cream is the order for dessert, or try the baked goods and specialty drinks from the full bar. No smoking is permitted. In the same locale, the Range has opened the Lizard Rodeo Lounge, a smoke-free, hoppin' place with Wild West decor that offers live music many nights a week. There's also a retail space that sells local art and New Mexico wines. Two other branches of the restaurant in Albuquerque have similar food offerings (4200 Wyoming Blvd. NE, ✆ **505/293-2633;** and 2200 Menaul Blvd. NE, ✆ **505/888-1660**).

925 Camino del Pueblo (P.O. Box 1780), Bernalillo. ✆ **505/867-1700.** Reservations accepted for 8 or more. Breakfast and lunch $4–$9, dinner $9–$20. AE, DISC, MC, V. Summer Sun–Thurs 7:30am–10pm; winter Sun–Thurs 7:30am–9:30pm; ½ hour later on Fri and Sat. Closed Thanksgiving and Christmas.

5 What to See & Do

Albuquerque's original town site, known today as Old Town, is the central point of interest for visitors. Here, grouped around the plaza, are the venerable Church of San Felipe de Neri and numerous restaurants, art galleries, and crafts shops.

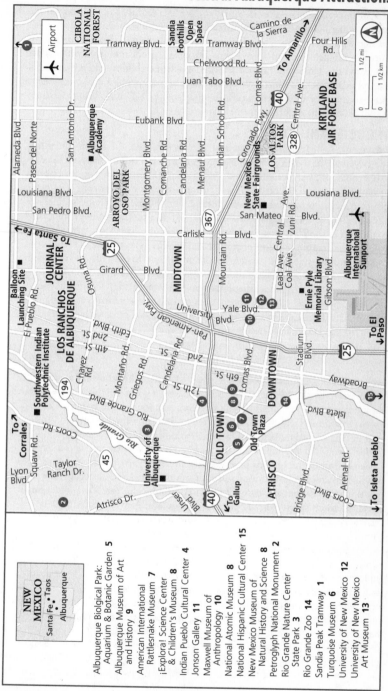

Central Albuquerque Attractions

Albuquerque Biolgical Park:
  Aquarium & Botanic Garden **5**
Albuquerque Museum of Art
  and History **9**
American International
  Rattlesnake Museum **7**
iExplora! Science Center
  & Children's Museum **8**
Indian Pueblo Cultural Center **4**
Jonson Gallery **11**
Maxwell Museum of
  Anthropology **10**
National Atomic Museum **8**
National Hispanic Cultural Center **15**
New Mexico Museum of
  Natural History and Science **8**
Petroglyph National Monument **2**
Rio Grande Nature Center
  State Park **3**
Rio Grande Zoo **14**
Sandia Peak Tramway **1**
Turquoise Museum **6**
University of New Mexico **12**
University of New Mexico
  Art Museum **13**

NEW
MEXICO
Santa Fe • Taos
    • Albuquerque

Several important museums are situated close by. Within a few blocks are the 25,000-square-foot Albuquerque Aquarium and the 50-acre Rio Grande Botanic Garden (near Central Ave. and Tingley Dr. NW), both well worth a visit.

But don't get stuck in Old Town. Elsewhere you'll find the Sandia Peak Tramway; the University of New Mexico, with its museums; and a number of natural attractions. Within day-trip range are several pueblos and monuments (see "Touring the Pueblos Around Albuquerque" and "Salinas Pueblo Missions National Monument," later in this chapter).

THE TOP ATTRACTIONS

Albuquerque Museum of Art and History (*Kids* Take an interesting journey down into the caverns of New Mexico's past in this museum on the outskirts of Old Town. Drawing on the largest U.S. collection of Spanish colonial artifacts, displays here include Don Quixote–style helmets, swords, and horse armor. You can wander through an 18th-century house compound with adobe floor and walls, and see gear used by *vaqueros*, the original cowboys who came to the area in the 16th century. A weaving exhibition allows kids to try spinning wool, and a trapping section provides them with pelts to touch. In an old-style theater, two films on Albuquerque history are shown. In the History Hopscotch area, kids can explore an old trunk or play with antique blocks and other toys. An Old Town walking tour originates here at 11am Tuesday to Sunday during spring, summer, and fall. The upper floors house permanent art collections and, best of all, a huge exhibit space where you'll find some extraordinary shows. A gift shop sells books and jewelry and has a nice selection of Navajo dolls.

2000 Mountain Rd. NW, Albuquerque, NM 87104. (*C*) **505/243-7255.** www.albuquerquemuseum.com. Admission $4 adults, $2 seniors 65 and older and children 4–12. Tues–Sun 9am–5pm. Closed major holidays.

Indian Pueblo Cultural Center (*Kids* Owned and operated as a nonprofit organization by the 19 pueblos of New Mexico, this is a fine place to begin an exploration of Native American culture. Located about a mile northeast of Old Town, this museum—modeled after Pueblo Bonito, a spectacular 9th-century ruin in Chaco Culture National Historic Park—consists of several parts.

Begin your exploration in the basement, where a permanent exhibit depicts the **evolution of the various pueblos** from prehistory to present, including displays of the distinctive handcrafts of each community. Note especially how pottery differs in concept and design from pueblo to pueblo. You'll also find a small screening room where you can see films of some of New Mexico's most noted Native American artists making their wares, including San Ildefonso potter María Martinez, firing her pottery with open flames.

The **Pueblo House Children's Museum,** located in a separate building, is a hands-on experience that gives children the opportunity to learn about and understand the evolution of Pueblo culture. There they can touch pot shards, play with *heishi* (shell) drills, and even don fox tails and dance.

Upstairs in the main building is an enormous **gift shop** featuring fine pottery, rugs, sand paintings, kachinas, drums, jewelry, Southwestern clothing, and souvenirs, among other things. Prices here are quite reasonable.

Every weekend throughout the year, **Native American dancers** perform at 11am and 2pm in an outdoor arena surrounded by original murals. Often, artisans demonstrate their crafts there as well. During certain weeks of the year, such as the Balloon Fiesta, dances are performed daily.

A restaurant serves traditional Native American foods. I wouldn't eat a full meal here, but it's a good place for some Indian fry bread and a bowl of *posole*.

2401 12th St. NW, Albuquerque, NM 87104. ℂ **800/766-4405** or 505/843-7270. www.indianpueblo.org. Admission $4 adults, $3 seniors, $1 students, free for children 4 and under. AE, DISC, MC, V. Daily 9am–4:30pm; restaurant 8am–3pm. Closed New Year's Day, Memorial Day, July 4, Labor Day, Thanksgiving, and Christmas.

National Hispanic Cultural Center ⍟   Located in the historic Barelas neighborhood on the Camino Real, this gem of Albuquerque museums offers a rich cultural journey through hundreds of years of history and across the globe. It explores Hispanic arts and lifeways with visual arts, drama, music, dance, and other programs. I most enjoyed the 11,000-square-foot gallery space, which exhibits exciting contemporary and traditional works. Look for photographs by Miguel Gandert. An exciting 2004 exhibit was *Corridos Sin Fronteras,* which re-creates the historical development of the *corrida* (a song portraying an adventure) in Mexico and the southwestern U.S. A restaurant offers New Mexican and American food. It's a good spot to sample authentic regional dishes such as tacos and enchiladas either from a buffet or by ordering from the menu. My favorite is the tortilla burger (a burger served in a flour tortilla, with all the fixin's). Plans are under way to incorporate a cultural cooking component into the center, which would allow visitors to sample Hispanic foods from all over the world.

1701 4th St. SW (corner of 4th St. and Avenida Cesar Chavez), Albuquerque, NM 87102. ℂ **505/246-2261.** Fax 505/246-2613. www.nhccnm.org. Admission Tues–Sat $3 adults, $2 seniors 60 and over, children 16 and under free; Sun $1 adults and seniors. AE, DISC, MC, V. Tues–Sun 10am–5pm; restaurant 8am–3pm. Closed New Year's Day, Easter, Memorial Day, Labor Day, and Christmas.

Old Town ⍟⍟   A maze of cobbled courtyard walkways leads to hidden patios and gardens, where many of Old Town's 150 galleries and shops are located. Adobe buildings, many refurbished in the Pueblo Revival style of the 1950s, are grouped around the tree-shaded plaza, created in 1780.

The buildings of Old Town once served as mercantile shops, grocery stores, and government offices, but the importance of Old Town as Albuquerque's commercial center declined after 1880, when the railroad came through 1¼ miles east of the plaza and businesses relocated to be closer to the trains. Old Town clung to its historical and sentimental roots, but the quarter fell into disrepair until the 1930s and 1940s, when artisans and other shop owners rediscovered it and the tourism industry burgeoned.

When Albuquerque was established in 1706, the first building the settlers erected was the **Church of San Felipe de Neri,** which faces the north side of the plaza. It's a cozy church with wonderful stained-glass windows and vivid *retablos* (religious paintings). It has been in almost continuous use for nearly 300 years.

Though you'll wade through a few trinket and T-shirt shops on the plaza, don't be fooled: Old Town is an excellent place to shop. Look for good buys from the Native Americans selling jewelry on the plaza, especially silver bracelets and strung turquoise. If you want to take something fun home and spend very little, buy a dyed corn necklace. Your best bet when wandering around Old Town is to just peek into shops, but there are a few places you'll definitely want to spend time. See "Shopping," later in this chapter, for a list of recommendations. An excellent Old Town historic walking tour originates at the Albuquerque Museum of Art and History (see above) at 11am Tuesday to Sunday during spring, summer, and fall. Plan to spend 2 to 3 hours strolling around.

Northeast of Central Ave. and Rio Grande Blvd. NW, Albuquerque, NM 87104. Old Town Visitor Center: 303 Romero St. NW, Albuquerque, NM 87104 (across the street from the Church of San Felipe de Neri). ℂ **505/ 243-3215.** Visitor Center daily 9am–5pm summer; 9:30am–4:30pm rest of the year.

Sandia Peak Tramway *(Kids* *(R(R)*   This fun and exciting half-day or evening outing allows incredible views of Albuquerque's landscape and wildlife. The Sandia Peak Tram is a "jigback"; in other words, as one car approaches the top, the other nears the bottom. The two pass halfway through the trip, in the midst of a 1½-mile "clear span" of unsupported cable between the second tower and the upper terminal.

Several hiking trails are available on Sandia Peak, and one of them—La Luz Trail—takes you on a steep and rigorous trek from the base to the summit. The views in all directions are extraordinary. *Note:* The trails on Sandia may not be suitable for children. There is a popular and expensive restaurant, High Finance Restaurant and Tavern, at Sandia's summit (see "Where to Dine," earlier in this chapter). Special tram rates apply with dinner reservations. Note that the tram does not operate on very windy days.

10 Tramway Loop NE, Albuquerque, NM 87122. ℂ **505/856-7325.** Fax 505/856-6335. www.sandiapeak. com. Admission $15 adults, $12 seniors, $10 children 5–12, free for children under 5. Memorial Day to Labor Day daily 9am–9pm; spring and fall Thurs–Tues 9am–8pm, Wed 5–8pm; ski season Thurs–Tues 9am–8pm, Wed noon–8pm. Closed 2 weeks each spring and fall for maintenance; check the website for details. Parking $1 daily. AE, DISC, MC, V. To reach the base of the tram, take I-25 north to Tramway Rd. (exit 234), then proceed east about 5 miles on Tramway Rd. (NM 556); or take Tramway Blvd., exit 167 (NM 556), north of I-40 approximately 8½ miles.

OTHER ATTRACTIONS
National Atomic Museum   "I am become death, the shatterer of worlds." Shortly after the successful detonation of the first atomic bomb, Robert Oppenheimer, who headed the Manhattan Project, said this, quoting from ancient Hindu texts. This and other valuable information highlight the 51-minute film *Ten Seconds That Shook the World,* which is shown daily (throughout the day) at this museum, an experience worth fitting into a busy schedule. The museum itself offers the next-best introduction to the nuclear age after the Bradbury Science Museum in Los Alamos, making for an interesting 1- to 2-hour perusal. It traces the history of nuclear-weapons development, beginning with the top-secret Manhattan Project of the 1940s, including a copy of the letter Albert Einstein wrote to President Franklin D. Roosevelt suggesting the possible need to beat the Germans at creating an atomic bomb—a letter that surprisingly went ignored for nearly 2 years. You'll find a permanent Marie Curie exhibit in the lobby and full-scale models of the "Fat Man" and "Little Boy" bombs, as well as displays and films on the peaceful application of nuclear technology—including nuclear medicine—and other alternative energy sources.

1905 Mountain Rd. NW (P.O. Box 5800, MS1490), Albuquerque, NM 87104. ℂ **505/245-2137.** Fax 505/ 242-4537. www.atomicmuseum.com. Admission $4 adults, $3 seniors and children 7–18, free for children 6 and under. Children under 12 not admitted without an adult. Group rates available. Daily 9am–5pm. Closed New Year's Day, Easter, Thanksgiving, and Christmas.

Petroglyph National Monument *(R* *(Kids*   These lava flows were once a hunting and gathering area for prehistoric Native Americans, who left a chronicle of their beliefs etched on the dark basalt boulders. Some 25,000 petroglyphs provide a nice outdoor adventure after a morning in a museum. You'll want to stop at the visitor center to get a map, check out the interactive computer, and, in summer, hook up with a ranger-led tour. From there, you can drive north to the Boca Negra area, where you have a choice of three trails. Mesa Point Trail (30 min.) climbs quickly up the side of a hill, offering many petroglyph sightings as well as an outstanding view of the Sandia Mountains. If you're traveling with your dog, you can bring her along on the Rinconada Trail. Hikers can have fun searching the rocks for more petroglyphs; there are many yet to be found. This trail (located a few miles south of the visitor center) runs for miles around a huge *rincon* (corner) at the base of the lava flow. Camping is not permitted in the park; it's strictly for day use, with picnic areas, drinking water, and restrooms provided.

6001 Unser Blvd. NW (3 miles north of I-40 at Unser and Western Trail), Albuquerque, NM 87120. © 505/899-0205. Fax 505/899-0207. www.nps.gov/petr. Admission $1 per vehicle weekdays, $2 weekends. DISC, MC, V. Visitor Center and Boca Negra area daily 8am–5pm. Closed New Year's Day, Thanksgiving, and Christmas.

Turquoise Museum *(Kids*   Don't be put off by the setting of this little gem of a museum in a strip mall west of Old Town. For those with curiosity, it's a real find that's been featured in *Smithsonian Magazine* and on *60 Minutes*. The passion of father and son Joe P. Lowry and Joe Dan Lowry, it contains "the world's largest collection of turquoise"—from 60 mines around the world. You start through a tunnel, where turquoise is embedded in the walls, and move on to exhibits that present the blue stone's geology, history, and mythology. You'll see maps showing where turquoise is mined, ranging from Egypt to Kingman, Arizona, and find out how to determine whether the turquoise you're hoping to buy is quality or not. Lowry Sr. will fill in any details and even tell you more about turquoise you're wearing. There's also a real lapidary shop; jewelry made there is sold in a gift shop that's open until 5pm. Plan to spend about 1 hour here.

2107 Central Ave. NW, Albuquerque, NM 87104. © 505/247-8650. Admission $4 adults, $3 children 7–17 and seniors 60 and over; free for children 6 and under; $10 family rate. AE, DISC, MC, V. Mon–Sat 10am–4pm.

University of New Mexico   The state's largest institution of higher learning stretches across an attractive 70-acre campus about 2 miles east of downtown Albuquerque, north of Central Avenue and east of University Boulevard. The five campus museums, none of which charges admission (like other UNM buildings) in a modified pueblo style. Popejoy Hall, in the south-central part of the campus, hosts many performing-arts presentations, including those of the New Mexico Symphony Orchestra; other public events are held in nearby Keller Hall and Woodward Hall.

The best way to see the museums and campus is on a walking tour, which can make for a nice 2- to 3-hour morning or afternoon outing. Begin on the west side of campus at the Maxwell Museum of Anthropology. You'll find parking meters there, as well as Maxwell Museum parking, for which you can get a permit inside.

The **Maxwell Museum of Anthropology,** situated on the west side of the campus on Redondo Drive, south of Las Lomas Road (© **505/277-4404;** www. unm.edu/~maxwell), is an internationally acclaimed repository of Southwestern anthropological finds. What's really intriguing here is not just the ancient pottery, tools, and yucca weavings, but the anthropological context within which these items are set. You'll see a reconstruction of an archaeological site, complete with string markers, brushes, and field notes, as well as microscope lenses you can examine to see how archaeologists perform temper analysis to find out where pots were made, and pollen analysis to help reconstruct past environments. There are two permanent exhibits: *Ancestors,* which looks at human evolution, and *People of the Southwest,* a look at the history of the Southwest from 10,000 years ago to the 16th century from an archeological perspective. It's open Tuesday to Friday 9am to 4pm, and Saturday 10am to 4pm; the museum is closed Sundays, Mondays, and holidays. From the Maxwell, walk east into the campus until you come to the Duck Pond and pass Mitchell Hall; then turn south (right) and walk down a lane until you reach Northrup Hall.

Cooking School

If you've fallen in love with New Mexican and Southwestern cooking during your stay (or if you did even before you arrived), you might like to sign up for cooking classes with Jane Butel, a leading Southwestern cooking authority, author of 14 cookbooks, and host of the national TV show *Jane Butel's Southwestern Kitchen.* At **Jane Butel Cooking School** *&*, at La Posada de Albuquerque, 125 Second St. NW (*©* **800/ 472-8229** or 505/243-2622; fax 505/243-8296; www.janebutel.com), you'll learn the history and techniques of Southwestern cuisine and have ample opportunity for hands-on preparation. If you choose the weeklong session, you'll start by learning about chiles and move on to native breads and dishes, appetizers, beverages, and desserts. Weekend sessions and special vegetarian sessions are also available, as are some sessions that include "culinary tours," including trips to Taos and Santa Fe. Call, fax, or check out Jane's website for current schedules and fees.

In **Northrup Hall** (*©* **505/277-4204**), about halfway between the Maxwell Museum and Popejoy Hall in the southern part of the campus, the adjacent **Geology Museum** (*©* **505/277-4204**) and **Meteorite Museum** (*©* **505/277-1644**) cover the gamut of recorded time from dinosaur bones to moon rocks. Within the Geology Museum, you'll see stones that create spectacular works of art, from black-on-white orbicular granite to brilliant blue dioptase. In the Meteorite Museum, 550 meteorite specimens comprise the sixth-largest collection in the United States. You'll see and touch a sink-size piece of a meteorite that weighs as much as a car, as well as samples of the many variations of stones that fall from the sky. Both museums are open Monday to Friday 9am to 4pm.

From here, you walk east, straight through a mall that takes you by the art building to the Fine Arts Center. The **University of New Mexico Art Museum** (*©* **505/277-4001;** http://unmartmuseum.unm.edu) is located here, just north of Central Avenue and Cornell Street. The museum features changing exhibitions of 19th- and 20th-century art. Its permanent collection includes Old Masters paintings and sculpture, significant New Mexican and Spanish-colonial artwork, the Tamarind Lithography Archives, and (my favorite part) one of the largest university-owned photography collections in the U.S. It's open Tuesday to Friday 9am to 4pm, Tuesday evening 5 to 8pm, and Sunday 1 to 4pm; it is closed holidays. A gift shop offers a variety of gifts and posters.

By now you'll probably want a break. Across the mall to the north is the Student Union Building, where you can get treats, from muffins to pizza. Campus maps can be obtained here, along with directions. Once you're refreshed, head out the north door of the Student Union Building and walk west through Smith Plaza, then turn north by the bus stop and walk to Las Lomas Road, where you'll turn right and walk a half block to the intimate **Jonson Gallery,** at 1909 Las Lomas Rd. NE (*©* **505/277-4967;** www.unm.edu/jonsong), on the north side of the central campus. This museum displays more than 2,000 works by the late Raymond Jonson, a leading modernist painter in early-20th-century New Mexico, as well as works by contemporary artists. If you're going to miss one of the campus museums, make it this one. It's open Tuesday to Friday 9am to 4pm and Tuesday evening 5 to 8pm. From the Jonson you can walk west on Las Lomas Road to Redondo Road, where you'll turn south and arrive back at the Maxwell Museum. Touring these museums takes a full morning or afternoon.

1 University Hill NE (north of Central Ave.), Albuquerque, NM 87131. © 505/277-0111. www.unm.edu.

6 Especially for Kids

Albuquerque Biological Park: Aquarium and Botanic Garden 🌟 *Kids*
For those of us born and raised in the desert, the aquarium quenches years of soul thirst. The self-guided tour begins with a beautifully produced 9-minute film that describes the course of the Rio Grande from its origin to the Gulf Coast. Then, you'll move on to the touch pool, where at certain times of day you can touch hermit crabs and starfish. You'll pass by a replica of a salt marsh, where a gentle tidal wave moves in and out, and you'll explore the eel tank, an arched aquarium you get to walk through. There's a colorful coral-reef exhibit, as well as the culminating show, in a 285,000-gallon shark tank, where many species of fish and 15 to 20 sand-tiger, brown, and nurse sharks swim around, looking ominous.

Within a state-of-the-art 10,000-square-foot conservatory, you'll find the botanical garden, split into two sections. The smaller one houses the desert collection and features plants from the lower Chihuahuan and Sonoran deserts, including unique species from Baja, California. The larger pavilion exhibits the Mediterranean collection and includes many exotic species native to the Mediterranean climates of southern California, South Africa, Australia, and the Mediterranean Basin. Allow at least 2 hours to see both parks. There is a restaurant on the premises.

In December, you can see the "River of Lights Holiday Light Display" Tuesday through Sunday; June through August you can attend Thursday evening concerts.

2601 Central Ave. NW, Albuquerque, NM 87104. © 505/764-6200. www.cabq.gov/biopark. Admission $7 adults ($10 with Rio Grande Zoo admission), $3 seniors 65 and over and children 12 and under ($5 with Rio Grande Zoo admission). Ticket sales stop a half-hour before closing. MC, V. Tues–Sun 9am–5pm (Sat–Sun to 6pm June–Aug). Closed New Year's Day, Thanksgiving, and Christmas.

American International Rattlesnake Museum *Finds* *Kids*   This unique museum, located just off Old Town Plaza, has living specimens of common, uncommon, and very rare rattlesnakes of North, Central, and South America in naturally landscaped habitats. Oddities such as albino and patternless rattlesnakes are included, as is a display popular with youngsters: baby rattlesnakes. More than 30 species can be seen, followed by a 7-minute film on this contributor to the ecological balance of our hemisphere. Throughout the museum are rattlesnake artifacts from early American history, Native American culture, medicine, the arts, and advertising. You'll also find a gift shop that sells a variety of items, all with an emphasis on rattlesnakes.

202 San Felipe St. NW, Albuquerque, NM 87104. © 505/242-6569. www.rattlesnakes.com. Admission $2.50 adults, $2 seniors, $1.50 children. AE, DISC, MC, V. Mon–Sat 10am–6pm; Sun noon–5pm.

¡Explora! Science Center and Children's Museum *Kids*   As a center for lifelong learning, ¡Explora! houses more than 250 hands-on scientific exhibits for visitors of all ages, on topics as diverse as water, the Rio Grande, light and optics, and energy. It features exhibits utilizing technology that is creatively accessible to the public and exhibits that engage visitors in creating all kinds of art.

1701 Mountain Rd., Albuquerque, NM 87104. ℂ **505/224-8300.** Fax 505/224-8325. www.explora.mus.nm. us. Admission $7 adults (age 12–64), $5 seniors 65 and over and children 1–11, free for children under 1. Mon–Sat 10am–6pm; Sun noon–6pm.

New Mexico Museum of Natural History and Science 🌟🌟 *Kids*   This museum will take you through 12 billion years of natural history, from the formation of the universe to the present day. Begin by looking at a display of stones and gems, then stroll through the "Age of Giants" display, where you'll see dinosaur skeletons cast from the real bones. Next, you come into the Cretaceous Period and learn of the progression of flooding in the southwestern United States, beginning 100 million years ago and continuing until 66 million years ago, when New Mexico became dry. This exhibit takes you through a tropical oasis, with aquariums of alligator gars, fish that were here 100 million years ago and still exist today. Next, step into the Evolator (kids love this!), a simulated time-travel ride that moves and rumbles, taking you 1.25 miles (2km) up (or down) and through 38 million years of history. Then, you'll feel the air grow hot as you walk into a cave and see the inner workings of a volcano, including simulated magma flow. Soon, you'll find yourself in the age of the mammoths and moving through the ice age. Other stops along the way include the Naturalist Center, where kids can peek through microscopes and make their own bear or raccoon footprints in sand, and FossilWorks, where paleontologists work behind glass, excavating bones of a seismosaurus. Be sure to check out the LodeStar Astronomy Center, a sophisticated planetarium with the Virtual Voyages Simulation theater. Those exhibits, as well as the DynaTheater, which surrounds you with images and sound, cost an additional fee. A gift shop sells imaginative nature games and other curios. This museum has good access for people with disabilities.

1801 Mountain Rd. NW, Albuquerque, NM 87104. ℂ **505/841-2800.** http://museums.state.nm.us/nmmnh/ nmmnh.html. Admission $5 adults, $4 seniors, $2 children 3–12, free for children under 3. DynaTheater, Planetarium, and Virtual Voyages cost extra, with prices in the $6 range for adults and the $3 range for children. Buying ticket combinations qualifies you for discounts. Daily 9am–5pm. Jan and Sept closed on Mon except major holidays; also closed Thanksgiving and Christmas.

Rio Grande Nature Center *Kids*   Whenever I'm in Albuquerque and want to get away from it all, I come here. The center, located just a few miles north of Old Town, spans 270 acres of riverside forest and meadows that include stands of 100-year-old cottonwoods and a 3-acre pond. Located on the Rio Grande Flyway, an important migratory route for many birds, it's an excellent place to see sandhill cranes, Canadian geese, and quail—more than 260 bird species have made this their temporary or permanent home. In a protected area where dogs aren't allowed (you can bring dogs on most of the 2 miles of trails), you'll find exhibits of native grasses, wildflowers, and herbs. Inside a building built half above and half below ground, you can sit next to the pond in a glassed-in viewing area and comfortably watch ducks and other birds in their avian antics. There are 21 self-guided interpretive exhibits as well as photo exhibits, a library, a small nature store, and a children's resource room. On Saturday mornings you can join a guided nature walk. Other weekend programs are available for adults and children, including nature photography and bird and wildflower identification classes.

2901 Candelaria Rd. NW, Albuquerque, NM 87107. ℂ **505/344-7240.** Fax 505/344-4505. www.frgnc.org. Admission $1 adults, 50¢ children 6–16, free for children under 6. DISC, MC, V. Daily 10am–5pm; store Mon–Fri 11am–3pm; Sat–Sun 10am–4pm. Closed New Year's Day, Thanksgiving, and Christmas.

Rio Grande Zoo 🌟 *Kids*   More than 1,200 animals from 300 species live on 60 acres of riverside bosque among ancient cottonwoods. Open-moat exhibits with animals in naturalized habitats are a treat for visitors. Major exhibits include polar bears, giraffes, sea lions (with underwater viewing), a bird show, and ape country. The zoo has an especially fine collection of elephants, mountain lions, koalas, reptiles, and native Southwestern species. A children's petting zoo is open during the summer. There are numerous snack bars on the zoo grounds, and La Ventana Gift Shop carries film and souvenirs. Also check out the seal and sea lion feeding at 10:30am and 3:30pm daily and the summer Zoo Music Concert Series.

903 10th St. SW, Albuquerque, NM 87102. ✆ **505/764-6200.** www.cabq.gov/biopark/zoo. Admission $7 adults ($10 with Aquarium and Botanic Garden admission), $3 seniors and children 3–12 ($5 with Aquarium and Botanic Garden admission), free for children 2 and under. Daily 9am–4:30pm (6pm summer weekends). Closed New Year's Day, Thanksgiving, and Christmas.

7 Outdoor Activities

BALLOONING
Visitors have a choice of several hot-air balloon operators; rates start at about $135 per person per hour. Call **Rainbow Ryders,** 11520 San Bernardino NE (✆ **505/823-1111**), or **World Balloon Corporation,** 1103 La Poblana NW (✆ **505/293-6800**). If you have your heart set on a balloon flight, reserve a time early in your trip because flights are sometimes canceled due to bad weather. That way, if you have to reschedule, you'll have enough time to do so.

If you'd rather just watch, go to the annual **Albuquerque International Balloon Fiesta** 🎈🎈, which is held the first through second weekends of October (see "New Mexico Calendar of Events," in chapter 2, for details).

BIKING
Albuquerque is a major bicycling hub in the summer, for both road racers and mountain bikers. For an excellent map of Albuquerque bicycle routes, call the **Albuquerque Parks & Recreation Department** at ✆ **505/768-3550** or visit **www.cabq.gov,** click on "Interactive Maps (GIS)," and then click on "Bike Paths." A great place to bike is **Sandia Peak** (✆ **505/242-9133;** www.sandia peak.com) in Cíbola National Forest. You can't take your bike on the tram, but a chairlift is available for uphill or downhill transportation with a bike. Bike rentals are available at the top and bottom of the chairlift. They cost $38 for adult bikes and $28 for junior ones. The lift costs $14 and runs on weekends, with Friday added in July and August, though you'll want to call to be sure. Helmets are mandatory. The clearly marked trails range from easy to very difficult.

Down in the valley, the **bosque trail** that runs along the Rio Grande is accessed through the Rio Grande Nature Center (see "Especially for Kids," earlier in this chapter). To the east, the **Foothills Trail** runs along the base of the mountains. It's a fun 7-mile-long trail that offers excellent views. Access it by driving east from downtown on Montgomery Boulevard, past the intersection with Tramway Boulevard. Go left on Glenwood Hills Drive and head north about a half-mile before turning right onto a short road that leads to the Embudito trail head.

Northeast Cyclery, 8305 Menaul Blvd. NE (✆ **505/299-1210**) rents bikes at the rate of $25 per day for front-suspension mountain bikes and $35 per day for road bikes. Multiday discounts are available. Unfortunately, the shop doesn't rent children's bikes. Rentals come with helmets.

BIRD-WATCHING
Bosque del Apache National Wildlife Refuge 🦅🦅 (✆ **505/835-1828**) is a haven for migratory waterfowl such as snow geese and cranes. It's located 90

miles south of Albuquerque on I-25, and it's well worth the drive. For details, see chapter 10.

FISHING

There are no real fishing opportunities in Albuquerque, but there is a nearby fishing area known as **Shady Lakes** (© **505/898-2568**). Nestled among cottonwood trees, it's located near I-25 on Albuquerque's north side. The most common catches are rainbow trout, black bass, bluegill, and channel catfish. To reach Shady Lakes, take I-25 north to the Tramway exit. Follow Tramway Road west for a mile and then go right on NM 313 for a half-mile. **Sandia Lakes Recreational Area** (© **505/897-3971**), also located on NM 313, is another popular fishing spot. It has a bait and tackle shop.

GOLF

There are quite a few public courses in the Albuquerque area. The **Championship Golf Course at the University of New Mexico,** 3601 University Blvd. SE (© **505/277-4546**), is one of the best in the Southwest and was rated one of the country's top 25 public courses by *Golf Digest.* **Paradise Hills Golf Course,** 10035 Country Club Lane NW (© **505/898-7001**), is a popular 18-hole golf course on the west side of town. Other Albuquerque courses are **Ladera,** 3401 Ladera Dr. NW (© **505/836-4449**); **Los Altos,** 9717 Copper Ave. NE (© **505/298-1897**); **Puerto del Sol,** 1800 Girard Blvd. SE (© **505/265-5636**); and **Arroyo del Oso,** 7001 Osuna Rd. NE (© **505/884-7505**).

If you're willing to drive a short distance just outside Albuquerque, you can play at the **Santa Ana Golf Club at Santa Ana Pueblo,** 288 Prairie Star Rd., Bernalillo, 87004 (© **505/867-9464**), which was rated by the *New York Times* as one of the best public golf courses in the country. Club rentals are available (call for information). In addition, **Isleta Pueblo,** 4001 Hwy. 47 (© **505/869-0950**), south of Albuquerque, has an 18-hole course.

HIKING

The 1.5-million-acre **Cíbola National Forest** offers ample hiking opportunities. Within town, the best hike is the **Embudito Trail,** which heads up into the foothills, with spectacular views down across Albuquerque. The 5.5-mile one-way hike is moderate to difficult. Allow 1 to 8 hours, depending on how far you want to go. Access it by driving east from downtown on Montgomery Boulevard past the intersection with Tramway Boulevard. Go left on Glenwood Hills Drive and head north about a half-mile before turning right onto a short road that leads to the trail head. The premier Sandia Mountain hike is **La Luz Trail,** a very strenuous journey from the Sandia foothills to the top of the Crest. It's a 15-mile round-trip jaunt, and it's half that if you take the Sandia Peak Tramway (see "The Top Attractions," earlier in this chapter) either up or down. Allow a full day for this hike. Access is off Tramway Boulevard and Forest Service Road 333. For more details contact the **Sandia Ranger Station,** Highway 337 south toward Tijeras (© **505/281-3304**).

HORSEBACK RIDING

If you want to get in a saddle and eat some trail dust, call the **Hyatt Regency Tamaya Resort and Spa,** 1300 Tuyuna Trail, Santa Ana Pueblo (© **505/771-6037**). The resort offers 2½-hour-long rides near the Rio Grande for $60 per person. Children must be over 7 years of age and over 4 feet tall. The resort is located about 15 miles north of Albuquerque. From I-25 take exit 242, following US 550 west to Tamaya Boulevard, and drive 1½ miles to the resort.

Getting Pampered: The Spa Scene

If you're looking to get pampered, you have a few options. **Mark Prado Salon & Spa** (*C* 800/363-7115) offers treatments at four locations: 1100 Juan Tabo Blvd. NE (*C* 505/298-2983), 8001 Wyoming Blvd. NE (*C* 505/856-7700), 3500 Central Ave. SE 7B (*C* 505/266-2400), and Cottonwood Mall, 10000 Coors Blvd. NE (*C* 505/897-2288).

Albuquerque's most luxurious spa experience is at the **Hyatt Regency Tamaya Resort & Spa,** 1300 Tuyuna Trail, Santa Ana Pueblo (*C* 505/867-1234). A vast array of treatments, and a sauna and steam room, are available in a refined atmosphere set near the Rio Grande, 15 minutes north of Albuquerque, near the village of Bernalillo.

RIVER RAFTING

River rafting is generally practiced farther north, in the area surrounding Santa Fe and Taos; however, Albuquerque is the home of **Wolf Whitewater,** 4626 Palo Alto SE (*C* 505/262-1099; www.wolfwhitewater.com), one of the best rafting companies in the region.

SKIING

Sandia Peak Ski Area is a good place for family skiing. There are plenty of beginner and intermediate runs. (However, if you're looking for more challenge or more variety, head north to Santa Fe or Taos.) The ski area has twin base-to-summit chairlifts to its upper slopes at 10,360 feet and a 1,700-foot vertical drop. There are 30 runs above the day lodge and ski-rental shop. Four chairs and two pomas accommodate 3,400 skiers an hour. All-day lift tickets are $38 for adults, $33 for teens ages 13 to 20, $29 for children ages 6 to 12 and seniors ages 62 to 71, and free for children 46 inches tall or less in ski boots and seniors ages 72 and over; rental packages are available. The season runs mid-December to mid-March. Contact the ski area, 10 Tramway Loop NE (*C* 505/242-9133), for more information, or call *C* 505/857-8977 for ski conditions.

Cross-country skiers can enjoy the trails of the Sandia Wilderness from Sandia Peak Ski Area, or they can venture an hour north to the remote Jemez Wilderness and its hot springs.

TENNIS

Albuquerque has 29 public parks with tennis courts. Because of the city's size, your best bet is to call the **Albuquerque Convention and Visitors Bureau** (*C* 800/284-2282) to find out which park is closest to your hotel.

8 Spectator Sports

BASEBALL

The **Albuquerque Isotopes** play 72 home games at Isotopes Park, as part of the Pacific Coast League. Tickets range from $5 to $10. For information, contact *C* 505/924-2255 or see **www.albuquerquebaseball.com.** Isotopes Park is located at 1601 Avenida Cesar Chavez SE. Take I-25 south to Avenida Cesar Chavez and go east, to the intersection with University Boulevard.

BASKETBALL

The University of New Mexico team, **"The Lobos,"** plays an average of 16 home games from late November to early March. Capacity crowds cheer the team at the 17,121-seat University Arena (fondly called "The Pit") at University and Stadium boulevards. The arena was the site of the NCAA championship tournament in 1983. For tickets and information call © **505/925-LOBO** (www.golobos.com).

FOOTBALL

The **UNM Lobos** football team plays a September-to-November season, usually with five home games, at the 30,000-seat University of New Mexico Stadium, opposite both Albuquerque Sports Stadium and University Arena at University and Stadium boulevards. For tickets and information call © **505/925-LOBO** (www.golobos.com).

HOCKEY

The **New Mexico Scorpions** play in the Western Professional Hockey League. Their home is at Tingley Coliseum, New Mexico State Fairgrounds, Central Avenue and Louisiana Boulevard (© **505/881-7825;** www.scorpionshockey. com).

HORSE RACING

The **Downs at Albuquerque Racetrack and Casino,** New Mexico State Fairgrounds (© **505/266-5555** for post times; www.abqdowns.com), is near Lomas and Louisiana boulevards NE. Racing and betting—on thoroughbreds and quarter horses—take place on weekends from April to July and during the State Fair in September. The Downs has a glass-enclosed grandstand and exclusive club seating. General admission is free. Seasonal live horse racing takes place March through June and during the New Mexico State Fair. Daily simulcast racing happens year-round. The 300-slot casino is open daily noon to midnight.

9 Shopping

Visitors seeking regional specialties will find many **local artists** and **galleries** of interest in Albuquerque, although not as many as in Santa Fe and Taos. The galleries and regional fashion designers around the plaza in Old Town comprise a kind of shopping center for travelers, with more than 40 merchants represented. The Sandia Pueblo runs its own **crafts market** at the reservation, off I-25 at Tramway Road, just beyond Albuquerque's northern city limits.

Albuquerque has three of the largest **shopping malls** in New Mexico, two within 2 blocks of each other on Louisiana Boulevard just north of I-40—Coronado Center and Winrock Center. The other is the Cottonwood Mall on the west mesa, at 10000 Coors Blvd. NW (© **505/899-SHOP**).

Business hours vary, but shops are generally open Monday to Saturday 10am to 6pm; many have extended hours; some have reduced hours; and a few, especially in shopping malls or during the high tourist season, are open on Sunday.

In Albuquerque the sales tax is 5.8125%.

BEST BUYS

The best buys in Albuquerque are Southwestern regional items, including **arts and crafts** of all kinds—traditional Native American and Hispanic as well as contemporary works. In local Native American art, look for silver and turquoise

Outback Shopping

While cruising the remote desert lands between Albuquerque and Santa Fe, you may want to stop in at **Traditions! A Festival Marketplace,** on I-25, exit 257 (© **505/867-9700**). The open-air mall offers shoppers the chance to sample many forms of New Mexico culture, from art to jewelry to food to entertainment. It's open daily 10am to 8pm.

jewelry, pottery, weavings, baskets, sand paintings, and Hopi kachina dolls. Hispanic folk art—hand-crafted furniture, tinwork and *retablos,* and religious paintings—is worth seeking out. The best contemporary art is in paintings, sculpture, jewelry, ceramics, and fiber art, including weaving.

Other items of potential interest are Southwestern fashions, gourmet foods, and unique local Native American and Hispanic creations.

By far the most **galleries** are in Old Town; others are spread around the city, with smaller groupings in the university district and the northeast heights. Consult the brochure published by the **Albuquerque Gallery Association,** *A Select Guide to Albuquerque Galleries,* or Wingspread Communications's annual *The Collector's Guide to Albuquerque,* widely distributed at shops. Once a month, usually from 5 to 9pm on the third Friday, the **Albuquerque Art Business Association** (© **505/244-0362** for information) sponsors an ArtsCrawl to dozens of galleries and studios. It's a great way to meet the artists.

You'll find some interesting shops in the Nob Hill area, which is just west of the University of New Mexico and has an Art Deco feel.

Following are some shopping recommendations for the Albuquerque area.

ARTS & CRAFTS

Amapola Gallery ⭐ Fifty artists and craftspeople show their talents at this lovely cooperative gallery off a cobbled courtyard. You'll find pottery, paintings, textiles, baskets, jewelry, and other items. 206 Romero St. © **505/242-4311.**

Bien Mur Indian Market Center ⭐ Sandia Pueblo's crafts market, on the reservation, sells turquoise and silver jewelry, pottery, baskets, kachina dolls, hand-woven rugs, sand paintings, and other arts and crafts. The market is open Monday through Saturday from 9am to 5:30pm and Sunday from 11am to 5pm. I-25 at Tramway Rd. NE. © **800/365-5400** or 505/821-5400.

Dartmouth Street Gallery ⭐ This gallery features vapor mirage works of Larry Bell, tapestries by Nancy Kozikowski, and a variety of work by 40 other contemporary artists, most from New Mexico. 3011 Monte Vista NE. © **800/474-7751** or 505/266-7751. www.dsg-art.com.

Gallery One This gallery features folk art, jewelry, contemporary crafts, cards and paper, and natural-fiber clothing. In the Nob Hill Shopping Center, 3500 Central Ave. SE. © **505/268-7449.**

Hispaniae in Old Town ⭐ *Finds* Day of the Dead people and Frida Kahlo faces greet you at this wild shop with everything from kitschy Mexican tableware to fine Oaxacan woodcarvings. 410 Romero St. NW. © **505/244-1533.**

La Piñata This shop features—what else?—piñatas, in shapes from dinosaurs to parrots to pigs, as well as paper flowers, puppets, toys, and crushable bolero hats decorated with ribbons. No. 2 Patio Market (Old Town). © **505/242-2400.**

Mariposa Gallery 🎨🎨 *Value*   Eclectic contemporary art, jewelry, blown glass, and sculpture fill this Nob Hill shop, with prices that even a travel writer can afford. In Nob Hill Shopping Center, 3500 Central Ave. SE. ℭ 505/268-6828.

Ortega's Indian Arts and Crafts   An institution in Gallup, adjacent to the Navajo Reservation, Ortega's now has this Albuquerque store. It sells, repairs, and appraises silver and turquoise jewelry. 6600 Menaul Blvd. NE, no. 359. ℭ 505/881-1231.

The Pueblo Loft (at Gallery One)   Owner Kitty Trask takes pride in the fact that all items featured here are crafted by Native Americans. For almost 15 years, her slogan has been, "Every purchase is an American Indian work of art." In the Nob Hill Shopping Center, 3500 Central Ave. SE. ℭ 505/268-8764.

R. C. Gorman Nizhoni Gallery Old Town 🎨   The painting and sculpture of famed Navajo artist Gorman, a resident of Taos, are shown here. Most works are available in limited-edition lithographs. 323 Romero NW, Suite 1. ℭ 505/843-7666.

Schelu Gallery 🎨🎨   Inventive pottery you'll want to use in your kitchen as well as bold textiles present a sojourn in color in this Old Town shop. 306 San Felipe NW. ℭ 800/234-7985 or 505/765-5869.

Skip Maisel's *Value*   If you want a bargain in Native American arts and crafts, this is the place to shop. You'll find a broad range of quality and price here in goods such as pottery, weavings, and kachinas. *Take note:* Adorning the outside of the store are murals painted in 1933 by notable Navajo painter Harrison Begay and Pueblo painter Pablita Velarde. 510 Central Ave. SW. ℭ 505/242-6526.

Tanner Chaney Galleries 🎨   In business since 1875, this gallery has fine jewelry, pottery, rugs, and more. 323 Romero NW, no. 4 (Old Town). ℭ 800/444-2242 or 505/247-2242.

Weyrich Gallery (Rare Vision Art Galerie)   Contemporary paintings, sculpture, textiles, jewelry, and ceramics by regional and nonregional artists are exhibited at this spacious midtown gallery. 2935D Louisiana Blvd. at Candelaria Rd. ℭ 505/883-7410.

Wright's Collection of Indian Art   This gallery, first opened in 1907, features a private museum and carries fine handmade Native American arts and crafts, both contemporary and traditional. 1100 San Mateo Blvd. NE. ℭ 505/266-0120.

BOOKS

Barnes & Noble   On the west side, just north of Cottonwood Mall, this huge bookstore offers plenty of browsing room and a Starbucks Cafe for lounging.

A Taste of the Grape

In addition to everything else New Mexico has to offer, wineries are springing up all over the state. Call to find out about their wine-tasting hours. Wineries in Albuquerque or within a short driving distance of the city include **Anderson Valley Vineyards**, 4920 Rio Grande Blvd. NW, Albuquerque, NM 87107 (ℭ 505/344-7266); **Sandia Shadows Vineyard and Winery**, 11704 Coronado NE, Albuquerque, NM 87122 (ℭ 505/856-1006; www.sandiawines.com); and **Gruet Winery**, 8400 Pan-American Hwy. NE, Albuquerque, NM 87113 (ℭ 505/821-0055; www.gruetwinery.com).

The store is known for its large children's section and weekly story-time readings. 3701 Ellison Dr. NW #A. 📞 **505/792-4234**. Or at the Coronado Center, 6600 Menaul Blvd. NE. 📞 **505/883-8200**.

Bookworks ⭐ This store, selling both new and used books, has one of the most complete Southwestern nonfiction and fiction sections in the region. A good place to linger, the store has a coffee bar and a stage area for readings. It also carries CDs and books on tape. 4022 Rio Grande Blvd. NW. 📞 **505/344-8139**.

Borders This branch of the popular chain provides a broad range of books, music, and videos, and hosts in-store appearances by authors, musicians, and artists. Winrock Center, 2100 Louisiana Blvd. NE. 📞 **505/884-7711**.

FOOD

The Candy Lady Having made chocolate for over 20 years, The Candy Lady is especially known for 21 varieties of fudge, including jalapeño flavor. 524 Romero NW (Old Town). 📞 **800/214-7731** or 505/243-6239.

La Mexicana This is a great place to shop if you're a die-hard fan of Mexican food. Many items are imported from Mexico, and others, such as tortillas, tamales, and pastries, are made fresh daily. 423 Atlantic Ave. SW. 📞 **505/243-0391**.

Rocky Mountain Chocolate Factory See old-fashioned candy made right before your eyes. 380 Coronado Center. 📞 **800/658-6151** or 505/888-3399.

FURNITURE

Ernest Thompson Furniture ⭐ Original-design, handcrafted furniture is exhibited in the factory showroom. Thompson is a fifth-generation furniture maker who still uses traditional production techniques. 4531 Osuna Rd. NE (¼ block west of I-25 and ½ block north of Osuna Rd.). 📞 **800/568-2344** or 505/344-1994.

Strictly Southwestern You'll find nice, solid pine and oak Southwestern-style furniture here. Lighting, art, pottery, and other interior items are also available. 1321 Eubank Blvd. NE. 📞 **505/292-7337**.

GIFTS/SOUVENIRS

Jackalope International ⭐⭐ Wandering through this vast shopping area is like an adventure to another land—to many lands, really. You'll find Mexican *trasteros* (armoires) next to Balinese puppets. The store sells sculpture, pottery, and Christmas ornaments as well. 834 US 550, Bernalillo. 📞 **505/867-9813**.

MARKETS

Flea Market Every Saturday and Sunday, year-round, the fairgrounds host this market from 8am to 5pm. It's a great place to browse for turquoise and silver jewelry and locally made crafts, as well as newly manufactured inexpensive goods such as socks and T-shirts. The place has a fair atmosphere. There's no admission charge. New Mexico State Fairgrounds. For information call the Albuquerque Convention and Visitors Bureau. 📞 **800/284-2282**.

SOUTHWESTERN APPAREL

Albuquerque Pendleton Cuddle up in this store's large selection of blankets and shawls. 1100 San Mateo NE, Suites 2 and 4. 📞 **505/255-6444**.

Western Warehouse Family Western wear, including an enormous collection of boots, is retailed here. This store claims to have the largest selection of work wear and work boots in New Mexico (8,000 pairs of boots altogether). 6210 San Mateo Blvd. NE. 📞 **505/883-7161**.

10 Albuquerque After Dark

Albuquerque has an active performing-arts and nightlife scene, as befits a city of 700,000 people. As also befits this area, the performing arts are multicultural, with Hispanic and (to a lesser extent) Native American productions sharing stage space with Anglo works, including theater, opera, symphony, and dance. Albuquerque also attracts many national touring companies. Nightclubs cover the gamut, with rock, jazz, and country predominant.

Complete information on all major cultural events can be obtained from the **Albuquerque Convention and Visitors Bureau** (© **800/284-2282** for recorded information after 5pm). Current listings appear in the two daily newspapers; detailed weekend arts calendars can be found in the Thursday evening *Tribune* and the Friday morning *Journal.* The monthly *On the Scene* also carries entertainment listings.

Tickets for nearly all major entertainment and sporting events can be obtained from **Ticketmaster,** 4004 Carlisle Blvd. NE (© **505/883-7800**). Discount tickets are often available for midweek and matinee performances; check with individual theater or concert hall box offices.

THE PERFORMING ARTS
CLASSICAL MUSIC
New Mexico Ballet Company   Founded in 1972, the state's oldest ballet company holds most of its performances at Popejoy Hall. Typically there is a fall production such as *Dracula,* a holiday one such as *The Nutcracker* or *A Christmas Carol,* and a contemporary spring production. 4200 Wyoming Blvd. NE, Suite B2 (P.O. Box 21518), Albuquerque, NM 87111. © 505/292-4245. www.nmballet.org. Tickets $20–$25 adults, $10–$20 children 12 and under.

New Mexico Symphony Orchestra 🞱   The NMSO first played in 1932 and has continued as a strong cultural force. The symphony performs classics and pops, as well as family and neighborhood concerts. It plays for more than 20,000 grade-school students and visits communities throughout the state in its annual tour program. Concert venues are generally Popejoy Hall and the Rio Grande Zoo, both of which are accessible to people with disabilities. Each season a few notable artists visit; recent years have included such guests as Yo Yo Ma and Guillermo and Ivonne Figueroa. I recommend the outdoor concerts at the band shell at the Rio Grande Zoo. 3301 Menaul Blvd. NE, Suite 4, Albuquerque, NM 87107. © 800/251-6676 for tickets and information, or 505/881-9590. www.nmso.org. Ticket prices vary with concert; call for details.

THEATER
Albuquerque Little Theatre   Albuquerque Little Theatre has been offering a variety of productions ranging from comedies to dramas to musicals since 1930. Seven plays are presented here annually during an August-to-May season. Located across from Old Town, Albuquerque Little Theatre offers plenty of free parking. 224 San Pasquale Ave. SW, Albuquerque, NM 87104. © 505/242-4750. www.swcp. com/~alt. Tickets $18, $16 students, $13 seniors. Box office Mon–Fri noon–6pm.

La Compañía de Teatro de Albuquerque *(Finds*   Productions given by the company can provide a focused view into New Mexico culture. One of the few major professional Hispanic companies in the United States and Puerto Rico, La Compañía stages a series of bilingual productions (most original New Mexican works) every year, late September to May. Comedies, dramas, and musicals are offered, along with an occasional Spanish-language play. Performances take

The Major Concert & Performance Halls

Journal Pavilion, 5601 University Blvd. NE (© **505/452-5100**).

Keller Hall, University of New Mexico, Cornell Street at Redondo Drive South NE (© **505/277-4569**).

KiMo Theatre, 423 Central Ave. NW (© **505/768-3544**).

Popejoy Hall, University of New Mexico, Cornell Street at Redondo Drive South NE (© **505/277-3824**).

South Broadway Cultural Center, 1025 Broadway Blvd. SE (© **505/848-1320**).

place in the National Hispanic Cultural Center, the South Broadway Cultural Center, and other venues. P.O. Box 884, Albuquerque, NM 87103. © **505/242-7929.** Tickets $12 adults, $8 students ages 18 and above and seniors, $7 children under 18.

Musical Theatre Southwest   Formerly known as the Albuquerque Civic Light Opera Association, this successful company has now condensed its name and expanded its season. From February to January, six major Broadway musicals, in addition to several smaller productions, are presented each year at either Popejoy Hall or the MTS's own 890-seat Hiland Theater. Most productions are staged for three consecutive weekends, including some Sunday matinees. 4804 Central Ave. SE, Albuquerque, NM 80178. © **505/262-9301.** www.hilandtheater.com. Tickets $15–$30 adults; students and seniors receive a $2 discount.

Vortex Theatre ⭐   A nearly 30-year-old community theater known for its innovative productions, the Vortex is Albuquerque's "Off-Broadway" theater, presenting a range of plays from classic to original. Performances take place on Friday and Saturday at 8pm and on Sunday at 6pm. The black-box theater seats 90. 2004½ Central Ave. SE, Albuquerque, NM 87106. © **505/247-8600.** Tickets $10 adults, $8 students and seniors, $8 for everyone on Sun.

THE CLUB & MUSIC SCENE
COMEDY CLUBS/DINNER THEATER

Laffs Comedy Cafe   Located on the west mesa, this club offers top acts from each coast, including comedians who have appeared on *The Late Show with David Letterman* and HBO. Shows are Wednesday through Sunday night. Call for times. San Mateo Blvd. and Osuna Rd., in the Fiesta del Norte Shopping Center. © **505/296-5653.** www.laffscomedy.com. $7 per person, with a 2-drink and/or menu-item minimum purchase.

Mystery Cafe *Finds*   If you're in the mood for a little interactive dinner theater, the Mystery Cafe might be just the ticket. You'll help the characters in this ever-popular, delightfully funny show solve the mystery as they serve you a four-course meal. Reservations are a must. Performances are Friday and Saturday evenings at 7:30pm; doors open at 7pm. 2600 Louisiana Blvd. NE (at Menaul Blvd. and Louisiana Blvd.). © **505/237-1385.** www.abqmystery.com. Approximately $33.

COUNTRY MUSIC

Midnight Rodeo/Gotham   The Southwest's largest nightclub, this place has bars in all corners; it even has its own shopping arcade, including a boutique and gift shop. A DJ spins records nightly until closing; the hardwood dance floor is so big (5,500 sq. ft.) that it resembles an indoor horse track. There's also a hip-hop and techno dance bar called Gotham here. Closed Monday and Tuesday. 4901 McLeod Rd. NE (near San Mateo Blvd.). ✆ 505/888-0100. $4 cover Fri–Sat,

ROCK/JAZZ

Brewsters Pub　Tuesday to Sunday, this downtown hot spot offers live blues, jazz, folk, or light rock entertainment in a sports bar–type setting. Sports fans can enjoy the game on a big-screen TV. Barbecue and burgers are served at lunch and dinner. 312 Central Ave. SW (Downtown). ✆ 505/247-2533.

Burt's Tiki Lounge　This club won the weekly paper *Alibi's* award for the best variety of drinks. The club offers live music Thursday to Sunday and charges no cover. 313 Gold Ave. ✆ 505/243-BURT.

Kelly's BYOB　Near the university, Kelly's is a local brewpub, set in a renovated auto body shop. The place has tasty pub fare, excellent brew specials, and live music Thursday to Saturday, usually with no cover. 3222 Central SE. ✆ 505/262-2739.

Martini Grille ⭐　On the eastern side of the Nob Hill district, this is the place for young professionals, who lush out on more than 30 flavors of martinis within a seductive Batman cave atmosphere. Live entertainment plays most weekends and some weeknights. 4200 Central SE. ✆ 505/255-4111.

O'niell's Pub　A favorite club in the University of New Mexico area, this Irish bar serves up good pub fare as well as live local music on Saturday nights and Celtic and bluegrass on Sunday evenings. 3211 Central NE. ✆ 505/256-0564.

MORE ENTERTAINMENT

Albuquerque's best nighttime attraction is the **Sandia Peak Tramway,** with the restaurant High Finance at the summit (see "What to See & Do" and "Where to Dine," earlier in this chapter). Here, you can enjoy a view nonpareil of the Rio Grande Valley and the city lights.

The best place to catch foreign films, art films, and limited-release productions is the **Guild Cinema,** 3405 Central Ave. NE (✆ 505/255-1848). For film classics, check out the **Southwest Film Center,** on the UNM campus (✆ 505/277-5608), which has double features, changing nightly (when classes are in session). In addition, Albuquerque has a number of first-run movie theaters whose numbers you can find in the local telephone directory.

If you want to include a little dice throw and slot machine play in your trip to New Mexico, you're in luck. The expansive **Sandia Casino,** north of I-25 and a quarter mile east on Tramway Boulevard (✆ 800/526-9366; www.sandia casino.com), is an $80 million structure that sits on Sandia Pueblo land and has outstanding views of the Sandia Mountains. Built in Pueblo architectural style, the graceful casino has a 3,650-seat outdoor amphitheater, three restaurants (one, **Bien Shur,** has excellent food made by the same folks who operate the acclaimed Artichoke Cafe, p. 83), a lounge, more than 1,350 slot and video poker machines, the largest poker room in the state, and blackjack, roulette, and craps tables. It's open from 8am to 4pm Sunday to Wednesday and 24 hours Thursday to Saturday. The **Isleta Gaming Palace,** 11000 Broadway SE (✆ 800/460-5686 or 505/724-3800; www.isletacasinoresort.com), is a luxurious, air-conditioned casino (featuring blackjack, poker, slots, bingo, and keno) with a full-service restaurant, nonsmoking section, and free bus transportation on request. Open Monday to Thursday 9am to 5am; Friday to Sunday 24 hours a day.

11 Touring the Pueblos Around Albuquerque

Ten Native American pueblos are located within an hour's drive of central Albuquerque. Two of them, Acoma and Laguna, are discussed in chapter 9, "Northwestern New Mexico." The others, from south to north, are discussed here, followed by Coronado and Jemez state monuments, which preserve ancient pueblo ruins. If you'd like to combine a tour of the archaeological sites and inhabited pueblos, consider driving the **Jemez Mountain Trail** 𝒜. Head north on Interstate 25 to Bernalillo, where you can visit the Coronado State Monument. Continue west on US 550 to Zia Pueblo. Six miles farther on US 550 takes you to NM 4, where you'll turn north and drive through orchards and along narrow cornfields of Jemez Pueblo. Farther north on NM 4, you'll find another archaeological site, the Jemez State Monument. You'll also find Jemez Springs, where you can stop for a hot soak. The road continues to the Los Alamos area, where you can see the spectacular ruins at Bandelier National Monument. From there you have the option of returning the way you came or via Santa Fe.

AREA PUEBLOS
ISLETA PUEBLO
Located just 14 miles south of Albuquerque, off I-25 or US 85, **Isleta Pueblo,** P.O. Box 1270, Isleta, NM 87022 (𝒞 **505/869-3111;** www.isletapueblo.com), is the largest of the Tiwa-speaking pueblos, comprising several settlements on the west side of the Rio Grande. The largest village, Shiaw-iba, contains the Mission of San Agustin de Isleta, one of the few mission churches not destroyed in the 17th-century Pueblo rebellion. Grasslands and wooded bosque along the river are gradually becoming part of Albuquerque's growing urban sprawl; already, some governmental agencies and commercial interests are leasing property from the Isleta. Most of the pueblo's 4,000-plus residents work in Albuquerque; others are employed in farming and ranching, private business, or in the pueblo's operations.

Isleta women potters make red wares distinctive for their red-and-black designs on white backgrounds. The tribe operates the **Isleta Casino and Resort** (𝒞 **877/747-5382** or 505/724-3800; www.isletacasinoresort.com) and fishing and camping areas at Isleta Lakes. A tent site costs $12, an RV site costs $15, and a fishing permit is $8 more. Permits can be purchased at the recreation area.

The Isleta hold an evergreen dance sometime in late February. The big day of the year is the feast day honoring St. Augustine, September 4, when a morning Mass and procession are followed by an afternoon harvest dance.

The pueblo is open to visitors daily during daylight hours. Admission is free. Photography is limited to the church.

SANDIA PUEBLO
Established about 1300, **Sandia Pueblo,** 481 Sandia Loop, Bernalillo, NM 87004 (𝒞 **505/867-3317**), is one of the few pueblos visited by Coronado's contingent in 1540. Remains of that village, known as Nafiat, or "sandy," are still visible near the present church. The Sandia people temporarily fled to Hopi country after the Pueblo rebellion of 1680, but they returned to the Rio Grande in 1742. Many of today's 300 Tiwa-speaking (Tanoan) inhabitants work in Albuquerque or at Pueblo Enterprises. They also run the **Bien Mur Indian Market Center** on Tramway Road (𝒞 **800/365-5400** or 505/821-5400) and **Sandia Casino** (𝒞 **800/526-9366;** www.sandiacasino.com). It's about 5 miles north of Albuquerque off I-25.

(*Tips* **Pueblo Etiquette: Do's & Don'ts**
_____

Those who are not Native American are welcome to visit Indian pueblos and reservations; however, there are some guidelines you should
follow as a guest on tribal land.

Native American reservations and pueblos have their own systems
of government and, therefore, their own laws and regulations. If you
don't follow their laws, you will be subject to punishment as outlined
by the American Indian government. The best thing that could happen
is that you'd simply be asked to leave.

Stay out of cemeteries and ceremonial rooms, such as kivas, as these
are sacred grounds. Remember, these are not museums or tourist
attractions in their own right; they are people's homes. Don't peek
into doors and windows, and don't climb on top of buildings.

Most pueblos require a permit to carry a camera or to sketch or
paint on location, and many prohibit photography at any time. If you
want to take pictures, make a video, or sketch anything on pueblo or
reservation land, find out about permits and fees in advance.

Do not wander around on your own if the residents have asked that
you visit the pueblo only by guided tour. If, on a guided tour, you are
asked not to take pictures of something, or are asked to stay out of a
certain area, please follow the guidelines. If you don't have to visit by
guided tour, don't go into private buildings without being escorted by
someone who lives there or who has the authority to take you inside.

Be respectful of ceremonial dances. Do not speak during dances
or ceremonies and don't applaud at the end of the dance—they
aren't dancing for your amusement; they are dancing as part of their
ceremony.

In short, be respectful and courteous and don't do anything you
wouldn't do in your own mother's house.

The pueblo celebrates its St. Anthony feast day on June 13, with a mid-
morning Mass, procession, and afternoon corn dance. Another dance honors
newly elected governors in January.

The pueblo is open to visitors weekdays during daylight hours, and admission
is free. No photographing, recording, or sketching is allowed.

SANTA ANA PUEBLO

Though partially abandoned, **Santa Ana Pueblo,** 2 Dove Rd., Santa Ana Pueblo,
NM 87004 (© **505/867-3301;** www.santaana.org), on the lower Jemez River,
claims a population of about 550. Many "residents" who maintain family homes
at the pueblo actually live nearer the stream's confluence with the Rio Grande, in
Ranchos de Santa Ana, near Bernalillo, where farming is more productive. A
handful of craftspeople in the old village produce pottery, wood carvings, ceremonial bands, red cloth belts, and unique wooden crosses with straw inlay.

Guests are normally welcomed only on ceremonial days. Pueblo members
perform the turtle and corn dances on New Year's Day; the eagle, elk, buffalo,
and deer dances on January 6; and several days of dances at Christmastime. Feast
Day celebrations honoring Saint Ann take place on July 26.

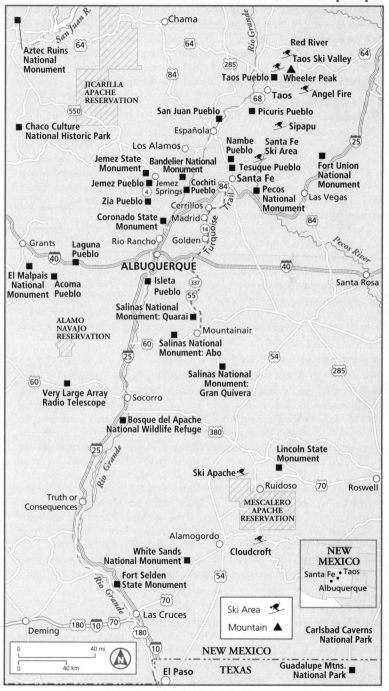

Aztec Ruins National Monument

San Juan R.

Chama

Rio Grande

64

64

285

84

Red River

Taos Ski Valley

64

Taos Pueblo

Wheeler Peak

JICARILLA APACHE RESERVATION

550

San Juan Pueblo

68

Taos

Angel Fire

Picuris Pueblo

Sipapu

Chaco Culture National Historic Park

Española

Nambe Pueblo

Santa Fe Ski Area

Los Alamos

Jemez State Monument

Bandelier National Monument

Tesuque Pueblo

Fort Union National Monument

25

Jemez Pueblo

Jemez Springs

4

Cochiti Pueblo

Santa Fe

Pecos National Monument

Las Vegas

Zia Pueblo

Cerrillos

84

Coronado State Monument

Madrid

Turquoise Trail

Pecos River

Grants

Rio Rancho

Golden

14

40

Laguna Pueblo

ALBUQUERQUE

40

Santa Rosa

El Malpais National Monument

Acoma Pueblo

Isleta Pueblo

337

55

ALAMO NAVAJO RESERVATION

Salinas National Monument: Quarai

Mountainair

60

25

Salinas National Monument: Abo

54

285

Very Large Array Radio Telescope

60

Socorro

Salinas National Monument: Gran Quivera

Bosque del Apache National Wildlife Refuge

380

25

Rio Grande

Lincoln State Monument

Ski Apache

Truth or Consequences

Ruidoso

70

Roswell

MESCALERO APACHE RESERVATION

Alamogordo

White Sands National Monument

Cloudcroft

NEW MEXICO

Santa Fe • Taos

Albuquerque

Fort Selden State Monument

54

Rio Grande

70

Deming

180

10

70

Las Cruces

180

| Ski Area | ✖ |
| Mountain | ▲ |

Carlsbad Caverns National Park

10

NEW MEXICO

El Paso

TEXAS

Guadalupe Mtns. National Park

0   40 mi
0   40 km

The pueblo is about 15 to 20 miles north of Albuquerque, reached via I-25 to Bernalillo, then 8 miles northwest on US 550. Admission is free and allowed only on dance days; photography is prohibited. Visitors can stay on Santa Ana Pueblo land at the **Hyatt Regency Tamaya Resort** (© **505/867-1234;** see "Where to Stay," earlier in this chapter). The **Santa Ana Star Casino** (© **505/ 867-0000;** www.santaanastar.com) offers all manner of gambling.

ZIA PUEBLO
Zia Pueblo, 135 Capitol Square Dr., Zia Pueblo, NM, 87053 (© **505/867-3304**), which has 720 inhabitants, blends in so perfectly with the soft tans of the stone and sand of the desertlike land around it that it's very hard to see—it's like a chameleon on a tree trunk. The pueblo is best known for its famous sun symbol—now the official symbol of the state of New Mexico—adapted from a pottery design showing three rays going in each of the four directions from a sun, or circle. It is hailed in the pledge to the state flag as "a symbol of perfect friendship among united cultures."

Zia has a reputation for excellence in pottery making. Its pottery is identified by its unglazed terra-cotta coloring, traditional geometric designs, and plant and animal motifs painted on a white slip. Paintings, weaving, and sculptures are also prized products of the artists of the Zia community. Their work can be viewed at the **Zia Cultural Center** located at the pueblo. Our Lady of the Assumption, the patron saint, is given a celebratory corn dance on her day, August 15.

The pueblo is about 8 miles northwest of Santa Ana Pueblo, just off of US 550. It's open to visitors daily during daylight hours, and admission is free. Photography is not permitted.

JEMEZ PUEBLO
The more than 3,400 **Jemez Pueblo** natives—including descendants of the Pecos Pueblo, east of Santa Fe, abandoned in 1838—are the only remaining people to speak the Towa dialect of the Tanoan group. The Jemez are famous for their excellent dancing and feast-making; their feast days attract residents from other pueblos, turning the celebrations into multitribal fairs. Two rectangular kivas are central points for groups of dancers. However, in recent years the pueblo has been closed to visitors. Though they are allowed to visit on dance days, the pueblo has become close-mouthed about when dances occur. However, visitors can partake of the crafts at local shops along NM 4 and at the Walatowa Visitor Center (see box below). The primary craft is Jemez pottery.

You can enjoy fishing and picnicking along the Jemez River on government forest lands and camping at the Dragonfly Recreation Area. Call about getting permits. The pueblo, P.O. Box 100, Jemez Pueblo, NM 87024 (© **877/733-5687** or 505/834-7235; www.jemezpueblo.org), is 55 miles northwest of Albuquerque via I-25 to Bernalillo, US 550 to San Ysidro, and NM 4 for 6 final miles.

SAN FELIPE PUEBLO
San Felipe Pueblo, a conservative pueblo of 2,500 people, located on a mesa on the west bank of the Rio Grande, is known for its beautiful ritual ceremonies. The plaza has been worn into the shape of a bowl by the feet of San Felipe's dancers over the centuries. In the grandest of these dances, hundreds of men, women, and children move through their rhythmic steps all day long in the spring corn dance on May 1, performed in honor of the pueblo's patron, St. Philip (San Felipe). The dancing is done to a great chorus of male singers intoning music that reaches back into prehistory and evokes strong emotions in participants and in visitors, too.

Other events here are a corn dance on January 6 and an arts-and-crafts fair in October or early December.

San Felipe Pueblo, P.O. Box 4339, San Felipe, NM 87001 (© **505/867-3381**), is 30 miles northeast of Albuquerque via I-25 and an access road. Admission is free. Photography and sketching are not permitted. The pueblo is open to visitors during daylight hours. **Casino Hollywood,** exit 252 off I-25 north of Albuquerque (© **505/867-6700;** www.sanfelipecasino.com), offers most types of gambling and an excellent fireworks display on July 4.

SANTO DOMINGO PUEBLO

One of New Mexico's largest pueblos, with 4,500 residents, this farming community on the east bank of the Rio Grande is also one of the state's most traditional. Craftspeople are known for their beautiful silver jewelry, unique necklaces of *heishi* (shell fragments), innovative pottery, and fine weaving.

At the dramatic **Santo Domingo Pueblo** feast day, August 4, the corn dance is performed as it is done nowhere else. It is a lavish production involving clowns, scores of singers and drummers, and 500 tireless and skilled dancers in imaginative traditional costumes. Other festive occasions during the year include the Easter spring corn dance and basket dance and an arts-and-crafts festival on Labor Day weekend, with more than 300 artisans in attendance.

Santo Domingo Pueblo, P.O. Box 99, Santo Domingo, NM 87052 (© **505/465-2214**), is 40 miles northeast of Albuquerque via I-25 north to NM 22. The pueblo is open daily to visitors during daylight hours. Admission is free, but no photography or sketching are permitted.

COCHITI PUEBLO

Occupied continuously since about the 13th century, **Cochiti Pueblo,** P.O. Box 70, Cochiti Pueblo, NM 87072 (© **505/465-2244**), the northernmost of the Keresan-speaking pueblos, stretches along the Rio Grande. Its Church of San Buenaventura, though rebuilt and remodeled since, still contains sections of its original 1628 structure.

Cochiti (pop. 1,300) is well known for its pottery, especially the famous "storyteller" figures created by Helen Cordero. Beadwork and soft leather moccasins are other craft specialties. The pueblo's double-headed dance drums, made from hollowed-out cottonwood logs and covered with leather, are used in ceremonies throughout the Rio Grande area.

San Buenaventura Feast Day is July 14, when the corn and rain dances are performed. Other events include a buffalo dance December 25, and other dances December 26 to 29.

The pueblo is about 40 miles north of Albuquerque, via I-25, then north on NM 22. It is open to visitors daily during daylight hours; admission is free. Photography, sketching, and tape recording are not permitted. Cochiti Lake, though fairly silty, is popular for watersports, especially windsurfing. Tent Rocks National Monument, on Cochiti Pueblo land, is a fun place to hike.

A STATE MONUMENT IN THE AREA

Coronado State Monument ⊛ When the Spanish explorer Coronado traveled through this region in 1540–41 while searching for the Seven Cities of Cíbola, he wintered at a village on the west bank of the Rio Grande—probably one located on the ruins of the ancient Anasazi Pueblo known as Kuaua. Those excavated ruins have been preserved in this state monument.

Hundreds of rooms can be seen, and a kiva has been restored so that visitors can descend a ladder into the enclosed space, once the site of sacred rites.

Unique multicolored murals, depicting human and animal forms, were found on successive layers of wall plaster in this and other kivas here; some examples are displayed in the monument's small archaeological museum.

485 Kuana Rd., Bernalillo, NM 87004. ℂ 505/867-5351. Admission $3 adults, free for children 16 and under. Wed–Mon 8am–5pm. Closed New Year's Day, Easter, Thanksgiving, and Christmas. To get to the site (20 miles north of Albuquerque), take I-25 to Bernalillo and US 550 west for 1 mile.

JEMEZ SPRINGS

A visit to this village along the Jemez River can provide a relaxing retreat and/or an exhilarating adventure. In the area are historic sites and relaxing hot springs, as well as excellent stream fishing, hiking, and cross-country skiing. You may want to combine a drive through this area with a visit to Los Alamos and Bandelier National Monument (see chapter 6).

North of town you'll come to the **Soda Dam,** a strange and beautiful mineral mass formed by travertine deposits—minerals that precipitate out of geothermal springs. Considered a sacred site by Native Americans, it has a gushing waterfall and caves. During the warm months it's a popular swimming hole.

Jemez State Monument 🗲   A stop at this small monument takes you on a journey through the history of the Jemez people. The journey begins in the museum, which tells the tale of Giusewa, "place of boiling waters," the original Tewa name of the area. Then it moves out into the mission ruins, whose story is told on small plaques that juxtapose the first impressions of the missionaries against the reality of the Jemez life. The missionaries saw the Jemez people as barbaric and set out to settle them. Part of the process involved hauling up river stones and erecting 6-foot-thick walls of the Mission of San José de los Jemez (founded in 1621) in the early 17th century. Excavations in 1921–22 and 1935–37 unearthed this massive complex through which you may wander. You enter through a broad doorway to a room that once held elaborate fresco paintings, the room tapering back to the nave, with a giant bell tower above. The setting is startling next to a creek, with steep mountains rising behind.

18160 NM 4 (P.O. Box 143), Jemez Springs, NM 87025. ℂ 505/829-3530. Admission $3 adults, free for children 17 and under. Wed–Mon 8:30am–5pm. Closed New Year's Day, Easter, Thanksgiving, and Christmas. From Albuquerque, take NM 550 (NM 44) to NM 4 and then continue on NM 4 for about 18 miles.

WHERE TO STAY & DINE

Cañon del Rio–Riverside Inn 🗲   "Eventually the watcher joined the river, and there was only one of us. I believe it was the river," wrote Norman Maclean in *A River Runs Through It.* That was my experience while sitting on a cottonwood-shaded bench at Cañon del Rio, on a long bow of the Jemez River, a

---

Historic Culture with a Hint of Honey

Jemez Pueblo, home to more than 3,000, no longer welcomes visitors except on selected days. However, visitors can get a taste of the Jemez culture at the **Walatowa Visitor Center,** on NM 4, 8 miles north of the junction with US 550 (ℂ 877/733-5687 or 505/834-7235; www.jemezpueblo. org). A museum and shop highlight the center, which also offers information about hiking and scenic tour routes. While in the area, you may encounter Jemez people sitting under *ramadas* (thatch-roofed lean-tos) selling home-baked native foods. If you're lucky, they may also be making fry bread, which you can smother with honey for one of New Mexico's more delectable treats.

Moments Sampling Nature's Nectars

When I was young, people often used to head out from Albuquerque to "the Jemez." That meant they were going to the hot springs. Back then, it was a place where the hippies hung out, naked, and it held a kind of foreboding allure for me. Today, the allure is one of comfort and beauty. My choice is to go to the naturally running springs (ask locally for directions), but if you prefer the more controlled environment of a bathhouse, that option is available, too. The waters running through the Jemez area are high in mineral content. In fact, the owner of **Jemez Springs Bath House,** 62 NM 4, on Jemez Springs Plaza (© 505/829-3303; www.jemezspringsbathhouse.com), says they are so healing, more than once she's had to run after visitors who walked off without their canes. This bathhouse was one of the first structures to be built in what is now Jemez Springs. Built in 1870 and 1878 of river rock and mud, it has thick walls and a richly herbal scent. You soak in individual tubs in either the men's side or the women's side. In back are a series of massage rooms, and outside is a hot tub within a wooden fence. In front is a gift shop packed with interesting soaps and soulful gifts. It is open daily 10am to 8pm.

At **Ponderosa Valley Vineyard & Winery,** 3171 Hwy. 290, Ponderosa, 87044 (© 800/WINE-MAKER or 505/834-7487; www.ponderosawinery.com), 3 miles off NM 4 south of Jemez Springs, you'll find a quaint country store with some of New Mexico's best wines. If you're lucky, the vintners will be presiding over the small curved bar and will pour you delectable tastes while telling stories of the history of wine in New Mexico and of the Jemez area, where they have lived and grown grapes for 30 years. Be sure to try the dry Vidal Blanc and the full-bodied Cabernet Sauvignon, both excellent, and both award winners at the New Mexico State Fair. The fruity zinfandel is like nothing you've ever tasted. This is the oldest wine-growing region in the United States, and the product definitely has its own spirit. A 10- to 15-minute tour will take your through the cellar and vineyards. You can purchase a bottle of wine for $8 to $20.

small, fast-flowing stream lined with cottonwoods. Built in 1994, the inn has clean lines and comfortable rooms, each named after a Native American tribe. I stayed in the Hopi room, a queen room that wasn't large but was well planned, with built-in drawers and many amenities. Each room has a sliding glass door that opens out to a patio where there's a fountain. The beds are comfortably firm, with good reading lights. The suites have private Jacuzzis and kitchens. The Great Room has a cozy, welcoming feel, with a big-screen TV, as well as a large table where breakfast is served family-style. A separate house is available for rent, the only option for children at the inn. Smoking is not allowed.

16445 Scenic Hwy. 4, Jemez Springs, NM 87025. © **505/829-4377.** www.canondelrio.com. 7 units. $99–$160 double, depending on the season; house $125–$150. Rates include full breakfast. AE, DISC, MC, V. **Amenities:** Jacuzzi; massage. *In room:* A/C, TV, hair dryer.

The Laughing Lizard Inn & Cafe ⋆ AMERICAN   This is the kind of small-town cafe that doesn't have to try to have a personality. It already has thick adobe walls, wood floors, and a wood-burning stove for its innate charm. Added touches are the brightly painted walls and funky old tables. If there were a Western version of the Whistle Stop Cafe, this would be it. Most dishes have a bit of an imaginative flair. The burritos come in a variety of types, such as fresh spinach with black beans, mushrooms, jack cheese, salsa, and guacamole. The pizzas feature ingredients such as pesto, sun-dried tomatoes, and feta, or more basic ones with red sauce as well. I had a Chinese stir-fry with tofu and peanut sauce that was a little overbearing but definitely sated my appetite. No alcohol is served, but there are daily dessert treats such as chocolate mousse and berry cobbler. The staff is friendly and accommodating. A small inn attached to the cafe provides inexpensive rooms that are clean but a bit timeworn.

17526 NM 4, Jemez Springs, NM 87025. © 505/829-3108. www.thelaughinglizard.com. Lunch or dinner $6.50–$8.50. DISC, MC, V. June–Oct Tues–Fri 11am–8pm, Sat 11am–8:30pm, Sun 11am–6pm; Nov–May Thurs–Fri 5–8pm, Sat 11am–8pm, Sun 9am–4pm.

12 Salinas Pueblo Missions National Monument ⋆

The rarely visited ruins of **Salinas Pueblo Missions National Monument** provide a unique glimpse into history. The Spanish conquistadors' Salinas Jurisdiction, on the east side of the Manzano Mountains (southeast of Albuquerque), was an important 17th-century trade center because of the salt the Native Americans extracted from the salt lakes. Franciscan priests, utilizing native labor, constructed missions of Abo red sandstone and blue-gray limestone for the native converts. The ruins of some of the most durable missions—along with evidence of preexisting ancestral Puebloan and Mogollon cultures—are the highlights of a visit here. The monument consists of three separate units: the ruins of Abo, Quarai, and Gran Quivira. They are situated around the quiet town of Mountainair, 75 miles southeast of Albuquerque at the junction of US 60 and NM 55.

Abo (© 505/847-2400), 9 miles west of Mountainair on US 60, boasts the 40-foot-high ruins of the **Mission of San Gregorio de Abo,** a rare example of medieval architecture in the United States. **Quarai** (© 505/847-2290), 8 miles north of Mountainair on NM 55, preserves the largely intact remains of the **Mission of La Purísima Concepción de Cuarac** (1630). Its vast size, 100 feet long and 40 feet high, contrasts with the modest size of the pueblo mounds. A small museum in the visitor center has a scale model of the original church, along with a selection of artifacts found at the site. **Gran Quivira** (© 505/847-2770), 25 miles south of Mountainair on NM 55, once had a population of 1,500. The pueblo has 300 rooms and seven kivas. Rooms dating back to 1300 can be seen. There are indications that an older village, dating to 800, may have previously stood here. Ruins of two churches (one almost 140 ft. long) and a *convento* (convent) have been preserved. The visitor center includes a museum with many artifacts from the site and shows a 40-minute movie about the excavation of some 200 rooms, plus a short history video of the pueblo.

All three pueblos and the churches that were constructed above them are believed to have been abandoned in the 1670s. Self-guided tour pamphlets can be obtained at the units' respective visitor centers and at the **Salinas Pueblo Missions National Monument Visitor Center** in Mountainair, on US 60, 1 block west of the intersection of US 60 and NM 55. The visitor center offers an audiovisual presentation on the region's history, a bookstore, and an art exhibit.

For more information, contact **Salinas Pueblo Missions National Monu-ment,** P.O. Box 517, Mountainair, NM 87036 (✆ **505/847-2585;** www.nps.gov/sapu). Admission is free. Sites are open in summer daily 9am to 6pm and the rest of the year 9am to 5pm. The visitor center in Mountainair is open daily (except New Year's Day, Thanksgiving, and Christmas) 8am to 5pm.

13 En Route to Santa Fe: Along the Turquoise Trail

THE TURQUOISE TRAIL

Known as "The Turquoise Trail," NM 14 begins about 16 miles east of down-town Albuquerque, at I-40's Cedar Crest exit, and winds some 46 miles to Santa Fe along the east side of the Sandia Mountains. This state-designated scenic and historic route traverses the revived ghost towns of Golden, Madrid, and Cerril-los, where gold, silver, coal, and turquoise were once mined in great quantities. Modern-day settlers, mostly artists and craftspeople, have brought a renewed frontier spirit to the old mining towns.

GOLDEN   Golden is approximately 10 miles north of the Sandia Park junc-tion on NM 14. Its sagging houses, with their missing boards and the wind whistling through the broken eaves, make it a purist's ghost town. There's a gen-eral store widely known for its large selection of well-priced jewelry, as well as a bottle seller's "glass garden." Nearby are the ruins of a pueblo called **Paako,** abandoned around 1670. Such communities of mud huts were all that the Spaniards ever found during their avid quest for the gold of Cíbola.

MADRID   Madrid (pronounced *mah*-drid) is about 12 miles north of Golden. Madrid and neighboring Cerrillos were in a fabled turquoise-mining area dating back to prehistory. Gold and silver mines followed, and when they faltered, there was coal. The Turquoise Trail towns supplied fuel for the loco-motives of the Santa Fe Railroad until the 1950s, when the railroad converted to diesel fuel. Madrid used to produce 100,000 tons of coal a year, but the mine closed in 1956. Today, this is a village of artists and craftspeople seemingly stuck in the 1960s: Its funky, ramshackle houses have many counterculture residents who operate several crafts stores and import shops.

The **Old Coal Mine Museum** (✆ **505/438-3780**) invites visitors to descend into a real mine that was saved when the town was abandoned. You can see the old mine's offices, steam engines, machines, and tools. It's called a living museum because blacksmiths, metalworkers, and leatherworkers ply their trades here in restoring parts and tools found in the mine. It's open daily; admission is $4 for adults, $3 for seniors, $1 for children 6 to 12, and free for children under 6.

Next door, the **Mine Shaft Tavern** (✆ **505/473-0743**) continues its colorful career by offering a variety of burgers and presenting live music Saturday nights and Sunday afternoons; it's open for dinner Friday to Sunday, and it attracts folks from Santa Fe and Albuquerque. Next door is the **Madrid Engine House Theater** (✆ **505/438-3780**), possibly the only such establishment on earth with a built-in steam locomotive on its stage. (The structure had been an engine repair shed; the balcony is made of railroad track.) The place to eat is **Native Grill** (✆ **505/474-5555**) on NM 14, in the center of town. You'll find food prepared with fresh ingredients, a broad range of choices, from pizza and burri-tos to a veggie bowl (steamed veggies with steak, chicken, or tofu). During the summer it's open from 11am to 6 or 7pm. In winter, it's open intermittently, so call ahead.

CERRILLOS Cerrillos, about 3 miles north of Madrid, is a village of dirt roads that sprawls along Galisteo Creek. It appears to have changed very little since it was founded during a lead strike in 1879; the old hotel, the saloon, and even the sheriff's office look very much like parts of an Old West movie set. It's another 15 miles to Santa Fe and I-25. If, like me, you're enchanted by the Galisteo Basin, you might want to stay a night or two in nearby Galisteo at the **Galisteo Inn** (© **866/404-8200** or 505/466-4000; www.galisteoinn.com). Set on grassy grounds under towering cottonwood trees, this 250-year-old hacienda has thick adobe walls and all the quiet a person could want. Rooms, all remodeled in 2004, are decorated with brightly painted walls and fun, bold-colored art. Most rooms are not sunny, but this means they stay very cool in summer. The inn serves a full breakfast daily for guests, as well as a prix-fixe dinner (at an extra cost) for guests and others on some nights. (At press time, there were plans for Tues–Sat and Sun brunch, but inquire ahead.) There's a lovely pool large enough to swim laps, a hot tub, and guided horseback riding. The inn is located on NM 41, 15 miles from Cerrillos via the dirt County Road 42.

6

Santa Fe

An odd city of 70,000 people living 7,000 feet above sea level, Santa Fe is an exotic and sophisticated place. The Native Americans enlighten the area with viewpoints and lifestyles deeply tied to nature and completely contrary to the American norm. Many of the Hispanics here still live within extended families and practice a devout Catholicism; they bring a slower pace to the city and an appreciation for deep-rooted ties. Meanwhile, a strong cosmopolitan element contributes cutting-edge cuisine, world-class opera, first-run art films, and some of the finest artwork in the world, seen easily while wandering on foot from gallery to gallery, museum to museum.

The city's history is told through its architecture. For its first 2 centuries, it was constructed mainly of adobe bricks. When the U.S. took over the territory from Mexico in 1846 and trade began flowing from the eastern states, new tools and materials began to change the face of the city. The old adobe took on brick facades and roof decoration in what became known as the Territorial style. But the flat roofs were retained so that the city never lost its unique, low profile, creating a sense of serenity found in no other U.S. city.

Bishop Jean-Baptiste Lamy, the inspiration for the character of Bishop Latour in Willa Cather's *Death Comes for the Archbishop,* built the French Romanesque St. Francis Cathedral shortly after he was appointed to head the diocese in 1851. Other structures still standing include what is claimed to be the oldest house in the United States. The San Miguel Mission is the oldest mission church in the country, while the state capitol, built in the circular form of a ceremonial Indian kiva, is among the newest in the U.S.

The city was originally named La Villa Real de la Santa Fe de San Francisco de Asis (The Royal City of the Holy Faith of St. Francis of Assisi) by its founder, Spanish governor Don Pedro de Peralta. He built the Palace of the Governors as his capitol on the central plaza; today it's an excellent museum of the city's 4 centuries of history. It is one of the major attractions in the Southwest, and under its portico, Native Americans sell their crafts to eager tourists, as they have done for decades.

The plaza is the focus of numerous bustling art markets and Santa Fe's early-September fiesta, celebrated annually since 1770. The fiesta commemorates the time following the years of the Pueblo revolt, when Spanish governor Don Diego de Vargas reconquered the city in 1692. The plaza was also the terminus of the Santa Fe Trail from Missouri, and of the earlier Camino Real (Royal Road) from Mexico, when the city thrived on the wool and fur of the Chihuahua trade. Today, a **new gazebo** makes a fun venue for summer concerts.

What captures me most now, though, is the city's setting, backed by the rolling hills and the blue peaks of the Sangre de Cristo Mountains. In the summer, thunderheads build into giant swirling structures above those peaks and move over the city, dropping cool rain. In the winter, snow often covers the many flat-roofed adobe homes, creating a poetic abstraction that at every glance convinces you that the place itself is exotic art.

1 Orientation

Part of the charm of Santa Fe is that it's so easy to get around. Like most cities of Hispanic origin, it was built around a parklike central plaza. Centuries-old adobe buildings and churches still line the narrow streets; many of them house shops, restaurants, art galleries, and museums.

Santa Fe sits high and dry at the foot of the Sangre de Cristo range. Santa Fe Baldy rises to more than 12,600 feet, a mere 12 miles northeast of the plaza. The city's downtown straddles the Santa Fe River, a tiny tributary of the Rio Grande that is little more than a trickle for much of the year. North is the Espanola Valley and, beyond that, the village of Taos, 66 miles distant (see chapter 7). South are ancient Indian turquoise mines in the Cerrillos Hills; southwest is metropolitan Albuquerque, 58 miles away (see chapter 5). To the west, across the Caja del Rio Plateau, is the Rio Grande, and beyond that, the 11,000-foot Jemez Mountains and Valle Grande, an ancient and massive volcanic caldera. Native American pueblos dot the entire Rio Grande valley; they're an hour's drive in any direction.

ARRIVING

BY PLANE   Many people choose to fly into the Albuquerque International Sunport. However, if you want to save time and don't mind paying a bit more, you can fly into the **Santa Fe Municipal Airport** (© 505/955-2900), just outside the southwestern city limits on Airport Road. In conjunction with United Airlines, commuter flights are offered via Denver, Colorado, by **United Express** (© 800/241-6522), which is operated by **Great Lakes Aviation** (© 800/473-4118).

If you fly into Albuquerque, you can rent a car or take one of the bus services. See "Getting There," in chapter 2, for details.

From the Santa Fe Municipal Airport, **Roadrunner Shuttle** (© 505/424-3367) meets every flight and takes visitors anywhere in Santa Fe.

BY TRAIN & BUS   For detailed information about train and bus service to Santa Fe, see "Getting There," in chapter 2.

BY CAR   I-25 skims past Santa Fe's southern city limits, connecting it along one continuous highway from Billings, Montana, to El Paso, Texas. I-40, the state's major east–west thoroughfare, which bisects Albuquerque, affords coast-to-coast access to Santa Fe. (From the west, motorists leave I-40 in Albuquerque and take I-25 north; from the east, travelers exit I-40 at Clines Corners and continue 52 miles to Santa Fe on US 285. *Note:* Diesel is scarce on US 285, so be sure to fill up before you leave Clines Corners.) For those coming from the northwest, the most direct route is via Durango, Colorado, on US 160, entering Santa Fe on US 84.

For information on car rentals in Albuquerque, see "Getting Around New Mexico," in chapter 2; for agencies in Santa Fe, see "Getting Around," below.

VISITOR INFORMATION

The **Santa Fe Convention and Visitors Bureau** is at 201 W. Marcy St., in Sweeney Center at the corner of Grant Street downtown (P.O. Box 909), Santa Fe, NM 87504-0909 (© 800/777-**CITY** or 505/955-6200). You can also log on to the bureau's website, at **www.santafe.org**. You might also try **www.visit santafe.com** for more information.

CITY LAYOUT

MAIN ARTERIES & STREETS   The limits of downtown Santa Fe are demarcated on three sides by the horseshoe-shaped Paseo de Peralta and on the west by St. Francis Drive, otherwise known as US 84/285. Alameda Street follows the north side of the Santa Fe River through downtown, with the State Capitol and other government buildings on the south side of the river, and most buildings of historic and tourist interest on the north, east of Guadalupe Street.

The plaza is Santa Fe's universally accepted point of orientation. Its four diagonal walkways meet at a central fountain, around which a strange and wonderful assortment of people of all ages, nationalities, and lifestyles can be found at nearly any hour of the day or night.

If you stand in the center of the plaza looking north, you'll be gazing directly at the Palace of the Governors. In front of you is Palace Avenue; behind you, San Francisco Street. To your left is Lincoln Avenue, and to your right is Washington Avenue, which divides the downtown avenues into east and west. St. Francis Cathedral is the massive Romanesque structure a block east, down San Francisco Street. Alameda Street is 2 full blocks behind you.

Near the intersection of Alameda Street and Paseo de Peralta, you'll find Canyon Road running east toward the mountains. Much of this street is one-way. The best way to experience it is to walk up or down, taking time to explore shops and galleries and even have lunch or dinner.

Running to the southwest from the downtown area, beginning opposite the state office buildings on Galisteo Avenue, is Cerrillos Road. Once the main north–south highway connecting New Mexico's state capital with its largest city, it is now a 6-mile-long motel and fast-food strip. St. Francis Drive, which crosses Cerrillos Road 3 blocks south of Guadalupe Street, is a far less tawdry byway, linking Santa Fe with I-25, located 4 miles southwest of downtown. The Old Pecos Trail, on the east side of the city, also joins downtown and the freeway. St. Michael's Drive connects the three arteries.

FINDING AN ADDRESS   The city's layout makes it difficult to know exactly where to look for a particular address. It's best to call ahead for directions.

MAPS   Free city and state maps can be obtained at tourist information offices. An excellent state highway map is published by the **New Mexico Department of Tourism,** 491 Old Santa Fe Trail, Lamy Building, Santa Fe, NM 87503 (© **800/733-6396** or 505/827-7307; to receive a tourism guide call © 800/ 777-CITY). There's also a Santa Fe visitor center in the same building. More specific county and city maps are available from the **State Highway and Transportation Department,** 1120 Cerrillos Rd., Santa Fe, NM 87504 (© **505/ 827-5100**). Members of AAA can obtain free maps from the **American Automobile Association office,** 1644 St. Michael's Dr. (© **505/471-6620**). Other good regional maps can be purchased at area bookstores.

2 Getting Around

The best way to see downtown Santa Fe is on foot. Free **walking-tour maps** are available at the **tourist information center** in Sweeney Center, 201 W. Marcy St. (© **800/777-CITY** or 505/984-6760), and information about several guided walking tours is included later in this chapter.

BY BUS

In 1993, Santa Fe opened **Santa Fe Trails** (© 505/955-2001), its first public bus system. There are seven routes, and visitors can pick up a map from the Convention and Visitors Bureau. Some buses operate Monday to Friday 6am to 11pm and Saturday 8am to 8pm. There is some service on Sunday, but no service on holidays. Call for a current schedule and fare information.

BY CAR

Cars can be rented from any of the following firms in Santa Fe: **Avis,** Santa Fe Airport (© **505/471-5892**); **Budget,** 1946 Cerrillos Rd. (© **505/984-1596**); **Enterprise,** 2641A Cerrillos Rd., 4450 Cerrillos Rd.(at the Auto Park), and the Santa Fe Hilton, 100 Sandoval St. (© **505/473-3600**); and **Hertz,** Santa Fe Airport (© **505/471-7189**).

If Santa Fe is merely your base for an extended driving exploration of New Mexico, be sure to give the vehicle you rent a thorough road check before starting out. There are a lot of wide-open desert and wilderness spaces here, so if you break down, you could be stranded for hours before someone passes by, and cellphones don't tend to work in these remote areas.

Make sure your driver's license and auto club membership (if you have one) are valid before you leave home. Check with your auto-insurance company to make sure you're covered when out of state and/or when driving a rental car.

Note: In 2002, the Santa Fe City Council imposed a law prohibiting use of cellphones while driving within the city limits, with strict fines imposed. If you need to make a call, be sure to pull off the road.

Street parking is difficult to find during summer months. There's a metered parking lot near the federal courthouse, 2 blocks north of the plaza; a city lot behind Santa Fe Village, a block south of the plaza; and another city lot at Water and Sandoval streets. If you stop by the Santa Fe Convention and Visitors Bureau, at the corner of Grant and Marcy streets, you can pick up a wallet-size guide to Santa Fe parking areas. The map shows both street and lot parking.

Unless otherwise posted, the speed limit on freeways is 75 mph; on most other two-lane open roads it's 60 to 65 mph. The minimum age for drivers is 16. Seat belts are required for drivers and all passengers ages 5 and over; children under 5 must use approved child seats.

Because Native American reservations enjoy a measure of self-rule, they can legally enforce certain designated laws. For instance, on the Navajo reservation, it is forbidden to transport alcoholic beverages, leave established roadways, or go without a seat belt. Motorcyclists must wear helmets. If you are caught breaking reservation laws, you are subject to reservation punishment—often stiff fines and, in some instances, detainment.

The **State Highway and Transportation Department** has a toll-free hot line (© **800/432-4269**) that provides up-to-the-hour information on road closures and conditions.

Warning: New Mexico has one of the highest per-capita rates of traffic deaths in the nation; although the number has actually been dropping in recent years, it's still a good idea to drive extra carefully!

BY TAXI

Cabs are difficult to flag from the street, but you can call for one. Expect to pay a standard fee of $2.40 for the service and an average of about $2.35 per mile. **Capital City Cab** (© **505/438-0000**) is the main company in Santa Fe.

BY BICYCLE

Riding a bicycle is an excellent way to get around town. Check with **Sun Mountain Bike Company,** 102 E. Water St., inside El Centro (© **505/982-8986**); **Bike-N-Sport,** 1829 Cerillos Rd. (© **505/820-0809**); or **Santa Fe Mountain Sports,** 607 Cerrillos Rd. (© **505/988-3337**), for rentals.

FAST FACTS: Santa Fe

Airport See "Orientation," above.

Area Code All of New Mexico is in area code **505.** However, at press time the state was initiating moves to add another area code, which may affect Santa Fe.

ATMs You can find ATMs (also known as *cash pueblos*) all over town, at supermarkets, banks, and drive-throughs.

Babysitters Most hotels can arrange for sitters on request. Alternatively, call professional, licensed sitters **Ida Rajotte** (© **505/471-6875**) or **Linda Iverson** (© **505/982-9327**).

Business Hours **Offices** and **stores** are generally open Monday to Friday, 9am to 5pm, with many stores also open Friday night, Saturday, and Sunday in the summer season. Most **banks** are open Monday to Thursday 9am to 5pm, and Friday 9am to 6pm. Some may also be open Saturday morning. Most branches have ATMs available 24 hours. Call establishments for specific hours.

Car Rentals See "Getting Around New Mexico," in chapter 2, or "Getting Around," above.

Climate See "When to Go," in chapter 2.

Currency Exchange You can exchange foreign currency at **Bank of America,** 1234 St. Michael's Dr. (© **505/473-8211**).

Dentists **Dr. Gilman Stenzhorn** (© **505/982-4317** or 505/983-4491) offers emergency service. He's located at 1496 St. Francis Dr., in the St. Francis Professional Center.

Doctors **The Lovelace Clinic,** 440 St. Michaels Dr. (© **505/995-2400**), is open Monday to Thursday 8am to 6pm; Fridays 8am to 5pm; and Saturdays 8am to 3pm. For physician and surgeon referral and information services, call the **American Board of Medical Specialties** (© **866/275-2267**).

Embassies & Consulates See "Fast Facts: For the International Traveler," in chapter 3.

Emergencies For police, fire, or ambulance emergencies, dial © **911.**

Etiquette & Customs Certain rules of etiquette should be observed when visiting the pueblos. For details, see "Touring the Pueblos Around Santa Fe" in this chapter.

Hospitals **St. Vincent Hospital,** 455 St. Michaels Dr. (© **505/983-3361,** or 505/995-3934 for emergency services), is a 248-bed regional health center. Patient services include urgent and emergency-room care and ambulatory surgery. Health services are also available at the **Women's Health Services Family Care and Counseling Center** (© **505/988-8869**). **Ultimed,** 707 Paseo de Peralta (© 505/989-8707), a new urgent care facility near the plaza, offers comprehensive health care.

Hot Lines The following hot lines are available in Santa Fe: **battered families** (© 505/473-5200), **poison control** (© 800/432-6866), **psychiatric emergencies** (© 888/920-6333 or 505/820-6333), and **sexual assault** (© 505/986-9111).

Information See "Visitor Information," under "Orientation," above.

Internet Access Head to the **Santa Fe Public Library** at 145 Washington Ave. (© 505/955-6780), or retrieve your e-mail at **FedEx Kinko's,** 301 N. Guadalupe (© 505/982-6311).

Libraries **The Santa Fe Public Library** is half a block from the plaza, at 145 Washington Ave. (© 505/955-6780). There are branch libraries at Villa Linda Mall and at 1730 Llano St., just off St. Michaels Drive. **The New Mexico State Library** is at 1209 Camino Carlos Rey (© 505/476-9700). Specialty libraries include the **Archives of New Mexico,** 1205 Camino Carlos Rey, and the **New Mexico History Library,** 120 Washington Ave.

Liquor Laws The legal drinking age is 21 throughout New Mexico. Bars may remain open until 2am Monday to Saturday and until midnight on Sunday. Wine, beer, and spirits are sold at licensed supermarkets and liquor stores, but there are no package sales on election days until after 7pm, and on Sundays before noon. It is illegal to transport liquor through most Native American reservations.

Lost Property Contact the **city police** at © 505/955-5030.

Newspapers & Magazines The *New Mexican*—Santa Fe's daily paper—is the oldest newspaper in the West. Its offices are at 202 E. Marcy St. (© 505/983-3303; www.santafenewmexican.com). The weekly *Santa Fe Reporter,* 132 E. Marcy St. (© 505/988-5541; www.sfreporter.com), published on Wednesday and available free at stands all over town, is often more willing to be controversial, and its entertainment listings are excellent. Regional magazines published locally are *New Mexico* magazine (monthly, statewide interest; www.nmmagazine.com) and the *Santa Fean* magazine (10 times a year, Southwestern lifestyles; www.santafean.com).

Pharmacies **Del Norte Pharmacy,** at 1691 Galisteo St. (© 505/988-9797), is open Monday to Friday 8:30am to 6pm, and Saturday 9am to noon. Emergency and delivery service are available.

Police In case of emergency, dial © 911. For all other inquiries, call the **Santa Fe Police Department,** 2515 Camino Entrada (© 505/428-3710). The **Santa Fe County Sheriff,** with jurisdiction outside the city limits, is located at 35 Camino Justicia (© 505/986-2400).

Post Offices The **main post office** is at 120 S. Federal Place (© 505/988-6351), 2 blocks north and 1 block west of the plaza. It's open from 7:30am to 5:30pm. The **Coronado Station branch,** 2071 S. Pacheco St. (© 505/438-8452), is open Monday to Friday 8am to 6pm and Saturday 9am to 1pm. Some of the major hotels have stamp machines and mailboxes. The zip code for central Santa Fe is 87501.

Radio Local radio stations are **BLU** (102.9), which plays contemporary jazz, and **KBAC** (98.1), which plays alternative rock and folk music.

Travel Tip: He who finds the best hotel deal has more to spend on facials involving knobbly vegetables.

Hello, the Roaming Gnome here. I've been nabbed from the garden and taken round the world. The people who took me are so terribly clever. They find the best offerings on Travelocity. For very little cha-ching. And that means I get to be pampered and exfoliated till I'm pink as a bunny's doodah.

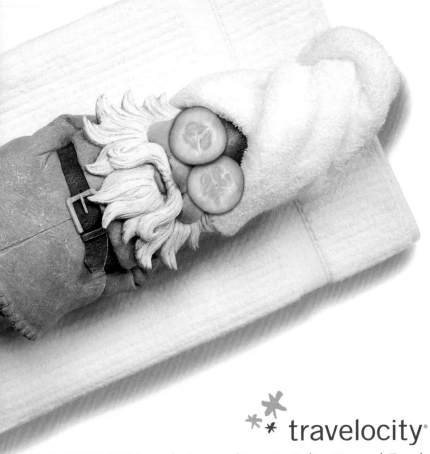

travelocity®

1-888-TRAVELOCITY / travelocity.com / America Online Keyword: Travel

travel · news · classifieds · health · personals · maps · autos · sp

Plan your vacation

- flights, hotels, car rentals
- cruises & vacation packages
- destination guides
- fare alerts
- go to yahoo.com, click travel

DO YOU YAHOO!?

Safety Although the tourist district appears very safe, Santa Fe is not on the whole a safe city; theft and the number of reported rapes have risen. The good news is that Santa Fe's overall crime statistics appear to be falling. Still, when walking the city streets, guard your purse carefully because there are many bag-grab thefts, particularly during the summer tourist months. Also, be aware of your surroundings, as you would in any other major city.

Taxes A tax of 6.43% is added to all purchases, with an additional 5% added to lodging bills.

Taxis See "Getting Around," above.

Television There are five Albuquerque network affiliates: **KOB-TV** (Channel 4, NBC), **KOAT-TV** (Channel 7, ABC), **KQRE-TV** (Channel 13, CBS), **KASA-TV** (Channel 2, FOX), and **KNME-TV** (Channel 5, PBS).

Time As is true throughout New Mexico, Santa Fe is on **Mountain Standard Time.** It's 2 hours earlier than New York, 1 hour earlier than Chicago, and 1 hour later than Los Angeles. Daylight saving time is in effect from early April to late October.

Useful Telephone Numbers Information on **road conditions** in the Santa Fe area can be obtained by calling the State Highway and Transportation Department (© **800/432-4269**). For **time and temperature,** call © **505/473-2211.**

Weather For **weather forecasts,** call © **505/988-5151.**

3 Where to Stay

It's difficult to find a bad place to stay in Santa Fe. From downtown hotels to Cerrillos Road motels, ranch-style resorts to quaint bed-and-breakfasts, the standard of accommodations is almost universally high.

You should be aware of the seasonal nature of the tourist industry in Santa Fe. Accommodations are often booked solid through the summer months, and most places raise their prices accordingly. Rates increase even more during Indian Market, the third weekend of August. For stays during these periods it's essential to make reservations well in advance.

Still, there seems to be little agreement on what constitutes the tourist season; one hotel may raise its rates July 1 and lower them again in mid-September, while another may raise its rates from May to November. Some hotels recognize a shoulder season, so it pays to shop around during the in-between seasons of May through June and September through October.

No matter the season, discounts are often available to seniors, affiliated groups, corporate employees, and others. If you have any questions about your eligibility for these lower rates, be sure to ask.

A combined city–state tax of about 11.5% is added to every hotel bill in Santa Fe. And unless otherwise indicated, all recommended accommodations come with a private bathroom.

RESERVATIONS SERVICES Year-round reservation assistance is available from **Santa Fe Central Reservations** (© 800/745-9910), the **Accommodation Hot Line** (© 800/338-6877), **All Santa Fe Reservations** (© 877/737-7366), and **Santa Fe Stay,** which specializes in casitas (© 800/995-2272). **Emergency**

Lodging Assistance is available free after 4pm daily (© 505/986-0038). All of the above are private companies and may have biases toward certain properties. Do your own research before calling.

HOTELS/MOTELS
DOWNTOWN

Everything within the horseshoe-shaped Paseo de Peralta and east a few blocks along either side of the Santa Fe River is considered downtown Santa Fe. All these accommodations are within walking distance of the plaza.

Very Expensive

Eldorado Hotel ⊛⊛ Since its opening in 1986, the Eldorado has been a model new hotel for the city. In a large structure, the architects managed to meld Pueblo Revival style with an interesting cathedral feel, inside and out. The lobby is grand, with a high ceiling that continues into the court area and the cafe, all adorned with well over $1 million worth of Southwestern art. The spacious, quiet rooms continue the artistic motif, with a warm feel created by the kiva fireplaces in many, as well as the custom-made furniture. You'll find families, businesspeople, and conference-goers staying here. Most of the rooms have views of downtown Santa Fe, many from balconies. If you're really indulging, join the ranks of Mick Jagger, Geena Davis, and King Juan Carlos of Spain and try the penthouse five-room presidential suite. The Eldorado also manages the nearby Zona Rosa condominiums, which are two-, three-, and four-bedroom suites with full kitchens. The innovative and elegant restaurant The Old House serves creative American cuisine (see "Where to Dine," later in this chapter).

309 W. San Francisco St., Santa Fe, NM 87501. © **800/286-6755** or 505/988-4455. Fax 505/995-4544. www.eldoradohotel.com. 219 units. High season $279–$1,500 double; low season $169–$900 double. Ski and other package rates are available. AE, DC, DISC, MC, V. Valet parking $16. Pets accepted. **Amenities:** 2 restaurants (p. 141); bar; heated rooftop pool; medium-size health club (with a view); Jacuzzi; his-and-hers saunas; concierge; business center; salon; room service; massage; laundry service; dry cleaning. *In room:* A/C, TV, dataport, minibar, coffeemaker, hair dryer, iron, safe.

Hilton of Santa Fe ⊛ With its landmark bell tower, the Hilton encompasses a full city block (1 block from the plaza) and incorporates most of the historic landholdings of the 350-year-old Ortiz family estate. It's built around a lovely courtyard pool and patio area, and it's a fine blend of ancient and modern styles. A renovation late in 2004 has brought more style to the rooms and common areas, with handcrafted furnishings and hip Southwestern decor. Rooms vary slightly in size; my favorites are a little smaller than some but have balconies opening onto the courtyard. The Hilton also has the Casa Ortiz de Santa Fe, luxury casitas with kitchens situated in a 1625 coach house adjacent to the hotel. Two restaurants on the Hilton's grounds occupy the premises of the early-18th-century Casa Ortiz. The Piñon Grill serves a variety of wood-fire-grilled items in a casual atmosphere, and the Chamisa Courtyard serves breakfast.

100 Sandoval St. (P.O. Box 25104), Santa Fe, NM 87501-2131. © **800/336-3676,** 800/HILTONS, or 505/988-2811. Fax 505/986-6439. www.hilton.com. 157 units. $159–$299 double; $239–$549 suite; $419–$559 casita, depending on time of year. Additional person $20. AE, DC, DISC, MC, V. Parking $10. **Amenities:** 2 restaurants; bar; outdoor pool; exercise room; Jacuzzi; concierge; car-rental desk; courtesy van; business center; room service; laundry service; dry cleaning. *In room:* A/C, TV, dataport, coffeemaker, hair dryer, iron, safe.

Hotel Plaza Real This New Orleans–meets–Santa Fe Territorial-style hotel built in 1990 provides comfortable rooms near the plaza. The construction and decor of the lobby are rustically elegant, built around a fireplace with balconies perched above. Clean and attractively decorated rooms have Southwestern-style

Where to Stay in Downtown Santa Fe

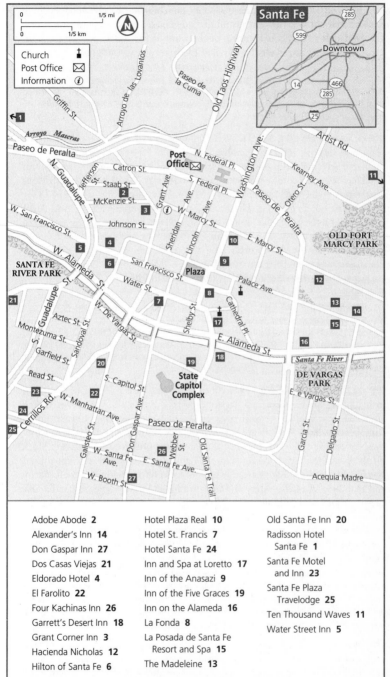

Adobe Abode **2**
Alexander's Inn **14**
Don Gaspar Inn **27**
Dos Casas Viejas **21**
Eldorado Hotel **4**
El Farolito **22**
Four Kachinas Inn **26**
Garrett's Desert Inn **18**
Grant Corner Inn **3**
Hacienda Nicholas **12**
Hilton of Santa Fe **6**

Hotel Plaza Real **10**
Hotel St. Francis **7**
Hotel Santa Fe **24**
Inn and Spa at Loretto **17**
Inn of the Anasazi **9**
Inn of the Five Graces **19**
Inn on the Alameda **16**
La Fonda **8**
La Posada de Santa Fe
   Resort and Spa **15**
The Madeleine **13**

Old Santa Fe Inn **20**
Radisson Hotel
   Santa Fe **1**
Santa Fe Motel
   and Inn **23**
Santa Fe Plaza
   Travelodge **25**
Ten Thousand Waves **11**
Water Street Inn **5**

furniture and accents such as *bancos* (adobe benches) and French doors opening onto balconies or terraces that surround a quiet courtyard decorated with *ristras*. Try the bar for an afternoon drink or the veranda for coffee. Service has been inconsistent since the Radisson acquired the hotel a few years ago.

125 Washington Ave., Santa Fe, NM 87501. 🕐 **877/901-7666** or 505/988-4900. Fax 505/983-9322. www. buynewmexico.com. 56 units. $149–$219 double, depending on time of year and type of room. Additional person $20. Children under 12 stay free in parent's room. AE, DC, DISC, MC, V. Parking $12. **Amenities:** Lounge; nearby health club access; laundry service; dry cleaning. *In room:* A/C, TV, dataport, coffeemaker, hair dryer, iron.

Inn & Spa at Loretto 🌟 This much-photographed hotel, 2 blocks from the plaza, was built in 1975 to resemble Taos Pueblo. Light and shadow dance on the five-level structure as the sun crosses the sky. With ongoing refinements, this hotel has become a comfortable and chic place to stay. Decor is Southwest/Montana ranch style, with faux painted walls and an interesting and cozy lobby lounge. The hotel's rooms and bathrooms are standard size, with the same decor as the rest of the hotel. Be aware that the Loretto likes convention traffic, so sometimes service lags for vacationers. Overall, it is fairly quiet and has nice views—especially on the northeast side, where you can see both the historic St. Francis Cathedral and the Loretto Chapel (see "More Attractions," later in this chapter). Spa Terre offers a range of treatments, in intimate, Southwest-meets-Asia rooms.

211 Old Santa Fe Trail (P.O. Box 1417), Santa Fe, NM 87501. 🕐 **800/727-5531** or 505/988-5531. Fax 505/ 984-7988. www.hotelloretto.com. 135 units. Jan–Mar $159–$265 double; Apr–June $185–$299 double; July–Oct $215–$499 double; Nov–Dec $185–$299 double. Additional person $25. Children 17 and under stay free in parent's room. AE, DC, DISC, MC, V. Valet parking $15. **Amenities:** Restaurant; lounge; outdoor pool (heated year-round); spa; concierge; business center with audiovisual conferencing equipment; room service; valet laundry. *In room:* A/C, TV, fridge, coffeemaker, hair dryer, iron.

Inn of the Anasazi 🌟🌟🌟 This fine luxury hotel has a feeling of grandness in a limited space. Vigas and flagstone floors create a warm and welcoming ambience that evokes the feeling of an Anasazi cliff dwelling. Oversize cacti complete the look. Accents are appropriately Navajo, in a nod to the fact that the Navajo live in the area the ancestral Puebloans once inhabited. A half block off the plaza, this hotel was built in 1991 to cater to travelers who know their hotels. On the ground floor are a living room and library with oversize furniture and replicas of Anasazi pottery and Navajo rugs. A library expansion and a new exercise room were completed in 2004. Even the smallest rooms are spacious, with pearl-finished walls and decor in cream tones accented by novelties such as iron candle sconces, original art, four-poster beds, gaslit kiva fireplaces, and humidifiers. All the rooms are quiet and comfortable, though none have dramatic views. The Anasazi Restaurant serves creative Southwestern cuisine.

113 Washington Ave., Santa Fe, NM 87501. 🕐 **800/688-8100** or 505/988-3030. Fax 505/988-3277. www. innoftheanasazi.com. 57 units. Jan 5–Feb 26 $205–$405; Feb 27–Apr 28 $225–$425; Apr 29–June 23 $255–$445; June 24–Jan 4 $295–$475 double. AE, DC, DISC, MC, V. Valet parking $13. **Amenities:** Restaurant; small exercise room; concierge; room service; in-room massage; laundry service; library/boardroom. *In room:* A/C, TV/VCR/DVD, coffeemaker, hair dryer, iron, safe.

The Inn of the Five Graces 🌟🌟 *(Finds)* Along historic Barrio de Analco in the center of downtown, this inn holds true to its stated theme: "Here the Orient and the Old West meet, surprisingly at home in each other's arms." With floral decked courtyards, elaborately decorated suites with kilim rugs, ornately carved beds, and often mosaic tile work in the bathrooms, this is truly a "sheik" place.

All but a few suites are medium-size, most with small bathrooms. The lower-priced rooms are smaller. Request one of the suites in the buildings on the north side of East de Vargas Street; they're more spacious and substantially built. Travelers seeking a fine and exotic stay will like this place; it's of the caliber of Inn of the Anasazi, though with more flair and fewer amenities. All rooms have robes, stocked fridges, patios, and CD players; some have kitchenettes.

150 E. de Vargas St., Santa Fe, NM 87501. © **505/992-0957.** www.fivegraces.com. 20 units. $295–$470 double, depending on the season and type of room. Price includes extended continental breakfast and afternoon treats. AE, MC, V. Free parking. Pets welcome with fee and deposit. **Amenities:** Concierge. *In room:* A/C, TV, CD player, fridge, coffeemaker, hair dryer, iron, microwave.

Inn on the Alameda ⭐

Across the street from the bosque-shaded Santa Fe River sits the Inn on the Alameda, a cozy stop for those who like the services of a hotel with the intimacy of an inn. Built in 1986, with additions over the years, it now rambles across four buildings. There are casita suites to the west, two three-story buildings at the center, and another one-story building that contains suites. All are Pueblo-style adobe, and most were built in the late 1980s. The owner, Joe Schepps, appreciates traditional Southwestern style; he's used red brick in the dining area and Mexican *equipae* (wicker) furniture in the lobby, as well as thick vigas and shiny *latillas* in a sitting area set around a grand fireplace. The rooms have similar good taste, some with fridges, CD players, safes, Jacuzzi tubs, and kiva fireplaces. The newer deluxe rooms and suites in the easternmost building are in the best shape. The traditional rooms are quaint, some with interesting angled bed configurations. The trees surrounding the inn make you feel as though you're in a treehouse when you step out on some of the balconies. If you're an art shopper, this is an ideal spot because it's a quick walk to Canyon Road. An elaborate continental "Breakfast of Enchantment" is served each morning in the Agoyo Room, in the outdoor courtyard, or in your room, and there is an afternoon wine and cheese reception. A full-service bar is open nightly.

303 E. Alameda St., Santa Fe, NM 87501. © **800/289-2122** or 505/984-2121. Fax 505/986-8325. www.innonthealameda.com. 69 units. $129–$209 queen; $142–$222 king; $210–$350 suite; reduced off-season rates are available. Rates include breakfast and afternoon wine and cheese reception. AE, DC, DISC, MC, V. Free parking. Pets welcome. **Amenities:** Bar; medium-size fitness facility; 2 open-air Jacuzzis; concierge; massage; child care by arrangement; coin-op laundry; same-day dry cleaning; pet amenities and a pet-walking map. *In room:* A/C, TV, dataport, hair dryer, iron.

La Fonda ⭐

Whether you stay in this hotel or not, it's worth strolling through just to get a sense of how Santa Fe once was—and in some ways still is. This was the inn at the end of the Santa Fe Trail; it saw trappers, traders, and merchants, as well as notables such as President Rutherford B. Hayes and General Ulysses S. Grant. The original inn was dying of old age in 1920 when it was razed and replaced by the current La Fonda. Its architecture is Pueblo Revival: imitation adobe with wooden balconies and beam ends protruding over the tops of windows. Inside, the lobby is rich and slightly dark, with people bustling about, sitting in the cafe, and buying jewelry from Native Americans.

The hotel has seen some renovation through the years, including a new wing, where you'll find deluxe suites and new meeting spaces. If you want a feel of the real Santa Fe, this is the place to stay. Overall, however, this hotel isn't the model of refinement. For that, you'd best go to the Hotel Santa Fe or other newer places. No two rooms are the same here, and while each has its own funky touch, some are more kitschy than quaint. Some have fridges, fireplaces, and private balconies. The spa offers a variety of treatments, from massages to salt glows, as well as a sauna and Jacuzzi. The French Pastry Shop is the place to get cappuccino and crepes; La Fiesta Lounge draws many locals to its economical New Mexican food lunch buffet; and La Plazuela offers some of the best new Southwestern cuisine in town, in a skylit garden patio. The Bell Tower Bar is the highest point in downtown Santa Fe—a great place for a cocktail and a view of the city.

100 E. San Francisco St. (P.O. Box 1209), Santa Fe, NM 87501. © **800/523-5002** or 505/982-5511. Fax 505/988-2952. www.lafondasantafe.com. 167 units. $219–$269 standard double; $239–$289 deluxe double; $349–$539 suite. Additional person $15. Children under 12 stay free in parent's room. AE, DC, DISC, MC, V. Parking $9 per day in a covered garage. **Amenities:** Restaurant; 2 bars; outdoor pool; exercise room; spa; 2 indoor Jacuzzis; concierge; tour desk; room service; massage room and in-room massage; babysitting; laundry service; dry cleaning. *In room:* A/C, TV, dataport, coffeemaker, hair dryer, iron, safe.

La Posada de Santa Fe Resort and Spa ⭐⭐ If you're in the mood to stay in a little New Mexico adobe village, you'll enjoy this recently renovated luxury hotel just 3 blocks from the plaza. The main building is an odd mix of architecture. The original part was a Victorian mansion built in 1882 by Abraham Staab, a German immigrant, for his bride, Julia. Later, an adobe structure was literally built around it, so now the Victorian presence is only within the charming bar and four rooms, which still maintain the original brick and high ceilings. It is said that Julia Staab, who died in 1896, continues to haunt the place. Mischievous but good-natured, she is Santa Fe's best-known and most frequently witnessed ghost. If you like Victorian interiors more than Santa Fe style, these rooms are a good bet.

The rest of the hotel follows in the pueblo-style construction and is quaint; it's especially nice in the summer, when surrounded by acres of green grass. Here, you get to experience squeaky maple floors, vigas and *latillas,* and, in many rooms, kiva fireplaces. Be aware that aside from the suites, most rooms are fairly small. The hotel benefited from a $23 million face-lift completed in 1999. Most notable are the Zen-Southwestern-style spa and pool and spacious spa rooms. Travelers who are reluctant to trust the whims of older adobe construction should reserve one of the spa rooms or any of the 40 other new rooms. The hotel attracts vacationers, a fair number of families, and conventioneers. Most rooms don't have views but have outdoor patios, and most are tucked back into the quiet compound.

330 E. Palace Ave., Santa Fe, NM 87501. © **800/727-5276** or 505/986-0000. Fax 505/982-6850. www.la posada zdesantafe.com. 157 units. $199–$359 double; suites $289 and way up, depending on the season. Various spa packages available. AE, DC, DISC, MC, V. Valet parking $14. **Amenities:** 2 restaurants; bar; outdoor pool; exercise room; spa with full treatments; Jacuzzi; bike rental; concierge; salon; room service; in-room massage; babysitting; dry cleaning. *In room:* A/C, TV, dataport, minibar, coffeemaker, hair dryer, iron, safe.

Ten Thousand Waves ⭐ *Moments* Longing for a little Zen in your life? This inn provides minimalist Japanese-adobe accommodations nestled within piñon trees below Ten Thousand Waves Japanese Health Spa (p. 166), a truly unique place renowned for its hot tubs and spa treatments. Inn guests receive complimentary use of communal baths. About a 10-minute drive from the plaza, the place is en route to Santa Fe Ski Area. Travelers seeking to enjoy the silence of their own being seek out this place. They need to be fit because the paths connecting the rooms with the spa have enough steps to make you gasp during your mantra. Rooms are aesthetically bare, medium-size, with clean lines and paper lamps, kimonos, and such hanging about. All have wood-burning fireplaces, robes, and balconies; four have full kitchens; and most have TV/VCRs. The High Moon is the most elaborate room, with a full kitchen, two balconies, and lots of space. More spartan and small is the Zen room, decorated in minimalist decor.

3451 Hyde Park Rd., Santa Fe, NM 87501. ☎ **505/982-9304** or 505/992-5025. Fax 505/989-5077. www.ten thousandwaves.com. 9 units. $190–$260 double. Additional person $20. Rates include use of communal baths. AE, DISC, MC, V. Free parking. One or more pets welcome, with advance notice, for $20 per night. **Amenities:** Spa with full treatments; coin-op laundry. *In room:* CD player, fridge, coffeemaker, hair dryer, iron, microwave.

Expensive

Don Gaspar Inn ★★ *Finds*   If you'd like to pretend that you live in Santa Fe during your vacation—that you're blessed with your very own Southwestern-style home, in a historic neighborhood, full of artful touches such as Native American tapestries and a kiva fireplace—this is your inn. A 10-minute walk from the plaza, the Don Gaspar occupies three homes, connected by brilliant gardens and brick walkways. Rooms vary in size, though all are plenty spacious, most with patios, some with kitchenettes, and there's even a full house for rent. Travelers looking for an adventure beyond a hotel stay, but without the close interaction of a B&B, enjoy this place. Though the rooms don't have views, all are quiet. The Courtyard Casita, with a kitchenette and a sleeper couch in its own room, is nice for a small family. The Territorial Suite, with carpet throughout and Italian marble in the bath, is perfect for a romantic getaway. All rooms have bathrobes and fireplaces. The friendly and dedicated staff serves a full breakfast, such as green chile stew with fresh baked items, on the patio under a peach tree (the fruit from which they make cobbler) in the warm months, and in the atrium in winter.

623 Don Gaspar, Santa Fe, NM 87505. ☎ **888/986-8664** or 505/986-8664. Fax 505/986-0696. www.don gaspar.com. 12 units. $115–$175 double; $145–$195 suite; $165–$295 casita or house. Rates include full breakfast. AE, MC, V. Free parking. **Amenities:** Babysitting; same-day laundry service. *In room:* A/C, TV/VCR, hair dryer, iron.

Hotel St. Francis ★   If you long for the rich fabrics, fine antiques, and slow pace of a European hotel, this is your place. The building was first constructed in the 1880s; it became fairly dilapidated but was renovated in 1986. Now elegantly redecorated, the lobby is crowned by a Victorian fireplace with hovering cherubs, a theme repeated throughout the hotel. The rooms continue the European decor, each with its own unique bent. You'll find a fishing room, a golf room, a garden room, and a music room, with each motif evoked by the furnishings: a vintage set of golf clubs here, a sheet of music in a dry flower arrangement there. The hotel, which attracts individual travelers as well as families and many Europeans, is well cared for by a concierge who speaks six languages. Enjoy high tea in the lobby 3 to 5:30pm daily. Request a room facing east, and you'll wake each day to a view of the mountains. Larger rooms have coffeemakers and hair dryers.

210 Don Gaspar Ave., Santa Fe, NM 87501. ☎ **800/529-5700** or 505/983-5700. Fax 505/989-7690. www. hotelstfrancis.com. 83 units. $92–$185 double; $205–$380 suite, depending on the season. Children under 12 stay free in parent's room. AE, DC, DISC, MC, V. Parking $5. **Amenities:** Restaurant; bar; access to nearby health club; concierge; room service; laundry service; dry cleaning; library and gaming tables. *In room:* A/C, TV, fridge, safe.

Hotel Santa Fe ★ *Finds*   About a 10-minute walk south of the plaza you'll find this newer three-story establishment, the only Native American–owned hotel in Santa Fe. It is a good choice for consistent, well-planned lodgings. Picuris Pueblo is the majority stockholder here, and part of the pleasure of staying here is the culture the Picuris bring to your visit. This is not to say that you'll get any sense of the rusticity of a pueblo in your accommodations; this sophisticated 14-year-old hotel is decorated in Southwestern style, with a few novel aspects such as an Allan Houser bronze buffalo dancer watching over the front desk and a fireplace surrounded by comfortable furniture in the lobby. The rooms are medium-size, with clean lines and comfortable beds, the decor accented with pine Taos-style furniture. Rooms on the north side get less street noise from Cerrillos Road and have better views of the mountains, but they don't have the sun shining onto their balconies. You will get a strong sense of the Native American presence on the patio during the summer, when Picuris dancers come to perform and bread bakers uncover the *horno* (oven) and prepare loaves for sale.

Opened in 2001, The Hacienda is a unique addition that features 35 luxurious rooms and suites, all with fireplaces, 10-foot ceilings, handcrafted Southwestern furnishings, and plush duvets. The restaurant serves a standard breakfast, but for lunch and dinner you can dine on Native American food from all over the Americas. Expect buffalo and turkey instead of beef and chicken.

1501 Paseo de Peralta, Santa Fe, NM 87501. © **800/825-9876** or 505/982-1200. Fax 505/984-2211. www. hotelsantafe.com. 163 units. $99–$199 double; $129–$269 junior suite, depending on the season. Hacienda rooms and suites $199–$459. Additional person $10. Children 17 and under stay free in parent's room. AE, DC, DISC, MC, V. Free parking. Pets accepted with $20 fee. **Amenities:** Restaurant; outdoor pool; Jacuzzi; concierge; car-rental desk; room service; in-room massage; babysitting; coin-op laundry; dry cleaning. *In room:* A/C, TV, dataport, minibar, iron, safe.

Moderate

Garrett's Desert Inn *(Value* Completion of this hotel in 1957 prompted the Historic Design Review Board to implement zoning restrictions throughout downtown. Apparently, residents were appalled by the huge air conditioners adorning the roof. Though they're still unsightly, the hotel makes up for them. First, with all the focus today on retro fashions, this hotel, located 3 blocks from the plaza, is totally in. It's a clean, two-story, concrete block building around a broad parking lot. The hotel underwent a complete remodel in 1994, with touch-ups through the years; it has managed to maintain some vintage touches, such as Art Deco tile in the bathrooms and plenty of space in the rooms, while being updated with larger windows and sturdy doors and wood accents. Rooms are equipped with tile vanities, and mini-suites have fridges and microwaves.

311 Old Santa Fe Trail, Santa Fe, NM 87501. © **800/888-2145** or 505/982-1851. Fax 505/989-1647. www. garrettsdesertinn.com. 83 units. $89–$165, depending on season and type of room. AE, DISC, MC, V. **Amenities:** Restaurant; bar; outdoor pool; concierge; room service; in-room massage; laundry service; dry cleaning. *In room:* A/C, TV, dataport, coffeemaker, hair dryer, iron.

Old Santa Fe Inn *(Finds (Kids* Want to stay downtown and savor Santa Fe–style ambience without wearing out your plastic? This is your hotel. A multi-million-dollar renovation to this 1930s court motel has created a comfortable, quiet inn just a few blocks from the plaza. Rooms verge on small but are decorated with such lovely handcrafted colonial-style furniture that you probably won't mind. All have small Mexican-tiled bathrooms, each with an outer vanity; most have gas fireplaces. You have a choice of king, queen, or twin bedrooms as well as suites. Though there's no pool or hot tub to wet you down, as there are at some of the other downtown moderately priced motels, this could still be a good choice for families because it has some adjoining rooms. Breakfast is served in an atmospheric dining room next to a comfortable library.

320 Galisteo St., Santa Fe, NM 87501. © **800/745-9910** or 505/995-0800. Fax 505/995-0400. www.old santafeinn.com. 43 units. Winter $89–$136 double, $119–$169 suite; summer $127–$149 double, $199–$249 suite. Rates include continental breakfast. AE, DC, DISC, MC, V. *In room:* A/C, TV/VCR, dataport, fridge, coffeemaker, CD player.

Kids Family-Friendly Hotels

The Bishop's Lodge (p. 130)   Riding lessons, tennis courts with instruction, a pool with a lifeguard, a stocked trout pond just for kids, a summer daytime program, horseback trail trips, and more make this a veritable day camp for all ages.

Old Santa Fe Inn (p. 128)   Although this inn doesn't have a pool or hot tub, it's a good-priced place downtown, and it has some adjoining rooms.

Santa Fe Motel and Inn   If you like walking to the plaza and restaurants but don't want to pay big bucks, this little compound is a good choice. Rooms here are larger than at the nearby Budget Inn and have more personality than those at the Travelodge. Ask for one of the casitas in back—you'll pay more but get a little turn-of-the-20th-century charm, plus more quiet and privacy. Some have vigas, others have skylights, fireplaces, and patios. The main part of the motel, built in 1955, is two-story Territorial style, with upstairs rooms that open onto a portal with a bit of a view. All guest rooms are decorated with a Southwestern motif and have very basic furnishings but comfortable beds. Some rooms have kitchenettes, with fridges, microwaves, stoves, coffeemakers, and toasters. Coffee is served each morning in the office, where a bulletin board lists Santa Fe activities.

510 Cerrillos Rd., Santa Fe, NM 87501. ℰ **800/930-5002** or 505/982-1039. Fax 505/986-1275. www.santafe motel.com. 23 units. $69–$139, depending on the season and type of room. Additional person $10. Rates include continental breakfast. AE, DC, MC, V. Free parking. *In room:* A/C, TV, hair dryer, iron.

Inexpensive

Santa Fe Budget Inn *(Value)*   If you're looking for a convenient, almost-downtown location at a reasonable price, this is one of your best bets. This two-story stucco adobe motel with portals is spread through three buildings and is about a 10-minute walk from the plaza. Built in 1985, it was remodeled in 1994 and has seen ongoing renovations. The rooms are plain, basic, and fairly small. The bathrooms and furniture could use some updating, but if you're a traveler who spends a lot of time out of the room, that probably won't matter to you. The motel is clean and functional, with comfortable beds and good reading lights. It's near McDonald's, and there's a small park in the back and an outdoor pool. To avoid street noise, ask for a room at the back of the property. An adjacent restaurant serves American and New Mexican food.

725 Cerrillos Rd., Santa Fe, NM 87501. ℰ **800/288-7600** or 505/982-5952. Fax 505/984-8879. www.santafe budgetinn.com. 160 units. $58–$72 double. Additional person $7. Rates include continental breakfast. AE, DC, MC, V. Free parking. Pets welcome. **Amenities:** Outdoor pool. *In room:* A/C, TV.

Santa Fe Plaza Travelodge   You can count on this motel near Hotel Santa Fe (6 blocks to the plaza) on busy Cerrillos Road for comfort, convenience, and a no-frills stay. The rooms are very clean, nicely lit, and, despite the busy location, relatively quiet. New mattresses and a pretty Southwestern ceiling border add to the comfort and decor.

646 Cerrillos Rd., Santa Fe, NM 87501. ℰ **800/578-7878** or 505/982-3551. Fax 505/983-8624. www.travel odge.com. 48 units. May–Oct $65–$88 double; Nov–Apr $39–$69 double. AE, DC, DISC, MC, V. Free parking. **Amenities:** Outdoor pool. *In room:* A/C, TV, fridge, coffeemaker.

NORTHSIDE

Within easy reach of the plaza, the north side encompasses the area that lies north of the loop of Paseo de Peralta.

Very Expensive

The Bishop's Lodge ★★ *Kids*   This resort holds special significance for me because my parents met in the lodge and were later married in the chapel. It's a place rich with history. More than a century ago, when Bishop Jean-Baptiste Lamy was the spiritual leader of northern New Mexico's Roman Catholic population, he often escaped clerical politics by hiking into this valley called Little Tesuque. He built a retreat and a humble chapel (now on the National Register of Historic Places) with vaulted ceilings and a hand-built altar. Today, Lamy's 1,000-acre getaway has become The Bishop's Lodge.

A recent $17 million renovation spruced up the place and added a spa and 10,000 square feet of meeting space. The guest rooms, spread through many buildings, feature handcrafted furniture and regional artwork. Standard rooms are spacious, and many have balconies, while deluxe rooms feature kiva fireplaces, a combination bedroom/sitting room, and private decks or patios. The newest rooms are luxurious, and some have spectacular views of the Jemez Mountains. The Bishop's Lodge is an active resort, with activities such as horseback riding, nature walks, and cookouts; in the winter, it takes on the character of a romantic country retreat. A children's program keeps kids busy for much of the day.

Bishop's Lodge Rd. (P.O. Box 2367), Santa Fe, NM 87504. © **505/983-6377.** Fax 505/989-8739. www. bishopslodge.com. 111 units. Summer $299–$399 double; fall and spring $249–$349 double; midwinter $189–$269 double. Additional person $15. Children 3 and under stay free in parent's room. Ask about packages that include meals. AE, DC, DISC, MC, V. Free parking. **Amenities:** Restaurant; outdoor pool; tennis courts; spa; Jacuzzi; sauna; steam room; concierge; courtesy shuttle; room service; in-room massage; babysitting; laundry service. *In room:* A/C, TV, coffeemaker, safe.

Moderate

Radisson Hotel Santa Fe   Set on a hill as you head north toward the Santa Fe Opera, this three-story hotel has recently benefited from a multi-million-dollar renovation that has made it a lovely place. I question the service, though. The theme here is Native American, with Anasazi-style stacked sandstone throughout the lobby and dining room. The guest rooms are medium-size, decorated in earth tones with bold prints, some with views of the mountains, others overlooking the pool. Premium rooms are more spacious, some with large living rooms and private balconies. Each parlor suite has a Murphy bed and kiva fireplace in the living room, a big dining area, a wet bar and fridges, and a jetted bathtub. The condo units nearby have fully equipped kitchens, fireplaces, and private decks.

750 N. St. Francis Dr., Santa Fe, NM 87501. © **800/333-3333** or 505/992-5800. Fax 505/992-5856. www. radisson.com. 128 units, 32 condos. $259 double; $225 suite; $309 condo. AE, DC, DISC, MC, V. Free parking. **Amenities:** Outdoor pool; free shuttle service to downtown. *In room:* A/C, TV, hair dryer, iron.

SOUTHSIDE

Santa Fe's major strip, Cerrillos Road, is US 85, the main route to and from Albuquerque and the I-25 freeway. It's about 5¼ miles from the plaza to the Villa Linda Mall, which marks the southern boundary of the city. Most motels are on this strip, although several of them are to the east, closer to St. Francis Drive (US 84) or the Las Vegas Highway.

Moderate

Best Western Inn of Santa Fe *Value*   This three-story hotel, a 15-minute drive from the plaza, offers clean cookie-cutter-type rooms at a reasonable price. It's a security-conscious hotel; rooms can be entered only from interior corridors, and there is a private safe in each room. Built in 1990, renovations are ongoing. The lobby is decorated in light pastels, with nice little tables where guests can eat their complimentary continental breakfast. The indoor Jacuzzi and pool are very clean, a good family spot to relax between outings. The somewhat narrow rooms have Aztec-motif bedspreads and blond furniture. Some doubles are more spacious, with couches. All have fairly small but functional bathrooms. Suites are larger, some with an in-room Jacuzzi; others have two rooms, with a sofa bed in one.

3650 Cerrillos Rd., Santa Fe, NM 87505. ⒞ **800/528-1234** or 505/438-3822. Fax 505/438-3795. www.best western.com. 97 units. $50–$100 double; $75–$145 suite, depending on the season. Children 12 and under stay free in parent's room. Rates include continental breakfast. AE, DC, DISC, MC, V. Free parking. Pets allowed with prior approval. **Amenities:** Indoor pool; Jacuzzi; laundry service. *In room:* A/C, TV, coffeemaker, hair dryer, safe.

El Rey Inn ⭐ *Finds* Staying at "The King" makes you feel like you're traveling the old Route 66 through the Southwest. The white stucco buildings of this court motel are decorated with bright trim around the doors and hand-painted Mexican tiles on the walls. Opened in the 1930s, it received additions in the 1950s, and remodeling is ongoing. The lobby has vigas and tile floors, and it is decorated with Oriental rugs and dark Spanish furniture. No two rooms are alike. The oldest section, nearest the lobby, feels a bit cramped, though the rooms have style, with Art Deco tile in the bathrooms and vigas on the ceilings. Some have little patios. Be sure to request a room as far back as possible from Cerrillos Road. The two stories of suites around the Spanish colonial courtyard are the sweetest deal I've seen in all of Santa Fe. These rooms make you feel like you're at a Spanish inn, with carved furniture and cozy couches. Some rooms have kitchenettes. To the north sit 10 deluxe units around the courtyard. These rooms offer more upscale amenities and gas fireplaces, as well as distinctive furnishings and artwork. A complimentary continental breakfast is served in a sunny room or on a terrace in the warmer months. There's also a sitting room with a library and game tables, as well as a picnic area, a playground, and an exercise room.

1862 Cerrillos Rd. (P.O. Box 4759), Santa Fe, NM 87502. ⒞ **800/521-1349** or 505/982-1931. Fax 505/989-9249. www.elreyinnsantafe.com. 85 units. $95–$165 double; $120–$225 suite. Rates include continental breakfast. AE, DC, DISC, MC, V. Free parking. **Amenities:** Outdoor pool; exercise room; Jacuzzi; sauna; coin-op laundry. *In room:* A/C, TV, fridge, coffeemaker, hair dryer, iron, safe.

Inexpensive

Super 8 Motel It's nothing flashy, but this pink stucco, boxy motel, which has received the "Pride of Super 8" award, attracts regulars who know precisely what to expect. You'll get a clean, comfortable room with double beds, a desk, and a few other amenities.

3358 Cerrillos Rd., Santa Fe, NM 87507. ⒞ **800/800-8000** or 505/471-8811. Fax 505/471-3239. www. super8.com. 96 units. $45–$80 double, depending on the season. Rates include continental breakfast. AE, DC, DISC, MC, V. Free parking. **Amenities:** Coin-op laundry. *In room:* A/C, TV, coffeemaker, safe.

BED & BREAKFASTS

If you prefer a homey, intimate setting to the sometimes impersonal ambience of a large hotel, one of Santa Fe's bed-and-breakfast inns may be right for you. All those listed here are located in or close to the downtown area and offer comfortable accommodations at expensive to moderate prices.

Adobe Abode ⭐ A short walk from the plaza, in the same quiet neighborhood as the Georgia O'Keeffe Museum, this is one of Santa Fe's most imaginative B&Bs. The living room is cozy, decorated with folk art. The creativity shines

Greater Santa Fe

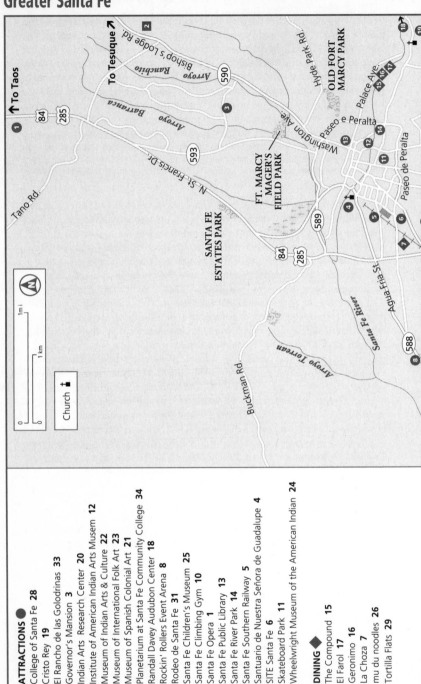

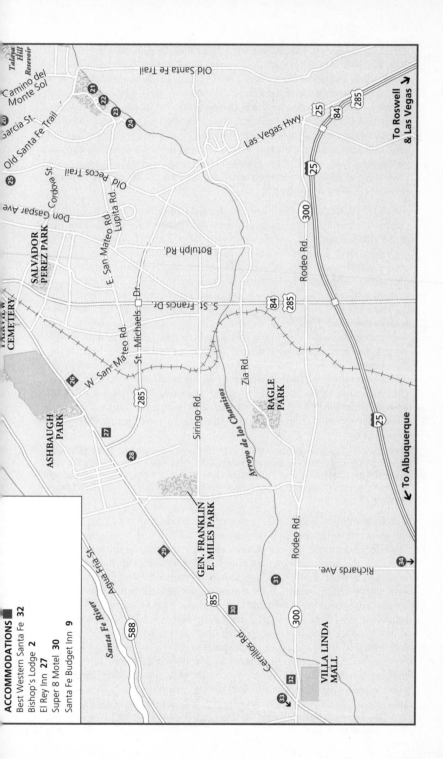

ACCOMMODATIONS
Best Western Santa Fe **32**
Bishop's Lodge **2**
El Rey Inn **27**
Super 8 Motel **30**
Santa Fe Budget Inn **9**

in each of the guest rooms as well, some located in the main house, which was built in 1907. Others, in back, are newer. The Provence Suite, decorated in sunny yellow and bright blue, offers a feel of France, while the Bronco Room is filled with cowboy paraphernalia: hats, Pendleton blankets, pioneer chests, and an entire shelf lined with children's cowboy boots. Two rooms have fireplaces, and several have private patios. Complimentary sherry, fruit, and cookies are served daily in the living room. Every morning a full breakfast of fresh fruit and a hot dish such as green chile corn soufflé is served in the country-style kitchen.

202 Chapelle St., Santa Fe, NM 87501. © **505/983-3133**. Fax 505/983-3132. www.adobeabode.com. 6 units. $135–$185 double. Rates include breakfast and afternoon snacks. DISC, MC, V. Limited free parking. *In room:* A/C, TV, coffeemaker, hair dryer, iron.

Alexander's Inn ★★   This inn, just 6 blocks from the plaza, continues to receive outstanding recommendations from such publications as *Glamour* ("one of the most romantic inns in the Southwest") and *Travel Holiday* ("a backdrop for a fairytale"). The 1903 Victorian/New England–style house, situated in a quiet residential area, is filled with delicious antiques, bedding, and draperies. The rooms have stenciling on the walls, hooked and Oriental rugs, muted colors such as apricot and lilac, and white iron or four-poster queen-size beds (there are some king-size beds as well). Separate from the inn are cottages, complete with kitchens (equipped with stove, oven, fridges, and swamp coolers, some with microwave) and living rooms with kiva fireplaces. Some have more Southwestern charm than others, so discuss your desires when making reservations. An extended continental breakfast of homemade baked goods is served in the dining room or on the veranda every morning, as are afternoon tea and cookies. Under the same excellent management, the **Hacienda Nicholas** ★★ (© **888/ 284-3170** or 505/992-8385; www.haciendanicholas.com), just a few blocks away, offers guests a delightful Southwestern stay in rooms gathered around a sunny patio.

529 E. Palace Ave., Santa Fe, NM 87501. © **888/321-5123** or 505/986-1431. Fax 505/982-8572. www. alexanders-inn.com. 10 units (8 with bathroom), 5 cottages. $85–$250 double. Additional person $25. Rates include extended continental breakfast and afternoon tea. AE, DISC, MC, V. Free parking. Pets accepted with $20 deposit. **Amenities:** Tennis club privileges; Jacuzzi; concierge; activities desk. *In room:* A/C, TV, dataport, hair dryer.

Dos Casas Viejas ★★★   These two old houses *(dos casas viejas),* not far from the plaza, offer the kind of luxury accommodations you'd expect from a fine hotel. Behind an old wooden security gate is a meandering brick lane along which are the elegant guest rooms. The innkeepers, Susan and Michael Strijek, maintain the place impeccably. The grounds are manicured, and the rooms, each with a patio and private entrance, are finely renovated and richly decorated. All rooms have Mexican-tile floors and kiva fireplaces; most have diamond-finished stucco walls and embedded vigas. They're furnished with Southwestern antiques and original art. Some have canopy beds, and one has a sleigh bed; all are covered with fine linens and down comforters. Guests can use the library and dining area (where a European breakfast is served each morning) in the main building. Breakfast can also be enjoyed on the patio alongside the elegant lap pool or (after you collect it in a basket) on your private patio.

610 Agua Fría St., Santa Fe, NM 87501. © **505/983-1636**. Fax 505/983-1749. www.doscasasviejas.com. 8 units. $195–$295 double. Additional person $20. Rates include breakfast. MC, V. Free parking. **Amenities:** Outdoor pool; concierge; same-day dry cleaning. *In room:* A/C, TV, dataport, fridge, coffeemaker, hair dryer, iron.

El Farolito ⭐⭐   The owners of this inn, which is within walking distance of the plaza, have created an authentic theme experience for guests in each room. The themes include the Native American Room, decorated with rugs and pottery; the South-of-the-Border Room, with Mexican folk art and a full-size sofa sleeper; and the elegant Santa Fe–style Opera Room, with hand-carved, lavishly upholstered furniture. A two-room suite has been added in the main building, with a queen-size iron bed and Southwestern decor. The walls of most of the rooms were rubbed with beeswax during plastering to give them a smooth, golden finish. All rooms (except for the new suite) have kiva fireplaces and private patios. The common area displays works by notable New Mexico artists. Part of the inn was built before 1912, and the rest is new, but the old-world elegance carries through. For breakfast, the focus is on healthy food with a little decadence thrown in. You'll enjoy fresh fruit and homemade breads and pastries. Under the same stellar ownership (but a little less expensive) is the nearby **Four Kachinas Inn** ⭐ (ℂ **888/634-8782** or 505/982-2550; www.fourkachinas. com), where Southwestern-style rooms sit around a sunny courtyard. A little less lavish than those at El Farolito, these rooms are sparkly clean, all with patios.

514 Galisteo St., Santa Fe, NM 87501. ℂ **888/634-8782** or 505/988-1631. Fax 505/988-4589. www. farolito.com. 8 units. $150–$280 casita. Rates include expanded continental breakfast. AE, DISC, MC, V. Free parking. **Amenities:** Babysitting by appointment; valet laundry. *In room:* A/C, TV, coffeemaker, hair dryer, iron.

Grant Corner Inn ⭐⭐   This early-20th-century manor, just 2 blocks west of the plaza and next door to the new Georgia O'Keeffe Museum, offers a quiet stay with a fanciful Victorian ambience. Each room is furnished with antiques, from brass or four-poster beds to armoires and quilts, and terry robes are available for those staying in rooms with shared bathrooms. All rooms have ceiling fans, and some are equipped with small fridges. Each room has its own character. For example, one has a hand-painted German wardrobe closet dating from 1772 and a washbasin with brass fittings in the shape of fish; another has a private outdoor deck that catches the morning sun; another has an antique collection of dolls and stuffed animals. Two rooms have kitchenettes, and two have laundry facilities. The inn's office doubles as a library and gift shop. Grant Corner Inn also offers accommodations in its hacienda, located at 604 Griffin St. It's a Southwestern-style condominium with two bedrooms and a full kitchen. Breakfast, for both the inn and the hacienda, is served in front of the living-room fireplace or on the front veranda in summer. The meals are so good that an enthusiastic public arrives for brunch here every Sunday (the inn is also open to the public for weekday breakfasts). Afternoon tea and snacks are complimentary.

122 Grant Ave., Santa Fe, NM 87501. ℂ **800/964-9003** or 505/983-6678 for reservations, 505/984-9001 for guest rooms. Fax 505/983-1526. www.grantcornerinn.com. 9 units, 1 hacienda. $130–$240 double. Hacienda: $145–$165 if the guest rooms are rented separately; $270–$310 for entire house. Additional person $20. Rates include full gourmet breakfast and afternoon tea. AE, MC, V. Free parking. Some rooms appropriate for children. **Amenities:** Restaurant (breakfast only); Jacuzzi; concierge; tour desk; in-room massage; laundry service. *In room:* A/C, TV, hair dryer, iron.

The Madeleine ⭐⭐   Lace, flowery upholstery, and stained glass surround you at this 1886 Queen Anne–style inn just 5 blocks east of the plaza. All rooms have terry robes, some have fireplaces, and there's a Jacuzzi for all to share. Two units share a bathroom. One of my favorite rooms is the Morning Glory, with a king-size bed, a corner fireplace, and lots of sun. An adjacent cottage built in 1987 received an award for compatible architecture from the Santa Fe Historical Association. The two rooms in the cottage are larger than the other rooms, with king-size beds and bay windows. In winter, a full breakfast (which often includes quiche or waffles) is served family-style in the dining room. In summer, it's served under apricot trees, on a flagstone patio surrounded by flowers. Tea, lemonade, cocoa, homemade cookies, and brownies are available throughout the day.

106 Faithway St., Santa Fe, NM 87501. (C) **888/877-7622** or 505/982-3465. Fax 505/982-8572. www. madeleineinn.com. 8 units (6 with bathroom), 2 cottages. $85–$110 double with shared bathroom; $130–$210 double with private bathroom. Additional person $25. Rates include full breakfast and all-day snacks. AE, DISC, MC, V. Free parking. **Amenities:** Access to nearby health club; Jacuzzi; concierge; business center. *In room:* A/C, TV/VCR, dataport, hair dryer.

Water Street Inn An award-winning adobe restoration 4 blocks from the plaza, this friendly inn features beautiful Mexican-tile bathrooms, several kiva fireplaces or wood stoves, and antique furnishings. Each room is packed with Southwestern art and books. In the afternoon, a happy hour, with quesadillas and margaritas, is offered in the living room or on the upstairs portal, where an extended continental breakfast is also served. All rooms are decorated in a Moroccan/Southwestern style. Room no. 3 provides a queen-size sofa bed to accommodate families. Room no. 4 features special regional touches in its decor and boasts a chaise longue, a fur rug, built-in seating, and a corner fireplace. Four new suites have elegant contemporary Southwestern furnishings and outdoor private patios with fountains. Most rooms have balconies or terraces.

427 Water St., Santa Fe, NM 87501. (C) **800/646-6752** or 505/984-1193. Fax 505/984-6235. www.water streetinn.com. 12 units. $100–$250 double. Rates include continental breakfast and afternoon hors d'oeuvres and refreshments. AE, DISC, MC, V. Free parking. Children and pets welcome with prior approval. **Amenities:** Jacuzzi; concierge; room service. *In room:* A/C, TV/VCR, dataport, hair dryer.

RV PARKS & CAMPGROUNDS
RV PARKS

Several private camping areas, mainly for recreational vehicles, are located within a few minutes' drive of downtown Santa Fe. Be sure to book ahead at busy times.

Los Campos RV Resort This resort has 95 spaces with full hookups, picnic tables, and a covered pavilion for use at no charge (with reservation). It's just 5 miles south of the plaza, so it's convenient, but it is surrounded by the city.

3574 Cerrillos Rd., Santa Fe, NM 87507. (C) **800/852-8160.** Fax 505/471-9220. $28–$33 daily; $169–$206 weekly; $450 monthly/winter; $470 monthly/summer. MC, V. Pets welcome. **Amenities:** Outdoor pool; concierge; coin-op laundry; restrooms; showers; grills; vending machines; free cable TV.

Rancheros de Santa Fe Campground Tents, motor homes, and trailers requiring full hookups are welcome here. The park's 130 sites are situated on 22 acres of piñon and juniper forest. Cabins are also available. It's located about 6 miles southeast of Santa Fe and is open March 15 to October 31.

736 Old Las Vegas Hwy. (exit 290 off I-25), Santa Fe, NM 87505. (C) **800/426-9259** or 505/466-3482. www. rancheros.com. Tent site $17–$19; RV hookup $25–$30. DISC, MC, V. **Amenities:** Outdoor pool; coin-op laundry; restrooms; showers; grills; cable TV hookups; grocery store; recreation room; tables; fireplaces; nature trails; playground; free nightly movies May–Sept; public telephones; propane.

Santa Fe KOA This campground, about 11 miles northeast of Santa Fe, sits among the foothills of the Sangre de Cristo Mountains, an excellent place to enjoy Northern New Mexico's pine-filled high desert. It offers full hookups, pull-through sites, and tent sites.

934 Old Las Vegas Hwy. (exit 290 or 294 off I-25), Santa Fe, NM 87505. (C) **800/KOA-1514** or 505/466-1419 for reservations. www.koa.com. Tent site $22–$25; RV hookup $26–$31. DISC, MC, V. **Amenities:** Coin-op laundry; restrooms; showers; store/gift shop; recreation room; playground; picnic tables; dataport; propane; dumping station.

CAMPGROUNDS

The forested sites along NM 475 on the way to Ski Santa Fe are all open from May to October. Overnight rates start at about $12.

Hyde Memorial State Park   About 8 miles from the city, this pine-surrounded park offers a quiet retreat. Seven RV pads with electrical pedestals and an RV dumping station are available. You can enjoy nature and hiking trails and a playground as well as a small winter skating pond.

740 Hyde Park Rd., Santa Fe, NM 87501. © 505/983-7175. www.nmparks.com. **Amenities:** Shelters; water; tables; vault toilets.

Santa Fe National Forest ☆☆   Black Canyon campground, with 44 sites, is located just before Hyde Memorial State Park. It is one of the only campgrounds in the state for which you can make a reservation; to do so you must go through a national reservation system (© 877/444-6777; www.reserveusa.com). The sites sit within thick forest, with hiking trails nearby. Big Tesuque, a first-come, first-served campground with 10 newly rehabilitated sites, is about 12 miles from town. The sites here are closer to the road and sit at the edge of aspen forests. Both Black Canyon and Big Tesuque campgrounds, located along the Santa Fe Scenic Byway, NM 475, are equipped with vault toilets.

P.O. Box 1689, Santa Fe, NM 87504. © 505/438-7840 or 505/753-7331. www.fs.fed.us/r3/sfe. **Amenities:** Water; vault toilets.

4 Where to Dine

Santa Fe abounds in dining options, with hundreds of restaurants in all categories. Competition among them is steep, and spots are continually opening and closing. Locals watch closely to see which ones will survive. Some chefs create dishes that incorporate traditional Southwestern foods with ingredients not indigenous to the region; their restaurants are referred to in the listings as "creative Southwestern." There is also standard regional New Mexican cuisine, and beyond that, diners can opt for excellent steak and seafood, as well as Continental, European, Asian, and, of course, Mexican menus. On the south end of town, Santa Fe has the requisite chain establishments such as **Outback Steakhouse,** 2574 Camino Entrada (© **505/424-6800**), **Olive Garden,** 3781 Cerrillos Rd. (© **505/438-7109**), and **Red Lobster,** 4450 Rodeo Rd. (© **505/473-1610**).

Especially during peak tourist seasons, dinner reservations may be essential. Reservations are always recommended at better restaurants.

DOWNTOWN

This area includes the circle defined by the Paseo de Peralta and St. Francis Drive, as well as Canyon Road.

EXPENSIVE

Cafe Pasqual's ☆☆ CREATIVE SOUTHWESTERN   "You have to become the food, erase the line between it as an object and you. You have to really examine its structure, its size, its color, its strength, its weakness, know who grew it, how long it's been out of the field," says Pasqual's owner Katharine Kagel. That attitude is completely apparent in this restaurant, where the walls are lined with murals depicting voluptuous villagers playing guitars, drinking, and even flying. Needless to say, it's a festive place, though it's also excellent for a romantic dinner. Service is jovial and professional. My favorite dish for breakfast or lunch is the *huevos motuleños* (two eggs over easy on blue-corn tortillas and black beans

topped with sautéed bananas, feta cheese, salsa, and green chile). Soups and salads are also served for lunch, and there's a delectable grilled-salmon burrito with
herbed goat cheese and cucumber salsa. The frequently changing dinner menu
offers grilled meats and seafood, plus vegetarian specials. Start with the Iroquois
corn tamale with roasted poblano, zucchini, and asadero cheese, and move on to
the spinach, jack cheese, and red onion enchiladas. There's a communal table for
those who would like to meet new people over a meal. Pasqual's offers imported
beers and wine by the bottle or glass. Try to go at an odd hour—late morning or
afternoon—or make a reservation for dinner; otherwise, you'll have to wait.

121 Don Gaspar Ave. ✆ 505/983-9340. Reservations recommended for dinner. Main courses $5.75–$13
breakfast, $6–$15 lunch, $16–$34 dinner. AE, MC, V. Mon–Sat 7am–3pm; Sun–Thurs 5:30–9:30pm; Fri–Sat
6–10pm; summer daily 6–10:30pm. Brunch Sun 8am–2pm.

The Compound ✿✿✿ NEW AMERICAN This reincarnation of one of
Santa Fe's classic restaurants serves some of the most flavorful and daring food
in town. During warm months, a broad patio shelters diners from the city bustle. With friendly, efficient service, this is an excellent place for a romantic dinner or a relaxing lunch. Chef/owner Mark Kiffin, after nearly 8 years as chef at
Coyote Café (see below), lets his creativity soar. You might start off with tuna
tartare topped with Osetra caviar. For an entree, a signature dish is the grilled
beef tenderloin with Italian potatoes and foie gras hollandaise. For lunch, monkfish chorizo with watercress is outrageously tasty. Finish with a bittersweet
chocolate torte. A carefully selected beer and wine list accompanies the menu.

653 Canyon Rd. ✆ 505/982-4353. Reservations recommended. Main courses $12–$20 lunch, $20–$31 dinner. AE, MC, V. Mon–Fri noon–2pm; daily 6–9pm; bar opens nightly at 5pm.

Coyote Café ✿✿ CREATIVE SOUTHWESTERN/LATIN World-
renowned chef and cookbook author Mark Miller has been "charged with single-handedly elevating the chile to haute status." That statement from the *New
York Times Magazine* sums up for me the experience of eating at this trendy nouveau Southwestern restaurant about a block from the plaza. The atmosphere is
urban Southwestern, with calfskin-covered chairs and a zoo of carved animals
watching from a balcony. The exhibition kitchen has lots of brass and tile, and
the waitstaff is efficient and friendly. It's the place to go for a fun night out, or
you can sample the great food for lunch at a fraction of the price. Some complain that on a busy night the space is noisy.

The menu changes seasonally, so the specific dishes I mention may not be
available. Start your meal with Coyote cocktails that might include a Brazilian
daiquiri or margarita del Maguey. Then look for delights such as chipotle tiger
prawns with griddled corn cakes or a duck tamale for appetizers. Move on to a
braised ancho lamb shank or horseradish-crusted Maine haddock. You can order
drinks from the full bar or wine by the glass. Smoking is not allowed.

Coyote Café has two adjunct establishments. In summer, the place to be seen
is the **Rooftop Cantina,** where light Latino/Cuban fare and cocktails are served
on a festively painted terrace. (Try the chicken skewers on sugarcane.) On the
ground floor is a new addition called **Cottonwoods,** offering a reasonably priced
menu in a new Southwestern diner ambience.

132 Water St. ✆ 505/983-1615. Reservations highly recommended. Main courses $6–$16 (Rooftop Cantina), $19–$36 (Coyote Café), $6–$15 (Cottonwoods). AE, DC, DISC, MC, V. Rooftop Cantina: daily
11:30am–9pm. Dining room: daily 6–9:30pm; daily 5:30–9pm during opera season.

El Farol ✿ SPANISH This is the place to head for local ambience and old-
fashioned flavor. El Farol (The Lantern) is the Canyon Road artists' quarter's

Where to Dine in Downtown Santa Fe

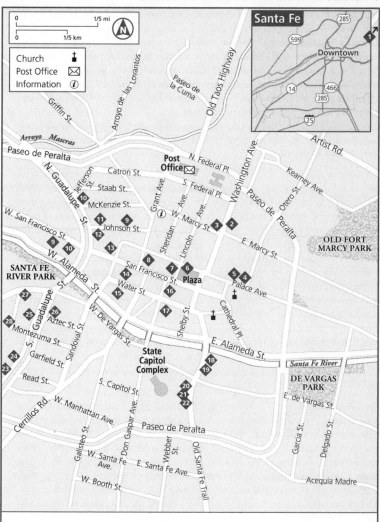

Blue Corn Café **14**
Bumble Bees Baja Grill **10**
Cafe Dominic **25**
Cafe Pasqual's **16**
Cafe San Estevan **27**
Cowgirl Hall of Fame **26**
Coyote Café **15**
El Nido **1**
Guadalupe Café **22**
Il Piatto Cucina Italiano **3**

India Palace **17**
La Casa Sena **4**
O'Keeffe Café **9**
The Old House **13**
Ore House on the Plaza **7**
The Palace **8**
The Pink Adobe **20**
Plaza Cafe **6**
Pranzo Italian Grill **28**
Rio Chama Steakhouse **21**

Rociada **12**
Santacafé **2**
Santa Fe Railyard
  Restaurant and Bar **23**
The Shed **5**
Shohko Cafe **11**
Tesuque Village Market **1**
Tomasita's Cafe **24**
315 **18**
Upper Crust Pizza **19**

original neighborhood bar. The restaurant has cozy low ceilings and hand-smoothed adobe walls. Thirty-five varieties of tapas are offered, including such delicacies as *gambas al ajillo* (shrimp with chile, garlic, Madeira, and lime) and *conejo y vino* (stewed rabbit). You can make a meal out of two or three tapas shared with your friends or order a full dinner, such as the paella or the grilled lamb chops with cranberry salsa. There is live entertainment 7 nights a week—including jazz/swing, folk, and Latin guitar music—starting at 9:30pm. In summer, two outdoor patios are open to diners.

808 Canyon Rd. ⓒ **505/983-9912.** Reservations recommended. Tapas $4.50–$12; main courses $8–$15 lunch, $26–$32 dinner. DC, DISC, MC, V. Daily 11:30am–3pm and 5:30–10pm (bar is open until 1am weekdays, 2am Friday and Saturday).

Geronimo ⭐⭐⭐ CONTINENTAL   This elegant restaurant offers one of Santa Fe's most delectable dining experiences. It occupies an old adobe structure known as the Borrego House, built by Geronimo Lopez in 1756 and now completely restored, but it still retains the feel of an old Santa Fe home. I especially recommend lunch here, when you can get a taste of this complex food for a fraction of the dinner price. Reserve a spot on the porch and watch the action on Canyon Road. My favorite at lunch is the house-smoked ruby trout salad, with crimson beluga lentils, organic grains, and a sweet sesame dressing. For a dinner appetizer, try the Maryland blue crab strudel and lime-toasted pepita and red onion salad. For an entree, the mesquite-grilled elk tenderloin with chestnut strudel is great, as is grilled Maine lobster with farmer's corn and leek compote. For dessert, you won't be disappointed by the trio of brûlées—espresso chocolate, Chambord, and orange—or the Belgian chocolate Grand Marnier cake. The menu changes seasonally, and there is an excellent wine list.

724 Canyon Rd. ⓒ **505/982-1500.** Reservations recommended. Main courses $10–$19 lunch, $20–$36 dinner. AE, MC, V. Tues–Sun 11:30am–2pm; daily 6–9:30pm.

La Casa Sena ⭐⭐ CREATIVE SOUTHWESTERN   Combining alluring ambience and tasty food, this is one of Santa Fe's favorite restaurants, though the food here isn't as precise and flavorful as at Santacafé or The Old House. It sits within the Sena compound, a prime example of a Spanish hacienda, in a Territorial-style adobe house built in 1867 by Civil War hero Major José Sena. The house, which surrounds a garden courtyard, is today a veritable art gallery, with museum-quality landscapes on the walls and Taos-style handcrafted furniture. The cuisine in the main dining room might be described as northern New Mexican with a continental flair. One of my favorite lunches is the flash-fried Baja sea bass fish tacos with mango salsa. In the evening, diners might start with a salad of garden greens and grilled mushrooms, and then move to a grilled lamb rack marinated with Dijon mustard and mint and accompanied by roasted root vegetables and green peppercorn sauce.

In the adjacent **La Cantina,** waiters and waitresses sing Broadway show tunes as they carry platters to the tables. The more moderately priced La Cantina menu offers the likes of cornmeal-breaded trout and grilled stuffed pork loin with peach-onion sauce. Both restaurants have exquisite desserts; try the black-and-white bittersweet chocolate terrine with raspberry sauce. The award-winning wine list features more than 850 selections. There's patio dining in summer.

125 E. Palace Ave. ⓒ **505/988-9232.** Reservations recommended. La Casa Sena main courses $8–$12 lunch, $21–$30 dinner; 5-course chef's tasting menu $42, with wine $58; La Cantina main courses $13–$23. AE, DC, DISC, MC, V. Mon–Sat 11:30am–3pm; Sunday brunch 11am–3pm; daily 5:30–10pm.

O'Keeffe Café ⚡ NEW AMERICAN   Following Georgia O'Keeffe's appreciation for sparse interiors, this restaurant has refined minimalist decor. It's a place of clean lines and innovative color use. Large black-and-white photographs of O'Keeffe stirring stew and serving tea adorn the walls. This is a good place to stop in between museums or, in the warm months, to sit on the open patio and watch the summer scene pass by. The food is excellent, but for a nice dinner (in winter), the atmosphere lags behind that of places in a similar price range, such as Santacafé and Geronimo. The menu is eclectic, with a good balance of chicken, lamb, fish, and vegetarian dishes, some in fancy salad and sandwich form (at lunch), along with more elaborate entree offerings. Most recently, I had crab cakes with chipotle aioli, and my friend tried smoked duck breast with dried grape risotto and almond cream—very rich. There's also a children's menu. The restaurant has a notable wine list and offers periodic wine tasting menus.

217 Johnson St. ✆ **505/946-1065.** Reservations recommended. Lunch $4–$21, dinner $6.50–$35. AE, MC, V. Mon–Sat 11am–3pm and 5:30–9:30pm (wine bar 3–5:30pm); Sunday brunch 11am–3pm.

The Old House ⚡⚡⚡ NEW AMERICAN/CONTINENTAL   This restaurant consistently rates as Santa Fe's best eatery in local publication's polls—and it's no wonder, with chef Martin Rios running the show. A native of Mexico, he worked his way up through some of Santa Fe's finest kitchens before embarking on a course at the Culinary Institute of America and returning to the City Different to turn The Old House into a nationally acclaimed restaurant, with a story running on PBS and a cover article in *Bon Appétit*. In a Southwestern atmosphere, rich with excellent Native American art, Rios serves quality meats, poultry, and seafood in refined sauces. The menu changes seasonally, with some signature dishes that remain year-round. Start with the lump crab cake, with grilled portobello and butternut squash salad. Move on to my favorite, the mustard-and-pepper–crusted lamb rack, with roasted shallot potato mash and red chile-Merlot lamb jus; or the sautéed Diver sea scallops with wild mushrooms, asparagus, and pumpkin seeds in a Xeres sherry reduction. My friend Michael says the crème brûlée here is the best dessert he's ever had, but my favorite is the warm-liquid-center chocolate cake. The wine list is a *Wine Spectator* award-winner.

In the Eldorado Hotel, 309 W. San Francisco St. ✆ **505/988-4455,** ext. 130. Reservations recommended. Main courses $23–$30. AE, DC, DISC, MC, V. Daily 5:30–10pm. Lounge 4:30–10pm.

Ore House on the Plaza ⚡ STEAK/SEAFOOD/NEW MEXICAN   The Ore House's second-story balcony, at the southwest corner of the plaza, is an ideal spot from which to watch the passing scene while you enjoy cocktails and hors d'oeuvres. In fact, it is *the* place to be between 4 and 6pm every afternoon. Inside, the decor is Southwestern, with plants and lanterns hanging amid white walls and booths. The menu offers fresh seafood and steaks, as well as some Nueva Latina dishes that incorporate interesting sauces. Daily fresh fish specials include salmon and swordfish (poached, blackened, teriyaki, or lemon), rainbow trout, lobster, and shellfish. The salmon with spinach pecan pesto has become a new favorite, and you can't go wrong with the Steak Ore House (wrapped in bacon and topped with crabmeat and béarnaise sauce). The Ore House offers vegetable platters for noncarnivores.

The bar, offering live music nightly Thursday to Sunday, serves more than 65 different margaritas. It offers a selection of domestic and imported beers and an excellent wine list. An appetizer menu is served from 2:30 to 10pm daily.

50 Lincoln Ave. ✆ **505/983-8687.** Reservations recommended. Main courses $5–$13 lunch, $16–$28 dinner. AE, MC, V. Daily 11:30am–10pm (bar until midnight or later).

The Palace ✿✿ ITALIAN/CONTINENTAL   On the site of this locals' spot, Santa Fe's 19th-century matriarch, Doña Tules, operated a thriving gambling hall and bordello. From the place's remains came a brass door knocker, half shaped like a horseshoe, and the other half like a saloon girl's stockinged leg, now the restaurant's logo. Hearkening back to those old days, The Palace serves flavorful food in a Victorian ambience, with a bit of bordello flair. Under new ownership in 2004, the restaurant, to locals' relief, still has a plush and comfortable feel, but with a new elegance. The food is well prepared and imaginative, though more conservative than that at The Compound and Geronimo. The Caesar salad—prepared tableside—is always good, as are the meat dishes, such as herb-crusted rack of lamb with mint couscous. A favorite fish dish at lunch is the Alaskan salmon scaloppini served with ratatouille. The pasta dishes are also tasty, as are the vegetarian ones and daily specials. The wine list is long and well considered. A lovely patio and a lively bar are locals' favorites. The bar has nightly entertainment including dancing on Saturday after 9pm, and it has its own menu from 3pm to midnight.

142 W. Palace Ave. ✆ 505/982-9891. Reservations recommended. Lunch $7–$16, dinner $16–$34. AE, DC, DISC, MC, V. Mon–Sat 11:30am–3pm; daily 5:30–10pm. Bar: Mon–Sat 11:30am–2am; Sun 5:30pm–midnight.

The Pink Adobe ✿ CONTINENTAL/SOUTHWESTERN   More show than flavor? Probably. This restaurant, located a few blocks off the plaza, offers a swirl of local old-timer gaiety and food that is more imaginative than flavorful, but The Pink Adobe has remained popular since it opened in 1944. The restaurant occupies an adobe home believed to be at least 350 years old. Guests enter through a narrow side door into a series of quaint, informal dining rooms with tile or hardwood floors. Stuccoed walls display original modern art and Priscilla Hoback pottery on built-in shelves. For lunch, I always have a chicken enchilada topped with an egg. The gypsy stew (chicken, green chile, tomatoes, and onions in sherry broth) sounds great but is on the bland side. At the dinner hour, The Pink Adobe offers the likes of escargot and shrimp rémoulade as appetizers. The local word here is that the steak Dunigan, with sautéed mushrooms and green chile, is "the thing" to order. You can't leave without trying the hot French apple pie.

Smoking is allowed only in The Dragon Room (p. 179), the lounge across the alleyway from the restaurant. Under the same ownership, the charming bar (a real local scene) has its own menu, offering traditional New Mexican food. Locals come to eat hearty green chile stew.

406 Old Santa Fe Trail. ✆ 505/983-7712. Reservations recommended. Main courses $4.75–$8.70 lunch, $14–$26 dinner. AE, DC, DISC, MC, V. Mon–Fri 11:30am–2pm; daily 5:30pm–closing. Bar: Mon–Fri 11:30am–2am; Sat 5pm–2am; Sun 5pm–midnight.

Rio Chama Steakhouse ✿✿ STEAK/SEAFOOD   Serving up tasty steaks in a refined ranch atmosphere, this is one of Santa Fe's best newer restaurants. It's a good spot for a business lunch or a fun-filled evening, and the patio is a bright spot during warm months. Service is efficient, and there's a full bar. My favorite for lunch is the buffalo patty, much more flavorful than beef. Lunch also brings a good selection of salads and sandwiches, as well as steaks at a reasonable price. Evenings, the prime rib is a big seller, as is the nightly seafood special. For dessert, try the chocolate cake.

414 Old Santa Fe Trail. ✆ 505/955-0765. Reservations recommended on weekend nights. Main courses $8–$22 lunch, $15–$35 dinner. AE, DC, DISC, MC, V. Daily 11am–3pm and 5–10pm; patio bar 5pm–closing.

Rociada ✫✫✫ FRENCH   Rated by *Condé Nast Traveler* as one of the world's 60 best new restaurants in 2000, Rociada continues to offer a country French dining experience with sophisticated flavors. In a classic 1883 Territorial-style building within walking distance of the plaza, the place has Nouveau-Deco decor, with clean lines, comfortable banquettes, and 1950s Thonet chairs. The menu changes seasonally. Start with a baby spinach salad with egg, crispy bacon, and red wine mustard vinaigrette; move on to the steak frites, chargrilled and served with french fries; or try the Halibut meunière (seared with lemon butter sauce), with zucchini, capers, and a lemon confit. For dessert, try the floral trio of crème brûlées: lavender, rose, and honey. Choose from the most comprehensive French wine list in New Mexico, with 350 selections. Beer is also available.

304 Johnson St. ✆ **505/983-3800.** Reservations recommended. Main courses $15–$28. AE, MC, V. Mon–Sat 5:30–10pm.

Santacafé ✫✫✫ *Moments* NEW AMERICAN/CREATIVE SOUTHWEST-ERN   When you eat at this fine restaurant, be prepared for spectacular bursts of flavor. The food combines the best of many cuisines, from Asian to Southwestern, served in an elegant setting with minimalist decor that accentuates the graceful architecture of the 18th-century Padre Gallegos House, 2 blocks from the plaza. The white walls are decorated only with deer antlers, and each room contains a fireplace. In warm months you can sit under elm trees in the charming courtyard. Be aware that on busy nights the rooms are noisy. The dishes change to take advantage of seasonal specialties, each served with precision. For a starter, try the shiitake and cactus spring rolls with Southwestern ponzu. One of my favorite main courses is the Alaskan halibut with English peas and saffron couscous. A heartier eater might try the bacon-wrapped black angus filet mignon with roasted garlic mashed potatoes. There's an extensive wine list, with wine by the glass as well. Desserts, as elegant as the rest of the food, are made in-house; try the warm chocolate upside-down cake with vanilla ice cream. Sunday brunch is served in summer and on Easter and Mother's Day.

231 Washington Ave. ✆ **505/984-1788.** Reservations recommended. Main courses $9–$15 lunch, $19–$40 dinner. AE, MC, V. Mon–Sat 11:30am–2pm; daily 6–10pm.

315 ✫✫ FRENCH   This classy French bistro enjoyed instant success when it opened in 1995 because the food is simply excellent. The elegant atmosphere provides a perfect setting for a romantic meal, and during warm months the patio is a popular place to people-watch. The menu changes seasonally; on my last visit, I started with a smooth and flavorful lobster bisque and moved on to lamb chops served with a tart mustard sauce and mashed potatoes. My favorite dessert here is the flourless chocolate cake: not too sweet, and luscious. Because 315 is so popular, reservations are an absolute must.

315 Old Santa Fe Trail. ✆ **505/986-9190.** www.315santafe.com. Reservations highly recommended. Main courses $9–$15 lunch, $20–$29 dinner. AE, DISC, MC, V. Summer Mon–Sat 11:30am–2pm, Sun–Thurs 5:30–9:00pm, Fri–Sat 5:30–9:30pm; winter daily 11:30am–2pm and 5:30–9pm.

MODERATE

Cafe San Estevan ✫ NEW MEXICAN/NATIVE AMERICAN WITH FRENCH ACCENTS   A Franciscan monk with a passion for saints, Estevan Garcia says he grew to love his art while cooking for friars and was inspired by angels to further his cooking skills. Thus was born this interesting twist on local cuisine. Though you can order an enchilada as you can at so many Santa Fe restaurants, here you'll find a little closer attention to sauce flavors and some innovation in food combinations. For instance, Garcia has on the menu one of my favorites, a veggie enchilada, which has *calabacitas* (squash cooked with corn and chile) inside. He also serves a rib-eye steak with potatoes, *calabacitas,* and *chile caribe* (red chile). If your party has varying needs, his menu can accommodate, with dishes such as *burguesa* (hamburger) or salmon served with *calabacitas* and *salsa tropical* (a salsa made with mango, jalapeno, and cilantro). The service is friendly and efficient, and the decor is casual Southwestern, a sort of hacienda feel, with vigas on the ceiling and woven tapestries on the walls. Best of all is the streetside dining, for which, during the warmer months, you might have to make a reservation. Wine (from an extensive list) and beer are served.

428 Agua Fria St. ✆ 505/995-1996. Reservations recommended for dinner. Main courses $6–$10 lunch, $10–$20 dinner. AE, MC, V. Tues–Fri 11am–2pm; Sat–Sun 10am–2pm; daily 5:30–9pm.

Cowgirl Hall of Fame REGIONAL AMERICAN/BARBECUE/CAJUN This raucous bar/restaurant serves decent food in a festive atmosphere. The main room is a bar—a hip hangout spot, and a good place to eat as well, if you don't mind the smoke. The back room is quieter, with wood floors and tables and plenty of cowgirl memorabilia. Best of all is sitting out on a brick patio lit with strings of white lights during the warm season. The service is at times brusque, and the food varies. In winter, my favorite is a big bowl of gumbo or crawfish étouffée, and the rest of the time I order Jamaican jerk chicken or pork tenderloin when it's a special. Careful—both can be hot. The daily blue-plate special is a real buy. There's even a special "kid's corral" that has horseshoes, a rocking horse, a horse-shaped rubber tire swing, hay bales, and a beanbag toss. Happy hour is from 3 to 6pm. There is live music almost every night.

319 S. Guadalupe St. ✆ 505/982-2565. Reservations recommended. Main courses $5–$10 lunch, $6–$22 dinner. AE, DISC, MC, V. Mon–Fri 11am–midnight; Sat 8:30am–midnight; Sun 8am–11pm. Bar: Mon–Sat until 2am; Sun until midnight.

Il Piatto Cucina Italiano ★★ (Value) NORTHERN ITALIAN This simple Italian cafe brings innovative flavors to thinner wallets. It's simple and elegant, with contemporary art on the walls—nice for a romantic evening. Service is efficient, though on a busy night, overworked. The menu changes seasonally but is complemented by a few perennial standards. For a starter, try the grilled calamari with shaved fennel and aioli. My favorite entree is the pancetta-wrapped trout with grilled polenta and wild mushrooms, though you can't go wrong with the jumbo scampi risotto with sweet peppers. The Gorgonzola-walnut ravioli is a favorite of many, though not quite enough food to fill me up. Wine and beer are served.

(Kids **Family-Friendly Restaurants**

Blue Corn Café (p. 146) A relaxed atmosphere and their own menu please kids, while excellent brewpub beer pleases parents.

Bumble Bee's Baja Grill (p. 146) A casual atmosphere allows parents to relax while their kids chow down on quesadillas and burritos.

Tortilla Flats (p. 149) Portions are gigantic, and the atmosphere is quite friendly at this southside restaurant.

Upper Crust Pizza (p. 148) Many people feel it has the best pizza in town, and it'll deliver it to tired tots and their families at downtown hotels.

95 West Marcy St. ⓒ **505/984-1091.** Reservations recommended. Main courses $10–$14. AE, DISC, MC, V. Mon–Fri 11:30am–2pm; daily 5:30–9pm. Closed New Year's Day, July 4, and Christmas.

India Palace ★ (Value INDIAN   Once every few weeks, I get a craving for the lamb vindaloo served at this restaurant in the center of downtown. A festive ambience, with pink walls painted with mosque shadows, makes this a nice place for a romantic meal. The service is efficient, and most of the waiters are from India, as is chef Amarjit Behal. The tandoori chicken, fish, lamb, and shrimp are rich and flavorful, as is the *baingan bhartha* (eggplant in a rich sauce). A lunch buffet provides an excellent selection of vegetarian and nonvegetarian dishes at a reasonable price. Beer and wine are available, or you might want some chai tea.

227 Don Gaspar Ave. (inside the Water St. parking compound). ⓒ **505/986-5859.** Reservations recommended. Main courses $9–$15; lunch buffet $9. AE, DC, DISC, MC, V. Daily 11:30am–2:30pm and 5–10pm. Closed Super Bowl Sunday.

Pranzo Italian Grill ★★ REGIONAL ITALIAN   Housed in a renovated warehouse and decorated in warm Tuscan colors, this sister of Albuquerque's Scalo restaurant has a contemporary atmosphere of modern abstract art and serves food prepared on an open grill. Homemade soups, salads, and creative thin-crust pizzas are among the less expensive menu items. *Bianchi e nere al capesante* (black-and-white linguine with bay scallops in seafood cream sauce) and *pizza ala pesto e gamberoni* (pizza with shrimp, pesto, goat cheese, and roasted peppers) are consistent favorites. Steak, chicken, veal, and fresh seafood grills—heavy on the garlic—dominate the dinner menu. The bar has the Southwest's largest collection of grappas, as well as a wide selection of wines and champagnes by the glass. The rooftop terrace is lovely for seasonal moon-watching over a glass of wine.

540 Montezuma St. (Sanbusco Center). ⓒ **505/984-2645.** Reservations recommended. Main courses $6–$10 lunch, $6–$24 dinner. AE, DC, DISC, MC, V. Mon–Sat 11:30am–3pm and 5pm–midnight; Sun 5–10pm.

Santa Fe Railyard Restaurant & Bar ★ (Finds NEW AMERICAN   Santa Fe locals' most talked-about new spot, the Railyard, is a fun and thoughtful addition to the restaurant scene. Set in one of the city's old railroad buildings, it offers a comfortable ambience and imaginative food at reasonable prices. The space has clean lines, with stained concrete floors and exposed ductwork, softened with maroon booths and wooden tables. Service is friendly and knowledgeable. If you like Cajun food, start with the Chesapeake crab cakes with shrimp bisque and jicama slaw. Move on to a fish special such as grilled swordfish with caper butter sauce, pasta, and a salad; or if you're really hungry, try the pork tenderloin sandwich, served with a mild "mojo" sauce that's a bit sweet and quite delectable. At dinner, a favorite is the all-day-roasted lamb shank, served with roasted garlic mashed potatoes. Desserts are made in-house, as is the ice cream, worth sampling. Select from a carefully considered wine list or from the full bar.

530 S. Guadalupe (¼ block north of Paseo de Peralta). ⓒ **505/989-8363.** Reservations recommended on weekend nights. Main courses $7.50–$10 lunch, $18–$22 dinner. Summer daily 11am–2:30pm and 5–9pm; winter Mon–Sat 11am–2:30pm, Thurs–Sat 5–9pm.

Shohko Cafe ★ JAPANESE/SUSHI   Santa Fe's favorite sushi restaurant serves fresh fish in a 150-year-old adobe building that was once a bordello. The atmosphere is sparse and comfortable, a blending of New Mexican decor with traditional Japanese decorative touches. Up to 30 fresh varieties of raw seafood, including sushi and sashimi, are served at plain pine tables in various rooms or at the sushi bar. Request the sushi bar, where the atmosphere is coziest, and you can watch the chefs at work. My mother likes the tempura combination with veggies, shrimp, and scallops. On an odd night, I'll order the salmon teriyaki, but most nights I have sushi, particularly the *anago* and spicy tuna roll—though if you're daring, you might try the Santa Fe roll (with green chile, shrimp tempura, and *masago*). Wine, imported beers, and hot sake are available.

321 Johnson St. ℂ **505/983-7288.** Reservations recommended. Main courses $4.25–$17 lunch, $8.50–$25 dinner. AE, DISC, MC, V. Mon–Fri 11:30am–2pm; Sun–Thurs 5:30–9pm; Fri–Sat 5:30–9:30pm.

INEXPENSIVE

Blue Corn Café (Kids) NEW MEXICAN/MICROBREWERY   If you're ready for a fun and inexpensive night out, eating decent New Mexican food, this is your place. Within a clean and breezy decor, you'll find a raucous and buoyant atmosphere, a good place to bring kids. The overworked waitstaff may be slow, but they're friendly. I recommend sampling dishes from the combination menu. You can get two to five items served with your choice of rice, beans, or one of the best *posoles* (hominy and chile) that I've tasted. I had the chicken enchilada, which I recommend, and the chalupa, which I don't because it was soggy. You can have tacos, tamales, and rellenos, too. Kids have their own menu and crayons to keep them occupied. There are nightly specials—the shrimp fajitas are tasty, served with nice guacamole and the usual toppings. Since this is also a brewery, you might want to sample the High Altitude Pale Ale or the Plaza Porter. My beverage choice is the prickly pear iced tea (black tea with enough cactus juice to give it a zing). The Spanish flan is tasty and large enough to share. **The Blue Corn Cafe & Brewery** (4056 Cerrillos Rd., Suite G; ℂ **505/438-1800**), on the south side at the corner of Cerrillos and Rodeo roads, has similar fare and atmosphere.

133 W. Water St. ℂ **505/984-1800.** Main courses $7–$18. AE, DC, DISC, MC, V. Daily 11am–10pm.

Bumble Bee's Baja Grill (Finds) (Kids) MEXICAN   This new "beestro" offers a refreshing twist on fast food. It's actually healthy! The secret? Tacos are made Mexican style, with a tortilla folded around quality meat, fish, and poultry grilled with veggies. You pick from an array of salsas. You can also sample from a selection of salads, including one with grilled chicken and avocado. Rotisserie chicken and burritos round out the main menu, and kids have their own options, such as quesadillas. Diners order at a counter, and a waiter brings the food. During warm months, I try to nab a patio table. Evenings often offer live jazz, when folks sit back and sip beer and wine. There's also a drive-through window.

301 Jefferson (from W. San Francisco St., take Guadalupe 2 blocks north). ℂ **505/820-2862.** Main courses $5–$11. AE, MC, V. Mon–Sat 11am–9pm.

Cafe Dominic AMERICAN/DELI   This cafe offers sophisticated flavors with casual ease in a comfortable urban environment. Diners order at a counter, and a waiter brings the food. The restaurant serves a variety of breakfasts as well as soups, salads, sandwiches, New Mexican food, grilled fish and meat, and pasta. My favorite is the cobb salad, which comes with crisp bacon, grilled chicken, Gorgonzola cheese, avocado, and egg wedges. For a real bargain, try the grilled salmon, served with beans, rice, salad, and grilled foccacia ($13). For dessert, you can feast on caramel turtle cheesecake or four-layer chocolate cake.

320 S. Guadalupe. ℂ **505/982-4743.** Main courses $5–$13. AE, MC, V. Mon 7:30am–3pm; Tues–Thurs 7:30am–8:30pm; Fri 7:30am–9pm; Sat 8am–9pm; Sun 8am–5pm.

Guadalupe Cafe NEW MEXICAN   When I want New Mexican food, I go to this restaurant, and like many Santa Feans, I go there often. This casually elegant cafe is in a white stucco building that's warm and friendly and has a nice-size patio for dining in warmer months. Service is generally friendly and conscientious. For breakfast, try the spinach-mushroom burritos or huevos rancheros, and for lunch, the chalupas or stuffed *sopaipillas*. At dinner, I'd start with fresh roasted ancho chiles (filled with a combination of Montrachet and Monterey Jack cheeses and piñon nuts, and topped with your choice of chile) and move on to the sour-cream chicken enchilada or any of the other South-western dishes. Order both red and green chile ("Christmas") so that you can sample some of the best sauces in town. Beware, though: The chile here can be hot, and the chef won't put it on the side. Diners can order from a selection of delicious salads. There are also traditional favorites, such as chicken-fried steak and turkey piñon meatloaf. Daily specials are available, and don't miss the chocolate-amaretto adobe pie for dessert. Beer, wine, and margaritas are served.

422 Old Santa Fe Trail. (*) **505/982-9762.** Breakfast $4.50–$8.75, lunch $6–$12, dinner $7–$15. DISC, MC, V. Tues–Fri 7am–2pm; Sat–Sun 8am–2pm; Tues–Sat 5:30–9pm.

Plaza Cafe 🎯 AMERICAN/DELI/NEW MEXICAN/GREEK   This cafe has excellent food in a bright and friendly atmosphere right on the plaza. I like to meet friends here, sit in a booth, eat, and laugh about life. A restaurant since the turn of the 20th century, it's been owned by the Razatos family since 1947. The decor has changed only enough to stay comfortable and clean, with red uphol-stered banquettes, Art Deco tile, and a soda-fountain–style service counter. Service is always quick and conscientious, and only during the heavy tourist seasons will you have to wait long for a table. Breakfasts are excellent and large, and the ham-burgers and sandwiches are good. I also like the soups and New Mexican dishes, such as the bowl of green-chile stew, or, if you're more adventurous, the pump-kin *posole.* Check out the Greek dishes, such as vegetable moussaka or beef and lamb gyros. Wash it down with an Italian soda, in flavors from vanilla to Amaretto. Alternatively, you can have a shake, a piece of coconut cream pie, or Plaza Cafe's signature dessert, *cajeta* (apple and pecan pie with Mexican caramel). Beer and wine are available.

54 Lincoln Ave. (on the plaza). (*) **505/982-1664.** No reservations. Main courses $8–$15. AE, DISC, MC, V. Daily 7am–9pm.

The Shed 🎯🎯 NEW MEXICAN   This longtime locals' favorite is so popular that during lunch, lines often form outside. Half a block east of the plaza, a lunch-eon institution since 1953, it occupies several rooms and the patio of a rambling hacienda built in 1692. Festive folk art adorns the doorways and walls. The food is delicious, some of the best in the state, and a compliment to traditional Hispanic and Pueblo cooking. The cheese enchilada is renowned in Santa Fe. Tacos and bur-ritos are good, too, all served on blue-corn tortillas, with pinto beans on the side. The green chile soup is a local favorite. The Shed's Joshua Carswell has added veg-etarian and low-fat Mexican foods to the menu, as well as a variety of soups and salads and grilled chicken and steak. The mocha cake is possibly the best dessert you'll ever eat. In addition to wine and beer, there is full bar service.

113½ E. Palace Ave. (*) **505/982-9030.** Reservations recommended, but accepted only at dinner. Lunch $5.75–$9.50, dinner $8–$17. AE, DC, DISC, MC, V. Mon–Sat 11am–2:30pm and 5:30–9pm.

Tomasita's Cafe 🎯 NEW MEXICAN   When I was in high school, I used to eat at Tomasita's, a little dive on a back street. I always ordered a burrito, and I think people used to bring liquor in bags. It's now in a modern building near the train station, and its food has become renowned. The atmosphere is simple— hanging plants and wood accents—with lots of families sitting at booths or tables and a festive spillover from the bar, where many come to drink margaritas. Service is quick, even a little rushed, which is my biggest gripe about Tomasita's. The food is still tasty, but unless you go at some odd hour, you'll wait for a table, and once you're seated, you may eat and be out again in less than an hour. The burritos are still excellent, though you may want to try the chile rellenos, a house specialty. Vegetarian dishes, burgers, steaks, and daily specials are also offered.

500 S. Guadalupe St. ✆ **505/983-5721.** Reservations not accepted, but large parties should call ahead. Lunch $5.25–$12, dinner $5.75–$13. DISC, MC, V. Mon–Sat 11am–10pm.

Upper Crust Pizza ✪ (Kids) PIZZA/ITALIAN Upper Crust serves Santa Fe's best pizzas, in an adobe house near the old San Miguel Mission. Meals-in-a-dish include the Grecian gourmet pizza (feta and olives) and the whole-wheat vegetarian pizza (topped with sesame seeds). You can either eat here or request free delivery (it takes about 30 min.) to your downtown hotel. Beer and wine are available, as are salads, calzones, sandwiches, and stromboli.

329 Old Santa Fe Trail. ✆ **505/982-0000.** Pizzas $7.25–$16. DISC, MC, V. Summer daily 11am–midnight; winter Sun–Thurs 11am–10pm, Fri–Sat 11am–11pm.

NORTHSIDE
EXPENSIVE
El Nido ✪ STEAK/SEAFOOD This is my favorite place to eat when I'm with my friend Carla. Her family is old Santa Fe, as is this restaurant. In the warm atmosphere, decorated with birdcages and smooth adobe partitions and *bancos,* we always encounter interesting characters, and since Carla eats here weekly, she knows what to order. In fact, during our last visit, she pointed to a corner of the front room (where two fires blaze in winter) and jokingly said she was born there. In the 1950s and 1960s, her parents used to party and dance at El Nido into the wee hours of the morning. Indeed, El Nido (the Nest) has been a landmark for many years. Built as a residence in the 1920s, it was a dance hall and Ma Nelson's brothel before it became a restaurant in 1939.

The food here is fresh and well prepared, with just a touch of fusion (European and Cajun influences) added to the specials. I suggest coming here if you're a bit overloaded by the seasonings at restaurants such as Santacafé and Coyote Café. El Nido is roomy, and the service is friendly and informal. Carla insists on oysters Rockefeller for an appetizer, though you can also start with a lighter ceviche. For entrees, she always has the salmon, which is broiled, with a light dill sauce on the side. I enjoy the broiled lamb chops, served with a light and tasty spinach mint sauce. All meals come with salad and baked potato, rice, or fries. For dessert, try the crème brûlée, or, if you're a chocolate lover, the chocolate piñon torte. There's a full bar, including a good selection of wines and local microbrewed beers.

Bishop's Lodge Rd., at the center of Tesuque Village. ✆ **505/988-4340.** Reservations recommended. Main courses $15–$26. AE, DC, MC, V. Tues–Sun 5:30–9:30pm.

MODERATE
Tesuque Village Market AMERICAN/SOUTHWESTERN You'll see shiny Range Rovers parked alongside beat-up ranch trucks in front of this charming market and restaurant, an indication that the food here has broad appeal. Located under a canopy of cottonwoods at the center of this quaint village, the restaurant doesn't have the greatest food but makes for a nice adventure 15 minutes north of town. During warmer months, you can sit on the porch; in other seasons, the interior is comfortable, with plain wooden tables next to a deli counter and upscale market. For me, this is a breakfast place, where blue-corn pancakes rule. Friends of mine like the breakfast burritos and huevos rancheros.

Lunch and dinner are also popular, and there's always a crowd (though, if you have to wait for a table, the wait is usually brief). For lunch, I recommend the burgers, and for dinner, one of the hearty specials, such as lasagna. For dessert, there's a variety of homemade pastries and cakes at the deli counter, as well as fancy granola bars and oversize cookies in the market. A kids' menu is available.

At the junction of Bishop's Lodge Rd. and NM 591, in Tesuque Village. *C* **505/988-8848.** Reservations recommended for holidays. Main courses $5–$8 breakfast, $6–$12 lunch, $8–$20 dinner. MC, V. Summer daily 7am–10pm; winter daily 7am–9pm.

SOUTHSIDE

Santa Fe's motel strip and other streets south of the Paseo de Peralta have their share of good, reasonably priced restaurants. See the map "Greater Santa Fe," on p. 132, for the location of the restaurants in this section.

MODERATE

mu du noodles *★★* PACIFIC RIM If you're ready for a light, healthy meal with lots of flavor, head to this small restaurant about an 8-minute drive from downtown. There are two rooms, with plain pine tables and chairs and sparse Asian prints on the walls. The carpeted back room is cozier, and a woodsy-feeling patio is definitely worth requesting during the warmer months. The waitstaff is friendly and unimposing. I almost always order the Malaysian *laksa,* thick rice noodles in a blend of coconut milk, hazelnuts, onions, and red curry, stir-fried with chicken or tofu and julienned vegetables and sprouts. If you're eating with others, you may each want to order a different dish and share. The pad Thai is lighter and spicier than most, served with a chile/vinegar sauce. A list of beers, wines, and sakes is available, tailored to the menu. I'm especially fond of the ginseng ginger ale. Menu items change seasonally.

1494 Cerrillos Rd. *C* **505/983-1411.** Reservations accepted for parties of 3 or more only. Main courses $9–$18. AE, DC, DISC, MC, V. Mon–Sat 5:30–9pm (sometimes 10pm in summer).

INEXPENSIVE

La Choza *★★* NEW MEXICAN This sister restaurant of The Shed (p. 147) offers some of the best New Mexican food in town, at a convenient location. When other restaurants are packed, you'll only wait a little while here. It's a warm, casual eatery with vividly painted walls; it's especially popular on cold days, when diners gather around the wood-burning stove and fireplace. Service is friendly and efficient. The menu offers enchiladas, tacos, and burritos on blue-corn tortillas, as well as green chile stew, chile con carne, and carne adovada. The portions are medium-size, so if you're hungry, start with guacamole or nachos. For years, I've ordered the cheese or chicken enchilada, two dishes I will always recommend. My new favorite, though, is the blue-corn burritos (tortillas stuffed with beans and cheese) served with *posole;* the dish can be made vegetarian if you'd like. For dessert, you can't leave without trying the mocha cake (chocolate cake with a mocha pudding filling, served with whipped cream). Vegetarians and children have their own menus. Beer and wine are available.

905 Alarid St. *C* **505/982-0909.** Lunch or dinner $7–$8.75. AE, DC, DISC, MC, V. Summer Mon–Sat 11am–9pm; winter Mon–Thurs 11am–8pm, Fri–Sat 11am–9pm.

Tortilla Flats *★* *Kids* NEW MEXICAN This casual restaurant takes pride in its all-natural ingredients and vegetarian menu offerings (its vegetarian burrito is famous around town). The atmosphere is a bit like Denny's, but the food is authentic. The blueberry pancakes are delicious, as are the fajitas and eggs with a side of black beans. I also like the blue-corn enchiladas and the chimichangas.

The Santa Fe Trail steak (8 oz. of prime rib-eye smothered with red or green chile and topped with grilled onions) will satisfy a big appetite. Above all, try the fresh tortillas and *sopaipillas*, made on the spot (you can even peek through a window into the kitchen and watch them being made). There's a full bar, with the legendary Ultimate Margarita, made with Grand Marnier and Cuervo Gold 1800 Tequila. A children's menu and a take-out service are available.

3139 Cerrillos Rd. ℂ 505/471-8685. Breakfast $2–$8, lunch $5–$10, dinner $6–$11. DISC, MC, V. Sun–Thurs 7am–9pm (10pm in summer); Fri–Sat 7am–10pm.

5 What to See & Do

One of the oldest cities in the United States, Santa Fe has long been a center for the creative and performing arts, so it's not surprising that most of the city's major sights are related to local history and the arts. The city's Museum of New Mexico, art galleries and studios, historic churches, and cultural sights associated with local Native American and Hispanic communities all merit a visit. It would be easy to spend a full week sightseeing in the city, without ever heading out to any nearby attractions. Of special note is the **Georgia O'Keeffe Museum.**

SUGGESTED ITINERARIES

If You Have 2 Days

Day 1 Start at the Palace of the Governors; as you leave you might want to peruse the crafts and jewelry sold by Native Americans beneath the portal facing the plaza. After lunch, take a self-guided walking tour of old Santa Fe, starting at the plaza.

Day 2 Spend the morning at the Museum of Fine Arts and the afternoon browsing in the galleries on Canyon Road.

If You Have 3 Days

Day 3 Visit the cluster of museums on Camino Lejo—in particular, the Museum of International Folk Art, the Museum of Indian Arts & Culture, and the Wheelwright Museum

of the American Indian. Then wander through the historic Barrio de Analco and spend the rest of the afternoon shopping.

If You Have 4 Days or More

Day 4 Explore the pueblos, including San Ildefonso Pueblo, with its broad plaza, and San Juan Pueblo, headquarters of the Eight Northern Indian Pueblos Council.

Day 5 Head out along the High Road to Taos, with a stop at El Santuario de Chimayo, and return down the Rio Grande Valley. If you have more time, take a trip to Los Alamos, birthplace of the atomic bomb and home of the Bradbury Science Museum and Bandelier National Monument.

THE TOP ATTRACTIONS

Museum of Fine Arts ⓡ   Located opposite the Palace of the Governors, this was one of the first Pueblo Revival–style buildings constructed in Santa Fe (in 1917).

The museum's permanent collection of more than 20,000 works emphasizes regional art and includes landscapes and portraits by all the Taos masters, *los Cincos Pintores* (a 1920s organization of Santa Fe artists), and contemporary artists. The museum also has a collection of photographic works by such masters as Ansel Adams, Edward Weston, and Elliot Porter. Modern artists are featured in

Downtown Santa Fe Attractions

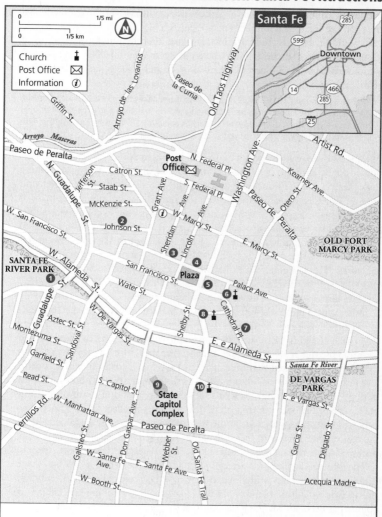

Catholic Museum & Lamy Garden **7**

Georgia O'Keeffe Museum **2**

Institute of American
  Indian Arts Museum **5**

Loretto Chapel Museum **8**

Mission of San Miguel **10**

Museum of Fine Arts **3**

New Mexico State Capitol
  (Roundhouse) **9**

Palace of the Governors **4**

Santuario de Nuestra Señora
  de Guadalupe **1**

St. Francis Cathedral **6**

temporary exhibits. Two sculpture gardens present a range of three-dimensional art, from the traditional to the abstract.

Graceful **St. Francis Auditorium,** patterned after the interiors of traditional Hispanic mission churches, adjoins the art museum (see "The Performing Arts," later in this chapter). A museum shop sells gifts, art books, prints, and postcards of the collection.

107 W. Palace (at Lincoln Ave.). © 505/476-5072. www.museumofnewmexico.org. Admission $7 adults, free for seniors Wed, free for children 16 and under, free for all Fri 5–8pm. 4-day pass (good at all 4 branches of the Museum of New Mexico and the Museum of Spanish Colonial Art) $15 for adults. Tues–Sun 10am–5pm (Fri until 8pm). Closed New Year's Day, Easter, Thanksgiving, and Christmas.

Palace of the Governors ★★   To fully appreciate this structure, it's important to know that this is where the only successful Native American uprising took place in 1680. Prior to the uprising, this was the local seat of power, and after de Vargas reconquered the natives, it resumed that position. Built in 1610 as the original capitol of New Mexico, the palace has been in continuous public use longer than any other structure in the United States. A watchful eye can find remnants of the conflicts this building has seen through the years. Begin out front, where Native Americans sell jewelry, pottery, and some weavings under the portal. This is a good place to buy, and it's a fun place to shop, especially if you visit with the artisans about their work. When you buy a piece, you may learn its history, a treasure as valuable as the piece itself.

Inside, a map illustrates 400 years of New Mexico history, from the 16th-century Spanish explorations through the frontier era and modern times. A rickety stagecoach contains tools, such as farm implements and kitchen utensils, used by early Hispanic residents. There's a replica of a mid-19th-century chapel, with a simple, bright-colored altarpiece made in 1830 for a Taos church by folk artist José Rafael Aragón. What I find most interesting are the period photos scattered throughout. The building's exterior seems elaborate now, but it was once a simple flat-topped adobe with thin posts. You can see a fireplace and chimney chiseled into the adobe wall, and, in the west section of the museum, a cutaway of the adobe floor. Farther in that direction, unearthed in a recent excavation, are storage pits where the Pueblo Indians kept corn, wheat, barley, and other goods.

The museum focuses little on regional Native American culture. (Most Native American artifacts previously housed here have been moved to the Museum of Indian Arts & Culture.) However, a world-class collection of pre-Columbian art objects has been added. You'll see South and Central American ceramics, gold, and stonework dating from 1500 B.C. to A.D. 1500. There's also an impressive 18th-century Segesser Hide painting collection and an exhibit called "Jewish Pioneers of America."

Governors' offices from the Mexican and 19th-century U.S. eras have been restored and preserved. My favorite display is a set of spurs ranging from the 16th to the late 19th centuries, including a spur with 5-inch rowels. Two shops are of particular interest. The bookstore has a fine selection of art, history, and anthropology books. The print shop and bindery produces limited-edition works on hand-operated presses.

The palace is the flagship of the Museum of New Mexico system; the main office is at 113 Lincoln Ave. (© **505/476-5060**). The system comprises five state monuments and four Santa Fe museums: the Palace of the Governors, the Museum of Fine Arts, the Museum of International Folk Art, and the Museum of Indian Arts & Culture.

North plaza. © 505/476-5100. www.palaceofthegovernors.org. Admission $7 adults, free for children 16 and under, free for all Fri. 4-day pass (good at all 4 branches of the Museum of New Mexico and the Museum of Spanish Colonial Art) $15 for adults. Tues–Sun 10am–5pm. Closed New Year's Day, Thanksgiving, and Christmas.

St. Francis Cathedral ✦   Santa Fe's grandest religious structure, with its French design, is an architectural anomaly in Santa Fe. A block east of the plaza, it was built between 1869 and 1886 by Archbishop Jean-Baptiste Lamy in the style of the great cathedrals of Europe. French architects designed the Romanesque building—named after Santa Fe's patron saint—and Italian masons assisted with its construction. The small adobe Our Lady of the Rosary chapel on the northeast side of the cathedral has a Spanish look. Built in 1807, it's the only portion that remains from Our Lady of the Assumption Church, founded along with Santa Fe in 1610. The new cathedral was built over and around the old church.

A wooden icon set in a niche in the wall of the north chapel, Our Lady of Peace, is the oldest representation of the Madonna in the United States. Rescued from the old church during the 1680 Pueblo Rebellion, it was brought back by Don Diego de Vargas on his (mostly peaceful) reconquest 12 years later—thus, the name. Today, Our Lady of Peace plays an important part in the annual Feast of Corpus Christi in June and July.

The cathedral's front doors feature 16 carved panels of historic note and a plaque memorializing the 38 Franciscan friars who were martyred during New Mexico's early years. There's also a large bronze statue of Bishop Lamy himself; his grave is under the main altar of the cathedral.

Cathedral Place at San Francisco St. © 505/982-5619. Donations appreciated. Open daily. Visitors may attend Mass Mon–Sat 7am and 5:15pm; Sun 8am, 10am, noon, and 5:15pm. Free parking in city lot next to the cathedral to attend church services.

MORE ATTRACTIONS
MUSEUMS

Catholic Museum and the Archbishop Lamy Commemorative Garden
This museum will be especially interesting if you've read Willa Cather's *Death Comes for the Archbishop,* a fictional account of Archbishop Lamy's experience in northern New Mexico. If you haven't read it, as you visit the St. Francis Cathedral, The Bishop's Lodge, and other areas around Santa Fe, take special note of tales of the archbishop because he is central to the area's history. The exhibition changes every few years, but you are likely to see a portrait of the determined, thin-lipped Frenchman—who resolutely battled what he felt was apostasy on the part of the Spanish clergy in New Mexico—and some of Lamy's personal items. All of the museum's changing exhibits feature objects and information about the 400-year-old history of the Catholic Church in New Mexico. The adjacent Lamy garden isn't much to see, but the gift shop has a nice collection of locally made religious articles.

223 Cathedral Place. © 505/983-3811. Donations appreciated. Mon–Fri 9am–4pm.

Georgia O'Keeffe Museum ✦   For years, anxious visitors to Santa Fe asked, "Where are the O'Keeffes?" Locals flushed and were forced to provide the answer: the Metropolitan Museum of Art in New York and the National Gallery of Art in Washington, D.C. Although this artist is known the world over for her haunting depictions of the shapes and colors of northern New Mexico, until rather recently, little of her work hung in the state.

This museum, inaugurated in July 1997, contains the largest collection of O'Keeffes in the world: currently 117 oil paintings, drawings, watercolors, and pastels, and more than 50 works by other artists of note. It is the only museum in the United States dedicated solely to one woman's work. You can see such killer O'Keeffes as *Jimson Weed,* painted in 1932, and *Evening Star No. VII,* from 1917. The rich and varied collection adorns the walls of a cathedral-like, 13,000-square-foot space—a former Baptist church with adobe walls. O'Keeffe's images are tied inextricably to local desert landscapes. She first visited New Mexico in 1917 and returned for extended periods from the '20s through the '40s.

217 Johnson St. ⓒ **505/946-1000.** www.okeeffemuseum.org. Admission $8, free for students, free for all Fri 5–8pm. July–Oct daily 10am–5pm (Fri until 8pm); Nov–June Thurs–Tues 10am–5pm (Fri until 8pm).

Indian Arts Research Center ⓡ
Having grown up in New Mexico, surrounded by Native American arts, I had a hodgepodge knowledge of whose work looked like what. The Center put my knowledge into an understandable framework. The School of American Research, of which the Indian Arts Research Center is a division, was established in 1907 as a center for advanced studies in anthropology and related fields. It sponsors scholarship, academic research, and educational programs, all in the name of keeping traditional arts alive.

The school has collected more than 10,000 objects, in the process compiling one of the world's finest collections of Southwest Indian pottery, jewelry, weavings, kachinas, paintings, baskets, and other arts that span from the prehistoric era (around 300–500 A.D.) to the present. You'll be led through temperature- and humidity-controlled rooms filled with items grouped by tribe. Admission is by tour only; see below for details.

School of American Research, 660 Garcia St. (off Canyon Rd.). ⓒ **505/954-7205.** www.sarweb.org/iarc/ iarc.htm. Free admission for Native Americans and SAR members, $15 fee for others. Public tours given most Fri 2pm (call for reservations). Group tours can also be arranged. Limited parking.

Institute of American Indian Arts Museum ⓡ
A visit to this museum (the most comprehensive collection of contemporary Native American art in the world) offers a profound look into the lives of a people negotiating two worlds: traditional and contemporary. Here, you'll see cutting-edge art that pushes the limits of many media, from creative writing to textile manufacturing to painting. One young artist says in a video, "I feel if I see one more warrior riding off into the sunset, I'm going to throw up." Much of the work originates from artists from The Institute of American Indian Arts (IAIA), the nation's only congressionally chartered institute of higher education devoted solely to the study and practice of the artistic and cultural traditions of all American Indian and Alaskan native peoples.

Exhibits change periodically, and a permanent collection of Allan Houser's monumental sculpture is on display in the museum's Art Park. The museum store has a broad collection of jewelry, pottery, books, and music.

108 Cathedral Place. ⓒ **505/983-8900.** www.iaiancad.org. Admission $4 adults, $2 seniors and students, free for children 16 and under. Oct–May Mon–Sat 10am–5pm, Sun noon–5pm; June–Sept daily 9am–5pm.

Museum of Indian Arts & Culture ⓡⓡ
An interactive permanent exhibit here has made this one of the most exciting Native American museum experiences in the Southwest. "Here, Now and Always" takes visitors through thousands of years of Native American history. More than 70,000 pieces of basketry, pottery, clothing, carpets, and jewelry—much of it quite old—are on continual rotating display. You begin by entering through a tunnel that symbolizes the *sipapu,* the ancestral Puebloan entrance into the upper worlds; you are greeted

Cultural Chow

If you get hungry while visiting the Museum of Indian Arts & Culture, the Museum of International Folk Art, the Wheelwright Museum of the American Indian, and the Museum of Spanish Colonial Art (all located together, southeast of the plaza), you can now feast on more than your fingernails. The **Museum Hill Café** (© **505/820-1776**) is open Tuesday through Saturday for beverages and snacks at 10am, and a tasty lunch from 11am to 3pm; it serves Sunday brunch 11am to 3pm.

by the sounds of trickling water, drums, and Native American music. Videos show Native Americans telling creation stories. Visitors can reflect on the lives of modern-day Native Americans by juxtaposing a traditional Pueblo kitchen with a modern kitchen. You can step into a Navajo hogan and stroll through a trading post. The rest of the museum houses a lovely pottery collection as well as changing exhibits.

Look for demonstrations of traditional skills by tribal artisans and regular programs in a 70-seat multimedia theater. Call for information on year-round lectures and classes on native traditions and arts, as well as performances of Native American music and dancing by tribal groups. In February, look for an annual fiber show, and in June, a presentation on oral traditions.

The laboratory, founded in 1931 by John D. Rockefeller, Jr., is itself a point of interest. Designed by the well-known Santa Fe architect John Gaw Meem, it is an exquisite example of Pueblo Revival architecture.

710 Camino Lejo. © **505/476-1250.** www.miaclab.org. Admission $7 adults, free for kids 16 and under. 4-day pass (good at all 4 branches of the Museum of New Mexico and the Museum of Spanish Colonial Art) $15. Tues–Sun 10am–5pm. Drive southeast on Old Santa Fe Trail (beware: Old Santa Fe Trail takes a left turn; if you find yourself on Old Pecos Trail, you missed the turn). Look for signs pointing right onto Camino Lejo.

Museum of International Folk Art ⊕⊕ *Kids*   This branch of the Museum

of New Mexico may not seem quite as typically Southwestern as other Santa Fe museums, but it's the largest of its kind in the world. With a collection of some 130,000 objects from more than 100 countries, it's my favorite city museum, well worth an hour or two of perusing. It was founded in 1953 by the Chicago collector Florence Dibell Bartlett, who said, "If peoples of different countries could have the opportunity to study each other's cultures, it would be one avenue for a closer understanding between men."

The special collections include Spanish colonial silver, traditional and contemporary New Mexican religious art, Mexican tribal costumes and majolica ceramics, Brazilian folk art, European glass, African sculptures, East Indian textiles, and the marvelous Morris Miniature Circus. Particularly delightful are numerous dioramas of people around the world at work and play in typical town, village, and home settings. Recent acquisitions include American weather vanes and quilts, Palestinian costume jewelry and amulets, and Bhutanese and Indonesian textiles.

Children love to look at the hundreds of toys on display, many of which are from a collection donated in 1982 by Alexander Girard, a notable architect and interior designer, and his wife, Susan. The couple spent their lives traveling the world collecting dolls, animals, fabrics, masks, and dioramas. They had a home in Santa Fe, where they spent many years before they died. Their donation included more than 100,000 pieces, 10,000 of which are exhibited at the museum.

The Hispanic Heritage Wing houses the country's finest collection of Spanish colonial and Hispanic folk art. Folk-art demonstrations, performances, and workshops are presented here. The 80,000-square-foot museum also has a lecture room, a research library, and a gift shop, where folk art is available for purchase.

706 Camino Lejo. (505/476-1200. www.moifa.org. Admission $7 adults, free for kids 16 and under. 4-day pass (good at all 4 branches of the Museum of New Mexico and the Museum of Spanish Colonial Art) $15. Tues–Sun 10am–5pm. The museum is located about 2 miles southeast of the plaza. Drive southeast on Old Santa Fe Trail (beware: Old Santa Fe Trail takes a left turn; if you find yourself on Old Pecos Trail, you missed the turn). Look for signs pointing right onto Camino Lejo.

Museum of Spanish Colonial Art ⊛

Beauty often follows in the tragic wake of imperialism. A good example of this point is Spanish colonial art, which has flourished from Europe across the Americas and even in the Philippines. This newer museum celebrates this art with a collection of 3,000 devotional and decorative works and utilitarian artifacts. Housed in a home built by noted architect John Gaw Meem, the museum displays *retablos* (religious paintings on wood), *bultos* (free-standing religious sculptures), furniture, metalwork, and textiles and, outside, an 18th-century wooden colonial house from Mexico.

750 Camino Lejo. (505/982-2226. www.spanishcolonial.org. Admission $6 adults, free for kids 16 and under. 4-day pass (good at all 4 branches of the Museum of New Mexico and the Museum of Spanish Colonial Art) $15. Tues–Sun 10am–5pm. The museum is located about 2 miles southeast of the plaza. Drive southeast on Old Santa Fe Trail (beware: Old Santa Fe Trail takes a left turn; if you find yourself on Old Pecos Trail, you missed the turn). Look for signs pointing right onto Camino Lejo.

SITE Santa Fe ⊛

This not-for-profit, 18,000-square-foot contemporary art space without a permanent collection has made a place for itself in the City Different, as well as in the international art scene. It's no wonder, with shows by some of the world's most noted contemporary artists—in 2005, Jim Campbell will present his interactive multimedia works here, for example. As well as bringing cutting-edge visual art to Santa Fe, SITE sponsors an art and culture series of lectures, multidisciplinary programs, and artist dialogues. SITE sponsors other events too, including a biennial exhibition that's well worth attending.

1606 Paseo de Peralta. (505/989-1199. www.sitesantafe.org. $5 adults, $2.50 students and seniors, free for SITE Santa Fe members, free for all Fri. Wed–Sun 10am–5pm (Fri until 7pm). Closed New Year's Day, Thanksgiving, Christmas Eve, Christmas, and New Year's Eve. Call for information about docent tours and tours in Spanish.

Wheelwright Museum of the American Indian ⊛ (Kids

This museum resembles a Navajo hogan, with its doorway facing east (toward the rising sun) and its ceiling formed in the interlocking "whirling log" style. It was founded in 1937 by Boston scholar Mary Cabot Wheelwright, in collaboration with a Navajo medicine man, Hastiin Klah, to preserve and document Navajo ritual beliefs and practices. Klah took the designs of sand paintings used in healing ceremonies and adapted them into the woven pictographs that are a major part of the museum's treasure. In 1976, the museum's focus was altered to include the living arts of all Native American cultures. The museum offers three or four exhibits per year. You may see a basketry exhibit, mixed-media Navajo toys, or amazing contemporary Navajo rugs. An added treat here is the Case Trading Post, an arts-and-crafts shop built to resemble the typical turn-of-the-20th-century trading post found on the Navajo reservation. Docent tours of the exhibition are Monday to Wednesday and Friday at 2pm and Saturday at 11am. Year-round each Saturday and Tuesday morning at 10:15am and Sunday at 2pm, the Trading Post presents a lively and informative introduction to Southwestern Indian art. The museum has excellent access for travelers with disabilities.

704 Camino Lejo. ⓒ **800/607-4636** or 505/982-4636. Fax 505/989-7386. www.wheelwright.org. Donations appreciated. Mon–Sat 10am–5pm; Sun 1–5pm. Closed New Year's Day, Thanksgiving, and Christmas. Drive southeast on Old Santa Fe Trail (beware: Old Santa Fe Trail takes a left turn; if you find yourself on Old Pecos Trail, you missed the turn). Look for signs pointing right onto Camino Lejo.

CHURCHES

Cristo Rey   This Catholic church ("Christ the King," in Spanish), a huge adobe structure, was built in 1940 to commemorate the 400th anniversary of Coronado's exploration of the Southwest. Parishioners did most of the construction work, even making adobe bricks from the earth where the church stands. The local architect John Gaw Meem designed the building, in missionary style, as a place to keep some magnificent stone *reredos* (altar screens) created by the Spanish during the colonial era and recovered and restored in the 20th century.

Upper Canyon Rd. ⓒ **505/983-8528.** Free admission. Mon–Fri 8am–5pm.

Loretto Chapel Museum ⋆   Though no longer consecrated for worship, the Loretto Chapel is an important site in Santa Fe. Patterned after the famous Sainte-Chapelle church in Paris, it was constructed in 1873—by the same French architects and Italian masons who were building Archbishop Lamy's cathedral—as a chapel for the Sisters of Loretto, who had established a school for young women in Santa Fe in 1852.

The chapel is especially notable for its remarkable spiral staircase: It makes two complete 360-degree turns, with no central or other visible support. The structure is steeped in legend: The building was nearly finished in 1878, when workers realized the stairs to the choir loft wouldn't fit. Hoping for a solution more attractive than a ladder, the sisters made a novena to St. Joseph and were rewarded when a mysterious carpenter appeared astride a donkey and offered to build a staircase. Armed with only a saw, a hammer, and a T-square, the master constructed this work of genius by soaking slats of wood in tubs of water to curve them and holding them together with wooden pegs. Then he disappeared without bothering to collect his fee.

207 Old Santa Fe Trail (between Alameda and Water sts.). ⓒ **505/982-0092.** www.lorettochapel.com. Admission $2.50 adults, $2 children 7–12 and seniors over 65, free for children 6 and under. Mon–Sat 9am–5pm; Sun 10:30am–5pm.

Mission of San Miguel   If you want to get the feel of colonial Catholicism, visit this church. Better yet, attend Mass here. Built in 1610, the church has massive adobe walls, high windows, an elegant altar screen (erected in 1798), and a 780-pound San José bell (now found inside), which was cast in Spain in 1356. If that doesn't impress you, perhaps the buffalo hide and deerskin Bible paintings used in 1630 by Franciscan missionaries to teach the Native Americans will. Anthropologists have excavated near the altar, down to the original floor that some claim to be part of a 12th-century pueblo. A small store sells religious articles.

401 Old Santa Fe Trail (at E. de Vargas St.). ⓒ **505/983-3974.** Admission $1, free for children under 6. Mon–Sat 9am–5pm; Sun 10am–4pm. Summer hours start earlier. Mass Sun 5pm.

Santuario de Nuestra Señora de Guadalupe ⋆   This church, built in 1776–96 at the end of El Camino Real by Franciscan missionaries, is believed to be the oldest shrine in the United States honoring the Virgin of Guadalupe. Better known as Santuario de Guadalupe, the shrine's adobe walls are almost 3 feet thick, and the deep-red plaster wall behind the altar was dyed with ox blood in traditional fashion when the church was restored early in the 20th century.

It is well worth a visit to see photographs of the transformation of the building over time; its styles have ranged from flat-topped Pueblo to New England town meeting and today's northern New Mexico style. On one wall is a famous oil painting, *Our Lady of Guadalupe,* created in 1783 by the renowned Mexican artist José de Alzibar. Painted expressly for this church, it was brought from Mexico City by mule caravan.

100 S. Guadalupe St. ℂ 505/988-2027. Donations appreciated. Mon–Sat 9am–4pm. Closed weekends Nov–Apr.

PARKS & REFUGES

Arroyo de los Chamisos Trail   This trail, which meanders through the southwestern part of town, is of special interest to those staying in hotels along Cerrillos Road. The 2.5-mile paved path follows a chamisa-lined *arroyo* (stream) and has mountain views. It's great for walking or bicycling; dogs must be leashed.

Begin at Santa Fe High School on Yucca St. or on Rodeo Rd. near Sam's Club. ℂ 505/955-2103.

Old Fort Marcy Park   Marking the 1846 site of the first U.S. military reservation in the Southwest, this park overlooks the northeast corner of downtown. Only a few mounds remain from the fort, but the Cross of the Martyrs, at the top of a winding brick walkway from Paseo de Peralta near Otero Street, is a popular spot for bird's-eye photographs. The cross was erected in 1920 by the Knights of Columbus and the Historical Society of New Mexico to commemorate the Franciscans killed during the Pueblo Rebellion of 1680. It has since played a role in numerous religious processions. It's open daily 24 hours.

617 Paseo de Peralta.

Randall Davey Audubon Center ⚘   Named for the late Santa Fe artist who willed his home to the National Audubon Society, this wildlife refuge occupies 135 acres at the mouth of Santa Fe Canyon. Just a few minutes' drive from the plaza, it's an excellent escape. More than 100 species of birds and 120 types of plants live here, and varied mammals have been spotted—including black bears, mule deer, mountain lions, bobcats, raccoons, and coyotes. Trails winding through more than 100 acres of the nature sanctuary are open to day hikers, but not to dogs. There's also a natural history bookstore on site.

1800 Upper Canyon Rd. ℂ 505/983-4609. Trail admission $1. Daily 9am–5pm. House tours (conducted by appointment and sporadically during the summer) $2 adults, $1 children under 12; call for hours. Gift shop daily 10am–4pm (call for winter hours). Free 1-hr. guided bird walk 1st Sat every month at 8:30am, 9am winter.

Santa Fe River Park   This is a lovely spot for an early morning jog, a midday walk beneath the trees, or a sack lunch at a picnic table. The green strip, which does not close, follows the midtown stream for about 4 miles as it meanders along Alameda from St. Francis Drive upstream beyond Camino Cabra, near its source.

Alameda St. ℂ 505/955-2103.

OTHER ATTRACTIONS

El Rancho de las Golondrinas ⚘ *(Kids*   This 200-acre ranch, about 15 miles south of the plaza via I-25, was once the last stopping place on the 1,000-mile El Camino Real from Mexico City to Santa Fe. Today, it's a living 18th- and 19th-century Spanish village, comprising a hacienda, a village store, a schoolhouse, and several chapels and kitchens. There's also a working molasses mill, wheelwright and blacksmith shops, shearing and weaving rooms, a threshing ground, a winery and vineyard, and four water mills, as well as dozens of farm animals. A walk around the entire property is 1¾ miles in length, with amazing scenery and plenty of room for the kids to romp.

The Spring Festival (the first full weekend of June) and the Harvest Festival (the first full weekend of Oct) are the year's highlights at Las Golondrinas (The Swallows). On these festival Sundays, the museum opens with a procession and Mass dedicated to San Ysidro, patron saint of farmers. Volunteers in authentic costumes demonstrate shearing, spinning, weaving, embroidery, wood carving, grain milling, blacksmithing, tinsmithing, soap making, and other activities. There's an exciting atmosphere of Spanish folk dancing, music, theater, and food.

334 Los Pinos Rd. © 505/471-2261. www.golondrinas.org. Admission $5 adults, $4 seniors and teens, $2 children 5–12, free for children under 5. Festival weekends $7 adults, $5 seniors and teens, $3 children 5–12. June–Sept Wed–Sun 10am–4pm; Apr–May and Oct open by advance arrangement. Closed Nov–Mar. From Santa Fe, drive south on I-25, taking exit 276; this leads to NM 599 going north; turn left on W. Frontage Rd.; drive 1/2 mile; turn right on Los Pinos Rd.; travel 3 miles to the museum.

New Mexico State Capitol (Roundhouse)   Some are surprised to learn that this is the only round capitol building in the U.S. Built in 1966, it's designed in the shape of a Zia Pueblo emblem (or sun sign, which is also the state symbol). It symbolizes the Circle of Life: four winds, four seasons, four directions, and four sacred obligations. Surrounding the capitol is a lush 6½-acre garden boasting more than 100 varieties of plants, including roses, plums, almonds, nectarines, Russian olive trees, and sequoias. Inside you'll find standard functional offices, with New Mexican art hanging on the walls. Check out the Governor's Gallery and the Capitol Art Collection. Self-guided tours are available 8am to 5pm Monday through Friday year-round; Memorial Day to Labor Day guided tours are available Monday through Saturday at 10am and 2pm.

Paseo de Peralta and Old Santa Fe Trail. © 505/986-4589. www.legis.state.nm.us. Free admission and tours. Mon–Sat 8am–5pm. Free parking.

Santa Fe Climbing Gym   The walls of this two-story, cavernous gym are covered with foot- and handholds, making it a perfect place to frolic, especially in winter. Rental gear is available.

825 Early St. © 505/986-8944. Daily passes $12 adults, $6 children under 12. Weekdays 5–10pm; Sat 1–8pm.

Santa Fe Southern Railway 👀   "Riding the old Santa Fe" always referred to riding the Atchison, Topeka & Santa Fe railroad. Ironically, the main route of the AT&SF bypassed Santa Fe, which probably forestalled some development for the capital city. A spur was run off the main line to Santa Fe in 1880, and today, an 18-mile ride along that spur offers views of some of New Mexico's most spectacular scenery.

The Santa Fe Depot is a well-preserved tribute to the Mission architecture that the railroad brought to the West in the early 1900s. Characterized by stuccoed walls, arched openings, and tile roofs, this style was part of an architectural revolution in Santa Fe when builders snubbed the traditional Pueblo style.

Inside the restored coach, passengers are surrounded by aged mahogany and faded velvet seats. The train snakes through Santa Fe and onto the New Mexico plains, broad landscapes spotted with piñon and chamisa, with views of the Sandia and Ortiz mountains. Arriving in the small track town of Lamy, you get another glimpse of a Mission-style station, this one surrounded by spacious lawns where passengers picnic. Check out the sunset rides on weekends and the specialty trains throughout the year.

410 S. Guadalupe St. 🕐 **888/989-8600** or 505/989-8600. Fax 505/983-7620. www.sfsr.com. Tickets range from $15 (children) to $25 (adults); $30–$80 Fri–Sat evening rides (Apr–Oct). Depending on the season, trains depart the Santa Fe Depot daily 9:30am–5pm (call to check schedule).

COOKING, ART & PHOTOGRAPHY CLASSES

If you're looking for something to do that's a little off the beaten tourist path, you might consider taking a class.

You can master the flavors of Santa Fe with an entertaining 3-hour demonstration cooking class at the **Santa Fe School of Cooking and Market** 🅰, on the upper level of the Plaza Mercado, 116 W. San Francisco St. (🕐 **505/983-4511;** fax 505/983-7540; www.santafeschoolofcooking.com). The class teaches about the flavors and history of traditional New Mexican and contemporary Southwestern cuisines. "Cooking Light" classes are available as well. Prices range from $40 to $88 and include a meal; call for a class schedule. The adjoining market offers a variety of regional foods and cookbooks, with gift baskets available.

If Southwestern art has you hooked, you can take a drawing and painting class led by Santa Fe artist Jane Shoenfeld. Students sketch such outdoor subjects as the Santa Fe landscape and adobe architecture. In case of inclement weather, classes are held in the studio. Each class lasts for 3 hours, and art materials are included in the fee, which ranges from $85 to $90. Private lessons can also be arranged. All levels of experience are welcome. Children's classes can be arranged. You can create your own personal art adventure with one of Shoenfeld's 1-day classes at Ghost Ranch in Abiquiu, or a 5-day intensive class (also held at Ghost Ranch). Contact Jane at **Sketching Santa Fe,** P.O. Box 5912, Santa Fe, NM 87502 (🕐 **505/986-1108;** fax 505/986-3845; www.skyfields.net).

Some of the world's most outstanding photographers convene in Santa Fe at various times during the year for the **Santa Fe Photography & Digital Workshops,** P.O. Box 9916, Santa Fe, NM 87504, at a delightful campus in the hills on the east side of town (🕐 **505/983-1400;** www.santafeworkshops.com). Most courses last a week. Food and lodging packages are available.

WINE TASTINGS

If you enjoy sampling regional wines, consider visiting the wineries within easy driving distance of Santa Fe: **Balagna Winery/Il Santo Cellars,** 223 Rio Bravo Dr., in Los Alamos (🕐 **505/672-3678**), north on US 84/285 and then west on NM 502; **Santa Fe Vineyards,** with a retail outlet at 235 Don Gaspar Avenue, in Santa Fe (🕐 **505/982-3474**), or the vineyard itself about 20 miles north of Santa Fe on US 84/285 (🕐 **505/753-8100**); **Madison Vineyards & Winery,** in Ribera (🕐 **505/421-8028**), about 45 miles east of Santa Fe on I-25 North; and the **Black Mesa Winery,** 1502 Hwy. 68, in Velarde (🕐 **800/852-6372**), north on US 84/285 to NM 68. Be sure to call in advance to find out when the wineries are open for tastings and to get specific directions.

ESPECIALLY FOR KIDS

Don't miss taking the kids to the **Museum of International Folk Art,** where they'll love the international dioramas and the toys (discussed earlier in this chapter). Also visit the tepee at the **Wheelwright Museum of the American Indian** (discussed earlier in this chapter), where storyteller Joe Hayes spins traditional Spanish *cuentos,* Native American folk tales, and Wild West tall tales on weekend evenings. **The Bishop's Lodge** has extensive children's programs during the summer. These include horseback riding, swimming, arts and crafts, and special activities, such as archery and tennis. Kids are sure to enjoy **El Rancho**

de las Golondrinas (discussed above), a living 18th- and 19th-century Spanish village comprising a hacienda, a village store, a schoolhouse, and several chapels and kitchens.

The **Genoveva Chavez Community Center** is a full-service family recreation center on the south side of Santa Fe (3221 Rodeo Rd.). The complex includes a 50-meter pool, a leisure pool, a therapy pool, an ice-skating rink, three gyms, a workout room, racquetball courts, and an indoor running track, as well as a spa and sauna. For hours and more information, call ✆ **505/955-4001.**

Planetarium at Santa Fe Community College *(Kids)*   The planetarium offers imaginative programs, combining star shows with storytelling and other interactive techniques. Among the planetarium's inventive programs: Rusty Rocket's Last Blast, in which kids launch a model rocket; and the Solar System Stakeout, in which kids build a solar system. There's also a 10-minute segment on the current night sky. Programs vary, from those designed for preschoolers to those for high school kids.

6401 Richards Ave. (south of Rodeo Rd.). ✆ **505/428-1677** or 505/428-1777, option 6, for the information line. www.sfccnm.edu/planetarium. Admission $5 adults, $3 seniors and children 12 and under. Live lecture 1st Wed of month 7–8pm; Celestial Highlights (live program mapping the night sky for that particular month) 1st Thurs of month 7–8pm; pre-recorded shows 2nd and 4th Thurs of month.

Rockin' Rollers Event Arena *(Kids)*   This roller rink offers public skating sessions and lessons as well as rentals. There's a concession area where kids can get snacks. In-line skates are allowed.

2915 Agua Fria St. ✆ **505/473-7755.** Public skating sessions summers only Mon–Fri 1–3pm and 3–5pm.

Rodeo de Santa Fe *(Kids)*   The rodeo is usually held sometime around June 21. It's a colorful and fun Southwestern event for kids, teens, and adults. (See "New Mexico Calendar of Events," in chapter 2, for details.)

3237 Rodeo Rd. ✆ **505/471-4300.**

Santa Fe Children's Museum *(Kids)*   This museum offers interactive exhibits and hands-on activities in the arts, humanities, and science. The most notable features include a 16-foot climbing wall that kids—outfitted with helmets and harnesses—can scale, and a 1-acre Southwestern horticulture garden, complete with animals, wetlands, and a greenhouse. This fascinating area serves as an outdoor classroom for ongoing environmental educational programs. Special performances and hands-on sessions with artists and scientists are regularly scheduled. Recently, *Family Life* magazine named this as one of the 10 hottest children's museums in the nation.

1050 Old Pecos Trail. ✆ **505/989-8359.** www.santafechildrensmuseum.org. Admission $4; children under 12 must be accompanied by an adult. Wed–Sat 10am–5pm; Sun noon–5pm.

Santa Fe Public Library *(Kids)*   Special programs, such as storytelling and magic shows, are held here weekly throughout the summer. The library is located in the center of town, 1 block from the plaza.

145 Washington Ave. ✆ **505/955-6780.** www.santafelibrary.org. Mon–Thurs 10am–9pm; Fri–Sat 10am–6pm; Sun 1–5pm. Call for additional information.

Skateboard Park *(Kids)*   Split-level ramps for daredevils, park benches for onlookers, and climbing structures for youngsters are located at this park near downtown.

At the intersection of de Vargas and Sandoval sts. ✆ **505/955-2100.** Free admission. Open 24 hr.

6 Organized Tours

BUS, CAR & TRAM TOURS

LorettoLine For an open-air tour of the city, contact LorettoLine. Tours last 1½ hours and are offered daily from April to October. Tour times are every hour on the hour during the day from 10am to 3pm.

At the Hotel Loretto, 211 Old Santa Fe Trail. ✆ **505/983-3701.** Tours $12 adults, $6 children.

WALKING TOURS

As with the independent strolls described earlier in this chapter, the following are the best way to get an appreciable feel for Santa Fe's history and culture.

A Foot in Santa Fe ⋒ Personalized 2-hour tours are offered year-round at 9:30am from the Hotel Loretto. Reservations are not required.

At the Hotel Loretto, 211 Old Santa Fe Trail. ✆ **505/983-3701.** Tours $10.

Storytellers and the Southwest: A Literary Walking Tour ⋒ Barbara Harrelson, a former Smithsonian museum docent and local writer, leads 2-hour literary walking tours of downtown, exploring the history, legends, characters, and authors of the region through its landmarks and historic sites. It's a great way to absorb the unique character of Santa Fe. Tours take place by appointment.

924 Old Taos Hwy. ✆ **505/989-4561.** www.sfaol.com/books/littour.html. Apr–Oct. Tours $15 per person, 2-person minimum.

Walking Tour of Santa Fe ⋒ One of Santa Fe's best walking tours begins under the T-shirt tree at Tees & Skis, 107 Washington Ave., near the northeast corner of the plaza (at 9:30am and 1:30pm). It lasts about 2½ hours.

54½ E. San Francisco St. (tour meets at 107 Washington Ave.). ✆ **800/338-6877** or 505/983-6565. Tours $10 adults, free for children under 12.

MISCELLANEOUS TOURS

Pathways Customized Tours ⋒ Don Dietz offers several planned tours, including a downtown Santa Fe walking tour, a full city tour, a trip to the cliff dwellings and native pueblos, a "Taos adventure," and a trip to Georgia O'Keeffe country (with a focus on the landscape that inspired the art now viewable in the O'Keeffe Museum). He will try to accommodate any special requests you might have. These tours last anywhere from 2 to 9 hours, depending on the one you choose. Don has extensive knowledge of the area's culture, history, geology, and flora and fauna, and will help you make the most of your precious vacation time.

161F Calle Ojo Feliz. ✆ **505/982-5382.** www.santafepathways.com. Tours $60–$200+ per day per couple. Credit cards not accepted.

Rain Parrish ⋒ A Navajo (or *Diné*) anthropologist, artist, and curator, Rain Parrish offers custom guide services focusing on cultural anthropology, Native American arts, and the history of the Native Americans of the Southwest. Some of these are true adventures to insider locations. Ms. Parrish includes visits to local Pueblo villages.

704 Kathryn St. ✆ **505/984-8236.** Tours $130 per couple for 4½ hr., $230 per couple for 7 hr.

Recursos de Santa Fe/Royal Road Tours This is a full-service destination management company, emphasizing custom-designed itineraries to meet the interests of any group. It specializes in the archaeology, art, literature, spirituality, architecture, environment, food, and history of the Southwest. Call or visit the website for a calendar and information about its annual writers' conferences and the international bead expo that it sponsors in Santa Fe on even years in March.

826 Camino de Monte Rey. ℂ **505/982-9301**. www.recursos.org.

Rojo Tours & Services   Customized and private tours are arranged to pueblos, cliff dwellings, ruins, hot-air ballooning, backpacking, or whitewater rafting. Rojo also provides planning services for groups.

2408 Calle Bella. ℂ **505/474-8333**. Fax 505/474-2992. www.rojotours.com.

Santa Fe Detours ⭐   Santa Fe's most extensive tour-booking agency accommodates almost all travelers' tastes, from bus and rail tours to river rafting, backpacking, and cross-country skiing. The agency can also facilitate hotel reservations, from budget to high end.

54½ San Francisco (summer tour desk, 107 Washington Ave.). ℂ **800/338-6877** or 505/983-6565. www. sfdetours.com.

Southwest Safaris ⭐⭐   This tour is one of the most interesting Southwestern experiences I've had. We flew in a small plane 1,000 feet off the ground from Santa Fe to the Grand Canyon while pilot Bruce Adams explained 300 million years of geologic history. We passed by the ancient ruins of Chaco Canyon and over the vivid colors of the Painted Desert, as well as over many land formations on Navajo Nation land so remote they remain nameless. Then there was the spectacular Grand Canyon, with ground transport to the South Rim and lunch on a canyonside bench. Trips to many Southwestern destinations are available, including Monument Valley, Mesa Verde, Canyon de Chelly, Arches/Canyonlands, as well as a trip to Capulin Volcano and the ruins at Aztec, New Mexico. Local 1- and 2-hour scenic flights are available as well, to places such as the Rio Grande Gorge, the back route in to Acoma Pueblo, and Abiquiu Valley—Georgia O'Keefe country. Tours depart from the Santa Fe Airport.

P.O. Box 945. ℂ **800/842-4246** or 505/988-4246. Tours $129–$699 per person.

7 Outdoor Activities

Set between the granite peaks of the Sangre de Cristo Mountains and the subtler volcanic Jemez Mountains, and with the Rio Grande flowing through, the Santa Fe area offers outdoor enthusiasts many opportunities to play. This is the land of high desert, where temperatures vary with the elevation, allowing for a full range of activities throughout the year.

BALLOONING

New Mexico is renowned for its spectacular Balloon Fiesta, which takes place annually in Albuquerque (p. 27). If you want to take a ride, you'll probably have to go to Albuquerque or Taos, but you can book your trip in Santa Fe through **Santa Fe Detours,** 54½ E. San Francisco St. (tour desk for summer, 107 Washington Ave.; ℂ **800/338-6877** or 505/983-6565). Flights take place early in the day. Rates begin at around $135 per flight.

BIKING

You can cycle along main roadways and paved country roads year-round in Santa Fe, but be aware that traffic is particularly heavy around the plaza—and all over town, motorists are not particularly attentive to bicyclists, so you need to be especially alert. Mountain biking interest has exploded here and is especially popular in the spring, summer, and fall; the high-desert terrain is rugged and challenging, but mountain bikers of all levels can find exhilarating rides. The Santa Fe Convention and Visitors Bureau can supply you with bike maps.

I recommend the following trails: West of Santa Fe, the **Caja del Rio** area has nice dirt roads and some light-to-moderate technical biking; the **railroad tracks south of Santa Fe** provide wide-open biking on beginner-to-intermediate technical trails; and the **Borrego Trail** up toward Santa Fe Ski Area is a challenging technical ride that links up with the **Windsor Trail,** a nationally renowned technical romp with plenty of verticality.

In Santa Fe bookstores, look for my book *Frommer's Great Outdoor Guide to Arizona and New Mexico, Mountain Biking in Northern New Mexico: Historical and Natural History Rides* by Craig Martin, and *The Mountain Biker's Guide to New Mexico* by Sarah Bennett. They are excellent guides to trails in Santa Fe, Taos, and Albuquerque, and outline tours for beginner, intermediate, and advanced riders. **Santa Fe Mountain Sports,** 606 Cerrillos Rd. (© **505/988-3337**), rents hard-tail mountain bikes ($20 for half a day and $25 for a full day) or full-suspension bikes ($35 for a full day). **Sun Mountain Bike Company,** 102 E. Water St. (© **505/982-8986**), rents quality front-suspension mountain bikes for $30 a day. Add $7 and they'll deliver to and pick up from your hotel (in the Santa Fe area). Multiday rentals are $22 per day. Both shops supply accessories such as helmets, locks, water, maps, and trail information. **Sun Mountain** also runs bike tours from April through October to some of the most spectacular spots in northern New Mexico. Trips range from an easy Glorieta Mesa tour to my favorite, the West Rim Trail, with prices from $60 to $109. All tours include bikes, transportation, and a snack.

FISHING

In the lakes and waterways around Santa Fe, anglers typically catch trout (there are five varieties in the area). Other local fish include bass, perch, and kokanee salmon. The most popular fishing holes are Cochiti and Abiquiu lakes as well as the Rio Chama, the Pecos River, and the Rio Grande. A world-renowned fly-fishing destination, the **San Juan River,** near Farmington, is worth a visit and can make for an exciting 2-day trip in combination with a tour around **Chaco Culture National Historic Park** (see chapter 9). Check with the **New Mexico Game and Fish Department** (© **800/862-9310** or 505/476-8000) for information (including maps of area waters), licenses, and fishing proclamations. **High Desert Angler,** 435 S. Guadalupe St. (© **505/988-7688**), specializes in fly-fishing gear and guide services.

GOLF

There are three courses in the Santa Fe area: the 18-hole **Santa Fe Country Club,** on Airport Road (© **505/471-2626**); the often praised 18-hole **Cochiti Lake Golf Course,** 5200 Cochiti Hwy., Cochiti Lake, about 35 miles southwest of Santa Fe via I-25 and NM 16 and 22 (© **505/465-2239**); and Santa Fe's newest 18-hole course, **Marty Sanchez Links de Santa Fe,** 205 Caja del Rio (© **505/955-4400**).

HIKING

It's hard to decide which of the 1,000 miles of nearby national forest trails to tackle. Four wilderness areas are nearby, most notably **Pecos Wilderness,** with 223,000 acres east of Santa Fe, and the 58,000-acre **Jemez Mountain National Recreation Area.** Information on these and other wilderness areas is available from the **Santa Fe National Forest,** P.O. Box 1689 (1474 Rodeo Rd.), Santa

Fe, NM 87504 (© **505/438-7840**). If you're looking for company on your trek, contact the Santa Fe branch of the **Sierra Club,** 621 Old Santa Fe Trail, Suite 10 (© **505/983-2703**). You can pick up a hiking schedule in the local newsletter outside the office. Some people enjoy taking a chairlift ride to the summit of the **Santa Fe Ski Area** (© **505/982-4429;** www.skisantafe.com) and hiking around up there during the summer. You might also consider purchasing *The Hiker's Guide to New Mexico* (Falcon Press) by Laurence Parent; it outlines 70 hikes throughout the state. *Frommer's Great Outdoor Guide to Arizona and New Mexico* (Wiley Publishing, Inc.), written by yours truly, details many of my favorite hikes. A popular guide with Santa Feans is *Day Hikes in the Santa Fe Area,* put out by the local branch of the Sierra Club. The most popular hiking trails are the **Borrego Trail,** a moderate 4-mile jaunt through aspens and ponderosa pines, ending at a creek; and **Aspen Vista,** an easy 1- to 5-mile hike through aspen forest with views to the east. Both are easy to find; simply head up Hyde Park Road toward Ski Santa Fe. The Borrego Trail is 8¼ miles up, while Aspen Vista is 10 miles. In recent years an energetic crew has cut the **Dale Ball Trails** (© **505/955-2103**), miles of hiking/biking trails throughout the Santa Fe foothills. The easiest access is off Hyde Park Road toward Ski Santa Fe. Drive 2 miles from Bishop's Lodge Road and watch for the trailhead on the left.

HORSEBACK RIDING

Trips ranging in length from a few hours to overnight can be arranged by **Santa Fe Detours,** 54½ E. San Francisco St. (summer tour desk, 107 Washington Ave.; © **800/338-6877** or 505/983-6565). You'll ride with "experienced wranglers" and can even arrange a trip that includes a cookout or brunch. Rides are also major activities at **The Bishop's Lodge** (see "Where to Stay," earlier in this chapter). The **Broken Saddle Riding Company** (© **505/424-7774**) offers rides through the stunning Galisteo Basin south of Santa Fe.

HUNTING

Elk and mule deer are taken by hunters in the Pecos Wilderness and Jemez Mountains, as are occasional black bears and bighorn sheep. Wild turkeys and grouse are frequently bagged in the uplands, geese and ducks at lower elevations. Check with the **New Mexico Game and Fish Department** (© **800/862-9310** or 505/476-8000) for information and licenses.

RIVER RAFTING & KAYAKING

Although Taos is the real rafting center of New Mexico, several companies serve Santa Fe during the April-to-October whitewater season. They include **Southwest Wilderness Adventures,** P.O. Box 9380, Santa Fe, NM 87504 (© **505/983-7262**); **New Wave Rafting,** 70 County Rd. 84B, Santa Fe, NM 87506 (© **800/984-1444** or 505/984-1444); **Santa Fe Rafting Co.,** 1000 Cerrillos Rd., Santa Fe, NM 87505 (© **800/467-RAFT** or 505/988-4914; www.santafe rafting.com); and **Wolf Whitewater,** 4626 Palo Alto SE, Albuquerque, NM 87108 (© **505/262-1099;** www.wolfwhitewater.com). You can expect the cost of a full-day trip to range from about $85 to $105.

RUNNING

Despite its elevation, Santa Fe is popular with runners, and hosts numerous competitions, including the annual **Old Santa Fe Trail Run** on Labor Day. Each Wednesday, Santa Fe runners gather at 6pm at the plaza and set out on foot for runs in the surrounding area. This is a great opportunity for travelers to find their way and to meet some locals. **Santa Fe Striders** (www.santafestriders. org) sponsors various runs during the year.

SKIING

There's something available for every ability level at **Ski Santa Fe,** about 16 miles northeast of Santa Fe via Hyde Park (Ski Basin) Road. Lots of locals ski here, particularly on weekends; if you can, go on weekdays. It's a good family area and fairly small, so it's easy to split off from and later reconnect with your party. Built on the upper reaches of 12,000-foot Tesuque Peak, the area has an average annual snowfall of 225 inches and a vertical drop of 1,650 feet. Seven lifts, including a 5,000-foot triple chair and a new quad chair, serve 39 runs and 590 acres of terrain, with a total capacity of 7,800 riders an hour. Base facilities, at 10,350 feet, center around **La Casa Mall,** with a cafeteria, lounge, ski shop, and boutique. Another restaurant, **Totemoff's,** has a mid-mountain patio.

Getting Pampered: The Spa Scene

If traveling, skiing, or other activities have left you weary, a great place to treat your body and mind is **Ten Thousand Waves** ★★, a Japanese-style health spa about 3 miles northeast of Santa Fe on Hyde Park Road (© 505/982-9304; www.tenthousandwaves.com). This serene retreat, nestled in a grove of piñon, offers hot tubs, saunas, and cold plunges, plus a variety of massage and other bodywork techniques. Bathing suits are optional in both the 10-foot communal hot tub (during the day) and the women's communal tub, where you can stay as long as you want for $14. Nine private hot tubs cost $20 to $27 an hour, with discounts for seniors and children. You can also arrange therapeutic massage, hot-oil massage, in-water *watsu* massage, herbal wraps, salt glows, facials, dry brush aromatherapy treatments, Ayurvedic treatments, and the much praised Japanese Hot Stone Massage. If you call far enough in advance, you may be able to find lodging at **Ten Thousand Waves** as well (see "Where to Stay," earlier in this chapter). The spa is open Sunday, Monday, Wednesday, and Thursday from 10am to 10pm; Tuesday from 4:30 to 10pm; and Friday and Saturday from 10am to 11pm (winter hours are shorter, so be sure to call). Reservations are recommended.

Decorated in Southwestern-cum-Asian style, with clean lines and lots of elegant stone, Santa Fe's most chic option is **Avanu** ★★ at the La Posada de Santa Fe Resort and Spa (© 505/986-0000). A full-service spa offering a range of treatments from massage to salt glows, this spot may initially seem expensive (about $95 for 50 min.), but treatments include full use of the steam room, hot tub, and grass-surrounded pool.

South of town, **Sunrise Springs Inn and Retreat,** 242 Los Pinos Rd. (© 505/471-3600), offers spa stays in a lovely pond-side setting. Some accommodations here retain a group-meeting feel; to avoid these, request their newest additions, which are lovely. Even if you don't stay here, plan a meal at the inn's **Blue Heron Restaurant** ★★, where you'll feast on delectable new American cuisine with a healthy flair.

The ski area is open daily from 9am to 4pm; the season often runs from Thanksgiving to early April, depending on snow conditions. Rates for all lifts are $47 for adults, $39 for teens (13–20 years), $35 for children and seniors, free for children less than 46 inches tall (in their ski boots), and free for seniors 72 and older. For more information, contact **Ski Santa Fe,** 2209 Brothers Rd., Suite 220 (© **505/982-4429;** www.skisantafe.com). For 24-hour reports on snow conditions, call © **505/983-9155. Ski New Mexico** (© **505/982-5300**) provides statewide reports. Ski packages are available through **Santa Fe Central Reservations** (© **800/745-9910**).

Cross-country skiers find seemingly endless miles of snow to track in the **Santa Fe National Forest** (© **505/438-7840**). A favorite place to start is at the Black Canyon campground, about 9 miles from downtown en route to the Santa Fe Ski Area. In the same area are the **Borrego Trail**, **Aspen Vista Trail,** and **Norski Trail,** all en route to the Santa Fe Ski Area as well. Other popular activities at the ski area in winter include snowshoeing, snowboarding, sledding, and inner-tubing. Snowshoe and snowboard rentals are available at a number of downtown shops and the ski area.

SWIMMING

There's a public pool at the **Fort Marcy Complex** (© **505/955-2500**) on Camino Santiago, off Bishop's Lodge Road. Admission is $1.85 for adults, $1.50 for ages 13 to 18, 75¢ for ages 8 to 12 and seniors, and 30¢ for children 7 and under.

TENNIS

Santa Fe has 44 public tennis courts and four major private facilities. The **City Recreation Department** (© **505/955-2100**) can help you locate indoor, out-door, and lighted public courts.

8 Shopping

Each time I head out to shop in northern New Mexico, I'm amazed by the number of handcrafts, pieces of art, and artifacts I find. There's a broad range of work, from very traditional Native American crafts and Hispanic folk art to extremely innovative contemporary work.

Some call Santa Fe one of the top art markets in the world. Galleries speckle the downtown area, and as an artists' thoroughfare, Canyon Road is preeminent. Still, the greatest concentration of Native American crafts is displayed beneath the portal of the Palace of the Governors.

Any serious arts aficionado should try to attend one or more of the city's great arts festivals—the Spring Festival of the Arts in May, the Spanish Market in July, the Indian Market in August, and the Fall Festival of the Arts in October.

Few visitors to Santa Fe leave the city without acquiring at least one item from the Native American artisans at the Palace of the Governors. When you are thinking of making such a purchase, keep the following pointers in mind:

Silver jewelry should have a harmony of design, clean lines, and neatly executed soldering. Navajo jewelry typically features large stones, with designs shaped around the stone. Zuni jewelry usually has patterns of small or inlaid stones. Hopi jewelry rarely uses stones; it's usually a silver-on-silver overlay, darkly oxidized so the image stands out.

Turquoise of a deeper color is usually higher quality, so long as it hasn't been color treated (undesirable because the process adds false color to the stone). Often, turquoise is "stabilized," which means it has resin baked into the stone.

This makes the stone less fragile but also prevents it from changing color with age and contact with body oils. Many people find the aging effect desirable. Beware of "reconstituted turquoise." In this process the stone is disassembled and reassembled; it usually has a uniformly blue color that looks very unnatural.

Pottery is traditionally hand-coiled and of natural clay, not thrown on a potter's wheel using commercial clay. It is hand-polished with a stone, hand-painted, and fired in an outdoor oven rather than an electric kiln. Look for an even shape; clean, accurate painting; a high polish (if it is a polished piece); and an artist's signature.

Navajo rugs are appraised according to tightness and evenness of weave, symmetry of design, and whether natural (preferred) or commercial dyes have been used.

The value of **kachina dolls** depends on the detail of their carving: fingers, toes, muscles, rib cages, feathers, and so on. Elaborate costumes are also desirable. Oil staining is preferred to the use of bright acrylic paints.

Sand paintings should display clean, narrow lines, even colors, balance, an intricacy of design, and smooth craftsmanship.

Local museums, particularly the Wheelwright Museum and the Institute of American Indian Arts Museum, can give you a good orientation to contemporary craftsmanship.

Contemporary artists are mainly painters, sculptors, ceramists, and fiber artists, including weavers. Peruse one of the outstanding **gallery catalogs** for an introduction to local dealers. They're available for free in many galleries and hotels. They include *The Collector's Guide to Art in Santa Fe and Taos* by Wingspread Incorporated (www.collectorsguide.com); *The Essential Guide* by Essential Guides, LLC (www.essentialguide.com); and *Performance de Santa Fe* by Cynthia Stearns (P.O. Box 8932, Santa Fe, NM 87504-8932). For a current listing of gallery openings, with recommendations for which ones to attend, purchase a copy of the monthly magazine the *Santa Fean* by Santa Fean, LLC (444 Galisteo, Santa Fe, NM 87501; www.santafean.com). Also check in the "Pasatiempo" section of the local newspaper, the *New Mexican* (www.santafenewmexican.com), every Friday.

Business hours vary quite a bit among establishments, but most are open at least weekdays from 10am to 5pm, with mall stores open until 8 or 9pm. Most shops are open similar hours on Saturday, and many also open on Sunday afternoon during the summer. Winter hours tend to be more limited.

After the high-rolling 1980s, during which art markets around the country prospered, came the penny-pinching 1990s and the fearful 2000s. Many galleries in Santa Fe have been forced to shut their doors. Those that remain tend to specialize in particular types of art, a refinement process that has improved the gallery scene here. Still, some worry that the lack of serious art buyers in the area leads to fewer good galleries and more T-shirt and trinket stores. The plaza has its share of those but still has a good number of serious galleries, appealing to those buyers whose interests run to accessible art—Southwestern landscapes and the like. On Canyon Road, the art is often more experimental and more diverse.

THE TOP GALLERIES
CONTEMPORARY ART

Adieb Khadoure Fine Art   This is a working artists' studio, featuring contemporary artists Steven Boone, Hal Larsen, Robert Anderson, and Barry Lee Darling. Their works are shown in the gallery daily from 10am to 6pm. Adieb

Khadoure also sells elegant rugs, furniture, and pottery from around the world. 610 Canyon Rd. ℭ 505/820-2666.

Canyon Road Contemporary Art   This gallery represents some of the finest emerging U.S. contemporary artists as well as internationally known artists. You'll find figurative, landscape, and abstract paintings, as well as raku pottery. 403 Canyon Rd. ℭ 505/983-0433.

Hahn Ross Gallery   Owners Tom Ross and Elizabeth Hahn, a children's book illustrator and surrealist painter, respectively, specialize in representing artists who create colorful, fantasy-oriented works. I'm especially fond of the wild party scenes by Susan Contreras. Check out the sculpture garden here. 409 Canyon Rd. ℭ 505/984-8434.

La Mesa of Santa Fe ✪ *Finds*   Step into this gallery and let your senses dance. Dramatically colored ceramic plates, bowls, and other kitchen items fill one room. Contemporary kachinas by Gregory Lomayesva—a real buy—line the walls, accented by steel lamps and rag rugs. An adventure. 225 Canyon Rd. ℭ 505/984-1688.

Leslie Muth Gallery   Here, you'll find "Outsider Art," wild works made by untrained artists in a bizarre variety of media, from sculptures fashioned from pop-bottle lids to portraits painted on flattened beer cans; this is also the place to find Navajo folk art. Much of the work here is extraordinary and affordable. By appointment only. 221 E. de Vargas St. ℭ 505/989-4620.

LewAllen Contemporary ✪ *Finds*   This is one of my favorite galleries. You'll find bizarre and beautiful contemporary works in a range of media, from granite to clay to twigs. There are always exciting works on canvas. 129 W. Palace Ave. ℭ 505/988-8997.

Linda Durham Contemporary Art ✪   The opening of this broad and bright art space in summer 2004 marks the return of one of Santa Fe's best galleries. Longtime gallery owner Linda Durham had moved her gallery 25 miles south of town, but has now returned with a strong roster of talent, including Greg Erf and Judy Tuwaletstiwa. 1101 Paseo de Peralta. ℭ 505/466-6600.

Peyton Wright Gallery ✪   Housed within the Historic Spiegelberg House, this excellent gallery offers contemporary, Spanish colonial, African, Russian, Native American, and pre-Columbian art and antiquities. In addition to representing such artists as Kellogg Johnson, Larry Fodor, and Darren Vigil Gray, the gallery features monthly exhibitions. 237 E. Palace Ave. ℭ 800/879-8898 or 505/989-9888.

Shidoni Foundry, Gallery, and Sculpture Gardens ✪✪ *Finds*   This is one of the area's most exciting spots for sculptors and sculpture enthusiasts. Visitors may take a tour through the foundry to view casting processes. In addition, Shidoni Foundry includes a 5,000-square-foot contemporary gallery, a bronze gallery, and a wonderful sculpture garden. Bishop's Lodge Rd., Tesuque. ℭ 505/988-8001.

Waxlander Gallery   Primarily featuring the whimsical acrylics and occasional watercolors of Phyllis Kapp, this is the place to browse if you like bold color. 622 Canyon Rd. ℭ 800/342-2202 or 505/984-2202.

NATIVE AMERICAN & OTHER INDIGENOUS ART

Andrea Fisher Fine Pottery ✪   This expansive gallery is a wonderland of authentic Southwestern Indian pottery. You'll find real showpieces here, including the work of renowned San Ildefonso Pueblo potter Maria Martinez. 100 W. San Francisco St. ℭ 505/986-1234.

Frank Howell Gallery If you've never seen the wonderful illustrative hand of the late Frank Howell, you'll want to visit this gallery. It displays a variety of works by contemporary American Indian artists, such as Pablo Antonio Milan, as well as the Southwestern impressionism of Paula Shaw. The gallery also features sculpture, jewelry, and graphics. 103 Washington Ave. ℂ 505/984-1074.

Morning Star Gallery ★★ *(Finds* This is one of my favorite places to browse. Throughout the rambling gallery are American Indian art masterpieces, all elegantly displayed. You'll see a broad range of works, from late-19th-century Navajo blankets to 1920s Zuni needlepoint jewelry. 513 Canyon Rd. ℂ 505/982-8187.

Ortega's on the Plaza A hearty shopper could spend hours here, perusing inventive turquoise and silver jewelry and especially fine strung beadwork, as well as rugs and pottery. An adjacent room showcases a wide array of clothing, all with a hip Southwestern flair. 101 W. San Francisco St. ℂ 505/988-1866.

PHOTOGRAPHY

Andrew Smith Gallery ★ I'm always amazed when I enter this gallery and see works I've seen reprinted in major magazines for years. There they are, photographic prints, large and beautiful, hanging on the wall. Here, you'll see famous works by Edward Curtis, Henri Cartier-Bresson, Ansel Adams, Annie Leibovitz, and others. 203 W. San Francisco St. ℂ 505/984-1234.

Photo-Eye Gallery You're bound to be surprised each time you step into this gallery a few blocks off Canyon Road. Dealing in contemporary photography, the gallery represents both internationally renowned and emerging artists. 370 Garcia St. ℂ 505/988-5152.

SPANISH & HISPANIC ART

Montez Gallery This shop is rich with New Mexican (and Mexican) art, decorations, and furnishings such as *santos* (saints), *retablos* (paintings), *bultos* (sculptures), and *trasteros* (armoires). Sena Plaza Courtyard, 125 E. Palace Ave., Suite 33. ℂ 505/982-1828.

TRADITIONAL ART

Altermann Galleries This gallery offers interesting traditional art, mostly American paintings and sculpture. It represents Remington and Russell, in addition to Taos founders, Santa Fe artists, and members of the Cowboy Artists of America and the National Academy of Western Art. The sculpture garden features whimsical bronzes of children and dogs. 225 Canyon Rd. ℂ 505/983-1590.

Gerald Peters Gallery ★★ The works in this two-story Pueblo-style building are so fine you'll feel as though you're in a museum. You'll find American painting and sculpture, featuring the art of Georgia O'Keeffe, William Wegman, and the founders of the Santa Fe and Taos artist colonies, as well as contemporary works. 1011 Paseo de Peralta. ℂ 505/954-5700.

The Mayans Gallery Ltd. Established in 1977, this is one of the oldest galleries in Santa Fe. You'll find 20th-century American and Latin American paintings, photography, prints, and sculpture. 601 Canyon Rd. ℂ 505/983-8068.

Nedra Matteucci Galleries ★ As you approach this gallery, note the elaborately crafted stone and adobe wall that surrounds it, merely a taste of what's to come. The gallery specializes in American art. Inside, you'll find a lot of high-ticket works such as those of early Taos and Santa Fe painters, as well as classic American Impressionism, historical Western modernism, and contemporary landscapes and sculpture. 1075 Paseo de Peralta. ℂ 505/982-4631.

Nouveau Shopping on the Plaza

Opened in 2004, the **Santa Fe Arcade,** 60 E. San Francisco St. (© **505/ 995-0219**), on the south side of the plaza, offers three stories of shops in a sleek, glassy European-style space. It's a far cry from the Woolworth's that once lived there. Showy Western wear, fine Indian jewelry, and hip clothing fill the display windows of some 60 spaces in the mall. Local favorite **Back at the Ranch** (suite 127; © **800/962-6687** or 505/989-8110; www.backattheranch.com) has a satellite shop in the arcade, where they display a portion of what they call the "largest selection of handmade cowboy boots in the country." Prima Fine Jewelry's **Oro Fino** (suite 218; © **505/983-9699**) has also opened up, selling contemporary and Southwestern inlaid jewelry in silver, gold, and platinum.

Owings-Dewey Fine Art These are treasure-filled rooms. You'll find 19th-, 20th-, and 21st-century American painting and sculpture, including works by Georgia O'Keeffe, Robert Henri, Maynard Dixon, Fremont Ellis, and Andrew Dasburg, as well as antique works such as Spanish colonial *retablos, bultos,* and tin works. Don't miss the Day of the Dead exhibition around Halloween. 76 E. San Francisco St., upstairs. © **505/982-6244.**

Zaplin Lampert Gallery Art aficionados as well as those who just like a nice landscape will enjoy this gallery, one of Santa Fe's classics. Hanging on old adobe walls are works by some of the region's early masters, including Bert Phillips, Gene Kloss, and Gustauve Baumann. 651 Canyon Rd. © **505/982-6100.**

MORE SHOPPING A TO Z
BELTS
Desert Son of Santa Fe *(Moments* From belts to mules, everything in this narrow little shop is hand-tooled, hand-carved, and/or hand-stamped. As well as leather items, look for cowboy hats and exotic turquoise jewelry. It's a slip of a shop with lots of character, presided over by the artist herself, Mindy Adler. 725 Canyon Rd. © **505/982-9499.**

BOOKS
Borders With close to 200 stores nationwide, this chain provides a broad range of books, music, and videos, and it hosts in-store appearances by authors, musicians, and artists. 500 Montezuma Ave. © **505/954-4707.**

Collected Works Bookstore This is a good downtown book source, with carefully recommended books up front and shelves of Southwest, travel, nature, and other books. 208B W. San Francisco St. © **505/988-4226.**

Horizons—The Discovery Store *(Kids* Here, you'll find adult and children's books, science-oriented games and toys, telescopes, binoculars, and a variety of unusual educational items. I always find interesting gifts for my little nieces in this store. 328 S. Guadalupe St. © **505/983-1554.**

Nicholas Potter, Bookseller This store handles rare and used books, as well as tickets to many local events. 211 E. Palace Ave. © **505/983-5434.**

CRAFTS

Davis Mather Folk Art Gallery   This shop is a wild animal adventure. You'll find New Mexican animal woodcarvings in shapes of lions, tigers, and bears, as well as other folk and Hispanic arts. 141 Lincoln Ave. ⓒ **505/983-1660.**

Nambe Outlets ⭐ *Finds*   Here, you'll find cooking, serving, and decorating pieces, fashioned from an exquisite sand-cast and handcrafted alloy. These items are also available at the Nambe Outlet stores at 104 W. San Francisco St. (ⓒ **505/ 988-3574**) and in Taos in Yucca Plaza, 113A Paseo del Pueblo Norte (ⓒ **505/ 758-8221**). 924 Paseo De Peralta. ⓒ **505/988-5528.**

FASHIONS

Judy's Unique Apparel   Judy's has eclectic separates made locally and imported from around the globe. You'll find a wide variety of items here, many at surprisingly reasonable prices. 714 Canyon Rd. ⓒ **505/988-5746.**

Origins ⭐ *Moments*   A little like a Guatemalan or Turkish marketplace, this store is packed with wearable art, folk art, and the work of local designers. Look for good buys on ethnic jewelry. Trunk shows offer opportunities to meet the artists. 135 W. San Francisco St. ⓒ **505/988-2323.**

Overland Sheepskin Company   The rich smell of leather will draw you in the door, and possibly hold onto you until you purchase a coat, blazer, hat, or other finely made leather item. 74 E. San Francisco St. ⓒ **505/983-4727.**

FOOD

The Chile Shop   This store has too many cheap trinketlike items for me, but many find novelty items to take back home. You'll find everything from salsas to cornmeal and tortilla chips. The shop also stocks cookbooks and pottery items. 109 E. Water St. ⓒ **505/983-6080.**

Cookworks   This is a fun place for browsing. You'll find inventive food products and cooking items spread across three shops. Cookworks also offers gourmet food and cooking classes. 316 S. Guadalupe St. ⓒ **505/988-7676.**

Señor Murphy Candy Maker   This candy store is unlike any you'll find in other parts of the country—everything here is made with local ingredients. The chile piñon-nut brittle is a taste sensation! Señor Murphy has another shop in the Villa Linda Mall (ⓒ **505/471-8899**). 100 E. San Francisco St. (La Fonda Hotel). ⓒ **505/982-0461.**

FURNITURE & DECOR

Asian Adobe   One of the Santa Fe Railyard district's newest treats, this shop marries the warmth of Southwestern decor with the austere grace of Asian decor. You'll find weathered wood tables and trasteros, colorful wall hangings, and moody rugs. 530 S. Guadalupe (in the Gross Kelly Warehouse). ⓒ **505/992-6846.**

Casa Nova   In the Santa Fe Railyard district, this colorful shop offers everything from dishware to furniture, all in bold and inventive colors. Those with whimsical natures will get happily lost here. 530 S. Guadalupe St. (in the Gross Kelly Warehouse). ⓒ **505/983-8558.**

El Paso Import Company ⭐   Whenever I'm in the vicinity of this shop, I always stop in. It's packed—and I mean packed—with colorful, weathered colonial and ranchero furniture. The home furnishings and folk art here are imported from Mexico. 418 Sandoval St. ⓒ **505/982-5698.**

Jackalope *(Kids) (Value)*   Spread over 7 acres, this is a wild place to spend a morning or an afternoon browsing through exotic furnishings from India and Mexico, as well as imported textiles, pottery, jewelry, and clothing. Kids love the new petting zoo and prairie dog village. 2820 Cerrillos Rd. ℭ **505/471-8539.**

Southwest Spanish Craftsmen   The Spanish colonial and Spanish provincial furniture, doors, and home accessories in this store are a bit too elaborate for my tastes, but if you find yourself dreaming of carved wood, this is your place. 328 S. Guadalupe St. ℭ **505/982-1767.**

Taos Furniture   Here you'll find classic Southwestern furnishings handcrafted in solid Ponderosa pine—both contemporary and traditional. Prices are a little better here than in downtown shops. 219 Galisteo St. ℭ **800/443-3448** or 505/988-1229.

GIFTS & SOUVENIRS

El Nicho *(Value)*   If you want to take a little piece of Santa Fe home with you, you'll likely find it at this shop. You'll find handcrafted Navajo folk art as well as jewelry and other items by local artisans, including woodcarvings (watch for the *santos*) by the renowned Ortega family. 227 Don Gaspar Ave. ℭ **505/984-2830.**

HATS

Montecristi Custom Hat Works *⊛*   This fun shop hand-makes fine Panama and felt hats in a range of styles, from Australian outback to Mexican bolero. 322 McKenzie St. ℭ 505/983-9598. www.montecristihats.com.

JEWELRY

Packards *⊛*   Opened by a notable trader, Al Packard, and later sold to new owners, this store on the plaza is worth checking out to see some of the best jewelry available. You'll also find exquisite rugs and pottery. 61 Old Santa Fe Trail. ℭ **505/ 983-9241.**

Tresa Vorenberg Goldsmiths   You'll find some wildly imaginative designs in this store, which represents more than 40 artisans. All items are handcrafted, and custom commissions are welcomed. 656 Canyon Rd. ℭ **505/988-7215.**

MALLS & SHOPPING CENTERS

de Vargas Center   This is Santa Fe's small, struggling mall, which has approximately 50 merchants and restaurants. Though there are fewer shops than at Villa Linda, this is where I shop because I don't tend to get the mall phobia I get in the more massive places. Open Monday to Friday 10am to 7pm, Saturday 10am to 6pm, and Sunday noon to 5pm. N. Guadalupe St. and Paseo de Peralta. ℭ **505/982-2655.**

Sanbusco Market Center *⊛*   Unique shops and restaurants occupy this remodeled warehouse near the old Santa Fe Railyard. Many of the shops are overpriced, but it's a fun place to windowshop. Open Monday to Saturday 10am to 6pm, Sunday noon to 5pm. 500 Montezuma St. ℭ **505/989-9390.**

Santa Fe Premium Outlets   Outlet shopping fans will enjoy this open-air mall on the south end of town. Anchors include Brooks Brothers, Jones New York, Nautica, and Coach. 8380 Cerrillos Rd. ℭ **505/474-4000.**

Villa Linda Mall   Santa Fe's largest mall is near the southwestern city limits, not far from the I-25 on-ramp. If you're from a major city, you'll probably find shopping here very provincial. Anchors include JCPenney, Sears, Dillard's, and Mervyn's. Open Monday to Saturday 10am to 9pm, Sunday noon to 6pm. 4250 Cerrillos Rd. (at Rodeo Rd.). ℭ **505/473-4253.**

MARKETS

Farmers' Market ⚮ *Finds*   The farmers' market has everything from fruits, vegetables, and flowers to cheeses, cider, and salsas. Great local treats! If you're an early riser, stroll through and enjoy good coffee and excellent pastries. Open April to mid-November, Saturday and Tuesday 7am to noon. In the Santa Fe Railyard, off S. Guadalupe behind Tomasita's. ⓒ **505/983-4098.**

Tesuque Flea Market ⚮ *Moments*   More than 500 vendors here sell everything from used cowboy boots (you might find some real beauties) to clothing, jewelry, books, and furniture, all against a big northern New Mexico view. Open March to late November, Friday to Sunday. Vendors start selling at about 7:30am and stay open until about 6:30pm, weather permitting. US 84/285 (about 8 miles north of Santa Fe). No phone.

NATURAL ART

Mineral & Fossil Gallery of Santa Fe   You'll find ancient artwork here, from fossils to geodes in all sizes and shapes. There is also natural mineral jewelry and decorative items for the home, including lamps, wall clocks, furniture, art glass, and carvings. Mineral & Fossil also has galleries in Taos, and in Scottsdale and Sedona, Arizona. 127 W. San Francisco St. ⓒ **800/762-9777** or 505/984-1682.

Stone Forest *Finds*   Proprietor Michael Zimber travels to China and other Asian countries every year to collaborate with the stone carvers who create the fountains, sculptures, and bath fixtures that fill this inventive shop and garden not far from the plaza. 833 Dunlap. ⓒ **505/986-8883.**

POTTERY & TILES

Artesanos Imports Company ⚮ *Moments*   This is like a trip south of the border, with all the scents and colors you'd expect on such a journey. You'll find a wide selection of Talavera tile and pottery, as well as light fixtures and many other accessories for the home. There's even an outdoor market where you can buy fountains, sculpture items, and outdoor furniture. A second store is located at 1414 Maclovia St. (ⓒ **505/471-8020**). 222 Galisteo St. ⓒ **505/983-1743.**

Santa Fe Pottery   The work of more than 120 master potters from New Mexico and the Southwest is on display here; you'll find everything from mugs to lamps. From June to December, the shop hosts a series of six one-man and -woman and group/theme shows, with openings for each. 323 S. Guadalupe St. ⓒ **505/989-3363.**

RUGS

Seret & Sons Rugs, Furnishings, and Architectural Pieces ⚮   If you're like me and find Middle Eastern decor irresistible, you need to wander through this shop. You'll find kilims and Persian and Turkish rugs, as well as some of the Moorish-style ancient doors and furnishings that you see around Santa Fe. 224 Galisteo St. ⓒ **505/988-9151** or 505/983-5008.

9 Santa Fe After Dark

Santa Fe is a city committed to the arts, so it's no surprise that the Santa Fe night scene is dominated by highbrow cultural events, beginning with the world-famous Santa Fe Opera. The club and popular music scene runs a distant second.

Information on all major cultural events can be obtained from the **Santa Fe Convention and Visitors Bureau** (ⓒ **800/777-CITY** or 505/955-6200) or from the **City of Santa Fe Arts Commission** (ⓒ **505/955-6707**). Current listings are published each Friday in the "Pasatiempo" section of *The New Mexican* (www. santafenewmexican.com), the city's daily newspaper, and in the *Santa Fe Reporter* (www.sfreporter.com), published every Wednesday.

Nicholas Potter, Bookseller, 211 E. Palace Ave. (© **505/983-5434**), sells tickets to select events. **Candyman,** 851 St. Michaels Dr. (© **505/983-5906**), and **CD Café,** 301 N. Guadalupe (© **505/986-0735**), sell tickets for Paramount Lounge events. You can also order by phone from **Ticketmaster** (© **505/883-7800**). Discount tickets may be available on the night of a performance; for example, the opera offers standing-room tickets on the day of the performance. Sales start at 10am.

A variety of free concerts, lectures, and other events are presented in the summer, co-sponsored by the City of Santa Fe and the Chamber of Commerce. Many of these musical and cultural events take place on the plaza; check in the "Pasatiempo" section for current listings and information.

THE PERFORMING ARTS

At least two dozen performing-arts groups flourish in this city of 65,000. Many of them perform year-round, but some are seasonal. The acclaimed Santa Fe Opera, for instance, has just a 2-month summer season: July and August.

Note: Many companies noted here perform at locations other than their listed addresses, so check the site of the performance you plan to attend.

MAJOR PERFORMING ARTS COMPANIES
OPERA & CLASSICAL MUSIC

Santa Fe Opera ★★★   Many rank the Santa Fe Opera second only to the Metropolitan Opera of New York in the United States. Established in 1957, it consistently attracts famed conductors, directors, and singers. At the height of the season, the company is 500 strong. It's noted for its performances of the classics, little-known works by classical European composers, and American premieres of 21st-century works. The theater, completed for the 1998 season, sits on a wooded hilltop 7 miles north of the city, off US 84/285. It's partially open-air, with open sides. A controversial structure, this new theater replaced the original, built in 1968, but preserved the sweeping curves attuned to the contour of the surrounding terrain. On a clear night, you can see the lights of Los Alamos in the distance.

The 40-performance opera season runs from late June through late August. Highlights for 2005 include the opera's first Spanish work in almost 30 years, Osvaldo Golijov's *Ainadamar,* based on the life of poet and playwright Federico García Lorca. Also slated are Puccini's arresting *Turandot,* Rossini's comic *The Barber of Seville,* Mozart's grand *Lucio Silla,* and Britten's tragic *Peter Grimes.* All

A Home for the Arts

The Santa Fe arts scene has gained an exciting addition: The **Lensic Performing Arts Center,** 211 W. San Francisco St. (© **505/988-7050**), now hosts many of the city's major performances, including the Santa Fe Chamber Music Festival and the Santa Fe Symphony Orchestra and Chorus, among others. The setting is wonderfully atmospheric; a multimillion-dollar face-lift brought out the 1931 movie palace's charm.

performances begin at 9pm, until the last 2 weeks of the season, when performances begin at 8:30pm. A screen in front of each seat shows the libretto during
the performance. A gift shop has been added, as has additional parking. The
entire theater is wheelchair accessible. P.O. Box 2408, Santa Fe, NM 87504-2408. ℂ 800/
280-4654 or 505/986-5900. www.santafeopera.org. Tickets $20–$130; standing room $10; Open-
ing Night Gala $1,000–$2,500. Backstage tours July–Aug Mon–Sat at noon; $5 adults, free for
children ages 5–17.

ORCHESTRAL & CHAMBER MUSIC

Santa Fe Pro Musica Chamber Orchestra & Ensemble   This chamber
ensemble performs everything from Bach to Vivaldi to contemporary masters.
During Holy Week, the Santa Fe Pro Musica presents its annual Mozart and
Hayden Concert at the St. Francis Cathedral. Christmas brings candlelight
chamber ensemble concerts. Pro Musica's season runs September to May. 430
Manhattan, Suite 10, Santa Fe, NM 87501. ℂ 505/988-4640. www.santafepromusica.com. Tickets $15–$50.

Santa Fe Symphony Orchestra and Chorus   This 60-piece professional
symphony orchestra has grown rapidly in stature since its founding in 1984.
Matinee and evening performances of classical and popular works are presented
in a subscription series at the Lensic Performing Arts Center from October to
May. There's a pre-concert lecture before each performance. During the spring,
the orchestra presents music festivals (call for details). P.O. Box 9692, Santa Fe, NM
87504. ℂ 800/480-1319 or 505/983-1414. www.sf-symphony.org. Tickets $15–$48 (5 seating
categories).

Serenata of Santa Fe   This professional chamber-music group specializes in
bringing lesser-known works of the masters to the concert stage. Concerts are
presented September to May. Call for location, dates, and details. P.O. Box 8410,
Santa Fe, NM 87504. ℂ 505/989-7988. Tickets $12 general admission, $15–$20 reserved seats.

MUSIC FESTIVALS & CONCERT SERIES

Santa Fe Chamber Music Festival ★★   An extraordinary group of international artists comes to Santa Fe every summer for this festival. Its season runs
mid-July to mid-August and is held in the St. Francis Auditorium and the Lensic
Performing Arts Center. Performances are Monday, Tuesday, Thursday, and Friday at 8pm; Saturday at various evening times; and Sunday at 6pm. Open
rehearsals, youth concerts, and pre-concert lectures are free to the public. 239
Johnson St., Suite B (P.O. Box 2227), Santa Fe, NM 87504. ℂ 505/983-2075 or 505/982-1890 for
box office (after June 22). www.sfcmf.org. Tickets $15–$40.

Santa Fe Concert Association   Founded in 1937, this oldest musical organization in northern New Mexico has a September-to-May season that includes
approximately 17 annual events. Among them are a "Great Performances" series
and an "Adventures" series, both featuring renowned instrumental and vocal
soloists and chamber ensembles. The association also hosts special holiday concerts
around Christmas. Performances are held at the Lensic Performing Arts Center
and the St. Francis Auditorium; tickets are available at the Lensic box office
(ℂ 505/988-1234) and at ℂ 800/905-3315 (www.tickets.com) or 505/984-
8759. 210 E. Marcy St. (P.O. Box 4626, Santa Fe, NM 87502), Santa Fe, NM 87501. Tickets $16–$75.

THEATER COMPANIES

Greer Garson Theater Center   In this graceful, intimate theater, the College
of Santa Fe's Performing Arts Department produces four plays annually, with six
presentations of each, given between October and May. Usually, the season

consists of a comedy, a drama, a musical, and a classic. The college also sponsors studio productions and various contemporary music concerts. College of Santa Fe, 1600 St. Michael's Dr., Santa Fe, NM 87505. (C) 505/473-6511. www.csf.edu. Tickets $8–$17 adults, $5 students.

Santa Fe Playhouse   Founded in the 1920s, this is the oldest extant theater group in New Mexico. Still performing in a historic adobe theater in the Barrio de Analco, it attracts thousands for its dramas, avant-garde theater, and musical comedy. Its popular one-act melodramas call on the public to boo the sneering villain and swoon for the damsel in distress. 142 E. de Vargas St., Santa Fe, NM 87501. (C) 505/988-4262. www.santafeplayhouse.org. Tickets "Pay What You Wish"–$20, depending on the show.

Santa Fe Stages ★★   International theater and dance troupes began coming to Santa Fe in 1994, with the founding of this theater. Year-round performances are presented at the Firestone Plaza and the Lensic Performing Arts Center. In recent years, the company has hosted such distinguished performances as the Tony Award–wining play *Copenhagen* and the Paul Taylor Dance Company. 422 N. W. San Francisco St., Santa Fe, NM 87501. (C) 505/982-6683. www.santafestages.org. Tickets $15–$52.

Theater Grottesco ★ *Finds*   This troupe combines the best of comedy, drama, and dance in its original productions performed each spring and summer in a renovated space at the Center for Contemporary Arts. Expect to be romanced, shocked, intellectually stimulated, and, above all, struck silly with laughter. Look for upcoming winter shows as well. 551 W. Cordova Rd. #8400, Santa Fe, NM 87505. (C) 505/474-8400. www.theatergrottesco.org. Tickets $7–$20.

Theaterwork Studio ★   A critic for the *Santa Fe New Mexican* called Theaterwork's performance of Chekhov's *Uncle Vanya* "the most rewarding experience I have yet had at a Santa Fe theater." That high praise is well deserved by this community theater that goes out of its way to present refreshing, at times risky, plays. In an intimate theater on the south end of town, Theaterwork offers seven main-stage productions a year, a broad variety including new plays and classics by regional and national playwrights. 1336 Rufina Circle (mail: P.O. Box 842, Santa Fe, NM 87504-0842). (C) 505/471-1799. www.theaterwork.org. Tickets $10–$15. Call for performance times.

DANCE COMPANIES

María Benitez Teatro Flamenco ★★ *Finds*   You won't want to miss this cultural treat. True flamenco is one of the most thrilling of dance forms, displaying the inner spirit and verve of the gypsies of Spanish Andalusia, and María Benitez, trained in Spain, is a fabulous performer. The Benitez Company's "Estampa Flamenca" summer series is performed nightly except Tuesday from late June to early September. The María Benitez Theater at the Radisson Hotel is modern and showy, and yet intimate enough that you're immersed in the art. Institute for Spanish Arts, P.O. Box 8418, Santa Fe, NM 87504-8418. For tickets call (C) 888/435-2636, or the box office (June 16–Sept 3) (C) 505/982-1237. www.mariabenitez.com. Tickets $18–$42.

MAJOR CONCERT HALLS & ALL-PURPOSE AUDITORIUMS

Center for Contemporary Arts and Cinematheque   CCA presents the work of internationally, nationally, and regionally known contemporary artists in art exhibitions, dance, new music concerts, poetry readings, performance-art events, theater, and video screenings. It screens films from around the world nightly, with special series presented regularly. CCA's galleries are open daily noon to 7pm. 1050 Old Pecos Trail. ℂ **505/982-1338.** www.ccasantafe.org. Film tickets $7.50. Art exhibitions are free; performances range broadly in price.

St. Francis Auditorium This atmospheric music hall, patterned after the interiors of traditional Hispanic mission churches, is noted for its excellent acoustics. The hall hosts a wide variety of musical events, including the Santa Fe Chamber Music Festival in July and August. Museum of Fine Arts, Lincoln and Palace aves. ℂ **505/476-5072.** Ticket prices vary; see above for specific performing-arts companies.

Sweeney Convention Center Santa Fe's largest indoor arena hosts a wide variety of trade expositions and other events during the year. The Berkshire Choral visits every year in May. 201 W. Marcy St. ℂ **800/777-2489** or 505/955-6200. Tickets $10–$30, depending on seating and performances. Tickets are never sold at Sweeney Convention Center; event sponsors handle ticket sales.

THE CLUB & MUSIC SCENE

In addition to the clubs and bars listed below, numerous hotel bars and lounges feature some type of entertainment (see "Where to Stay," earlier in this chapter).

COUNTRY, JAZZ & LATIN

Cowgirl Hall of Fame It's difficult to categorize what goes on in this bar and restaurant, but there's live entertainment nightly. Some nights it's blues guitar, other nights it's folk music; you might also find "progressive rock," comedy, or cowboy poetry. In the summer, this is a great place to sit under the stars and listen to music. 319 S. Guadalupe St. ℂ **505/982-2565.** No cover for music Sun, Mon, and Wed. Tues and Thurs–Sat $3 cover. Special performances $10.

Eldorado Hotel In a grand lobby-lounge full of fine art, classical guitarists and pianists perform nightly. 309 W. San Francisco St. ℂ **505/988-4455.**

El Farol This original neighborhood bar of the Canyon Road artists' quarter (its name means "the lantern") is the place to head for local ambience. Its low ceilings and dark brown walls are home to Santa Fe's largest and most unusual selection of tapas. Jazz, swing, folk, and ethnic musicians—some of national note—perform most nights. 808 Canyon Rd. ℂ **505/983-9912.** Cover $7.

La Fiesta Lounge 🟡 Set in the notable La Fonda hotel on the plaza, this nightclub offers excellent country bands on weekends, with old- and new-timers two-stepping across the floor. This lively lobby bar offers cocktails, an appetizer menu, and live entertainment nightly. It's a great authentic Santa Fe spot. La Fonda Hotel, 110 E. San Francisco St. ℂ **505/982-5511.**

Rodeo Nites A real locals' spot, this club offers dancing to a variety of types of music, including New Mexican, Mexican, and, on weekends, country. Open Wednesday through Sunday. 2911 Cerrillos Rd. ℂ **505/473-4138.** Cover varies, averaging $6.

ROCK & DISCO

Catamount Bar and Grille The post-college crowd hangs out at this bar, where there's live rock and blues music on weekends. Food is served until midnight, and there is also a billiards room. 125 E. Water St. ℂ **505/988-7222.**

Paramount Lounge and Night Club This hip nightspot presents an ambitious array of entertainment—from live music to comedy to weekly DJ dance nights. "Trash Disco" on Wednesday nights (a blend of disco hits from the '70s and more contemporary "house" music) is especially popular and always draws an eclectic crowd. On other nights, the dance floor transforms into a listening room for live music; recent performances included J. J. Cale and Buckwheat Zydeco.

In the back of the building you'll find Bar B, a much smaller room with more of an intimate, martini-lounge atmosphere. Along with a happy hour Monday to Friday, weekly live jazz, and changing art shows, Bar B hosts many musical acts—often "unplugged" singer-songwriters.

The **Candyman** (© 505/983-5906) and the **CD Café** (© 505/986-0735) sell tickets for Paramount Lounge events. 331 Sandoval St. © 505/982-8999. Cover $5 for dance nights; call for music performances.

THE BAR SCENE

The Dragon Room ⭐ A number of years ago, *International Newsweek* named the Dragon Room at The Pink Adobe (see "Where to Dine" earlier in this chapter) one of the top 20 bars in the world. The reason is its spirited but comfortable ambience, which draws students, artists, politicians, and even an occasional celebrity. The decor theme is dragons, which you'll find carved on the front doors as well as hanging from the ceiling, all within low-lit, aged elegance akin to The Pink Adobe's interior. Live trees also grow through the roof. In addition to the tempting lunch and bar menu, there's always a complimentary bowl of popcorn close at hand. 406 Old Santa Fe Trail. © 505/983-7712.

El Paseo Bar and Grill You can almost always catch live music at this casual, unpretentious place (yet it's not a "sports bar"). The crowd here is somewhat younger than at most other downtown establishments, and on certain nights, the bar is completely packed. In addition to the open-mike night on Tuesdays, a variety of local bands play here regularly—cranking out many types of music, from blues to rock to jazz to bluegrass. 208 Galisteo St. © 505/992-2848. Cover $3–$5 weekends.

Evangelo's A popular downtown hangout, this bar can get raucous at times. It's an interesting place, with tropical decor and a mahogany bar. More than 60 varieties of imported beer are available, and pool tables are an added attraction. On Friday and Saturday nights starting at 9pm and Wednesdays at 7:30pm, live bands play (jazz, rock, or reggae). Evangelo's is extremely popular with the local crowd. Open Monday to Saturday noon to 1:30am and Sundays until midnight. 200 W. San Francisco St. © 505/982-9014. Cover for special performances only.

Swig ⭐ *Finds* Santa Fe's most happening club stirs a splash of '60s retro in with a good shot of contemporary chic. The result? A smooth sip of fun. Catering to a broad clientele, this martini bar serves classic and cutting-edge drinks along with delectable small plates of Asian food. The lounge serves until 11pm on weekdays and midnight on weekends, making it one of the few Santa Fe spots for late-night food. Open Tuesday through Saturday from 5pm to 2am. 135 W. Palace Ave., level 3. © 505/955-0400.

Vanessie of Santa Fe ⭐ This is Santa Fe's most popular piano bar. The talented Doug Montgomery and Charles Tichenor have a loyal local following. Their repertoire ranges from Bach to Billy Joel, Gershwin to Barry Manilow. They play nightly from 8pm until closing, which could be anywhere from midnight to 2am. There's an extra microphone, so if you're daring (or drunk), you can stand up and accompany the piano and vocals (though this is *not* a karaoke scene). National celebrities have even joined in—including Harry Connick, Jr. Vanessie's offers a great bar menu. 434 W. San Francisco St. © 505/982-9966.

10 Touring the Pueblos Around Santa Fe

Of the eight northern pueblos, Tesuque, Pojoaque, Nambe, San Ildefonso, San Juan, and Santa Clara are within about 30 miles of Santa Fe. Picuris (San Lorenzo) is on the High Road to Taos (see "Taking the High Road to Taos," later in this chapter), and Taos Pueblo is just outside the town of Taos (p. 233).

The six pueblos described in this section can easily be visited in a single day's round-trip from Santa Fe, though I suggest visiting just the two that really give a feel of the ancient lifestyle: San Ildefonso, with its broad plaza, and San Juan, including its arts cooperative. In an easy day trip from Santa Fe you can take in both, with some delicious New Mexican food in Española en route. If you're in the area at a time when you can catch certain rituals, that's when you should see some of the other pueblos.

TESUQUE PUEBLO

Tesuque (te-*soo*-keh) **Pueblo** is located about 9 miles north of Santa Fe on US 84/285. You will know that you are approaching the pueblo when you see a large store near the highway. If you're driving north and you get to the unusual Camel Rock and a large roadside casino, you've missed the pueblo entrance.

The 400 pueblo dwellers at Tesuque are faithful to their traditional religion, rituals, and ceremonies. Excavations confirm that a pueblo has existed here at least since the year A.D. 1200; accordingly, this pueblo is now on the National Register of Historic Places. When you come to the welcome sign at the pueblo, turn right, go a block, and park on the right. You'll see the plaza off to the left. There's not a lot to see; in recent years renovation has brought a new look to some of the homes around it. There's a big open area where dances are held, and the **San Diego Church,** completed in 2004 on the site of an 1888 structure that burned down recently. It's the fifth church on the pueblo's plaza since 1641. Visitors are asked to remain in this area.

Some Tesuque women are skilled potters; Ignacia Duran's black-and-white and red micaceous pottery and Teresa Tapia's miniatures and pots with animal figures are especially noteworthy. You'll find many crafts at a gallery on the plaza's southeast corner. The **San Diego Feast Day,** which may feature harvest, buffalo, deer, flag, or Comanche dances, is November 12.

The Tesuque Pueblo address is Route 5, Box 360T, Santa Fe, NM 87501 (© **505/983-2667**). Admission to the pueblo is free; however, there is a $20 charge for use of still cameras; special permission is required for movie cameras, sketching, and painting. The pueblo is open daily 9am to 5pm. **Camel Rock**

Pueblo Etiquette

When you visit pueblos, it is important to observe certain rules of etiquette. These are personal dwellings and/or important historic sites and must be respected as such. Don't climb on the buildings or peek into doors or windows. Don't enter sacred grounds, such as cemeteries and kivas. If you attend a dance or ceremony, remain silent while it is taking place and refrain from applause when it's over. Many pueblos prohibit photography or sketches; others require you to pay a fee for a permit. If you don't respect the privacy of the Native Americans who live at the pueblo, you'll be asked to leave.

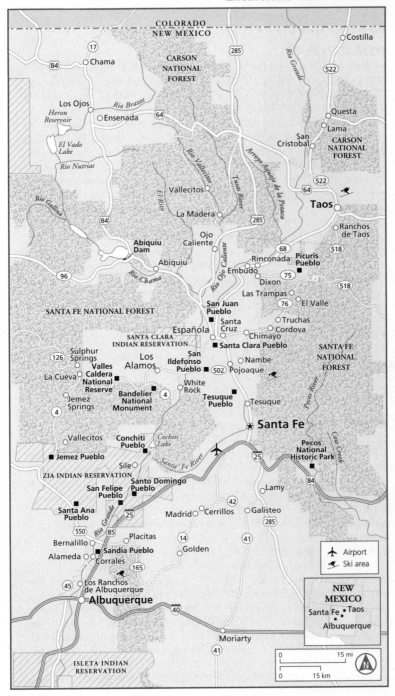

Excursions from Santa Fe

Casino (© 505/984-8414) is open Sunday to Wednesday 8am to 4am, Thursday to Saturday 24 hours; it has a snack bar on the premises.

POJOAQUE PUEBLO

About 6 miles north of Tesuque Pueblo on US 84/285, at the junction of NM 502, **Pojoaque** (Po-*hwa*-keh) **Pueblo** provides a roadside peek into Pueblo arts. Though small (pop. 200) and without a definable village (more modern dwellings exist now), Pojoaque is important as a center for traveler services; in fact, Pojoaque, in its Tewa form, means "water-drinking place." The historical accounts of the Pojoaque people are sketchy, but we do know that in 1890, smallpox took its toll on the Pojoaque population, forcing most of the pueblo residents to abandon their village. Since the 1930s, the population has gradually increased, and in 1990, a war chief and two war captains were appointed. Today, visitors won't find much to look at, but the **Poeh Cultural Center and Museum,** on US 84/285, operated by the pueblo, features a museum, a cultural center, and artists' studios. It's situated within a complex of adobe buildings, including the three-story Sun Tower. There are frequent artist demonstrations, exhibitions, and, in the warmer months, traditional ceremonial dances. Indigenous pottery, embroidery, silverwork, and beadwork are available for sale at the Pojoaque Pueblo Visitor Center nearby.

If you leave US 84/285 and travel on the frontage road back to where the pueblo actually was, you'll encounter lovely orchards and alfalfa fields backed by desert and mountains. A modern community center is located near the site of the old pueblo and church. On December 12, the annual feast day of **Our Lady of Guadalupe** features a buffalo dance.

The pueblo's address is Rt. 11, Box 71, Santa Fe, NM 87506 (© **505/455-2278**). The pueblo is open daily during daylight hours. The Poeh Center is at 78 Cities of Gold Rd. (© **505/455-3334**). Admission is free. Open daily 8am to 5pm. Sketching, cameras, and video cameras are prohibited.

NAMBE PUEBLO

On US 84/285, continue north from Pojoaque about 3 miles until you come to NM 503; turn right, and travel until you see the Bureau of Reclamation sign for Nambe Falls; turn right on NP 101. Approximately 2 miles farther is **Nambe** ("mound of earth in the corner"), a 700-year-old Tewa-speaking pueblo (pop. 450), with a solar-powered tribal headquarters, at the foot of the Sangre de Cristo range. Only a few original pueblo buildings remain, including a large round kiva, used today in ceremonies. Pueblo artisans make woven belts, beadwork, and brown micaceous pottery. One of my favorite reasons for visiting this pueblo is to see the small herd of bison that roam on 179 acres set aside for them.

Nambe Falls makes a stunning three-tier drop through a cleft in a rock face about 4 miles beyond the pueblo. You can reach the falls via a 15-minute hike on a rocky, clearly marked path that leaves from the picnic area. A recreational site at the reservoir offers fishing, boating (non-motor boats only), hiking, camping, and picnicking. The **Waterfall Dances** on July 4 and the **Saint Francis of Assisi Feast Day** on October 4, which has buffalo and deer dances, are observed at the pueblo. Dry weather has caused cancellations; before setting out, call the pueblo.

The address is Route 1, Box 117BB, Santa Fe, NM 87501 (© **505/455-2036,** or 505/455-2304 for the Ranger Station). Admission to the pueblo is free, but there is a $10 charge for still cameras, $20 for movie cameras, and $25 for sketching. The pueblo is open daily 8am to 5pm. The recreational site is open in March 7am to 6pm, in April and May 7am to 8pm, in June to August 6am to 8pm, and in September and October 7am to 7pm.

SAN ILDEFONSO PUEBLO 😽😽

Pox Oge, as **San Ildefonsos Pueblo** is called in its own Tewa language, means "place where the water cuts down through," possibly because of the way the Rio Grande cuts through the mountains nearby. Turn left on NM 502 at Pojoaque, and drive about 6 miles to the turnoff. This pueblo has a broad, dusty plaza, with a kiva on one side, ancient dwellings on the other, and a church at the far end. It's nationally famous for its matte-finish, black-on-black pottery, developed by tribeswoman María Martinez in the 1920s. One of the most visited pueblos in northern New Mexico, San Ildefonso attracts more than 20,000 visitors a year.

The San Ildefonsos could best be described as rebellious because this was one of the last pueblos to succumb to the reconquest spearheaded by Don Diego de Vargas in 1692. Within view of the pueblo is the volcanic Black Mesa, a symbol of the San Ildefonsos people's strength. Through the years, each time San Ildefonso felt itself threatened by enemy forces, the residents, along with members of other pueblos, would hide out up on the butte, returning to the valley only when starvation set in. Today, a visit to the pueblo is valuable mainly in order to see or buy rich black pottery. A few shops surround the plaza, and the **San Ildefonso Pueblo Museum** is tucked away in the governor's office beyond the plaza. I especially recommend visiting during ceremonial days. **San Ildefonso Feast Day,** on January 23, features the buffalo and Comanche dances in alternate years. **Corn dances,** held in late August or early September, commemorate a basic element in pueblo life, the importance of fertility in all creatures and plants.

The pueblo has a 4½-acre fishing lake that is surrounded by *bosque,* open April to October. Picnicking is encouraged; look at the sites before you decide on one because some are nicer than others. Camping is not allowed.

The pueblo's address is Route 5, Box 315A, Santa Fe, NM 87506 (© **505/ 455-3549**). Admission is $3 per car. The charge for using a still camera is $10; you'll pay $20 to use a video camera and $25 for sketching. If you plan to fish, the charge is $10 for adults and $8 for seniors and children under 12, but you'll want to call to be sure the lake is open. In summer, the pueblo is open weekdays 8am to 5pm; call for weekend hours. In the winter, it is open Monday to Friday 8am to 4:30pm. It's closed for major holidays and tribal events.

SAN JUAN PUEBLO 😽

If you continue north on US 84/285, you will reach **San Juan Pueblo** via NM 74, a mile off NM 68, about 4 miles north of Española.

The largest (pop. 1,950) of the Tewa-speaking pueblos and headquarters of the Eight Northern Indian Pueblos Council, San Juan is located on the east side of the Rio Grande—opposite the 1598 site of San Gabriel, the first Spanish settlement west of the Mississippi River and the first capital of New Spain. In 1598, the Spanish, impressed with the openness and helpfulness of the people of San Juan, decided to establish a capital there (it was moved to Santa Fe 10 years later), making San Juan Pueblo the first to be subjected to Spanish colonization. The Indians were generous, providing food, clothing, shelter, and fuel—they even helped sustain the settlement when its leader Conquistador Juan de Oñate became preoccupied with his search for gold and neglected the needs of his people. Unfortunately, the Spanish subjugation of the Indians left them virtual slaves, forced to provide the Spanish with corn, venison, cloth, and labor. They were compelled to participate in Spanish religious ceremonies and to abandon their own religious practices. Indian ceremonies were not allowed; those caught participating in them were punished. In 1676, several Indians were accused of sorcery and jailed in Santa Fe. Later they were led to the plaza and flogged or hanged. This despicable incident became a turning point in Indian–Spanish relations, generating an overwhelming feeling of rage in the Indian community. One of the accused, a San Juan Pueblo Indian named Po'Pay, became a leader in the Great Pueblo Revolt, which led to freedom from Spanish rule for 12 years.

The past and present cohabit here. Though many of the tribe members are Catholics, most of the San Juan tribe still practices traditional religious rituals. Thus, two rectangular kivas flank the church in the main plaza, and *caciques* (pueblo priests) share power with civil authorities. The annual **San Juan Fiesta** is held June 23 and 24; it features buffalo and Comanche dances. Another annual ceremony is the **turtle dance** on December 26. The **Matachine dance,** performed here Christmas day, vividly depicts the subjugation of the Native Americans by the Catholic Spaniards.

The address of the pueblo is P.O. Box 1099, San Juan Pueblo, NM 87566 (© **505/852-4400** or 505/852-4210). Admission is free. Photography or sketching may be allowed with prior permission from the governor's office. For information, call the number above. The charge for fishing is $8 for adults and $5 for children and seniors. The pueblo is open daily during daylight hours.

The **Eight Northern Indian Pueblos Council** (© **505/852-4265**) is a sort of chamber of commerce and social-service agency.

A crafts shop, **Oke Oweenge Arts and Crafts Cooperative** (© **505/852-2372**), specializes in local wares. This is a fine place to seek out San Juan's distinctive red pottery, a lustrous ceramic incised with traditional geometric symbols. Also displayed for sale are seed, turquoise, and silver jewelry; wood and stone carvings; indigenous clothing and weavings; embroidery; and paintings. Artisans often work on the premises, allowing visitors to watch. The co-op is open Monday through Saturday 9am to 4:30pm in winter, until 5pm in summer (but is closed San Juan Feast Day, June 24). **Sunrise Crafts,** another crafts shop, is located to the right of the co-op. There, you'll find one-of-a-kind handcrafted pipes, beadwork, and burned and painted gourds.

Fishing and picnicking are encouraged at the **San Juan Tribal Lakes. Ohkay Casino** (© **505/747-1668**) offers table games and slot machines, as well as live music nightly Tuesday through Saturday. It's open daily, 24 hours.

SANTA CLARA PUEBLO

Close to Española (on NM 5), **Santa Clara Pueblo,** with a population of about 1,800, is one of the largest pueblos, and it's the one most special to me. I've spent a good bit of time here, writing about the Santa Clara people. You'll see the village sprawling across the river basin near the beautiful Black Mesa, rows of tract homes surrounding an adobe central area. Although it's in an incredible setting, the pueblo itself is not much to see; however, a trip through it will give you a real feel for the contemporary lives of these people. Though stories vary, the Santa Clarans teach their children that their ancestors once lived in cliffside dwellings named Puye and migrated down to the river bottom in the 13th century. This pueblo is noted for its language program. Artisan/elders work with children to teach them their native Tewa language, on the brink of extinction because so many now speak English. This pueblo is also the home of noted potter Nancy Youngblood, who comes from a long line of famous potters and now does alluring contemporary work.

Follow the main route to the old village, where you come to the visitor center, also known as the neighborhood center. There you can get directions to small shops that sell distinctive black, incised Santa Clara pottery, red burnished pottery, baskets, and other crafts. One stunning sight here is the cemetery. Stop on the west side of the church and look over the 4-foot wall. It's a primitive site, with plain wooden crosses and some graves adorned with plastic flowers.

There are corn and harvest dances on **Santa Clara Feast Day** (Aug 12); information on other special days (including the corn or harvest dances, as well as children's dances) can be obtained from the pueblo office.

The famed **Puye Cliff Dwellings** (see below) are on the Santa Clara reservation.

The pueblo's address is P.O. Box 580, Española, NM 87532 (© **505/753-7326**). Admission is free. The charge for still cameras is $5; video cameras and sketching are not allowed. The pueblo is open daily 9am to 4pm; the visitor center is open Monday to Friday 8am to 4:30pm.

PUYE CLIFF DWELLINGS ★★

Well worth visiting, the Puye Cliff Dwellings offer a view of centuries of culture so well preserved you can almost hear ancient life clamoring around you. Unfortunately, recent fires devastated the area, so Santa Clara has closed the ruins and recreation area indefinitely. Call before setting out for opening times and admissions information (© **505/753-7326**).

11 A Side Trip to Pecos National Historical Park ★★

About 15 miles east of Santa Fe, I-25 meanders through **Glorieta Pass,** site of an important Civil War skirmish. In March 1862, volunteers from Colorado and New Mexico, along with Fort Union regulars, defeated a Confederate force marching on Santa Fe, thereby turning the tide of Southern encroachment in the West.

Follow NM 50 east to **Pecos** for about 7 miles. This quaint town, well off the beaten track since the interstate was constructed, is the site of a noted **Benedictine monastery.** About 26 miles north of here on NM 63 is the village of **Cowles,** gateway to the natural wonderland of the **Pecos Wilderness.** There are many camping, picnicking, and fishing locales en route.

Pecos National Historical Park (© **505/757-6414;** www.nps.gov/peco), about 2 miles south of the town of Pecos off NM 63, contains the ruins of a 15th-century pueblo and 17th- and 18th-century missions that jut up spectacularly from a high meadow. Coronado mentioned Pecos Pueblo in 1540: "It is feared through the land," he wrote. The approximately 2,000 Native Americans here farmed in irrigated fields and hunted wild game. Their pueblo had 660 rooms and many kivas. By 1620, Franciscan monks had established a church and convent. Military and natural disasters took their toll on the pueblo, and in 1838, the 20 surviving Pecos went to live with relatives at the Jemez Pueblo.

The **E. E. Fogelson Visitor Center** tells the history of the Pecos people in a well-done, chronologically organized exhibit, complete with dioramas. A 1.5-mile loop trail begins at the center and continues through Pecos Pueblo and the **Misión de Nuestra Señora de Los Angeles de Porciuncula** (as the church was formerly called). This excavated structure—170 feet long and 90 feet wide at the transept—was once the most magnificent church north of Mexico City.

Pecos National Historical Park is open Memorial Day to Labor Day, daily 8am to 6pm; the rest of the year, daily 8am to 5pm. It's closed January 1 and December 25. Admission is $3 per person over age 16.

12 Los Alamos & the Ancient Cliff Dwellings of Bandelier National Monument

Pueblo tribes lived in the rugged Los Alamos area for well over 1,000 years, and an exclusive boys' school operated atop the 7,300-foot plateau from 1918 to 1943. Then, the **Los Alamos National Laboratory** was established here in secrecy, code-named Site Y of the Manhattan Project, the hush-hush wartime program that developed the world's first atomic bombs.

Project director J. Robert Oppenheimer, later succeeded by Norris E. Bradbury, worked along with thousands of scientists, engineers, and technicians in research, development, and production of those early weapons. Today, more than 10,000 people work at the Los Alamos National Laboratory, making it the largest employer in northern New Mexico. Operated from the beginning by the University of California, currently under a contract through the U.S. Department of Energy, its 2,200 individual facilities and 47 separate technical areas occupy 43 square miles of mesa-top land.

Today the lab is one of the world's foremost scientific institutions. While primarily focused on nuclear weapons research—the Trident and Minuteman strategic warheads were designed here, for example—it has many other interdisciplinary research programs, including international nuclear safeguards and nonproliferation, space, and atmospheric studies; supercomputing; theoretical physics; biomedical and materials science; and environmental restoration.

Current plans call on Los Alamos National Laboratory, in 2007, to begin building a limited number of replacement plutonium pits for use in the enduring U.S. nuclear weapons stockpile. The lab has the only plutonium-processing facility in the United States that is capable of producing those components.

ORIENTATION & USEFUL INFORMATION

Los Alamos is located about 35 miles west of Santa Fe and about 65 miles southwest of Taos. From Santa Fe, take US 84/285 north approximately 16 miles to the Pojoaque junction, then turn west on NM 502. Driving time is only about 50 minutes.

Los Alamos is a town of 18,000, spread over the colorful, fingerlike mesas of the Pajarito Plateau, between the Jemez Mountains and the Rio Grande Valley. As NM 502 enters Los Alamos from Santa Fe, it follows Trinity Drive, where accommodations, restaurants, and other services are located. Central Avenue parallels Trinity Drive and has restaurants, galleries, and shops, as well as the **Los Alamos Historical Museum** (1921 Juniper St.; *©* **505/662-4493;** free) and the **Bradbury Science Museum** (15th St. and Central Ave.; *©* **505/667-4444;** free). In the spring of 2000, the town was evacuated due to a forest fire that destroyed 400 families' homes. Though no lives were lost, the appearance of Los Alamos and particularly the forest surrounding it—47,000 acres of which burned—were forever changed.

The **Los Alamos Chamber of Commerce,** P.O. Box 460, Los Alamos, NM 87544 (*©* **505/662-8105;** fax 505/662-8399), runs a visitor center that is open Monday to Friday 9am to 5pm, Saturday 9am to 4pm, and Sunday 10am to 3pm. It's located at 109 Central Park Square (across from the Bradbury Science Museum).

EVENTS

The Los Alamos events schedule includes the **Sports Skiesta** in mid-March; **arts-and-crafts fairs** in May, August, and November; a **county fair, rodeo, and arts festival** in August; and a **triathlon** in August/September.

WHAT TO SEE & DO

Aside from the sights described below, Los Alamos offers the **Pajarito Mountain ski area,** Camp May Road (P.O. Box 155), Los Alamos, NM 87544 (✆ **505/662-5725**), with five chairlifts; it's only open Friday through Sunday and federal holidays. It's an outstanding ski area that rarely gets crowded; many trails are steep and have moguls. Los Alamos also offers the **Los Alamos Golf Course,** 4250 Diamond Dr. (✆ **505/662-8139**), at the edge of town, where greens fees are around $20; and the **Larry R. Walkup Aquatic Center,** 2760 Canyon Rd. (✆ **505/662-8170**), the highest-altitude indoor Olympic-size swimming pool in the United States. Not far from downtown is an outdoor ice-skating rink, with a snack bar and skate rentals, open Thanksgiving to late February (✆ **505/662-4500**). It's located at 4475 West Rd. (take Trinity Dr. to Diamond St., turn left and watch for the sign on your right). There are no outstanding restaurants in Los Alamos, but if you get hungry, you can stop at the **Blue Window,** 800 Trinity Dr. (✆ **505/662-6305**), a country-style restaurant serving pasta, sandwiches, and salads, with a view of the Sangre de Cristo Mountains. The Chamber of Commerce has maps for self-guided historical walking tours, and you can find self-guided driving-tour tapes at stores and hotels around town.

The Art Center at Fuller Lodge
This is a public showcase for work by visual artists from the northern New Mexico region. Annual arts-and-crafts fairs are also held here in August and October. The gallery shop sells local crafts at good prices.

In the same building is the **Los Alamos Arts Council** (✆ 505/663-0477), a multidisciplinary organization that sponsors two art fairs (May and Nov), as well as evening and noontime cultural programs.

2132 Central Ave. ✆ 505/662-9331. www.artfulnm.org. Free admission. Mon–Sat 10am–4pm.

Black Hole (Finds)
This store/museum is an engineer's dream world, a creative photographer's heaven, and a Felix Unger nightmare. Owned and run by Edward Grothus, it's an old grocery store packed to the ceiling with the remains of the nuclear age, from Geiger counters to giant Waring blenders. If you go, be sure to visit with Grothus. He'll point out an A-frame building next door that he's christened the "First Church of High Technology," where he says a "critical mass" each Sunday. In this business for over 50 years, Grothus has been written about in *Wired* magazine and has supplied props for the movies *Silkwood, Earth II,* and *The Manhattan Project.*

4015 Arkansas. ✆ 505/662-5053. Free admission. Mon–Sat 10am–5pm.

Bradbury Science Museum ✦
This is a great place to get acquainted with what goes on at a weapons production facility after nuclear proliferation. Though the museum is run by Los Alamos National Laboratory, which definitely puts a positive spin on the business of producing weapons, it's a fascinating place to explore and includes more than 35 hands-on exhibits. Begin in the History Gallery, where you'll learn about the evolution of the site from the Los Alamos Ranch School days through the Manhattan Project to the present, including a 1939 letter from Albert Einstein to President Franklin D. Roosevelt, suggesting research into uranium as a new and important source of energy. Next, move into the Research and Technology Gallery, where you can see work that's been done on the Human Genome Project, including a computer map of human DNA. You can try out a laser and learn about the workings of a particle accelerator. Meanwhile, listen for announcement of the film *The Town That*

Never Was, an 18-minute presentation on this community that grew up shrouded in secrecy (shown in the auditorium). Further exploration will take you to the Defense Gallery, where you can test the heaviness of plutonium against that of other substances, see an actual 5-ton Little Boy nuclear bomb (like the one dropped on Hiroshima), and see firsthand how Los Alamos conducts worldwide surveillance of nuclear explosions. The museum has added a new exhibit on national defense. It presents issues related to nuclear weapons: why we have them, how they work, how scientists ensure that aging weapons will still work, what treaties govern them, and what environmental problem sites resulted from their production. It includes a 16-minute film, computer-based activities for visitors, and displays of bombs, a cruise missile, and warhead casings.

15th St. and Central Ave. ⓒ **505/667-4444.** Free admission. Tues–Fri 9am–5pm; Sat–Mon 1–5pm. Closed New Year's Day, Thanksgiving, and Christmas.

Los Alamos Historical Museum ⭐   Fuller Lodge, a massive vertical-log building built by John Gaw Meem in 1928, is well worth the visit. The log work is intricate and artistic, and the feel of the old place is warm and majestic. It once housed the dining and recreation hall for the Los Alamos Ranch School for boys and is now a National Historic Landmark. It is accessible to people with disabilities. Its current occupants include the museum office and research archives and The Art Center at Fuller Lodge (see above). The museum, located in the small log-and-stone building to the north of Fuller Lodge, depicts area history from prehistoric cliff dwellers to the present. Exhibits range from Native American artifacts to school memorabilia and an excellent Manhattan Project exhibit that offers a more realistic view of the devastation resulting from use of atomic bombs than is offered at the Bradbury Science Museum.

1921 Juniper St. ⓒ **505/662-4493.** Free admission. Summer Mon–Sat 9:30am–4:30pm, Sun 11am–5pm; winter Mon–Sat 10am–4pm, Sun 1–4pm. Closed Thanksgiving, Christmas, and Easter.

NEARBY

Bandelier National Monument ⭐⭐⭐   Less than 15 miles south of Los Alamos along NM 4, this National Park Service area contains stunningly preserved ruins of the ancient cliff-dwelling ancestral Puebloan culture within 46 square miles of canyon-and-mesa wilderness. The national monument is named after the archaeologist Adolph Bandelier, who explored here in the 1880s. During busy summer months, head out early; there can be a waiting line for parking.

After an orientation stop at the visitor center and museum to learn about the culture that flourished here between 1100 and 1550, most visitors follow a trail along Frijoles Creek to the principal ruins. The pueblo site, including an underground kiva, has been stabilized. The biggest thrill for most folks is climbing hardy ponderosa pine ladders to visit an alcove—140 feet above the canyon floor—that was once home to prehistoric people. Tours are self-guided or led by a National Park Service ranger. Be aware that dogs are not allowed on trails.

On summer nights, rangers offer campfire talks about the history, culture, and geology of the area. The guided night walks offered some summer evenings reveal a different, spooky aspect of the ruins and cave houses, outlined in the two-dimensional chiaroscuro of the thin light from the starry sky. During the day, nature programs are sometimes offered for adults and children. The small museum at the visitor center displays artifacts found in the area.

Elsewhere in the monument area, 70 miles of maintained trails lead to more tribal ruins, waterfalls, and wildlife habitats. A recent fire has decimated parts of this area, so periodic closings take place in order to allow the land to reforest.

The separate **Tsankawi** section, reached by an ancient 2-mile trail close to **White Rock,** has a large unexcavated ruin on a high mesa overlooking the Rio Grande Valley. The town of White Rock, about 10 miles southeast of Los Alamos on NM 4, offers spectacular panoramas of the river valley in the direction of Santa Fe; the **White Rock Overlook** is a great picnic spot. Within Bandelier, areas have been set aside for picnicking and camping.

While you're in the area, check out the **Valles Caldera National Preserve,** past Bandelier National Monument on NM 4, beginning about 15 miles from Los Alamos. The reserve is all that remains of a volcanic caldera created by a collapse after eruptions nearly a million years ago. When the mountain spewed ashes and dust as far away as Kansas and Nebraska, its underground magma chambers collapsed, forming this great valley—one of the largest volcanic calderas in the world. Lava domes that pushed up after the collapse obstruct a full view across the expanse, but the beauty of the place is still within grasp. Visitors have many guided options for exploring the preserve, from sleigh rides in winter to fly-fishing in summer. For more information check out www.vallescaldera.gov.

NM 4 (HCR 1, Box 1, Suite 15, Los Alamos, NM 87544-9701). (C) **505/672-3861,** ext 517. www.nps.gov/ band. Admission $10 per vehicle. Open daily during daylight hours. No pets allowed on trails. Closed New Year's Day and Christmas.

13 Taking the High Road to Taos (★(★

Unless you're in a hurry to get from Santa Fe to Taos, the High Road—also called the Mountain Road or the King's Road—is by far the most fascinating route between the two cities. It begins in lowlands of mystically formed pink and yellow stone, passing by apple and peach orchards and chile farms in the weaving village of **Chimayo.** Then it climbs toward the highlands to the village of **Cordova,** known for its woodcarvers, and higher still to **Truchas,** a renegade arts town where Hispanic traditions and ways of life continue much as they did a century ago. Though I've described this tour from south to north, the most scenic way to see it is from north to south, on your return from Taos.

CHIMAYO

About 28 miles north of Santa Fe on NM 76/285 is the historic weaving center of **Chimayo.** It's approximately 16 miles past the Pojoaque junction, at the junction of NM 520 and NM 76 via NM 503. In this small village, families still maintain the tradition of crafting hand-woven textiles initiated by their ancestors seven generations ago, in the early 1800s. The Ortegas are one such family, and both the **Ortega's Weaving Shop** ((C) **505/351-4215**) and **Galeria Ortega** ((C) **505/351-2288**), both at the corner of NM 520 and NM 76, are fine places to take a close look at this ancient craft. A more humble spot is **Trujillo Weavings** ((C) **505/351-4457**) on NM 76. If you're lucky enough to find the proprietors in, you might get a weaving history lesson. You can see an 80-year-old loom and a 100-year-old shuttle carved from apricot wood. The weavings you'll find are some of the best of the Rio Grande style, with rich patterns, many made from naturally dyed wool. Also on display are some fine Cordova woodcarvings.

One of the best places to shop in Chimayo, **Chimayo Trading and Mercantile** ((C) **505/351-4566**), on Highway 76, is a richly cluttered store carrying local arts and crafts as well as select imports. It has a good selection of kachinas and Hopi corn maidens, as well as specialty items such as elaborately beaded cow skulls. Look for George Zarolinski's "smoked porcelain."

Many people come to Chimayo to visit **El Santuario de Nuestro Señor de Esquipulas (The Shrine of Our Lord of Esquipulas)** ⚡⚡, better known simply as "El Santuario de Chimayo." Ascribed with miraculous powers of healing, this church has attracted thousands of pilgrims since its construction in 1814 to 1816. Up to 30,000 people participate in the annual Good Friday pilgrimage, many of them walking from as far away as Albuquerque.

Although only the earth in the anteroom beside the altar is presumed to have the gift of healing powers, the entire shrine radiates true serenity. A National Historic Landmark, the church has five beautiful *reredos* (panels of sacred paintings)—one behind the main altar and two on each side of the nave. Each year during the fourth weekend in July, the military exploits of the 9th-century Spanish saint Santiago are celebrated in a weekend fiesta, including the historic play **Los Moros y Los Cristianos** *(The Moors and the Christians)*.

A good place to stop for a quick bite, **Leona's Restaurante de Chimayo** (© **505/351-4569**) is right next door to the Santuario de Chimayo. Leona herself presides over this little taco and burrito stand with plastic tables inside and, during warm months, out. Leona has gained national fame for her flavored tortillas—such delicacies as raspberry and chocolate really are tasty. Burritos and soft tacos made with chicken, beef, or veggie-style with beans will definitely tide you over en route to Taos or Santa Fe. Open Thursday through Monday 11am to 5pm.

Nearby **Santa Cruz Lake** provides water for Chimayo Valley farms and also offers a recreation site for trout fishing and camping at the edge of the Pecos Wilderness. During busy summer months, trash might litter its shores. To reach the lake from Chimayo, drive 2 miles south on NM 520, then turn east on NM 503 and travel 4 miles.

WHERE TO STAY & DINE IN CHIMAYO

Casa Escondida ⚡   On the outskirts of Chimayo, this inn offers a lovely retreat and a good home base for exploring the Sangre de Cristo Mountains and their many soulful farming villages. This hacienda-feeling place has a cozy living room with a large kiva fireplace. Decor is simple and classic, with Mission-style furniture lending a colonial feel. The breakfast room is a sunny atrium with French doors that open out in summer to a grassy yard spotted with apricot trees. The rooms are varied; all of my favorites are within the main house. The Sun Room catches all that passionate northern New Mexico sun upon its red brick floors and on its private flagstone patio. It has an elegant feel and connects with a smaller room, so it's a good choice for families. The Vista is on the second story. Its dormer windows give it an oddly shaped roofline. It has a wrought-iron queen bed as well as a twin, and it opens out onto a large deck, offering spectacular sunset views. The casita adjacent to the main house has a kiva fireplace, a stove, and a minifridge, as well as nice meadow views.

Off County Road 0100 (P.O. Box 142), Chimayo, NM 87522. © **800/643-7201** or 505/351-4805. Fax 505/351-2575. www.casaescondida.com. 8 units. $85–$145 double. Rates include full breakfast. MC, V. Pets welcome for a small fee; prearrangement required. **Amenities:** Jacuzzi; in-room massage; laundry service.

Restaurante Rancho de Chimayo ⚡ NEW MEXICAN   For as long as I can remember, my family and many of my friends' families have scheduled trips into northern New Mexico to coincide with lunchtime or dinnertime at this fun restaurant. Located in an adobe home built by Hermenegildo Jaramillo in the 1880s, it is now run as a restaurant by his descendants. Unfortunately, the restaurant has become so famous that tour buses now stop here. However, the food has suffered only a little. In the warmer months, you can dine on the terraced patio. During winter, you'll be seated in one of a number of cozy rooms. The food is prepared from generations-old Jaramillo family recipes. You can't go wrong with the enchiladas, served layered, northern New Mexico style, rather than rolled. For variety you might want to try the *combinación picante* (carne adovada, tamale, enchilada, beans, and posole). Each plate comes with two *sopaipillas*. With a little honey, who needs dessert? The full bar serves delicious margaritas.

Couty Road 98 (P.O. Box 11), Chimayo, NM 87522. 📞 505/351-4444. Reservations recommended. Lunch $7.50–$13, dinner $10–$15. AE, DC, DISC, MC, V. Daily 11:30am–9pm; Sat–Sun breakfast 8:30–10:30am. Closed Mon Nov 1–Apr 30.

CORDOVA

Just as Chimayo is famous for its weaving, **Cordova,** about 7 miles east on NM 76, is noted for its woodcarvers. It's easy to whiz by this village, nestled below the High Road, but don't. Just a short way through this truly traditional northern New Mexico town is a gem: **The Castillo Gallery** ⭐ (📞 505/351-4067), a mile into the village of Cordova, carries moody and colorful acrylic paintings by Paula Castillo, as well as her found-art welded sculptures. It also carries the work of Terry Enseñat Mulert, whose contemporary woodcarvings are treasures of the high country. En route to the Castillo, you may want to stop in at two other local carvers' galleries. The first you'll come to is that of **Sabinita Lopez Ortiz;** the second belongs to her cousin, **Gloria Ortiz.** Both are descendants of the well-noted José Dolores Lopez. Carved from cedar wood and aspen, the works range from simple statues of saints *(santos)* to elaborate scenes of birds.

TRUCHAS

Robert Redford's 1988 movie *The Milagro Beanfield War* featured the town of **Truchas** (which means "trout"). A former Spanish colonial outpost built on top of an 8,000-foot mesa, 4 miles east of Cordova, it was chosen as the site for the film in part because traditional Hispanic culture is still very much in evidence. Subsistence farming is prevalent here. The scenery is spectacular: 13,101-foot Truchas Peak dominates one side of the mesa, and the broad Rio Grande Valley dominates the other.

Be sure to find your way into **The Cordovas' Handweaving Workshop** (📞 505/689-2437). Located in the center of town, this tiny shop is run by Harry Cordova, a fourth-generation weaver with a unique style. His works tend to be simpler than many Rio Grande weavings, utilizing mainly stripes in the designs.

Just down the road from the Cordovas' is **Hand Artes Gallery** (📞 800/689-2441 or 505/689-2443), a definite surprise in this remote region. Here you'll find an array of contemporary as well as representational art from noted regional artists. Look for Sheila Keeffe's worldly painted panels, Susan Christie's monoprints and subtly textured paintings, and Norbert Voelkel's colorful paintings.

About 6 miles east of Truchas on NM 76 is the small town of **Las Trampas,** noted for its **San José Church,** which, with its thick walls and elegant lines, might possibly be the most beautiful of all New Mexico churches built during the Spanish colonial period.

PICURIS (SAN LORENZO) PUEBLO

Near the regional education center of Peñasco, about 24 miles from Chimayo, near the intersection of NM 75 and NM 76, is **Picuris (San Lorenzo) Pueblo** (📞 505/587-2519). The 375 citizens of this 15,000-acre pueblo, native Tewa speakers, consider themselves a sovereign nation: Their forebears never made a treaty with any foreign country, including the U.S. Thus, they observe a traditional form of tribal council government. A few of the original mud-and-stone houses still stand, as does a lovely church. A striking aboveground ceremonial kiva called "the Roundhouse," built at least 700 years ago, and some historic excavated kivas and storerooms are located on a hill above the pueblo and are open to visitors. The **annual feast days** at San Lorenzo Church are August 9 and 10.

The people here are modern enough to have fully computerized their public showcase operations as Picuris Tribal Enterprises. Besides running the Hotel Santa Fe in the state capital, they own the **Picuris Pueblo Museum and Visitor's Center,** where weaving, beadwork, and distinctive reddish-brown clay cooking pottery are exhibited daily 9am to 6pm. Self-guided tours through the old village ruins begin at the museum and cost $5; the camera fee is $6; sketching and video camera fees are $25. There is also an information center, a crafts shop, and a restaurant. Fishing permits ($11 for adults, $8 for seniors, and $7 for children) are available, as are permits to camp ($8) at Tu-Tah Lake, which is stocked with trout.

About a mile east of Peñasco on NM 75 is **Vadito,** the former center for a conservative Catholic brotherhood, the Penitentes, early in the 20th century. You'll see a small adobe chapel on the left. Also watch for Penitente crosses scattered about the area, often on hilltops.

DIXON & EMBUDO

Taos is about 24 miles north of Peñasco via NM 518, but day-trippers from Santa Fe can loop back to the capital by taking NM 75 west from Picuris Pueblo. Dixon, approximately 12 miles west of Picuris, and its twin village Embudo, a mile farther on NM 68 at the Rio Grande, are home to many artists and craftspeople who exhibit their works during the annual **autumn show** sponsored by the Dixon Arts Association. If you get to Embudo at mealtime, stop in at **Embudo Station** (© **800/852-4707** or 505/852-4707), a restaurant right on the banks of the Rio Grande. From mid-April to October—the only time it's open—you can sit on the patio under giant cottonwoods and sip the restaurant's own microbrewed beer (try the green-chile ale, its most celebrated) and signature wines while watching the peaceful Rio flow by. The specialty here is Southwestern food, but you'll find other tantalizing tastes as well. Try the rainbow trout roasted on a cedar plank. The restaurant is generally open Tuesday to Sunday noon to 9pm, but call before making plans. It is especially known for its Jazz on Sunday, an affair that PBS once featured. For more taste of the local grape, you can follow signs to **La Chiripada Winery** (© **505/579-4437**), whose product is surprisingly good, especially to those who don't know that New Mexico has a long winemaking history. Local pottery is also sold in the tasting room. The winery is open Monday to Saturday 10am to 5pm, Sunday noon to 5pm.

Two more small villages lie in the Rio Grande Valley at 6-mile intervals south of Embudo on NM 68. **Velarde** is a fruit-growing center; in season, the road here is lined with stands selling fresh fruit or crimson chile ristras and wreaths of native plants. **Alcalde** is the site of Los Luceros, an early-17th-century home that is to be refurbished as an arts and history center. The unique **Dance of the Matachines,** a Moorish ritual brought from Spain, is performed here on holidays and feast days.

ESPAÑOLA

The commercial center of Española (pop. 7,000) no longer has the railroad that led to its establishment in the 1880s, but it may have New Mexico's greatest

Georgia O'Keeffe & New Mexico: A Desert Romance

In June 1917, during a short visit to the Southwest, the painter Georgia O'Keeffe (born 1887) visited New Mexico for the first time. She was immediately enchanted by the stark scenery; even after her return to the energy and chaos of New York City, her mind wandered frequently to New Mexico's arid land and undulating mesas. However, not until coaxed by the arts patron and "collector of people" Mabel Dodge Luhan 12 years later did O'Keeffe return to the multihued desert of her daydreams.

O'Keeffe was reportedly ill, both physically and emotionally, when she arrived in Santa Fe in April 1929. New Mexico seemed to soothe her spirit and heal her physical ailments almost magically. Two days after her arrival, Mabel Dodge Luhan persuaded O'Keeffe to move into her home in Taos. There, she would be free to paint and socialize as she liked.

In Taos, O'Keeffe began painting what would become some of her best-known canvases—close-ups of desert flowers and objects such as cow and horse skulls. "The color up there is different . . . the blue-green of the sage and the mountains, the wildflowers in bloom," O'Keeffe once said of Taos. "It's a different kind of color from any I've ever seen—there's nothing like that in north Texas or even in Colorado." Taos transformed not only her art, but her personality as well. She bought a car and learned to drive. Sometimes, on warm days, she ran naked through the sage fields. That August, a new, rejuvenated O'Keeffe rejoined her husband, photographer Alfred Stieglitz, in New York.

The artist returned to New Mexico year after year, spending time with Mabel Dodge Luhan as well as staying at the isolated Ghost Ranch. She drove through the countryside in her snappy Ford, stopping to paint in her favorite spots along the way. Until 1949, O'Keeffe always returned to New York in the fall. Three years after Stieglitz's death, though, she relocated permanently to New Mexico, spending each winter and spring in Abiquiu and each summer and fall at Ghost Ranch. Georgia O'Keeffe died in Santa Fe in 1986.

A great way to see Ghost Ranch is on a hike that climbs above the mystical area. Take US 84 north from Española about 36 miles to Ghost Ranch and follow the road to the Ghost Ranch office. The ranch is managed by the Presbyterian Church, and the staff will supply you with a primitive map for the **Kitchen Mesa** and **Chimney Rock** hikes.

concentration of **low riders.** These are late-model customized cars, so called because their suspension leaves them sitting quite close to the ground.

Sights of interest in Española include the **Bond House Museum** (© 505/747-8535), a Victorian-era adobe home that exhibits local history and art; and the **Santa Cruz Church,** built in 1733 and renovated in 1979, which houses many fine examples of Spanish colonial religious art. The **Convento,** built to resemble a colonial cathedral, on the Española Plaza (at the junction of NM 30 and US 84), houses a variety of shops, including a trading post and an antique gallery, as well as a display room for the Historical Society. Major events include the July **Fiesta de Oñate,** commemorating the valley's founding in 1596; the October **Tri-Cultural Art Festival** on the Northern New Mexico Community College campus; the weeklong **Summer Solstice** celebration staged in June by the nearby Ram Dass Puri ashram of the Sikhs (© **888/346-2420** or 505/367-1310); and **Peace Prayer Day,** an outdoor festival in mid-June—featuring art, music, food, guest speakers, and more—in the Jemez Mountains (© **877/707-3223**).

Complete information on Española and the vicinity can be obtained from the **Española Valley Chamber of Commerce,** 710 Paseo de Onate, Española, NM 87532 (© **505/753-2831**).

If you admire the work of Georgia O'Keeffe, try to plan a short trip to **Abiquiu,** a tiny town at a bend of the Rio Chama, 14 miles south of Ghost Ranch and 22 miles north of Española on US 84. When you see the surrounding terrain, it will be clear that this was the inspiration for many of her startling landscapes. **O'Keeffe's adobe home** (where she lived and painted) is open for public tours. However, a reservation must be made in advance; the minimum requested donation is $22 for a 1-hour tour. A number of tours are given each week—on Tuesday, Thursday, and Friday (Mar–Nov only)—and a limited number of people are accepted per tour. Visitors are not permitted to take pictures. Fortunately, O'Keeffe's home remains as it was when she lived there (until 1986). Call several months in advance for reservations (© **505/685-4539**).

WHERE TO STAY & DINE IN ESPAÑOLA

El Paragua NORTHERN NEW MEXICAN This Española restaurant is a great place to stop en route to Taos, though some Santa Feans make a special trip here. Every time I enter El Paragua (which means "the umbrella"), with its red tile floors and colorful Saltillo-tile trimmings, I feel as though I've stepped into Mexico. The restaurant opened in 1958 as a small taco stand owned by two brothers, and through the years it has flourished. It has received praise from many sources, including *Gourmet Magazine* and N. Scott Momaday, writing for the *New York Times.* You can't go wrong ordering the enchilada suprema, a chicken and cheese enchilada with onion and sour cream. Also on the menu are fajitas and a variety of seafood dishes and steaks, including the *churrasco Argentino.* Served at your table in a hot brazier, it's cooked in a green herb *salsa chimichurri.* There's a full bar from which you may want to try Don Luis's Italian coffee, made with a coffee-flavored liquor called Tuaca. For equally excellent but faster food, go next door to **El Parasol** and order a chicken taco—the best ever.

603 Santa Cruz Rd., Española (off the main drag; turn east at Long John Silver's). © **505/753-3211.** Reservations recommended. Main courses $9–$20. AE, DISC, MC, V. Daily 11am–9pm.

Rancho de San Juan   Located between Española and Ojo Caliente, this inn provides an authentic northern New Mexico desert experience with the comfort of a luxury hotel. It's the passion of architect and chef John Johnson, responsible for the design and cuisine, and interior designer David Heath, responsible for the elegant interiors. The original part of the inn comprises four rooms around a central courtyard. Thirteen additional casitas have been added in the outlying hills. The original rooms are a bit small but very elegant, with European antiques and spectacular views of desert landscapes and distant, snow-capped peaks. The Kiva suite is the most innovative, with a round bedroom and a skylight just above the bed, perfect for stargazing.

Tuesday through Saturday evenings, a four-course prix fixe dinner is served. The meal ranges in price from $45 per person on up, depending on the wine.

A few minutes' hike from the inn is the **Grand Chamber,** an impressive shrine that the innkeepers commissioned to be carved into a sandstone outcropping, where weddings and other festivities are held.

US 285 (en route to Ojo Caliente), P.O. Box 4140, Fairview Station, Española, NM 87533. ℂ 505/753-6818. www.ranchodesanjuan.com. 17 units. $175–$400 double; $25 added for single-night lodging. AE, DISC, MC, V. **Amenities:** Restaurant; concierge; in-room massage and other spa treatments; laundry service. *In room:* Stocked fridge, coffeemaker, hair dryer.

OJO CALIENTE & CHAMA

Many locals from the area like to rejuvenate at **Ojo Caliente Mineral Springs,** Ojo Caliente, NM 87549 (ℂ **800/222-9162** or 505/583-2233); it's on US 285, 50 miles (a 1-hr. drive) northwest of Santa Fe and 50 miles southwest of Taos. This National Historic Site was considered sacred by prehistoric tribes. When Spanish explorer Cabeza de Vaca discovered and named the springs in the 16th century, he called them "the greatest treasure that I found these strange people to possess." No other hot spring in the world has Ojo Caliente's combination of iron, soda, lithium, sodium, and arsenic. If the weather is warm enough, the outdoor mud bath is a real treat. The dressing rooms are fairly new and in good shape; however, the whole place has an earthy feel. If you're a fastidious type, you won't be comfortable here. The resort offers herbal wraps and massages, lodging, and meals. It's open daily 8am to 8pm (9pm Fri–Sat).

If you find yourself enamored with this part of New Mexico, you may want to explore farther north to the **Chama** area, where, between late May and mid-October, you can ride the **Cumbres and Toltec Scenic Railroad** (ℂ **505/756-2151**). Built in 1880, America's longest and highest narrow-gauge steam railroad operates on a 64-mile track between Chama and Antonito, Colorado.

New Mexico's favorite arts town sits in a masterpiece setting. It's wedged between the towering peaks of the Rocky Mountains and the plunging chasm of the Rio Grande Gorge.

Located about 70 miles north of Santa Fe, this town of 5,000 residents combines 1960s hippiedom (thanks to communes set up in the hills back then) with the ancient culture of Taos Pueblo (some people still live without electricity and running water, as their ancestors did 1,000 years ago). It can be an odd place, where some completely eschew materialism and live "off the grid" in half-underground houses called *earthships*. But there are plenty of more mainstream attractions as well—Taos boasts some of the best restaurants in the state, a hot and funky arts scene, and incredible outdoors action, including world-class skiing.

Its history is rich. Throughout the Taos valley, ruins and artifacts attest to a Native American presence dating back 5,000 years. The Spanish first visited this area in 1540, colonizing it in 1598. In the last 2 decades of the 17th century, they put down three rebellions at Taos Pueblo. During the 18th and 19th centuries, Taos was an important trade center: New Mexico's annual caravan to Chihuahua, Mexico, couldn't leave until after the annual midsummer **Taos Fair.** French trappers began attending the fair in 1739. Even though the Plains tribes often attacked the pueblos at other times, they would attend the market festival under a temporary annual truce. By the early 1800s, Taos had become a meeting place for American mountain men, the most famous of whom, Kit Carson, made his home in Taos from 1826 to 1868.

Taos remained loyal to Mexico during the U.S.–Mexican War of 1846. The town rebelled against its new U.S. landlord in 1847, even killing newly appointed Governor Charles Bent in his Taos home. Nevertheless, the town was eventually incorporated into the Territory of New Mexico in 1850. During the Civil War, Taos fell into Confederate hands for 6 weeks; afterward, Carson and two other men raised the Union flag over Taos Plaza and guarded it day and night. Since that time, Taos has had the honor of flying the flag 24 hours a day.

Taos's population declined when the railroad bypassed it in favor of Santa Fe. In 1898, two East Coast artists—Ernest Blumenschein and Bert Phillips—discovered the dramatic, varied effects of sunlight on the natural environment of the Taos valley and depicted them on canvas. By 1912, thanks to the growing influence of the **Taos Society of Artists,** the town had gained a worldwide reputation as a cultural center. Today, it is estimated that more than 15% of the population are painters, sculptors, writers, or musicians, or in some other way earn their income from artistic pursuits.

The town of Taos is merely the focal point of the rugged 2,200-square-mile Taos County. Two features dominate this sparsely populated region: the high desert mesa, split in two by the 650-foot-deep chasm of the **Rio**

Grande; and the **Sangre de Cristo** range, which tops out at 13,161-foot Wheeler Peak, New Mexico's highest mountain. From the forested uplands to the sage-carpeted mesa, the county is home to a large variety of wildlife. The human element includes Native Americans who are still living in ancient pueblos and Hispanic farmers who continue to irrigate their farmlands using centuries-old methods.

Taos is also inhabited by many people who have chosen to retreat from, or altogether drop out of, mainstream society. There's a laid-back attitude here, even more pronounced than the general *mañana* attitude for which New Mexico is known. Most Taoseños live here to play here—and that means outdoors. Many work at the ski area all winter (skiing whenever they can) and work for raft companies in the summer (to get on the river as much as they can). Others are into rock climbing, mountain biking, and backpacking. That's not to say that Taos is just a resort town. With the Hispanic and Native American populations' histories in the area, there's a richness and depth here that most resort towns lack.

1 Orientation

ARRIVING

BY PLANE The **Taos Municipal Airport** (© 505/758-4995) is about 8 miles northwest of town on US 64. **Rio Grande Air** (© 877/435-9742 or 505/737-9790; www.riograndeair.com) runs daily flights between Albuquerque and Taos. Most people opt to fly into Albuquerque International Sunport, rent a car, and drive up to Taos from there. The drive takes approximately 2½ hours. If you'd rather be picked up at Albuquerque International Sunport, call **Faust's Transportation, Inc.** (© 505/758-3410), which offers daily service, as well as taxi service between Taos and Taos Ski Valley.

BY BUS The **Taos Bus Center** is located 5 miles south of the plaza at 1386 Paseo del Pueblo Sur (© 505/758-1144). **TNM&O** (© 505/242-4998) arrives and departs from this depot several times a day. For more information on this and other bus services to and from Albuquerque and Santa Fe, see "Getting There," in chapter 2.

BY CAR Most visitors arrive in Taos via either NM 68 or US 64. Northbound travelers should exit I-25 at Santa Fe, follow US 285 as far as San Juan Pueblo, and then continue on the divided highway when it becomes NM 68. Taos is about 79 miles from the I-25 junction. Southbound travelers from Denver on I-25 should exit about 6 miles south of Raton at US 64 and then follow it about 95 miles to Taos. Another major route is US 64 from the west (214 miles from Farmington).

VISITOR INFORMATION

The **Taos County Chamber of Commerce,** at the junction of NM 68 and NM 585 (P.O. Drawer I), Taos, NM 87571 (© 800/732-TAOS or 505/758-3873; www.taoschamber.com), is open in summer, daily 9am to 5pm. It's closed on major holidays. **Carson National Forest** also has an information center in the same building.

CITY LAYOUT

The **plaza** is a short block west of Taos's major intersection—where US 64 (Kit Carson Rd.) from the east joins NM 68, **Paseo del Pueblo Sur.** US 64 proceeds north from the intersection as **Paseo del Pueblo Norte. Camino de la Placita**

(Placitas Rd.) circles the west side of downtown, passing within a block of the other side of the plaza. Many of the streets that join these thoroughfares are winding lanes lined by traditional adobe homes, many of them over 100 years old.

Most of the art galleries are located on or near the plaza, which was paved over with bricks several years ago, and along neighboring streets. Others are located in the **Ranchos de Taos** area a few miles south of the plaza.

MAPS   To find your way around town, pick up a free Taos map from the **Chamber of Commerce at Taos Visitor Center,** 1139 Paseo del Pueblo Sur (© **505/758-3873**). Good, detailed city maps can be found at area bookstores as well (see "Shopping," later in this chapter).

2 Getting Around

BY CAR

With offices at the Taos airport, **Enterprise** (© **800/369-4226** or 505/751-7490) is reliable and efficient. Other car-rental agencies are available out of Albuquerque. See "Getting Around," in chapter 5, for details.

PARKING   Parking can be difficult during the summer rush, when the stream of tourists' cars moving north and south through town never ceases. If you can't find parking on the street or in the plaza, check out some of the nearby roads (Kit Carson Rd., for instance); there are plenty of metered and unmetered lots in Taos.

ROAD CONDITIONS   Information on highway conditions throughout the state can be obtained from the **State Highway Department** (© **800/432-4269**).

BY BUS & TAXI

If you're in Taos without a car, you're in luck because there is now a local bus service, provided by **Chile Line Town of Taos Transit** (© **505/751-4459**). It operates on the half-hour Monday to Saturday 7am to 7pm in summer, 7am to 6pm in winter, and on the hour Sunday 8am to 5pm. Two simultaneous routes run southbound from Taos Pueblo and northbound from the Ranchos de Taos Post Office. Each route makes stops at the casino and various hotels in town, as well as at Taos RV Park. Bus fares are 50¢ one-way, $1 round-trip, $5 for a 7-day pass, and $20 for a 31-day pass.

In addition, **Faust's Transportation** (© **505/758-3410**) has a taxi service linking town hotels and Taos Ski Valley. Faust's Transportation also offers shuttle service and on-call taxi service daily from 7am to 9pm, with fares of about $8 anywhere within the city limits for up to two people ($2 per additional person).

⌒*Warning* Warning for Drivers

En route to many recreation sites, reliable paved roads often give way to poorer forest roads. When you get off the main roads, you don't find gas stations or cafes. Four-wheel-drive vehicles are recommended on snow and much of the unpaved terrain of the region. If you're doing some off-road adventuring, it's wise to go with a full gas tank, extra food and water, and warm clothing—just in case. At the higher-than-10,000-foot elevations of northern New Mexico, sudden summer snowstorms are not unheard of.

BY BICYCLE

Bicycle rentals are available from **Gearing Up Bicycle Shop,** 129 Paseo del Pueblo Sur (© **505/751-0365**). Daily rentals run $35 for a full day and $25 for a half day for a mountain bike with front suspension. From April to October, **Native Sons Adventures,** 1033A Paseo del Pueblo Sur (© **800/753-7559** or 505/758-9342), rents no-suspension bikes ($15 for a half day and $20 for a full day), front-suspension bikes ($25 for a half day and $35 for a full day), and full-suspension bikes ($35 for a half day and $45 for a full day). It also rents car racks for $5. Each shop supplies helmets and water bottles with rentals.

FAST FACTS: Taos

Airport See "Orientation," above.

Area Code The telephone area code for all of New Mexico is **505**; however, at press time, plans were in the works to add new codes.

ATMs You can find ATMs (also known as *cash pueblos*) all over town, at supermarkets, banks, and drive-throughs.

Business Hours Most **businesses** are open at least Monday to Friday 10am to 5pm, though some may open an hour earlier and close an hour later. Many **tourist-oriented shops** are also open on Saturday morning, and some **art galleries** are open all day Saturday and Sunday, especially during peak tourist seasons. **Banks** are generally open Monday to Thursday 9am to 5pm and often for longer hours on Friday. Some may be open Saturday morning. Most branches have ATMs available 24 hours. Call establishments for specific hours.

Car Rentals See "Getting Around New Mexico," in chapter 2, or "Getting Around," above.

Climate Taos's climate is similar to that of Santa Fe. Summer days are dry and sunny, except for frequent afternoon thunderstorms. Winter days are often bracing, with snowfalls common but rarely lasting too long. Average **summer temperatures** range from 50°F to 87°F (10°–31°C). **Winter temperatures** vary between 9°F and 40°F (-13°–4°C). **Annual rainfall** is 12 inches; annual snowfall is 35 inches in town and 300 inches at Taos Ski Valley, where the elevation is 9,207 feet. (A foot of snow is equal to an inch of rain.)

Currency Exchange Foreign currency can be exchanged at the **Centinel Bank of Taos,** 512 Paseo del Pueblo Sur (© **505/758-6700**).

Dentists Try **Dr. Walter Jakiela,** 1392 Weimer Rd. (© **505/758-8654**); **Dr. Michael Rivera,** 107 Plaza Garcia, Suite E (© **505/758-0531**); or **Dr. Tom Simms,** 1392 Weimer Rd. (© **505/758-8303**).

Doctors Members of the **Taos Medical Group,** on Weimer Road (© **505/758-2224**), are highly respected. Also recommended are **Family Practice Associates of Taos,** 630 Paseo del Pueblo Sur, Suite 150 (© **505/758-3005**).

Embassies & Consulates See "Fast Facts: For the International Traveler," in chapter 3.

Emergencies Dial © **911** for police, fire, and ambulance.

Hospital **Holy Cross Hospital,** 1397 Weimer Rd., off Paseo del Canyon (© 505/758-8883), has 24-hour emergency service. Serious cases are transferred to Santa Fe or Albuquerque.

Hot Lines The **crisis hot line** (© 505/758-9888) is available for emergency counseling.

Information See "Visitor Information," under "Orientation," above.

Internet Access You can retrieve your e-mail at **Magic Circle Bagels,** 710 Paseo del Pueblo Sur (© 505/758-0045).

Library The **Taos Public Library** is at 402 Camino de la Placita (© 505/758-3063 or 505/737-2590).

Liquor Laws The legal drinking age is 21 in New Mexico, as it is throughout the United States. Bars may remain open until 2am Monday to Saturday and until midnight on Sunday. Wine, beer, and spirits are sold at licensed supermarkets and liquor stores, but there are no package sales on election days until after 7pm. It is illegal to transport liquor through most Native American reservations.

Lost Property Check with the **Taos police** at © 505/758-2216.

Newspapers & Magazines **The Taos News** (© 505/758-2241; www.taos news.com) and the **Sangre de Cristo Chronicle** (© 505/377-2358; www. sangrechronicle.com) are published every Thursday. *Taos Magazine* is also a good source of local information. The **Albuquerque Journal** (www.abq journal.com) and the **New Mexican** (from Santa Fe; www.santafenew mexican.com) are easily obtained at book and convenience stores.

Pharmacies **Raley's Pharmacy** (© 505/758-1203), **Smith's Pharmacy** (© 505/758-4824), and **Wal-Mart Pharmacy** (© 505/758-2743) are all located on Pueblo Sur and are easily seen from the road.

Police In case of emergency, dial © 911. All other inquiries should be directed to the **Taos police,** Civic Plaza Drive (© 505/758-2216). The **Taos County Sheriff,** with jurisdiction outside the city limits, is located in the county courthouse on Paseo del Pueblo Sur (© 505/758-3361).

Post Offices The main **Taos post office** is at 318 Paseo del Pueblo Norte (© 505/758-2081), a few blocks north of the plaza traffic light. There are smaller offices in **Ranchos de Taos** (© 505/758-3944) and at **El Prado** (© 505/758-4810). The zip code for Taos is 87571.

Radio A local station is **KTAO-FM** (101.7), which broadcasts an entertainment calendar daily (© 505/758-1017); National Public Radio can be found on **KUNM-FM** (98.5) from Albuquerque.

Taxes Gross receipts tax for the city of Taos is 7%, and for Taos County it's 6.31%. There is an additional local bed tax of 4.5% in the city of Taos and 5% on hotel rooms in Taos County.

Taxis See "Getting Around," above.

Television **Channel 2,** the local access station, is available in most hotels. For a few hours a day it shows local programming. Cable networks carry Santa Fe and Albuquerque stations.

Time As is true throughout New Mexico, Taos is on **Mountain Standard Time.** It's 2 hours earlier than New York, 1 hour earlier than Chicago, and

1 hour later than Los Angeles. Daylight saving time is in effect from early April to late October.

Useful Telephone Numbers For **emergency road service** in the Taos area, call the state police at 𝄐 **505/758-8878**; for **road conditions** dial 𝄐 **800/ 432-4269** (within New Mexico) for the state highway department. **Taos County offices** are at 𝄐 **505/737-6300**.

Weather For **weather forecasts,** Taos has no number to call, but if you're online, check **www.taoschamber.com**.

3 Where to Stay

A tiny town with a big tourist market, Taos has thousands of rooms in hotels, motels, condominiums, and bed-and-breakfasts. Many new properties have recently opened, turning this into a buyer's market. In the slower seasons, in January through early February and April through early May, when competition for travelers is steep, you may even want to try bargaining your room rate down. Most of the hotels and motels are located on Paseo del Pueblo Sur and Norte, with a few scattered just east of the town center, along Kit Carson Road. The condos and bed-and-breakfasts are generally scattered throughout Taos's back streets.

During peak seasons, visitors without reservations may have difficulty finding vacant rooms. **Taos Central Reservations,** P.O. Box 1713, Taos, NM 87571 (𝄐 **800/821-2437**), might be able to help.

Fifteen hundred or so of Taos County's beds are in condominiums and lodges at or near Taos Ski Valley. The **Taos Valley Resort Association,** P.O. Box 85, Taos Ski Valley, NM 87525 (𝄐 **800/776-1111** or 505/776-2233; fax 505/776-8842; www.visitnewmexico.com), can book these, as well as rooms in Taos and all the rest of northern New Mexico, and it can book private home rentals.

Reservations of Taos, 1033A Paseo del Pueblo Sur, Taos, NM 87571 (𝄐 **505/751-1292**), will help you find accommodations from bed-and-breakfasts to home rentals, hotels, RV parks, and cabins throughout Taos and the rest of northern New Mexico. It'll also help you arrange package prices for outdoor activities such as whitewater rafting, horseback riding, hot-air ballooning, snowmobiling, fishing, and skiing.

There are two high seasons in Taos: winter (the Christmas-to-Easter ski season, except for Jan, which is notoriously slow) and summer. Spring and fall are shoulder seasons, often with lower rates. The period between Easter and Memorial Day is also slow in the tourist industry here, and many proprietors of restaurants and other businesses take their annual vacations at this time. Book well ahead for ski holiday periods (especially Christmas) and for the annual arts festivals (late May to mid-June and late Sept to early Oct). A tax of 11.5% in Taos proper and 11.31% in Taos County will be added to every hotel bill.

TAOS
HOTELS/MOTELS
Expensive
El Monte Sagrado ★★★ *(Moments)* For those, like me, who are blessed (or cursed) with sensitive senses, El Monte Sagrado (the Sacred Mountain), Taos's new resort near the center of town, is pure heaven. Often while traveling I find

I'm accosted by sounds, scents, even sights, but at this resort my senses rejoice. Water running over falls, clear air, and delicious food and drink lull guests into a sweet *samadhi,* or state of relaxation, while the eyes luxuriate in the beauty of rooms impeccably decorated. These range in theme from the Caribbean Casita, a medium-size room with a medium-size bathroom, which evokes the feel of an African jungle; to the China Casita, a large two-bedroom suite with two large bathrooms, all bathed in gold, with its own patio and outdoor hot tub; to the Kamasutra Suite, with suggestive carvings throughout, a room resort owner Tom Worrell describes as "the first honeymoon suite to come with instructions." All rooms are quiet and lovely, with patios or balconies and views. In line with Worrell's plan to preserve the earth's environment through responsible development and sustainable technologies, the resort recycles its water and makes much of its own electricity. All rooms rim a grassy, cottonwood-shaded "Sacred Circle," which also has trout and koi ponds. The intimate spa offers a full range of treatments in softly shaped rooms. The **Anaconda Bar** (see "Taos After Dark" later in this chapter) and **De La Tierra restaurant** (see "Where to Dine," later in this chapter) combine a contemporary feel with elegant Asian touches.

317 Kit Carson Rd., Taos, NM 87571. ℂ 800/828-TAOS or 505/758-3502. www.elmontesagrado.com. 36 units. $245–$375 historic 1-bedroom casita; $295–$395 1-bedroom junior suite; $395–$795 1-bedroom exclusive casita; $1,095–$1,495 2-bedroom global suite. AE, DC, DISC, MC, V. Free parking. **Amenities:** Restaurant (p. 213); bar (p. 238); indoor pool; well-equipped health club & spa; Jacuzzi; concierge; babysitting; laundry service. *In room:* A/C, TV, dataport, hair dryer, safe.

Fechin Inn ★★

This masterfully created luxury hotel provides comfort, quiet, and lots of amenities. Built next door to Russian artist Nicolai Fechin's 1927 home (see the discussion of the Taos Art Museum later in this chapter), the hotel features elegantly carved wood furniture and artwork by Jeremy Morelli of Santa Fe. The hotel is located right next to Kit Carson Park, a short walk from the plaza. The two-story lobby is airy, with a bank of windows and French doors looking south to a portal where diners can eat breakfast in the warmer months. The spacious rooms have Southwestern decor with nice touches such as guest robes, hickory furniture, and flagstone-topped tables; some have balconies or patios. Suites have kiva fireplaces. The bathrooms are delightful, with Italian tile. There's a library where you can play chess or backgammon. For an additional cost, you can eat an elaborate continental breakfast. In the evenings, drinks are available.

227 Paseo del Pueblo Norte, Taos, NM 87571. ℂ 800/811-2933 or 505/751-1000. Fax 505/751-7338. www. fechininn.com. 84 units. $114–$177 double; $282–$512 suite. Rates vary according to season. Additional person $15. AE, DC, DISC, MC, V. Free parking. Pets accepted with some restrictions and extra fee. **Amenities:** Medium-size health club; Jacuzzi; car-rental desk; room service; massage; coin-op laundry; same-day drycleaning and laundry service. *In room:* A/C, TV, dataport, fridge, coffeemaker, hair dryer.

The Historic Taos Inn ★

It's rare to see a hotel that has withstood the years with grace. The Historic Taos Inn has. Here, you'll be surrounded by 20th-century luxury without ever forgetting that you're within the thick walls of a number of 19th-century Southwestern homes. Dr. Thomas Paul Martin, the town's first physician, purchased the complex in 1895. In 1936, a year after the doctor's death, his widow, Helen, enclosed the plaza—now the inn's darling two-story lobby—and turned it into a hotel. In 1981–82, the inn was restored; it's now listed on both the State and National Registers of Historic Places.

The lobby doubles as the **Adobe Bar,** a popular local gathering place, with adobe *bancos* (benches) and a sunken fireplace, all surrounding a wishing well that was once the old town well. A number of rooms open onto a balcony that

Where to Stay in the Taos Area

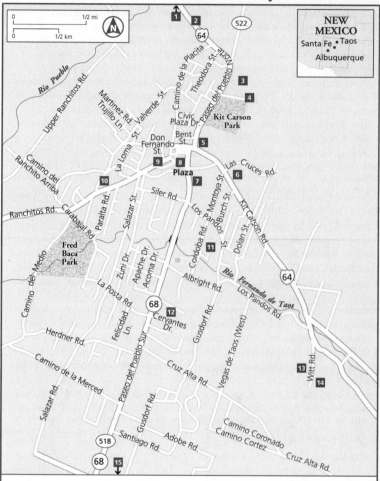

Adobe and Pines Inn **15**
Adobe Sun God Lodge **12**
Best Western Kachina Lodge **3**
Carson National Forest **1**
Casa de las Chimeneas **11**
Comfort Suites **15**
El Monte Sagrado **6**
Fechin Inn **4**
Hacienda del Sol **2**
The Historic Taos Inn **5**
Hotel La Fonda de Taos **8**

Indian Hills Taos Plaza **7**
Inger Jirby's Guest Houses **9**
Inn on La Loma Plaza **10**
Little Tree Bed & Breakfast **1**
Old Taos Guesthouse Bed & Breakfast **13**
Questa Lodge **1**
Sagebrush Inn **15**
San Geronimo Lodge **14**
Taos RV Park **15**
Taos Valley RV Park and
    Campground **15**

overlooks this area. If you like community and don't mind the sound of jazz and flamenco drifting up toward your room, these rooms are for you. However, if you appreciate solitude and silence, request one of the courtyard rooms downstairs. All the rooms are unique and comfortable, decorated with Spanish colonial art, Taos-style furniture, and interesting touches; many rooms have fireplaces.

In recent years I've had complaints from guests about the temperamental nature of these old buildings. You may encounter problems such as windows not staying open or not having screens. I've also had complaints about the service here.

Doc Martin's, with good nouveau Southwestern cuisine and a hint of Asia, is a good bet for dinner (see "Where to Dine," later in this chapter).

125 Paseo del Pueblo Norte, Taos, NM 87571. © **800/TAOS-INN** or 505/758-2233. Fax 505/758-5776. www. taosinn.com. 36 units. $65–$225, depending on the type of room and season. AE, DISC, MC, V. **Amenities:** Restaurant (p. 213); bar; seasonal outdoor pool; Jacuzzi; room service; coffee or refreshments in lobby. *In room:* A/C, TV, VCR on request, hair dryer, iron.

Hotel La Fonda de Taos ⚡

Finally, Taos has a recommendable hotel on the plaza. A $3 million renovation to this historic property built in 1880 has turned it into a comfortable, fun spot with a stellar location. The charismatic Taos figure Saki Kavaras put this hotel on the society map in the 1930s, when, most notably, British author D. H. Lawrence frequented it. His legacy is preserved in a unique D. H. Lawrence Forbidden Art Museum, where some of his risqué paintings hang—a must-see even if you don't stay here (free for guests; $3 for nonguests). Rooms are set off broad hallways, each styled in earth tones, Southwestern furnishings, and tile bathrooms. Standards are small, each with a queen-size bed. Your better bet is to reserve a plaza or deluxe plaza room, or a suite. These are larger, with king beds. My favorite rooms are 201 and 301, which overlook the plaza. Groups can rent the whole top floor, which includes a full kitchen suite.

108 South Plaza, Taos, NM 87571. © **800/833-2211** or 505/758-2211. Fax 505/758-8508. www.hotella fonda.com. 24 units. $99–$169 standard double; $129–$219 plaza and deluxe double; $169–$229 suite. AE, DC, DISC, MC, V. Free parking. **Amenities:** Restaurant; coffee shop; bar. *In room:* A/C, TV, hair dryer, iron.

Inger Jirby's Guest Houses ⚡⚡

You can't have a better address in Taos than this artist has, 2 blocks from the plaza, between the R. C. Gorman Gallery and the Ernest L. Blumenschein Museum. Inger Jirby has chosen this for her gallery space as well as a home for travelers. From the remains of a 400-year-old adobe, she's carved and added these lively dwellings and adorned them with her unique style. Full of rich Mexican and Balinese art, and then accented by her own vivid landscapes of the Southwest and beyond, the casitas are artsy and comfortable. Each has a full kitchen, with range, dishwasher, microwave, and washer/dryer. The larger two have flagstone floors, large windows, and sleeping lofts. (Very big people might have trouble maneuvering the spiral staircases in these.) These also have sofa beds. The third casita has a large kitchen, a smaller bedroom, and an atrium. All are equipped with stereos and robes. More than anywhere else in town, these casitas provide a real home away from home.

207 Ledoux St., Taos, NM 87571. © 505/758-7333. www.jirby.com. 3 units. $125–$175 double; $175–$250 double during holidays. Rates include self-prepared breakfast. Additional person $25. *In room:* TV/VCR, kitchen, hair dryer.

Moderate

Best Western Kachina Lodge & Meeting Center ⚡ *Kids*

Built in the early 1960s, this lodge on the north end of town, within walking distance of the plaza, has a lot of charm despite the fact that it's really a motor hotel. Though it

Kids   Family-Friendly Hotels

The Bavarian Lodge (p. 209)   Just feet from the slopes and with sleeping lofts in the rooms, this is a fun spot for kids.

Best Western Kachina Lodge & Meeting Center (p. 204)   An outdoor swimming pool and Pueblo Indian presentations keep kids well entertained.

Indian Hills Inn Taos Plaza (p. 206)   With a pool, picnic tables, barbecue grills, and acres of grass, this inn offers plenty of room for families to spread out.

has traditionally been a good spot for families and travelers, in recent years management has begun catering so much to convention traffic that the service has suffered for others. Remodeling is ongoing in the solidly built Southwestern-style rooms—some have couches and most have Taos-style *trasteros* (armoires) that hold the TVs. Rooms are placed around a grassy courtyard studded with huge blue spruce trees, allowing kids room to run. In the center is a stage where a family from Taos Pueblo builds a bonfire and dances nightly in the summer and explains the significance of the dances—a real treat.

413 Paseo del Pueblo Norte (P.O. Box NM), Taos, NM 87571. © **800/522-4462** or 505/758-2275. Fax 505/758-9207. www.kachinalodge.com. 118 units. $59–$129 double. Additional person $10. Children under 12 stay free in parent's room. AE, DC, DISC, MC, V. **Amenities:** 2 restaurants; lounge; outdoor pool; salon; coin-op laundry. *In room:* A/C, TV, coffeemaker, hair dryer, iron.

Comfort Suites   New, clean, and predictable is what you'll get here. Each room has a small living/dining area with a sleeper sofa and a bedroom with handcrafted wood furniture and a comfortable king- or queen-size bed. If you have kids, you might want a ground-floor poolside room. The pool is warm, roomy, and accompanied by a hot tub.

1500 Paseo del Pueblo Sur (P.O. Box 1268), Taos, NM 87571. © **888/751-1555** or 505/751-1555. Fax 505/751-1991. www.comfortsuites.com. 62 units. $69–$149 double. Rates include continental breakfast. AE, DC, DISC, MC, V. **Amenities:** Outdoor pool; Jacuzzi; sauna; car-rental desk; in-room massage; same-day dry cleaning. *In room:* A/C, TV, dataport, fridge, microwave, coffeemaker, hair dryer.

Sagebrush Inn   Three miles south of Taos, surrounded by acres of sage, this inn is housed in an adobe building that has been added on to decade after decade, creating an interesting mix of accommodations. The original structure was built in 1929. It had three floors and 12 rooms, hand-sculpted from adobe; the roof was held in place with hand-hewn vigas. That part still remains, and the rooms are small and cozy and have the feel of old Taos—in fact, Georgia O'Keeffe lived and worked here for 10 months in the late 1930s. But to those more accustomed to refined style, it might feel dated.

The treasure of this place is the large grass courtyard dotted with elm trees, where visitors sit and read in the warm months. Some of the rooms added in the '50s through '70s have a tackiness not overcome by the vigas and tile work. More recent additions (to the west) are more skillful; these suites away from the hotel proper are spacious and full of amenities, but they have noisy plumbing.

The lobby-cum-cantina has an Old West feel that livens at night when it becomes a venue for country/western dancing and one of Taos's most active nightspots for live music (see "Taos After Dark," later in this chapter). Traditionally, this has been a family hotel, but with a new convention center and the addition of a Comfort Suites hotel on the property, management is working to appeal to convention guests as well.

1508 Paseo del Pueblo Sur (P.O. Box 557), Taos, NM 87571. ✆ **800/428-3626** or 505/758-2254. Fax 505/758-5077. www.sagebrushinn.com. 100 units. $70–$95 double; $90–$155 deluxe or small suite; $105–$185 executive suite. Additional person $10. Children under 18 stay free in parent's room. Rates include breakfast. AE, DC, DISC, MC, V. Pets welcome. **Amenities:** 2 restaurants; bar (p. 240); 2 outdoor pools; tennis courts; Jacuzzi; courtesy shuttle; business center; in-room massage; same-day dry cleaning; executive-level rooms. *In room:* A/C, TV, dataport, fridge, coffeemaker, hair dryer, iron.

Inexpensive

Adobe Sun God Lodge   For a comfortable, economical stay with a northern New Mexico ambience, this is a good choice. This hotel, a 5-minute drive from the plaza, has three distinct parts spread across 1½ acres of landscaped grounds. The oldest was solidly built in 1958 and has some court-motel charm, with a low ceiling and large windows. To update the rooms, the owners added tile sinks, Taos-style furniture, and new carpeting. To the south is a section built in 1988. The rooms are small but have little touches that make them feel cozy, such as little *nichos* (niches) and hand-carved furnishings. In back to the east are the newest buildings, built in 1994. These are two-story structures with portal-style porches and balconies. Some rooms have kitchenettes, which include microwaves, fridges, and stoves; others have kiva fireplaces. The two suites on the northeast corner of the property are the quietest and have the best views.

919 Paseo del Pueblo Sur, Taos, NM 87571. ✆ **800/821-2437** or 505/758-3162. Fax 505/758-1716. www.sungodlodge.com. 53 units. $49–$99 double; $69–$139 suite. AE, DISC, MC, V. Pets allowed for $10 per day. **Amenities:** Jacuzzi. *In room:* A/C, TV, dataport, coffeemaker.

Indian Hills Inn Taos Plaza (Kids)   With its close location to the plaza (3 blocks), this is a good choice if you're looking for a decent, functional night's stay. There are two sections to the hotel: one built in the 1950s, the other completed in 1996. The older section has received a major face-lift. However, for a few more dollars you can stay in the newer section, where the rooms are larger, with gas-log fireplaces, and the bathrooms are fresher, though noise can travel from nearby guest rooms. Both sections sit on a broad lawn studded with towering blue spruce trees. Picnic tables and barbecue grills add to the place's charm and functionality and provide families a bit of respite from the restaurant scene. The hotel offers golf, ski, and rafting packages at reduced rates, as well as Cumbres & Toltec Scenic Railroad tickets (see chapter 9).

233 Paseo del Pueblo Sur (P.O. Box 1229), Taos, NM 87571. ✆ **800/444-2346** or 505/758-4293. www.taosnet.com/indianhillsinn. 55 units. $49–$99 double. Group and package rates available. Rates include continental breakfast. AE, DC, DISC, MC, V. Small pets welcome with prior arrangements. **Amenities:** Outdoor pool; tour desk. *In room:* A/C, TV.

BED & BREAKFASTS
Expensive

Adobe & Pines Inn (★★)   This inn seeks to create a magical escape. It succeeds. Much of it is located in a 150-year-old adobe directly off NM 68, less than half a mile south of St. Francis Plaza (about a 10-min. drive from Taos Plaza). The inn is set around a courtyard marked by an 80-foot-long grand portal and surrounded by pine and fruit trees. Each room has a private entrance and fireplace (three even have fireplaces in their bathrooms), and each is uniquely decorated. The theme here is the use of colors, which are richly displayed on the walls and in the furnishings. Puerta Azul is a cozy blue room with thick adobe walls, and Puerta Turquese is a separate whimsically painted guest cottage with a full kitchen. The two newest rooms, completed in 1996, have bold maroon and copper-yellow themes. The walls have handprint and petroglyph motifs, and each room is furnished with rich and comfortable couches. Most of the inn's rooms also have Jacuzzi tubs. Since this inn is near the highway, at times cars can be heard, but the rooms themselves are quiet. Morning brings a delicious full gourmet breakfast in the glassed-in breakfast room.

NM 68, Ranchos de Taos, NM 87557. (800/723-8267 or 505/751-0947. Fax 505/758-8423. www.adobe pines.com. 7 units, 3 casitas. $95–$195 double. Rates include full gourmet breakfast. MC, V. Pets accepted with prior arrangements. **Amenities:** In-room massage; complimentary laundry facility available evenings. *In room:* TV, no phone.

Casa de las Chimeneas *ααα*

This 82-year-old adobe home has, since its opening in 1988, been a model of Southwestern elegance. Now, with new additions, it has become a full-service luxury inn as well. The addition includes a spa with a small fitness room and sauna, as well as complete massage and facial treatments for an additional charge. I highly recommend the Rio Grande and Territorial rooms, which are air-conditioned. Both of these rooms have heated Saltillo-tile floors, gas kiva fireplaces, and Jacuzzi tubs. If you prefer a more antique-feeling room, try the delightful older section, especially the Library Suite. Each room in the inn is decorated with original works of art and has elegant bedding, a private entrance, robes, and a minifridge stocked with complimentary soft drinks, juices, and mineral water. All rooms have kiva fireplaces, and most look out on flower and herb gardens. Breakfasts are delicious. Specialties include an artichoke heart and mushroom omelet or ricotta cream-cheese blintz, plus innkeeper Susan Vernon's special fruit frappé. In the evening she serves a light supper. During one evening I had canapés with avocado, cheese, and tomato; a spicy broccoli soup; and moonshine cake. End the day in the large hot tub in the courtyard. Smoking is not permitted. Ask about the spa specials.

405 Cordoba Rd., at Los Pandos Rd. (5303 NDCBU), Taos, NM 87571. (877/758-4777 or 505/758-4777. Fax 505/758-3976. www.visittaos.com. 8 units. $165–$290 double; $325 suite. Rates include breakfast and supper. AE, DC, DISC, MC, V. **Amenities:** Small exercise room; spa; Jacuzzi; sauna; concierge; car-rental desk; in-room massage; coin-op laundry; laundry service; all nonsmoking. *In room:* TV/VCR, dataport, free stocked minibar, coffeemaker, hair dryer, iron.

Hacienda del Sol *αα*

What's unique about this B&B is its completely unobstructed view of Taos Mountain. Because the 1¼-acre property borders Taos Pueblo, the land is pristine. The inn also has a rich history. It was once owned by arts patron Mabel Dodge Luhan, and it was here that author Frank Waters wrote *The People of the Valley.* You'll find bold splashes of color—from the gardens, where in summer tulips, pansies, and flax bloom, to the rooms themselves, where woven bedspreads and original art lend a Mexican feel. The main house is nearly 200 years old, so it has the wonderful curves of adobe as well as thick vigas. Some guest rooms are in this section. Others range from 3 to 10 years in age. These newer rooms are finely constructed, and I almost recommend them over the others because they're a little more private and the bathrooms are more refined. All rooms have robes and CD players, most have fireplaces, three have private Jacuzzis, and three have private steam rooms. Some have minifridges. A full and delicious breakfast as well as evening hors d'oeuvres are served in the Spanish-hacienda-style dining area. The outdoor hot tub has a mountain view and is available for private guest use in half-hour segments.

109 Mabel Dodge Lane (P.O. Box 177), Taos, NM 87571. ℂ **505/758-0287**. Fax 505/758-5895. www.taos haciendadelsol.com. 11 units. $85–$245 double. Rates include full breakfast and evening hors d'oeuvres. AE, DISC, MC, V. **Amenities:** Jacuzzi; sauna; concierge; in-room massage. *In room:* TV, CD player, dataport, fridge, hair dryer.

Inn on La Loma Plaza 🌟🌟

Named by *American Historic Inns* as one of the 10 most romantic inns in America, the Inn on La Loma Plaza provides the comfortable intimacy of a B&B with the service and amenities of an inn. It's located on a historic neighborhood plaza, complete with dirt streets and a tiny central park, which was once a 1796 neighborhood stronghold—adobe homes built around a square, with thick outer walls to fend off marauders. The building, a 10-minute walk from Taos Plaza, is a 200-year-old home, complete with aged vigas and maple floors, decorated tastefully with comfortable furniture and Middle Eastern rugs. Each room is unique, most with sponge-painted walls and Talavera tile in the bathrooms to provide an eclectic ambience. All have robes, slippers, lighted makeup mirrors, bottled water, and fireplaces, and most have balconies or terraces and views. Some have special touches, such as the Happy Trails Room, with knotty pine paneling, a brass bed, old chaps, and decorative hanging spurs. Some rooms have kitchenettes. Guests dine on such delights as breakfast burritos or green-chile casserole in a plant-filled sunroom or on the patio.

315 Ranchitos Rd., Taos, NM 87571. ℂ **800/530-3040** or 505/758-1717. Fax 505/751-0155. www.vacation taos.com. 7 units. $125–$225 double; $250–$325 artist's studio; $475–$550 suite. Additional person $20. Children 12 and under stay free in parent's room. Discounts available. Rates include full breakfast. AE, DISC, MC, V. **Amenities:** Pool and spa privileges at nearby Taos Spa; Jacuzzi. *In room:* TV/VCR, hair dryer, iron.

Little Tree Bed & Breakfast 🌟🌟 (Finds)

Little Tree is one of my favorite Taos B&Bs, partly because it's located in a beautiful, secluded setting, and partly because it's constructed with real adobe that's been left in its raw state, lending the place an authentic hacienda feel. Located 2 miles down a country road, about midway between Taos and the ski area, it's surrounded by sage and piñon. The charming and cozy rooms have radiant heat under the floors, queen-size beds (one with a king), nice medium-size baths (one with a Jacuzzi tub), and access to the portal and courtyard garden, at the center of which is the little tree for which the inn is named. The Piñon (my favorite) and Juniper rooms have fireplaces and private entrances. The Piñon and Aspen rooms offer sunset views. The Spruce Room, Victorian in ambience, is decorated with quilts. In the main building, the living room has a traditional viga-and-*latilla* ceiling and *tierra blanca* adobe (adobe that's naturally white; if you look closely at it, you can see little pieces of mica and straw). Guests enjoy a scrumptious breakfast on the portal during warmer months. On arrival, guests are treated to refreshments.

County Road B-143 (P.O. Box 509), Taos, NM 87513. ℂ **800/334-8467** or 505/776-8467. www.littletree bandb.com. 4 units. $105–$175 double. Rates include breakfast and afternoon snack. MC, V. *In room:* TV/VCR.

Moderate

Old Taos Guesthouse Bed & Breakfast 🌟

Less than 2 miles from the plaza, this 180-year-old adobe hacienda sits on 7½ acres and provides a cozy northern New Mexico rural experience. Once a farmer's home and later an artist's estate, it's been restored by owners and incorrigible ski bums Tim and Leslie Reeves, who, for more than 15 years, have carefully maintained the country charm, including vigas, Mexican tile in the bathrooms, and kiva-style fireplaces in most of the rooms. Each room has an entrance from the outside, some off the broad portal that shades the front of the hacienda, some from a grassy lawn in the back, with a view toward the mountains. Some rooms are more utilitarian, some quainter. One of my favorites is the Taos Suite, with a king-size bed, a big picture window, and a full kitchen that includes an oven, a stove, a minifridge, and a microwave. A nature path and healthy breakfast complete the experience.

1028 Witt Rd., Taos, NM 87571. © 800/758-5448 or 505/758-5448. www.oldtaos.com. 9 units. $85–$160 double. Rates include expanded continental breakfast. DISC, MC, V. Pets accepted in some rooms with $25 fee. **Amenities:** Jacuzzi; concierge; tour desk; in-room massage; babysitting. *In room:* Hair dryer, iron.

San Geronimo Lodge ☽ Built in 1925 in the style of a grand old lodge, this inn has high ceilings and rambling verandas, all situated on 2½ acres of grounds with views of Taos Mountain, yet it's a 5-minute drive from the plaza. The lodge received a major renovation in 1994. Common areas are filled with artwork for sale, from landscapes to portraits. The guest rooms are cozy and comfortable, eight with kiva fireplaces, all with furniture hand-built by local craftspeople and Mexican tile in the bathrooms. Guests feast on a full breakfast and afternoon snacks in the grand dining room, which looks out on elaborate gardens. There's an outdoor swimming pool, unusual for a B&B.

1101 Witt Rd., Taos, NM 87571. © 800/894-4119 or 505/751-3776. Fax 505/751-1493. www.sangeronimo lodge.com. 18 units. $95–$150 double. Rates include full breakfast and afternoon snack. AE, DISC, MC, V. Pets accepted with prior arrangements. **Amenities:** Outdoor pool (summer only); Jacuzzi; concierge; massage. *In room:* TV, hair dryer.

TAOS SKI VALLEY

For information on the skiing and the facilities offered at Taos Ski Valley, see "Skiing," below.

EXPENSIVE
Hotels

The Bavarian Lodge ☽ *Kids* This getaway offers the quintessence of Bavaria at the base of Taos Ski Valley's back bowls. At an elevation of 10,200 feet, the lodge has interesting accommodations and excellent food. The first-floor restaurant/reception area is a study in Bavaria—lots of aged pine paneling accented by an antler chandelier. Upstairs, the rooms combine antique and modern elements—not always successfully, but with good intent. All are fairly spacious, with large bathrooms, and most with lofts to accommodate kids. The rooms aren't cozy, and some have odd configurations, but they all utilize faux painting to evoke old Europe; some have kitchenettes and balconies. The sun deck is the place to be on sunny ski days, and The Bavarian Restaurant (see "Where to Dine," below) is worth visiting even if you aren't a guest. The lodge offers nature hikes in summer.

100 Kachina Rd. (P.O. Box 653), Taos Ski Valley, NM 87525. © 888/205-8020 or 505/776-8020. Fax 888/304-5301. www.thebavarian.com. 4 units. Dec 15–Jan 8 and Feb 10–Apr 6 $335–$395 double; late Nov–Dec 15 and Jan 9–Feb 9 $285–$350; summer $155–$195. AE, MC, V. Free parking. **Amenities:** Restaurant (p. 219); bar; courtesy shuttle to and from the ski area. *In room:* TV, coffeemaker, microwave, no phone.

Chalet Montesano ☽☽ This chalet, constructed from a turn-of-the-20th-century miner's cabin, is a romantic ski vacation retreat. A 5-minute walk from restaurants and the lift, it's a woodsy and secluded place, just what innkeepers Victor and Karin Frohlich, who have been in Taos Ski Valley since the 1960s, set out to create. All rooms have a Bavarian feel, with nice touches such as CD players, VCRs, coffeemakers, and minifridges; some have fireplaces. In the studio apartments, you'll find Murphy beds that fold into hand-crafted chests to leave plenty of room for daytime living. These and the one-bedroom apartment have kitchenettes or full kitchens, with stoves, ovens, microwaves, and dishwashers. On the west side of the building are a picturesque lap pool, health club, and Jacuzzi, banked by windows, with views of the runs and forest. Smoking is not allowed here.

Pattison Loop #3 (P.O. Box 77), Taos Ski Valley, NM 87525. ℂ **800/723-9104** or 505/776-8226. Fax 505/776-8760. www.chaletmontesano.com. 7 units. Ski season $170–$220 double, $135–$330 apt (for 2 people); summer $85–$120 double; $120–$140 apt (for 2 people). Weekly rates $1,190–$2,560 during ski season, depending on type of room and number of people. AE, DISC, MC, V. Children under 14 not accepted. **Amenities:** Indoor pool; exercise room; Jacuzzi; sauna; in-room massage; coin-op laundry; all units nonsmoking. *In room:* TV/VCR, dataport, fridge, coffeemaker, hair dryer, iron, safe, CD player.

Edelweiss Lodge & Spa

Set to open in 2005, this lodge at the very base of the mountain is a remake of a 1960s classic. Now, it's a brand-new condo-hotel, with the only full spa facility in Taos Ski Valley. At press time, it had yet to open, so I can't rate its quality. However, the owners have been excellent hosts since they purchased the property in 1997, so I'm confident it will be well planned and run. The condominiums are upscale, each with a fireplace and full kitchen with stainless-steel appliances, and many with balconies; the hotel rooms are planned to be more standard. Check their website for a glimpse of rooms and other facilities.

106 Sutton Place, Taos Ski Valley, NM 87525. ℂ **800/I-LUV-SKI** or 505/776-2301. Fax 505/776-2533. www.edelweisslodgeandspa.com. 46 units. Ski week includes gourmet meals, lift tickets, and lessons: $1,145–$1,590 per person double; per-day rates: winter $145–$270, summer $100–$150. AE, DISC, MC, V. **Amenities:** Restaurant; bar; health club & full spa; 2 Jacuzzis; sauna; concierge; massage. *In room:* TV, fridge, coffeemaker, hair dryer.

Inn at Snakedance ★★

With all the luxuries of a full-service hotel, this inn can please most people. Skiers will appreciate the inn's location, just steps from the lift, as well as amenities such as ski storage and boot dryers. The original structure that stood on this site (part of which has been restored for use today) was known as the Hondo Lodge. Before there was a Taos Ski Valley, Hondo Lodge served as a refuge for fishermen, hunters, and artists. Constructed from enormous pine timbers that had been cut for a copper mining operation in the 1890s, it was literally nothing more than a place for the men to bed down for the night. The Inn at Snakedance today offers comfortable guest rooms; many feature wood-burning fireplaces, and all have humidifiers. All the furnishings are modern, the decor stylish, and the windows (many of which offer views) open to let in the mountain air. Some rooms adjoin, connecting a standard hotel room with a fireplace room—perfect for families. Smoking is prohibited in the guest rooms and most public areas. The Hondo Restaurant and Bar offers dining and entertainment daily during the ski season (off-season schedules vary) and sponsors wine tastings and wine dinners. Grilled items, salads, and snacks are available on an outdoor deck. The hotel also offers shuttle service to and from nearby shops and restaurants.

110 Sutton Place (P.O. Box 89), Taos Ski Valley, NM 87525. ℂ **800/322-9815** or 505/776-2277. Fax 505/776-1410. www.innsnakedance.com. 60 units. Christmas holiday $270 double; rest of ski season $225 double; value season $165 double; summer $75 double. AE, DC, DISC, MC, V. Children 6 and under not accepted. Free parking at Taos Ski Valley parking lot. Closed mid-Apr to mid-June and mid-Oct to mid-Nov. **Amenities:** Restaurant; bar; exercise room; spa; Jacuzzi; sauna; massage; convenience store (with food, sundries, video rental, and alcoholic beverages); all units nonsmoking. *In room:* Satellite TV, fridge, coffeemaker, hair dryer, humidifier.

Powderhorn Suites and Condominiums ★★ *(Finds*

A cozy, homelike feel and Euro-Southwestern ambience make this inn one of the best buys in Taos Ski Valley, just a 2-minute walk from the lift. You'll find consistency and quality here, with impeccably clean medium-size rooms, mountain views, vaulted ceilings, spotless bathrooms, and comfortable beds. The larger suites have stoves, balconies, and fireplaces. Adjoining rooms are perfect for families. You can expect conscientious and expert service as well. There's no elevator, so if stairs are a problem for you, be sure to ask for a room on the ground floor.

5 Ernie Blake Rd. (P.O. Box 69), Taos Ski Valley, NM 87525. ℭ **800/776-2346** or 505/776-2341. Fax 505/776-2341 ext. 103. www.taoswebb.com/powderhorn. 17 units. Ski season $99–$165 double, $130–$200 suite, $195–$400 condo; summer $69 double, $79–$89 suite, $109–$129 condo. MC, V. Valet parking. **Amenities:** 2 Jacuzzis; massage. *In room:* TV, dataport, kitchenette.

Moderate

Alpine Village Suites 𝄞   Alpine Village is a small village within Taos Ski Valley, a few steps from the lift. Owned by John and Barbara Cottam, the complex also houses a ski shop and bar/restaurant. The Cottams began with seven rooms, still nice rentals, above their ski shop. Each has a sleeping loft for the agile who care to climb a ladder, as well as sunny windows. The newer section has nicely decorated rooms, with attractive touches such as Mexican furniture and inventive tile work done by locals. Like most other accommodations at Taos Ski Valley, the rooms are not especially soundproof. Fortunately, most skiers go to bed early. All rooms have VCRs, stoves, microwaves, and minifridges. In the newer building, rooms have fireplaces and private balconies. Request a south-facing room for a view of the slopes. The Jacuzzi has a fireplace and a view of the slopes.

100 Thunderbird Rd. (P.O. Box 98), Taos Ski Valley, NM 87525. ℭ **800/576-2666** or 505/776-8540. Fax 505/776-8542. www.alpine-suites.com. 29 units. Ski season $70–$145 suite for 2, $265–$335 suite for up to 6; summer $65–$120 suite for 2 (includes continental breakfast). AE, DISC, MC, V. Covered valet parking $10. **Amenities:** Jacuzzi; sauna; massage. *In room:* TV/VCR, kitchenette.

Thunderbird Lodge 𝄞   Owners Elisabeth and Tom Brownell's goal at this Bavarian-style lodge is to bring people together, and they accomplish it—sometimes a little too well. The lodge sits on the sunny side of the ski area. The lobby has a stone fireplace, raw pine pillars, and tables accented with copper lamps. There's a sun-lit room ideal for breakfast and lunch, with a bank of windows looking out toward the notorious Al's Run and the rest of the ski village. Adjoining is a large bar/lounge with booths, a grand piano, and a fireplace, where live entertainment plays during the evenings through the winter. The rooms are small, some tiny, and noise travels up and down the halls, giving these three stories a dormitory atmosphere. I suggest when making reservations that you request their widest room; otherwise, you may feel as though you're in a train car.

Across the road, the Thunderbird also has a chalet with larger rooms and a brilliant sun porch. Food is the big draw at the Thunderbird. Gourmet breakfast and dinner are included in your stay—you'll be dining on some of the best food available in the region. For breakfast, we had blueberry pancakes and bacon, with our choice from a table of continental breakfast accompaniments; and for dinner, we had four courses highlighted by rack of lamb Provençal. You can eat at your own table or join the larger communal one and get to know the guests, some of whom have been returning for as many as 30 years.

3 Thunderbird Rd. (P.O. Box 87), Taos Ski Valley, NM 87525. ℭ **800/776-2279** or 505/776-2280. Fax 505/776-2238. www.thunderbird-taos.com. 32 units. $126–$147 per person. 7-day ski week package $1,190–$1,260 per person double (7 days room, 14 meals, 6 lift tickets, and ski lessons), depending on season and type of accommodation. Rates include 2 full meals per day. AE, MC, V. Free valet parking. **Amenities:** Jacuzzi; his-and-hers saunas; game room; business center; massage; babysitting by prior arrangement; laundry service.

CONDOMINIUMS

Expensive

Sierra del Sol Condominiums ☆   I have wonderful memories of these condominiums, which are just a 2-minute walk from the lift; family friends used to invite me to stay with them here when I was about 10. The units, built in the 1960s, with additions through the years, have been well maintained. Though they're privately owned, and therefore decorated at the whim of the owners, management does inspect them every year and make suggestions. They're smartly built and come in a few sizes: studio, one-bedroom, and two-bedroom. The one- and two-bedroom units have big living rooms with fireplaces and porches that look out on the ski runs. The bedrooms are spacious, and some have sleeping lofts. Each has a full kitchen, with a dishwasher, stove, oven, and fridge. Most units also have microwaves and humidifiers. Two-bedroom units sleep up to six. Grills and picnic tables on the grounds sit near a mountain river.

13 Thunderbird Rd. (P.O. Box 84), Taos Ski Valley, NM 87525. ℂ **800/523-3954** or 505/776-2981. Fax 505/776-2347. www.sierrataos.com. 32 units. Prices range from $70 (studio) in summer to $395 (2-bedroom condo) in high season. AE, DISC, MC, V. Free parking. **Amenities:** 2 Jacuzzis; 2 saunas; massage; babysitting; coin-op laundry. *In room:* TV/VCR, kitchen, hair dryer upon request, iron upon request, safe.

Moderate

Taos Mountain Lodge (Value   About a mile west of Taos Ski Valley on the road from Taos, these loft suites, which can each accommodate up to six people, provide comfortable lodging for a good price. Built in 1990, the place has undergone some renovation over the years. Don't expect a lot of privacy in these condominiums, but they're good for a romping ski vacation. Each unit has a small bedroom downstairs and a loft bedroom upstairs, as well as a sofa bed or futon couch in the living room. Regular rooms have kitchenettes, with minifridges and stoves, and deluxe rooms have full kitchens, with fridges, stoves, and ovens.

Taos Ski Valley Road (P.O. Box 202), Taos Ski Valley, NM 87525. ℂ **866/320-8267** or 505/776-2229. Fax 505/776-3982. www.taosmountainlodge.com. 10 units. Ski season $119–$280 suite; May–Oct $80–$100 suite. Ski packages available. AE, DISC, MC, V. *In room:* Kitchen or kitchenette.

RV PARKS & CAMPGROUNDS

Carson National Forest   There are nine national-forest camping areas within 20 miles of Taos; these developed areas are open from Memorial Day to Labor Day. They range from woodsy, streamside sites on the road to Taos Ski Valley to open lowlands with lots of sage. Call the Forest Service to discuss the best location for your needs.

208 Cruz Alta Rd., Taos, NM 87571. ℂ **505/758-6200.** www.fs.fed.us/r3/carson. Fees range from $7–$15 per night. No credit cards.

Questa Lodge   On the banks of the Red River, this RV camp is just outside the small village of Questa. It's a nice pastoral setting. The cabins aren't in the best condition, but the RV and camping accommodations are pleasant—all with amazing mountain views.

Lower Embargo Road #8 (P.O. Box 155), Questa, NM 87556. ℂ **505/586-0300.** 24 sites. Full RV hookup $20 per day, $200 per month. 4 cabins for rent in summer. AE, DISC, MC, V. Closed Nov–Apr.

Taos RV Park   This RV park, located on the edge of town, offers a convenient location with a city atmosphere. It has very clean and nice bathrooms and showers. Two tepees rent for around $25 each, but beware: They're right on the main drag and may be noisy. The park is located on a local bus line. Senior discounts are available.

1802 NM 68, Taos, NM 87557. $\mathcal{C}$ **800/323-6009** or 505/758-1667. Fax 505/758-1989. www.taosbudget host.com. 33 spaces. $17 without RV hookup; $25 with RV hookup. DISC, MC, V.

Taos Valley RV Park and Campground   Just 2½ miles south of the plaza, this campground is surrounded by sage and offers views of the surrounding mountains. Each site has a picnic table and grill. The place has a small store, a laundry room, a playground, and tent shelters, as well as a dump station and very clean restrooms. Pets are welcome.

120 Este Rd., off NM 68 (7204 NDCBU), Taos, NM 87571. $\mathcal{C}$ **800/999-7571** or 505/758-4469. Fax 505/758-4469. www.camptaos.com/rv. 92 spaces. $18 without RV hookup; $24–$27 with RV hookup. MC, V.

4 Where to Dine

Taos is one of my favorite places to eat. Informality reigns; at a number of restaurants you can dine on world-class food while wearing jeans or even ski pants. Nowhere is a jacket and tie mandatory. This informality doesn't extend to reservations, however; especially during the peak season, it is important to make reservations well in advance and keep them or else cancel. Also, be aware that Taos is not a late-night place; most restaurants finish serving at about 9pm.

TAOS
EXPENSIVE
De La Tierra ★★★ REGIONAL AMERICAN   This hot spot not far from the plaza always leaves me with an exotic and buoyant sense that I attribute to its setting and cuisine. Located at the new eco-resort El Monte Sagrado, this restaurant creates an elegance of old world Orient, with an open, high ceiling and comfortable black silk chairs, while serving imaginative American fare with an emphasis on wild game. Service is excellent, even down to the master sommelier overseeing the wine selections. The chef utilizes seasonal and local ingredients, including organic ones when he can. For starters, I recommend the Dungeness crab cake, or, for a more exotic treat, try the yak satay, the meat from the resort owner's high-mountain animals. For a main course, I've enjoyed the venison medallions, served over garlic mashed potatoes and with roasted spring mushrooms. My mother likes the rosemary skewered shrimp, served with white-corn polenta and chard. Tasty food is served during the day at The Gardens, a more casual spot, with lots of exotic plants and a lovely patio (try the yak cheese frittata). Tapas are served at the Anaconda Bar.

In the El Monte Sagrado hotel, 317 Kit Carson Rd. $\mathcal{C}$ **800/828-TAOS** or 505/758-3502. Reservations recommended. The Gardens breakfast $5–$11, lunch $8–$16; De La Tierra dinner $19–$34. AE, DC, DISC, MC, V. The Gardens daily 7–10am and 11am–2:30pm; De La Tierra daily 5:30–10pm.

Doc Martin's ★ NEW AMERICAN   Doc Martin's serves innovative food in a historic setting. The restaurant comprises Dr. Thomas Paul Martin's former home, office, and delivery room. In 1912, painters Bert Philips (Doc's brother-in-law) and Ernest Blumenschein hatched the concept of the Taos Society of Artists in the dining room. Art still predominates here, in both the paintings that adorn the walls and the cuisine. The food is often good here, but it can be inconsistent.

The wine list has received numerous "Awards of Excellence" from *Wine Spectator* magazine. In a rich atmosphere, with bins of yellow squash, eggplants, and red peppers set near the kiva fireplace, diners feast on Southwestern breakfast fare such as huevos rancheros (fried eggs on a blue-corn tortilla smothered with chile and Jack cheese). Lunch might include the house specialty, the Doc chile relleno, or chipolte shrimp on corn cake. For dinner, a good bet is the piñon-encrusted salmon or the Southwest lacquered duck served with *posole* and mango relish. There's always a nice selection of desserts—try the chocolate mousse cake or the *capirotada* (New Mexican bread pudding). Brunch is served on Sundays from 7:30am to 2:30pm. The Adobe bar has live jazz with no cover charge.

In the Historic Taos Inn, 125 Paseo del Pueblo Norte. Ⓒ **505/758-1977.** www.taosinn.com. Reservations recommended. Breakfast $5–$8, lunch $5.50–$11, dinner $14–$28, fixed-price menu $23. AE, DISC, MC, V. Daily 7:30–11am, 11:30am–2:30pm, and 5:30–9pm.

Joseph's Table ⚘⚘ *Finds* NEW AMERICAN/MEDITERRANEAN Taos funk meets European flair at this intimate restaurant on the plaza. Recently moved to the renovated Hotel La Fonda de Taos, this notable eatery now occupies a larger space, but it can still fill up. Chef/owner Joseph Wrede (once selected as one of the 10 "Best New Chefs" in America by *Food and Wine Magazine*) creates such delicacies as six-way duck and a lovely steak au poivre, inventively prepared and served. The duck is literally cooked six different ways, ranging from roasted to sliced thinly, prosciutto style, and paired with a delicate corn crème brûlée. Meanwhile, the steak sits atop a layer of smooth mashed potatoes and is crowned with an exotic mushroom salad. The offerings are not for the faint of palate, though. Wrede likes complex flavors, so those who prefer more conservative food might opt for Lambert's (below). The servers can help guide you through the complex menu, so be sure to ask. For dessert, try such delicacies as the mescal chocolate bar with lime sorbet or the black-pepper-roasted pineapple bread pudding. An eclectic selection of beers and wines by the bottle and glass is available. Be aware that in winter, parts of the restaurant can be cold.

In the Hotel La Fonda de Taos, 108A South Taos Plaza. Ⓒ **505/751-4512.** www.josephstable.com. Reservations recommended. Main courses $8–$18 lunch, $18–$35 dinner. AE, DISC, MC, V. May–Aug daily 11:30am–2:30pm and 5:30–10pm; ski season 4:30–10pm; rest of the year 5:30–10pm.

Lambert's of Taos ⚘⚘ CONTEMPORARY AMERICAN Zeke Lambert, once the head chef at Doc Martin's, opened this fine dining establishment in 1989 in the historic Randall Home near Los Pandos Road. It's a sparsely decorated place with contemporary art on the walls—a nice spot for a romantic evening. The service is friendly and efficient, and the meal begins with a complimentary aperitif. The house salad is nicely prepared, with butter lettuce and radicchio. Appetizers include a Mediterranean olive plate and chile-dusted rock shrimp. The restaurant's signature dish is pepper-crusted lamb. If you like strong flavors, this is your dish—very peppery, served with a red wine demi-glace and linguine. Others I've spoken to have enjoyed the grilled salmon with tomato-sage sauce. For dessert, the white chocolate ice cream and Zeke's chocolate mousse with raspberry sauce are delicious. Espresso coffees, beers, and wine are served.

309 Paseo del Pueblo Sur. Ⓒ **505/758-1009.** Reservations recommended. Main courses $17–$30. AE, DC, DISC, MC, V. Daily 5pm–closing, usually 9pm or so.

Momentitos de la Vida ⚘⚘ NEW AMERICAN For years, this personable adobe building housed Casa Cordova, where, in the '60s and '70s, the jet-set après ski crowd hung out, drinking martinis. Well, as long as martinis are back in style, why not revamp this spot on the outskirts of Arroyo Seco and once again make it the place to be? That was what owner/chefs Chris and Kelly Maher had in mind for this restaurant. The atmosphere is moody; the service is refined and attentive. Though locals call the place too pricey, the food is very thoughtfully prepared, with real attention to imaginative detail: The excellent sourdough bread comes with a squash butter spread, and the dishes' ingredients include

Where to Dine in the Taos Area

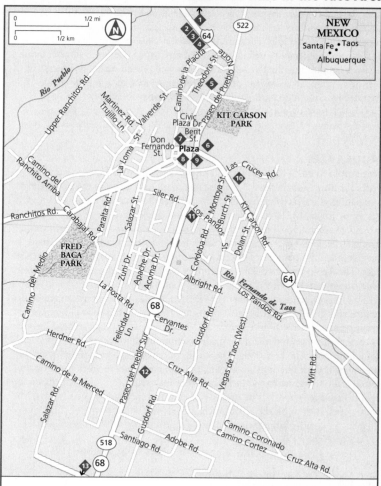

The Apple Tree **7**
The Bavarian Restaurant **1**
Bent Street Cafe & Deli **7**
Bravo **12**
De La Tierra **10**
Doc Martin's **6**
Guadalajara Grill **3, 13**
Gypsy 360° **1**
Joseph's Table **8**

Lambert's of Taos **11**
Michael's Kitchen **5**
Momentitos de la Vida **1**
Ogelvie's Bar & Grill **9**
Old Blinking Light **1**
Orlando's New Mexican Café **2**
Taos Pizza Out Back **4**
Trading Post Café **13**

such novelties as parsnips and purple potatoes. You might start with a smoked trout éclair or grilled habañero prawns. One of the most popular main courses is the blackened filet mignon, served with root mashed potatoes (a tasty mixture of rutabaga and parsnip), wilted greens, and asparagus. The vegan shepherd's pie is also a tasty option. There are fish dishes as well. Finish with a hot berry cobbler or tiramisu. In warm months, you can enjoy your meal on the patio, surrounded by a plum orchard. Jazz plays fireside Friday to Sunday.

5 miles north of the intersection of NM 150 and NM 522, Arroyo Seco. ✆ 505/776-3333. Reservations recommended on weekends. Bistro menu $8–$15; main dining room $19–$36. AE, MC, V. Tues–Sun 5:30–10pm; bar 4:30pm–closing.

MODERATE

The Apple Tree ⭐ SOUTHWESTERN/AMERICAN Eclectic music pervades the four adobe rooms of this restaurant, a block north of the plaza. Original paintings by Taos masters watch over the candlelit service indoors. Outside, diners sit at wooden tables beneath a spreading apple tree.

This restaurant is popular among locals and travelers, but it isn't my favorite. Though the chefs use fresh and tasty ingredients, the recipes often try too hard. I suggest ordering what looks simplest, either from the menu or from the daily specials. The Apple Tree salad (greens sprinkled with dried cranberries, walnuts, and blue cheese, served with vinaigrette) is very good, as is the *calabasa* (squash) quesadilla. A popular dish is mango chicken enchiladas (chicken simmered with onions and spices, layered between blue corn tortillas with mango chutney, sour cream, and salsa fresca, and smothered with green chile), but beware: They're sweet. I prefer the salmon alfredo, made with sun-dried tomatoes and New Mexico goat cheese. The best thing here is the chile-jalapeño bread, served with the meal. The brunch offerings are worth sampling, even more so when eaten on the lovely patio under the restaurant's namesake. Such standards as French toast and eggs Benedict are good, but the specials usually outshine them, especially the fresh fruit crepes, such as blueberry or peach, served with whipped cream. The Apple Tree has an award-winning wine list, and the desserts are prepared fresh daily.

123 Bent St. ✆ 505/758-1900. Reservations recommended. Main courses $5–$11 brunch, $6–$12 lunch, $12–$30 dinner. AE, DC, DISC, MC, V. Mon–Sat 11:30am–3pm; daily 5:30–9pm; brunch Sun 11am–3pm.

Bent Street Cafe & Deli ⭐ CAFE/INTERNATIONAL This popular cafe, a short block north of the plaza, has inventive, reliable food in a country-home atmosphere. Outside, a flower box surrounds sidewalk seating that is heated in winter. Inside, baskets and bottles of homemade jam accent wooden tables. The menu features breakfast burritos and homemade granola in the morning; for lunch, you can choose from 18 deli sandwiches, plus a "create-your-own" column, as well as a nice selection of salads. At dinner, select a special such as beef tenderloin medallions served over fettuccine with chipotle-Fontina cream sauce, or, from the menu, *camarones di pesto* (tiger prawns with sun-dried tomatoes, artichoke hearts, and green chile pesto). The deli offers carryout service for great picnics.

120 Bent St. ✆ 505/758-5787. Breakfast $2–$8, lunch $2.50–$8, dinner $11–$20. MC, V. Mon–Sat 8am–9pm.

Bravo ⭐ AMERICAN/CAFE This bustling cafe on the south end of town offers a refreshing big-city mix of atmosphere and flavors. As well as a restaurant, it is a specialty wine and beer shop, package liquor store, and gourmet deli. There's a large communal table at the restaurant's heart. The menu is eclectic, offering good-size portions of very tasty food. With owner/chef Lionel Garnier's French background lending magic, the flavors are refined. Locals rave about the

---

Kids Family-Friendly Restaurants

Michael's Kitchen (p. 219)   With a broad menu, comfy booths, and a very casual, diner-type atmosphere, both kids and parents feel at home.

Orlando's New Mexican Café (p. 219)   Kids love the relaxed atmosphere and playfully colorful walls almost as much as the tacos and quesadillas made especially for them.

Taos Pizza Out Back (p. 217)   The pizza will please both parents and kids, and so will all the odd decorations, such as the chain with foot-long links hanging over the front counter.

---

three-cheese pizza; my favorite is the Bravo, with roasted vegetables. The Caesar salad with chicken is also popular, as is the elaborate salad bar, complete with pasta and bean concoctions. A variety of sandwiches fills the menu as well, and in the evening you can order Continental dishes. During busy hours, service is slow but congenial. There's also a martini and beer bar here, with specials, such as a beer sampler and enough types of martinis to make you really wonder how many things you should mix with gin or vodka.

1353A Paseo del Pueblo Sur, Ranchos de Taos. ☏ 505/758-8100. Lunch $6–$12, dinner $8–$18. AE, DISC, MC, V. Mon–Sat 11am–9pm.

Ogelvie's Bar & Grille INTERNATIONAL   The only real reason to go to this restaurant is to have a cocktail right on the plaza. In the warm months, there's a nice balcony where diners can sit and drink margaritas and indulge in chips or other appetizers, such as potato skins, or even burgers. Otherwise, the food here is not flavorful, and the atmosphere inside is dated.

103E. Plaza Suite I. ☏ 505/758-8866. Lunch $6–$12, dinner $8.50–$25. AE, DC, DISC, MC, V. Daily 11am–9pm dining, 10pm bar.

Old Blinking Light ✯ AMERICAN   This restaurant on the Ski Valley Road provides tasty American food in a casual atmosphere. Decorated with Spanish colonial furniture and an excellent art collection, this is a good place to stop after skiing. The service is friendly and efficient. To accompany the free chips and house-made salsa, order a margarita and sip it next to the patio bonfire, open evenings year-round. The menu is broad, ranging from salads and burgers to steaks, seafood, and Mexican food. I say head straight for the fajitas, especially the jumbo shrimp wrapped in bacon and stuffed with poblano peppers and jack cheese. Leave room for the Old Blinking Light mud pie, made with local Taos Cow Ice Cream. Live music plays Monday and Friday nights.

US 150, mile marker 1. ☏ 505/776-8787. Reservations recommended weekends and Mon nights. Main courses $9–$26. AE, MC, V. Wine shop daily 11:30am–10pm. Restaurant daily 5–10pm.

Taos Pizza Out Back ✯ Kids PASTA AND GOURMET PIZZA   My kayaking buddies always go here after a day on the river. That will give you an idea of the level of informality (very), as well as the quality of the food and beer (great), and the size of the portions (large). It's a raucous old hippie-decorated adobe restaurant, with a friendly and eager waitstaff. What to order? PIZZA. Sure, the spicy Greek pasta is good, as is the Veggie Zone (a calzone filled with stir-fried veggies and two cheeses)—but, why? The pizzas are incredible. All come with a delicious thin crust (no sogginess here) that's folded over on the edges and sprinkled with sesame seeds. The sauce is unthinkably tasty, and the variations are broad. There's Thai chicken pizza (pineapple, peanuts, and a spicy sauce); The Killer, with sun-dried tomatoes, Gorgonzola, green chile, and black olives; and my favorite, pizza Florentine (spinach, basil, sun-dried tomatoes, chicken breast, mushrooms, capers, and garlic, sautéed in white wine). Don't leave without trying either a Dalai Lama bar (coconut, chocolate, and caramel) or the Taos Yum (a "mondo" chocolate-chip cookie with ice cream, whipped cream, and chocolate sauce). Check out the small selection of wines and the large selection of microbrews.

712 Paseo del Pueblo Norte (just north of Allsup's). © 505/758-3112. Reservations recommended weekends and holidays. Pizza $12–$26, pasta and calzone $7–$12. MC, V. Summer daily 11am–10pm; winter Sun–Thurs 11am–9pm, Fri–Sat 11am–10pm.

Trading Post Café 🎿🎿 Finds NORTHERN ITALIAN/INTERNATIONAL
One of my tastiest writing assignments was doing a profile of this restaurant for the *New York Times*. Chef/owner René Mettler spent 3 hours serving course after course of dishes prepared especially for us. If you think this gastronomical orgy might color my opinion, just ask anyone in town where they most like to eat. Even notables such as R. C. Gorman, Dennis Hopper, and Gene Hackman will likely name the Trading Post. What draws the crowds is a gallery atmosphere, where rough plastered walls washed with an orange hue are set off by sculptures, paintings, and photographs. The meals are also artistically served. "You eat with your eyes," says Mettler. If you show up without reservations, be prepared to wait for a table, and don't expect quiet romance here: The place bustles. A bar—a fun place to sit—encloses an open-exhibition kitchen. Although the focus is on the fine food, diners can feel comfortable here, even if trying three appetizers and skipping the main course. The outstanding Caesar salad has an interesting twist—garlic chips. If you like pasta, you'll find a nice variety on the menu. The fettuccine alla carbonara is tasty, as is the seafood pasta. Heartier appetites might like the New Zealand lamb chops with tomato-mint sauce. There's also a fresh fish of the day and usually some nice stews and soups, at very reasonable prices. A good list of beers and wines round out the experience. For dessert, try the tarts.

4179 Paseo del Pueblo Sur, Ranchos de Taos. © 505/758-5089. Reservations recommended. Menu items $6–$28. AE, DC, DISC, MC, V. Tues–Sat 11:30am–9:30pm; Sun 5–9pm.

INEXPENSIVE

Guadalajara Grill 🎿 MEXICAN My organic-lettuce-farmer friend, Joe, introduced me to this authentic Mexican restaurant; then he disappeared into Mexico, only communicating occasionally by e-mail. Did the incredible food lure him south? I wonder. The restaurant shares a building with a car wash, but don't let that put you off; the food here is excellent. It's Mexican rather than New Mexican, a refreshing treat. I recommend the tacos, particularly pork or chicken, served in soft homemade corn tortillas, the meat artfully seasoned and grilled. The burritos are large and smothered in chile. *Platos* are served with rice and beans, and half orders are available for smaller appetites. There are also some seafood dishes available—try the *mojo de ajo* (shrimp cooked with garlic), served with rice, beans, and guacamole. Beer and wine are served.

1384 Paseo del Pueblo Sur. © 505/751-0063. All items under $15. MC, V. Mon–Sat 10:30am–9pm; Sun 11am–9pm. A second location, at 1822 Paseo del Pueblo Norte (© 505/737-0816), is open Mon–Sat 10:30am–9pm; Sun 11am–8:30pm.

Michael's Kitchen *(Kids)* NEW MEXICAN/AMERICAN   A couple blocks north of the plaza, this eatery provides big portions of okay food in a relaxed atmosphere. Between its hardwood floor and viga ceiling are various knick-knacks: a deer head here, a Tiffany lamp there. Seating is at booths and tables. Breakfast dishes, including a large selection of pancakes and egg preparations (with names like the "Moofy," and "Omelette Extra-ordinaire") are served all day, as are lunch sandwiches (including Philly cheesesteak, tuna melt, and a veggie sandwich). Some people like the generically (and facetiously) titled "Health Food" meal, a double order of fries with red or green chile and cheese. Dinners range from veal cordon bleu to plantation-fried chicken. For breakfast, try one of the excellent doughnuts served from Michael's bakery.

304 C Paseo del Pueblo Norte. © **505/758-4178.** Reservations not accepted. Breakfast $3–$8, lunch $4–$9.50, dinner $6–$14. AE, DISC, MC, V. Daily 7am–8:30pm. Closed major holidays.

Orlando's New Mexican Café *(★) (Kids)* NEW MEXICAN   Festivity reigns in this spicy little cafe on the north end of town. Serving some of northern New Mexico's best chile, this place has colorful tables set around a bustling open kitchen and airy patio dining during warmer months. Service is friendly but minimal. Try the Los Colores, their most popular dish, with three enchiladas (chicken, beef, and cheese) smothered in chile and served with beans and *posole*. The taco salad is another favorite. Portions are big here, and you can order a Mexican or microbrew beer, or a New Mexican or California wine.

114 Don Juan Valdez Lane. (1¾ miles north of the plaza, off Paseo del Pueblo Norte). © **505/751-1450.** Reservations not accepted. Main courses under $10. No credit cards. Daily 10:30am–9pm.

NORTH OF TOWN

The Bavarian Restaurant *(★) (Finds)* BAVARIAN   Enter through 300-year-old castle doors into a high alpine world full of Bavaria. This restaurant, sitting high above Taos Ski Valley at an elevation of 10,200 feet, creates, with beamed ceilings, aged pine paneling, and an antler lamp all set around an authentic *kachelofe*, a Bavarian-style stove, a feel both rustic and elegant. Service is uneven but well intentioned. At lunch, the porch fills with sun-worshipers. Dishes include traditional foods such as goulash (a hearty beef and paprika stew) and spaetzle (Bavarian-style pasta) at lunch. Dinnertime brings classic dishes such as Wiener schnitzel (Viennese veal cutlet) and sauerbraten (beef roast). Most dishes come with a potato dish and fresh vegetable. For dessert try the apple strudel. Accompany your meal with a selection from the well-chosen European wine list or with a beer, served in an authentic stein. The road to The Bavarian is easily driveable in summer. In winter, most diners ski here or call to arrange for a shuttle to pick them up at the Taos Ski Valley parking lot. Proust!

In The Bavarian Lodge, Taos Ski Valley. © **888/205-8020** or 505/776-8020. Reservations recommended at dinner. Lunch $7.50–$15, dinner $17–$35. AE, MC, V. Daily ski season 11:30am–3pm and 6–9pm; summer Thurs–Sun 11:30am–3:30pm and 5:30pm–closing.

Gypsy 360° *(★) (Finds)* ASIAN/AMERICAN   This funky cafe on a side street is as cute as the village of Arroyo Seco where it resides. And the food is tasty and inventive. During the winter diners sit in a sunny atrium or a more enclosed space, all casual with lawn-style furnishings and bright colors. In warm months, a sunny patio opens up the place. Service is accommodating though at times overworked. The food ranges from sushi to Thai to sandwiches. My Berkley Bowl salad had lots of spring greens and crisp goodies such as carrots and jicama, and the chef accommodated my request for grilled salmon on top. The pesto dressing is now my all-time favorite. My mother's angus burger was thick and juicy, topped with crisp bacon and bleu cheese; her potato salad had fresh dill. Other times I've enjoyed the noodle bowls, such as a Sri Lankan red curry or pad Thai. If you're staying in Taos, this spot makes for a great destination, with plenty of fun shops to peruse when your tummy's full.

480 NM 150, Seco Plaza, Arroyo Seco. ✆ 505/776-3166. Main courses $7.50–$15. MC, V. Tues–Wed and Sat 8am–4pm; Thurs–Fri 8am–8pm; Sun 9am–3pm.

5 What to See & Do

With a history shaped by pre-Columbian civilization, Spanish colonialism, and the Wild West; outdoor activities that range from ballooning to world-class skiing; and a clustering of artists, writers, and musicians, Taos has something to offer almost everybody. Its pueblo is the most accessible in New Mexico, and its museums represent a world-class display of regional history and culture.

SUGGESTED ITINERARIES

If You Have Only 1 Day

Spend at least 2 hours at Taos Pueblo. You'll also have time to see the Millicent Rogers Museum and to browse in some of the town's fine art galleries. Try to make it to Ranchos de Taos to see the San Francisco de Asis Church and to shop on the plaza there.

If You Have 2 Days

On the second day, explore the Taos Historic Museums—the Martinez Hacienda, the Kit Carson Home, and the Ernest L. Blumenschein

Home. Then head out of town to enjoy the view from the Rio Grande Gorge Bridge.

If You Have 3 Days or More

On your third day, drive the "Enchanted Circle" through Red River, Eagle Nest, and Angel Fire or head to the Taos Art Museum. You may want to allow a full day for shopping or perhaps drive up to Taos Ski Valley for a chairlift ride or a short hike. Of course, if you're here in the winter with skis, the mountain is your first priority.

THE TOP ATTRACTIONS

Millicent Rogers Museum of Northern New Mexico ⑆ This museum will give you a glimpse of some of the finest Southwestern arts and crafts anywhere, but it's small enough to avoid being overwhelming. It was founded in 1953 by Millicent Rogers's family members after her death. Rogers was a wealthy Taos émigré who in 1947 began acquiring a magnificent collection of beautiful Native American arts and crafts. Included are Navajo and Pueblo jewelry, Navajo textiles, Pueblo pottery, Hopi and Zuni kachina dolls, paintings from the Rio Grande Pueblo people, and basketry from a wide variety of Southwestern tribes. The museum also presents exhibitions of Southwestern art, crafts, and design.

Since the 1970s, the scope of the museum's permanent collection has been expanded to include Anglo arts and crafts and Hispanic religious and secular arts and crafts, from Spanish and Mexican colonial to contemporary times. Included are *santos* (religious images), furniture, weavings, *colcha* embroideries, and decorative tinwork. Agricultural implements, domestic utensils, and craftspeople's tools dating from the 17th and 18th centuries are also displayed.

The museum gift shop has a fine collection of superior regional art. Classes and workshops, lectures, and field trips are held throughout the year.

Taos Attractions

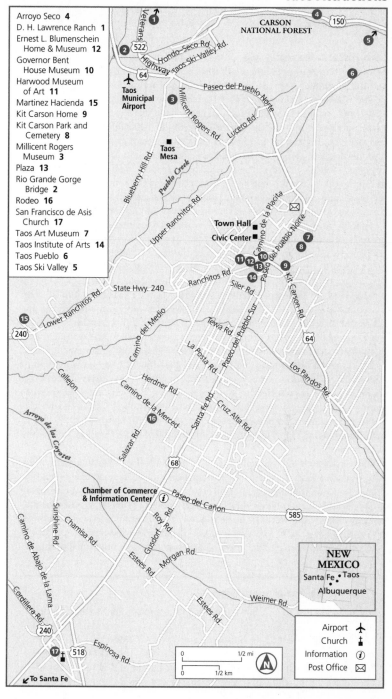

Arroyo Seco **4**
D. H. Lawrence Ranch **1**
Ernest L. Blumenschein
  Home & Museum **12**
Governor Bent
  House Museum **10**
Harwood Museum
  of Art **11**
Martinez Hacienda **15**
Kit Carson Home **9**
Kit Carson Park and
  Cemetery **8**
Millicent Rogers
  Museum **3**
Plaza **13**
Rio Grande Gorge
  Bridge **2**
Rodeo **16**
San Francisco de Asis
  Church **17**
Taos Art Museum **7**
Taos Institute of Arts **14**
Taos Pueblo **6**
Taos Ski Valley **5**

CARSON
NATIONAL FOREST

Veterans
522
Highway
Hondo-Seco Rd.
Taos Ski Valley Rd.
64
Paseo del Pueblo Norte
150

Taos
Municipal
Airport

Millicent Rogers Rd.
Lucero Rd.

Taos
Mesa

Blueberry Hill Rd.
Pueblo Creek

Upper Ranchitos Rd.

Camino de la Placita
Town Hall
Civic Center
Camino del Pueblo Norte
Paseo del Pueblo Norte
Kit Carson Rd.

Lower Ranchitos Rd.
State Hwy. 240
240
Ranchitos Rd.
Siler Rd.
Tewa Rd.
Paseo del Pueblo Sur
Los Pandos Rd.
64

Callejon
Camino del Medio
La Posta Rd.
Santa Fe Rd.
Cruz Alta Rd.

Herdner Rd.
Camino de la Merced
Salazar Rd.

Arroyo de los Coyotes

68

Chamber of Commerce
& Information Center
Paseo del Cañon
Roy Rd.
585

Sunshine Rd.
Chamisa Rd.
Gusdorf Rd.
Morgan Rd.
Estees Rd.

Camino de Abajo de la Lama
Cordillera Rd.
240
Espinosa Rd.
518
Estees Rd.
Weimer Rd.

To Santa Fe

NEW
MEXICO
Santa Fe · Taos
Albuquerque

Airport ✈
Church ♁
Information ⓘ
Post Office ✉

0   1/2 mi
0   1/2 km
N

Off NM 522, 4 miles north of Taos Plaza, on Millicent Rogers Rd. © 505/758-2462. www.millicentrogers. org. Admission $6 adults, $5 students and seniors, $15 family rate, $1 children 6–16. Daily 10am–5pm. Closed Mon Nov–Mar, New Year's Day, Easter, Thanksgiving, and Christmas. Self-parking.

Taos Historic Museums ⭐⭐ Two historical homes are operated as museums, affording visitors a glimpse of early Taos lifestyles. The Martinez Hacienda and Ernest Blumenschein Home each has unique appeal.

The **Martinez Hacienda,** Lower Ranchitos Road, Highway 240 (© **505/ 758-1000**), is the only Spanish colonial hacienda in the United States that's open to the public year-round. This was the home of the merchant, trader, and *alcalde* (mayor) Don Antonio Severino Martinez, who bought it in 1804 and lived here until his death in 1827. His eldest son was Padre Antonio José Martinez, northern New Mexico's controversial spiritual leader from 1826 to 1867. Located on the west bank of the Rio Pueblo de Taos, about 2 miles southwest of the plaza, the museum is remarkably beautiful, with thick, raw adobe walls. The hacienda has no exterior windows—this was to protect against raids by Plains tribes.

Twenty-one rooms were built around two *placitas,* or interior courtyards. They give you a glimpse of the austerity of frontier lives, with only a few pieces of modest period furniture in each. You'll see bedrooms, servants' quarters, stables, a kitchen, and a large fiesta room. Exhibits tell the story of the Martinez family and life in Spanish Taos between 1598 and 1821, when Mexico gained control.

Taos Historic Museums has developed the Martinez Hacienda into a living museum with weavers, blacksmiths, and woodcarvers. Demonstrations are scheduled daily, and during the **Taos Trade Fair** (held in late Sept) they run virtually nonstop. The Trade Fair commemorates the era when Native Americans, Spanish settlers, and mountain men met here to trade with each other.

The **Ernest L. Blumenschein Home & Museum,** 222 Ledoux St. (© **505/ 758-0505**), 1½ blocks southwest of the plaza, re-creates the lifestyle of one of the founders of the Taos Society of Artists (founded 1915). An adobe home with garden walls and a courtyard, parts of which date from the 1790s, it became the home and studio of Blumenschein (1874–1960) and his family in 1919. Period furnishings include European antiques and handmade Taos furniture in Spanish colonial style.

Blumenschein was born and raised in Pittsburgh. In 1898, after training in New York and Paris, he and fellow painter Bert Phillips were on assignment for *Harper's* and *McClure's* magazines of New York when a wheel of their wagon broke 30 miles north of Taos. Blumenschein drew the short straw and thus was obliged to bring the wheel by horseback to Taos for repair. He later recounted his initial reaction to the valley he entered: "No artist had ever recorded the New Mexico I was now seeing. No writer had ever written down the smell of this air

---

Tips **A Tip for Museumgoers**

If you would like to visit five museums that comprise the Museum Association of Taos—Blumenschein Home, Martinez Hacienda, Harwood Museum, Millicent Rogers Museum, and Taos Art Museum—you'll save money by purchasing a combination ticket for $20. The ticket allows one-time entry to each museum during a 1-year period and is fully transferable. You can purchase the pass at any of the five museums. For more information, call © 505/758-0505.

The Kit Carson Home

Previously, the Kit Carson Home and Museum, East Kit Carson Road, located a block east of the plaza intersection, was the town's general museum of Taos history. The 12-room adobe home was built in 1825 and purchased in 1843 by Carson, the famous mountain man, Indian agent, and scout, as a wedding gift for his young bride, Josefa Jaramillo. It remained their home for 25 years, until both died (exactly a month apart) in 1868. At press time, the owners of the home, the Masonic Lodge, had closed it, with the intent of reopening it as a new museum. The Kit Carson collection, however, remains in the hands of the Taos Historic Museums, many pieces of which are now on display at the Martinez Hacienda.

or the feel of that morning sky. I was receiving . . . the first great unforgettable inspiration of my life. My destiny was being decided."

That spark later led to the foundation of Taos as an art colony. An extensive collection of works by early-20th-century Taos artists, including some by Blumenschein's daughter, Helen, is on display in several rooms of the home.

222 Ledoux St. ℂ 505/758-0505 (information for both museums can be obtained at this number). www.taoshistoricmuseums.com. Admission for each museum $5 adults, $3 children ages 6–16, free for children under 6, $10 families. Summer daily 9am–5pm; call for winter hours.

Taos Pueblo ★★★   It's amazing that in our frenetic world, more than 100 Taos Pueblo residents still live much as their ancestors did 1,000 years ago. When you enter the pueblo, you'll see two large buildings, both with rooms piled on top of each other, forming structures that echo the shape of Taos Mountain (which sits to the northeast). Here, a portion of Taos residents live without electricity and running water. The remaining 2,000 residents of Taos Pueblo live in conventional homes on the pueblo's 95,000 acres.

The main buildings' distinctive flowing lines of shaped mud, with a straw-and-mud exterior plaster, are typical of Pueblo architecture throughout the Southwest. It's architecture that blends in with the surrounding land. Bright blue doors are the same shade as the sky that frames the brown buildings.

The northernmost of New Mexico's 19 pueblos, Taos Pueblo has been home to the Tiwa tribes for more than 900 years. Many residents here still practice ancestral rituals. The center of their world is still nature; women use hornos to bake bread, and most still drink water that flows down from the sacred Blue Lake. Meanwhile, arts and crafts and other tourism-related businesses support the economy, along with government services, ranching, and farming.

The village looks much the same today as it did when a regiment from Coronado's expedition first came upon it in 1540. Though the Tiwa were essentially a peaceful agrarian people, they are perhaps best remembered for spearheading the only successful revolt by Native Americans in history. Launched by Pope (poh-*pay*) in 1680, the uprising drove the Spanish from Santa Fe until 1692 and from Taos until 1698.

As you explore the pueblo, you can visit the residents' studios, sample home-made bread, look into the **San Geronimo Chapel,** and wander past the fascinating ruins of the old church and cemetery. You're expected to ask permission from individuals before taking their photos; some will ask for a small payment. Do not trespass into kivas (ceremonial rooms) and other areas marked as restricted.

The **Feast of San Geronimo** (the patron saint of Taos Pueblo), on September 29 and 30, marks the end of the harvest season. The feast day is reminiscent of an ancient trade fair for the Taos Indians, when tribes from as far south as South America and as far north as the Arctic would come and trade for wares, hides, clothing, and harvested crops. The day is filled with foot races, pole climbing done by traditional Indian clowns, and artists and craftspeople mimicking the early traders. Dances are performed the evening of September 29. Other annual events include a **turtle dance** on New Year's Day, **deer or buffalo dances** on Three Kings Day (Jan 6), and **corn dances** on Santa Cruz Day (May 3), San Antonio Day (June 13), San Juan Day (June 24), Santiago Day (July 25), and Santa Ana Day (July 26). The annual **Taos Pueblo Powwow,** a dance competition and parade that brings together tribes from throughout North America, is held the second weekend of July on tribal lands off NM 522 (see "New Mexico Calendar of Events," in chapter 2). The pueblo Christmas celebration begins on Christmas Eve, with bonfires and a procession with children's dances. On Christmas day, the **deer** or **Matachine dances** take place.

During your visit to the pueblo you will have the opportunity to purchase traditional fried and oven-baked bread as well as a variety of arts and crafts. If you would like to try traditional feast-day meals, the **Tiwa Kitchen,** near the entrance to the pueblo, is a good place to stop. Close to Tiwa Kitchen is the **Oo-oonah Children's Art Center,** where you can see the creative works of pueblo children.

As with many of the other pueblos in New Mexico, Taos Pueblo has opened a casino. **Taos Mountain Casino** (© 888/WIN-TAOS) is located on the main road to Taos Pueblo and features slot machines, blackjack, and poker.

Veterans Hwy. (P.O. Box 1846), Taos Pueblo. © 505/758-1028. www.taospueblo.com. Admission cost, as well as camera, video, and sketching fees, subject to change annually; be sure to ask about telephoto lenses and digital cameras; photography not permitted on feast days. Daily 8am–4:30pm, with a few exceptions. Guided tours available. Closed for 45 consecutive days every year late winter or early spring (call ahead). Also, because this is a living community, you can expect periodic closures. From Paseo del Pueblo Norte, travel north 2 miles on Veterans Hwy.

MORE ATTRACTIONS

D. H. Lawrence Ranch   A trip to this ranch north of Taos leads you into odd realms of devotion for the controversial early-20th-century author who lived and wrote in the area in the early 1920s. A short uphill walk from the ranch home (not open to visitors), is the D. H. Lawrence Memorial, a shedlike structure that's a bit of a forgotten place, where people have left a few mementos such as juniper berries and sticks of gum. The guest book is also interesting: One couple wrote of trying for 24 years to get here from England.

Lawrence lived in Taos on and off between 1922 and 1925. The ranch was a gift to his wife, Frieda, from the art patron Mabel Dodge Luhan. Lawrence repaid Luhan the favor by giving her the manuscript of *Sons and Lovers.* When Lawrence died in southern France in 1930 of tuberculosis, his ashes were returned here for burial. The grave of Frieda, who died in 1956, is outside the memorial. The memorial is the only public building at the ranch, which is operated today by the University of New Mexico as an educational and recreational retreat.

NM 522, San Cristobal. © 505/776-2245. Free admission. Daily 8am–5pm. To reach the site, head north from Taos about 15 miles on NM 522, then another 6 miles east into the forested Sangre de Cristo range via a well-marked dirt road.

Governor Bent House Museum *(Kids)*   Located a short block north of the plaza, this residence of Charles Bent, New Mexico Territory's first American governor, offers an interesting peek into the region's sometimes brutal history. Bent, a former trader who established Fort Bent, Colorado, was murdered during the 1847 Native American and Hispanic rebellion, while his wife and children escaped by digging through an adobe wall into the house next door. The hole is still visible. Period art and artifacts are on display.

117 Bent St. ℂ **505/758-2376.** Admission $2 adults, $1 children 8–15, free for children under 8. MC, V. Summer daily 9:30am–5pm; winter daily 10am–5pm. Closed Easter, Thanksgiving, Christmas, and New Year's Day. Street parking.

Harwood Museum of Art of the University of New Mexico *(★)*   With its high ceilings and broad wood floors, this recently restored museum is a lovely place to wander among New Mexico–inspired images. A cultural and community center since 1923, the museum displays paintings, drawings, prints, sculpture, and photographs by Taos-area artists from 1800 to the present. Featured are paintings from the early days of the art colony by members of the Taos Society of Artists, including Oscar Berninghaus, Ernest Blumenschein, Herbert Dunton, Victor Higgins, Bert Phillips, and Walter Ufer. Also included are works by Emil Bisttram, Andrew Dasburg, Agnes Martin, Larry Bell, and Thomas Benrimo.

Upstairs are 19th-century pounded-tin pieces and *retablos,* religious paintings of saints that have traditionally been used for decoration and inspiration in the homes and churches of New Mexico. The permanent collection includes sculptures by Patrociño Barela, one of the leading Hispanic artists of 20th-century New Mexico—well worth seeing, especially his 3-foot-tall "Death Cart," a rendition of Doña Sebastiána, the bringer of death.

The museum also schedules more than eight changing exhibitions a year, many of which feature works by celebrated artists currently living in Taos.

238 Ledoux St. ℂ **505/758-9826.** www.harwoodmuseum.org. Admission $5. Tues–Sat 10am–5pm; Sun noon–5pm.

Kit Carson Park and Cemetery   Major community events are held in the park in summer. The cemetery, established in 1847, contains the graves of Carson, his wife, Governor Charles Bent, the Don Antonio Martinez family, Mabel Dodge Luhan, and many other noted historical figures and artists. Their lives are described briefly on plaques.

Paseo del Pueblo Norte. ℂ **505/758-8234.** Free admission. Daily 24 hr.

Rio Grande Gorge Bridge *(★) (Kids)*   This impressive bridge, west of the Taos airport, spans the Southwest's greatest river. At 650 feet above the canyon floor, it's one of America's highest bridges. If you can withstand the vertigo, it's interesting to come more than once, at different times of day, to observe how the changing light plays tricks with the colors of the cliff walls. A curious aside is that the wedding scene in the movie *Natural Born Killers* was filmed here.

US 64, 10 miles west of Taos. Admission free. Daily 24 hr.

San Francisco de Asis church *(★★)*   On NM 68, about 4 miles south of Taos, this famous church appears as a modern adobe sculpture with no doors or windows, an image that has often been photographed and painted. Visitors must walk through the garden on the east side to enter the two-story church and get a full perspective of its massive walls, authentic adobe plaster, and beauty.

A video presentation is given in the church office every hour on the half-hour. Also, displayed on the wall is an unusual painting, *The Shadow of the Cross,* by

Henri Ault (1896). Under ordinary light it portrays a barefoot Christ at the Sea of Galilee; in darkness, however, the portrait becomes luminescent, and the perfect shadow of a cross forms over the left shoulder of Jesus' silhouette. The artist reportedly was as shocked as everyone else to see this. The reason for the illusion remains a mystery. A few crafts shops surround the square.

Ranchos de Taos Plaza. ℂ **505/758-2754**. Admission $3 for video and mystery painting. Mon–Sat 9am–4pm. Visitors may attend Mass Mon–Fri 5:30pm, Sat 6pm (Mass rotates from this church to the 3 mission chapels), Sun 7 (in Spanish), 9, and 11:30am. Closed to the public 1st 2 weeks in June, when repairs are done; however, services still take place.

Taos Art Museum ⚸ *(Finds*   Set in the home of Russian artist Nicolai Fechin (*Feh*-shin), this collection displays works of the Taos Society of Artists, which give a sense of what Taos was like in the late 19th and early 20th centuries. The works are rich and varied, including panoramas and images of the Native American and Hispanic villagers. The setting in what was Fechin's home from 1927 until 1933 is truly unique. The historic building commemorates his career. Born in Russia in 1881, Fechin came to the United States in 1923, already acclaimed as a master of painting, drawing, sculpture, architecture, and woodwork. In Taos, he renovated the home and embellished it with hand-carved doors, windows, gates, posts, fireplaces, and other features of a Russian country home. Fechin died in 1955.

227 Paseo del Pueblo Norte. ℂ **505/758-2690**. www.taosmuseums.org. Admission $6 adults, $3 children 6–16, free for under age 6. Summer Thurs–Sun 10am–5pm; call for winter hours.

ART CLASSES

If you'd like to pursue an artistic adventure of your own in Taos, check out the weeklong classes in such media as writing, sculpting, painting, jewelry making, photography, clay working, and textiles that are available at the **Taos Institute of Arts,** 108B Civic Plaza Dr. (ℂ **800/822-7183** or 505/758-2793; www.tia taos.com). Class sizes are limited, so if you're thinking about giving these workshops a try, call for information well in advance. The fees vary from class to class and usually don't include the cost of materials.

ORGANIZED TOURS

An excellent opportunity to explore the historic downtown area of Taos is offered by **Taos Historic Walking Tours** (ℂ **505/758-4020**). Tours cost $10 and take 1½ to 2 hours, leaving from the Mabel Dodge Luhan house at 10:30am Monday to Saturday (May–Sept). Closed Sundays and holidays. Call to make an appointment during the off season.

If you'd really like a taste of Taos history and drama, call **Enchantment Dreams Walking Tours** ⚸ (ℂ **505/776-2562**). Roberta Courtney Meyers, a theater artist, dramatist, and composer, will tour you through Taos's history while performing a number of characters, such as Georgia O'Keeffe and Kit Carson. Walking tours cost $20 per person.

6 Skiing ⚸⚸⚸

DOWNHILL SKIING

Five alpine resorts are within an hour's drive of Taos; all offer complete facilities, including equipment rentals. Although exact opening and closing dates vary according to snow conditions, the season usually begins around Thanksgiving and continues into early April.

Ski clothing can be purchased, and ski equipment can be rented or bought, from several Taos outlets. Among them are **Cottam's Ski & Outdoor Shops,** with four locations (call ✆ **800/322-8267** or 505/758-2822 for the one nearest you), and **Taos Ski Valley Sportswear, Ski & Boot Co.,** in Taos Ski Valley (✆ **505/776-2291**).

TAOS SKI VALLEY

Taos Ski Valley ⭐⭐⭐, P.O. Box 90, Taos Ski Valley, NM 87525 (✆ **505/776-2291;** www.skitaos.org), is the preeminent ski resort in the southern Rocky Mountains. It was founded in 1955 by a Swiss-German immigrant, Ernie Blake. According to local legend, Blake searched for 2 years in a small plane for the perfect location for a ski resort comparable to what he was accustomed to in the Alps. He found it at the abandoned mining site of Twining, high above Taos. Today, under the management of two younger generations of Blakes, the resort has become internationally renowned for its light, dry powder (as much as 320 in. annually), its superb ski school, and its personal, friendly service.

Taos Ski Valley can best be appreciated by the more experienced skier. It offers steep, high-alpine, high-adventure skiing. The mountain is more intricate than it might seem at first glance, and it holds many surprises and challenges—even for the expert. The *London Times* called the valley "without any argument the best ski resort in the world. Small, intimate, and endlessly challenging, Taos simply has no equal." And, if you're sick of dealing with yahoos on snowboards, you will be pleased to know that they're not permitted on the slopes of Taos Ski Valley, at least for now: You may see a number of "Free Taos" bumper stickers on your trip, part of a campaign by snowboarders to open up the slopes (go to www.freetaos. com for more information). The quality of the snow here (light and dry) is believed to be due to the dry Southwestern air and abundant sunshine.

Between the 11,819-foot summit and the 9,207-foot base are 72 trails and bowls, more than half of them designated for expert and advanced skiers. Most of the remaining trails are suitable for advanced intermediates; there is little flat terrain for novices to gain experience and mileage. However, many beginning skiers find that after spending time in lessons they can enjoy the **Kachina Bowl,** which offers spectacular views as well as wide-open slopes.

The area has an uphill capacity of 15,000 skiers per hour on its five double chairs, one triple, four quads, and one surface tow. Full-day lift tickets, depending on the season, cost $33 to $51 for adults, $21 to $31 for children 7 to 12, $19 to $40 for teens ages 13 to 17, $38 for seniors ages 65 to 69, and are free for seniors over 70 and for children 6 and under with an adult ticket purchase. Full rental packages are $20 for adults and $13 for children. Taos Ski Valley is open daily 9am to 4pm from Thanksgiving to around the second week of April.

Kids Skiing with Kids

With its children's ski school, Taos Ski Valley has always been an excellent location for skiing families, but with the 1994 addition of an 18,000-square-foot children's center (Kinderkäfig Center), skiing with your children in Taos is even better. Kinderkäfig offers every service imaginable, from equipment rental for children to babysitting services. Call ahead for more information.

Note: Taos Ski Valley has one of the best ski schools in the country, specializing in teaching people how to negotiate steep and challenging runs.

Taos Ski Valley has many lodges and condominiums, with nearly 1,500 beds. (See "Where to Stay," earlier in this chapter for details on accommodations.) All offer ski-week packages; four of them have restaurants. There are three restaurants on the mountain in addition to the many facilities of Village Center at the base. For reservations, contact the **Taos Valley Resort Association** (© 800/776-1111 or 505/776-2233; www.visitnewmexico.com).

RED RIVER SKI & SNOWBOARD AREA

Not far from Taos Ski Valley is **Red River Ski & Snowboard Area,** P.O. Box 900, Red River, NM 87558 (© **800/331-7669** for reservations; 505/754-2223 for information; www.redriverskiarea.com). One of the bonuses of this ski area is that lodgers at Red River can walk out their doors and be on the slopes. Two other factors make this 40-year-old, family-oriented area special: First, most of its 57 trails are geared toward the intermediate skier, though beginners and experts also have some trails; and second, good snow is guaranteed early and late in the year by snowmaking equipment that can work on 87% of the runs, more than any other in New Mexico. However, be aware that this human-made snow tends to be icy, and the mountain is full of inexperienced skiers, so you really have to watch your back. Locals in the area refer to this as "Little Texas" because it's so popular with Texans and other southerners. A very friendly atmosphere, with a touch of redneck attitude, prevails.

There's a 1,600-foot vertical drop here to a base elevation of 8,750 feet. Lifts include four double chairs, two triple chairs, and a surface tow, with a capacity of 7,920 skiers per hour. The cost of a lift ticket for all lifts is $47 for adults for a full day, $37 for a half day; $42 for teens 13 to 17 for a full day, $32 for a half day; $33 for children ages 7 to 12 and seniors 65 and over, $24 for a half day. All rental packages start at $17 for adults, $14 for children. Lifts run daily 9am to 4pm Thanksgiving to about March 28.

ANGEL FIRE RESORT

Also quite close to Taos is **Angel Fire Resort** ⓕ, P.O. Drawer B, Angel Fire, NM 87710 (© **800/633-7463** or 505/377-6401; www.angelfireresort.com). If you (or your kids) don't feel up to skiing steeper Taos Mountain, Angel Fire is a good choice. The 62 trails are heavily oriented to beginner and intermediate skiers and snowboarders, with a few runs for more advanced skiers and snowboarders. The mountain has received over $7 million in improvements in past years. This is not an old village like you'll find at Taos and Red River. Instead, it's a Vail-style resort, built in 1960, with a variety of activities other than skiing (see "A Scenic Drive Around the Enchanted Circle," later in this chapter). The snow-making capabilities here are excellent, and the ski school is good, though I hear it's so crowded that it's difficult to get in during spring break. With the only two high-speed quad lifts in New Mexico, you can get to the top fast and have a long ski to the bottom. There are also three double lifts and one surface lift. Also here are a large snowboard park (with a banked slalom course, rails, jumps, and other obstacles) and some new hike-access advanced runs; note, however, that the hike is substantial. Cross-country skiing, snowshoeing, and snowbiking are also available. All-day lift tickets cost $48 for adults, $31 for teens (ages 13–17), and $26 for children (ages 7–12). Kids 6 and under and seniors 70 and over ski free. Open from approximately Thanksgiving to March 29 (depending on the weather) daily 9am to 4pm.

SIPAPU SKI AND SUMMER RESORT

The oldest ski area in the Taos region, founded in 1952, **Sipapu Ski and Summer Resort,** NM 518, Route Box 29, Vadito, NM 87579 (© **505/587-2240;** www.sipapunm.com), is 25 miles southeast of Taos, on NM 518 in Tres Ritos Canyon. It prides itself on being a small local ski area, especially popular with schoolchildren. It has two triple chairs and two surface lifts, with a vertical drop of 1,025 feet to the 8,200-foot base elevation. There are 31 trails, half classified as intermediate, and two terrain park trails have been added. It's a nice little area, tucked way back in the mountains, with excellent lodging rates. Be aware that because the elevation is fairly low, runs get very icy. Lift tickets are $35 for adults for a full day, $26 half-day; $26 for children under 12 for a full day, $22 half-day; $23 for seniors age 65 to 69 for a half or full day; and free for seniors age 70 and over, as well as children 5 and under. A package including lift tickets, equipment rental, and a lesson costs $49 for adults and $42 for children. Sipapu is open from about December 12 to April 1st, and lifts run daily from 9am to 4pm.

CROSS-COUNTRY SKIING

Numerous popular Nordic trails exist in **Carson National Forest.** If you call or write ahead, the ranger will send you a booklet titled *Where to Go in the Snow,* which offers cross-country skiers details about the maintained trails. One of the more popular trails is **Amole Canyon,** off NM 518 near the Sipapu Ski Area, where the Taos Nordic Ski Club maintains set tracks and signs along a 3-mile loop. It's closed to snowmobiles, a comfort to lovers of serenity.

Just east of Red River, with 16 miles of groomed trails (in addition to 6 miles of trails strictly for snowshoers) in 400 acres of forestlands atop Bobcat Pass, is the **Enchanted Forest Cross Country Ski Area** (© 505/754-6112; www. enchantedforestxc.com). Full-day trail passes, good 9am to 4:30pm, are $10 for adults; $8 for teens 13 to 17 and seniors 62 to 69; $3 for children age 7 to 12; and free for seniors age 70 and over, as well as for children 6 and under. In addition to cross-country ski and snowshoe rentals, the ski area also rents pulk sleds—high-tech devices in which children are pulled by their skiing parents. The ski area offers a full snack bar. Equipment rentals and lessons can be arranged either at Enchanted Forest or at **Miller's Crossing** ski shop at 417 W. Main St. in Red River (© **505/754-2374**). Nordic skiers can get instruction in cross-country classic as well as freestyle skating.

Taos Mountain Outfitters, 114 S. Plaza (© **505/758-9292**), offers telemark and cross-country sales, rentals, and guide service, as does **Los Rios Whitewater Ski Shop** (© **800/544-1181** or 505/776-8854).

Southwest Nordic Center (© **505/758-4761;** www.southwestnordic center.com) offers rentals of five *yurts* (Mongolian-style huts), four of which are in the Rio Grande National Forest near Chama; each of these yurts accommodates up to six people. The fifth and newest addition is located outside the Taos Ski Valley (offering access to high Alpine terrain) and is much larger than the others; this yurt accommodates up to 10 people. These are insulated and fully equipped accommodations, each with a stove, cookware, dishes, silverware, mattresses, pillows, a table and benches, and wood-stove heating. Skiers trek into the huts, carrying their clothing and food in backpacks. Guide service is provided, or people can go in on their own, following directions on a map. The yurts are rented by the night and range from $65 to $125 per group. Call for reservations as much in advance as possible as they do book up. The season is mid-November through April, depending on snow conditions.

7 Other Outdoor Activities

Taos County's 2,200 square miles embrace a great diversity of scenic beauty, from New Mexico's highest mountain, 13,161-foot **Wheeler Peak,** to the 650-foot-deep chasm of the **Rio Grande Gorge** ☆☆. Carson National Forest, which extends to the eastern city limits of Taos and cloaks a large part of the county, contains several major ski facilities as well as hundreds of miles of hiking trails through the Sangre de Cristo range.

Recreation areas are mainly in the national forest, where pine and aspen provide refuge for abundant wildlife. Forty-eight areas are accessible by road, including 38 with campsites. There are also areas on the high desert mesa, carpeted by sagebrush, cactus, and, frequently, wildflowers. Two beautiful areas within a short drive of Taos are the **Valle Vidal Recreation Area,** north of Red River, and the **Wild Rivers Recreation Area,** near Questa. For complete information, contact **Carson National Forest,** 208 Cruz Alta Rd. (© **505/758-6200**), or the **Bureau of Land Management,** 226 Cruz Alta Rd. (© **505/758-8851**).

BALLOONING

As in many other towns throughout New Mexico, hot-air ballooning is a top attraction. Recreational trips over the Taos Valley and Rio Grande Gorge are offered by **Paradise Hot Air Balloon Adventure** (© **505/751-6098**). The company also offers ultra-light rides.

The **Taos Mountain Balloon Rally,** P.O. Box 3096 (© **800/732-8267**), is held each year in October. (See "New Mexico Calendar of Events," in chapter 2.)

BIKING

Even if you're not an avid cyclist, it won't take long for you to realize that getting around Taos by bike is preferable to driving. You won't have the usual parking problems, and you won't have to sit in the line of traffic as it snakes through the center of town. If you feel like exploring the surrounding area, Carson National Forest rangers recommend several biking trails in the greater Taos area. Head to the **Taos Box West Rim** for a scenic and easy ride. To reach the trail, travel NM 68 south for 17 miles to Pilar; turn west onto NM 570. Travel along the river for 6¼ miles, cross the bridge, and drive to the top of the ridge. Watch for the trail marker on your right. For a more technical and challenging ride, go to **Devisadero Loop:** From Taos, drive out of town on US 64 to your first pull-out on the right, just as you enter the canyon at El Nogal Picnic Area. To ride the notorious **South Boundary Trail,** a 20-mile romp for advanced riders, contact Native Sons Adventures (below). Native Sons can arrange directions, a shuttle, and a guide, if necessary. The **U.S. Forest Service** office, 208 Cruz Alta Rd. (© **505/758-6200**), has excellent trail information. Also look for the *Taos Trails* map (created jointly by Carson National Forest, Native Sons Adventures, and Trails Illustrated) at area bookstores.

Bicycle rentals are available from the **Gearing Up Bicycle Shop,** 129 Paseo del Pueblo Sur (© **505/751-0365**); daily rentals run $35 for a mountain bike with front suspension. **Native Sons Adventures,** 1033A Paseo del Pueblo Sur (© **800/753-7559** or 505/758-9342), rents bikes ranging from regular (unsuspended) to full-suspension bikes for $15 to $35/half-day and $20 to $45/full-day; it also rents some car racks. All these prices include use of helmets and water bottles.

Annual touring events include Red River's **Enchanted Circle Century Bike Tour** (© **505/754-2366**) on the weekend following Labor Day.

FISHING

In many of New Mexico's waters, fishing is possible year-round, though due to conditions, many high lakes and streams are fishable only during the warmer months. Overall, the best fishing is in the spring and fall. Naturally, the Rio Grande is a favorite fishing spot, but there is also excellent fishing in the streams around Taos. Taoseños favor the Rio Hondo, Rio Pueblo (near Tres Ritos), Rio Fernando (in Taos Canyon), Pot Creek, and Rio Chiquito. Rainbow, cutthroat, German brown trout, and kokanee (a freshwater salmon) are commonly stocked and caught. Pike and catfish have been caught in the Rio Grande as well. Jiggs, spinners, or woolly worms are recommended as lure, or worms, corn, or salmon eggs as bait; many experienced anglers prefer fly-fishing.

Licenses are required, of course, and are sold, along with tackle, at several Taos sporting-goods shops. For backcountry guides, try **Deep Creek Wilderness Outfitters and Guides,** P.O. Box 721, El Prado, NM 87529 (© **505/776-8423** or 505/776-5901), or **Taylor Streit Flyfishing Service,** 405 Camino de la Placita (© **505/751-1312;** www.streitflyfishing.com).

FITNESS FACILITIES

The **Taos Spa and Tennis Club,** 111 Dona Ana Dr., across from Sagebrush Inn (© **505/758-1980;** www.taosspa.com), is a fully equipped fitness center that rivals any you'd find in a big city. It has a variety of cardiovascular machines, bikes, and weight-training machines, as well as saunas, indoor and outdoor Jacuzzis, a steam room, and indoor and outdoor pools. Classes range from yoga to Pilates to water fitness. In addition, it has tennis and racquetball courts. Therapeutic massage, facials, and physical therapy are available daily by appointment. Children's programs include a tennis camp and swimming lessons, and babysitting programs are available in the morning and evening. The spa is open weekdays 5am to 9pm, weekends 7am to 8pm. Monthly memberships are available for individuals and families, as are summer memberships and punch cards. For visitors, there's a daily rate of $12.

The **Northside Health and Fitness Center,** at 1307 Paseo del Pueblo Norte (© **505/751-1242**), is also a full-service facility, featuring top-of-the-line Cybex equipment, free weights, and cardiovascular equipment. Aerobics classes are scheduled daily (Jazzercise classes weekly), and there are indoor/outdoor pools and four tennis courts, as well as children's and seniors' programs. Open weekdays 6am to 9pm, weekends 8am to 8pm. The daily visitors' rate is $10.

GOLF

Since the summer of 1993, the 18-hole golf course at the **Taos Country Club,** 54 Golf Course Dr., Ranchos de Taos (© **800/758-7375** or 505/758-7300), has been open to the public. Located on Country Road 110, just 6 miles south of the plaza, it's a first-rate championship golf course designed for all levels of play. It has open fairways and no hidden greens. The club also features a driving range, practice putting and chipping green, and instruction by PGA professionals. Greens fees are seasonal and start at $48; cart and club rentals are available. The country club has also added a clubhouse, featuring a restaurant and full bar. It's always advisable to call ahead for tee times 1 week in advance, but it's not unusual for people to show up unannounced and still manage to find a time to tee off.

The par-72, 18-hole course at the **Angel Fire Resort Golf Course** (© **800/ 633-7463** or 505/377-3055) is PGA endorsed. Surrounded by stands of ponderosa pine, spruce, and aspen, at 8,500 feet, it's one of the highest regulation golf courses in the world. It also has a driving range and putting green. Carts and clubs can be rented at the course, and the club pro provides instruction. Greens fees range from $45 to $65.

HIKING

There are hundreds of miles of hiking trails in Taos County's mountain and high-mesa country. The trails are especially well traveled in the summer and fall, although nights turn chilly and mountain weather may be fickle by September.

Free materials and advice on all **Carson National Forest** trails and recreation areas can be obtained from the **Forest Service Building,** 208 Cruz Alta Rd. (② **505/758-6200**), open weekdays 8am to 4:30pm. Detailed USGS topographical maps of backcountry areas can be purchased from **Taos Mountain Outfitters,** South Plaza (② **505/758-9292**).

The 19,663-acre **Wheeler Peak Wilderness** is a wonderland of alpine tundra, encompassing New Mexico's highest peak (13,161 ft.). A favorite (though rigorous) hike to Wheeler Peak's summit (15 miles round-trip, with a 3,700-ft. elevation gain) makes for a long but fun day. The trailhead is at Taos Ski Valley. For year-round hiking, head to the **Wild Rivers Recreation Area** (② **505/770-1600**), near Questa (see "A Scenic Drive Around the Enchanted Circle," later in this chapter).

HORSEBACK RIDING

The sage meadows and pine-covered mountains around Taos make it one of the West's most romantic places to ride. **Taos Indian Horse Ranch** 🐎🐎, on Pueblo land off Ski Valley Road, just before **Arroyo Seco** (② **505/758-3212**), offers a variety of guided rides. Open by appointment, the ranch provides horses for all types of riders (English, Western, Australian, and bareback) and ability levels. Call ahead to reserve and for prices, which will likely run about $85 for a 2-hour trail ride.

Horseback riding is also offered by **Rio Grande Stables,** P.O. Box 2122, El Prado (② **505/776-5913;** www.lajitasstables.com/taos.htm), with rides taking place during the summer months at Taos Ski Valley. Most riding outfitters offer lunch trips and overnight trips. Call for prices and further details.

HUNTING

Hunters in **Carson National Forest** bag deer, turkey, grouse, band-tailed pigeons, and elk by special permit. Hunting seasons vary year to year, so it's important to inquire ahead with the New Mexico **Game and Fish Department** in Santa Fe (② **505/476-8101**).

ICE-SKATING AND SKATEBOARDING

If a latent Michelle Kwan or Brian Boitano dwells in you, try your blades at **Taos Youth Family Center,** 406 Paseo del Cañon, 2 miles south of the plaza and about ¾ mile off Paseo del Pueblo Sur (② **505/758-4160**). The rink is open daily from early November thorough mid-March. Call for hours. Skate rentals are available for adults and children. Admission is $4. Also at the center is an in-line skate and skateboarding park, open when there's no snow or ice. Admission is free.

JOGGING

The paved paths and grass of Kit Carson Park (see "More Attractions," earlier in this chapter) provide a quiet place to stretch your legs.

LLAMA TREKKING

For a taste of the unusual, you might want to try letting a llama carry your gear and food while you walk and explore, free of any heavy burdens. They're friendly, gentle animals that have keen senses of sight and smell. Often, other animals, such as elk, deer, and mountain sheep, are attracted to the scent of the llamas and will venture closer to hikers if the llamas are present. **El Paseo Llama Expeditions** ✦✦ (© **800/455-2627** or 505/758-3111; www.elpaseollama. com) utilizes U.S. Forest Service–maintained trails that wind through canyons and over mountain ridges. The llama expeditions are scheduled May to mid-October, and day hikes are scheduled year-round. Gourmet meals are provided. Half-day hikes cost $59, day hikes $79, and 2- to 8-day hikes run $249 to $989.

Wild Earth Llama Adventures ✦✦ (© **800/758-LAMA** [5262] or 505/586-0174; www.llamaadventures.com) offers a "Take a Llama to Llunch" day hike—a full day of hiking into the Sangre de Cristo Mountains, complete with a gourmet lunch for $75. Wild Earth also offers a variety of custom multiday wilderness adventures tailored to trekkers' needs and fitness levels for $125 per person per day. Children under 12 receive discounts. Camping gear and food are provided. On the trips, experienced guides provide information about native plants and local wildlife, as well as natural and regional history of the area. The head guide has doubled as a chef in the off season, so the meals on these treks are quite tasty.

RIVER RAFTING

Half- or full-day whitewater rafting trips down the Rio Grande and Rio Chama originate in Taos and can be booked through a variety of outfitters in the area. The wild **Taos Box** ✦✦✦, a steep-sided canyon south of the Wild Rivers Recreation Area, offers a series of class IV rapids that rarely let up for some 17 miles. The water drops up to 90 feet per mile, providing one of the most exciting 1-day white-water tours in the West. May and June, when the water is rising, is a good time to go. Experience is not required, but you will be required to wear a life jacket (provided), and you should be willing to get wet.

Most of the companies listed run the **Taos Box** ($99–$109 per person) and **Pilar Racecourse** ($40–$48 per person per half-day) on a daily basis.

I highly recommend **Los Rios River Runners** ✦ in Taos, P.O. Box 2734 (© **800/544-1181** or 505/776-8854; www.losriosriverrunners.com). Other safe bets are **Native Sons Adventures,** 1033A Paseo del Pueblo Sur (© **800/753-7559** or 505/758-9342; www.nativesonsadventures.com); and **Far Flung Adventures,** P.O. Box 707, El Prado (© **800/359-2627** or 505/758-2628; www.farflung.com).

Safety warning: Taos is not the place to experiment if you are not an experienced rafter. Check with the **Bureau of Land Management** (© **505/758-8851**) to make sure you're fully equipped to go white-water rafting without a guide.

Getting Pampered: The Spa Scene

Taos doesn't have the spa scene that Tucson and Phoenix do, but you can get pampered at **Taos Spa and Tennis Club** (see "Fitness Facilities," above).

If you'd like to stay at a spa, **El Monte Sagrado,** 317 Kit Carson Rd. (© **800/828-TAOS** or 505/758-3502; www.elmontesagrado.com) and **Casa de las Chimineas,** 405 Cordoba Rd. (© **877/758-4777** or 505/758-4777; www.visittaos.com), offer a variety of treatments to their guests (see "Where to Stay" earlier in this chapter).

Have them check your gear to ensure that it's sturdy enough—this is serious rafting!

ROCK CLIMBING

Mountain Skills, P.O. Box 206, Arroyo Seco, NM 87514 (© **505/776-2222;** www.climbingschoolusa.com), offers rock-climbing instruction for all skill levels, from beginners to more advanced climbers who would like to fine-tune their skills or just find out about the best area climbs.

SNOWMOBILING AND ATV RIDING

Native Sons Adventures, 1033A Paseo del Pueblo Sur (© **800/753-7559** or 505/758-9342), runs fully guided tours in the Sangre de Cristo Mountains. Rates run $64 to $150. Advanced reservations required.

SWIMMING

The **Don Fernando Pool** (© **505/737-2622**), on Civic Plaza Drive at Camino de la Placita, opposite the new Convention Center, admits swimmers over age 8 without adult supervision.

TENNIS

Quail Ridge Inn (© **800/624-4448** or 505/776-2211; www.quailridgeinn.com) on Ski Valley Road has outdoor tennis courts available to those staying in Quail Ridge condos. **Taos Spa and Tennis Club** (see "Fitness Facilities," above) has four courts, and the **Northside Health and Fitness Center** (see "Fitness Facilities," above) has three tennis courts. In addition, there are four free public courts in Taos, two at **Kit Carson Park,** on Paseo del Pueblo Norte, and two at **Fred Baca Memorial Park,** on Camino del Medio, south of Ranchitos Road.

8 Shopping

Given the town's historical associations with the arts, it isn't surprising that many visitors come to Taos to buy fine art. Fifty or so galleries are located within easy walking distance of the plaza, and a couple dozen more are just a short drive from downtown. Galleries and shops are generally open 7 days a week during summer and closed Sundays during winter. Hours vary but generally run from 10am to 5 or 6pm. Some artists show their work by appointment only.

The best-known artist in modern Taos is R. C. Gorman, a Navajo from Arizona who has made his home in Taos for more than 2 decades. He is internationally acclaimed for his bright, somewhat surrealistic depictions of Navajo women. His **Navajo Gallery,** at 210 Ledoux St. (© 505/758-3250), is a showcase for his widely varied work: acrylics, lithographs, silk screens, bronzes, tapestries, hand-cast ceramic vases, etched glass, and more.

My favorite new spot to shop is the village of **Arroyo Seco** ✦ on NM 150, about 5 miles north of Taos en route to Taos Ski Valley. Not only is there a lovely 1834 church, La Santísima Trinidad, but a few cute little shops line the winding lane through town. My favorites are the **Taos Sunflower** (© 505/776-5644), selling specialty yarns and fibers, just off the highway near the Gypsy 360° cafe and **Arroyo Seco Mercantile** (© 505/776-8806) at 488 NM 150, which is full of cowboy hats, antiques, and country home items.

ART

Act I Gallery   This gallery has a broad range of works in a variety of media. You'll find watercolors, *retablos,* furniture, paintings, Hispanic folk art, pottery, jewelry, and sculpture. 218 Paseo del Pueblo Norte. © 800/666-2933 or 505/758-7831.

Fenix Gallery   The Fenix Gallery focuses on Taos artists with national and/or international collections and reputations who live and work in Taos. The work is primarily non-objective and very contemporary. Some "historic" artists are represented as well. Recent expansion has doubled the gallery space. 228B N. Pueblo Rd. ✆ 505/758-9120.

Franzetti Metalworks   This gallery's designs are surprisingly whimsical for metalwork. Much of the work is functional; you'll find laughing-horse switch plates and "froggie" earthquake detectors. 120G Bent St. ✆ 505/758-7872.

Gallery A   The oldest gallery in town, Gallery A has contemporary and traditional paintings and sculpture, including Gene Kloss etchings, watercolors, and oils, as well as regional and national collections. 105–107 Kit Carson Rd. ✆ 505/758-2343.

Inger Jirby Gallery ⊛ *Finds*   The word *expressionist* could have been created to define the work of internationally known artist Inger Jirby. Full of bold color and passionate brush strokes, Jirby's oils record the lives and landscapes of villages from the southwestern U.S. to Guatemala to Bali. This gallery, which meanders back through a 400-year-old adobe house, is a feast for the eyes and soul. 207 Ledoux St. ✆ 505/758-7333.

Lumina of New Mexico ⊛⊛ *Finds*   Located in the historic Victor Higgins home, next to the Mabel Dodge Luhan estate, Lumina is one of the loveliest galleries in New Mexico. You'll find a large variety of fine art, including paintings, sculpture, and photography. This place is as much a tourist attraction as any of the museums and historic homes in town. Look for the wonderful paintings and sculpture of Enrico Embrilo, and take a stroll through the new 2-acre Ridhwan sculpture garden with a pond and waterfall—where you'll find large outdoor pieces from all over the United States. About 8 minutes from town is **Lumina North** in Arroyo Seco, which features 3 acres of Buddhist sculpture and a tea house. 239 Morada Rd. (off Kit Carson Rd.). ✆ 505/758-7282. Lumina North: 11 Des Moines Rd. ✆ 505/776-3957.

Michael McCormick Gallery ⊛ *Finds*   Nationally renowned artists dynamically play with Southwestern themes in the works hanging at this gallery, steps from the plaza. Especially notable are the bright portraits by Miguel Martinez and the moody architectural pieces by Margaret Nes. If the gallery's namesake is in, strike up a conversation about art or poetry. 106C Paseo del Pueblo Norte. ✆ 800/279-0879 or 505/758-1372.

New Directions Gallery   Here you'll find a variety of contemporary abstract works such as the beautiful blown glasswork of Tony Jojola. My favorites, though, are the impressionist works depicting northern New Mexico villages by Tom Noble. 107 North Plaza Suite B. ✆ 800/658-6903 or 505/758-2771.

Nichols Taos Fine Art Gallery   Here you will find traditional works in all media, including Western and cowboy art. 403 Paseo del Pueblo Norte. ✆ 505/758-2475.

Parks Gallery ⊛   Some of the region's finest contemporary art decks the walls of this gallery just off the plaza. Some of the top artists here include Melissa Zink, Jim Wagner, Susan Contreres, and Erin Currier. 127 Bent St. ✆ 505/751-0343.

Philip Bareiss Gallery   The works of some 30 leading Taos artists, including sculptor and painter Ron Davis, sculptor Gray Mercer, and watercolorist Patricia Sanford, are exhibited here. 15 Rt. 150. ✆ 505/776-2284. bareiss@taosartappraisal.com.

R. B. Ravens   A trader for many years, including 21 on the Ranchos Plaza, R. B. Ravens is skilled at finding incredible period artwork. Here, you'll see (and have the chance to buy) Navajo rugs, and pottery, all in the setting of an old home with raw pine floors and hand-sculpted adobe walls. 4146 NM 68 (across from the St. Francis Church Plaza), Ranchos de Taos. ℂ **505/758-7322.**

Shriver Gallery   This gallery sells traditional paintings, drawings, etchings, and bronze sculptures. 401 Paseo del Pueblo Norte. ℂ **505/758-4994.**

BOOKS

Brodsky Bookshop   This shop has an exceptional inventory of fiction, non-fiction, Southwestern and Native American–studies books, children's books, used books, cards, tapes, and CDs. 226 Paseo del Pueblo Norte. ℂ **888/223-8730** or 505/758-9468.

Moby Dickens Bookshop ✸   This is one of Taos's best bookstores. You'll find children's and adults' collections of Southwest, Native American, and out-of-print books. The shop has comfortable places to sit and read. 124A Bent St. ℂ **888/442-9980** or 505/758-3050.

CRAFTS

Clay & Fiber Gallery   Clay & Fiber represents more than 150 artists from around the country. Merchandise changes frequently, but you should expect to see a variety of ceramics, fiber arts, jewelry, and wearables. 201 Paseo del Pueblo Sur. ℂ **505/758-8093.**

Southwest Moccasin & Drum ✸ *Kids*   Home of the All One Tribe Drum, this favorite local shop carries a large variety of drums in all sizes and styles, handmade by master Native American drum makers from Taos Pueblo. The shop also has the country's second-largest selection of moccasins, as well as an impressive inventory of indigenous world instruments and tapes, sculpture, weavings, rattles, fans, fetishes, bags, decor, and many handmade one-of-a-kind items. Kids enjoy the instruments as well as other colorful goods. A percentage of the store's profits support Native American causes. 803 Paseo del Pueblo Norte. ℂ **800/447-3630** or 505/758-9332. www.swnativecrafts.com.

Taos Artisans Cooperative Gallery *Value*   This seven-member cooperative gallery, owned and operated by local artists, sells local handmade jewelry, wearables, clay work, glass, leather work, and garden sculpture. You'll always find an artist in the shop. 107C Bent St. ℂ **505/758-1558.**

Taos Blue   This gallery has fine Native American and contemporary handcrafts. 101A Bent St. ℂ **505/758-3561.**

Twining Weavers and Contemporary Crafts   Here, you'll find an interesting mix of hand-woven wool rugs and pillows by owner Sally Bachman, as well as creations by other gallery artists in fiber, basketry, and clay. 133 Kit Carson Rd. ℂ **505/758-9000.**

Weaving Southwest   Contemporary tapestries by New Mexico artists, as well as one-of-a-kind rugs, blankets, and pillows, are the woven specialties found here. 216B Paseo del Pueblo Norte. ℂ **505/758-0433.**

FASHIONS

Artemisia   Wearable art in bold colors defines this little shop a block from the plaza. Goods are pricey but unique, most hand-woven or hand-sewn, all for women. 115 Bent St. ℂ **505/737-9800.**

Mariposa Boutique   What first caught my eye in this little shop were bright chile-pepper-print overalls for kids. Closer scrutiny brought me to plenty of finds for myself, such as suede and rayon broomstick skirts and Mexican-style dresses, perfect for showing off turquoise jewelry. 120F Bent St. ✆ 505/758-9028.

Overland Sheepskin Company ⭐ *Finds*   You can't miss the romantically weathered barn sitting on a meadow north of town. Inside, you'll find anything you can imagine in leather: coats, gloves, hats, slippers. The coats here are exquisite, from oversize ranch styles to tailored blazers in a variety of leathers from sheepskin to buffalo hide. NM 522 (a few miles north of town). ✆ 505/758-8820.

FOOD

Cid's Food Market   This store has the best selection of natural and gourmet foods in Taos. It's a great place to stock your picnic basket with such items as roasted chicken and barbecued brisket, or with lighter fare, such as sushi, Purple Onion–brand sandwiches, black-bean salad, and fresh hummus and tabbouleh. 623 Paseo del Pueblo Norte. ✆ 505/758-1148.

Xocoatl   Set in a cozy enclave connected to Michael McCormick Gallery, this fun chocolate and wine shop offers some of the tastiest truffles I've had. Tim Van Rixel makes such delicacies as mango truffles and pineapple coconut truffles. A bar serves Italian sodas, and plans are in the works for contemporary snacks such as cracker-crust pizzas and salads. 107B Juan Largo Lane. ✆ 505/751-7549.

FURNITURE

Country Furnishings of Taos   Here, you'll find unique hand-painted folk-art furniture. The pieces are as individual as the styles of the local folk artists who make them. There are also home accessories, unusual gifts, clothing, and jewelry. 534 Paseo del Pueblo Norte. ✆ 505/758-4633.

Lo Fino   With a name meaning "the refined," you know that this expansive showroom is worth taking time to wander through. You'll find a variety of home furnishings, from driftwood lamps and finely painted *trasteros* (armoires) to handcrafted traditional and contemporary Southwestern furniture. Lo Fino specializes in custom-built furniture. 201 Paseo del Pueblo Sur. ✆ 505/758-0298. lofino@ newmex.com.

The Taos Company   This interior-design showroom specializes in unique Southwestern and contemporary furniture and decorative accessories. Especially look for graceful stone fountains, iron-and-wood furniture, and custom jewelry. 124K John Dunn Plaza, Bent St. ✆ 800/548-1141 or 505/758-1141.

GIFTS & SOUVENIRS

Chimayo Trading del Norte   Specializing in Navajo weavings, pueblo pottery, and other types of pottery, this is a fun spot to peruse on the Ranchos de Taos Plaza. Look especially for the Casas Grandes pottery from Mexico. #1 Ranchos de Taos Plaza. ✆ 505/758-0504.

El Rincón Trading Post *Finds*   This shop has a real trading-post feel. It's a wonderful place to find turquoise jewelry, whether you're looking for contemporary or antique. In the back of the store is a museum full of Native American and Western artifacts. 114 Kit Carson Rd. ✆ 505/758-9188.

San Francisco de Asis Gift Shop   Local devotional art fills this funky little shop behind the San Francisco de Asis church. *Retablos* (altar paintings), rosary beads, and hand-carved wooden crosses appeal to a range of visitors, from the deeply religious to the pagan power shopper. Ranchos de Taos Plaza. ✆ 505/758-2754.

JEWELRY

Artwares Contemporary Jewelry   The gallery owners here call their contemporary jewelry "a departure from the traditional." True to this slogan, each piece here offers a new twist on traditional Southwestern and Native American design, by artists such as John Hardy and Diane Malouf. 129 N. Plaza. © **800/527-8850** or 505/758-8850.

Taos Gems & Minerals   In business for over 30 years, Taos Gems & Minerals is a fine lapidary showroom. This is a great place to explore; you can buy jewelry, carvings, and antique pieces at reasonable prices. 637 Paseo del Pueblo Sur. © **505/758-3910.**

MUSICAL INSTRUMENTS

Taos Drum Company   Drum-making is an age-old tradition to which local artisans give continued life in Taos. The drums are made of hollowed-out logs stretched with rawhide, and they come in all different shapes, sizes, and styles. Taos Drums has the largest selection of Native American log and hand drums in the world. In addition to drums, the showroom displays Southwestern and wrought-iron furniture, cowboy art, and more than 60 styles of rawhide lampshades, as well as a constantly changing selection of South American imports, primitive folk art, ethnic crafts, Native American music tapes, books, and other information on drumming. Ask about the tour that demonstrates the drum-making process. To find Taos Drum Company, look for the tepees and drums off NM 68, 5 miles south of Taos Plaza. © **505/758-3796.**

POTTERY & TILES

Stephen Kilborn Pottery   Visiting this shop in town is a treat, but for a real adventure, go 17 miles south of Taos toward Santa Fe to Stephen Kilborn's studio in Pilar, open Monday to Saturday 10am to 5pm and noon to 4pm on Sunday. There, you'll see where the pottery is made. 136A Paseo del Pueblo Norte. © **800/758-0136** or 505/758-5760. www.kilbornpottery.com.

Vargas Tile Co.   Vargas Tile has a great little collection of hand-painted Mexican tiles at good prices. You'll find beautiful pots with sunflowers on them and colorful cabinet doorknobs, as well as inventive sinks. South end of town on NM 68. © **505/758-5986.**

9 Taos After Dark

For a small town, Taos has its share of top entertainment. The resort atmosphere and the arts community attract performers, and the city enjoys annual programs in music and literary arts. State troupes, such as the New Mexico Repertory Theater and New Mexico Symphony Orchestra, make regular visits.

Many events are scheduled by the **Taos Center for the Arts** (TCA), 133 Paseo del Pueblo Norte (© **505/758-2052;** www.taoscenterforthearts.org), at the **Taos Community Auditorium** (© **505/758-2052**). The TCA imports local, regional, and national performers in theater, dance, and concerts (Robert Mirabal, among others, has performed here, and The Vagina Monologues has been presented). Also, look for a weekly film series offered year-round.

You can obtain information on current events in the *Taos News,* published every Thursday. The **Taos County Chamber of Commerce** (© **800/732-TAOS** or 505/758-3873; www.taoschamber.com) publishes semiannual listings of *Taos County Events,* as well as the annual *Taos Country Vacation Guide* that also lists events and happenings around town.

The Major Concert & Performance Halls

Taos Civic Plaza and Convention Center, 121 Civic Plaza Dr. ((C) **505/ 758-4160**). This convention space has an exhibit center where presentations, lectures, and concerts are held.

Taos Community Auditorium, Kit Carson Memorial State Park ((C) **505/ 758-4677**). A comfortable, small-town space, this community auditorium makes a nice venue for films, concerts, and lectures.

THE PERFORMING ARTS

Fort Burgwin   This historic site (of the 1,000-year-old Pot Creek Pueblo), located about 10 miles south of Taos, is a summer campus of Dallas's Southern Methodist University. From mid-May through mid-August, the SMU-in-Taos curriculum (including studio arts, humanities, and sciences) includes courses in music and theater. There are regularly scheduled orchestral concerts, guitar and harpsichord recitals, and theater performances available to the community, without charge, throughout the summer. 6580 NM 518, Ranchos de Taos. (C) **505/758-8322.**

Music from Angel Fire   This acclaimed program of chamber music begins in mid-August, with weekend concerts, and continues up to Labor Day. Based in the small resort community of Angel Fire (located about 21 miles east of Taos, off US 64), it also presents numerous concerts in Taos, Las Vegas, and Raton. P.O. Box 502, Angel Fire, NM 87710. (C) **505/377-3233** or 505/989-4772.

Taos School of Music   Founded in 1963, this music summer school offers excellent concerts by notable artists. The school is located at the Hotel St. Bernard in Taos Ski Valley. From mid-June to mid-August there is an intensive 8-week study and performance program for advanced students of violin, viola, cello, and piano. The 8-week **Chamber Music Festival,** an important adjunct of the school, offers 16 concerts and seminars for the public; performances are given by pianist Robert McDonald, the Chicago String Quartet, the Brentano String Quartet, Michael Tree, and the international young student artists. Performances are held at the Taos Community Auditorium and the Hotel St. Bernard. P.O. Box 1879. (C) **505/776-2388.** www.taosschoolofmusic.com. Tickets for chamber music concerts $15 for adults, $10 for children under 16.

THE CLUB & MUSIC SCENE

Adobe Bar   A favorite gathering place for locals and visitors, the Adobe Bar is known for its live music series (nights vary) devoted to the eclectic talents of Taos musicians. The schedule offers a little of everything—classical, jazz, folk, Hispanic, and acoustic. The Adobe Bar features a wide selection of international beers, wines by the glass, light New Mexican dining, desserts, and an espresso menu. In the Historic Taos Inn, 125 Paseo del Pueblo Norte. (C) **505/758-2233.** Noon–10:30pm.

Alley Cantina ★ *Moments*   This bar that touts its location as the oldest house in Taos has become the hot late-night spot. The focus is on interaction, as well as TV sports. Patrons playing shuffleboard, pool, chess, and backgammon listen to live music 4 to 5 nights a week. Burgers, fish-and-chips, and other informal dishes are served until 11pm. 121 Teresina Lane. (C) **505/758-2121.** Cover for live music only.

Anaconda Bar 👁★ Set in the new eco-resort El Monte Sagrado, this is Taos's happening night spot, with live entertainment—jazz, blues, Native American flute, or country—playing nightly. An anaconda sculpture snaking across the ceiling and an 11,000-gallon fish tank set the contemporary tone of the place, where a variety of delectable tapas are served. In the El Monte Sagrado hotel, 317 Kit Carson Rd. ✆ 505/758-3502.

Hideaway Lounge This hotel lounge, built around a large adobe fireplace, offers live entertainment and an extensive hors d'oeuvre buffet. Call for schedule. Don Fernando de Taos, 1005 Paseo del Pueblo Sur. ✆ 505/758-4444.

Momentitos de la Vida 👁★ This low-lit, moody bar, with thick pine tables and comfortable chairs, serves up martinis and jazz in bluesy doses. Other drinks and music selections also play here, with live music on Friday and Saturday nights. The restaurant cum club serves a bistro menu with prices from $8.50 to $14. Nonsmoking. Open Tuesday through Sunday 5–10:30pm or so (later on weekends). 4¾ miles north of the intersection of NM 150 and NM 522 (P.O. Box 505), Arroyo Seco. ✆ 505/776-3333.

Sagebrush Inn ★ This is a real hot spot for locals. The atmosphere is Old West, with a rustic wooden dance floor and plenty of smoke. Dancers generally two-step to country music nightly, year-round, starting at 9pm. Paseo del Pueblo Sur (P.O. Box 557). ✆ 505/758-2254.

Thunderbird Lodge Throughout the winter, the Thunderbird offers a variety of nightly entertainment at the foot of the ski slopes. You'll also find wine tastings. Taos Ski Valley. ✆ 505/776-2280. Cover occasionally on holidays, with the cost varying widely.

10 A Scenic Drive Around the Enchanted Circle

If you're in the mood to explore, take this 90-mile loop north of Taos, through the old Hispanic villages of Arroyo Hondo and Questa, into a pass that the Apaches, Kiowas, and Comanches once used to cross the mountains to trade with the Taos Indians. You'll come to the Wild West mining town of Red River, pass through the expansive Moreno Valley, and travel along the base of some of New Mexico's tallest peaks. Then, you'll skim the shores of a high mountain lake at Eagle Nest, pass through the resort village of Angel Fire, and head back to Taos along the meandering Rio Fernando de Taos. Although one can drive the entire loop in 2 hours from Taos, most folks prefer to take a full day, and many take several days.

ARROYO HONDO

Traveling north from Taos via NM 522, it's a 9-mile drive to this village, the remains of an 1815 land grant along the Rio Hondo. Along the dirt roads that lead off NM 522, you may find a windowless *morada* or two, marked by plain crosses in front—places of worship for the still active Penitentes, a religious order known for self-flagellation. This is also the turnoff point for trips to the Rio Grande Box, an awesome 1-day, 17-mile white-water run for which you can book trips in Santa Fe, Taos, Red River, and Angel Fire. (See the "Other Outdoor Activities" sections in chapter 6 and earlier in this chapter for booking agents in Santa Fe and Taos, respectively.)

Arroyo Hondo was also the site of the New Buffalo commune in the 1960s. Hippies flocked here, looking to escape the mores of modern society. Over the years, the commune members have dispersed throughout northern New Mexico,

Taos Area (Including Enchanted Circle)

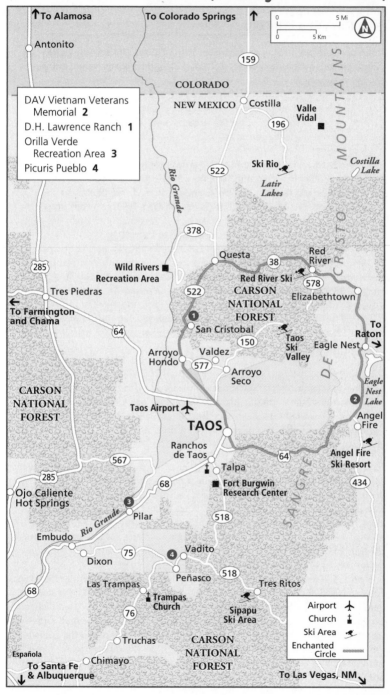

↑ To Alamosa

To Colorado Springs ↑

0 — 5 Mi
0 — 5 Km

N

Antonito

159

COLORADO
NEW MEXICO   Costilla   Valle Vidal

196   Costilla Lake

DAV Vietnam Veterans
Memorial **2**
D.H. Lawrence Ranch **1**
Orilla Verde
Recreation Area **3**
Picuris Pueblo **4**

522   Ski Rio   *Latir Lakes*

Rio Grande

378

285   Questa   38   Red River

Wild Rivers
Recreation Area   Red River Ski   578

Tres Piedras   522   **CARSON NATIONAL FOREST**   Elizabethtown

←
To Farmington
and Chama   64   ① San Cristobal   150   Taos Ski Valley   Eagle Nest   To Raton →

Arroyo Hondo   Valdez   577   Arroyo Seco   *Eagle Nest Lake*

Taos Airport ✈   ② Angel Fire

TAOS

Ranchos de Taos   Angel Fire Ski Resort

567   Talpa

285   68   Fort Burgwin Research Center   434

Ojo Caliente Hot Springs   ③ Pilar   518

Embudo   *Rio Grande*

Dixon   75   ④ Vadito

68   Peñasco   518   Tres Ritos

Las Trampas   Trampas Church

76   Sipapu Ski Area

Truchas   **CARSON NATIONAL FOREST**

Española   Chimayo
To Santa Fe & Albuquerque
↓   To Las Vegas, NM ↘

Airport ✈
Church ♦
Ski Area ⚞
Enchanted Circle ----

SANGRE DE CRISTO MOUNTAINS

A Sojourn on the Green Shore

A sweet spot en route to Taos from Santa Fe, the **Orilla Verde** (green shore) **Recreation Area** offers just what its name implies: lovely green shores along the Rio Grande. It's an excellent place to camp or to simply have a picnic. If you're adventurous, the flat water in this section of the river makes for scenic canoeing, kayaking, rafting, and fishing. Hiking trails thread through the area as well. Along them, you may come across ancient cultural artifacts, but be sure to leave them as you find them.

While traveling to the area, you'll encounter two places of note. The village of **Pilar** is a charming farming village, home to apple orchards, corn fields, and artists. The **Rio Grande Gorge Visitor Center** (at the intersection of NM 570 and NM 68; ✆ **505/751-4899**) provides information about the gorge and has very clean restrooms. It's open daily during business hours from Memorial Day to Labor Day.

The day use fee for Orilla Verde is $3; camping is $7 per night, and RV camping is $15 per night. All campsites have picnic tables, grills, and restrooms. For information contact the **Orilla Verde Visitor Station** (✆ **505/758-4060**; www.nm.blm.gov/tafo/rafting/rio_grande/ovra/ovra_info.html), at the campground. To reach the recreation area, travel north from Santa Fe 50 miles or southwest from Taos 15 miles on NM 68; turn north on NM 570 and travel 1 mile.

bringing an interesting creative element to the food, architecture, and philosophy of the state. En route north, the highway passes near **San Cristobal,** where a side road turns off to the **D. H. Lawrence Ranch** (see "More Attractions," earlier in this chapter) and **Lama,** site of an isolated spiritual retreat.

QUESTA

Next, Highway 522 passes through Questa, most of whose residents are employed at a molybdenum mine about 5 miles east of town. Mining molybdenum (an ingredient in lightbulbs, television tubes, and missile systems) in the area has not been without controversy. The process has raked across hillsides along the Red River, and though Molycorp, the mine's owner, treats the water it uses before returning it to the river, studies show that it has adversely affected the fish life. Still, the mine is a major employer in the area, and locals are grateful for the income it generates.

If you turn west off NM 522 onto NM 378 about 3 miles north of Questa, you'll travel 8 miles on a paved road to the Bureau of Land Management–administered **Wild Rivers Recreation Area** (✆ **505/770-1600**). Here, where the Red River enters the gorge, you'll find 22 miles of trails, some suited for biking and some for hiking, a few trails traveling 800 feet down into the gorge to the banks of the Rio Grande. Forty-eight miles of the Rio Grande, which extend south from the Colorado border, are protected under the national Wild and Scenic River Act of 1968. Information on geology and wildlife, as well as hikers' trail maps, can be obtained at the visitor center here.

The village of **Costilla,** near the Colorado border, is 20 miles north of Questa. This is the turnoff point for four-wheel-drive jaunts and hiking trips into **Valle Vidal,** a huge U.S. Forest Service–administered reserve with 42 miles of roads and many hiking trails. A day hike in this area can bring you sightings of hundreds of elk.

RED RIVER

To continue on the Enchanted Circle loop, turn east at Questa onto NM 38 for a 12-mile climb to Red River, a rough-and-ready 1890s gold-mining town that has parlayed its Wild West ambience into a pleasant resort village that's especially popular with families from Texas and Oklahoma.

This community, at 8,750 feet, is a center for skiing, snowmobiling, fishing, hiking, off-road driving, horseback riding, mountain biking, river rafting, and other outdoor pursuits. Frontier-style celebrations, honky-tonk entertainment, and even staged shootouts on Main Street are held throughout the year.

Though it can be a charming and fun town, Red River's food and accommodations are mediocre at best. Its patrons are down-home folks, happy with a bed and a diner-style meal. If you decide to stay, try **The Lodge at Red River,** P.O. Box 189, Red River, NM 87558 (© **800/91-LODGE** or 505/754-6280; www.redrivernm.com/lodgeatrr), in the center of town. It offers hotel rooms ranging in price from $84 to $106. Knotty pine throughout, the accommodations are clean and comfortable. Downstairs, the restaurant serves three home-style meals daily.

If you're passing through and want a quick meal, the **Main Street Deli,** 316 E. Main St., Red River, NM 87558 (© **505/754-3400**), has brought some excellent flavors to the little village. You'll find tasty meatloaf and chicken-and-dumpling specials, as well as home-baked muffins, soups, and sub sandwiches under $9. Don't leave without trying a macadamia-nut white-chocolate-chip cookie. Open Monday through Saturday 8am to 8pm, Sunday 8am to 2pm.

The **Red River Chamber of Commerce,** P.O. Box 870, Red River, NM 87558 (© **800/348-6444** or 505/754-2366; www.redrivernewmexico.com), lists more than 40 accommodations, including lodges and condominiums. Some are open winters or summers only.

EAGLE NEST

About 16 miles southeast of Red River, on the other side of 9,850-foot Bobcat Pass, is the village of Eagle Nest, resting on the shore of Eagle Nest Lake in the Moreno Valley. Gold was mined in this area as early as 1866, starting in what is now the ghost town of **Elizabethtown** about 5 miles north; Eagle Nest itself (pop. 200) wasn't incorporated until 1976. The 4-square-mile **Eagle Nest Lake** (© **888-NM-PARKS** or 505/476-3355; www.nmparks.com) recently became a New Mexico state park. At press time, work was under way to build a visitor center and upgrade facilities. The lake is considered one of the top trout producers in the United States and attracts ice fishermen in winter as well as summer anglers. It's too cold for swimming, but sailboaters and windsurfers ply the waters.

If you're heading to Cimarron or Denver, proceed east on US 64 from Eagle Nest. But if you're circling back to Taos, continue southwest on US 38 and US 64 to Agua Fría and Angel Fire.

Shortly before the Agua Fría junction, you'll see the **DAV Vietnam Veterans Memorial.** It's a stunning structure with curved, white walls soaring high against the backdrop of the Sangre de Cristo range. Consisting of a chapel and an underground visitor center, it was built by Dr. Victor Westphall in memory of his son, David, a marine lieutenant killed in Vietnam in 1968. The chapel has a changing gallery of photographs of Vietnam veterans who lost their lives in the Southeast Asian war, but no photo is as poignant as this inscription written by young David Westphall, a promising poet:

> Greed plowed cities desolate.
> Lusts ran snorting through the streets.
> Pride reared up to desecrate
> Shrines, and there were no retreats.
> So man learned to shed the tears
> With which he measures out his years.

ANGEL FIRE

If you like the clean efficiency of a resort complex, you may want to plan a night or two here—any time of year. Angel Fire is approximately 150 miles north of Albuquerque and 21 miles east of Taos. Opened in the late 1960s, this resort offers a hotel with spacious, comfortable rooms, as well as condominiums and cabins. Winter is the biggest season. This medium-size beginner and intermediate mountain is an excellent place for families to roam about (see "Skiing," earlier in this chapter). Two high-speed quad lifts zip skiers to the top quickly while allowing them a long ski down. The views of the Moreno Valley are awe inspiring. Fourteen miles of Nordic trail have been added at the top of the mountain; visitors can also snowmobile and take sleigh rides, including one out to a sheepherder's tent with a plank floor and a wood stove where you can eat dinner cooked over an open fire. Contact **Roadrunner Tours** (© **505/377-6416** or 505/377-1811).

During spring, summer, and fall, **Angel Fire Resort** offers golf, tennis, hiking, mountain biking (you can take your bike up on the quad lift), fly-fishing, river rafting, and horseback riding. There are other fun family activities, such as the Human Maze, 5,200 square feet of wooden passageways within which you can let loose your inner rat. There is a video arcade, a miniature golf course, theater performances, and, throughout the year, a variety of festivals, including a hot-air balloon festival, Winterfest, and concerts of both classical and popular music.

The unofficial community center is **Angel Fire Resort,** North Angel Fire Road (P.O. Drawer B), Angel Fire, NM 87710 (© **800/633-7463** or 505/377-6401; www.angelfireresort.com), a 155-unit hotel with spacious, comfortable rooms, some with fireplaces and some with balconies. Rates range from $85 to $199.

For more information on the Moreno Valley, including full accommodations listings, contact the **Angel Fire Chamber of Commerce,** P.O. Box 547, Angel Fire, NM 87710 (© **800/446-8117** or 505/377-6661; fax 505/377-3034; www. angelfirechamber.org).

You may want to try a 1-hour, 1-day, or overnight horseback riding trip with **Roadrunner Tours,** P.O. Box 274, Angel Fire, NM 87710 (© **505/377-6416;** www.rtours.com). One-hour rides run year-round for $30, but if you'd like a little more adventure, try an overnight. From Angel Fire, Nancy and Bill Burch guide riders through private ranchland of ponderosa forests and meadows of asters and sunflowers, often including wildlife sightings. Once at camp, riders bed down in an authentic mountain cowboy cabin. Call for prices.

8

Northeastern New Mexico

Much of my growing up took place on the oft-dusty, oft-lush plains of northeastern New Mexico, the region north of I-40 and east of the Sangre de Cristo Mountains, where dinosaurs and buffalo once roamed. My family has a ranch here, along the Cimarron cutoff of the Santa Fe Trail. I grew up with the ghost of Samuel Watrous, who once had a store on that historic trade route. For a time, I slept in the room where Watrous was said to have committed suicide, though he was found with not one but two bullet holes in his head.

The long miles through the mountains from Las Vegas to Cimarron, or across the plains from Raton to Clayton, are worth it. The history is everywhere, from evidence of Coronado's passage during his 16th-century search of Cíbola, to the Santa Fe Trail ruts on the prairie made some 300 years later. In Cimarron you'll see evidence of the holdings of cattle baron Lucien Maxwell, who controlled most of these prairies as his private empire in the latter half of the 19th century. During his era, this was truly the Wild West. Cimarron attracted nearly every gunslinger of the era, from Butch Cassidy to Clay Allison, Black Jack Ketchum to Jesse James. Bullet holes still decorate the ceiling of the St. James Hotel.

Established long before its Nevada namesake, **Las Vegas** was the largest city in New Mexico at the turn of the 20th century, with a fast-growing, cosmopolitan population. Doc Holliday, Bat Masterson, and Wyatt Earp walked its wild streets in the 1880s. A decade later, it was the headquarters of Teddy Roosevelt's Rough Riders, and early in the 20th century, it was a silent film capital and the site of a world heavyweight boxing match. Today, with a population of approximately 17,000, it is the region's largest city and the proud home of 900 historic properties. **Raton** (pop. 7,500), on I-25 in the Sangre de Cristo foothills, is the gateway to New Mexico from the north. **Clayton** (pop. 2,500), **Tucumcari** (pop. 6,831), and **Santa Rosa** (pop. 2,500) are all transportation hubs and ranching centers.

Two national monuments are particular points of interest. **Fort Union,** 24 miles north of Las Vegas, was the largest military installation in the Southwest in the 1860s and 1870s. **Capulin Volcano,** 33 miles east of Raton, last erupted 60,000 years ago; visitors can now walk inside the crater. Also of note are the **Kiowa and Rita Blanca National Grasslands** preserves: 136,000 acres of pure prairie.

Drained by the Pecos and Canadian rivers, northeastern New Mexico is otherwise notable for the number of small lakes that afford opportunities for fishing, hunting, boating, camping, and even scuba diving. Eleven state parks and about a half dozen designated wildlife areas are within the region. **Philmont Scout Ranch,** south of Cimarron, is known by Boy Scouts throughout the world.

1 The Great Outdoors in Northeastern New Mexico

Northeastern New Mexico encompasses a variety of Southwestern landscapes. The undulating grasslands of the eastern portion of the region eventually give way to the cliffs, canyons, and forests of the mighty Sangre de Cristo Mountains, which offer some of the best hiking and camping in the state. The area is drained by the Pecos and Canadian rivers and has many small streams and lakes, including Ute Lake, the second-largest in the state, that afford opportunities for fishing, including some great fly-fishing, boating, and other recreational pursuits in this seemingly arid region.

BIRD-WATCHING Las Vegas National Wildlife Refuge (© 505/425-3581), 5 miles southeast of Las Vegas, is a great place for bird-watching. Species spotted year-round include prairie falcons and hawks; during late fall and early winter, migratory birds such as sandhill cranes, snow geese, Canada geese, and bald and golden eagles frequent the refuge. In all, more than 240 species can be sighted in the area. The **Maxwell National Wildlife Refuge** (© 505/375-2331), near Raton, also boasts a rich population of resident and migratory birds, including raptors and bald eagles.

BOATING You'll find opportunities for boating, windsurfing, and swimming throughout this region. Two of the most popular boating areas are **Storrie Lake State Park** (© 505/425-7278), 6 miles north of Las Vegas, and **Conchas Lake State Park** (© 505/868-2270), near Tucumcari. Storrie Lake is especially popular among **windsurfers,** who favor its consistent winds. To find information on New Mexico state parks, go to **www.nmparks.com**.

FISHING Isolated and primitive **Morphy Lake State Park** is a favorite destination for serious anglers. The lake is regularly stocked with rainbow trout. **Cimarron Canyon State Park** is also popular with fishers. Lake Alice in **Sugarite Canyon State Park,** just north of Raton at the Colorado border, is a good spot for fly-fishing. For more information on the best fishing opportunities in the area, see chapters 6 and 7.

GOLF Duffers can get in a few holes in or near virtually every town covered in this section. I recommend the following courses: **New Mexico Highlands University Golf Course,** East Mills Avenue and Country Club Drive, Las Vegas, NM 87701 (© 505/425-7711); **Raton Municipal Golf Course,** 510 Country Club Rd., Raton NM 87740 (© 505/445-8113); **Pendaries Lodge and Country Club,** in Rociada (© 505/425-3561; www.pendaries.net), 13 miles south of Mora and 27 miles northwest of Las Vegas; and **Tucumcari Municipal Golf Course,** Old US 66, Tucumcari, NM 88401 (© 505/461-1849).

HIKING Northeastern New Mexico abounds in great places to hike, including the trails at Capulin Volcano; however, the best places are in the mountains to the north of Las Vegas and west of Santa Fe and Taos. **Clayton Lake, Coyote Creek, Morphy Lake, Santa Rosa Lake, Sugarite Canyon,** and **Villanueva** state parks all have hiking trails, which range from fairly informal to clearly marked. For information about them, contact (© **888/NM-PARKS** or 505/476-3355; www.emnrd.state.nm.us/nmparks). The region's premier hike takes you to the top of **Hermit's Peak,** a lovely but strenuous 8-mile round-trip foray onto a stunning precipice. Take NM 65 about 15 miles northwest of Las Vegas to the El Porvenir Campground. It's probably best to acquire equipment and supplies in Albuquerque before you set out. Try **REI-Albuquerque,** 1550 Mercantile Ave. NE (© **505/247-1191;** www.rei.com).

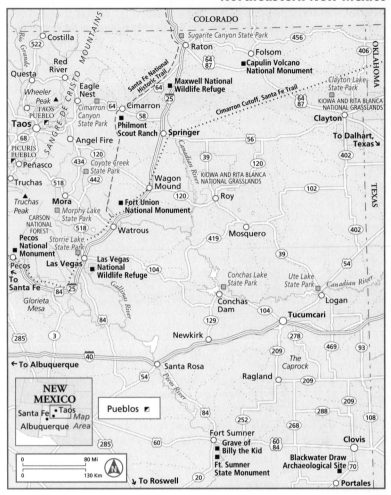

COLORADO

Sugarite Canyon State Park — 456

Costilla — 522

Raton — 64 / 87

Folsom

Capulin Volcano National Monument — 406 OKLAHOMA

Red River

Questa

Santa Fe National Historic Trail

Wheeler Peak ▲

Eagle Nest — 64

Maxwell National Wildlife Refuge — 64

Clayton Lake State Park

TAOS PUEBLO

Cimarron Canyon State Park — 64 — Cimarron — 25

Cimarron Cutoff, Santa Fe Trail — 64 / 87

KIOWA AND RITA BLANCA NATIONAL GRASSLANDS

Taos

Philmont Scout Ranch — Springer

Clayton

68

Angel Fire — 120 — 56

To Dalhart, Texas ↘

PICURIS PUEBLO

Peñasco

434 — Coyote Creek State Park — 39 — 120 — 402

Truchas — 518 — 442

Wagon Mound

KIOWA AND RITA BLANCA NATIONAL GRASSLANDS — 102

Truchas Peak ▲

Mora

120 — Roy

CARSON NATIONAL FOREST

Morphy Lake State Park — 518

Fort Union National Monument

Mosquero — 419

Pecos National Monument

Storrie Lake State Park

Watrous

Conchas Lake State Park

Ute Lake State Park — Canadian River

39

54

Pecos

To Santa Fe — 84 / 25

Las Vegas

Las Vegas National Wildlife Refuge — 104

Conchas Dam — 104

Logan

Glorieta Mesa

Gallinas River

Conchas Dam — 129

Tucumcari

84

285 — 3

40

Newkirk

278

209 — 469 — 93

← To Albuquerque

54

Santa Rosa

Ragland — 209

The Caprock

NEW MEXICO

Santa Fe • Taos Map Area

Albuquerque

Pueblos ▱

Pecos River

209

84 — 252 — 288 — 108

285 — 60

Fort Sumner

Grave of Billy the Kid — 60 / 84

Clovis

0 — 80 Mi
0 — 130 Km

Ft. Sumner State Monument

Blackwater Draw Archaeological Site — 70

↘ To Roswell — 20

Portales

HOT SPRINGS In this region look for **Montezuma Hot Springs,** located on the campus of the Armand Hammer United World College of the American West, near Las Vegas (see "Exploring Las Vegas," below).

HORSEBACK RIDING If you'd like to try your spurs at some real ranch riding, moving cattle, and spitting on the plains and such, contact the **Hartley Guest Ranch,** 50 Guest Ranch Lane, Roy (✆ **800/OUR-DUDE** or 505/673-2244; www.hartleyranch.com). The ranch offers 3- and 5-night packages from April through September.

SCUBA DIVING There couldn't possibly be scuba diving in this dry, landlocked state, could there? Yes, there is, with the best at Santa Rosa, where you'll find the **Blue Hole,** an 81-foot-deep artesian well that's a favorite of divers from around the world. The best place to rent equipment is at the **Santa Rosa Dive Center** on Blue Hole Road (✆ **505/472-3370**).

SWIMMING Swimming is best (although chilly) at **Clayton, Conchas, Morphy, Storrie,** and **Ute lakes.** (You can find directions to and specifics about these lakes at various points in the rest of this chapter.) In addition, though it's an indoor rather than outdoor experience, the **Las Vegas Recreation Center's** (© **505/426-1739**) swimming pool, located at 1751 North Grand Ave., is an especially good place to take kids. It's Olympic-size and has an incredible slide that will keep kids busy for hours. Call for more information.

2 Las Vegas & Environs *★*★

Once known as the "gateway to New Mexico," **Las Vegas,** a pleasant town in the foothills of the Sangre de Cristo Mountains, was founded with a land grant from the Mexican government in 1835. A group of 29 Spanish colonists planted crops in the area and built a central plaza, which started out as a meeting place and a defense against Indian attack but soon became a main trading center on the Santa Fe Trail. Las Vegas boomed with the advent of the Atchison, Topeka, and Santa Fe Railway in 1879; almost overnight the town became the most important trading center and gathering place in the state and one of the largest towns in the Rocky Mountain West, rivaling Denver, Tucson, and El Paso in size.

Town settlers who arrived by train in the late 19th century shunned the indigenous adobe architecture, favoring instead building styles more typical of the Midwest or New England. They put up scores of fancy Queen Anne and Victorian-style houses and hotels, and the town is noted to this day for its dazzling diversity of architectural styles. Some 900 buildings in Las Vegas are on the National Register of Historic Places.

ESSENTIALS

GETTING THERE From Santa Fe, take I-25 northeast 60 miles (1¼ hr.); from Raton, take I-25 south 105 miles (1¾ hr.); from Taos, follow NM 518 southeast 78 miles through Mora (2 hr.); from Tucumcari, follow NM 104 west 112 miles (2 hr.). **Las Vegas Municipal Airport** handles private flights and charters but has no regularly scheduled commercial service.

VISITOR INFORMATION The **Las Vegas & San Miguel County Chamber of Commerce** is at 701 Grand Ave. (P.O. Box 128), Las Vegas, NM 87701 (© **800/832-5947** or 505/425-8631; www.lasvegasnm.org). It is open weekdays from 9am to 5pm.

EXPLORING LAS VEGAS
THE RAILROAD DISTRICT

When you first enter Las Vegas, you may want to take a brief driving tour through the railroad district and "east Las Vegas" to get a sense of how the railroad's arrival in the 1870s shaped that side of the city. Turn east on Douglas Avenue, which will take you to Railroad Avenue. In this district are turn-of-the-20th-century brick buildings housing such businesses as Moonlite Welding and Blue Dart Upholstery Shop. The center of the railroad district is the old Fred Harvey **Castañeda Hotel** at 510 Railroad. Built in 1898, it is one of the early Harvey Houses to be built in the Mission Revival style. It no longer operates as a hotel; however, you'll want to stop and take a peek into the lobby, which is still elegant, with a molded tin ceiling and arched windows.

THE HISTORIC DISTRICT

The chamber of commerce on Grand Avenue (see "Essentials," above) has a map of a self-guided tour of this area. What's most notable is the town's early Spanish history; adobe buildings going back to the first Spanish visits in the 16th century are still standing alongside the ornate structures of the late 1800s. In addition, it's hard to find such a well-preserved collection of Territorial-style buildings. Most of the interesting structures can be found in the Plaza–Bridge Street area.

In particular, don't miss the **Plaza Hotel,** 230 Old Town Plaza, the finest hotel in the New Mexico Territory back in 1881. Its three-story facade, topped with a fancy broken pediment decoration, was the town's pride and joy, and it has been happily restored. (See "Where to Stay in Las Vegas," below.)

Another highlight is the **Dice Apartments,** 210 Old Town Plaza. Although the low adobe building is unimpressive, its history is distinguished—it is the sole building on the plaza that predates the U.S.–Mexican War of 1846. In that year, Gen. Stephen Kearny, commander of the Army of the West, stood on a one-story building on the north side of the plaza (probably this one) to address the town's population, claiming New Mexico for the United States.

For shopping, be sure to browse through **Rough Rider Antiques,** at 158 Bridge St. (© 505/454-8063). You'll find Southwestern furniture, eclectic Western art, and quilts here. Another good shopping stop is **Plaza Antiques,** 1805 Old Town Plaza (© 505/454-9447), a fun place to browse for antique clothing and kitchen tables.

Housed in a 1940s-era Work Projects Administration (WPA) building, the **Las Vegas City Museum and Rough Riders Memorial Collection,** 727 Grand Ave. (© 505/454-1401, ext. 283), is a fun spot to spend about an hour. The largest contingent of Rough Riders was recruited from New Mexico to fight in the 1898 Spanish–American War. This museum chronicles their contribution to U.S. history and also contains artifacts relating to the history of the city. Another exhibit documents the history of Las Vegas. Admission is free. The museum is open weekdays from 9am to noon and 1 to 4pm, and by appointment.

New to the plaza area, the **Santa Fe Trail Interpretive Center,** 127 Bridge St. (© 505/425-8803; www.worldplaces.com/cchp/pwap.htm), offers a glimpse into efforts to restore the town's 918 historic buildings as well as information about the Santa Fe Trail. Set in the 1890s Winternitz Building, it's a fun stop, if you find it open. Hours vary greatly, as it is staffed by volunteers.

OTHER ATTRACTIONS NEAR TOWN

Las Vegas has two colleges. **New Mexico Highlands University** (© 505/425-7511; www.nmhu.edu), a 4-year liberal arts school of almost 3,000 students, was established in 1893. In 1971, it hired the nation's first Hispanic college president. Located on University Avenue, just west of US 85, it is especially strong in its minority education curriculum, and it fields outstanding athletic teams.

Value Weaving Magic

You can watch weavers at work at **Tapetes de Lana** on the Las Vegas Plaza. Appropriately set in a late-1800s textile shop, this fun shop and weavers' studio offers a peek into the art as well as lovely works to buy. Hanging from antique stone walls are scarves, shawls, and Rio Grande–style rugs woven as part of a job-training program for people with low income, many of whom have mastered the art beautifully. It's located at 1814 Plaza (© 505/426-8638; www.tapetesdelana.com) and is open Monday through Friday 8am to 5pm and Saturday 10am to 5pm. Prices are uncommonly reasonable.

The **Armand Hammer United World College,** 5 miles west of Las Vegas via NM 65 (© **505/454-4200;** www.uwc.org), is an international school with students from more than 70 countries. It is housed in the former **Montezuma Hotel,** a luxury resort built by the Santa Fe Railroad in the 1880s and now a historic landmark. Three U.S. presidents, Germany's Kaiser Wilhelm II, and Japan's Meiji Emperor Mutsuhito stayed in the multistoried, turreted, 270-room "Montezuma Castle," as it came to be known. It was abandoned during the Depression and purchased in 1981 by Armand Hammer, philanthropist and former chair of the Occidental Petroleum Corporation. Call for information about occasional private tours. Also on the campus are the **Montezuma Hot Springs.** Free and open to the public, the springs have attracted health-seekers for more than 1,000 years; legend has it that ancient Aztecs, including chief Montezuma II, journeyed here from Mexico in the early 16th century, long before the arrival of the Spanish. Open daily from 8am to midnight.

EXPLORING THE AREA

Mora, a small village 31 miles north of Las Vegas via NM 518, is the main center between Las Vegas and Taos, and it's the seat of sparsely populated Mora County. The 15-mile-long Mora Valley is one of New Mexico's prettiest but most economically depressed regions, where families have for centuries lived by subsistence farming and are only recently having to adapt to other means of earning income.

Cleveland Roller Mill ★ One vestige of a more prosperous past is this two-story adobe mill, which ground out 50 barrels of wheat flour a day, virtually every day, from 1901 to 1947. It was the last flour mill to be built in New Mexico and the last to stop running, and it is the only roller mill in the state to have its original milling works intact. Today, it's been converted into a museum with exhibits on local regional history and culture. The Millfest, on Labor Day weekend, features the mill in operation, dances, arts and crafts, music, and more. It's advisable to call ahead because the mill is closed from time to time. Plan to spend 1 to 2 hours exploring.

NM 518, about 2 miles west of Mora, Cleveland, NM 87715. © **505/387-2645.** Admission $2 adults, $1 children 7–17, free for ages 6 and under. Open weekends only, Memorial Day–Labor Day 10am–3pm, or by appointment.

La Cueva National Historic Site and Salman Ranch ★ *Finds* Each fall, I make a bit of a pilgrimage to this spot in a lush valley along the Mora River. Its history is rich, dating from the early 1800s, when a man named Vicente Romero began farming and raising sheep here. He completed an elegant two-story northern New Mexico home that still stands, as well as a mill that ground flour and supplied electricity for the area (the real draw). Just north of these historic sites is the San Rafael Mission Church, with exquisite French Gothic windows. Recently restored by local people, it's now painted blue and white. The trip through these sites is worth the time during any season, but in the fall, the raspberries ripen and turn this into a must-do trip. The ranch's current owner, Frances Salman, planted 20 acres of the delectable fruit and now sells it by the basket or crate, as well as in jams and over soft vanilla ice cream. Delicious.

NM 518, 6 miles east of Mora, Buena Vista, NM 87712. © **505/387-2900.** Free admission. Summer Mon–Sat 9am–5pm, Sun 10am–5pm; winter hours limited (call first).

Victory Ranch *Kids* Few things surprise me in this strange part of the state, where images of Jesus are known to appear on stucco walls and ghosts are said to inhabit the old haciendas, but I must say that my head turned when I saw alpacas grazing in a meadow here. I stopped immediately and stepped out of my car just in time for a tour. With a small cup of feed I purchased, I followed a young boy out to some lush pens where the odd South American Andean creatures greeted us with a harmonica-like hum. Very friendly, they ate from our hands while the babies roamed about, heads held high, marble-clear brown eyes looking quizzical. Also on site is a store that sells sweaters and shawls made from alpaca wool, as well as a loom where visitors can try weaving. Weaving and spinning demonstrations are available on request. Group tours are also available.

1 mile north of Mora on NM 434, Mora, NM 87732. (C) **505/387-2254.** Fax 505/387-9005. www.victory ranch.com. Admission for feeding tour $3 adults, $2 children under age 12. Daily 10am–4pm, with tours at 11am, 1pm, and 3pm.

GETTING OUTSIDE: OFF-THE-BEATEN-PATH STATE PARKS & OTHER SCENIC HIGHLIGHTS

A short drive north of the Montezuma Hot Springs takes you to a pond on the Gallinas River that provides winter skating and summer fishing.

Other nearby parklands include **Las Vegas National Wildlife Refuge** ((C) **505/425-3581;** http://southwest.fws.gov/refuges/newmex/lasvegas), 5 miles southeast via NM 104 and NM 281, open Monday through Friday from 8am to 4:30pm, boasting 220 species of birds and other animals on 8,672 acres of wetland; and **Storrie Lake State Park** ((C) **505/425-7278**), 4 miles north via NM 518 and open daily during daylight hours year-round, which offers fishing, swimming, windsurfing, waterskiing, camping, a visitor center with historic exhibits, and a playground.

Villanueva State Park ((C) **505/421-2957**), 31 miles southwest via I-25 and NM 3 and open daily from 7am to 9pm (until 7pm in winter), offers excellent hiking, camping, and picnicking between red sandstone bluffs in the Pecos River Valley. Nearby are the Spanish colonial villages **Villanueva** and **San Miguel del Vado;** the latter is a national historic district built around an impressive 1805 church.

Isolated **Morphy Lake State Park** ((C) **505/387-2328**), which is reached via NM 518 to Mora and NM 94 south for 4 miles, is open daily 24 hours. The pretty lake is set in a basin of pine forest; it offers primitive camping, swimming (though in mossy conditions), and trout fishing. Check on driving conditions before going; the road to the park is rough and best suited for four-wheel-drive vehicles, though usually passable by cars. Fourteen miles north of Mora via NM 434 is another always open, out-of-the-way beauty, **Coyote Creek State Park** ((C) **505/387-2328**), with fully developed and primitive campsites beside a stream. The fishing is good, and a few well-marked hiking trails head into the mountains.

If you prefer your nature a little less primitive, head for the **Pendaries Lodge and Country Club,** P.O. Box 820, Rociada, NM 87742 ((C) **505/425-3561;** www.pendaries.net), located 13 miles south of Mora and 27 miles northwest of Las Vegas, on NM 105 off NM 94. This lovely foothills lodge boasts the region's finest 18-hole golf course and fishing. It also has overnight accommodations and a restaurant/lounge.

FORT UNION NATIONAL MONUMENT 🐾

Established in 1851 to defend the Santa Fe Trail against attacks from Plains Indians, Fort Union was expanded in 1861 in anticipation of a Confederate invasion, which was subsequently thwarted at Glorieta Pass, 20 miles southeast of Santa Fe. Fort Union's location on the Santa Fe Trail made it a welcome way station for travelers, but when the railroad replaced the trail in 1879, the fort was on its way out. It was abandoned in 1891. Today, Fort Union, the largest military installation in the 19th-century Southwest, is in ruins. Though it offers little to see but adobe walls and chimneys, the very scope of the fort is impressive. Santa Fe Trail wagon ruts can still be seen nearby. Follow the 1½-mile self-guided interpretive trail that wanders through the ruins and imagine yourself a weary 19th-century wagon traveler stopping for rest and supplies.

The national monument has a small visitor center and museum with exhibits and booklets on the fort's history. Visitors should allow 2 hours to tour the ruins.

JUST THE FACTS   To reach the site from Las Vegas, drive 18 miles north on I-25 to the Watrous exit, and then another 8 miles northwest on NM 161. Admission is $3 per person. Fort Union National Monument is open Memorial Day to Labor Day daily from 8am to 6pm; during the rest of the year, it is open daily from 8am to 4pm. It's closed Thanksgiving, Christmas, and New Year's Day.

A gift shop carries a wide selection of books on New Mexico history and women's history, and frontier military books. Camping is not available at the monument, but facilities are available in nearby Las Vegas.

For more information on the monument, contact Fort Union National Monument, P.O. Box 127, Watrous, NM 87753 (© **505/425-8025;** www.nps.gov/foun).

WHERE TO STAY IN LAS VEGAS

Most motels are on US 85 (Grand Ave.), the main north–south highway through downtown Las Vegas. (An exception is the Plaza Hotel, below.)

Inn on the Santa Fe Trail ✪   Built in the 1920s as a court motel, this inn has been remodeled in a hacienda style, with all rooms looking out onto the central courtyard, creating a quiet, intimate, and sophisticated retreat just off busy Grand Avenue. Although it's not as historical as the Plaza Hotel (see below), the rooms are a bit more up-to-date and functional, and you can park your car right outside. Rooms are medium-size with nice accents, such as handcrafted iron light fixtures, towel racks, and hand-carved pine furniture—even *trasteros* (armoires) to conceal the televisions. The beds are comfortably firm, and each room has a table with two chairs and a desk. The bathrooms are small but very clean. Suites have sofa beds and minifridges. Be sure to read about the motel's restaurant, Blackjack's Grill, in "Where to Dine in Las Vegas," below. The heated outdoor pool, open seasonally, is lovely. Ask about the regional cultural events that the inn helps organize.

1133 Grand Ave., Las Vegas, NM 87701. © **888/448-8438** or 505/425-6791. www.innonthesantafetrail. com. 42 units. $79 double. Rates include continental breakfast. Extra person $5. AE, DISC, MC, V. Pets permitted for $5 fee. **Amenities:** Restaurant (p. 254); outdoor heated pool. *In room:* A/C, TV, coffeemaker.

Plaza Hotel ✪   A stay in this hotel offers a romantic peek into the past, with a view of the plaza. The windows look out on the spot where, in 1846, a ceremony led by Gen. Stephen Kearny marked the takeover of New Mexico by the United States. The inn was built in Italianate bracketed style in 1882, in the days when Western towns, newly connected with the East by train, vied with one another in constructing fancy "railroad hotels," as they were known. Considered the finest hotel in the New Mexico Territory when it was built, it underwent a $2 million renovation exactly 100 years later. Stately walnut staircases frame the lobby and conservatory (with its piano); throughout the hotel, the architecture is true to its era.

As with most renovations in northern New Mexico, don't expect to see the elegance of the Ritz. Instead, expect a more frontier style, with antiques a bit worn and old rugs a bit torn. Rooms vary in size, but most are average size, with elegantly high ceilings, antique furnishings, comfortably firm beds, and armoires concealing the televisions. The bathrooms also range in size; most are small, with lots of original tile but up-to-date fixtures. The rooms either have windows facing outward toward the plaza and surrounding streets or inward toward an atrium. The inward-facing rooms are quieter but a bit claustrophobic. All rooms open onto spacious hallways with casual seating areas.

The hotel offers limited room service from its Landmark Grill, which has good food, especially the New Mexican dishes, in a period setting. Notice the walls of the Landmark: The original 19th-century stenciling has been restored. The restaurant is open for lunch and dinner. Byron T's 19th-century saloon often features live music on Friday and Saturday evenings.

230 Plaza, Las Vegas, NM 87701. (℃) **800/328-1882** or 505/425-3591. Fax 505/425-9659. www.plazahotel-nm.com. 36 units. $96–$116 double; $138–$146 suite. Rates includes hot cooked-to-order breakfast. AE, DC, DISC, MC, V. **Amenities:** Restaurant; bar. *In room:* A/C, TV, wireless Internet, coffeemaker.

Star Hill Inn 🌟 *(Finds*   Located "in the Orion Spiral Arm of the Milky Way Galaxy," 12 miles northwest of Las Vegas, this inn is a haven for astronomers, stargazers, and anyone else in search of a peaceful mountain retreat. Owner Phil Mahon picked the site in the late 1980s for its nighttime darkness and frequently clear skies. On 195 pine-covered acres at the base of the Sangre de Cristo Mountains, this property has seven cottages with plenty of space between them. Each unit is furnished with a fully equipped kitchen, a covered porch, and a small fireplace. Comfortable beds and clean, functional bathrooms round out the experience. The cottages are decorated with photos, taken on site, of Comet Hale-Bopp. The recently added three-bedroom house has two bathrooms and similar amenities and furnishings as the cottages. Meal service is not provided, but grocery stores and restaurants are 20 minutes away in Las Vegas.

Star Hill rents a variety of astronomical observing equipment. Telescopes can be rented by the night or the week, and camera mounts and tripods are also available. One-hour "sky tours" are available to demonstrate the telescopes and introduce visitors to the intricacies of the night sky.

County Road A-3. P.O. Box 707, Sapello, NM 87745. (℃) **505/425-5605**. www.starhillinn.com. 7 cottages and 1 house. $165–$230 double (cottage); $375 for 4 people (house). Rates include star tour or telescope use. $10 each additional guest over age 12. Minimum 2-night stay. AE, MC, V. Nonsmoking. *In room:* Kitchen.

CAMPING

There's plenty of camping available in and around Las Vegas. I recommend the **Las Vegas KOA** (℃ **800/562-3423** or 505/454-0180; www.koa.com), which has 60 sites, 15 with full hookups, 26 with water and electricity. Laundry, grocery, ice, and recreational facilities (including a pool) are available, as is a large gift shop. Seasonal cookouts are offered. From I-25, go 1 block southeast on US 84, then half a mile southwest on Frontage Road (also called Sheridan Rd.).

Also in Las Vegas is **Vegas RV Park** (℃ 505/425-5640), which offers 40 sites, 33 with full hookups, and cable TV availability. It's located at 504 Harris Rd. in Las Vegas.

If you'd rather camp at a state park, try **Storrie Lake State Park** (℃ 505/425-7278), which offers 20 sites with electricity, 23 sites without it, and primitive camping in an open area close to the lake. Developed sites have water, picnic tables, and grills, and a visitor center is nearby.

Camping is also allowed in the secluded **Morphy Lake State Park** as well as in **Coyote Creek State Park** ✰. Each of these parks offers sites with picnic tables, fire rings, and pit toilets, as well as primitive camping. In addition, Coyote Creek has 17 sites with hookups, some with shelters, and a bathhouse with showers. Morphy Lake's campground does not have drinking water available. For more information about either park, call ✆ **505/387-2328.**

WHERE TO DINE IN LAS VEGAS

Blackjack's Grill ✰✰ STEAKS/SEAFOOD   Las Vegas needed a fancier restaurant for a long time, and now it has one. The main dining room at Blackjack's is small and cozy, done in brilliant colors with mood lighting. In the warmer months, diners can sit on a patio under white cloth umbrellas. As befits the area, it's a fairly informal restaurant that does fill up, so try to make reservations. Each night the chef serves some special dishes. Most are fairly traditional. I've enjoyed beef medallions in wine sauce served with garlic mashed potatoes. The pasta dishes, such as fettuccine Alfredo, can also be good. Most meals come with bread, a choice of salad or soup, and a vegetable. A variety of dessert specials are available. Beer and wine are served.

At the Inn on the Santa Fe Trail, 1133 Grand Ave. ✆ **888/448-8438** or 505/425-6791. Reservations recommended. Main courses $13–$20. AE, MC, V. Daily 5–8:30pm.

El Rialto Restaurant & Lounge ✰ (Kids) NEW MEXICAN   Since I was a young girl, this has been one of my favorite restaurants. In fact, my mother still asks owner Ralph Garcia to cater any big parties she has. The food is simply excellent. It's a locals' place, full of families, old Hispanic farmers, and students from the United World College. The decor is cheesy pastels, but it can be overlooked for the comfort, especially of the booths. The lounge still retains the original red upholstery, which is more to my liking. Service is friendly and efficient. The chile, especially the green, is outstanding here (order anything smothered with it). My favorite is the chicken enchilada plate. The beef is good, too, and the rellenos are quite tasty. There are a variety of stuffed sopaipillas, and steaks, too, as well as sandwiches and a kids' menu. For dessert, I usually smother my sopaipilla with honey, though you can order pie or flan. There's a full bar and outdoor patio here.

141 Bridge St. ✆ **505/454-0037.** Reservations recommended. Main courses $5–$10 lunch, $7–$23 dinner. AE, DC, DISC, MC, V. Mon–Sat 10:30am–9pm.

Pastime Café ✰ (Finds) AMERICAN   In a comfortable, earthy atmosphere, steps from the plaza, this restaurant serves healthy and delicious food. The menu offers more sophistication than most northeastern New Mexico eateries, and yet diners can find many small-town standards as well. Low-carb seekers can savor a grilled chicken breast on crisp greens, while their indulgent alter egos can feast on a triple-decker club (with turkey, bacon, and avocado on toasted potato bread). Either will enjoy the spinach and feta quiche.

113 Bridge St. ✆ **505/454-1755.** Reservations accepted. Main courses $4–$8. MC, V. Mon–Fri 11:30am–2:30pm.

3 Cimarron & Raton: Historic Towns on the Santa Fe Trail

CIMARRON ✰

Few towns in the American West have as much lore or legend attached to them as Cimarron, 41 miles southwest of Raton via US 64. Nestled against the eastern slope of the Sangre de Cristo Mountains, the town (its name is Spanish for "wild" or "untamed") achieved its greatest fame as a "wild and woolly" outpost on the Santa Fe Trail between the 1850s and 1880s and a gathering place for area ranchers, traders, gamblers, gunslingers, and other characters.

ESSENTIALS

GETTING THERE   From Fort Union National Monument, head north on I-25, then west on US 58 to Cimarron.

VISITOR INFORMATION   The **Cimarron Chamber of Commerce,** 104 N. Lincoln Ave. (P.O. Box 604), Cimarron, NM 87714 (© **505/376-2417;** www.cimarronnm.com), has complete information on the region. It is open in summer Thursday through Monday from 8:30am to 4:30pm; in winter Monday through Friday from 10am to 3pm.

EXPLORING THE WILD WEST TOWN

Frontier personalities such as Kit Carson and Wyatt Earp, Buffalo Bill Cody and Annie Oakley, Bat Masterson and Doc Holliday, Butch Cassidy and Jesse James, painter Frederic Remington and novelist Zane Grey all passed through and stayed in Cimarron—most of them at the **St. James Hotel** (see "Where to Stay & Dine in Cimarron," below). Even if you're not planning an overnight stay here, it's a fun place to visit for an hour or two.

Land baron Lucien Maxwell founded the town in 1848 as the base of operations for his 1.7-million-acre empire. In 1857, he built a mansion at his **Maxwell Ranch,** furnishing it opulently with heavy draperies, gold-framed paintings, and two grand pianos. In the gaming room, the tables saw high stakes, as guests bet silver Mexican pesos or pokes of yellow gold dust. Gold was struck in 1867 on Maxwell's land, near Baldy Mountain, and the rush of prospectors that followed caused him to sell out 3 years later.

The ranch isn't open for viewing today, but Maxwell's 1864 stone gristmill, built to supply flour to Fort Union, is. The **Old Mill Museum** (© **505/376-2417**), a grand, three-story stone structure that's well worth visiting, houses an interesting collection of early photos, as well as memorabilia ranging from a saddle that belonged to Kit Carson to dresses worn by Virginia Maxwell. It's open in May and September, Saturday from 9am to 5pm and Sunday from 1 to 5pm; Memorial Day to Labor Day, Friday through Wednesday from 9am to 5pm. It's closed October through April. Admission is $2 for adults, $1 for seniors and children.

Cimarron has numerous other buildings of historic note, and a walking tour to see them only takes about a half-hour. A walking-tour map is included in the Old Mill Museum brochure, which you can pick up at the museum, or, if that's closed, at the chamber of commerce, 104 N. Lincoln Ave.

NEARBY ATTRACTIONS

Cimarron is the gateway to the **Philmont Scout Ranch** (© **505/376-2281;** www.philmont.com), a 137,500-acre property donated in pieces, beginning in 1938, to the Boy Scouts of America by Texas oilman Waite Phillips. Scouts from all over the world use the ranch for backcountry camping and leadership training in the summer and for conferences the remainder of the year. On one of my visits, after touring the incredible Villa (worth seeing even if you have no interest in scouting), I got a flat tire. If you're going to get a flat tire anywhere in the West, this is the place to do it. Two young scouts, an Eagle Scout, and two girls who were working at the camp for the summer came to my rescue, and I was back on the road in a half-hour. All three museums on the ranch are open to the public.

GETTING OUTSIDE: CIMARRON CANYON STATE PARK

US 64 from Cimarron leads west 24 miles to Eagle Nest, passing en route the popular and often crowded **Cimarron Canyon State Park** (© 505/377-6271). A 32,000-acre designated state wildlife area, it sits at the foot of crenelated granite cliffs, 800 feet high in some areas, known as the Palisades. Rock climbing is allowed throughout the park except in the Palisades area. The river and the two park lakes attract anglers; for the best fishing, move away from the heavily populated campgrounds.

Just east of Cimarron, County Road 204 offers access to the Carson National Forest's **Valle Vidal** recreation area (see chapter 7), an incredible place to hike, backpack, and see hundreds of elk.

WHERE TO STAY & DINE IN CIMARRON

Casa del Gavilan 🕊 *Finds* This sprawling adobe villa, built in 1910 on a broad hill overlooking Philmont and the mountains beyond, provides a quiet Southwestern ranch-style experience. The common areas have high ceilings with thick vigas (beams) and wooden floors. The rooms surround a central courtyard, a nice place to sit and relax in the cool evenings. The rooms are spacious, with comfortably firm beds and plenty of antiques. The bathrooms are medium-size and maintain an old-style charm. The two-bedroom suite, which is housed in what's called the Guest House, is good for families, though lower ceilings give it a slightly newer feel. There isn't a television on the premises, but a hiking trail just off the courtyard leads to amazing vistas. Breakfast is served in a big, sunny dining room; you'll find such specialties as baked French toast with ham and fruit salad and a baked apple pancake served with sausage.

6 miles south of Cimarron on NM 21 (P.O. Box 518), Cimarron, NM 87714. © 800/GAVILAN or 505/376-2246. Fax 505/376-2247. www.casadelgavilan.com. 5 units. $75–$137 per unit. Rates include full breakfast. Extra adult $20, extra child 5–10 $10. AE, DISC, MC, V. *In room:* Coffeemaker, no phone.

Kit Carson Motel and Restaurant AMERICAN/STEAKS This unassuming place offers decent diner-style food at reasonable prices. Breakfast offerings include plenty of eggs and pancakes. Lunch brings sandwiches and burgers. My favorite dinner here is the breaded trout with a salad. Be sure to leave room for strawberry shortcake. Locals enjoy the daily specials, such as enchilada casserole. During summer in the same building, the **Cimarron Steak and Chop House** offers tasty steaks with all the fixin's. Behind the restaurant, the motel offers decent rooms.

31036 US 64 E. © 505/376-2288. Reservations recommended in summer. Main courses: $4–$7 breakfast, $5–$10 lunch, $7–$18 dinner. AE, DISC, MC, V. Summer daily 6am–9:30pm; winter daily 7am–2pm and 5–8:30pm.

St. James Hotel 🕊 This landmark hotel offers travelers a romantically historic stay in this Old West town. It looks much the same today as it did in 1873, when it was built by Henri Lambert, previously a chef for Napoleon, Abraham Lincoln, and Ulysses S. Grant. In its early years, it was a rare luxury hotel on the Santa Fe Trail, with a dining room, a saloon, gambling rooms, and lavish guest rooms outfitted with Victorian furniture. Today, you will find lace and cherrywood in the bedrooms, though like the Plaza in Las Vegas, the feel is frontier elegance rather than lavishness. Rooms don't have televisions or phones—the better to evoke the days when famous guests such as Zane Grey, who wrote *Fighting Caravans* at the hotel, were residents. Annie Oakley's bed is here, and a glass case holds a register with the signatures of Buffalo Bill Cody and the notorious Jesse James. The beds are comfortably soft, and the bathrooms are small and basic.

One room just off the lobby is left open so that those not staying the night can have a peek.

The St. James was a place of some lawlessness: 26 men were said to have been killed within the 2-foot-thick adobe walls, and owner Perry Champion can point out bullet holes in the pressed-tin ceiling of the dining room. The ghosts of some are believed to inhabit the hotel still.

Next door are 12 more rooms in a motel. These rooms are narrow and not sturdily made, though they do have recently renovated bathrooms. They also provide TV and telephone for those who prefer the 21st century.

During summer months, Lambert's at the St. James serves good food in an atmosphere that doesn't quite bridge the century gap. The molded tin ceiling and textured wallpaper are lovely, but the tables and chairs are contemporary. The menu is short, but good, with dishes such as pasta primavera and filet mignon, priced from $14 to $28. A separate coffee shop serves three meals daily in summer, purveying large portions of tasty New Mexican food. The hotel also offers a tour desk, an outdoor patio, and a gift shop.

17th St. and Collinson, Cimarron, NM 87714. (✆ **866/472-5019** or 505/376-2664. Fax 505/376-2623. 23 units. Hotel $60–$100 double, $120 suite; motel $60 double. AE, DISC, MC, V. **Amenities:** Restaurant; bar; coffee shop; billiards room. *In room:* No phone in some rooms.

RATON

Raton was founded in 1879 at the site of Willow Springs, a watering stop on the Santa Fe Trail. Mountain man "Uncle Dick" Wooton, a closet entrepreneur, had blasted a pass through the Rocky Mountains just north of the spring and began charging tolls. When the railroad bought Wooton's road, Raton developed as the railroad, mining, and ranching center for this part of the New Mexico Territory. Today it has a well-preserved historic district and the finest shooting facility in the United States.

East of Raton is Capulin Mountain, home to Capulin Volcano National Monument. The volcanic crater of the majestic 8,182-foot peak, inactive for 60,000 years, is open to visitors. See below for more about Capulin Volcano National Monument.

ESSENTIALS
GETTING THERE   From Santa Fe, take I-25 north; from Taos, take US 64 east.

VISITOR INFORMATION   The tourist information center is at the **Raton Chamber and Economic Development Council,** 100 Clayton Rd., at the corner of 2nd Street (P.O. Box 1211), Raton, NM 87740 (✆ **800/638-6161** or 505/445-3689; www.raton.info). Memorial Day to Labor Day, the center is open daily from 8am to 6pm; hours are 8am to 5pm during the rest of the year.

A WALKING TOUR OF HISTORIC RATON
Five blocks of Raton's original town site are listed on the National Register of Historic Places, with some 70 significant buildings. It's best to explore the historic district by foot, allowing 1 to 2 hours. Start at the **Raton Museum,** 216 S. 1st St. (✆ **505/445-8979**), where you can pick up a walking-tour map. The museum, open Tuesday through Saturday from 9am to 5pm, displays a wide variety of mining, railroad, and ranching items from the early days of the town.

NEARBY ATTRACTIONS
The **NRA Whittington Center** (✆ **505/445-3615;** www.nrawc.org), off US 64 about 10 miles south of Raton, is considered the most complete nonmilitary

shooting and training facility in the world. Operated by the National Rifle Association, it spans 50 square miles of rolling hills. It has 16 instructional and competitive ranges, a handful of log cabins, and hookups for campers. Classes in pistol, rifle, and shotgun shooting; firearm safety; and conservation are offered. National championship events are held annually. A gift shop is open Monday through Friday 8am to 5pm. The shooting range is open daily from dawn until dusk.

In the little town of **Springer** (pop. 1,300), 39 miles south of Raton via I-25, the **Santa Fe Trail Museum,** in the center of town on Maxwell Avenue (© **505/483-5554**), is housed in the old three-story 1881 Colfax County Courthouse. It contains pioneer artifacts and memorabilia from travelers along the Santa Fe Trail and early residents of the area, as well as a livery stable and New Mexico's only electric chair, which was used to execute seven convicted murderers between 1933 and 1956. Hours are Thursday through Saturday from 10am to 4pm and Sunday 1 to 4pm from Memorial Day to the end of September. Admission is $3 for adults, $2 for seniors, and $1 for children 12 to 18; free for children under 12. The **Colfax County Fair** takes place in Springer annually in mid-August, with a rodeo and 4-H fair. Call © **505/445-8071** for more information.

If you want to stay or dine in Springer, stop in at the **Brown Hotel & Café,** 302 Maxwell Ave. (© **505/483-2269**). This old-time place has photos of area ranchers on the walls and sweet country-style rooms upstairs. The food is diner-style, with plenty of pancakes, burritos, and, of course, chicken-fried steak.

About 24 miles east of Springer, via US 56 and 12 miles on a dirt road, is the **Dorsey Mansion Ranch,** a two-story log-and-stone home built in the 1880s by U.S. senator and cattleman Stephen Dorsey. With 29 rooms, hardwood floors, Italian marble fireplaces, a hand-carved cherry staircase, and a dining room table that sat 60, it was quite a masterpiece! Public tours are offered by appointment (© **505/375-2222;** www.dorseymansion.com) Monday through Saturday from 10am to 4pm, Sunday from 1 to 5pm, and may be arranged during other hours. Admission is $3 for adults and $1 for children under age 6 (with a $5 minimum per tour).

GETTING OUTSIDE
Sugarite Canyon State Park (© **505/445-5607**), 10 miles northeast of Raton via NM 72 and NM 526, offers historic exhibits, camping, boating, and excellent fishing at three trout-stocked lakes. Lake Alice is the best place in the park for fly-fishing. Numerous hiking trails meander through the park, and a museum at the visitor center traces the canyon's mining history.

Heading down I-25, **Maxwell National Wildlife Refuge** (© **505/375-2331**), on the Canadian River 24 miles southwest of Raton, has a rich resident and migratory bird population (including many hawks) and numerous native mammals (including three black-tail prairie dog towns). More than 344 species have been recorded in the refuge, which offers some of the best bird-watching in this part of the state. You'll find primitive camping by Lake 13, which has some of the best seasonal trout fishing in the state.

South of US 56 via NM 39 is the westernmost of the two parcels that comprise the **Kiowa and Rita Blanca National Grasslands** (© **505/374-9652**). The 263,954-acre area is a project to reclaim once-barren prairie land, the result of over-farming in the late 19th and early 20th centuries, and the Great Plains Dustbowl of the 1930s. Today the plains are irrigated and green, and the area provides food, cover, and water for a wide variety of wildlife, such as antelope, bear, Barbary sheep, mountain lion, wild turkey, pheasant, and quail. Another portion of the grasslands is located east of here, along US 56/412, near the town of Clayton, just west of the Oklahoma border.

WHERE TO STAY IN RATON

Best Western Sands *(Kids)*   Rooms in this hotel, equidistant between downtown and the interstate, are so clean and roomy that reservations are a must during summer months. Built in 1959, the hotel updates rooms periodically. All rooms are decorated with Southwestern prints, with nice touches such as ceramic lamps and finely made oak furniture. In the luxury wing, rooms have minifridges, recliners, hair dryers, and Institute Swiss soaps. All rooms have comfortably firm beds and down pillows. The standard rooms are more than adequate and provide plenty of space and parking right outside your door. Families enjoy a "lenders library" and a selection of family games. The hotel also offers an assistive telephone kit for the hearing impaired.

300 Clayton Hwy., Raton, NM 87740. © 800/518-2581, 800/528-1234, or 505/445-2737. Fax 505/445-4053. www.bestwestern.com/sandsraton. 50 units. $44–$99 double. Extra person $3. AE, DC, DISC, MC, V. **Amenities:** Outdoor heated pool in summer; Jacuzzi; business center. *In room:* A/C, TV, dataport, coffeemaker, hair dryer, iron.

Heart's Desire Bed & Breakfast *(Finds)*   Set in the Raton Historic District, this little crystal of history was built in 1885 to serve as a boarding house during Raton's railroad heyday. In 1997, Barbara Riley restored it, bringing splendor to the Victorian building. Guest rooms are medium-size, all decorated with Victorian touches, all with a shared bath. Each room has a sink and a comfortable bed. There's also a suite with a full kitchen and its own bath. Over an awesome breakfast such as eggs Benedict with fresh fruit, Barbara will regale you with tales of the area, where she grew up out on the plains. Be sure to ask about her father's part in a train robbery, from which she retains a stolen relic.

301 S. 3rd St., Raton, NM 87740. © 866/488-1028 or 505/445-1000. www.heartsdesireraton.com. 3 units, 1 suite. $75–$90 double with shared bathroom, $130 double suite. Rates include full breakfast. AE, DISC, MC, V. **Amenities:** Access to health club across the street. *In room:* Hair dryer, iron upon request.

Camping

Quite a few campgrounds are in the Raton area, including the **Raton KOA,** in town at 1330 S. 2nd St. (© **800/562-9033** or 505/445-3488; www.koa.com), with 54 sites, grocery and laundry facilities, and picnic tables and grills.

   Summerland RV Park, at 1900 S. Cedar/I-25 and US 87 (© **505/445-9536**), which is convenient to the interstate, has 42 sites (plus 16 monthly sites), laundry and grocery facilities, and picnic tables.

WHERE TO DINE IN RATON

Oasis Restaurant *(Kids)*   At mealtime, area residents crowd this bright, open cafe on the south end of town. With comfortable American decor and tables and booths adequately spaced, the restaurant provides a good setting for locals to chat and gossip. "You gettin' old?" one man asked another. "Naw," his neighbor said. "I'm *already* old." All ages fill this place, though—they seem to enjoy the burgers (hand-patted) and fries (hand-cut). Soups are homemade, as are rolls, tortillas, and sopaipillas. Each day brings a special such as green chile chicken casserole. Breakfasts are hearty, with lots of egg and pancake options.

1445 S. 2nd St. (from Clayton road, turn south). © 505/445-2221. Reservations not needed. $4–$7 breakfast, $5–$13 lunch or dinner. AE, DISC, MC, V. Winter daily 6am–8pm; summer daily 6am–8:30pm.

Pappas' Sweet Shop Restaurant STEAKS/SEAFOOD   Founded almost 78 years ago, this restaurant still seems to draw praise from most locals. It's an interesting place, with counters full of chocolate up front. A big dining room, recently remodeled after a fire, has a comfortable tearoom feel, with only one window. Though the food isn't sophisticated, it is carefully prepared and tasty. Best known are the beef dishes, with prime rib a big seller here. I've enjoyed a filet that was perfectly prepared and served with nicely cooked vegetables. Meals come with homemade bread, a salad, and choice of potato dish or pasta. The broiled breast of chicken is also popular. A full-service lounge adjoins the restaurant. There is also a gift shop.

1201 S. 2nd St. ⓒ 505/445-9811. Reservations suggested at dinner in summer. Main courses $6–$10 lunch, $9–$33 dinner. AE, DISC, MC, V. Mon–Sat 11am–2pm and 5–9pm.

4 Capulin Volcano National Monument ★★

Capulin Volcano National Monument offers visitors the rare opportunity to walk inside a volcanic crater. A 2-mile road spirals up from the visitor center more than 600 feet to the crater of the 8,182-foot peak, where two self-guided trails leave from the parking area: an energetic and spectacular 1-mile hike around the crater rim and a 100-foot descent into the crater to the ancient volcanic vent. One of the most interesting features here is the symmetry of the main cinder cone. The volcano was last active about 60,000 years ago, when it sent out the last of four lava flows. Scientists consider it dormant, with a potential for future activity, rather than extinct. As far back as 1891, Congress prohibited public settlement on Capulin Mountain. In 1916, it was protected by presidential proclamation as Capulin Mountain National Monument for its scientific and geologic interest. The final name change came in 1987.

Because of the elevation, wear light jackets in the summer and layers during the rest of the year. Be aware that the road up to the crater rim is frequently closed due to weather conditions. Plan on spending 1 to 3 hours at the volcano; a more in-depth exploration could take several days, but camping is not permitted.

A short nature trail behind the center introduces plant and animal life of the area and is great for kids and accessible to people with disabilities. A longer hike starts at park headquarters up to the parking lot at the crater rim. The crater rim offers magnificent panoramic views of the surrounding landscape, the Sangre de Cristo Mountains, and, on clear days, portions of four contiguous states: Kansas, Texas, Colorado, and Oklahoma. During the summer, the volcano attracts swarms of ladybird beetles (ladybugs).

ESSENTIALS

GETTING THERE The monument is located 30 miles east of Raton via US 64/87 and north 3 miles on NM 325.

VISITOR INFORMATION The visitor center, located at the base of the western side of the volcano, is open daily Memorial Day to Labor Day from 7:30am to 6:30pm, the rest of the year daily 8am to 4pm. An audiovisual program discusses volcanism, and park personnel will answer questions. Admission is $5 per car. For more information, contact **Capulin Volcano National Monument,** P.O. Box 40, Capulin, NM 88414 (ⓒ **505/278-2201;** www.nps.gov/cavo).

CAMPING

Camping is not permitted inside the monument; however, camping facilities are available 24 hours a day only 3 miles away, in Capulin (try the **Capulin RV**

Park, at © **505/278-2921;** www.capulinrvpark.com), as well as in the neighboring towns of Raton and Clayton.

5 The Clayton Highway: Dinosaurs, Outlaws & Folsom Man

FOLSOM

Near here, cowboy George McJunkin discovered the 10,000-year-old remains of "Folsom Man." The find, excavated by the Denver Museum of Natural History in 1926, represented the first association of the artifacts of prehistoric people (spear points) with the fossil bones of extinct animals (a species of bison). The site is on private property and is closed to the public, but some artifacts (prehistoric as well as from the 19th century) are displayed at the **Folsom Museum,** Main Street, Folsom (© **505/278-2122** in summer, 505/278-3616 in winter; http://folsommuseum.netfirms.com). The museum does not, however, contain any authentic Folsom prints, only copies. The museum has limited exhibits on prehistoric and historic Native Americans of the area, as well as Folsom's settlement by whites. Hours are daily 10am to 5pm from Memorial Day to Labor Day, winter by appointment. Open weekends only in May and September. Admission is $1.50 for adults, 50¢ for children 6 to 12, and free for children under age 6. To get to Folsom, take NM 325 off the Clayton Highway (US 64/87, running 83 miles east–southeast from Raton to Clayton) for 7 miles.

CLAYTON

Clayton (pop. 2,500) is a ranching center just 9 miles west of the Texas and Oklahoma panhandle borders. Rich prairie grasses, typical of nearby **Kiowa and Rita Blanca National Grasslands** (© **505/374-9652**), led to its founding in 1887 at the site of a longtime cowboy resting spot and watering hole. In the early 19th century, the Cimarron Cutoff of the Santa Fe Trail passed through here. This area was also the site of numerous bloody battles between Plains Indians and Anglo settlers and traders. Clayton is most known as the town where the notorious train robber Thomas "Black Jack" Ketchum was inadvertently decapitated while being hanged in 1901 (a doctor carefully reunited head and body before Ketchum was buried here).

Tracks from eight species of dinosaurs can be clearly seen in **Clayton Lake State Park** ⋒, 12 miles north of town off NM 370, near the distinctive Rabbit Ears Mountains (© **505/374-8808**). The lake is crystalline blue and is strange to come upon after driving across these pale prairies. It offers fishing, swimming, boating, hiking, and camping. A half-mile trail on the southeast side of the lake leads across the dam to an exhibit describing the types of dinosaurs that roamed this area. From there, you can wander along a boardwalk to the amazingly intact dinosaur tracks. Another trail starts on the north side of the lake and is 1½ miles long; if you wish, you can follow it farther to the dinosaur tracks, making for a 3½-mile hike.

Lay your head for the night at the **Best Western Kokopelli Lodge,** 702 S. 1st St., Clayton, NM 88415 (© **800/528-1234** or 505/374-2589; www.bestwestern. com). And if you're hungry, head for the decent food and Old West atmosphere at **Eklund Hotel Dining Room and Saloon,** 15 Main St. (© **505/374-2551**). It's open daily for lunch and dinner.

VISITOR INFORMATION   For information on other area attractions, as well as more lodging and dining options, contact the **Clayton–Union County Chamber of Commerce,** 1103 S. 1st St. (P.O. Box 476), Clayton, NM 88415 (© **505/374-9253;** www.claytonnewmexico.org).

6 The I-40 Corridor

The 216 freeway miles on I-40 from Albuquerque to the Texas border cross featureless prairie and very few towns. But the valleys of the Pecos River (site of Santa Rosa) and the Canadian River (Tucumcari is on its banks) have several attractions, including natural lakes. There's not a lot to explore here unless you're a bird-watcher or a fisher, but both towns can make a day's stopover worthwhile.

ESSENTIALS

GETTING THERE   Travel time from Albuquerque to Tucumcari via I-40 is 2 hours, 40 minutes; to Santa Rosa, 1 hour, 45 minutes. There's no regularly scheduled commercial service into either Tucumcari or Santa Rosa. Private planes can land at **Tucumcari Municipal Airport** (© 505/461-3229).

VISITOR INFORMATION   Contact the **Tucumcari–Quay County Chamber of Commerce,** 404 W. Tucumcari Blvd. (P.O. Drawer E), Tucumcari, NM 88401 (© **888-664-7255** or 505/461-1694; www.tucumcarinm.com) or the **Santa Rosa City Information Center,** 486 Parker Ave., Santa Rosa, NM 88435 (© **505/472-3763**).

SEEING THE SIGHTS

The **Mesalands Community College's Dinosaur Museum,** 222 East Laughlin (© **505/461-3466;** www.mesalands.edu/museum/museum.htm), half a block east off 1st Street, is open from March 1 to Labor Day, Tuesday through Saturday 10am to 6pm (noon to 5pm the rest of the year). Admission is $5.50 for adults, $3 for children 5 to 11, free for children under 5, $4.50 for seniors 65 and older, and $3.50 for educators and students. This is the home of the largest collection of life-size bronze prehistoric skeletons in the world.

The **Tucumcari Historical Museum,** 416 S. Adams (© **505/461-4201**), 1 block east of 1st Street, is open from 9am to 6pm Monday through Saturday in summer and from 9am to 5pm Tuesday through Saturday in winter. Admission is $2.11 for adults and 53¢ for children 6 to 15; it's free for kids under age 6. Renovated in 1999, the museum showcases Route 66 memorabilia, an old sheriff's office, an authentic Western schoolroom, and other set exhibits, as well as oddities such as a late-1800s slot machine called "The Owl" (it's elaborately carved and painted with owls), a tightly woven Mexican vaquero hat, and a finely tooled sidesaddle that looks terribly uncomfortable.

The moonlike **Mesa Redondo,** a round mesa rising 11 miles south of town via NM 209, was once train robber "Black Jack" Ketchum's hideout—he was eventually captured and executed in Clayton in 1901.

To the northwest, 34 miles distant from Tucumcari over NM 104, is **Conchas Lake State Park** (© **505/868-2270**), with a reservoir 25 miles long. I spent a lot of my growing-up years water-skiing and diving off cliffs at this lake. Though the water is a beautiful aqua, it sits within a desert environment, with lots of sand and little shade. A marina on the northern side provides facilities for boating, fishing, and waterskiing, while nearby you'll find a store, cafe, RV park with hookups, and trailers available to rent. The south side of the lake, which is managed by the private concessionaire **South Conchas Resort** (© **505/868-2988**), contains a lodge, campgrounds, and boat-launch facilities.

Ute Lake State Park (© **505/487-2284**) is 22 miles northeast of Tucumcari on US 54, near the town of Logan. It has a full-service marina, docking facilities, picnic tables, campsites, and rental boats.

Quay County around Tucumcari is noted for its blue-quail hunting, said to be the best anywhere in the United States.

Santa Rosa calls itself "the city of natural lakes." Those bodies of water include **Blue Hole** ⚲, a crystal-clear, 81-foot-deep artesian well just east of downtown. Fed by a subterranean river that flows 3,000 gallons per minute at a constant 61°F (16°C), it's a favorite of scuba divers (equipment can be rented at a nearby shop), and it's deep enough to merit open-water certification. Divers must either be certified or be with a certified instructor, and they must purchase a permit from the Santa Rosa Police Department. In fact, I got my certification here. For those accustomed to diving in the ocean, Blue Hole doesn't provide much room for exploration. The experience reminds me of swimming in a fish bowl, often with a number of other fish (divers) swimming about. No permit is required for swimming or snorkeling, however, and a bathhouse is on site. **Park Lake** (© 505/472-3763), in the middle of town, serves as the town's municipal pool. It's a lovely spot to take the kids. They can swim with the geese while you cool off under the elm trees. The lake offers free swimming, picnicking, and fishing, as well as a softball field and playground. **Santa Rosa Lake State Park,** P.O. Box 384, Santa Rosa, NM 88435 (© 505/472-3110), on a dammed portion of the Pecos River, has camping, hiking, boating, and excellent fishing. Ten miles south of town via NM 91, the village of **Puerto de Luna** is a 19th-century county seat with a mid-1800s courthouse and church, Nuestra Señora del Refugio. Francisco Vásquez de Coronado was believed to have camped here as he traveled en route to Kansas. For insight into village life here, read Rudolfo Anaya's *Bless Me, Ultima,* a tale of growing up on the *llano* (plains) of the area.

WHERE TO STAY

Major chain hotels are at I-40 interchanges in both Tucumcari and Santa Rosa. Smaller "Ma and Pa" motels can be found along the main streets through town that were once segments of legendary Route 66—Tucumcari Boulevard in Tucumcari and Will Rogers Drive in Santa Rosa.

IN TUCUMCARI

Best Western Discovery Inn   This pink Mission-style motel has large quiet rooms and provides an oasis in the somewhat barren eastern part of the state. It's located off the strip, but near I-40; take exit 332. Opened in 1985, remodeling is ongoing. Rooms are decorated in earth tones, with comfortable beds. Bathrooms are small but each has an outer sink/vanity and dressing room. Everything is very clean. Complimentary morning coffee is an added touch. K-Bob's restaurant is right next door.

200 E. Estrella Ave. (at I-40 exit 332), Tucumcari, NM 88401. © 800/528-1234 or 505/461-4884. Fax 505/461-2463. www.bestwestern.com/discoveryinn. 107 units. May–Oct $66–$74 double; Nov–Apr $52–$58 double. AE, DC, DISC, MC, V. Pets additional $5 per day. **Amenities:** Seasonal outdoor pool; fitness center; Jacuzzi; coin-op laundry. *In room:* A/C, TV.

Camping Near Tucumcari

There are three good campgrounds around Tucumcari. **Tucumcari KOA** (© 800/562-1871 or 505/461-1841; www.koa.com) has 111 sites, laundry and grocery facilities, RV supplies, picnic tables, and grills. It also offers a recreation hall with video games, a heated swimming pool, a basketball hoop, a playground, horseshoes, and shuffleboard, along with lots of elm trees for shade. To get there from I-40, get off the interstate at Exit 335, and then go ¼ mile east on South Frontage Road.

Moments **Route 66 Revisited: Rediscovering New Mexico's Stretch of the Mother Road**

As the old Bobby Troupe hit suggests: Get your kicks on Route 66. The highway that once stretched from Chicago to California was hailed as the road to freedom. During the Great Depression, it was the way west for farmers escaping Dust Bowl poverty out on the plains. If you found yourself in a rut in the late 1940s and 1950s, all you had to do was hop in the car and head west on Route 66.

Of course, the road existed long before it gained such widespread fascination. Built in the late 1920s and paved in 1937, it was the lifeblood of communities in eight states. Nowadays, however, US 66 is as elusive as the fantasies that once carried hundreds of thousands west in search of a better life. Replaced by other roads, covered up by interstates (mostly I-40), and just plain out of use, Route 66 still exists in New Mexico, but you'll have to do a little searching and take some extra time to find it.

Motorists driving west from Texas can take a spin (make that a slow spin) on a 20-mile gravel stretch of the original highway running from Glenrio (Texas) to San Jon. From San Jon to Tucumcari, you can enjoy nearly 24 continuous paved miles of vintage 66. In Tucumcari, the historic route sliced through the center of town along what is now Tucumcari Boulevard. Santa Rosa's Will Rogers Drive is that city's 4-mile claim to the Mother Road. In Albuquerque, US 66 follows Central Avenue for 18 miles, from the 1936 State Fairgrounds, past original 1930s motels and the historic Nob Hill district, on west through downtown.

One of the best spots to pretend you are a 1950s road warrior crossing the desert—whizzing past rattlesnakes, tepees, and tumbleweeds—is along NM 124, which winds 25 miles from Mesita to Acoma in northwestern New Mexico. You can next pick up old Route 66 in Grants, along the 6-mile Santa Fe Avenue. In Gallup, a 9-mile segment of US 66 is lined with restaurants and hotels reminiscent of the city's days as a Western film capital from 1929 to 1964. Just outside Gallup, the historic route continues west to the Arizona border as NM 118.

For more information about Route 66, contact the **Grants/Cíbola County Chamber of Commerce** (© 800/748-2142) or the **New Mexico Department of Tourism** (© 800/545-2040).

Mt. Road RV Park (© 505/461-9628) has 60 sites with full hookups, tenting, laundry facilities, and picnic tables. From I-40, take Exit 333 to Mountain Road; the park is on the US 54 bypass.

The campground in **Conchas Lake State Park** (© 505/868-2270) has 104 sites, 40 full hookups, lake swimming, boating, and fishing.

IN SANTA ROSA
La Quinta Perched on a hill above Santa Rosa, this newer white-washed chain hotel offers clean and very functional rooms. All are medium-size, decorated in tasteful earth tones. Each has a small bathroom with an outer sink/vanity. Beds

are comfy and are accompanied by a table and chairs. The place is inventively landscaped with a rock grotto patio where the hot tub sits.

1701 Will Rogers Dr., Santa Rosa, NM 88435. (*C*) 800/531-5900 or 505/472-4800. www.laquinta.com. Fax: 505/472-4809. 60 units. $72–$81 double. Rates include continental breakfast. AE, DC, DISC, MC, V. **Amenities:** Indoor pool; outdoor Jacuzzi. *In room:* A/C, TV, dataport, coffeemaker, hair dryer, safe.

Camping Near Santa Rosa

The **Santa Rosa Campground** ((*C*) 505/472-3126) offers 94 sites, 33 full hookups, laundry and grocery facilities, fire rings, grills, a heated swimming pool, and a playground for the kids. Situated in a piñon and juniper forest near town, the campground has a few small elm trees on the grounds. Coming from the east on I-40, take exit 277 and go 1 mile west on Business Loop; coming from the west on I-40, take exit 275 and go ¼ mile east on Business Loop.

Also in the area is **Santa Rosa Lake State Park** ((*C*) 505/472-3110), with year-round camping featuring 75 sites (about a third with electric hookups) as well as grills, boating, fishing, and hiking trails. Swimming in the lake is permitted but not encouraged because of the lake's uneven bottom and lack of beaches; children would be safer swimming in Park Lake in Santa Rosa.

TWO GOOD PLACES TO EAT IN THE AREA

Del's Family Restaurant AMERICAN/MEXICAN   The big cow atop Del's neon sign is not only a Route 66 landmark, it also points to the fine steaks inside. The restaurant has big windows along most every wall, letting in plenty of daylight or neon light at night. It's a casual, diner-style eatery with lots of plants. Breakfast brings big plates of dishes such as scrambled eggs and pancakes. At lunch, sample sandwiches and salads. The roast beef is a big seller here at dinnertime, served with a scoop of mashed potatoes and a trip to the salad bar. You can also order a grilled chicken breast. The New Mexican food is good but not great. Del's is not licensed for alcoholic beverages.

1202 E. Route 66, Tucumcari. (*C*) 505/461-1740. Reservations not accepted. Main courses $4–$7 breakfast, $5–$9 lunch, $7–$15 dinner. MC, V. Mon–Sat 7am–9pm.

Joseph's Restaurant & Cantina ℱ AMERICAN/NEW MEXICAN   You may want to plan your drive so that you can eat a meal at "Joe's." In business since 1956, it's a real Route 66 diner, with linoleum tables, comfortable booths, and plenty of memorabilia, from license plates to vintage RC Cola posters. The locals all eat here: You'll see Hispanic grandmothers, skinny cowboys in straw hats, and dusty farmhands just in from the fields. The varied menu offers excellent fare. Breakfast brings eggs and bacon or omelets. At lunch, I've enjoyed a salad topped with juicy grilled chicken. The New Mexican dishes are large and chile-smothered, and the burgers are juicy, with a variety of toppings, from the Rio Pecos topped with green chile to the Acapulco, with guacamole. Steaks are a big seller, also, at a good price. For dessert, try a piece of pie or a shake. Also on the premises are a bakery, a full-service bar, and a gift shop.

865 Will Rogers Dr., Santa Rosa. (*C*) 505/472-3361. Reservations not accepted. Main courses $4–$7 breakfast, $6–$9 lunch, $6–$12 dinner. AE, DC, DISC, MC, V. Summer daily 6am–10pm; winter daily 6am–9pm.

9

Northwestern New Mexico

Here in New Mexico's "Indian Country," adventures in my home state rival ones in "exotic" places I've traveled, such as Borneo or Bolivia.

At **Acoma,** I peeked through a hole in the wall of an ancient cemetery on a mesa hundreds of feet above the ground. It had been left there so that the spirits of some children who were taken from the pueblo could return. In **Grants** (pop. 8,900), a former uranium-mining boomtown, I traveled deep into a mine. In **Gallup** (pop. 20,000), self-proclaimed "Indian capital of the world" and a mecca for silver jewelry shoppers, I jogged along Route 66 and up on top of a pink mesa overlooking the city. In **Farmington** (pop. 36,000), center of the fertile San Juan valley and gateway to the Four Corners region, I slept in a cave. And in **Chama** (pop. 1,000), I rode on the Cumbres & Toltec Railroad—the longest and highest narrow-gauge steam railroad in the country.

Each was an adventure in its own right, but what really made them special for me was the people I encountered along the way. The biggest presence here is the Native American culture, old and new. Each time I travel to this area, I'm pleasantly surprised by the number of Pueblos, Navajos, and Apaches who inhabit it. Truly, they are the majority, and they set the pace and tone of the place. The Zuni, Acoma, and Laguna pueblos are each located within a short distance of I-40. Acoma's "Sky City" has been continually occupied for more than 9 centuries.

A huge chunk of the northwest is taken up by a part of the Navajo Reservation, the largest in America; and the Jicarilla Apache Reservation stretches 65 miles south from the Colorado border. All share their arts and crafts as well as their distinctive cultures with visitors, but they ask that their personal privacy and religious traditions be respected.

The past lives here, too. The Pueblo people believe that their ancestors' spirits still inhabit the ruins. **Chaco Culture National Historical Park,** with 12 major ruins and hundreds of smaller ones, represents the development of ancient Puebloan civilization, which reached its peak in the 11th century. **Aztec Ruins National Monument** and the nearby **Salmon Ruins** are similarly spectacular Pueblo preservations. It's interesting to note that the contemporary Pueblo tribes no longer want to use the word *Anasazi* to refer to the people who once inhabited the ruins of Chaco, Salmon, Aztec, Mesa Verde, and others. *Anasazi* is a Navajo word meaning "ancient ones," or possibly "ancient enemies." The Pueblo tribes, believed to be the descendants of the "Anasazi," prefer the term *ancestral Puebloan people.*

Two other national monuments in northwestern New Mexico also speak of the region's history. **El Morro** is a sandstone monolith known as "Inscription Rock," where travelers and explorers documented their journeys for centuries; **El Malpais** is a volcanic badland with spectacular cinder cones, ice caves, and lava tubes.

Northwestern New Mexico

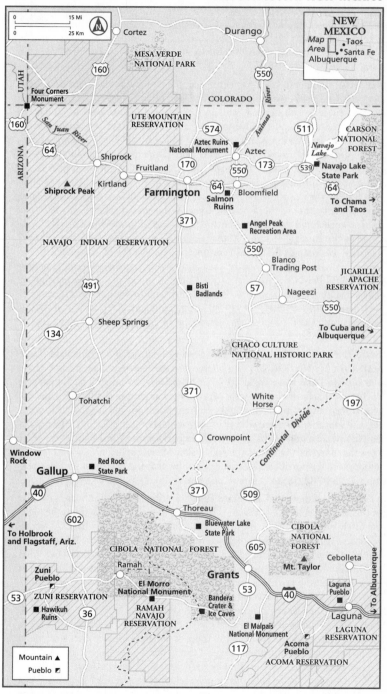

1 The Great Outdoors in Northwestern New Mexico

Like the rest of New Mexico, the northwestern region offers much in the way of outdoor recreation. If you're an outdoor enthusiast, you could spend months here.

BIKING Mountain biking is permitted in parts of **Cíbola National Forest** (© **505/346-2650;** www.fs.fed.us/r3/cibola), which, in this region, is located on both sides of I-40 in the Grants to Gallup area. The national forest has six districts; call the number above for a referral to the district you want to visit. Some of the best biking is in Farmington, which is where the "Durangatangs" come during the winter to train and ride (Durango is a mountain-biking mecca). **Bicycle Express,** 103 North Main Ave. (© **505/334-4354**) in Aztec will give trail directions, as will **Cottonwood Cycles,** 4370 E. Main (© **505/ 326-0429;** www.cottonwoodcycles.com), in Farmington. Cottonwood also rents bikes. Be sure to check out the **Lions Wilderness Park,** where you'll find its renowned **Road Apple Trail** on the north end of town. Bikers are also welcome at the **Bureau of Land Management Conservation Area** just off NM 117 near **El Malpais National Monument** (see "Acoma & Laguna Pueblos," below). For equipment rental in that area, try calling **Scoreboard Sporting Goods,** 107 West Coal Ave. (© **505/722-6077**) in Gallup; or you may opt to rent something before you leave Albuquerque at **Rio Mountain Sport,** 1210 Rio Grande NW (© **505/766-9970**). At Chaco Canyon, check out the Wijiji Ruin trail, nice and easy but through beautiful country leading to an Anasazi ruin.

BOATING If you're towing a boat, good places to stop are **Bluewater Lake State Park** (© **505/876-2391**), a reservoir located between Gallup and Grants, and **Navajo Lake State Park** (© **505/632-2278**), located about 25 miles east of Bloomfield. Both of these state parks have boat ramps, and Navajo Lake has several marinas (from which visitors can rent boats), picnic areas, a visitor center, and groceries for those who plan to make a day of it. (To find information on New Mexico state parks, go to **www.nmparks.com.**) **Zuni Lakes,** six bodies of water operated by the Zuni tribe, also offers opportunities for boating, although you're not allowed to use gasoline motors and you must receive a permit (© **505/782-5851**) before setting out.

FISHING **Bluewater Lake State Park** (mentioned above for boating) is one of the best places to fish in the area. In fact, some people believe it has the highest catch rate of all New Mexico lakes. Look to catch trout here. A world-renowned fishing destination, the **San Juan River** ★★, just below Navajo Dam, can be a fly-fisher's heaven and hell. For those good enough to know their flies and glean what the large and wily trout are eating, trophy catching is easy. For those like me who are more on the beginner end of the scale, it's a bit frustrating watching the big fish swim around your ankles while they ignore your fly. Fortunately, the scenery is outstanding enough to make up for the empty creel, and excellent guides in the area can help you fill it. **Navajo Lake State Park** (see "Boating," above) features about 150 miles of shoreline where fishers go to catch trout, bass, catfish, and pike. Navajo Lake is one of the largest lakes in New Mexico, and the park is very heavily trafficked, so if crowds aren't your thing, look for another fishing hole. Just 4 miles south of Kirtland is **Morgan Lake,** a quiet spot for largemouth bass and catfish. If you need fishing gear or want to hire a guide while in the area, contact **Duranglers on the San Juan,** 1003 NM

511, Navajo Dam (© **505/632-5952;** www.duranglers.com), or the nearby **Abe's Motel and Fly Shop,** 1791 US 173, Navajo Dam (© **505/632-2194**). In Farmington, contact **Dad's Boat Parts and Backyard Boutique,** 210 E. Piñon St. (© **505/326-1870**), or **Zia Sporting Goods,** 500 E. Main (© **505/327-6004;** www.ziasportinggoods.com).

GOLF   A few years back, *Golf Digest* rated **Piñon Hills Golf Course,** 2101 Sunrise Pkwy., in Farmington (© **505/326-6066**), the "best public golf course" in the United States. Also in Farmington is the **Civitan Golf Course,** 2100 North Dustin (© **505/599-1194**). In Kirtland (approximately 7 miles west of Farmington), your only golf option is **Riverview Golf Course,** located on US 64 (© **505/598-0140**).

HIKING   This part of the state has some great hiking trails. You'll get to see ancient archaeological ruins in places such as Aztec Ruins and Chaco Canyon. In **Cíbola National Forest** (© **505/287-8833;** www.fs.fed.us/r3/cibola), the hike to the summit of Mount Taylor is excellent. In cooler months, but not winter, try hiking around **El Malpais National Monument** (© **505/285-4641;** www.nps.gov/elma). Two good hikes to try in El Malpais are the Zuni–Acoma Trail (this one is extremely taxing, so if you're not in shape, don't expect to make the 15-mile round-trip hike) and the Big Lava Tubes Trail (1 mile round-trip). For quiet hiking in state parks, head to **Bluewater Lake State Park** (© **505/876-2391**), **Red Rock State Park** (© **505/722-3839**), or **Angel Peak Recreation Area** (© **505/599-8900**).

Sporting goods stores where you can get hiking gear include **REI-Albuquerque,** at 1550 Mercantile Ave. NE in Albuquerque (© **505/247-1191;** www.rei.com), **Frontier Sports,** at 300 NE Aztec Blvd. in Aztec (© **505/334-0009**), and **Zia Sporting Goods,** at 500 E. Main in Farmington (© **505/327-6004;** www.ziasportinggoods.com).

HORSEBACK RIDING   You'll find lots of riding opportunities around Chama. A good bet is **5M Outfitters,** which charges approximately $60 for a half-day ride and $95 for a full day. Contact Bruce Maker at P.O. Box 361, Chama, NM 87520 (© **505/588-7003;** www.5moutfitters.com).

RAFTING & KAYAKING   The Chama River Canyon Wilderness begins just below El Vado Dam and runs past the Monastery of Christ in the Desert, usually an overnight trip, though some last up to 3 nights. The river snakes through one of the most spectacular canyons I've ever seen, at one point rising 1,500 feet above your head. Rapids are mostly Class II (on a scale from I to VI), but there are some big waves. Water is released on most weekends throughout the summer, so you can count on enough to make the trip exciting. Half-day trips are $47.50 for adults, $37.50 for kids. Full-day trips are $90 to $100 for adults; $90 for kids. Contact **Far Flung Adventures,** P.O. Box 707, El Prado, NM 87529 (© **800/359-2627** or 505/758-2628; www.farflung.com).

SKIING   Some of the best cross-country skiing in the state is in the Chama area. Lots of broad bowls make the area a favorite of backcountry skiers as well as day-touring skiers. If you're up for an overnight adventure, contact **Southwest Nordic Center** (© **505/758-4761;** www.southwestnordiccenter.com), a company that rents five *yurts* (Mongolian-style huts), four of which are in the Rio Grande National Forest near Chama; the fifth, and newest addition, is located outside the Taos Ski Valley. These are insulated and fully equipped accommodations. Skiers trek into the huts, carrying their clothing and food in backpacks.

Guide service is provided, or you can go in on your own, following directions on a map. The yurts are rented by the night and range from $65 to $125 per group. Call for reservations as much in advance as possible as they do book up. The season is from mid-November to April, depending on snow conditions.

Some like to ski the old logging roads of Mount Taylor in **Cíbola National Forest** near Grants. Contact the Ranger Station in Grants at © **505/287-8833** for more information. If you need to rent ski equipment, try **Chama Ski Service** (© **505/756-2492**), which also offers snow reports and trail information.

SNOWMOBILING   Chama is an excellent place to ride those mean machines. Contact **Tricky Dickie's Snowmobile Tours,** 2733 Dallas St. NE, Albuquerque, NM 87110 (© **505/588-7657**).

SWIMMING   Good swimming is available at **Navajo Lake State Park** (© **505/632-2278**). Before diving in at other lakes in state parks, make sure swimming is permitted.

2 Acoma & Laguna Pueblos

Your best base for exploring the Acoma and Laguna pueblos, as well as the El Malpais and El Morro National Monuments (see "El Malpais & El Morro National Monuments," later in this chapter), is the town of Grants, 1¼ hours west of Albuquerque on I-40 west.

ACOMA PUEBLO ✸✸✸

The spectacular Acoma Sky City, a walled adobe village perched high atop a sheer rock mesa 367 feet above the 6,600-foot valley floor, is said to have been inhabited at least since the 11th century—it's the longest continuously occupied community in the United States. Native history says it has been inhabited since before the time of Christ. Both the pueblo and its mission church of **San Esteban del Rey** are National Historic Landmarks. When Coronado visited in 1540, he suggested that Acoma was "the greatest stronghold in the world"; those who attempt to follow the cliff-side footpath down after their guided tour, rather than take the bus back down, may agree.

About 50 to 75 Keresan-speaking Acoma (pronounced *Ack*-oo-mah) reside year-round on the 70-acre mesa top. Many others maintain ancestral homes and occupy them during ceremonial periods. The terraced three-story buildings face south for maximum exposure to the winter sun. Most of Sky City's permanent residents make their living off the throngs of tourists who flock here to see the magnificent church, built in 1639 and containing numerous masterpieces of Spanish colonial art, and to purchase the thin-walled white pottery with brown-and-black designs for which the pueblo is famous.

Many Acomas work in Grants, 15 miles west of the pueblo; in Albuquerque; or for one of Acoma's business enterprises, such as Sky City Casino. Others are cattle ranchers and farm individual family gardens.

ESSENTIALS

GETTING THERE   To reach Acoma from Grants, drive east 15 miles on I-40 to McCartys, then south 13 miles on paved tribal roads to the visitor center. From Albuquerque, drive west 65 miles to the Acoma–Sky City exit (102), then 15 miles southwest.

VISITOR INFORMATION   For additional information before you leave home, contact the pueblo at P.O. Box 309, Acoma, NM 87034 (© **800/747-0181** or 505/469-1052; www.puebloofacoma.org).

ADMISSION FEES & HOURS   Admission is $10 for adults, $9 for seniors 60 and over, $7 for children 6 to 17, and free for children under 6. Group discounts apply to parties of 15 or more, and there's also a discount for Native American visitors. The charge to take still photographs is $10; no videotaping, sketching, or painting is allowed except by special permission. The pueblo is open daily in the summer from 8am to 6pm and daily the rest of the year from 8am to 4pm.

SEEING THE HIGHLIGHTS

You absolutely cannot wander freely around Acoma Pueblo, but you can start your tour of Acoma at the visitor center at the base of the mesa. One-hour tours begin every 30 minutes, depending on the demand; the last tour is scheduled 1 hour before closing. The pueblo is closed to visitors on Easter weekend (some years), June 24 and 29, July 10 to 13, and the first or second weekend in October. It's best to call ahead to make sure that the tour is available when you're visiting.

While waiting, peruse the excellent little **museum** of Acoma history and crafts, or buy snacks at the nearby **concession stand.** Then board the tour bus, which climbs through a rock garden of 50-foot sandstone monoliths and past precipitously dangling outhouses to the mesa's summit. With no running water or electricity in this medieval-looking village, it's a truly unique place. A small reservoir collects rainwater for most uses, and drinking water is transported up from below. Wood-hole ladders and mica windows are prevalent among the 300-odd adobe structures. As you tour the village, you'll have many opportunities to buy pottery and other pueblo treasures. Pottery is expensive here, but you're not going to find it any cheaper anywhere else, and you'll be guaranteed that it's authentic if you buy it directly from the craftsperson. Along the way, be sure to sample some Indian fry bread topped with honey.

DANCES & CEREMONIES

The annual San Esteban del Rey feast day is September 2, when the pueblo's patron saint is honored with a mid-morning Mass, a procession, an afternoon corn dance, and an arts-and-crafts fair. The Governor's Feast is held annually in February; and 4 days of Christmas festivals run from December 25 to 28. Still cameras are allowed for a $10 fee, and guided tours do not operate on the mesa during feast days.

Other celebrations are held in low-lying pueblo villages at Easter (in Acomita), the first weekend in May (Santa Maria feast at McCartys), and August 10 (San Lorenzo Day in Acomita).

LAGUNA PUEBLO

This major Keresan-speaking pueblo consists of a central settlement and five smaller villages not far from Acoma Pueblo and just over a half-hour from Grants. In fact, Lagunas are closely related to the Acomas who live just 14 miles away. Founded after the 1680 revolt by refugees from the Rio Grande Valley, Laguna is the youngest of New Mexico's pueblos and has about 7,000 residents. Today, many Lagunas are engaged in agriculture or private business, including a tribal-operated commercial center. Federal funds brought modern housing facilities and scholarship programs, one of which helped start the career of famous Laguna author Leslie Marmon Silko. The employment rate here is high, and this is widely considered one of New Mexico's wealthiest pueblos.

ESSENTIALS

GETTING THERE   From Grants, take I-40 east for 32 miles. The pueblo is 50 miles west of Albuquerque along I-40.

VISITOR INFORMATION   For information about Laguna before you leave home, contact the **tribal governor's office** at P.O. Box 194, Laguna Pueblo, NM 87026 (℃ **505/552-6654;** www.lagunapueblo.org.)

ADMISSION FEES & HOURS   No admission or photo fee is charged, but some restrictions apply from village to village. No video or cassette recorders are allowed. Visitors are welcome during daylight hours year-round.

SEEING THE HIGHLIGHTS

Organized tours of the pueblo and surrounding area are available; call ℃ **505/552-9771** for information. You can also wander around (respecting the fact that this is home to thousands of people) on your own. The outlying villages of Mesita, Paguate, Paraje, Encinal, and Seama are interesting, but the best place to visit is the old pueblo, where you can see the massive stone church, San Jose de Laguna, built in 1699, and famous for its interior. It was restored in the 1930s.

DANCES & CEREMONIES

Pueblo and Navajo people from throughout the region attend St. Joseph's Feast Day (Sept 19) at Old Laguna Village. The fair begins in the morning with a Mass and procession, followed by a harvest dance, sports events, and a carnival. New Year's Day and Three Kings Day (Jan 6) are also celebrated at the pueblo with processions and dances. Each smaller village has its own feast day between July 26 and October 17; call the pueblo office for details.

AN ATTRACTION NEAR LAGUNA

Seboyeta, the oldest Hispanic community in western New Mexico, is 3½ miles north of Paguate, outside Laguna Pueblo. Still in view are ruins of adobe fortress walls built in the 1830s to protect the village from Navajo attack. The Mission of Our Lady of Sorrows was built in the 1830s, as was the nearby Shrine of Los Portales, built in a cave north of town.

GRANTS

If you've ever wondered what a "boom and bust town" looks like, come to Grants and find out. Grants first boomed with the coming of the railroad in the late 19th century, when 4,000 workers descended on the tiny farm town. When the railroad was completed, the workers left, and the town was bust. Next, Grants saw high times in the 1940s, growing carrots and sending them to the East Coast, but when packaging became more advanced, Grants lost its foothold in the market and busted again. Then came the 1950s, when a Navajo sheep rancher named Paddy Martinez discovered some strange yellow rocks near Haystack Mountain, northwest of town. The United States was in need of uranium, and his find led to the biggest boom in the area. By the early 1980s, demand for uranium had dropped, and so went the big wages and big spenders that the ore's popularity had produced. Today, the city is little more than a segment of Route 66 with some interesting old buildings.

You'll see dilapidated court motels and store signs. Note the Uranium Cafe, with a sign in the window that reads "OUR FOOD WILL BLOW YOUR MINE."

The city is the seat of expansive Cíbola County, which stretches from the Arizona border nearly to the Albuquerque area. For more information, contact the **Grants/Cíbola County Chamber of Commerce** at 100 N. Iron Ave. (P.O. Box

297), Grants, NM 87020 (© **800/748-2142** or 505/287-4802; www.grants. org). It's located in the same building as the Mining Museum.

AN ATTRACTION IN GRANTS

New Mexico Mining Museum ★ *(Kids)*   This enormously interesting little museum primes you for the underground adventure of traveling into a re-creation of a mine shaft by showing you, on ground level, some geology, such as a fossilized dinosaur leg bone and a piece of Malpais lava. The world's only underground uranium-mining museum also gives you a sense of the context within which uranium was mined, through photos of the uranium-mining pioneers. Thus, the stage is set for your walk into a mine-shaft-like doorway adorned with rusty metal hats. An elevator takes you down into a spooky, low-lit place with stone walls. You begin in the station where uranium was loaded and unloaded and travel down into the earth through places defined on wall plaques. While exploring, you get a sense of the dark and dirty work that mining can be. Those with claustrophobia may have to content themselves with visiting the exhibits *above* ground.

100 N. Iron Ave., at Santa Fe Avenue © **800/748-2142** or 505/287-4802. Fax 505/287-8224. www.grants. org/mining/mining.htm. Admission $3 adults, $2 seniors over age 60 and children 7–18; free for children 6 and under. Mon–Sat 9am–4pm.

WHERE TO STAY IN GRANTS

Grants hotels are all on or near Route 66, with major properties near I-40 interchanges, and smaller or older motels nearer downtown. Lodger's tax is 5%, which is added to the gross receipts tax of 6.8125%, for a total room tax of just under 12%. Parking is usually free.

Best Western Inn & Suites   Built in 1976 with remodeling ongoing, this is one of four New Mexico hotels owned by Southwest Innkeepers, providing spacious rooms and good amenities, though you have to like to walk. Rooms are built around a huge quadrangle with an indoor pool in a sunny, plant-filled courtyard at the center. Request a room at one of the four corner entrances to avoid trudging down the long hallways. Also, request a room that is facing outside rather than in toward the courtyard, where noise from the pool carries. Though not quite as efficient as the Holiday Inn Express (see below), more amenities are provided here. Rooms are bright; they're done in floral prints with Aztec trim. Beds are firm, and bathrooms are medium-size and clean.

1501 E. Santa Fe Ave. (I-40 exit 85), Grants, NM 87020. © **800/528-1234** or 505/287-7901. Fax 505/285-5751. www.bestwestern.com. 126 units. $49–$69 double. Rates include breakfast. AE, DC, DISC, MC, V. Pets are welcome. **Amenities:** Indoor pool; exercise room; Jacuzzi; men's and women's saunas; video arcade; coin-op laundry. *In room:* A/C, TV, coffeemaker, hair dryer, iron.

Holiday Inn Express   Located just off the interstate, this two-story motel provides large, well-conceived rooms with a comfortable atmosphere. Ground-floor rooms open both off an inner corridor and from an outside door where your car is parked. Rooms are spacious, with high ceilings and large bathrooms.

1496 E. Santa Fe Ave., Grants, NM 87020. © **800-HOLIDAY** or 505/285-4676. Fax 505/285-6998. www.hi express.com. 58 units. $90 double. Rates include continental breakfast. AE, DC, DISC, MC, V. Pets are welcome. **Amenities:** Small indoor pool; Jacuzzi. *In room:* A/C, TV, dataport, coffeemaker, hair dryer, iron.

Sands Motel *(Finds)*   At first glance, you might wonder why anyone would rather stay at this older place than at the newer chain hotels near the interstate, and yet the Sands draws crowds. Rates are generally good, and the rooms are clean— though the furnishings and carpet aren't as new as those at more recent competitors. Located a block from Route 66 in the center of town, it gives travelers a break from the noise of the interstate. Rooms are spacious, each with a table and chairs. The beds are comfortable, and the bathrooms are clean. The parking area is enclosed by a wall, and you can park right in front of your room.

112 McArthur St. (P.O. Box 1437), Grants, NM 87020. ℂ 800/424-7679 or 505/287-2996. Fax 505/287-2996. 24 units. $38 double. Continental breakfast included. AE, DISC, MC, V. Pets welcome for a $5 1-time fee. *In room:* A/C, TV, dataport, fridge.

CAMPING

Grants has three decent campgrounds with both tent and RV facilities. All range in price from $9 to $14 for tent camping and $13 to $19 for full hookups. **Blue Spruce RV Park** (ℂ **505/287-2560**) has 25 sites and 16 full hookups and is open year-round. It has enough trees to block the wind, it has some grass, and the roads and parking spaces are gravel, so dust is minimized. Cable television hookups are available, as are laundry facilities and a recreation room. To reach the park, take I-40 to Exit 81 and then go ¼ mile south on NM 53.

    Lavaland RV Park (ℂ **505/287-8665;** www.lavalandrvpark.com), the closest site to Grants, has 51 sites and 39 full hookups. Located near a lava outcropping, the site is clean, though a little desolate and dusty, with a few pine trees to block the wind. Air-conditioning and heating hookups are available, as are some free cable and telephone hookups. In addition, you'll find cabins, laundry, limited grocery facilities, picnic tables and grills, and recreation facilities. Lavaland is open year-round. From I-40, get off at exit 85 and continue 100 yards south on Access Road.

WHERE TO DINE IN GRANTS

In general, you won't find places to eat at pueblos or national monuments, so you're best off looking for a restaurant in Grants.

El Cafecito (Value) (Kids) MEXICAN/AMERICAN   This real locals' spot serves up tasty food in a relaxed atmosphere. At mealtime, the brightly lit space with Saltillo tile floors bustles with families eating huevos rancheros (eggs over tortillas, smothered in chile) for breakfast, and enchiladas, stuffed *sopaipillas,* and burgers for lunch and dinner. All meals are large and inexpensive. Kids enjoy their own menu selections.

820 E. Santa Fe Ave. ℂ 505/285-6229. Main courses $3–$6 breakfast, $5–$10 lunch or dinner. AE, DISC, MC, V. Mon–Fri 7am–9pm; Sat 7am–8pm.

La Ventana NEW MEXICAN/STEAKS   This is where the Grants locals go for a big dinner or lunch out. With one large room that seats about 50 people, the restaurant is done in a cheesy Southwestern decor, with a two-horse sculpture and some dancing kachinas. The place is dark, with few windows, so if you can catch Grants on a nonwindy day, opt for the patio. Service is friendly and varies in its efficiency. You can't go wrong with one of the salads, such as the chicken fajita, or with the prime rib. You'll also find sandwiches such as turkey and guacamole served on seven-grain bread. There's a full bar.

110½ Geis St., Hillcrest Center. ℂ 505/287-9393. Reservations recommended. Main courses $4.50–$10 lunch, $8–$20 dinner. AE, DC, DISC, MC, V. Mon–Sat 11am–11pm.

3 El Malpais & El Morro National Monuments

Northwestern New Mexico has two national monuments that are must-sees for anyone touring this region: El Malpais and El Morro. The region is also home to the Cíbola National Forest, with its stately Mount Taylor, visible from miles away and an excellent place to hike and backcountry ski.

EL MALPAIS: EXPLORING THE BADLANDS ⊛

Designated a national monument in 1987, El Malpais (Spanish for "badlands") is an outstanding example of the volcanic landscapes in the United States. El Malpais contains 115,000 acres of cinder cones, vast lava flows, hundreds of lava tubes, ice caves, sandstone cliffs, natural bridges and arches, Anasazi ruins, ancient Native American trails, and Spanish and Anglo homesteads.

ESSENTIALS

GETTING THERE   You can take one of two approaches to El Malpais, via NM 117 or NM 53. NM 117 exits I-40 7 miles east of Grants.

VISITOR INFORMATION   Admission to El Malpais is free (unless you're visiting the privately owned Ice Caves), and it's open to visitors year-round. The **visitor center,** located off Route 53 between mile markers 63 and 64, is open daily from 8:30am to 4:30pm. Here you can pick up maps of the park, leaflets on specific trails, and other details about exploring the monument. For more information, contact **El Malpais National Monument,** NPS, P.O. Box 939, Grants, NM 87020 (℃ **505/285-4641;** www.nps.gov/elma).

SEEING THE HIGHLIGHTS

From **Sandstone Bluffs Overlook** (10 miles south of I-40 off NM 117), many craters are visible in the lava flow, which extends for miles along the eastern flank of the Continental Divide. The most recent flows are only 1,000 years old; Native American legends tell of rivers of "fire rock." Seventeen miles south of I-40 is **La Ventana Natural Arch,** the largest accessible natural arch in New Mexico.

From NM 53, which exits I-40 just west of Grants, visitors have access to the **Zuni–Acoma Trail,** an ancient Pueblo trade route that crosses four major lava flows in a 7½-mile (one-way) hike. A printed trail guide is available. **El Calderon,** a forested area 20 miles south of I-40, is a trail head for exploring a cinder cone, lava tubes, and a bat cave. (*Warning:* Hikers should not enter the bat cave or otherwise disturb the bats.)

The largest of all Malpais cinder cones, **Bandera Crater** is on private property 25 miles south of I-40. The National Park Service has laid plans to absorb this commercial operation, known as **Ice Caves Resort** (℃ **888/ICE-CAVE** or 505/783-4303; www.icecaves.com). For a fee ($8 for adults and $4 for children 5–12), visitors hike up the crater or walk to the edge of an ice cave. It's open daily from 8am to 7pm in summer and from 8am to 4pm in winter (generally closing 1 hr. before sunset).

Perhaps the most fascinating phenomenon of El Malpais is the lava tubes, formed when the outer surface of a lava flow cooled and solidified. When the lava river drained, tunnel-like caves were left. Ice caves within some of the tubes have delicate ice-crystal ceilings, ice stalactites, and floors like ice rinks.

HIKING & CAMPING

El Malpais has several hiking trails, including the above-mentioned Zuni–Acoma Trail. Most are marked with rock cairns; some are dirt trails. The best times to hike this area are spring and fall, when it's not too hot. You are pretty much on your own when exploring this area, so prepare accordingly. Carry plenty of water with you; do not drink surface water. Carrying first-aid gear is always a good idea; the lava rocks can be extremely sharp and inflict nasty cuts. Never go into a cave alone. The park service advises wearing hard hats, boots, protective clothing, and gloves, and carrying three sources of light when entering lava tubes. The weather can change suddenly, so be prepared; if lightning is around, move off the lava as quickly as possible.

Primitive camping is allowed in the park, but you must first obtain a free backcountry permit from the visitor center.

EL MORRO NATIONAL MONUMENT ✈

Travelers who like to look history straight in the eye are fascinated by "Inscription Rock," 43 miles west of Grants along NM 53. Looming up out of the sand and sagebrush is a bluff 200 feet high, holding some of the most captivating messages in North America. Its sandstone face displays a written record of the many who inhabited and traveled through this land, beginning with the ancestral Puebloans, who lived atop the formation around 1200. Carved with steel points are the signatures and comments of almost every explorer, conquistador, missionary, army officer, surveyor, and pioneer emigrant who passed this way between 1605, when Gov. Don Juan de Oñate carved the first inscription, and 1906, when it was preserved by the National Park Service. Oñate's inscription, dated April 16, 1605, was perhaps the first graffiti any European left in America.

A paved walkway makes it easy to walk to the writings, and a stone stairway leads up to other treasures. One entry reads: "Year of 1716 on the 26th of August passed by here Don Feliz Martinez, Governor and Captain General of this realm to the reduction and conquest of the Moqui." Confident of success as he was, Martinez actually got nowhere with any "conquest of the Moqui," or Hopi, peoples. After a 2-month battle, they chased him back to Santa Fe.

Another special group to pass by this way was the U.S. Camel Corps, trekking past on their way from Texas to California in 1857. The camels worked out fine in mountains and deserts, outlasting horses and mules 10 to 1, but the Civil War ended the experiment. When Peachy Breckinridge, fresh out of the Virginia Military Academy, came by with 25 camels, he noted the fact on the stone here.

El Morro was at one time as famous as the Blarney Stone of Ireland: Everybody had to stop by and make a mark. But when the Santa Fe Railroad was laid 25 miles to the north, El Morro was no longer on the main route to California, and from the 1870s, the tradition began to die out.

Atop Inscription Rock via a short, steep trail, Anasazi ruins occupy an area 200 by 300 feet. Inscription Rock's name, Atsinna, suggests that carving one's name here is a very old custom indeed: The word, in Zuni, means "writing on rock."

ESSENTIALS
GETTING THERE   El Morro is located 43 miles west of Grants on NM 53.

VISITOR INFORMATION   For information, contact **El Morro National Monument,** Route 2, Box 43, Ramah, NM 87321-9603 (© **505/783-4226;** www.nps.gov/elmo). Admission to El Morro is $3 per person 17 and older. Self-guided trail booklets are available at the visitor center (turn off NM 53 at the El Morro sign and travel approximately a half mile), open year-round from 9am to 5pm. Trails are also open year-round; check with the **visitor center** for hours. A **museum** at the visitor center features exhibits on the 700 years of human activity at El Morro. A 15-minute video gives a good introduction to the park. Also within the visitor center is a **bookstore** where you can pick up souvenirs and informational books. It takes between 2 and 4 hours to visit the museum and hike a couple of trails. The park is closed on Christmas and New Year's Day.

CAMPING

Though it isn't necessary to camp here in order to see most of the park, a nine-site campground at El Morro is open from around Memorial Day to Labor Day, and it costs $5 per night. No supplies are available within the park, so if you're planning on spending a night or two, be sure to arrive well equipped.

One nearby private enterprise, **El Morro RV Park,** HC 61, Box 44, Ramah, NM 87321 (✆ **505/783-4612;** www.elmorro-nm.com), has cabins, RV and tent camping, and a cafe.

EXPLORING THE AREA: CÍBOLA NATIONAL FOREST

Cíbola National Forest is actually a combination of parcels of land throughout the state that total more than 1.6 million acres. Elevation varies from 5,000 to 11,301 feet, and the forest includes the Datil, Gallinas, Bear, Manzano, Sandia, San Mateo, and Zuni mountains.

Two major pieces of the forest flank I-40 on either side of Grants, near the pueblos and monuments described above. To the northeast of Grants, NM 547 leads some 20 miles into the San Mateo Mountains. The range's high point, and the highest point in the forest, 11,301-foot Mount Taylor, is home of the annual Mount Taylor Winter Quadrathlon in February. The route passes two campgrounds: Lobo Canyon and Coal Mine Canyon. Hiking and enjoying magnificent scenery are popular in summer, cross-country skiing in winter.

JUST THE FACTS   For more information about this section of Cíbola National Forest, contact the **Mount Taylor Ranger District,** 1800 Lobo Canyon Rd., Grants, NM 87020 (✆ **505/287-8833**). For general information about all six districts of the National Forest, contact **Cíbola National Forest,** 2113 Osuna Rd. NE, Suite A, Albuquerque, NM 87113-1001 (✆ **505/346-2650;** www.fs. fed.us/r3/cibola).

A modern road stop on I-40 heading west, 17 miles before Gallup, is the **Giant Travel Center** (✆ **505/722-6655**). This is my idea of what a space station would be like. Not only can you get gas here, you can also fill up at a Pizza Hut, Taco Bell, or A&W Root Beer. There's also a full restaurant with a salad bar and hot food bar. The center has plenty of pay phones, clean bathrooms, a post office, and a video arcade.

4 Gallup: Gateway to Indian Country ⭐

For me, **Gallup** has always been a mysterious place, home to many Native Americans, with dust left from its Wild West days, and with an unmistakable Route 66 architectural presence; it just doesn't seem to exist in this era. The best way to get a sense of the place is by walking around downtown, wandering through the trading posts and pawnshops and by the historic buildings. In doing so, you'll probably encounter many locals and get a real feel for this "Heart of Indian Country."

Gallup began as a town when the railroad from Arizona reached this spot in 1881. At that time, the town consisted of a stagecoach stop and a saloon, the Blue Goose. Within 2 years, coal mining had made the town boom, and some 22 saloons (including the Bucket of Blood) and an opera house filled the town, most of which was inhabited by immigrants from mining areas in eastern Europe, England, Wales, Germany, and Italy.

When the popularity of the railroads declined, Gallup turned briefly to the movie business as its boom ticket. The area's red-rock canyons and lonely deserts were perfect for Westerns of the era, such as *Big Carnival,* with Kirk Douglas; *Four Faces West,* with Joel McCrea; and *The Bad Man,* starring Wallace Beery, Lionel Barrymore, and Ronald Reagan. These stars and many others stayed in a Route 66 hotel built by R. E. Griffith in 1937. Today, the El Rancho Hotel and Motel is one of Gallup's most notable landmarks and worth strolling through (see "Where to Stay in Gallup," and "Where to Dine in Gallup," below). Gallup's next income generator was trade and tourism. Its central location within the Navajo Reservation and the Zuni lands, as well as its proximity to the ancient ruins at Chaco, make it a crossroads for trade and travel.

Gallup's most notable special event is the **Inter-Tribal Indian Ceremonial** held every August. Native Americans converge on the town for a parade, dances, and an all-Indian rodeo east of town, at Red Rock State Park. It's a busy time in Gallup, and reservations must be made way in advance. If you're not in town for the Ceremonial, try hitting Gallup on a Saturday, when many Native Americans come to town to trade; the place gets busy. Best of all on this day is the **Flea Market,** located north of town just off US 491. Here you can sample fry bread, Zuni bread, and Acoma bread, eat real mutton stew, and shop for anything from jewelry to underwear. After the Flea Market, most Gallup-area residents, native and nonnative alike, go to Earl's (see "Where to Dine in Gallup," below) to eat.

ESSENTIALS

GETTING THERE   From Albuquerque, take I-40 west (2½ hr.). From Farmington, take US 64 west to Shiprock, then US 491 south (2½ hr.). From Flagstaff, Arizona, take I-40 east (3 hr.). Gallup is not served by any commercial airlines at this time.

VISITOR INFORMATION   The **Gallup Convention and Visitors Bureau,** 103 W. US 66, Gallup, NM 87301 (© 800/242-4282 or 505/863-3841; www. gallupnm.org), is just south of the main I-40 interchange for downtown Gallup. Or you can contact the **Gallup–McKinley County Chamber of Commerce,** 103 W. US 66, Gallup, NM 87301 (© 505/722-2228; www.gallupchamber. com).

WHAT TO SEE & DO
EXPLORING GALLUP

Gallup has 20 buildings that are either listed on or have been nominated to the National Register of Historic Places. Some hold trading posts worth visiting. A good place to start your visit is at the **Santa Fe Railroad Depot,** which also houses the **Gallup Cultural Center** (for details see "Sunset Dances" below) at East 66 Avenue and Strong Street. Built in 1923 in modified Mission style, it has been renovated into a community transportation and cultural center, with a small museum worth visiting, as well as a gift shop and diner. Across the highway, the **Drake Hotel** (later the Turquoise Club but now abandoned), built of blond brick in 1919, had the Prohibition-era reputation of being controlled by bootleggers, with wine running in the faucets in place of water.

The 1928 **White Cafe,** 100 W. 66 Ave., is an elaborate decorative brick structure that catered to the early auto tourist traffic. Now it's the **All Tribes Indian Center** (© 505/722-6272), with some interesting stone carvings, finished jewelry, as well as innovative use of stones such as charolite and lapis, and some big fetishes (charms).

The **Rex Hotel,** 300 W. 66 Ave., constructed of locally quarried sandstone, was once known for its "ladies of the night." It's now the **Rex Museum** (© 505/ 863-1363), a somewhat random display of items from the Gallup Historical

Society Collection, but fun for history buffs. It's open daily but with unpredictable hours. Call before setting out.

Gallup's architectural gems include the **Chief Theater,** 228 W. Coal Ave. This structure was built in 1920; in 1936, it was completely redesigned in Pueblo–Deco style, with zigzag relief and geometric form, by R. E. "Griff" Griffith (who also built the El Rancho Hotel), brother of Hollywood producer D. W. Griffith. Now this is **City Electric Shoe Shop** (© **505/863-5252**), where the Native Americans go to buy feathers, leather, and other goods to make ceremonial clothing. It is known to locals simply as "City Electric," so called because it was the first shop in town to have an automated shoe repair machine. Also visit the 1928 **El Morro Theater,** 207 W. Coal Ave., built in Spanish colonial revival style with Spanish baroque plaster carving and bright polychromatic painting; it's where locals come to see movies and dance performances.

GETTING OUTSIDE: A NEARBY STATE PARK

Six miles east of downtown Gallup, **Red Rock State Park,** NM 566 (P.O. Box 10), Church Rock, NM 87311 (© **505/722-3839**), is not part of the New Mexico State Park system, so it doesn't have the fine services you'd expect in those parks. It does have a natural amphitheater set against elegantly shaped red sandstone buttes. It includes an auditorium/convention center, a historical museum, a post office, a trading post, stables, and modern campgrounds.

The 8,000-seat arena is the site of numerous annual events, including the Intertribal Indian Ceremonial in mid-August. Red Rock Convention Center accommodates 600 for trade shows or concert performances.

A nature trail leads up into these stone monuments and makes for a nice break after hours on the road. See "Where to Stay in Gallup," below, for camping information. The park also has a playground, horseback riding trails, and a sports field.

The **Red Rock Museum** has displays on prehistoric Anasazi and modern Zuni, Hopi, and Navajo cultures, including an interesting collection of very intricate kachinas. A gallery features changing exhibits, often locally made crafts such as prayer and dancing fans, pottery, or weavings. In the summer, the museum is open Monday through Saturday from 8am to 6pm, Sunday from 8am to 4:30pm; winter hours are Monday through Saturday from 8am to 4:30pm, closed Sundays. There is a suggested donation of $2 for adults, $1 for seniors, and 50¢ for children.

Also at this site, in early December, is the **Red Rock Balloon Rally,** a high point on the sporting balloonist's calendar. For information, call the Gallup–McKinley County Chamber of Commerce (see "Visitor Information," above).

SHOPPING: BEST BUYS ON JEWELRY & CRAFTS

Nowhere are the jewelry and crafts of Navajo, Zuni, and Hopi tribes less expensive than in Gallup. The most intriguing places to shop are the trading posts and pawnshops, which provide a surprising range of services for their largely Native American clientele and have little in common with the pawnshops of large U.S. cities.

Navajoland **pawnbrokers** in essence are bankers, at least from the Navajo and Zuni viewpoint. Pawnshops provide safekeeping of valuable personal goods and make small-collateral loans. The trader will hold on to an item for months or even years before deeming it "dead" and putting it up for sale. Fewer than 5% of items ever go unredeemed, but over the years traders do accumulate a selection, so the shops are worth perusing.

If you're shopping for jewelry, look for silver concho belts, worn with jeans and Southwestern skirts; cuff bracelets; and necklaces, from traditional squash blossoms to silver beads to *heishi,* which are very fine beads worn in several strands. Earrings may be only silver, or they may be decorated with various stones.

Also be on the lookout for bolo ties and belt buckles of silver or turquoise. Silver concho hatbands go great on Stetson hats. Silver or gold handcrafted earrings, sometimes decorated with turquoise, are a big seller.

Handwoven Native American rugs may be draped on couches, hung on walls, or used on floors. Also look for pottery, kachinas, and sculpture.

Most shops are open Monday through Saturday from 9am to 5pm. For a look at everything from pawn jewelry to Pendleton robes and shawls to enamel and cast-iron kitchenware, visit **Ellis Tanner Trading Company** (© **505/863-4434**), Highway 602 Bypass, south from I-40 on Highway 602 about 2 miles; it's at the corner of Nizhoni Boulevard; and **Perry Null-Tobe Turpen's Indian Trading Company,** 1710 S. Second St. (© **505/722-3806**), farther out on Second Street, a big free-standing brick building full of jewelry, rugs, kachinas, and pottery.

SUNSET DANCES

Every evening Memorial Day to Labor Day, dancers from a variety of area tribes sing, drum, and twirl in a stunning display of ritual from 7 to 8pm. The dances take place at the **Gallup Cultural Center** (© **505/863-4131**) on East 66 Avenue and Strong Street. The center is open weekdays from 9am to 5pm, often with extended hours in the summer. Also at the center are a gift shop, a cafe, and a museum with a permanent exhibit on regional history, and other changing art exhibits. Admission to the center and dances is free.

WHERE TO STAY IN GALLUP

Virtually every accommodation in Gallup is somewhere along Route 66, either near the I-40 interchanges or on the highway through downtown.

MODERATE

El Rancho Hotel and Motel ⟨ꝑ⟩   This historic hotel owes as much to Hollywood as to Gallup. Built in 1937 by R. E. "Griff" Griffith, brother of movie mogul D. W. Griffith, it became the place for film companies to set up headquarters when filming here. Between the 1940s and 1960s, a who's who of Hollywood stayed here. Their autographed photos line the walls of the hotel's cafe. Spencer Tracy and Katharine Hepburn stayed here during production of *The Sea of Grass;* Burt Lancaster and Lee Remick were guests when they made *The Hallelujah Trail.* The list goes on and on: Gene Autry, Lucille Ball, Jack Benny, Humphrey Bogart, James Cagney, Errol Flynn, Henry Fonda, the Marx Brothers, Ronald Reagan, Rosalind Russell, James Stewart, John Wayne, and Mae West all stayed here.

In 1986, Gallup businessman Armand Ortega, a longtime jewelry merchant, bought the then run-down El Rancho and restored it to its earlier elegance. The lobby staircase rises to the mezzanine on either side of an enormous stone fireplace, while heavy ceiling beams and railings made of tree limbs give the room a hunting-lodge ambience. The hotel is on the National Register of Historic Places.

Rooms in El Rancho differ from one to the next and are named for the stars that stayed in them. Most are long and medium-size, with wagon-wheel headboards and good, heavy pine furniture stained dark. Bathrooms are small, some with showers, others with shower/bathtub combos. All have lovely small white hexagonal tiles. Many rooms have balconies. Two suites with kitchenettes are also available. Light sleepers should be aware that the train can be heard from all rooms in the hotel.

1000 E. 66 Ave., Gallup, NM 87301. ☎ **800/543-6351** or 505/863-9311. Fax 505/722-5917. www.elrancho hotel.com. 100 units. $47–$86 double; $105 suite. AE, DISC, MC, V. Pets are welcome. **Amenities:** Restaurant (below); lounge; seasonal outdoor pool; coin-op laundry. *In room:* A/C, TV.

Holiday Inn Express ☆   The challenge in Gallup is to find a quiet place to sleep. With busy train tracks running right through town, most accommodations stay noisy through the night. Sitting north of town, this is the quietest place I've found. Though highway noise persists in the night, it's not as intrusive as the train's roar and whistle. Rooms are medium-size, with high ceilings and lots of amenities. They're very well maintained and have comfortable beds and fairly spacious baths. Cookies upon arrival and a hot breakfast add to the appeal. You may pay an extra $10 or $20 to stay here, but for me, a good night's sleep is easily worth that.

1500 W. Maloney Ave., Gallup, NM 87301. ☎ **800/HOLIDAY** or 505/726-1000. Fax 505/722-4954. www.hi express.com. 70 units. $75–$119 double, depending on season and type of room. Rates include hot breakfast. AE, DC, DISC, MC, V. **Amenities:** Indoor pool; Jacuzzi; sauna. *In room:* A/C, TV, coffeemaker, hair dryer, iron.

CAMPING

As in the rest of the state, the Gallup area offers plenty of places to pitch a tent or hook up your RV. **USA RV Park** (☎ **505/863-5021**) has 145 sites, 50 full hookups (cable TV costs extra), and cabins, as well as grocery and laundry facilities. Recreation facilities include coin games, a seasonal heated swimming pool, and a playground. An outdoor breakfast and dinner are served at an extra cost. Sites range from $21 for tents to $27 for full hookups. Cabins are $35. To reach the campground, take I-40 to the US 66/Business I-40 junction (exit 16); go 1 mile east on US 66/Business I-40.

Red Rock State Park campground (☎ **505/722-3839**) has 106 sites—50 with no hookups and 56 with water and electricity. Tent sites are available. The campground offers dry camping for $10 and camping with water and electrical hookups for $18. The sites are right against the buttes, though in the spring they will surely be dusty because of little protection from the wind. Also accessible are a convenience store, picnic tables, and grills. For more information on Red Rock State Park, see "Getting Outside: A Nearby State Park," above.

WHERE TO DINE IN GALLUP

The Coffee House BAKED GOODS/SANDWICHES   This cafe in a historic building in the center of town offers a little big-city flair. Sparse decor with wood tables under an old tin ceiling is accented by local art shows. The espresso and cappuccino are delicious, as are the homemade cookies and muffins. For lunch or dinner, try the turkey and Swiss sandwich, the Waldorf chicken salad, or the homemade red chile chicken posole.

203 W. Coal Ave. ☎ 505/726-0291. All menu items under $8. No credit cards. Mon–Thurs 7am–9:30pm; Fri 7am–11pm; Sat 8am–11pm; Sun 10am–4pm.

El Rancho ☆ *Moments* *Kids* NEW MEXICAN/AMERICAN   Set in the historic El Rancho Hotel (see above), this restaurant has fans all across the Southwest. They come to experience the Old West decor—with well-spaced, heavy wooden furniture and movie memorabilia on the walls—and the sense of the many movie stars who once ate here. The food is fine-diner-style, with dishes such as steak and eggs or hot cakes for breakfast, as well as regional delights, such as *atole* (hot blue-corn cereal) or a breakfast taco. At lunch you can always count on a good burger here or select from a cast of sandwiches, such as the Doris Day (sirloin steak on French bread), or salads. At dinner, steaks are a big hit, as is the grilled salmon, both served with soup or salad, vegetable, and choice of potato or rice. The New Mexican food is also good. Kids can select from the "little buckaroos" menu. A full bar is available.

In the El Rancho Hotel and Motel, 1000 E. 66 Ave. ✆ **800/543-6351** or 505/863-9311. Main courses $4–$10 breakfast, $7–$9 lunch, $8–$16 dinner. AE, DISC, MC, V. Daily 6:30am–10pm.

Earl's *(Finds) (Kids)* NEW MEXICAN/AMERICAN   This is where the locals come to eat, particularly on weekends, en route to and from trading in Gallup. The place fills up with a variety of clientele, from college students to Navajo grandmothers. A Denny's-style diner, with comfortable booths and chairs, the restaurant allows Native Americans to sell their wares to you while you eat; however, you have the option of putting up a sign asking not to be disturbed. Often on weekends, vendors set up tables out front, so the whole place takes on a bustling bazaar atmosphere. And the food is good. I recommend the New Mexican dishes such as huevos rancheros, the enchilada plate, or the smothered grande burrito. Earl's offers a kids' menu and half-portion items for smaller appetites, as well as some salads and a "baked potato meal." Open since 1947, Earl's continues to please.

1400 E. 66 Ave. ✆ **505/863-4201.** Reservations accepted except Fri–Sat. Most menu items under $10. AE, MC, V. Sat–Thurs 6am–9pm; Fri 6am–9:30pm.

Jerry's Cafe *(Value) (Kids)* NEW MEXICAN/AMERICAN   This is where the locals go to eat New Mexican food. It's a narrow and cozy space with booths on both walls and dark wood paneling. Usually it's packed with all manner of people, filling up on big plates of food smothered in chile sauces. You can't go wrong with any of the New Mexican dishes; try the scrambled eggs with chile for breakfast. For lunch or dinner order the flat enchiladas topped with an egg and served with a flour tortilla and sopaipilla, or the stuffed sopaipilla, with guacamole, beans, and beef, smothered in chile. Jerry's has a children's menu as well as burgers and basic sandwiches. It serves no alcohol.

406 W. Coal Ave. ✆ **505/722-6775.** Main courses $4–$6 breakfast, $6.50–$10 lunch and dinner. MC, V. Mon–Sat. 8am–9pm.

Oasis Mediterranean Restaurant & Hookah Lounge *(R) (Finds)* MEDITERRANEAN   A gallery in the center of downtown provides the setting for this new restaurant that serves some of the best food in western New Mexico. Though the setting feels a little sterile, with white floors and walls, some good art in cases is fun to peruse while you wait for your food (although the service is good). The meal starts with a medley of tasty olives, pickles, and peppers. The menu has all the Mediterranean standards—baba gannouj and hummus for appetizers, falafel sandwiches and meat shwarmas for a light lunch or dinner, all carefully made with fresh ingredients. Rather than going with those, though, have the waitress guide you to the best choices. She recommended to me the chicken gallaba, which has become my favorite—richly spiced chicken with mushrooms and bell peppers, served with a choice of rice, hummus, or salad. The baklava and rice pudding are both good finishers. The restaurant also serves steaks, shrimp, and barbecued chicken. Beer and wine are available. An upstairs lounge is still in the development stages.

100 E. 66 Ave., Gallup, NM 87301. ✆ **505/722-9572.** Main courses $5–$17 lunch or dinner. AE, DISC, MC, V. Mon–Sat 10am–10pm.

5 Zuni Pueblo & the Navajo Reservation

ZUNI PUEBLO

Because of its remoteness and its fierce clinging to its roots, Zuni is one of the most interesting pueblos in New Mexico. When the Spanish first arrived, approximately 3,000 Zunis lived in six different villages, and they had occupied the region for more than 300 years.

One of the main villages amid the high pink and gold sandstone formations of the area was **Hawikuh.** It was the first Southwestern village to encounter Europeans. In 1539, Fray Marcos de Niza, guided by the Moor Esteban (who had accompanied Cabeza de Baca in his earlier roaming of the area), came to New Mexico in search of the Seven Cities of Cíbola, cities that Baca had said were made of gold, silver, and precious stones. Esteban antagonized the inhabitants and was killed. de Niza was forced to retreat without really seeing the pueblo, although he described it in exaggerated terms on his return to Mexico, and the legend of the golden city was fueled.

The following year Coronado arrived at the village. Though the Zunis took up arms against him, he conquered the village easily, and the Zunis fled to *Towayalane* (Corn Mountain), a noble mile-long sandstone mesa near the present-day pueblo, as they would later do during the 1680 Pueblo Revolt.

At the time, the Zunis had a sophisticated civilization, with a relationship to the land and to each other that had sustained them for thousands of years. Today, the tribe continues efforts to preserve its cultural heritage. It has recovered valuable seed strains once used for dryland farming, it is teaching the Zuni language in schools, and it is taking measures to preserve area wildlife that's critical to the Zuni faith.

The Zunis didn't fully accept the Christianity thrust upon them. Occasionally, they burned mission churches and killed priests. Though the Catholic mission, dedicated to Our Lady of Guadalupe, sits in the center of their village, clearly their primary religion is their own ancient one, and it's practiced most notably during the days of **Shalako,** an elaborate ceremony that takes place in late November or early December, reenacting the creation and migration of the Zuni people to Heptina, or the "Middle Place," which was destined to be their home.

ESSENTIALS

GETTING THERE   Zuni Pueblo is located about 38 miles south of Gallup via NM 602 and NM 53.

VISITOR INFORMATION   For advance information, contact the **Zuni Tribal Office,** P.O. Box 339, Zuni, NM 87327 (© **505/782-7238;** www. experiencezuni.com). As at all Indian reservations, visitors are asked to respect tribal customs and individuals' privacy. No sketching or painting is allowed, but still photography and videotaping are permitted, with a $10 fee for each. Although the pueblo is never completely closed to outside visitors, certain areas may be off-limits during ceremonies, and photography may be prohibited at times.

ADMISSION FEES & HOURS   Admission is free, and visitors are welcome daily from dawn to dusk.

SEEING THE HIGHLIGHTS

Most of the pueblo consists of modern housing, so there isn't really that much to see; nevertheless, you'll get a feeling for time gone by if you take a walk through the old pueblo. Make a stop at the Catholic mission, dedicated to Our Lady of Guadalupe. Within you'll find a series of murals that depict events in the Zuni ceremonial calendar. In addition, some Native American archaeological ruins on Zuni land date from the early 1200s, but you must obtain permission from the Tribal Office well in advance of your visit in order to see them. The **A:shiwi Awan Museum and Heritage Center,** 1222 NM 53 (**505/782-4403**), offers a glimpse into traditional Zuni culture. An exhibit under the auspices of the museum, "Echoes from the Past," set in a building in the heart of Zuni, presents artifacts from Hawikuh (on loan from the Smithsonian Institute). The main museum is open weekdays, year-round, from 9am to 5:30pm (same hours on Sat during the summer). Admission is free. Call for exhibit hours and directions.

Today, Zuni tribal members are widely acclaimed for their jewelry, made from turquoise, shell, and jet, set in silver in intricate patterns called "needlepoint." The tribe also does fine beadwork, carving in shell and stone, and some pottery. Jewelry and other crafts are sold at the tribally owned **Pueblo of Zuni Arts and Crafts,** 1222 NM 53 (℃ **505/782-5531**). Look especially for the hand-carved fetishes as well as the acclaimed needlepoint jewelry.

If you're planning your visit for late August, call ahead and find out if you're going to be around during the pueblo's annual fair and rodeo.

WHERE TO STAY IN ZUNI

Inn at Halona *(Finds)*   When checking in to this inn, I felt as though I were on an adventure in a foreign land. Situated in the center of Zuni, its front desk is at an old trading post/store. The inn itself fills two homes—one built in 1920, the other in 1940. I recommend the main house (built in 1920) as it is the brighter of the two and was remodeled in 1998. Both are filled with local art and decorated with handcrafted furniture. Most rooms are fairly small, and some rooms share bathrooms, so you'll want to reserve accordingly. All rooms have good linens and comfortably firm beds. My favorite, the Penthouse Room, is small but very sunny and quaint. Over a full and delicious breakfast served family-style in the dining room or out on the lovely patio, innkeepers Roger Thomas and Elaine Dodson Thomas will delight you with stories of living at Zuni, where Elaine's Dutch family started the first trading post in 1903. Basic food is available in the trading post store.

23B Pia Mesa Rd. (P.O. Box 446), Zuni, NM 87327-0446. ℃ **800/752-3278** or 505/782-4547. Fax 505/782-2155. www.halona.com. 8 units. $84 double. $10 for each extra person. Rates include full breakfast. MC, V.

NAVAJO INDIAN RESERVATION

Navajos comprise the largest Native American tribe in the United States, with more than 200,000 members. Their reservation, known to them as Navajoland, spreads across 24,000 square miles of Arizona, Utah, and New Mexico. The New Mexico portion, extending in a band 45 miles wide from just north of Gallup to the Colorado border, comprises only about 15% of the total area.

Until the 1920s, the Navajo Nation governed itself with a complex clan system. When oil was discovered on reservation land, the Navajos established a tribal government to handle the complexities of the 20th century. Today, the Navajo Tribal Council has 88 council delegates representing 110 regional chapters, some two dozen of which are in New Mexico. They meet at least four times a year as a full body in Window Rock, Arizona, capital of the Navajo Nation, near the New Mexico border, 24 miles northwest of Gallup.

Natural resources and tourism are the mainstays of the Navajo economy. Coal, oil, gas, and uranium earn much of the Navajo Nation's money, as does tourism, especially on the Arizona side of the border, which contains or abuts

Grand Canyon National Park, Petrified Forest National Park, Canyon de Chelly National Monuments, Wupatki National Monuments, Navajo National Monument, and Monument Valley Navajo Tribal Park; and in Utah, Glen Canyon National Recreation Area, Rainbow Bridge National Monuments, Hovenweep National Monument, and Four Corners Monument.

The Navajos, like their linguistic cousins the Apaches, belong to the large family of Athapaskan Indians found across Alaska and northwestern Canada and in parts of the Northern California coast. They are believed to have migrated to the Southwest around the 14th century. In 1864, after nearly 2 decades of conflict with the U.S. Army, the entire tribe was rounded up and forced into internment at an agricultural colony near Fort Sumner, New Mexico—an event still recalled as "The Long March." Four years of near-starvation later, the experiment was declared a failure, and the Navajos returned to their homeland.

During World War II, 320 Navajo young men served in the U.S. Marine Corps as communications specialists in the Pacific. The code they created, 437 terms based on the extremely complex Navajo language, was never cracked by the Japanese. Among those heroes was artist Carl Gorman, coordinator of the Navajo Medicine Man Organization and father of internationally famed painter R. C. Gorman. The 2002 movie *Windtalkers,* starring Nicholas Cage, was based on their story.

Although Navajos express themselves artistically in all media, they are best known for their work in silversmithing, sand painting, basketry, and weaving. Distinctive styles of handwoven rugs from Two Grey Hills, Ganado, and Crystal are known worldwide.

ESSENTIALS

GETTING THERE   From Gallup, US 491 goes directly through the Navajo Indian Reservation up to Shiprock. From there you can head over to Farmington (see "Farmington: Gateway to the Four Corners Region," below) on US 64. *Warning:* US 491, previously labeled US 666, running between Gallup and Shiprock, has been called America's "most dangerous highway" by *USA Today.* In hopes of changing the fate of what many called the "Devil's Highway," the name was changed to a more benign set of numbers. Even with the new designation, you'll want to drive carefully!

VISITOR INFORMATION   For information before your trip, contact the **Navajo Tourism Department,** P.O. Box 663, Window Rock, AZ 86515 (© **928/871-6436;** www.discovernavajo.com).

WHAT TO SEE & DO

Attractions in Window Rock, Arizona, include the Navajo Nation Council Chambers; the Navajo Nation Arts and Crafts Enterprise; the huge new Navajo Museum, Library, and Visitor's Center; and Window Rock Tribal Park, containing the natural red-rock arch after which the community is named.

Nearby attractions include **Hubbell Trading Post National Historic Site** (© **928/755-3475**), on Arizona 264, half a mile west of AZ 191, at Ganado, 30 miles west of Window Rock, and **Canyon de Chelly National Monument** (© **928/674-5500**), 39 miles north of Ganado on U.S. 191, at Chinle.

From September 6 to 10, the annual 5-day **Navajo Nation Fair** (© **928/871-6478**) attracts more than 100,000 people to Window Rock for a huge rodeo, parade, carnival, Miss Navajo Nation contest, arts-and-crafts shows, intertribal powwow, concerts, country dancing, and agricultural exhibits. It's the country's largest Native American fair. A smaller but older and more traditional annual tribal fair is the early-October **Northern Navajo Nation Fair** (© **928/871-6436**), held 90 miles north of Gallup in the town of Shiprock.

The **Crownpoint Rug Weavers Association** ℱ has 12 public auctions a year, normally on Friday evening, about 5 weeks apart. Travelers come from all over the world to sit in the stuffy Crownpoint Elementary School gymnasium (drive 20 miles north of I-40 on NM 371, turn west on Indian Route 9, and drive half a mile) and bid on lovely rugs made throughout the Southwest. Prices are good, and the bidding can get exciting. Indian tacos and sodas are offered for sale outside. For more information, call © **505/786-5302**.

WHERE TO STAY & DINE ON THE NAVAJO INDIAN RESERVATION

The place to stay on the reservation is the **Quality Inn Navajo Nation Capital,** 48 W. Highway 264 (P.O. Box 2340), Window Rock, AZ 86515 (© **928/871-4108**). The modern guest rooms are comfortable and moderately priced (a double costs $68), and the restaurant offers Navajo specialties.

6 Chaco Culture National Historical Park ℱℱℱ

A combination of a stunning setting and well-preserved ruins makes the long drive to **Chaco Culture National Historic Park,** often referred to as Chaco Canyon, worth the trip. Whether you come from the north or south, you drive in on a dusty (and sometimes muddy) road that seems to add to the authenticity and adventure of this remote New Mexico experience.

When you finally arrive, you walk through stark desert country that seems perhaps ill suited as a center of culture. However, the ancient Anasazi people successfully farmed the lowlands and built great masonry towns, which connected with other towns over a wide-ranging network of roads crossing this desolate place.

What's most interesting here is how changes in architecture—beginning in the mid-800s, when the Anasazi started building on a larger scale than they had previously—chart the area's cultural progress. The Anasazi used the same masonry techniques that tribes had used in smaller villages in the region (walls one-stone thick, with generous use of mud mortar), but they built stone villages of multiple stories with rooms several times larger than in the previous stage of their culture. Within a century, six large pueblos were underway. This pattern of a single large pueblo with oversize rooms, surrounded by conventional villages, caught on throughout the region. New communities built along these lines sprang up. Old villages built similarly large pueblos. Eventually there were more than 75 such towns, most of them closely tied to Chaco by an extensive system of roads.

This progress led to Chaco becoming the economic center of the San Juan Basin by A.D. 1000. As many as 5,000 people may have lived in some 400 settlements in and around Chaco. As masonry techniques advanced through the years, walls rose more than four stories in height. Some of these are still visible today.

Chaco's decline after 1½ centuries of success coincided with a drought in the San Juan Basin between A.D. 1130 and 1180. Scientists still argue vehemently over why the site was abandoned and where the Chacoans went. Many believe that an influx of outsiders may have brought new rituals to the region, causing a schism among tribal members. Most agree, however, that the people drifted away to more hospitable places in the region and that their descendants live among the Pueblo people today.

This is an isolated area, and **no services** are available within or close to the park—no food, gas, auto repairs, firewood, lodging (besides the campground), or drinking water (other than at the visitor center) are available. Overnight camping is permitted year-round. If you're headed towards Santa Fe after a day at the park and looking for a place to spend the night, one nice option is the **Casa del Rio–Riverside Inn,** 16445 Scenic Highway 4, Jemez Springs, NM 87025 (© **505/829-4377;** www.canondelrio.com).

ESSENTIALS

GETTING THERE To get to Chaco from Santa Fe, take I-25 south to Bernalillo, then US 550 northwest. Turn off US 550 at C.R. 7900 (3 miles southeast of Nageezi and about 50 miles west of Cuba at mile 112.5). Follow the signs from US 550 to the park boundary (21 miles). This route includes 5 miles of paved road (C.R. 7900) and 16 miles of rough dirt road (C.R. 7950). This is the recommended route. Highway 57 from Blanco Trading Post is closed. The trip takes about 3½ to 4 hours. Farmington is the nearest population center, a 1½-hour drive away. The park can also be reached from Grants via I-40 west to NM 371, then north on NM 57 (with the final 19 miles ungraded dirt). This route is rough to impassable and is not recommended for RVs.

Whichever way you come, call ahead to inquire about **road conditions** (© **505/786-7014**) before leaving the paved highways. The dirt roads can get extremely muddy and dangerous after rain or snow, and afternoon thunderstorms are common in late summer. Roads often flood when it rains.

VISITOR INFORMATION Ranger-guided walks and campfire talks are available in the summer at the visitor center where you can get self-guided trail brochures and permits for the overnight campground (see "Camping," below). If you want information before you leave home, write to the Superintendent, Chaco Culture National Historical Park, 1808 County Rd. 7950, Nageezi, NM 87037 (© **505/786-7014;** www.nps.gov/chcu).

ADMISSION FEES & HOURS Admission is $8 per car; a campsite is $10 extra. The visitor center is open daily 8am to 5pm. Trails are open from sunrise to sunset.

SEEING THE HIGHLIGHTS

Exploring the ruins and hiking are the most popular activities here. A series of pueblo ruins stand within 5 or 6 miles of each other on the broad, flat, treeless canyon floor. Plan to spend at least 3 to 4 hours here driving to and exploring the different pueblos. A one-way road from the visitor center loops up one side of the canyon and down the other. Parking lots are scattered along the road near the various pueblos; from most, it's only a short walk to the ruins.

You may want to focus your energy on seeing **Pueblo Bonito,** the largest prehistoric Southwest Native American dwelling ever excavated. It contains giant kivas and 800 rooms covering more than 3 acres. Also, the **Pueblo Alto Trail** is a nice hike that takes you up on the canyon rim so that you can see the ruins from above—in the afternoon, with thunderheads building, the views are spectacular. If you're a cyclist, stop at the visitor center to pick up a map outlining ridable trails.

Aerial photos show hundreds of miles of roads connecting these towns with the Chaco pueblos, one of the longest running 42 miles straight north to Salmon Ruins and the Aztec Ruins (see below). It is this road network that leads some scholars to believe that Chaco was the center of a unified Anasazi society.

CAMPING

Gallo Campground, located within the park, is quite popular with hikers. It's located about 1 mile east of the visitor center; fees are $10 per night. The camp-ground has 47 sites (group sites are also available), with fire grates (bring your own wood or charcoal), central toilets, and nonpotable water. Drinking water is available only at the visitor center. The campground cannot accommodate trail-ers over 30 feet.

As I said above, there's no place to stock up on supplies once you start the arduous drive to the canyon, so if you're camping, make sure you're well sup-plied, especially with water, before you leave home base.

7 Farmington: Gateway to the Four Corners Region

Farmington has historic and outdoor finds that can keep you occupied for at least a day or two. A town of 36,500 residents, it sits at the junction of the San Juan, Animas, and La Plata rivers. Adorned with arched globe willow trees, it's a lush place by New Mexico standards. A system of five parks along the San Juan River and its tributaries is its pride and joy. What's most notable for me, how-ever, is the quaint downtown area, where century-old buildings still house thriv-ing businesses and some trading posts with great prices. It's also an industrial center (coal, oil, natural gas, and hydroelectricity) and a shopping center for people within a 100-mile radius.

For visitors, Farmington is a takeoff point for explorations of the Navajo Reser-vation and Chaco Culture National Historical Park. For outdoor lovers, it's the spot to head to the Bisti/De-Na-Zin Wilderness; world-class fly-fishing on the San Juan River; lovely scenery at the Angel Peak Recreation Area; and even a trip up to Durango to enjoy some rafting, kayaking, skiing, and mountain biking. The nearby towns of Aztec and Bloomfield offer a variety of attractions as well.

ESSENTIALS

GETTING THERE   From Albuquerque, take US 550 (through Cuba) from the I-25 Bernalillo exit, then head west on US 64 at Bloomfield (45 min.). From Gallup, take US 491 north to Shiprock, and then head east on US 64 (2¼ hr.). From Taos, follow US 64 all the way (4½ hr.). From Durango, Colorado, take US 500 south (1 hr.).

All commercial flights arrive at busy **Four Corners Regional Airport** on West Navajo Drive (✆ **505/599-1395**). The principal carriers are **United Express** (✆ **800/241-6522**), with flights from Denver and other Colorado cities; and **America West Airlines** (✆ **800/235-9292**), with flights from Phoenix and other Arizona cities.

Car-rental agencies at Four Corners Regional Airport include **Avis** (✆ **800 331-1212** or 505/327-9864), **Budget** (✆505/327-7304), and **Hertz** (✆ **800/ 654-3131** or 505/327-6093).

VISITOR INFORMATION   The **Farmington Convention and Visitors Bureau,** 3041 E. Main St. (✆ **800/448-1240** or 505/326-7602; www.farmingtonnm.org), is the clearinghouse for tourist information for the Four Corners region. For more information, contact the **Farmington Chamber of Commerce,** 105 N. Orchard Ave. (✆ **505/325-0279;** www.gofarmington.com).

SEEING THE SIGHTS IN THE AREA
IN FARMINGTON
Farmington Museum and Gateway Center   Small-town museums can be completely precious, and this one and its neighbor in Aztec (see below) typify a tiny part of the world, and yet the truths they reveal span continents. Here you get to see the everyday struggle of a people to support themselves within a fairly inhospitable part of the world, spanning boom and bust years of agriculture, oil and gas production, and tourism. Now located in the slick new Gateway Visitor Center, exhibits vary, utilizing over 7,000 objects. You may walk through displays of a 1930s trading post, with an old enameled scale, cloth bolts, and even a vintage box of Cracker Jacks. Next, you may get a look at the oil and gas history of the area, including a photo of the lethally named Rattlesnake Refinery, a desolate place, in operation in 1925. Excellent changing exhibits rotate through as well. While at the Gateway Center, ask about other local exhibits in other parts of the city, such as the Harvest Grove Farm and Orchards, the E3 Children's Museum and Science Center, and the Riverside Nature Center, all located at Animas Park. A gift shop sells fun local art and some nice New Mexico–made treats.

3041 E. Main St. © 505/599-1174. Fax 505/326-7572. www.farmingtonmuseum.org. Free admission. Mon–Sat 8am–5pm.

IN NEARBY AZTEC
VISITOR INFORMATION   The **Aztec Chamber of Commerce,** 110 N. Ash St. (© **505/334-9551;** www.aztecchamber.com), is a friendly place with a wealth of information about the area.

Aztec Museum and Pioneer Village *Kids*   A real treat for kids, this museum and village transport visitors back a full century to a place populated by strangely ubiquitous mannequins. The museum is crammed with memorabilia, but the outer exhibit of replicas and real buildings, with all the trimmings, is what will hold interest. You'll walk through the actual 1912 Aztec jail—nowhere you'd want to live—into the sheriff's office, where a stuffed Andy of Mayberry lookalike is strangely lethargic. The blacksmith shop has an anvil and lots of dusty, uncomfortable-looking saddles, even some oddly shaped burro shoes. The Citizens Bank has a lovely oak cage and counter, and it's run by attentive mannequin women. You'll see an authentic 1906 church and a schoolhouse where mannequins Dick and Jane lead a possibly heated discussion.

125 N. Main Ave., Aztec. © 505/334-9829. www.aztecnm.com/museum/museum_index.htm. Admission $3 adults, $1 children 11–17, free for children 10 and under. Summer Mon–Sat 9am–5pm; winter Mon–Sat 10am–4pm.

IN NEARBY BLOOMFIELD
Salmon Ruins *Kids*   What really marks the 150 rooms of these ruins 11 miles west of Farmington near Bloomfield is their setting on a hillside, surrounded by lush San Juan River bosque. You'll begin in the museum, though, where a number of informative displays range from one showing the variety of types of ancestral Puebloan vessels, from pitchers to canteens, to wild plants. Like the ruins at Aztec, two strong architectural influences are visible here. First the Chacoan, who built the village around the 11th century, with walls of an intricate rubble-filled core with sandstone veneer. The more simple Mesa Verde masonry was added in the 13th century. A trail guide will lead you to each site. There is a marvelous elevated ceremonial chamber, or "tower kiva," and a Great Kiva, now a low-lying ruin, but with some engaging remains, such as the central

fire pit and an antechamber possibly used by leaders for storage of ceremonial goods. There is also a photograph exhibit of Navajo pueblitos and rock art.

One of the most recently excavated ruins in the West, the site is only 30% excavated, by design. It's being saved for future generations of archaeologists, who, it's assumed, will be able to apply advanced research techniques. For now, the archaeological research center studies regional sites earmarked for natural-resource exploitation.

Built in 1990, **Heritage Park,** on an adjoining plot of land, comprises a series of reconstructed ancient and historic dwellings representing the area's cultures, from a paleoarchaic sand-dune site to an Anasazi pit house, from Apache wick-iups and tepees to Navajo hogans, and an original pioneer homestead. Visitors are encouraged to enter the re-creations.

In the visitor center, you'll find a gift shop and a scholarly research library.

6131 US 64 (P.O. Box 125), Bloomfield, NM 87413. © **505/632-2013.** Fax 505/632-8633. www.salmonruins. com. Admission $3 adults, $1 children 6–16, $2 seniors, free for children under 6. Summer Mon–Fri 8am–5pm, Sat–Sun 9am–5 pm; winter Mon–Fri 8am–5pm, Sat 9am–5pm, and Sun noon–5pm.

AZTEC RUINS NATIONAL MONUMENT ℛ

What's most striking about these ruins is the central kiva, which visitors can enter and sit within, sensing the site's ancient history. The ruins of this 450-room Native American pueblo, left by the ancestral Puebloans 7 centuries ago, are located 14 miles northeast of Farmington, in the town of Aztec on the Animas River. Early Anglo settlers, convinced that the ruins were of Aztec origin, misnamed the site. Despite the fact that this pueblo was built long before the Aztecs of central Mexico lived, the name persisted.

The influence of the Chaco culture is strong at Aztec, as evidenced in the pre-planned architecture, the open plaza, and the fine stone masonry in the old walls. But a later occupation shows the influence of Mesa Verde (which flourished 1200–1275). This second group of settlers remodeled the old pueblo and built others nearby, using techniques less elaborate and decorative than those of the Chacoans.

Aztec Ruins is best known for its Great Kiva, the only completely reconstructed Anasazi great kiva in existence. About 50 feet in diameter, with a main floor sunken 8 feet below the surface of the surrounding ground, this circular ceremonial room rivets the imagination. It's hard not to feel spiritually impressed, and perhaps to feel the presence of people who walked here nearly 1,000 years ago. (However, be aware that doubt has been cast on the reconstruction job performed by archaeologist Earl H. Morris in 1934; some believe the structure is much taller than the original.)

Visiting Aztec Ruins National Monument will take you approximately 1 hour, even if you take the ¼-mile self-guided trail and spend some time in the visitor center, which displays some outstanding examples of Anasazi ceramics and basketry. Add another half-hour if you plan to watch the video that imaginatively documents the history of native cultures in the area.

ESSENTIALS

GETTING THERE   Aztec Ruins is approximately a half mile north of US 550 on Ruins Road (C.R. 2900) on the north edge of the city of Aztec. Ruins Road is the first street immediately west of the Animas River Bridge on Highway 516 in Aztec.

VISITOR INFORMATION For more information, contact **Aztec Ruins National Monument,** 84 County Rd. 2900, Aztec, NM 87410-0640 (© **505/334-6174,** ext. 30; www.nps.gov/azru).

ADMISSION FEES & HOURS Admission is $4 for adults; children under 17 are admitted free. The monument is open daily from 8am to 6pm Memorial Day through Labor Day and 8am to 5pm the rest of the year; it's closed Thanksgiving, Christmas, and New Year's Day.

CAMPING

Camping is not permitted at the monument. Nearby, **Bloomfield KOA** (© **800/562-8513** or 505/632-8339; www.koa.com), on Blanco Boulevard, offers 83 sites, 73 full hookups, tenting, cabins, laundry and grocery facilities, picnic tables, grills, and firewood. The recreation room/area has coin games, a heated swimming pool, a basketball hoop, a playground, horseshoes, volleyball, and a hot tub.

Camping is also available at **Navajo Lake State Park** (© **505/632-2278**).

SHOPPING

Downtown Farmington shops are generally open from 10am to 6pm Monday through Saturday. Native American arts and crafts are best purchased at trading posts, either downtown on Main or Broadway streets, or west of Farmington on US 64/550 toward Shiprock. You may want to check out the following stores.

Foutz Indian Room, 301 W. Main St. (© **505/325-9413**), has some affordable jewelry, as well as whimsical Navajo folk art such as painted carvings of pickups carrying sheep and chickens. The store also sells wool and leather to artisans.

Hogback Trading Company, 3221 US 64, Waterflow, 17 miles west of Farmington (© **505/598-5154**), has large displays of Indian jewelry, rugs, and folk art.

Navajo Trading Company, 126 E. Main St. (© **505/325-1685**), is an actual pawnshop, with lots of exquisite old jewelry, including the most incredible concho belt I've ever seen, priced at $2,500; you can peruse bracelets and necklaces while listening to clerks speaking Navajo.

GETTING OUTSIDE: NEARBY PARKS & RECREATION AREAS
SHIPROCK PEAK

This distinctive landmark, located on the Navajo Indian Reservation southwest of Shiprock, 29 miles west of Farmington via US 64, is known to the Navajo as *Tse bidá hi,* "Rock with wings." Composed of igneous rock flanked by long upright walls of solidified lava, it rises 1,700 feet off the desert floor to an elevation of 7,178 feet. There are scenic viewing points off US 491, 6 to 7 miles south of the town of Shiprock. You can get closer by taking the tribal road to the community of Red Rock, but you must have permission to get any nearer to this sacred Navajo rock. Climbing is not permitted.

The town named after the rock is a gateway to the Navajo reservation and the Four Corners region. There's a tribal visitor center here.

From Shiprock, you may want to make the 32-mile drive west on US 64 to Teec Nos Pos, Arizona, and then north on US 160, to the **Four Corners Monument.** A concrete slab here sits astride the only point in the United States where four states meet: New Mexico, Colorado, Utah, and Arizona. Kids especially like the idea of standing at the center and occupying four states at once. It's a primitive place with no visitor center, but booths sell crafts and food. With no view to speak of, some find a visit here not worth the trip or cost. For information, call

© **928/871-6647.** Open daily 7am to 7pm Memorial Day to Labor Day and 8am to 5pm the rest of the year. The cost is $3 per person for adults, and $2 for kids 6 and under.

NAVAJO LAKE STATE PARK

The **San Juan River, Pine River,** and **Sims Mesa recreation sites,** all with camping, fishing, and boating, make this the most popular water-sports destination for residents of northwestern New Mexico. Trout, northern pike, largemouth bass, and catfish are caught in lake and river waters, and the surrounding hills attract hunters seeking deer and elk. A visitor center at Pine River Recreation Area has interpretive displays on natural history and on the construction and purposes of the dam.

Navajo Lake, with an area of 15,000 acres, extends from the confluence of the San Juan and Los Pinos rivers 25 miles north into Colorado. Navajo Dam, an earthen embankment, is ¾ of a mile long and 400 feet high. It provides Farmington-area cities, industries, and farms with their principal water supply. It's also the main storage reservoir for the Navajo Indian Irrigation Project, designed to irrigate 110,000 acres.

Anglers come from all over the world to fish the San Juan below the dam, a pastoral spot bordered by green hills, where golden light reflects off the water. Much of the water is designated "catch and release" and is teeming with rainbow, brown, and cutthroat trout. Experts will be heartily challenged by these fish that are attuned to the best tricks, while amateurs may want to hire a guide. For more information, see "The Great Outdoors in Northwestern New Mexico," earlier in this chapter.

The park is located 40 miles east of Farmington on NM 511. For more information, call *©* **505/632-2278.**

ANGEL PEAK RECREATION AREA

The distinctive pinnacle of 6,991-foot Angel Peak can often be spotted from the hillsides around Farmington. The area offers a short nature trail and a variety of unusual, colorful geological formations and canyons to explore on foot. The Bureau of Land Management has developed a primitive campground with nine campsites and provided picnic tables in a few spots, but no drinking water is available here. The park is located about 35 miles south of Farmington on US 550; the last 6 miles of access, after turning off US 550, are over a graded dirt road. For more information on the park, call *©* **505/599-8900.**

BISTI/DE-NA-ZIN WILDERNESS

Often referred to as Bisti Badlands (pronounced bist-*eye*), this barren region may merit that name today, but it was once very different. Around 70 million years ago, large dinosaurs lived near what was then a coastal swamp, bordering a retreating inland sea. Today, their bones, and those of fish, turtles, lizards, and small mammals, are eroding slowly from the low shale hills.

Kirtland Shale, containing several bands of color, dominates the eastern part of the Wilderness and caps the mushroom-shaped formations found there. Along with the spires and fanciful shapes of rock, hikers may find petrified wood sprinkled in small chips throughout the area, or even an occasional log. Removing petrified wood, fossils, or anything else from the wilderness is prohibited.

Hiking in the Bisti is fairly easy; from the small parking lot, follow an arroyo east 2 or 3 miles into the heart of the formations, which you'll see on your right (aim for the two red hills). The De-Na-Zin Wilderness to the east requires more climbing and navigational skills. It has no designated trails, bikes and motorized vehicles are prohibited, and it has no water or significant shade. The hour just after sunset or, especially, just before sunrise is a pleasant and quite magical time to see this starkly beautiful landscape. Primitive camping is allowed, but bring plenty of water and other supplies.

Bisti/De-Na-Zin Wilderness is located just off NM 371, 37 miles south of Farmington. For more information, call the **Bureau of Land Management** at ⓒ **505/599-8900.**

WHERE TO STAY IN FARMINGTON & AZTEC
MODERATE
Best Western Inn and Suites   This is where my brother stays when he's doing business in Farmington. Built in 1976, it provides spacious rooms and good amenities, though you have to like to walk because the rooms are built around a huge quadrangle with an indoor pool in a sunny, plant-filled courtyard. Request a room at one of the four corner entrances to avoid trudging down the long hallways. Also request a room that is facing outside rather than in toward the courtyard, where noise from the pool carries. This is a good choice for winter, when you can enjoy the courtyard. Rooms are bright and decorated with Southwest accents. Beds are firm, and bathrooms are medium-size and clean. Suites have microwaves, wet bars, extra phones at desks, and sofa beds. Best of all, the hotel is just steps away from the Riverwalk, a great place to get your morning or evening exercise.

The hotel's restaurant, the Riverwalk Patio and Grille, offers a wide selection of New Mexican and Southwest Italian cuisine. Rookie's Sports Bar, which features pool tables and televised sporting events and specials, always offers a drink special.

700 Scott Ave., Farmington, NM 87401. ⓒ **800/528-1234,** 800/600-5221, or 505/327-5221. Fax 505/327-1565. www.bestwestern.com. 194 units. $79–$84 double. Rates include breakfast. AE, DC, DISC, MC, V. Pets are welcome. **Amenities:** Restaurant; bar; indoor pool; exercise room; Jacuzzi; sauna; game room; car-rental desk; business center; limited room service; coin-op laundry; laundry service. *In room:* A/C, TV/VCR w/pay movies, dataport, fridge, coffeemaker, hair dryer, iron.

Step Back Inn ⓡ   This inn offers Victorian charm in a newer building with modern conveniences. Though it's a fair-size hotel, it has a cozy inn feel and plenty of amenities. The building was designed by the same architect who built the Inn of the Anasazi in Santa Fe, and the tastefulness and functionality are apparent in the layout of the large rooms and good-size baths, as well as in the quietness, which is due to good insulation. The rooms have pretty touches such as wallpaper and early American antique replica armoires, which hold the television. Each is named after an early pioneer family of the area, some of whom are the ancestors of the hotel's owner, and each room includes a small booklet that tells their stories. The beds are firm, and the linens are good. Breakfast brings a warm, delicious cinnamon roll as large as a plate, served in a quiet tearoom.

103 W. Aztec Blvd., Aztec, NM 87410 ⓒ **800/334-1255** or 505/334-1200. 39 units. May 15–Nov 1 $68–$78 double; Nov 2–May 14 $58–$68 double. Rates include cinnamon roll, juice, and coffee. AE, MC, V. *In room:* A/C, TV, hair dryer.

INEXPENSIVE
Enchantment Lodge   Lots of fishers, including my mother and me when we go angling on the San Juan, enjoy this pleasant and very reasonable small roadside motel, marked by pink neon lights reminiscent of the late 1950s, when it was built. With remodeling ongoing, the simple, medium-size rooms have

Southwest touches and 1950s tile in the bathrooms. A small pool offers a nice respite at the end of the day. Request a room toward the back to avoid highway noise.

1800 W. Aztec Blvd., Aztec, NM 87410. © **800/847-2194** for reservations only, or 505/334-6143. Fax 505/334-9234. www.enchantmentlodge.com. 20 units. $44–$52 double. Rates include continental breakfast. AE, DC, DISC, MC, V. **Amenities:** Small outdoor pool; coin-op laundry; laundry service. *In room:* A/C, TV, fridge.

BED & BREAKFASTS

Casa Blanca 🐾🐾 *Finds*　Recent renovation has turned this B & B into a travel destination. Located in a quiet residential neighborhood just a few blocks from the shops and restaurants of Main Street, this inn built in the 1940s was once the home of a wealthy family that traded with the Navajos. In 2004, new owners expanded it, adding patios and fountains, creating a lovely oasis. The large rooms, decorated in an elegant Southwestern style, have original artwork and plenty of amenities. Travelers with disabilities are treated especially well here (two large suites especially for them), as are business travelers (high-speed Internet and a meeting room). The full breakfast is always gourmet.

505 E. La Plata St., Farmington, NM 87401. © **800/550-6503** or 505/327-6503. Fax 505/326-5680. www.4cornersbandb.com. 9 units. $95–$165 double; $20 single traveler discount. Rates include full breakfast. AE, MC, V. *In room:* A/C, TV, high-speed Internet, fridge, coffeemaker, hair dryer, iron.

Kokopelli's Cave 🐾🐾　After a long day of sightseeing, I lay on a queen bed under 200 feet of sandstone, listening to Beethoven, with a sliding glass door open to a view hundreds of feet down to a river snaking across a valley. It began to rain, slow big drops that made the air smell like wet sage. It suddenly struck me: I was staying in a cave. I can't quite stress how cool an experience it was.

Here's the story: Retired geologist Bruce Black wanted to build an office in a cave, so he gave some laid-off Grants miners $20,000 to bore as deeply as they could into the side of a cliff face. This luxury apartment was the result. Through time, it worked better as a living space than a work space, and that is what it remains. Built in a semicircle, both the entry hall and the bedroom have wide sliding glass doors leading to little balconies beyond which the cliff face drops hundreds of feet below. This really is a cliff dwelling, and you must hike a bit down to it, though good guardrails guide you.

The apartment is laid out around a broad central pillar, and the ceilings and walls are thick, undulating stone. Golden eagles nest in the area, and ring-tail cats tend to wander onto the balcony. A grill is outside, as are chairs where you can relax in the mornings and evenings. Fruit, juice, coffee, and pastries make up a self-serve breakfast.

3204 Crestridge Dr., Farmington, NM 87401. © **505/326-2461**. Fax 505/325-9671. www.bbonline.com/nm/kokopelli. 1 unit. $220 double; $260 for 3–4 people. Closed Dec–Feb. AE, MC, V. **Amenities:** Jacuzzi. *In room:* TV/VCR, kitchen, hair dryer, iron.

CAMPING

Downs RV Park (© **800/582-6427**) has 33 sites, 31 of them with full hookups. Tenting space is also available. The park has a playground, an arcade, and a game room. It's located 5 miles west of Farmington on US 64. **Mom and Pop RV Park** (© **505/327-3200**) has 36 sites, 35 of them with full hookups, tenting, a bathhouse, and a toy soldier shop. The sites are a bit desolate, around an asphalt central area, but a little grassy spot at the office has an incredible electric train set that Pop runs at certain times during the day. Mom and Pop RV Park is located at 901 Illinois Ave., in Farmington (just off US 64).

WHERE TO DINE IN FARMINGTON & AZTEC

EXPENSIVE

The Bluffs ★★ *Finds* STEAKS/SEAFOOD/SANDWICHES   Finally, Farmington has fine dining. Ten minutes east of town center, The Bluffs serves inventive food with attention to detail. A large room is sectioned off by wooden partitions crowned with elegantly glazed glass shaped like the bluffs prominent in the surrounding area. It's a comfortable atmosphere with roomy booths and stacked sandstone accents. Service is efficient. The outdoor patio is a nice spot on not-so-hot days. For lunch, my pick is the turkey bacon club, served on ciabatta bread. The Thai beef salad is also tasty. At dinner, try your favorite steak cut of Angus beef or sesame-crusted ahi tuna. Dinners come with salad and a choice of vegetable or potato. There's a full bar here, but for a real treat, before dining, slip into the package store next door, owned by the same folks, where you'll find some very fine wines. In the restaurant, you'll pay a corking fee but still save a bundle.

3450 E. Main St. © 505/325-8155. Reservations recommended on weekend nights. Main courses $7–$11 lunch, $13–$30 dinner. AE, DISC, MC, V. Mon–Sat 11am–2pm; Mon–Thurs 5–9pm; Fri–Sat 4–10pm. Lounge daily 3–9 or 10pm.

MODERATE

3 Rivers Eatery & Brewhouse AMERICAN   After a long day of traveling, I went to this brewpub on an elegant corner in the center of downtown. One sip of their Papa Bear's Golden Honey, and I was ready to recommend the place. It's set in a big two-story brick building that once housed the Farmington Drug Store and the Farmington *Times-Hustler* newspaper. Wood floors and vintage items, such as period bottles and posters found in the renovation, complete the experience. It's a comfortable place where the owner might just sit down in one of the comfy booths with you and chat about his passion, beer brewing. I recommend the burgers, which come in a variety of flavors, from grilled onion and Swiss to jack and green chile. You'll also find barbecue pork ribs, steaks, and seafood. The waiter brought me another beer flavor to sample, Arroyo Amber Ale, which I liked as well as the first. For dessert, try the brewmaster's root beer float.

101 E. Main St., Farmington. © 505/324-2187. www.threeriversbrewery.com. Main courses $5–$22 lunch and dinner. AE, DISC, MC, V. Mon–Thurs 11am–10pm; Fri–Sat 11am–11pm; Sun 11am–9pm.

INEXPENSIVE

Bagel Conspiracy BAGELS AND SANDWICHES   If you find yourself in east Farmington's strip and shopping mall never-never land and want to stop in for a quick bite, head to this spot. The interior isn't much—industrial, with a few tables and an eating counter looking out on a parking lot—but the food is fresh and tasty. Bagels are baked daily in a variety of flavors, served with a range of spreads and made into sandwiches such as an egg and cheese with bacon for breakfast or chicken salad for lunch. Wash it down with a cappuccino, an espresso, or an Italian soda.

3554 E. Main St., Suite H (in the little mall in front of Home Depot). © 505/564-8888. All menu items under $6. AE, DC, DISC, MC, V. Mon–Fri 6am–5pm; Sat 7am–5pm; Sun 7am–2pm.

Main Street Bistro ★ CAFE/BAKERY   In all my travels across New Mexico I've stumbled upon a quiet quest—finding good coffee and such things as home-baked muffins and veggie sandwiches. In states with a lot of people, this would be a small task, but out here, where hundreds of miles separate gas stations, it becomes almost quixotic. Each time I find a little gem like this one, I revel in it and visit it as many times as I can while I'm in the vicinity. The place reels with imagination. The walls and floors are brightly colored, and the menu changes at the whim of the chefs. The service is friendly and decent, and the place bustles during peak hours; so if you want quiet time, go midmorning or later in the afternoon. You can't go wrong with the daily soup special, a salad, a sandwich (try the Ultimate—turkey, bacon, avocado, and sprouts), or the quiche, made fresh daily.

122 N. Main St., Aztec. ℂ 505/334-0109. All menu items under $8. DISC, MC, V. Mon–Sat 7am–4pm.

Something Special Bakery and Tea Room GOURMET HOME COOK-ING/VEGETARIAN   Ask people in Farmington where to eat and they'll recommend this little shop. In a quaint Victorian home, it has wooden floors and tables and an open, friendly atmosphere. Best of all is the vine-draped, arbor-shaded patio in back. Breakfast is decadent pastries, such as a blueberry cream cheese or a spinach and feta croissant, all made with wholesome ingredients. Each day, diners have a choice of two lunch entrees, such as a vegetable quiche or a mild Thai chicken served over veggies and rice. Every day brings 20 plus dessert options, including such delicacies as blueberry/raspberry chocolate cake or a strawberry napoleon. A lighter option is the white chocolate macadamia nut cookie. Believe it or not, amid all this richness are low-fat "heart smart" menu options as well.

116 N. Auburn Ave., near Main St., Farmington. ℂ 505/325-8183. Breakfast $3–$6; lunch main course $10; desserts $5. AE, DC, DISC, MC, V. Tues–Fri 7am–2pm (lunch served 11:30am–2pm).

FARMINGTON AFTER DARK

Black River Traders, an annual outdoor historical drama, depicts 1910 trading-post life in the Four Corners region. Presented in the Lions Wilderness Park Amphitheater (off College Blvd.) against a sandstone backdrop, the drama tells of the struggle for survival by both Navajos and whites as two cultures fought to understand each other. This play, using dance and mime, was written by Mark R. Sumner. A Southwestern-style dinner is also available. The production company also presents other musicals at the amphitheater. For information and advance ticket sales, call ℂ **505/599-1148,** or you can purchase tickets at the gate. Shows are Wednesday through Saturday from late June to mid-August, with dinner at 6:30pm and the performance at 8pm.

A new night spot, **3 Rivers Tap & Game Room,** 113 E. Main St. (ℂ **505/ 325-6605;** www.threeriversbrewery.com), is a big hit with locals. This brew-pub/game room has the feel of the bar from the television show *Cheers,* with wood floors, high ceilings, and lots of laughter and brew flowing. Pool tables, foosball, and shuffleboard fill patrons' time in this nonsmoking space, while they munch on popcorn and peanuts, and, some nights, listen to live music jam. Patrons can order from the next-door brewpub/restaurant of the same name (see above).

8 The Jicarilla Apache Reservation

About 3,200 Apaches live on the Jicarilla Apache Indian Reservation along US 64 and NM 537. Its 768,000 acres stretch from the Colorado border south 65 miles to US 550 near Cuba, New Mexico.

The word *jicarilla* (pronounced hick-ah-*ree*-ah) means "little basket," so it's no surprise that tribal craftspeople are noted for their basket weaving and bead-work. See their work, both contemporary and of museum quality, at the **Jicar-illa Apache Arts and Crafts Shop and Museum,** a green building along US 64 west of the central village on the reservation (ℂ **505/759-4274**). In the back rooms here I found women listening to 1950s rock while they wove baskets and strung beads. Two isolated pueblo ruins, open to the public, are found on the reservation: **Cordova Canyon** ruins on tribal Road 13 and **Honolulu** ruins on Road 63.

Though the area is lovely, there's not much else to do unless you're interested in hunting and fishing. Tribe members guide fishers and trophy hunters, most of whom seek elk, mule deer, or bear, into the reservation's rugged wilderness backcountry. Fishing permits for seven reservation lakes and the Navajo River run $10 per day for adults, $5 for seniors and children under age 12. Rainbow, cutthroat, and brown trout are regularly stocked.

Just south of Chama on Jicarilla's northeastern flank is **Horse Lake Mesa Game Park,** P.O. Box 313, Dulce, NM 87528 (© **505/759-3442**), a 20,000-acre reserve surrounded by a predator-proof fence. At an altitude of around 8,500 feet, this is the home of Rocky Mountain elk, mule deer, bobcats, bears, and coyotes.

Highlights of the Jicarilla calendar are the **Little Beaver Celebration** (mid-July), which features a rodeo, a 5-mile run, a draft-horse pull, and a powwow. The **Stone Lake Fiesta** (Sept 14–15 annually) includes a rodeo, ceremonial dances, and a footrace.

Admission to Jicarilla Apache Reservation is free, and visitors are welcome year-round. For information on outdoor activities, contact the tribal Game and Fish office at the number above, or for general information (if they answer), the Tribal Office at P.O. Box 507 (© **505/759-3242**).

The **Best Western Jicarilla Inn and Casino** on US 64 (P.O. Box 233), Dulce, NM 87528 (© **800/742-1938** or 505/759-3663; www.bestwestern.com/jicarillainn), offers decent rooms, though you'll find better accommodations in Chama (see below).

9 Chama: Home of the Cumbres & Toltec Scenic Railroad

Some of my best outdoor adventuring has taken place in the area surrounding this pioneer village of 1,250 people at the base of the 10,000-foot Cumbres Pass. With backpack on, I cross-country skied high into the mountains and stayed the night in a *yurt* (Mongolian hut), waking the next day to hundreds of acres of snowy fields to explore. Another time, we headed down **Rio Chama,** an official wild and scenic river, on rafts and in kayaks following the course that Navajos, Utes, and Comanches once traveled to raid the Pueblo Indians downriver. The campsites along the way were pristine, with mule deer threading through the trees beyond our tents. In my most recent visit to the village, it was summertime, and I'd just come from Durango, which was packed with tourists, to hike, raft, and ride the train. Chama was still quiet, and I realized Chama is New Mexico's undiscovered Durango, without the masses. Now, with some new additions, the town is really looking up. A park, clock-tower, and, drumroll please...sidewalks (!) give it a more friendly tone.

Bordered by three wilderness areas, the Carson, Rio Grande, and Santa Fe national forests, the area is indeed prime for hunting, fishing, cross-country skiing, snowmobiling, snowshoeing, and hiking.

Another highlight here is America's longest and highest narrow-gauge coal-fired steam line, the **Cumbres & Toltec Scenic Railroad,** which winds through valleys and mountain meadows 64 miles between Chama and Antonito, Colorado. The village of Chama boomed when the railroad arrived in 1881. A rough-and-ready frontier town, the place still maintains that flavor, with lumber and ranching making up a big part of the economy.

Landmarks to watch for are the **Brazos Cliffs** and waterfall and **Heron and El Vado lakes.** Tierra Amarilla, the Rio Arriba County seat, is 14 miles south, and is at the center—along with Los Ojos and Los Brazos—of a wool-raising and weaving tradition where local craftspeople still weave masterpieces. Dulce, governmental seat of the Jicarilla Apache Indian Reservation, is 27 miles west.

ESSENTIALS

GETTING THERE   From Santa Fe, take US 84 north (2 hr.). From Taos, take US 64 west (2½ hr.). From Farmington, take US 64 east (2¼ hr.).

VISITOR INFORMATION   The **New Mexico Visitor Information Center,** P.O. Box 697, Chama, NM 87520 (✆ **505/756-2235**), is at 2372 NM 17. It's open daily from 8am to 6pm in the summer, from 8am to 5pm in the winter. At the same address is the **Chama Valley Chamber of Commerce** (✆ **800/ 477-0149** or 505/756-2306).

ALL ABOARD THE HISTORIC C&T RAILROAD

Cumbres & Toltec Scenic Railroad   If you have a passion for the past and for incredible scenery, climb aboard America's longest and highest narrow-gauge steam railroad, the historic C&T. It operates on a 64-mile track between Chama and Antonito, Colorado. Built in 1880 as an extension of the Denver and Rio Grande line to serve the mining camps of the San Juan Mountains, it is perhaps the finest surviving example of what once was a vast network of remote Rocky Mountain railways.

The C&T passes through forests of pine and aspen, past striking rock formations, and over the magnificent Toltec Gorge of the Rio de los Pinos. It crests at the 10,015-foot Cumbres Pass, the highest in the United States used by scheduled passenger trains.

Halfway through the route, at Osier, Colorado, the *New Mexico Express* from Chama meets the *Colorado Limited* from Antonito. They stop to exchange greetings, engines, and through passengers. Round-trip day passengers return to their starting point after enjoying a picnic or catered lunch beside the old water tank and stock pens in Osier. Through passengers continue on to Antonito and return by van. Be aware that both trips are nearly full-day events. Ask about their Parlor Car, a more luxurious alternative to coach seating. Those who find it uncomfortable to sit for long periods may instead want to opt for hiking or skiing in the area.

A walking-tour brochure, describing 23 points of interest in the Chama railroad yards, can be picked up at the 1899 depot in Chama. A registered National Historic Site, the C&T is owned by the states of Colorado and New Mexico. Special cars with lifts for people with disabilities are available with a 7-day advance reservation.

After all the sitting while on the train, you may want to stroll a while, hitting a few of the shops in Chama. One of note is the **Local Color Gallery** (✆ **888/ 756-2604** or 505/756-2604) in the center of town. Here you'll find all kinds of locally made arts and crafts, from flashy broomstick skirts to moody candles painted with petroglyph symbols to picturesque watercolors of the Chama area.

P.O. Box 789, Chama, NM 87520. ✆ **888/CUMBRES** or 505/756-2151. Fax 505/756-2694. www.cumbres andtoltec.com. Lunch is included with all fares. Round-trip to Osier: adults $69.75, children 11 and under $37. Through trip to Antonito, return by van (or to Antonito by van, return by train): adults $64.75, children $34.50. Reservations highly recommended. Memorial Day to mid-Oct trains leave Chama daily at 10am; vans depart for Antonito at 8am.

WHERE TO STAY IN CHAMA

Most accommodations in this area are found on NM 17 or south of the US 64/84 junction, known as the "Y."

HOTELS/LODGES

Chama Trails Inn   This stucco building adorned with chile *ristras* (decorative strung chiles) houses nice motel-style rooms at a reasonable price. The place is impeccably kept; all rooms, some with suitelike configurations, include queen-size beds, custom-made pine furnishings, and minifridges. Be aware that ceilings are fairly low and rooms are a bit dark. A few rooms have ceiling fans, gas fireplaces, and/or Mexican-tile bathroom floors. Some have newer mattresses than others, so ask for a new one.

2362 NM 17 (P.O. Box 975), Chama, NM 87520. ℭ 800/289-1421 or 505/756-2156. Fax 505/756-2855. www.chamatrailsinn.com. 15 units. $50–$85 double, depending on the season. AE, DC, DISC, MC, V. Pets accepted with $10 fee. **Amenities:** Exercise room; Jacuzzi; sauna. *In room:* TV, dataport, fridge, coffeemaker, iron.

River Bend Lodge   Set on a bend of the Chama River, this lodging offers the best cabins in town and clean motel rooms. If you can reserve cabins number 40, 50, or 60 at the back of the property, you'll have a sweet riverside stay. Some of these cabins are split-level, with a queen sleeping loft and a bedroom—not great for privacy, but good for a family that doesn't mind sharing space. Others are similar, but without the loft. Every cabin has a fold-out futon in the living room, an efficient little kitchen, and a small bathroom. The motel rooms are medium-size, with basic furnishings.

2625 US 64/285, Chama, NM 87520. ℭ 800/288-1371 or 505/756-2264. Fax: 505/756-2664; www.chama riverbendlodge.com. 20 units. Motel rooms $65–$78 double; cabins $89–$129 double. Additional person $10. Children under 13 stay free in parent's room. AE, DC, DISC, MC, V. Pets accepted with $10 fee. **Amenities:** Jacuzzi; river for fishing and wading. *In room:* A/C, TV, fridge, coffeemaker (upon request), microwave (upon request).

The Timbers at Chama ⭐   This luxury lodge, set on 400 acres of meadow, with only streams, birds, and elk to disturb your sleep, is one of the region's real gems. Designed as a hunting and fishing lodge, the place has an elegant great room on the first floor, with vaulted ceilings, a giant stone fireplace, and a big-screen TV. One wall is devoted to a vast display of game heads, a detail that non-hunters may find disturbing. Outside is a broad deck with a hot tub and outdoor fireplace overlooking a little pond. The rooms, all decorated in an elegant Montana ranch style, are medium-size (the suite is large) with heavy pine furniture, views, and medium-size bathrooms. The beds are comfortably firm and have fine linens. All rooms have VCRs, jet tubs, and robes, and are decorated with original art. An adjacent guesthouse has a kitchen—a great place for families. Hunting and fishing guides are available, as are horses for guests to ride, all for an additional charge.

Off NM 512 to the Brazos (HC 75, Box 136), Chama, NM 87520. ℭ 505/588-7950. Fax 505/588-7051. www. thetimbersatchama.com. 5 units. $100–$175 double. Guest house $200 double. Rates include full breakfast, except for guest house. DISC, MC, V. **Amenities:** Jacuzzi. *In room:* TV/VCR, coffeemaker, hair dryer, safe.

BED & BREAKFASTS

Gandy Dancer Bed & Breakfast Inn ⭐   Located in a 1912 two-story Victorian from the early railroad era, this B&B offers an old-world feel with up-to-date amenities. New owners have added color and a cozy atmosphere to the place. Rooms range in size, all with medium-size bathrooms and comfortable beds. Attractive antiques make each room—all named with railroad lingo—unique. The upstairs Caboose, with a king bed, sky-blue walls, and lots of light from all directions, is one pick of the place, but my favorite is the downstairs Main Line, a large room with a king bed and a purple iris theme. The full breakfast is well worth waking up for. The spinach quiche served with Canadian bacon and an almond French pancake from my last stay is still memorable. Ask about their winter packages, including home-cooked German dinners.

299 Maple Ave. (P.O. Box 810), Chama, NM 87520. © 800/424-6702 or 505/756-2191. Fax 505/756-2649. www.gandydancerbb.com. 7 units. Summer $95–$125 double; winter $85 double. Additional person $15. Rates include full breakfast. AE, DISC, MC, V. **Amenities:** Jacuzzi. *In room:* A/C, TV/VCR.

CAMPING

At **Rio Chama RV Campground** (© **505/756-2303**), you're within easy walking distance of the Cumbres & Toltec Scenic Railroad depot. This shady campground with 94 sites along the Rio Chama is ideal for RVers and tenters who plan to take train rides. The campground also offers great photo opportunities of the old steam trains leaving the depot. Hot showers, a dump station, and complete hookups are available. It's open from mid-May to mid-October only. The campground is located 2¼ miles north of the US 84/64 junction on NM 17.

Twin Rivers Trailer Park (© **505/756-2218;** www.twinriversonline.net) has 50 sites and 40 full hookups; phone hookups are offered. Tenting is available, as are laundry facilities, ice, and picnic tables. River swimming and fishing are popular activities; other sports facilities include basketball, volleyball, badminton, and horseshoes. Twin Rivers is open from April 15 to November 15 and is located 100 yards west of the junction of NM 17 and US 84/64.

WHERE TO DINE IN CHAMA

High Country Restaurant and Saloon ⭐ STEAKS/SEAFOOD/NEW MEXICAN This is definitely a country place, with functional furniture, orange vinyl chairs, brown carpet, and a big stone fireplace. But it's *the* place innkeepers recommend, and one traveling couple I spoke to had eaten lunch and dinner here every day of their weeklong stay. The steaks are a big draw here. More sophisticated appetites may like the *trucha con piñon,* trout dusted in flour and cooked with pine nuts, garlic, and shallots. Meals are served with a salad and choice of potato. The New Mexican food is also good. The attached saloon has a full bar and bustles with people eating peanuts and throwing the shells on the floor. Breakfast on Sunday is country-style, with offerings such as steak and eggs and biscuits and gravy topping the menu, as well as pancakes and huevos rancheros (eggs atop tortillas smothered in chile sauce).

Main St. (⅒ mile north of the "Y"). © 505/756-2384. Main courses: $4–$10 breakfast, $6–$12 lunch, $6–$17 dinner. AE, DISC, MC, V. Mon–Sat 11am–10pm; Sun 8am–10pm. Closed Easter, Thanksgiving, and Christmas.

Village Bean ⭐ BAKERY/SANDWICHES Sunny colored walls and lots of space encourage coffee lovers to linger in this new cafe in the center of town. The owner roasts his own coffee beans, so you can count on your espresso, cappuccino, or just plain Joe being tasty. The food follows in the same thoughtful vein. For breakfast, select from a variety of home-baked goods. At lunch, creations such as the Hot and Spicy Pastrami (with cream cheese, provolone, green chiles, and red onions) and the Blue Spruce (with three cheeses, cucumbers, avocado, and sprouts) come on home-baked bread. A variety of soups and salads round out the menu. You can even get boxed lunches to take on Chama outings. Call to see if a Monday night open mic is happening (until 8pm).

425 Terrace Ave. © 505/756-1663. All menu items under $7. No credit cards. Daily 7am–4pm.

Viva Vera's Mexican Kitchen NEW MEXICAN/AMERICAN   A locals' favorite, Vera's serves tasty sauces over rich enchiladas and burritos, followed by fluffy sopaipillas soaked with honey. Some complain that the chile is too hot, but I say bring it on. The setting is pastoral, with fields of gazing horses stretching to the river. The porch is *the* place to sit on warmer days. Inside, the restaurant has a vaulted ceiling, and typical Mexican memorabilia hangs on the walls—even sequined sombreros. The tables are well spaced, and a TV rests in the corner. Beer and wine are served, but the favorite seems to be wine margaritas, frothy and frozen, served in big glasses. For breakfast try the huevos rancheros (eggs atop corn tortillas smothered in chile sauce).

2202 NM 17. © 505/756-2557. Main courses $4–$7 breakfast, $4–$12 lunch and dinner. AE, MC, V. Daily 8am–8pm.

CHAMA AFTER DARK

Summer evenings in Chama now include entertainment beyond watching the river flow in its banks or the beer flow in the local tavern. The Elkhorn Lodge, 2663 S. US 84 (© **800/532-8874** or 505/756-2105; www.elkhornlodge.net), sponsors a **Chuckwagon Cowboy Dinner** Saturday and Sunday evenings. Guests chow down on beef brisket, beans, and corn bread while watching a historical western narrative told through guitar music and singing. Kids like the food and the fun story. Reservations required; contact Elkhorn Lodge. Performances start at 6:30pm, and prices run $16 for adults and $9 for children under 14; under 2 eat free.

ON THE ROAD: WHAT TO SEE & DO ON US 84 SOUTH

Note: For a map of this area, see "Touring the Pueblos Around Santa Fe," in chapter 6.

Distinctive yellow earth provided a name for the town of **Tierra Amarilla,** 14 miles south of Chama at the junction of US 84 and US 64. Throughout New Mexico, this name is synonymous with a continuing controversy over the land-grant rights of the descendants of the original Hispanic settlers. But the economy of this community of 1,000 is dyed in the wool—literally.

The organization *Ganados del Valle* (Livestock Growers of the Valley) is at work to save the longhaired Spanish churro sheep from extinction, to introduce other unusual wool breeds to the valley, and to perpetuate a 200-year-old tradition of shepherding, spinning, weaving, and dyeing. Many of the craftspeople work in conjunction with **Tierra Wools** ⊛, P.O. Box 229, Los Ojos, NM 87551 (© **505/588-7231;** www.handweavers.com), which has a showroom and work-shop in a century-old mercantile building just north of Tierra Amarilla. One-of-a-kind blankets and men's and women's apparel are among the products displayed and sold.

Just down the street, across from the Los Ojos General Store, is an interesting little art studio worth checking out. **Yellow Earth Studio** (© **505/588-7807**), the passion of Paul Trachtman, the resident artist, is a great place to see and purchase enchanting scenes of the Los Ojos area in the form of paintings and monotype, woodcut, and metal engraving prints. His work is part of the permanent collection of the New Mexico State Capitol. Paul will likely be working away in his studio in back, and if you're fortunate, he'll guide you through some of his techniques.

Two state parks are a short drive west from Tierra Amarilla. **El Vado Lake State Park,** 14 miles southwest on NM 112 (© **505/588-7247**), offers boating and water-skiing, fishing, and camping in summer; cross-country skiing and ice fishing in winter. **Heron Lake State Park,** 11 miles west on US 64 and NM 95 (© **505/588-7470**), has a no-wake speed limit for motor vessels, adding to its appeal for fishing, sailing, windsurfing, canoeing, and swimming. The park has an interpretive center, plus camping, picnic sites, hiking trails, and cross-country skiing in the winter. The 5½-mile Rio Chama trail connects the two lakes.

East of Tierra Amarilla, the Rio Brazos cuts a canyon through the Tusas Mountains and around 11,403-foot Brazos Peak. Just north of Los Ojos, NM 512 heads east 7½ miles up the **Brazos Box Canyon.** High cliffs that rise straight from the valley floor give it a Yosemite-like appearance—which is even more apparent from an overlook on US 64, 18 miles east of Tierra Amarilla en route to Taos. **El Chorro,** an impressive waterfall at the mouth of the canyon, usually flows only from early May to mid-June. Several resort lodges are in the area.

About 37 miles south of Tierra Amarilla on US 84, and 3 miles north of Ghost Ranch, is **Echo Canyon Amphitheater** (© **505/684-2486**), a U.S. Forest Service campground and picnic area. The natural "theater," hollowed out of sandstone by thousands of years of erosion, is a natural work of art, with layers of stone in colors ranging from pearl to blood red. The walls send back eerie echoes and even clips of conversations. It's a 10-minute walk from the parking area. The fee is $3. Some 13 miles west of here, via the dirt Forest Service Road 151 into the Chama River Canyon Wilderness, is the isolated **Monastery of Christ in the Desert** (www.christdesert.org), built in 1964 by Benedictine monks. The chapel is a graceful structure set against bold cliffs, worth visiting if you like a taste of solemnity. The brothers produce crafts, sold at a small gift shop, and operate a guesthouse.

Along the same road (FS 151) is access to the Chama River, a good place to hike, mountain bike, kayak, and camp. The **Rim Vista Trail** will take you to the top of the rim, with vast views out across Abiquiu Lake and Ghost Ranch. Primitive campsites can be found all along the river.

A 3-mile drive from there is **Ghost Ranch,** a collection of adobe buildings that make up a study center maintained by the United Presbyterian Church. A number of hauntingly memorable hikes originate from this place, which gets its name from the *brujas,* or witches, said to inhabit the canyons. Most notable among the hikes is **Kitchen Mesa,** directions for which can be obtained at the visitor center. World-renowned painter Georgia O'Keeffe spent time at Ghost Ranch painting these canyons and other land formations. Eventually she bought a portion of the ranch and lived in a humble adobe house there. The ranch now offers seminars on a variety of topics that are open to all.

The **Florence Hawley Ellis Museum of Anthropology** has interpretative exhibits of a Spanish ranch house and Native American anthropology, and the **Ruth Hall Paleontology Museum** (for both museums, contact © **505/685-4333;** www.ghostranch.org) displays fossils of the early dinosaur named coelophysis found on the ranch. A lightly built creature, it was very fast when chasing prey. It roamed the area 250 million years ago, making it the oldest dinosaur found in New Mexico.

Celebrated artist Georgia O'Keeffe spent most of her adult life in **Abiquiu,** a tiny town in a bend of the Rio Chama 14 miles south of the Ghost Ranch, and

22 miles north of Española, on US 84. The inspiration for O'Keeffe's startling landscapes (many of which can now be seen in the Georgia O'Keeffe Museum; p. 153) is clear in the surrounding terrain. **O'Keeffe's adobe home** (where she lived and painted until her death in 1986) is open for public tours, but reservations are required 1 to 2 months in advance (call ✆ **505/685-4539**). The charge is $22 for a 1-hour tour. A number of tours are given each week—on Tuesday, Thursday, and Friday—and a limited number of people are accepted per tour. Visitors are not permitted to take pictures. Fortunately, O'Keeffe's home remains as it was when she lived there.

Many dinosaur skeletons have been found in rocks along the base of cliffs near **Abiquiu Reservoir** (✆ **505/685-4371**), a popular boating and fishing spot formed by the Abiquiu Dam.

A good place to stay in the area is the **Abiquiu Inn,** a small country inn, restaurant, art gallery, and gift shop, half a mile north of the village of Abiquiu (✆ **505/685-4378**). The casitas are especially nice. Rates are $109 to $189.

Heading south from Abiquiu, watch for **Dar al Islam** (✆ **505/685-4515**), a spiritual center with a circular Middle Eastern–style mosque made of adobe; the small community of **Mendanales,** where you'll find the shop of renowned weaver Cordelia Coronado; and **Hernandez,** the village immortalized in Ansel Adams's famous 1941 photograph *Moonrise, Hernandez, New Mexico.*

10

Southwestern New Mexico

The lonely drive from Grants down through Quemado and Reserve to Silver City takes you along excellent but winding roads through the 3.3-million-acre **Gila National Forest,** which contains one of the nation's largest and most spectacular wilderness areas. For me, ruggedness and remoteness define this part of the state—and make it an undiscovered wonder.

It was and still is a good place to hide out. Billy the Kid lived here; so did Geronimo. You'll stumble upon relics of their past at many junctures. You'll see thousands of snow geese taking flight at the **Bosque del Apache National Wildlife Refuge.** You can even contemplate the vastness of space at the **Very Large Array (VLA),** the world's most powerful radio telescope.

Though no large cities are within the area, the most settled part is down the center of the state, where the Rio Grande marks a distinct riparian line. Throughout history, this river has nourished the Native American, Hispanic, and Anglo settlers who have built their homes beside its banks. The river land was especially fertile around modern Las Cruces; the settlement of La Mesilla was southern New Mexico's major center for 3 centuries.

West of the river, the Black Range and Mogollon Mountains rise in the area now cloaked by Gila National Forest. This was the homeland of the Mogollon Indians 1,000 years ago. **Gila Cliff Dwellings National Monument** preserves one of their great legacies. This was also the homeland of the fiercely independent Chiricahua Apaches in the 19th century. Considered the last North American Indians to succumb to the whites, they counted Cochise and Geronimo among their leaders.

Mining and outdoor recreation, centered in historic **Silver City** (pop. 11,508), are now the economic stanchions of the region. But dozens of mining towns have boomed and busted in the past 140 years, as a smattering of ghost towns throughout the region attest.

Las Cruces, at the foot of the Organ Mountains, is New Mexico's second largest city, with 73,600 people. It's a busy agricultural and education center. North up the valley are **Truth or Consequences** (pop. 7,500), a spa town named for the 1950s radio and TV game show, and **Socorro** (pop. 9,000), a historic city with Spanish roots. West, on the I-10 corridor to Arizona, are the ranching centers of **Deming** (pop. 14,500) and **Lordsburg** (pop. 3,010).

1 The Great Outdoors in Southwestern New Mexico

Rugged, remote, forested, and fascinating all describe southwestern New Mexico, where few tourists venture—lucky for you if you're looking for backcountry adventure.

BIKING   A popular cycling area is located in the Socorro area, at **Bosque del Apache National Wildlife Refuge** (© 505/835-1828), where cyclists enjoy the

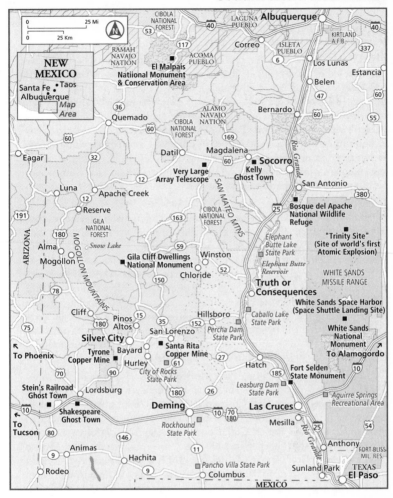

12-mile loop tour. Bikes are not allowed in the Gila Wilderness, but they are permitted on trails in other parts of **Gila National Forest** (© **505/388-8201;** www.fs.fed.us/r3/gila). Refer to "Other Adventures in Gila National Forest," later in this chapter, for some specific ride suggestions and contact **Gila Hike and Bike** (© **505/388-3222**) in Silver City for rentals and guidebooks to riding in the Gila National Forest.

BIRD-WATCHING   **Bosque del Apache National Wildlife Refuge** (© **505/ 835-1828**) is a refuge for migratory waterfowl such as snow geese and cranes. It's located 16 miles south of Socorro. **North Monticello Point** (© **505/744-5421**), located on Elephant Butte Lake, is a great place to see pelicans, bald eagles, and a variety of waterfowl, while **Water Canyon** (© **505/854-2281**), 14 miles west of Socorro in the **Cíbola National Forest,** is home to golden eagles. The **Sevilleta National Wildlife Refuge** (© **505/864-4021**), north of Socorro between La Joya and Chamizal, is a long-term ecological research site under the direction of the National Science Foundation. Its visitor center is open 7:30am to 4pm weekdays, and 9am to 3pm Saturday (closed Sun, Christmas, and New Year's Day) and has exhibits about the refuge. The refuge offers free tours during its open house, the second Saturday in October.

BOATING   In the Gila National Forest, both **Lake Roberts** (© 505/536-2250), about 40 miles north of Silver City on NM 15, and **Snow Lake** (© 505/533-6231), north on US 180 from Silver City and then east on NM 159, allow boating. Lake Roberts features motorboat rentals, whereas Snow Lake only permits canoes, rowboats, and other boats without gas motors.

Elephant Butte Lake State Park (© 505/744-5923) boasts the largest body of water in New Mexico. The lake is 43 miles long and popular with boating enthusiasts. Three ramps provide boating access to the lake, and there are launching areas for smaller vessels. (To find information on New Mexico state parks, go to **www.nmparks.com**.)

FISHING   **Caballo Lake State Park** (© 505/743-3942), located about 18 miles south of Truth or Consequences, offers smallmouth and largemouth bass, stripers, bluegill, crappie, catfish, and walleye fishing in its 11,500-acre lake. **Elephant Butte Lake State Park** (© 505/744-5923), also near Truth or Consequences, is another great fishing location. Look to catch white bass, black bass, catfish, walleye, crappie, and stripers here. **Lake Roberts** (© 505/536-2250), located about 40 miles north of Silver City in the Gila National Forest, is prime rainbow trout fishing waters. A fishing license and habitat stamp are both required. You'll find fly-fishing in the **Gila River** year-round, but the best seasons are spring and fall. Mainly rainbow trout swim these waters, with catfish on the lower Gila. For more information, contact the **New Mexico Game and Fish Department** (© 505/476-8000; www.wildlife.state.nm.us).

GOLF   In Socorro, the 18-hole **New Mexico Tech Golf Course** (© 505/835-5335) offers tree-lined fairways and water on more than half of its holes. The **Truth or Consequences Golf Course** (© 505/894-2603) offers 9 fairly traditional holes in a desert setting. A more contemporary course is in Las Cruces, at the 18-hole **Sonoma Ranch Golf Course** (© 505/521-1818; www.sonomaranchgolf.com), which opened in 2000. Las Cruces also has the **New Mexico State University Golf Course** (© 505/646-3219; www.nmsu.edu/~golf), built with collegiate golf in mind. With wide-spanning views and undulating terrain, this Cal Olsen–designed course has much to offer. Deming has the 18-hole **Rio Mimbres Country Club** (© 505/546-9481), while Silver City golfers go to the 18-hole **Silver City Golf Course** (© 505/538-5041), home to the annual Billy Casper Golf Tournament, where the legend himself returns each year in September (usually Labor Day) to participate.

HIKING   It goes without saying that there's great hiking available in the **Gila National Forest** (© 505/388-8201), which has approximately 1,500 miles of trails, ranging in length and difficulty. Your best bet for hiking in the area is to purchase a guidebook devoted entirely to hiking the Gila National Forest, but popular areas include the Crest Trail, the West Fork Trail, and the Aldo Leopold Wilderness. One favorite day hike in the forest is The Catwalk, a moderately strenuous hike along a series of steel bridges and walkways suspended over Whitewater Canyon. See "Other Adventures in Gila National Forest," later in this chapter, for more hiking suggestions. Whenever and wherever you go hiking, be sure to carry plenty of water.

HORSEBACK RIDING   If you want to go horseback riding in this area, the **Double E Guest Ranch** (© 505/535-2048; www.doubleeranch.com) offers authentic ranch riding in the southwestern New Mexico desert and forest lands. Because the ranch is also a working cattle ranch, it has an authentic feel, and a guest capacity of only 12 adds to the authenticity. Trail rides and cattle drives range across 30,000 acres, which adjoin the legendary 3-million-acre Gila Wilderness. About a half-hour from Silver City, the ranch sits on a shady bend of Bear Creek, a place that draws plenty of wildlife. The accommodations are in old ranch buildings, which range from cozy to expansive. My favorite has old saddles hanging from the rafters. These are not luxury rooms; instead, they're real ranch lodgings. The ranch does not have a separate children's program but does accept kids.

HOT SPRINGS   This is hot springs country. For locations in Truth or Consequences, call © **800/831-9487** or 505/894-3536, or see "Truth or Consequences," later in this chapter for my choices of bathhouses. Near City of Rocks State Park is **Faywood Hot Springs,** 2 miles east of NM 180 (© **505/536-9663;** www.faywood.com), where you can soak in outdoor pools (clothing is required in only one of the pools); massage, camping, and small cabins are available. It's a bit of a hippie kind of place, so if you're a Felix Unger type, you might cringe here. **Lightfeather Hot Spring** is a spring near the Gila Cliff Dwellings National Monument visitor center.

SWIMMING   Swimming is permitted at **Elephant Butte Lake State Park** (© **505/744-5923**) and **Caballo Lake State Park** (© **505/743-3942**), but not at some others. Be sure to ask first.

2 Socorro: Gateway to Bosque del Apache & the VLA

Socorro, a quiet, pleasant town of about 9,000, is an unusual mix of the 19th, 20th, and 21st centuries. Established as a mining settlement and ranching center, its downtown area is dominated by numerous mid-1800s buildings and the 17th-century San Miguel Mission. **The New Mexico Institute of Mining and Technology** (New Mexico Tech) is a major research center. Socorro is also the gateway to a vast and varied two-county region that includes the **Bosque del Apache National Wildlife Refuge,** the **Very Large Array National Radio Astronomy Observatory (VLA),** and three national forests.

ESSENTIALS

GETTING THERE   From Albuquerque, take I-25 south (1¼ hr.). From Las Cruces, take I-25 north (2¾ hr.).

VISITOR INFORMATION   The **Socorro County Chamber of Commerce,** which is also the visitor information headquarters, is located at 101 Plaza (P.O. Box 743), Socorro, NM 87801 (© **505/835-0424;** www.socorro-nm.com).

EXPLORING SOCORRO

The best introduction to Socorro is a walking tour of the historic district. A brochure with a map and guidebook, available at the chamber of commerce on the **plaza,** where the tour begins, points out several historic buildings, many on the National Register of Historic Places. A decent spot to break for lunch, a snack, or just a cup of coffee is **Martha's Black Dog Coffeehouse** (© **505/838-0311**).

You'll definitely want to check out the old **Val Verde Hotel.** Although the hotel is no longer in operation, a restaurant still operates there. If it's lunchtime or dinnertime, the **Val Verde Steak House** (see "Where to Dine in the Socorro Area," below) is a good place to stop.

OTHER ATTRACTIONS

Mineral Museum   Run by the New Mexico Bureau of Geology and Mineral Resources, this museum has the largest geological collection in the state. Its more than 10,000 specimens include mineral samples from all over the world, fossils, mining artifacts, and photographs.

Campus Rd., New Mexico Tech campus. (C) **505/835-5420.** Free admission. Mon–Fri 8am–5pm; Sat–Sun 10am–3pm.

Old San Miguel Mission ★★   Built during the period from 1615 to 1626 but abandoned during the Pueblo Revolt of 1680, this graceful church was subsequently restored, and a new wing was built in 1853. It boasts thick adobe walls, large carved vigas (rafters), and supporting corbel arches. English-language Masses are Saturday at 6pm and Sunday at 9:30 and 11am.

403 El Camino Real NW, 2 blocks north of the plaza. (C) **505/835-1620.** Free admission. Summer Mon–Fri 8am–7:30pm; winter 8am–6:30pm.

SEEING THE SIGHTS NEAR SOCORRO

SOUTH OF SOCORRO   The village of **San Antonio,** the boyhood home of Conrad Hilton, is 10 miles from Socorro via I-25. During the financial panic of 1907, his merchant father, Augustus Hilton, converted part of his store into a rooming house. This gave Conrad his first exposure to the hospitality industry, and he went on to worldwide fame as a hotelier. Only ruins of the store/boardinghouse remain.

WEST OF SOCORRO   US 60, running west to Arizona, is the avenue to several points of interest. **Magdalena,** 27 miles from Socorro, is a mining and ranching town that preserves an 1880s Old West spirit. In mid-November, this little town holds its Fall Festival, which includes a variety of studio tours, artist demonstrations, and a silent auction. If you want to stay in Magdalena, I recommend the **Western Bed and Breakfast & RV Park,** 404 First St. ((C) **505/ 854-2417** or 505/854-2412; www.thewesternmotel.com), a rustic and quaint motel, with pine walls decorating most rooms. Be sure to stop in at **Evetts Cafe** on US 60 ((C) **505/854-2449**) for one of the best milkshakes in New Mexico; order yours made from hand-packed ice cream.

Three miles south, the ghost town of **Kelly** produced more than $40 million worth of lead, zinc, copper, silver, and gold in the late 19th and early 20th centuries. Today, the ghost town is a fun site for a hike.

Thirty-two miles north of Magdalena, on a dead-end road, is the home of the **Alamo Navajo Nation.** On special occasions (particularly during the month of Oct), the public may be allowed to visit the band of 1,400 Navajo who live on this reservation; inquire with the Alamo Chapter office ((C) **505/854-2686**).

Southeast of Magdalena, atop 10,783-foot South Baldy Mountain, the **Langmuir Research Laboratory** studies thunderstorms and atmospheric electricity from June to August. It has a visitor center with exhibits. The research center can be reached by high-clearance vehicles only; visitors should call (C) **505/835-5423** in advance to check on road conditions.

Fifty-four miles west of Socorro via US 60 is the **Very Large Array National Radio Astronomy Observatory (VLA).** (The Socorro office is at 1003 Lopezville Rd. NW; (C) **505/835-7000;** www.nrao.edu.) Here, 27 dish-shaped antennas, each 82 feet in diameter, are spread across the plains of San Agustin, forming a single gigantic radio telescope. Many recognize the site from the 1997 movie *Contact,* starring Jodie Foster. Photographs taken with this apparatus are similar to those taken with the largest optical telescopes, except that radio telescopes are

sensitive to low-frequency radio waves. All types of celestial objects are photographed, including the sun and its planets, stars, quasars, galaxies, and even the
faint remains of the "big bang" that scientists believe occurred some 10 billion
years ago. You begin in the visitor center, viewing an informational film about the
VLA. In the museum, you can see how radio waves can be transformed into space
pictures and why this is such an effective method of exploration. On the outdoor,
self-guided walking tour, you'll have a chance to get a closer look at the massive
antennas. Don't miss the whispering display, where you can sample firsthand how
a dish collects and transmits sound. Admission is free, and visitors are welcomed
daily from 8:30am to sunset.

WHERE TO STAY IN THE SOCORRO AREA

Most accommodations are along California Street, the main highway through
town, or the adjacent I-25 frontage road. Most lodgings provide free parking.

Casa Blanca   The ideal situation in this part of the world is to be just a few
minutes away from the Bosque del Apache. That way, you only have to get out
of bed a half-hour or so before sunup in order to get to the wildlife refuge and
see the morning flight (see "Oasis in the Desert: Bosque del Apache National
Wildlife Refuge," below). Casa Blanca is the place to stay for this reason. It's a
cozy Victorian farmhouse and home to proprietor Phoebe Wood, a former
schoolteacher. The place has a genuine homelike quality—comfortable and well
maintained. The best room is the Crane, light and airy, with a queen-size bed
and private bathroom. Breakfast is simple and can be eaten early, on the way out
to the Bosque, or later, upon your return. Fruit, cereals, and home-baked
muffins are served in a homey kitchen. Smoking is not permitted.

13 Montoya St. (P.O. Box 31), San Antonio, NM 87832. 📞 **505/835-3027.** www.casablancabedand
breakfast.com. 3 units. $70–$90 double. Rates include generous continental breakfast. MC, V. Closed Memorial Day to Labor Day. Pets welcome.

Holiday Inn Express   Like most of the accommodations of this newer chain
of hotels, this two-story inn offers clean, functional rooms and plenty of amenities. Guests can select from two types of rooms here: hotel-style ones opening
off corridors or motel-style ones in which you park your car near your door. All
rooms are medium-size with medium-firm beds and standard-size bathrooms.

1100 California Ave. NE, Socorro, NM 87801. 📞 **888/526-4567** or 505/838-0556. Fax 505/838-0598. www.
hiexpress.com. 120 units. $90 double. Rates include continental breakfast. AE, DISC, MC, V. Pets are welcome
for a $10 1-time fee. **Amenities:** Indoor pool; 2 exercise rooms; indoor/outdoor Jacuzzis. *In room:* A/C, TV,
fridge, coffeemaker, hair dryer, iron, microwave.

CAMPING

Casey's Socorro RV Park (📞 **800/674-2234** or 505/835-2234) offers mountain
and valley views and plenty of shade, as well as 100 sites and 30 full hookups.
Tenting is available, as are picnic tables, grills, and ice. A playground and swimming pool are open year-round. To reach Casey's, take I-25 to exit 147, go 1
block west on Business I-25 and then 1 block south on West Frontage Road.

WHERE TO DINE IN THE SOCORRO AREA

El Sombrero 🉐 NEW MEXICAN   This is a real locals' place. My Socorran
friends call it "the Hat" and always request the garden room, where tables surround a small fountain. This is some of the best New Mexican food around. I
especially enjoy the chicken enchiladas, though my friend Dennis always orders
the spinach ones. They come rolled, with beans, rice, and a sopaipilla. Most popular on the menu are the fajitas, beef or chicken, served with rice, beans, tortillas,

and guacamole. The restaurant is known for its trademark sauces, especially the poblano chile and mole sauces, which are served over enchiladas or meats such as chicken. For dessert, try the churro, a cinnamon sugared stick with vanilla ice cream. Beer and wine are available.

210 Mesquite NE., Socorro. ⟨ 505/835-3945. Main courses $4–$11 lunch and dinner. AE, DC, DISC, MC, V. Daily 11am–9pm.

Owl Bar and Cafe AMERICAN   A low-lit tavern in a one-story adobe building, 7 miles south of Socorro, the Owl was once *the* place to stop for a green chile cheeseburger. Unfortunately, this is no longer the case. The burgers are mediocre, at best, but it's a decent refreshment stop en route. Breakfasts offer such standards as eggs and pancakes.

NM 1 and US 380, San Antonio. ⟨ 505/835-9946. Main courses $3–$8 breakfast and lunch, $6–$14 dinner. AE, DISC, MC, V. Mon–Sat 8am–9:30pm.

Socorro Springs Brewing Company ⟨ PIZZA/SANDWICHES/SALADS This little pocket of sophistication is a nice addition to small-town Socorro. On most any day, the place is full of happy diners sampling the brew and eating some pretty tasty wood-oven cuisine. It's a casual place with a brewpub atmosphere. The service is congenial though not quick. You may choose from salads and sandwiches, calzones and pizzas. I sampled the "tomato del sol," which isn't the best choice as it lacked zest. A better choice is the "bandido," with pepperoni, Italian sausage, prosciutto, and jalapeños, or the "vigilante," with artichoke hearts, chicken, and Kalamata olives. The beer is nice, with a bit of a smoky taste.

115 Abeyta Ave., Socorro. (at this writing, the restaurant was slated to move; call for the new address). ⟨ 505/838-0650. Reservations accepted. Main courses $5–$7 lunch and dinner. AE, DISC, MC, V. Daily 11am–10pm.

Val Verde Steak House ⟨ AMERICAN   Whenever my dad is traveling south, this is where he stops to eat; he has very good taste, so I often follow his recommendations. The restaurant is housed in the horseshoe-shaped Val Verde Hotel, a National Historic Landmark, built in 1919 in California Mission style. The hotel has been converted to apartments, but the public can still enjoy the old dining room. Lunch menu items are simple but tasty: homemade soups, salads, and sandwiches, plus steaks and seafood. A lunch buffet offers a different theme every day, from Mexican to country-style barbecue. Dinner is more elaborate, with dishes such as a 10-oz. top sirloin or an extravagant 16-oz. chateaubriand. Gourmet Southwestern dishes are also served. The nightclub is open daily until midnight, depending on the crowd, and until 1am on Friday and Saturday, when there's live music.

203 Manzanares Ave., Socorro. ⟨ 505/835-3380. Reservations recommended. Main courses $4.50–$13 lunch, $9–$39 dinner. AE, DC, DISC, MC, V. Mon–Fri 11am–2pm; Sun–Thurs 5:30–9pm; Fri–Sat 5–9:30pm. Closed Christmas and July 4.

3 Oasis in the Desert: Bosque del Apache National Wildlife Refuge

By Ian Wilker

The barren lands to either side of I-25 south of Albuquerque seem hardly fit for rattlesnakes, much less one of the Southwest's greatest concentrations of wildlife. The plants that do find purchase in the parched washes and small canyons along the road—forbiddingly named hardies such as creosote bush, tarbush, and white thorn—serve notice that you are indeed within the northernmost finger of the great Chihuahuan Desert, which covers southern New Mexico and southwestern Texas, and runs deep into Mexico.

However, to the east of the interstate is the green-margined Rio Grande. In the midst of such a blasted landscape, the river stands out as an inviting beacon to wildlife, and nowhere does it shine more brightly than at Bosque del Apache's 7,000 acres of carefully managed riparian habitat, which includes marshlands, meadows, agricultural fields, arrow-weed thickets on the riverbanks, and big old-growth cottonwoods lining what were once the oxbows of the river. The refuge supports a riot of wildlife, including all the characteristic mammals and reptiles of the Southwest (mule deer, jackrabbits, and coyotes are common) and about 377 species of birds.

A visit here during the peak winter season—from November to March—is one of the most consistently thrilling wildlife spectacles you can see anywhere in the lower 48 states, especially if you're an avid bird-watcher. Bosque del Apache is, you might say, the LAX of the Central Flyway, one of four paths that migratory birds follow every year between their summer breeding grounds in the tundral north and wintering grounds in the southern United States, Mexico, even as far away as South America—and many of these birds either stop over here to recharge their batteries or settle down for the winter.

It is not enough to say that hundreds of species of birds are on hand. The wonder is in the sheer numbers of them: In early December the refuge may harbor as many as 45,000 snow geese, 57,000 ducks of many different species, and 18,000 sandhill cranes—huge, ungainly birds that nonetheless have a special majesty in flight, pinkish in the sun at dawn or dusk. Plenty of raptors are also about—numerous red-tailed hawks and northern harriers (sometimes called marsh hawks), Cooper's hawks and kestrels, and even bald and golden eagles—as well as Bosque del Apache's many year-round avian residents: pheasants and quail, wild turkeys, and much mythologized roadrunners (*El Paisano,* in Mexican folklore). The interest of experienced birders will be whetted by the presence of Mexican mallards, Chihuahuan ravens, burrowing owls, rare grebes, beautiful, long-billed American avocets, and especially whooping cranes (a very few remain from an experiment to imprint the migratory path of sandhills on whoopers). Everyone will be mesmerized by the huge societies of sandhills, ducks, and geese, going about their daily business of feeding, gabbling, quarreling, honking, and otherwise making an immense racket.

The refuge has a 12-mile auto tour loop, which you should drive very slowly; the south half of the loop travels past numerous water impoundments, where the majority of the ducks and geese hang out, and the north half has the meadows and farmland, where you'll see the roadrunners and other land birds, and where the cranes and geese feed from midmorning through the afternoon.

A few special experiences bear further explanation. Dawn is definitely the best time to be here—songbirds are far more active in the first hours of the day, and the cranes and geese take flight en masse. This last is not to be missed. Dusk, when the birds return to the water, is also a good time. At either dawn or dusk, find your way to one of the observation decks and wait for what birders call the "fly out" (off the water to the fields) or "fly in" (from the fields to the water).

Don't despair if you can't be at the Bosque del Apache during the prime winter months, for it's a special place any time of year. By April, the geese and ducks have flown north, and the refuge drains the water impoundments to allow the marsh plants to regenerate; the resulting mud flats are an ideal feeding ground for the migrating shorebirds that arrive in April and May.

If you'd like to stretch your legs a bit, check out the **Chupadera Peak Trail,** which follows a 2-mile loop or a 9.5-mile loop to a high point overlooking the refuge. Ask for directions at the visitor center.

JUST THE FACTS   The Bosque del Apache National Wildlife Refuge is about a 1½-hour drive from Albuquerque. Follow I-25 for 9 miles south of Socorro, then take the San Antonio exit. At the main intersection of San Antonio, turn south onto NM 1. In 3 miles, you'll be on refuge lands, and another 4 miles will bring you to the excellent visitor center, which has a small museum with inter-pretive displays and a large shelf of field guides, natural histories, and other books of interest for visitors to New Mexico. The visitor center is open from 7:30am to 4pm weekdays, and from 8am to 4:30pm weekends. The refuge itself is open daily year-round from 1 hour before sunrise to 1 hour after sunset. Admission is $3 per vehicle. For more information, contact **Bosque del Apache National Wildlife Refuge,** P.O. Box 1246, Socorro, NM 87801 (© **505/835-1828**).

4 Truth or Consequences

Originally known as Hot Springs, after the therapeutic mineral springs bubbling up near the river, the town took the name Truth or Consequences—usually shortened to "T or C"—in 1950. That was the year that Ralph Edwards, pro-ducer of the popular radio and television program *Truth or Consequences,* began his weekly broadcast with these words: "I wish that some town in the United States liked and respected our show so much that it would like to change its name to Truth or Consequences." The reward to any city willing to do so was to become the site of the 10th-anniversary broadcast of the program, which would put it on the national map in a big way. The locals voted for the name change, which has survived three protest elections over the years.

Although the TV program was canceled decades ago, Ralph Edwards continued to return for the annual **Truth or Consequences Fiesta,** the first weekend of May. (Now that he's in his 90s, he no longer attends.) Another popular annual festival is **Geronimo Days,** the second weekend of October. Despite its festive roots, T or C seems to have an identity crisis—perhaps a consequence of giving up your name for the fame and fortune of television. The city displays a forlorn quality, possibly due to the struggling economy. However, in recent years, a few of the bathhouses have undergone renovation, so there may be hope. Overall, you'll want to visit here to explore the strangeness of a town that traded away its identity.

ESSENTIALS

GETTING THERE   From Albuquerque, take I-25 south (2½ hr.). From Las Cruces, take I-25 north (1¼ hr.). Though no commercial flight service exists, those who fly themselves may contact the **Truth or Consequences Municipal Airport,** Old North Highway 85 (© **505/894-6199**).

VISITOR INFORMATION   The **visitor information center** is at the corner of Main Street (Business Loop 25) and Foch Street in downtown Truth or Con-sequences. Also located there is the **Truth or Consequences & Sierra County Chamber of Commerce,** P.O. Drawer 31, Truth or Consequences, NM 87901 (© **505/894-3536;** www.truthorconsequencesnm.net).

CITY LAYOUT   This year-round resort town and retirement community of 7,500 is spread along the Rio Grande between the Elephant Butte and Caballo reservoirs, two of the three largest bodies of water in the state. Business Loop 25 branches off from I-25 to wind through the city, splitting into Main Street (one-way west) and South Broadway (one-way east) in the downtown area. Third Avenue connects T or C with the Elephant Butte resort community, 5 miles east.

TAKING THE WATERS AT THE HISTORIC HOT SPRINGS

The town's "original" attraction is its hot springs. The entire downtown area is located over a table of odorless hot mineral water, 98°F to 115°F (37°–46°C), that bubbles to the surface through wells or pools. The first bathhouse was built in the 1880s; most of the half-dozen historic spas operating today date from the 1930s. Generally open from morning to early evening, these spas welcome visitors for soaks and massages. Baths of 20 minutes or longer start at $5 per person.

The chamber of commerce has information on all the local spas (see "Essentials," above). Among them is **Sierra Grande Lodge & Spa,** 501 McAdoo St. (© **505/894-6976;** www.sierragrandelodge.com), where Geronimo himself is rumored to have taken a break. (See "Where to Stay in & Around Truth or Consequences," below.) **Artesian Bath House,** 312 Marr St. (© **505/894-2684**), is quite clean and has an RV park on the premises.

I highly recommend the **Hay-Yo-Kay Hot Springs** ✦, 300 Austin St. (© **505/894-2228;** www.hay-yo-kay.com). It has natural-flow pools (versus tubs filled with spring water). The tub rooms are private and gracefully tiled. The Long House, a cooler tub, is the largest in town and can hold up to 20 people. Hay-Yo-Kay is open in the summer Wednesday through Friday 4 to 8pm, weekends from noon to 8pm. Winter hours (September to May) are Wednesday through Friday 10am to 7pm, weekends from noon to 7pm. Hours on Monday holidays are from noon to 7pm. Massages and reflexology are also available.

A MUSEUM IN T OR C

Geronimo Springs Museum   Outside this museum is Geronimo's Spring, where the great Apache shaman is said to have taken his warriors to bathe their battle wounds. Turtleback Mountain, looming over the Rio Grande east of the city, is believed to have been sacred to Native Americans.

Exhibits include prehistoric Mimbres pottery (A.D. 950–1250); the Spanish Heritage Room, updated and renovated, featuring artifacts of the first families of Sierra County; and artists' work, including historical murals and sculptured bronzes. An authentic miner's cabin has been moved here from the nearby mountains. The Ralph Edwards Wing contains the history and highlights of the annual fiestas and celebrates the city's name change, including television footage from the shows filmed in T or C. The museum is geothermally heated.

211 Main St. © 505/894-6600. Admission $3 adults, $1.50 students; family rates available. DISC, MC, V. Mon–Sat 9am–5pm.

GETTING OUTSIDE

Elephant Butte Lake State Park encompasses New Mexico's largest body of water, with 36,500 lake surface acres. It is one of the most popular state parks in New Mexico, attracting watersports enthusiasts and fishers from throughout the south and central regions of the state. Fishing for white bass, black bass, catfish, walleye, crappie, and stripers goes on year-round. Trout are stocked in the Rio Grande below Elephant Butte Dam. The park has sandy beaches for tanning and swimming (though don't expect the white sands of the Cayman Islands here). My favorite beach, called Cow Camp, has a small pier that's good for diving. You can also find boating, sailing, water-skiing, windsurfing, jet-skiing, scuba diving, nature trails, and camping. Beware of going to the lake on summer weekends—4th of July and Labor Day weekend in particular—when the crowds are overwhelming. However, in the other seasons and during the week in summer, it's a quiet place.

Bird-watchers also enjoy the park, spotting hundreds of species, including bald eagles, great blue herons, and more than 20 species of duck during migrations in spring and fall. The lake was named for a huge rock formation that makes an island; before the inundation that created the lake, it clearly looked like an elephant. Today, it's partially submerged.

The park is about 5 miles north of Truth or Consequences via I-25. For more information on the park, call ℂ **505/744-5923.**

About 18 miles south of Truth or Consequences via I-25 is another recreation area, **Caballo Lake State Park** (ℂ **505/743-3942**), which, like Elephant Butte, has year-round watersports, fishing, swimming, and campsites. The lofty ridge of the Caballo Mountains just to the east of the lake makes a handsome backdrop. Park facilities include a full-service marina with a shop for boaters and full hookups for recreational vehicles.

Reached from the same exit off I-25 is yet another recreation area, **Percha Dam State Park** (ℂ **505/743-3942**), a lovely shaded spot under great cottonwood trees, part of the ancient *bosque,* or woods, the Spanish found bordering the Rio Grande when they first arrived in this area in the 1530s. The dam here diverts river water for irrigation. The park offers campsites, restrooms and showers, hiking trails, and access to fishing.

EXPLORING THE GHOST TOWNS IN THE AREA

NORTH OF TRUTH OR CONSEQUENCES   About 40 miles from Truth or Consequences are the precarious remains of Winston and Chloride, two so-called ghost towns—abandoned mining centers that nevertheless do have a few residents. Exploring these towns makes for a nice side trip off I-25. You may want to include a visit to the Very Large Array and the old mining town of Magdalena in the trip (see "Socorro: Gateway to Bosque del Apache & the VLA," earlier in this chapter). However, be aware that if you do, much of the journey from Winston to the VLA is on graded dirt road.

Winston, 37 miles northwest of Truth or Consequences on NM 52, was abandoned in the early 1900s when silver prices dropped and local mining became unprofitable. Some of the original structures from that era are still standing. A similar fate befell **Chloride,** 5 miles west of Winston on a side road off NM 52, where famed silver mines had such names as Nana, Wall Street, and Unknown. Chloride also figured in many battles in the turn-of-the-20th-century war between cattle-ranching and sheep-ranching interests. In the very center of town is the "hanging tree," where the town used to tie drunks to "dry" in the sun.

SOUTH OF TRUTH OR CONSEQUENCES   Thirty-two miles from Truth or Consequences, via I-25 south to NM 152, then west, is **Hillsboro** ⊛, another ghost town that's fast losing its ghosts to a small invasion of artists and craftspeople, antiques shops, and galleries. This town boomed after an 1877 gold strike nearby, and during its heyday it produced $6 million in silver and gold. It was the county seat from 1884 to 1938. Hillsboro's Labor Day weekend **Apple Festival** is famous throughout the state.

The **Black Range Historical Museum** (ℂ **505/895-5233** or 505/895-5685) contains exhibits and artifacts from Hillsboro's mining boom. Located in the former Ocean Grove Hotel, a turn-of-the-20th-century brothel operated by Sadie Orchard, the museum collection includes some of the madam's effects. This volunteer-staffed museum is supposed to be open Wednesday through Saturday from 11am to 4pm, Sunday from 1 to 5pm, but it isn't always. It's closed most major holidays. Suggested donation is $2 for adults, $1 for children, and $5 for a family.

The **Enchanted Villa** bed-and-breakfast inn, ¼ mile west of Hillsboro on NM 152 (no street address), P.O. Box 456, Hillsboro, NM 88042 (☎ **505/895-5686**), is a 1941 adobe that offers decent accommodations. The rates, $84 for a double and $55 for a single, include full hot breakfasts.

Nine miles west of Hillsboro on NM 152, just after you've entered the Gila National Forest, is **Kingston,** born with a rich silver strike in 1880 and reputed to have been among the wildest mining towns in the region, with 7,000 people, 22 saloons, a notorious red-light district (conveniently located on Virtue Ave.), and an opera house. Kingston was also once the home of Albert Fall, a U.S. secretary of state who gained notoriety for his role in the Teapot Dome Scandal.

Your headquarters in Kingston should be the **Black Range Lodge,** 119 Main St., Kingston, NM 88042 (☎ **505/895-5652;** www.blackrangelodge.com), a rustic stone lodge that dates from the 1880s, and over the years has housed miners and soldiers, as well as Pretty Sam's Casino and the Monarch Saloon. The lodge has seven rooms—all with private bathrooms and some with private balconies—a large game room with a pool table and video games, and family suites, as well as a new luxury guesthouse. I recommend the rooms on the north side of the building because they have windows that open to the outside rather than the greenhouse. Life here is relaxed and homey. You may want to bring your own food to prepare in the family-style kitchen. Breakfast is provided—fresh-baked bread, cereals, and health-conscious additions such as soy milk and herbal teas. Rates are $69 for a double, with multiple-night discounts; the guest house is $120 per night. Well-behaved pets are welcome for a $5 one-time fee.

Among historic buildings in Kingston are the brick assay office, the **Victorio Hotel,** and the **Percha Bank,** now a museum open by appointment—ask at Black Range Lodge. The town bell in front of the Volunteer Fire Department was once used to warn residents of Native American attacks. Nearby, **Camp Shiloh** has a public outdoor swimming pool that's open in summer (again, ask at the lodge). Also ask about the mountain bike and hiking trails in the area. I biked two of them, one going north, which climbed through the pines, and another that followed a creek to the west. **Emory Pass** (20 min. on NM 152) is your driving route to a 10-mile round-trip Hillsboro Peak hike.

WHERE TO STAY IN & AROUND TRUTH OR CONSEQUENCES

Best Western Hot Springs Inn   This freeway-exit motel lives up to the Best Western standard, with spacious, comfortable rooms in a quiet setting. All accommodations are medium-size, with up-to-date furnishings, medium-size baths, and plenty of amenities. K-Bob's steakhouse is adjacent.

2270 N. Date St. (at I-25 Exit 79), Truth or Consequences, NM 87901. ☎ 800/528-1234 or 505/894-6665. Fax 505/894-6665. www.bestwestern.com. 41 units. Winter $55–$58 double; summer $58–$64 double. AE, DC, DISC, MC, V. **Amenities:** Outdoor seasonal pool. *In room:* A/C, TV, fridge, coffeemaker.

Elephant Butte Inn ✿   This hotel offers a comfortable stay and a unique experience. It sits above Elephant Butte Lake and has panoramic views as well as a relaxing resortlike feel. Recent years have brought a complete face-lift to the whole place. It caters to boaters, fishers, and other relaxation lovers. Rooms are standard size, furnished with medium-firm king- or queen-size beds. Bathrooms are small but functional. I recommend the lakeside view, where a big grassy lawn stretches down to tennis courts. The pool was recently remodeled and is now heated. For golfers, packages are available that include greens fees at the nearby Truth or Consequences Golf Course.

NM 195 (P.O. Box 996), Elephant Butte, NM 87935. ℂ **505/744-5431.** Fax 505/744-5044. www.elephant butteinn.com. 48 units. Mid-Sept to Apr $70–$100 double; May to early Sept $75–$90 double. AE, DC, DISC, MC, V. **Amenities:** Restaurant; outdoor pool; limited room service. *In room:* A/C, TV, coffeemaker, hair dryer, iron.

Sierra Grande Lodge & Spa 🐾🐾   This resort provides a sensual oasis in southern New Mexico. The biggest draw is the springs. Nowhere else in the state can you stay in luxury while partaking of warm, healing waters rich in minerals. The medium-size rooms in this renovated 1920s lodge have refined, handcrafted furnishings, and many have balconies. Suites have in-room Jacuzzis. A special casita with its own outdoor tub is so popular it's reserved months in advance. When it opened, *Condé Nast Traveler* placed the lodge's restaurant (open seasonally) on its list of the world's 50 top new restaurants. It serves bistro-style cuisine in a city-chic atmosphere (see "Where to Dine in & Around Truth or Consequences," below).

501 McAdoo St., Truth or Consequences, NM 87901. ℂ **505/894-6976.** www.sierragrandelodge.com. 17 units. $65–$95 double Tues–Thurs; $95–$125 double Fri–Mon; $200 suite. AE, DISC, MC, V. **Amenities:** Restaurant (p. 317); 4 hot mineral baths; spa; massage. *In room:* A/C, TV, DVD player upon request, dataport, hair dryer.

CAMPING

Elephant Butte Lake State Park (ℂ **505/744-5923**) welcomes backpackers and RVs alike, with 200 developed campsites, 150 RV hookups, picnic tables, and access points for swimming, hiking, boating, and fishing. Kids love the playground.

Not far from Elephant Butte Lake is **Monticello Point RV Park** (ℂ **505/894-6468**), which offers tenting and 69 sites with full hookups. Laundry and grocery facilities are also on the premises, as are restrooms with showers. To reach Monticello Point, take I-25 to exit 89, and proceed 5½ miles east on the paved road—follow the signs.

Lakeside RV Park and Lodging (ℂ **505/744-5996**), also near Elephant Butte, has 50 sites, two overflow sites (all 52 are full hookups), as well as a recreation room with cable and laundry facilities. When you are headed south on I-25, the RV park is located 4 miles southeast of the I-25 and NM 195 junction (exit 83) on NM 195. To reach the RV park when you're headed north on I-25, take I-25 to exit 79, go half a mile east on the paved road, 1½ miles north on NM 181, then 1½ miles east on NM 171, and finally ¼ mile south on NM 195.

Camping is also available at **Caballo Lake State Park** and **Percha Dam State Park.** For information on either park, call ℂ **505/743-3942** or visit **www.nm parks.com**.

WHERE TO DINE IN & AROUND TRUTH OR CONSEQUENCES

La Cocina 🧒 NEW MEXICAN/AMERICAN   A real locals' place, this restaurant serves decent New Mexican food in a festive atmosphere. The *tostadas* (crispy tortillas covered with beans and meat) and chile rellenos are tasty, but my favorite is the cheese enchiladas. Even better still are the huge sopaipillas. Kids like the big booths and their own quesadillas and tacos.

1 Lakeview Dr. (at Date St.). ℂ **505/894-6499.** Reservations recommended on weekends. Main courses $7–$19 lunch and dinner. DISC, MC, V. Mon–Thurs 10:30am–10pm in summer, 10:30am–9pm in winter; Fri–Sun 10:30am–10pm year-round.

Los Arcos Steak & Lobster 🐾 AMERICAN   A favorite of my father's, this spacious hacienda-style restaurant fronted by a lovely desert garden is intimate and friendly in atmosphere, as if you're at an old friend's home. Its steaks are regionally famous; my choice is always the filet mignon, served with salad and choice of potato or rice. The fish dishes are also good. You may want to try a fresh catch, such as walleye pike or catfish, served on the weekends. The restaurant also has a fine dessert list and cordial selection. During warmer months, diners enjoy the outdoor patio.

1400 Date St. ⓒ **505/894-6200.** Main courses $10–$40. AE, DC, DISC, MC, V. Sun–Thurs 5–9:30pm, Fri–Sat 5–10:30pm.

Pacific Grill *(Finds (Kids* SEAFOOD   In a festive tropical atmosphere, with palms and ceiling fans, this restaurant serves decent fish prepared inventively. It's a good family spot or a fun place for a night out with friends. Service is friendly but overworked. Though the fish is brought to the restaurant frozen, the preparations make it seem fresh. I enjoyed lemon pepper salmon, and my friend opted for island-style sweet-and-sour chicken (the menu has some chicken, beef, and pork selections).

304 S. Pershing St. (behind the State National Bank). ⓒ **505/894-7687.** Main courses $5–$18 lunch and dinner. AE, DISC, MC, V. Mon–Sat 11am–2pm and 5–8pm.

Sierra Grande ⭐⭐⭐ NEW AMERICAN/BISTRO   Amazing! That's my reaction to finding this oasis in the middle of New Mexico's sparse Sonoran desert. Saltillo tile floors, contemporary wall sconces, and a stained-glass mural of Elephant Butte Dam give the place, set in the Sierra Grande Lodge & Spa, a warm and refreshingly sophisticated feel. The eclectic menu changes seasonally. Try delicacies such as achiote shrimp salad or a crawfish cake for starters. For entrees I've enjoyed the pistachio-crusted rack of lamb served with root vegetable mashed potatoes. I've also liked the olive-crusted salmon with herbed Mediterranean couscous. If you're looking for a lighter meal, you can order entrees "simply grilled." Service is attentive and, some nights, a tarot card reader will do a reading for you (for an extra fee). For dessert, try the Mexican pressed chocolate cake, with a hint of red chile in it. A good wine list accompanies the menu.

In the Sierra Grande Lodge & Spa, 501 McAdoo St. ⓒ **505/894-6976.** www.sierragrandelodge.com. Main courses $15–$25. AE, DISC, MC, V. Wed–Sun 5–10pm.

5 Las Cruces

Picture a valley full of weathered wooden crosses marking graves of settlers brutally murdered by Apaches, behind them mountains with peaks so jagged they resemble organ pipes. Such was the scene that caused people to begin calling this city Las Cruces, meaning "the crosses." Even today, the place has a mysterious presence, its rich history haunting it still. Reminders of characters such as Billy the Kid, who was sentenced to death in this area, and Pancho Villa, who spent time here, are present throughout the region.

Established in 1849 on El Camino Real, the "royal highway" between Santa Fe and Mexico City, Las Cruces became a supply center for miners prospecting the Organ Mountains and soldiers stationed at nearby Fort Selden. Today, it is New Mexico's second-largest urban area, with 73,600 people. It is noted as an agricultural center, especially for its cotton, pecans, and chiles; as a regional transportation hub; and as the gateway to the White Sands Missile Range and other defense installations.

Las Cruces manages to survive within a desert landscape that gets only 8 inches of moisture a year, pulling enough moisture from the Rio Grande, which runs through, to irrigate a broad swath of valley.

ESSENTIALS

GETTING THERE From Albuquerque, take I-25 south (4 hr.). From El Paso, take I-10 north (¾ hr.). From Tucson, take I-25 east (5 hr.).

Las Cruces International Airport (© **505/524-2762;** www.las-cruces.org/ airport), 8 miles west, has service several times daily to and from Albuquerque on **Mesa Airlines** (© **800/MESA-AIR** or 505/326-3338; www.mesa-air.com). **El Paso International Airport** (© **915/772-4271;** www.elpasointernational airport.com), 47 miles south, has daily flights to Albuquerque, Phoenix, Dallas, and Houston, among other cities. The **Las Cruces Shuttle Service,** P.O. Box 3172, Las Cruces, NM 88003 (© **800/288-1784** or 505/525-1784; www.las crucesshuttle.com), provides service between the El Paso airport and Las Cruces. It leaves Las Cruces 12 times daily between 5am and 9:30pm for a charge of $30 one-way or $46 round-trip per person, with large discounts for additional pas-sengers traveling together. A $7 charge is added for pickup or drop-off at places other than its regular stops at major hotels. Connections can also be made three times a day from Las Cruces to Deming and Silver City.

VISITOR INFORMATION The **Las Cruces Convention and Visitors Bureau** is at 211 N. Water St., Las Cruces, NM 88001 (© **877/266-8252** or 505/541-2444; www.lascrucescvb.org). The **Greater Las Cruces Chamber of Commerce,** 760 W. Picacho St., can be reached by writing P.O. Drawer 519, Las Cruces, NM 88004; calling © **505/524-1968;** or visiting **www.lascruces.org**.

WHAT TO SEE & DO IN LAS CRUCES

On a hot day, when the church bells are ringing and you're wandering the brick streets of **Mesilla** 🟊🟊, you may for a moment slip back into the late 16th cen-tury—or certainly feel as though you have. This village on Las Cruces's south-western flank was established in the late 1500s by Mexican colonists. It became the crossroads of El Camino Real and the Butterfield Overland Mail route. The Gads-den Purchase, which annexed Mesilla to the United States and fixed the current international boundaries of New Mexico and Arizona, was signed here in 1854.

Mesilla's most notorious resident, William Bonney, otherwise known as Billy the Kid, was sentenced to death at the county courthouse here. He was sent back to Lincoln, New Mexico, to be hanged, but escaped before the sentence was car-ried out. Legendary hero Pat Garrett eventually tracked down and killed The Kid at Fort Sumner; later, Garrett was mysteriously murdered in an arroyo just outside Las Cruces. He is buried in the local Masonic cemetery.

Thick-walled adobe buildings, which once protected residents against Apache attacks, now house art galleries, restaurants, museums, and gift shops. Through-out Mesilla, colorful red-chile ristras decorate homes and businesses. On Sunday during the summer locals sell crafts and baked goods, and mariachi bands play.

A WALKING TOUR OF MESILLA

This is a fun and easy jaunt that will familiarize you with the history and archi-tecture of this interesting village. Depending on how curious you are, it could take from a half-hour to 2 hours. Begin at the **San Albino Church** (see "Other Attractions," below). From here you can get a view of the plaza and even peek down the side streets leading away, where some of the old adobe houses have been restored and painted bold pinks and greens. Head east on Calle de Santi-ago until you come to **Silver Assets** (© **505/523-8747**). Located in the old Valles Gallegos building (1850s), it was once a carpentry shop and now sells jew-elry and native crafts.

Turn south on Avenida de Mesilla and go to the **Mesilla Visitor Center,** 2340 Avenida de Mesilla (✆ **505/647-9698**), where you'll find period photos and plenty of brochures on the area, as well as clean public restrooms. Continue south to Boutz Street. Turn east, and you'll come to the **Gadsden Museum,** a grand old house full of memorabilia but only open intermittently (see "Other Attractions," below). In the back of the museum parking lot is a replica of the old Mesilla jail, a dismal storage shed with original jail doors that once helped to incarcerate Billy the Kid.

Travel back west along Boutz Street and you'll come to a little cluster of shops at the corner of Avenida de Mesilla and Calle de Parian. This 1860s building housed the customs house for the area. The shops in the complex are great for browsing.

Continuing west on Calle de Parian, you'll come to the **William Bonney Gallery** (✆ **505/526-8275**). Here you'll find some nice local paintings as well as lovely pottery and kachinas. Across the street is **La Posta de Mesilla** restaurant, a decent place to stop for a meal (see "Where to Dine in & Around Las Cruces," later in this section), though not the best in the area. The building dates from the mid-18th century and is the only surviving stagecoach station of the Butterfield Overland Mail route from Missouri to San Francisco. Kit Carson, Pancho Villa, and Billy the Kid were all here.

Then continue west around the plaza to the **Nambé Showroom** (✆ **505/527-4623**), a shop displaying handcrafted tableware by Nambé Mills in Santa Fe. It's a great place to shop for gifts. On the southwest corner of the plaza is the oldest documented brick building in New Mexico, built by Augustin Maurin in 1860. It has a sad history of its proprietors being murdered by robbers.

Continue north along the plaza and be sure to stop at the **Bowlin's Mesilla Book Center** (✆ **505/526-6220**). Housed in a historic mercantile building (ca. 1856), the building has tall ceilings with elaborate vigas and latillas. The bookstore has a strong selection of Southwestern books and children's titles. A few doors down is **El Platero** (✆ **505/523-5561**), a store that sells mostly tourist trinkets but also large snow cones, perfect to cool you off after a walking tour. If you'd like a more adult treat, head across the plaza to **Stahmann's on the Plaza,** 2329 Calle de Guadalupe (✆ **505/527-0667**). A retail outlet for the notable Stahmann Farms goods, the shop sells cookies, pecan candy, and just plain, but delicious, pecans. Chocolate lovers will find hand-dipped bon bons and homemade ice cream at **J. Eric Chocolatier,** 2379 Calle de Guadalupe (✆ **505/526-2744**).

If you prefer a guided historic walking tour, contact **Preciliana Sandoval,** 2488 Calle Principal (behind El Patio Bar) (✆ **505/647-2639**). This bold artist/historian, a fifth-generation Mesilla Valley native, will regale you with stories of ghosts and historic battles in the area. Tours cost $10 per person and take about one hour.

PLACES OF NOTE IN HISTORIC LAS CRUCES

Though it has a much less romantic atmosphere than Mesilla, downtown Las Cruces has a few historical buildings, which make visiting it worthwhile. If you'd like to do a walking tour of the area, pick up a map at the **Las Cruces Convention and Visitors Bureau** at 211 N. Water St.

Central to the area is the **Bicentennial Log Cabin,** Main Street and Lucero Avenue, Downtown Mall (✆ **505/541-2155**). The cabin, which was built around 1850 and moved to Las Cruces from the Black Range Mountains, contains authentic furnishings and artifacts. This municipal museum is open year-round by appointment. Nearby is the **Branigan Cultural Center,** 500 N. Water

St. (© 505/541-2155). This museum features traveling and local exhibits of art and local history, and it presents performing arts, educational programs, and special events. Next door, on the mall, is the **Museum of Fine Arts and Culture,** 490 N. Water St. (© 505/541-2137), which houses galleries, art studios, and classrooms. The museum is open Tuesday through Friday from 10am to 2pm and Saturday from 9am to 1pm. The rest of the mall doesn't offer much except on Saturday in summer, when one of the best growers' markets in the area sets up—well worth browsing through.

OTHER ATTRACTIONS

Gadsden Museum   A famous painting of the signing of the Gadsden Purchase is a highlight of this collection, from the Albert Jennings Fountain family. The museum, 3 blocks east of the Old Mesilla Plaza in the 1875 Fountain family home, also houses Indian and Civil War relics and Old West artifacts. All visitors go on the museum's guided tour.

1875 Boutz Rd. © 505/526-6293. Admission $2 adults, $1 children 6–12; free for children under 6. Call for hours.

Las Cruces Museum of Natural History *(Kids*   This small city-funded museum offers a variety of exhibits, changed quarterly, that emphasize science and natural history. The museum features live animals of the Chihuahuan Desert, hands-on science activities, and a small native plant garden. The Cenozoic Shop offers scientific toys and books about the region. Exhibits, such as "Insects and Bugs," change every few months. In summer 2004, the museum hosted an exhibit titled "Our Vanishing Sky."

Mesilla Valley Mall, 700 S. Telshor. © 505/522-3120. Free admission. Mon–Thurs and Sat 10am–5pm; Fri 10am–8pm; Sun 1–5pm.

New Mexico Farm and Ranch Heritage Museum   Having grown up on a New Mexico ranch, I was anxious to see how the Western lifestyle would be presented in this museum. This is a 47-acre interactive museum that brings to life the 3,000-year history of farming, ranching, and rural living in New Mexico. It's housed within a huge structure that's well designed to look like a hacienda-style barn, with a U-shaped courtyard in back and exhibits surrounding it on expansive grounds. The museum lacks a really exciting draw, but for someone like my brother who loves farm and ranch equipment, it would appear like Disneyland, with such relics as a 1937 John Deere tractor and a number of examples of how ranchers "make do," ingeniously combining tools such as a tractor seat with a milk barrel to come up with a chair. Most interesting are the art exhibits—in particular, pencil drawings by Robert Shufelt, which are on rotational display.

You may want to plan your visit around a meal at the Purple Sage restaurant here, with upscale versions of Mexican dishes and burgers served in an elegant new Southwest atmosphere—very Santa Fe, if I do say so. Annual events at the museum are the La Fiesta de San Ysidro in May and the Cowboy Days on the third weekend in October.

4100 Dripping Springs Rd. (follow University Ave. east beyond the edge of town). © 505/522-4100. www. frhm.org. Admission $3 adults, $2 seniors 60 and over, $1 children 6–17; free for children 5 and under. Mon–Sat 9am–5pm; Sunday noon–5pm.

New Mexico State University   Established in 1888, this institution of 24,000 students is especially noted for its schools of engineering and agriculture. Its facilities include the Solar Energy Institute and the Water Resources Institute of New Mexico. **University Museum** in Kent Hall (© 505/646-3739) has exhibits of historic and prehistoric Native American culture and art. It's open Tuesday through Saturday from 12 to 4pm; admission is free. The **University Art Gallery** (© 505/646-2545) features monthly exhibits of contemporary and historical art, and a permanent collection of prints, photographs, and *retablos*— Mexican devotional paintings on tin. **Corbett Center Gallery,** in the student center (© 505/646-3235), has various exhibits throughout the year; a 12-foot copper-alloy triangle outside has a notch that symbolizes the transition from youth to adulthood. Clyde Tombaugh Observatory, named for the discoverer of the planet Pluto (who was a resident of Las Cruces), has a high-powered telescope open for public viewing one evening a month.

University Ave. and Locust St. © 505/646-0111. www.nmsu.edu.

San Albino Church ★★   This is one of the oldest churches in the Mesilla valley. The present structure was built in 1906 on the foundation of the original church, constructed in 1851. It was named for St. Albin, a medieval English bishop of North Africa, on whose day an important irrigation ditch from the Rio Grande was completed. The church bells date from the early 1870s; the pews were made in Taos of Philippine mahogany.

North side of Old Mesilla Plaza. © 505/526-9349. Free admission; donations appreciated. Usually open Mon–Sat 1–3pm (call ahead). English-language Mass Sat 5:30pm and Sun 11am; Spanish Mass Sun 8am, weekdays 7am.

SPECTATOR SPORTS

New Mexico State University football, basketball, baseball, softball, and volleyball teams play intercollegiate schedules in the Big West Conference, against schools from California, Nevada, and Utah. The Aggies play their home games on the NMSU campus, south of University Avenue on Locust Street. Football is played in the Chili Bowl, basketball in the Pan Am Center arena. For information about the games, call the **Pan Am Ticket Office** (© 505/646-1420; http://panam.nmsu.edu/tickets.html).

Fans of motor sports will find sprint and stock car racing at **The Speedway,** at Southern New Mexico State Fairgrounds, 11 miles west of Las Cruces via I-10 (© 505/524-7913; www.snmspeedway.com), open Saturday nights from May to September.

New Mexico's longest horse-racing season takes place 45 miles south of Las Cruces at **Sunland Park Racetrack and Casino** (© 505/874-5200; www.sunland-park.com). Live races run Friday, Saturday, Sunday, and Tuesday, from November to April. The Casino, which features 700 slot machines, is open daily from noon to midnight.

SHOPPING

Shoppers should be aware that in Las Cruces, Monday is a notoriously quiet day. Some stores close for the day, so it's best to call ahead before traveling to a specific store.

For art, visit **Lundeen's Inn of the Arts,** 618 S. Alameda Blvd. (© 505/526-3326), displaying the works of about 30 Southwest painters, sculptors, and potters; **Rising Sky Artworks,** 415 E. Foster (© 505/525-8454), which features works in clay by local and Western artists; and the **William Bonney Gallery,** 2060 Calle de Parian, just off the southeast corner of Old Mesilla Plaza (© 505/526-8275), with a variety of Southwestern art.

For books, try **Bowlin's Mesilla Book Center,** in an 1856 mercantile building on the west side of Old Mesilla Plaza (© 505/526-6220).

For native crafts and jewelry, check out **Silver Assets,** 1948 Calle de Santiago (© **505/523-8747**), 1½ blocks east of San Albino Church in Mesilla.

Mesilla Valley Mall is a full-service shopping center at 700 S. Telshor Blvd., just off the I-25 interchange with Lohman Avenue (© **505/522-1001**), with well over 100 stores. The mall is open Monday through Saturday from 10am to 9pm and Sunday from noon to 6pm.

The Las Cruces area has two wineries. **Blue Teal Vineyards** (© **877/669-4637** or 505/524-0390; www.blueteal.com) has a tasting room next to the historic Fountain Theater, 2461 Calle de Guadalupe, south of Old Mesilla Plaza. It's open Monday through Thursday 11am to 6pm, Friday and Saturday 11am to 8pm, and Sunday 12 to 6pm. The tasting room at **La Viña Winery** (© **505/882-7632**), south of Las Cruces off NM 28, is open daily from noon to 5pm, and by appointment.

LAS CRUCES AFTER DARK

National recording artists frequently perform at NMSU's **Pan Am Center** (© **505/646-1420**). The **NMSU Music Department** (© **505/646-2421**) offers free jazz, classical, and pop concerts from August to May, and the **Las Cruces Symphony Orchestra** (© **505/646-3709;** www.lascrucessymphony. com) often performs here as well.

Hershel Zohn Theater (© **505/646-4515**), at NMSU, presents plays of the professional/student **American Southwest Theatre Company** from September to May, featuring dramas, comedies, musicals, and original works. Visit **http://theatre.nmsu.edu/astc** for information.

The **Las Cruces Community Theatre** (© **505/523-1200;** www.lcctnm.org) mounts six productions a year at its own facility on the downtown mall.

The **Mesilla Valley Film Society** (© **505/524-8287**) runs a good selection of contemporary and vintage art films at the Fountain Theatre (www.fountain theatre.org), 2469 Calle de Guadalupe, a half-block south of the plaza in Mesilla, nightly at 7:30pm and sometimes 9:45pm, and Sunday at 2:30pm and sometimes 5pm.

EXPLORING THE AREA

NORTH OF LAS CRUCES   The town of **Hatch,** 39 miles north via I-25 or 34 miles north via NM 185, calls itself the "chile capital of the world." It is the center of a 22,000-acre agricultural belt that grows and processes more chile than anywhere else in the world. The annual Hatch Chile Festival over Labor Day weekend celebrates the harvest. For information, call the **Hatch Chamber of Commerce** (© **505/267-5050**).

Fort Selden State Monument is located 15 miles north of Las Cruces between I-25 (exit 19) and NM 185. Founded in 1865, Fort Selden housed the famous Black Cavalry, the "Buffalo Soldiers" who protected settlers from marauding natives. It was subsequently the boyhood home of Gen. Douglas MacArthur, whose father, Arthur, was in charge of troops patrolling the U.S.–Mexico border in the 1880s. The fort closed permanently in 1891. Today, only eroding ruins remain. Displays in the visitor center tell Fort Selden's story, including photos of young Douglas and his family. The monument is open from 8:30am to 5pm Wednesday to Monday; admission is $3 for adults and free for children age 16 and under. For more information, call © **505/526-8911** or visit **www.nm monuments.org**. Adjacent to the state monument, **Leasburg Dam State Park** (© **505/524-4068**) offers picnicking, camping, canoeing, and fishing.

SOUTH OF LAS CRUCES **Stahmann Farms,** 10 miles south of La Mesilla on NM 28, is one of the world's largest single producers of pecans. Several million pounds are harvested, mostly during November, from orchards in the bed of an ancient lake. **Stahmann's Country Store** (© **800/654-6887** or 505/526-8974; www.stahmanns.com) sells pecans, pecan candy, and other specialty foods, and it has a small cafe. It's open Monday through Saturday from 9am to 6pm, Sunday from 11am to 5pm.

War Eagles Air Museum ⊛ (© **505/589-2000;** www.war-eagles-air-museum.com), at the Santa Teresa Airport, about 35 miles south of Las Cruces via I-10 (call or check the website for directions), has an extensive collection of historic aircraft from World War II and the Korean War, plus automobiles and a tank. The aircraft include a beautifully restored P-38 Lightning, P-51 Mustang, F-86 Sabre, and several Russian MIG-15s. Most of the museum's 28 planes are in flying condition, and are kept inside a well-lit, 64,000-square-foot hangar. The museum is open Tuesday through Sunday from 10am to 4pm; admission is $5 for adults, $4 for senior citizens age 65 and over; free for children under age 12.

EAST OF LAS CRUCES The **Organ Mountains,** so-called because they resemble the pipes of a church organ, draw inevitable comparisons to Wyoming's Grand Tetons. Organ Peak, at 9,119 feet, is the highest point in Doña Ana County.

The **Aguirre Springs Recreation Area** (© **505/525-4300**), off US 70 on the western slope of the Organ Mountains, is one of the most spectacular places I've ever camped. Operated by the Bureau of Land Management, the camping and picnic sites sit at the base of the jagged Organ Mountains. Visitors to the area can hike, camp, picnic, or ride horseback (no horse rentals on site). If you'd like to hike, don't miss the **Baylor Pass** trail, which crosses along the base of the Organ peaks, up through a pass, and over to the Las Cruces side. Though the hike is 6 miles one-way, just over 2 miles will get you to the pass, where there's a meadow with amazing views.

WHERE TO STAY IN & AROUND LAS CRUCES

La Quinta ⊛ Five minutes from Old Mesilla, this chain hotel provides relatively quiet and very comfortable rooms with plenty of amenities. The clean and well-designed rooms range from medium to large, all with desks, and medium-size bathrooms. An outdoor pool sits within a comfortable courtyard, an important addition in this warm climate. Guests eat their continental breakfast in a bright garden room off the lobby. Though this hotel doesn't have a restaurant, a Best Western across the street does. (It's a noisier hotel without the refinement of this one, but the food there is decent.)

790 Avenida de Mesilla, Las Cruces, NM 88005. © **800/531-5900** or 505/524-0331. Fax 505/525-8360. www.laquinta.com. $72–$81 double. Rates include continental breakfast. AE, DISC, MC, V. Pets welcome. **Amenities:** Outdoor pool; small fitness room. *In room:* A/C, TV, coffeemaker, hair dryer, iron.

Las Cruces Hilton ⊛ South-of-the-border romance and elegance define this seven-story hotel on the east side of town, about a 15-minute drive from Mesilla, with an incredible view of the city and the Organ Mountains. The hotel was built in 1986, with remodeling ongoing. The lobby has a fountain, lots of colorful Mexican tile, and plenty of ferns. Rooms are spacious, with the same south-of-the border feel, and outfitted with sturdy pine furniture. Baths are medium-size and very clean. Some rooms flank the pool and have little patios. The Ventana Terrace serves breakfast, lunch, and dinner.

705 S. Telshor Blvd., Las Cruces, NM 88011. ℂ 800/284-0616 or 505/522-4300. Fax 505/521-4707. www.hilton.com. 203 units. $89–$149 double; $125–$309 suite. Rates include full breakfast. Golf packages available. AE, DC, DISC, MC, V. **Amenities:** Restaurant; lounge; heated outdoor pool; exercise room; Jacuzzi; car rental; courtesy van; limited room service; valet laundry. *In room:* A/C, TV, coffeemaker, dataport, hair dryer, iron.

BED & BREAKFASTS

The Lundeen Inn of the Arts ✿
This inn is a late-1890s adobe home, with whitewashed walls, narrow alleys, and arched doorways. It's a complex composite of rooms stretching across 14,000 square feet of floor space. There's a wide range of rooms, each named for an artist. My favorites are in the main part of the house, set around a two-story garden room, with elegant antiques and arched windows. Most rooms are medium-size with comfortably firm beds dressed in fine linens. Bathrooms are generally small and simple but clean. My favorite rooms are the Maria Martinez (the only room without a TV), which has wood floors and a working fireplace, and gets lots of sun; and the Frederic Remington, which has a more masculine feel and includes a kitchenette with a microwave, minifridge, stove, and coffeemaker. Other rooms have similarly equipped kitchenettes. The inn is also an art gallery, displaying the works of about 30 Southwestern painters, sculptors, and potters. Breakfast includes fresh fruit and such specialties as pumpkin waffles and huevos rancheros.

618 S. Alameda Blvd., Las Cruces, NM 88005. ℂ 888/526-3326 or 505/526-3326. Fax 505/647-1334. www.innofthearts.com. 18 units. $75–$85 double; $85–$105 suite. Rates include breakfast. AE, DC, DISC, MC, V. Pets welcome. **Amenities:** Secretarial service; babysitting; laundry service. *In room:* A/C, TV, hair dryer, iron.

Mesón de Mesilla Hotel & Gourmet Restaurant
The closest lodging to Old Mesilla, this inn provides decent rooms that have a motel feel. Built in the early 1980s, with remodeling ongoing, the rooms range greatly in size and price, giving the place broad appeal. What's most notable here is the lovely outdoor swimming pool with a view of the Organ Mountains. Each of the medium-size rooms is uniquely decorated, with medium-firm beds and basic bathrooms. Most rooms have Southwestern and antique furniture, as well as ceiling fans. Almost all rooms have balconies. A full breakfast is served in the garden atrium of the inn's restaurant (see "Where to Dine in & Around Las Cruces," below).

1803 Avenida de Mesilla, Mesilla, NM 88046. ℂ 800/732-6025 or 505/525-9212. Fax 505/527-4196. www.mesondemesilla.com. 16 units. $65–$70 double. Rates include a full breakfast. AE, DC, DISC, MC, V. Pets are welcome with $10 1-time fee. **Amenities:** Restaurant (p. ###); outdoor pool. *In room:* A/C, TV, dataport.

CAMPING

Quite a few campgrounds are located within or near Las Cruces. All the ones listed here include full hookups for RVs, tenting areas, and recreation areas. **Best View RV Park** (ℂ **505/526-6555**) also offers cabins and laundry and grocery facilities. From the junction of I-10 and US 70 (exit 135), go 1½ miles east on US 70, then half a block south on Weinrich Road.

Another option is **Dalmont's RV Park** (ℂ **505/523-2992**). If you're coming from the west, when you reach the junction of I-25 and I-10, go 2½ miles northwest on I-10 to the Main Street exit, then go 2 blocks west on Valley Drive. If you're coming from the east, at the junction of I-10 and Main Street, go ¼ mile north on Main Street and then 1 block west on Valley Drive. To reach **Siesta RV Park** (ℂ **505/523-6816**), at the junction of I-10 and NM 28, take exit 140 and go half a mile south on NM 28. **Leasburg Dam State Park** (ℂ **505/524-4068**) is a smaller park that also offers RV and tent camping, but it has no laundry or grocery facilities. A general country store is about 1 mile down the road, and hiking and fishing are available.

WHERE TO DINE IN & AROUND LAS CRUCES
EXPENSIVE

Double Eagle 🎭🎭 CONTINENTAL   When I was a kid, whenever we went to Las Cruces, we always made a special trip to this elegant restaurant imbued with Old West style. I'm pleased to say that it's still a quality place to dine. This 150-year-old Territorial-style hacienda is on the National Register of Historic Places. Built around a central courtyard, it has numerous rooms, one of which is said to be frequented by a woman's ghost. Another room has a 30-foot-long bar with Corinthian columns in gold leaf, Gay Nineties oil paintings, and 18-armed brass chandeliers hung with Baccarat crystals. The menu is quite varied and includes pasta, chicken, fish, and steak dishes. My favorite is the filet mignon bordelaise, served on a French rusk with a rich red-wine sauce. The Columbia River salmon, served with a triple citrus-chipotle chile sauce, is also delicious. All entrees come with salad, vegetable, and choice of potato or pasta. There's a full bar, and for dessert you can end it all with the Death by Chocolate Cake.

2355 Calle de Guadalupe, on the east side of Old Mesilla Plaza. ℂ **505/523-6700.** Reservations recommended. Main courses $5.25–$11.50 lunch, $11–$27 dinner. AE, DC, DISC, MC, V. Mon–Sat 11am–10pm; Sun 11am–9pm.

Mesón de Mesilla 🎭🎭 CONTINENTAL   A few blocks from Old Mesilla, this friendly restaurant, situated in the Mesón de Mesilla Hotel, offers quality food with a touch of elegance. The dining room and covered patio have hand-carved Spanish chairs and ceramic wall sconces, lending a south-of-the border feel. You can order two ways: what they call a la carte or a four-course meal, either one fairly reasonable, considering what you get. A la carte entrees include two side offerings, while the four-course meal includes soup, salad, a main course with sides, and dessert. The restaurant's signature dish is chateaubriand. I enjoy the rack of lamb, served with a vegetable and mashed potatoes, or the Chilean sea bass in lemon caper sauce with a vegetable and rice pilaf. For dessert, try the apple crisp a la mode. A full bar and excellent wine list complement the menu.

In Mesón de Mesilla Hotel, 1803 Avenida de Mesilla. ℂ **800/732-6025** or 505/525-9212. Main courses: $21–$26 a la carte; $28–$32 four-course meal. AE, DC, DISC, MC, V. Tues–Thurs and Sun 5:30–9:30pm; Fri–Sat 5:30–10:30pm.

MODERATE

Peppers SOUTHWESTERN   This restaurant shares a building and the same ownership with the Double Eagle, but the resemblance ends there. The Eagle has age and grace; Peppers has youthful exuberance. Hispanic folk art, including traditional masks and *santos,* greets guests in the entryway, and diners can sit within a lush atrium central courtyard (a great place to sit and drink margaritas) around which the Double Eagle dining rooms reside. The cuisine is Santa Fe–style Southwestern, the chef adding interesting touches to traditional dishes. The service here tends to be slow; come only if you have time to lounge. For starters, try the green chile and cheese wontons, a house specialty. The most popular dish is the grilled chicken Mesilla, topped with sautéed onions and Mennonite cheese, served with guacamole and black beans. For dessert, the banana enchiladas sound weird but are actually delicious crepes with ice cream and Mesilla Valley Pecan praline sauce.

2335 Calle Guadalupe, on the east side of Old Mesilla Plaza. ℂ **505/523-4999.** Fax 505/523-0051. Reservations for large parties only. Tapas $4–$7.50; lunch main courses $5.25–$11.50; dinner main courses $7–$15. AE, DC, DISC, MC, V. Mon–Sat 11am–10pm; Sun noon–9pm.

INEXPENSIVE

Chope's Bar & Cafe ⭐ (Finds) (Kids) NEW MEXICAN   This is one of those legendary spots, a requisite weekly pilgrimage for many. Drive 15 minutes south of Old Mesilla through pecan orchards to its door, and you'll encounter a real locals' scene. The dining rooms are plain. Set in an old house, they have tile floors, faux wood paneling, and closely set tables, usually full of families, business people, and college students. You'll feast on chile rellenos, enchiladas, and burritos. Whatever you order, make sure it's smothered with red or green chile, if you can handle the heat. If not, opt for tacos or a hamburger. Kids like the place because it's casual and they have their own menu. Service is friendly but very overworked. With your meal, order up margaritas or a Mexican beer, or, if you really wish to partake, head next door to the cantina, a dark and raucous place reminiscent of a border-town bar.

NM 28 (in the center of town in La Mesa; no street address). ℂ **505/233-3420** or 505/233-9976. Main courses $4.50–$8 lunch and dinner. MC, V. Tues–Sat 11:30am–1:30pm and 5:30–8:30pm; cantina Tues–Sat 11:30am–9:30pm.

La Posta de Mesilla (Kids) MEXICAN/STEAKS   If you're on the Old Mesilla Plaza and want to eat New Mexican food for not much money, walk in here. The restaurant occupies a mid-18th-century adobe building that is the only surviving stagecoach station of the Butterfield Overland Mail route from Tipton, Missouri, to San Francisco. Kit Carson, Pancho Villa, General Douglas MacArthur, and Billy the Kid were all here at one time. The entrance leads through a jungle of tall plants beneath a Plexiglas roof, past a tank of piranhas and a noisy aviary of macaws and Amazon parrots, to nine dining rooms with bright, festive decor. (Kids love this and their own menu selections.) You may want to request the atrium, where you can dine under ficus trees. The tables are basic, however, with vinyl and metal chairs, giving it a cheap air. Such is an indication of the food quality. If you want really good New Mexican food, go to Nellie's (see below). If you come here, try the enchiladas, which come with a nice chile sauce. Avoid the dry rellenos and the soggy tacos. The tostadas (tortilla cups filled with beans and topped with chile and cheese) are a house specialty. There's a full-service bar.

2410 Calle de San Albino (southeast corner of Old Mesilla Plaza). ℂ **505/524-3524.** Reservations recommended. Main courses $4–$13 lunch and dinner. AE, DC, DISC, MC, V. Sun and Tues–Thurs 11am–9pm; Fri–Sat 11am–9:30pm.

Lorenzo's Restaurante Italiano de Old Messilla SICILIAN   The main walls of this little restaurant just off the Mesilla Plaza are covered with bold murals of Mesilla Valley farming, giving the place a paisano charm, a good indication of the food here. Rather than refined Italian food like you find in many cities, this restaurant serves traditional Sicilian meals, with lots of red sauces and homemade pasta. It's big with locals, and it fills up, so you may want to make reservations. The atmosphere is jovial and the service is good, though it may be a bit slow because the food is cooked in-house. You can't go wrong with standards such as spaghetti marinara or lasagna, or for something more adventurous, try the linguini and clams. Meals are served with focaccia so good you'll have a tough time stopping yourself from eating it all, and a small salad of freshly tossed greens. Wash it down with a carafe of Chianti.

1750 Calle de Mercado #4 (Onate Plaza, a block from Old Mesilla Plaza). ℂ **505/525-3174.** Reservations recommended. Main courses $6–$14 lunch and dinner. AE, DISC, MC, V. Mon–Thurs 11am–9pm; Fri–Sat 11am–9:30pm; Sun 4–8:30pm.

Nellie's ⓡ NEW MEXICAN   A good indication of the quality of food at this restaurant that serves "chile with an attitude" is that at 10:45am on a Monday the place was full. I told three young guys wearing baseball caps at the next table where I was from and one said, "This is the best damn New Mexican food in the world—too bad Santa Fe doesn't have a place this good." If I weren't so fond of my home-town, I'd have agreed. It's a small cafe with two rooms, totally unassuming, with big windows up front that let in lots of light. There's a jukebox and, on the walls, R. C. Gorman prints. Order anything on the menu and you'll be pleased. At breakfast, order up eggs and bacon or huevos rancheros (eggs over tortillas, smoth-ered with chile). For lunch or dinner, the sopaipilla compuesta (sopaipilla topped with beans, meat, lettuce, tomatoes, and cheese) is amazing. The combination plate gives you a sampling of a number of delicacies. As should be the case with any true New Mexican restaurant, you can also have menudo, what they call the "breakfast of champions" (beef tripe and hominy in red chile), and though I didn't dare, I heard it, too, is tasty. No alcoholic beverages are served.

1226 West Hadley. ⓒ 505/524-9982 or 505/526-6816. Reservations not accepted. Main courses $3–$7 breakfast, $5–$7.50 lunch and dinner. No credit cards. Tues–Sat 8am–4pm. Closed one or two weeks in July.

Spirit Winds Coffee Bar (Finds) CAFE/BAKERY   This little find not far from the university offers a breath of sophistication in southern New Mexico. The brightly painted walls and inventive coffee drinks and sandwiches attract lots of students and artist types, as well as local businesspeople. If you're hungry, you may want to try a fresh-baked scone or blueberry muffin (the way I like them, not very sweet), or any variety of soups and sandwiches, such as spicy black beans rolled up in a tortilla with veggies and olives, or a roast beef sandwich with tomatoes, cheddar cheese, and Dijon/mayo spread.

2260 Locust St. ⓒ 505/521-0222. All menu items around $5. MC, V. Summer Mon–Sat 7:30am–8pm, Sun 9am–6pm; winter Mon–Sat 7:30am–10pm, Sun 9am–7pm.

6 Deming & Lordsburg

New Mexico's least populated corner is this one, which includes the "boot heel" of the Gadsden Purchase, which pokes 40 miles down into Mexico (a great place for backpacking). These two railroad towns, an hour apart on I-10, see a lot of traffic; but whereas **Deming** (pop. 14,500) is thriving as a ranching and retire-ment center, **Lordsburg** has had a steady population of about 3,000 for years. This is a popular area for rockhounds, aficionados of ghost towns, and history buffs: **Columbus,** 32 miles south of Deming, was the site of the last foreign incursion on continental American soil, by the Mexican bandit-revolutionary Pancho Villa in 1916.

ESSENTIALS
GETTING THERE   From Las Cruces, take I-10 west (1 hr. to Deming, 2 hr. to Lordsburg). From Tucson, take I-10 east (3 hr. to Lordsburg, 4 hr. to Deming).

The **Grant County Airport** (ⓒ **505/388-4554**), 15 miles south of Silver City, is served by **Mesa Airlines** (ⓒ **800/MESA-AIR** or 505/326-3338; www.mesa-air.com), with daily flights to Albuquerque. The **Las Cruces Shuttle Serv-ice,** P.O. Box 3172, Las Cruces, NM 88003 (ⓒ **800/288-1784** or 505/525-1784; www.lascrucesshuttle.com), runs several times daily between Deming and the El Paso airport by way of Las Cruces.

VISITOR INFORMATION   The **Deming–Luna County Chamber of Com-merce** is located at 800 E. Pine St., Deming (ⓒ **800/848-4955** or 505/546-2674;

www.demingchamber.com). You can write to them at P.O. Box 8, Deming, NM 88031. The **Lordsburg–Hidalgo County Chamber of Commerce** is located at 117 E. 2nd St., Lordsburg, NM 88045 (© **505/542-9864;** www.hidalgocounty. org/lordsburgcoc).

WHAT TO SEE & DO NEAR DEMING

Deming Luna Mimbres Museum   Deming was the meeting place of the second east–west railroad to connect the Pacific and Atlantic coasts, and that heritage is recalled in this museum, run by the Luna County Historical Society. It has a military room that contains exhibits from the Indian wars, Pancho Villa's raid, WWI and WWII, and the Korean and Vietnam wars; a room featuring the John and Mary Alice King Collection of Mimbres pottery; and a doll room with more than 800 dolls. A 5,000-square-foot adjacent space displays transportation-related exhibits, including a replica of a railroad depot, a Harvey House, and vintage fire trucks.

Across the street is the Custom House, a turn-of-the-century adobe home that has been turned into a walk-through exhibit. You can see a period bedroom, kitchen, and living room, inhabited by mannequins. Most interesting here are the customs books from that era, showing what goods were brought from Mexico.

301 S. Silver Ave., Deming. © 505/546-2382. Fax 505/544-0121. Admission $2, children with parents free. Mon–Sat 9am–4pm; Sun 1:30–4pm.

GETTING OUTSIDE

At **Rockhound State Park** ✯, 14 miles southeast of Deming via NM 11, visitors are encouraged to pick up and take home with them as much as 15 pounds of minerals—jasper, agate, quartz crystal, flow-banded rhyolite, and others. Located at the base of the Little Florida Mountains, the park is a lovely, arid, cactus-covered land with paths leading down into dry gullies and canyons. (You may have to walk a bit, as the more accessible minerals have been largely picked out.)

The campground ($10 for non-electric hookup; $14 with electric hookup), which has shelters, restrooms, and showers, offers a distant view of mountain ranges all the way to the Mexican border. The park also has one marked hiking trail and a playground. Admission is $5 per vehicle, and the park is open year-round from dawn to dusk. For more information, call © **505/546-6182.**

Some 35 miles south of Deming is the tiny border town of **Columbus,** which looks across at Mexico. The **Pancho Villa State Park** here marks the last foreign invasion of American soil. A temporary fort, where a tiny garrison was housed in tents, was attacked in 1916 by 600 Mexican revolutionaries, who cut through the boundary fence at Columbus. Eighteen Americans were killed, 12 wounded; an estimated 200 Mexicans died. The Mexicans immediately retreated across their border. An American punitive expedition, headed by Gen. John J. Pershing, was launched into Mexico but got nowhere. Villa restricted his banditry to Mexico after that, until his assassination in 1923.

The state park includes ruins of the old fort and a visitor center with exhibits and a film. The park also has a strikingly beautiful desert botanical garden, worth the trip alone, plus campsites, restrooms, showers, an RV dump station, and a playground. There's a $5-per-vehicle entrance fee; the park is staffed from 8am to 5pm daily. For more information, call © **505/531-2711.**

Across the street from the state park is the old Southern Pacific Railroad Depot, which has been restored by the Columbus Historical Society and now houses the **Columbus Historical Museum** (© **505/531-2620**), which contains railroad memorabilia and exhibits on local history. Call for hours, which vary.

Three miles south across the border in Mexico is **Las Palomas, Chihuahua** (pop. 1,500). The port of entry is open 24 hours. A few desirable restaurants and tourist-oriented businesses are located in Las Palomas. Mostly, though, it's a drug-trafficking town. Beware of barhopping in Palomas at night, as it can be dangerous.

WHAT TO SEE & DO NEAR LORDSBURG

Visitors to Lordsburg can go **rockhounding** in this area rich in minerals of many kinds. Desert roses can be found near Summit, and agate is known to exist in many abandoned mines locally. Mine dumps, southwest of Hachita, contain lead, zinc, and gold; the Animas Mountains have manganese. Volcanic glass can be picked up in Coronado National Forest, and you can pan for gold in Gold Gulch.

Rodeo, 30 miles southwest via I-10 and NM 80, is the home of the **Chiricahua Gallery** (© **505/557-2225**), open Monday through Saturday from 10am to 4pm. Regional artists have joined in a nonprofit, cooperative venture to exhibit works and offer classes in a variety of media. Many choose to live on the high-desert slopes of the Chiricahua Range. The gallery is on NM 80 en route to Douglas, Arizona.

Shakespeare Ghost Town *(Kids)*   A national historic site, Shakespeare was once the home of 3,000 miners, promoters, and dealers of various kinds. Under the name Ralston, it enjoyed a silver boom in 1870. This was followed by a notorious diamond fraud in 1872, in which a mine was salted with diamonds in order to raise prices on mining stock; many notables were sucked in, particularly William Ralston, founder of the Bank of California. It enjoyed a mining revival in 1879 under its new name, Shakespeare. It was a town with no church, no newspaper, and no local law. Some serious fights resulted in hangings from the roof timbers in the Stage Station.

Since 1935, it's been privately owned by the Hill family, which has kept it uncommercialized, with no souvenir hype or gift shops. Six original buildings and two reconstructed buildings survive in various stages of repair. Two-hour guided tours are offered on a limited basis, and reenactments and living history are staged on the fourth weekends of April, June, August, and October, if performers are available. Phone to confirm the performances.

2.5 miles south of Lordsburg (no street address), P.O. Box 253, Lordsburg, NM 88045. © **505/542-9034**. www.shakespeareghostown.com. Admission $3 adults, $2 children 6–12; for shoot-outs and special events $4 adults, $3 children. Open 10am and 2pm on the 2nd Sun and preceding Sat of each month. Special tours by appointment. To reach Shakespeare, drive 1½ miles south from I-10 on Main St. Just before the town cemetery, turn right, proceed ½ mile, and turn right again. Follow the dirt road another ½ mile into Shakespeare.

Stein's Railroad Ghost Town *(Kids)*   This settlement 19 miles west of Lordsburg started as a Butterfield Stage stop and then was a railroad town of about 1,000 residents from 1880 to 1955. It was so isolated that water, hauled from Doubtful Canyon, brought $1 a barrel!

Today there remain 12 buildings, with 16 rooms filled with artifacts and furnishings from the 19th and early 20th centuries. There is also a petting zoo for kids and the Steins Mercantile shop.

Exit 3, I-10 (P.O. Box 2185), Road Forks, NM 88045. © **505/542-9791**. Admission $2.50 age 12 and over, free for under age 12. Daily 9am–dusk.

WHERE TO STAY IN DEMING & LORDSBURG
IN DEMING

Grand Hotel *(Kids)*   Looking like a redbrick Colonial Williamsburg manor and situated close to town, the Grand isn't quite as refined as the Holiday Inn (see below), but its construction is older (1967) and more substantial. It's built around a central lawn and shrubbery garden, with a large pool for adults and a small one for children. The quiet, medium-size rooms have antique-style furnishings and firm mattresses. Bathrooms are medium-size, each with an outer vanity and dressing area.

US 70/180 east of downtown (P.O. Box 309), Deming, NM 88031. ✆ **505/546-2631.** Fax 505/546-4446. 60 units. $41 double. AE, DC, DISC, MC, V. **Amenities:** Restaurant; lounge; 2 outdoor pools; courtesy shuttle; coin-op laundry. *In room:* A/C, TV.

Holiday Inn 🐾   This hotel just off I-10 brings a bit of style to dusty Deming. Though from the outside the 1974 two-story white brick structure appears basic, the rooms—with renovations ongoing—tell another story. Each is medium-size with light pine furniture and decorated in Aztec prints, with bold expressionist paintings on the walls. Bathrooms are small but each has a vanity and dressing area. Some of the suites come with Jacuzzis. The large pool is surrounded by lush grass; request a poolside room and you'll have a bit of a resort feel. The hotel's restaurant is open for breakfast, lunch, and dinner, serving New Mexican and American cuisine.

Off I-10, Exit 85 (P.O. Box 1138), Deming, NM 88031. ✆ **800/HOLIDAY** or 505/546-2661. Fax 505/546-6308. www.ichotels.com. 116 units. $50–$68 double. AE, DC, DISC, MC, V. Pets are welcome. **Amenities:** Restaurant; outdoor heated pool; exercise room; Jacuzzi; limited room service; coin-op laundry; laundry service; dry cleaning. *In room:* A/C, TV, dataport, fridge, coffeemaker, hair dryer, iron.

IN LORDSBURG

Best Western Western Skies Inn   This redbrick motel built in 1990 at the I-10 interchange offers comfortable rooms on well-landscaped grounds. Remodeling is ongoing and well done. The large rooms have oak furnishings and medium-firm beds. Bathrooms are medium-size, and each has an outer vanity with a sink. Many have minifridges. The motel has a small outdoor pool, and Kranberry's Family Restaurant (see "Where to Dine in Deming & Lordsburg," below) is next door. The motel is reachable by Greyhound and Amtrak. Light sleepers beware: Trains pass by this motel during the night.

1303 S. Main St. at I-10 (exit 22), Lordsburg, NM 88045. ✆ **800/528-1234** or 505/542-8807. Fax 505/542-8895. www.bestwestern.com. 40 units. $62 double. AE, DC, DISC, MC, V. Pets $5–$10 fee, depending on size. **Amenities:** Outdoor pool. *In room:* A/C, TV, coffeemaker, hair dryer, iron.

Martha's Place Bed & Breakfast   If you'd like to add a little Mexico adventure to your southern New Mexico stay, head south of Deming 30 miles and stay with Martha. She has a two-story stucco Pueblo-style adobe painted cream and green, with Victorian touches inside. Built in 1991, it's just 3 miles from the Mexican border town of Las Palomas. The place is furnished with some nice antiques as well as furniture made in Martha's family's *maquilladora* (manufacturing plant) across the border. The medium-size rooms have comfortably firm beds and good bedding. Each has French doors and a balcony. Bathrooms are medium-size and basic, with showers, and very clean. This is not a luxury B&B, nor is great care taken in making your stay perfect, but Martha is a character and enjoys being a host, which is worth a lot. She'll fill you with stories of border town life and tell you exactly when and how to see what. Breakfasts are simple and filling. I've enjoyed fruit, eggs and toast, and Canadian bacon. If you're lucky, you'll arrive on one of the 2 weeks of the year when the Tumbleweed Theater has a melodrama performance, held in back of the inn, with Martha presiding.

Main and Lima sts., Columbus, NM 88029. ✆ **505/531-2467.** Fax 505/531-7177. 6 units. $60 double. Rates include breakfast. DISC, MC, V. Pets are welcome. **Amenities:** Laundry service. *In room:* A/C, TV, iron.

CAMPING IN & AROUND DEMING & LORDSBURG

City of Rocks State Park, in Deming (© **505/536-2800**), has 52 campsites, 10 with electric hookups; tenting is available, and picnic tables and a hiking trail are nearby. **Dreamcatcher RV Park** (© **505/544-4004**), also in Deming (take exit 85, Motel Dr., off I-10 and go 1 block south on Business I-10), has 92 sites, all with full hookups. It also offers free access to a nearby swimming pool and on-site laundry facilities. **Little Vineyard RV Park** (© **505/546-3560**) in Deming (from I-10 take exit 85 and go 1 mile southwest on Business I-10 toward Deming) is larger than those already mentioned. It offers the same facilities as Dreamcatcher RV Park, with the addition of limited groceries, an indoor pool and hot tub, cable TV hookups, e-mail access, and a small RV parts store. The campground at **Rockhound State Park** (© **505/546-6182**) is picturesque and great for rockhounds who can't get enough of their hobby. RV sites with hookups and tenting are both available, as are shelters, restrooms, and showers.

If you'd rather camp near Lordsburg, try **Lordsburg KOA** (© **800/562-5772** or 505/542-8003; www.koa.com). It's in a desert setting but with shade trees, and tenting is permitted. Grocery and laundry facilities are available, in addition to a recreation room/area, a swimming pool, a playground, and horseshoes. To reach the campground, take I-10 to Exit 22 and then go 1 block south; next, turn right at the Chevron station and follow the signs to the campground.

WHERE TO DINE IN DEMING & LORDSBURG

Kranberry's Family Restaurant AMERICAN/MEXICAN A friendly, casual Denny's-style family restaurant decorated with Southwestern art, Kranberry's offers American favorites, including eggs and pancakes for breakfast; and burgers, chicken, beef, and salads, as well as Mexican selections for lunch and dinner. Baked goods are made on the premises daily. My favorite is the corn bread, served with the soup special.

1405 S. Main St., Lordsburg. © **505/542-9400.** Main courses $3–$6 breakfast, $4–$15 lunch and dinner. AE, DC, DISC, MC, V. Daily 6am–10pm.

Si Señor ✦ MEXICAN As one local put it, this place gets packed. Locals crowd this basic downtown cafe to eat platters full of tasty New Mexican food. The plain interior has functional furniture and a few woodcarved pictures on the wall. Smoking is allowed in one section of the restaurant, but the nonsmoking section seems airy enough. At breakfast try the huevos rancheros (eggs over corn tortillas, smothered in chile). The big seller here for lunch and dinner is the deluxe combination, with a chile relleno, a tamale, a cheese enchilada, a taco, refried beans, Spanish rice, and red or green chile. The menu also sports salads, hamburgers, and chicken and fish dishes. All come with chips and salsa, and wine and beer are served.

200 E. Pine, Deming. © **505/546-3938.** Main courses $4–$8 breakfast, $5–$10 lunch and dinner. DISC, MC, V. Mon–Sat 9am–8:30pm; Sun 9am–3pm.

7 Silver City: Gateway to the Gila Cliff Dwellings ✦✦

Silver City (pop. 10,545) is an old mining town, located in the foothills of the Pinos Altos Range of the Mogollon Mountains, and gateway to the Gila Wilderness and the Gila Cliff Dwellings. Early Native Americans mined turquoise from these hills, and by 1804, Spanish settlers were digging for copper. In 1870, a group of prospectors discovered silver, and the rush was on. In 10 short months, the newly christened Silver City grew from a single cabin to more than 80 buildings. Early visitors included Billy the Kid, Judge Roy Bean, and William Randolph Hearst.

This comparatively isolated community kept pace with every modern convenience: telephones in 1883, electric lights in 1884 (only 2 years after New York City installed its lighting), and a water system in 1887. Typically, the town should have busted with the crash of silver prices in 1893. But unlike many Western towns, Silver City did not become a picturesque memory. It capitalized on its high dry climate to become today's county seat and trade center. Copper mining and processing are still the major industry. But Silver City also can boast a famous son: The late Harrison (Jack) Schmitt, the first civilian geologist to visit the moon, and later a U.S. senator, was born and raised in nearby Santa Rita.

ESSENTIALS

GETTING THERE From Albuquerque, take I-25 south, 15 miles past Truth or Consequences; then west on NM 152 and US 180 (5 hr.). From Las Cruces, take I-10 west to Deming, then north on US 180 (2 hr.).

Mesa Airlines (© **800/MESA-AIR** or 505/326-3338; www.mesa-air.com) flies daily from Albuquerque to **Grant County Airport** (© **505/388-4554**), 15 miles south of Silver City near Hurley. **Silver Stage Lines** (© **800/522-0162**) offers daily shuttle service to the El Paso airport, and charter service to Tucson. The **Las Cruces Shuttle Service** (© **800/288-1784** or 505/525-1784; www.las crucesshuttle.com) runs several times daily from Silver City to the El Paso airport, by way of Las Cruces.

VISITOR INFORMATION The **Silver City–Grant County Chamber of Commerce,** at 201 N. Hudson St., Silver City, NM 88061 (© **800/548-9378** or 505/538-3785; www.silvercity.org), maintains a visitor information headquarters at 201 N. Hudson Ave. The chamber produces extremely useful tourist publications.

WHAT TO SEE & DO IN SILVER CITY

Silver City's downtown **Historic District** ⋇, the first such district to receive National Register recognition, is a must for visitors. The downtown core is marked by the extensive use of brick in construction: Brick clay was discovered in the area soon after the town's founding in 1870, and an 1880 ordinance prohibited frame construction within the town limits. Mansard-roofed Victorian houses, Queen Anne and Italianate residences, and commercial buildings show off the cast-iron architecture of the period. Some are still undergoing restoration.

An 1895 flood washed out Main Street and turned it into a gaping chasm, which was eventually bridged over; finally, the **Big Ditch,** as it's called, was made into a green park in the center of town. Facing downtown, in the 500 block of North Hudson Street, was a famous red-light district from the turn-of-the-century until the late 1960s.

Billy the Kid lived in Silver City as a youth. You can see his cabin site a block north of the Broadway Bridge, on the east side of the Big Ditch. The Kid (William Bonney) waited tables at the Star Hotel, at Hudson Street and Broadway. He was jailed (at 304 N. Hudson St.) in 1875 at the age of 15, after being convicted of stealing from a Chinese laundry, but he escaped—a first for The Kid. The grave of Bonney's mother, Catherine McCarty, is in Silver City Cemetery, east of town on Memory Lane, off US 180. She died of tuberculosis about a year after the family moved here in 1873.

Silver City Museum ⋇ This very well-presented museum of city and regional history contains collections relating to Southwestern New Mexico history, mining,

Native American pottery, and early photographs. Exhibits include a southwestern New Mexico history timeline; a parlor displaying Victorian decorative arts; and a chronicle of commerce in early Silver City. A local history research library is available to visitors also. The main gallery features changing exhibits. The museum is lodged in the 1881 H. B. Ailman House, a former city hall and fire station, remarkable for its cupola and Victorian mansard roof. Ailman came to Silver City penniless in 1871, made a fortune in mining, and went on to start the Meredith and Ailman Bank. Guided historic district walking tours are offered on Memorial Day and Labor Day. There is also a museum store.

312 W. Broadway. (© **505/538-5921.** Fax 505/388-1096. Free admission. Tues–Fri 9am–4:30pm; Sat–Sun 10am–4pm. Closed Mon except Memorial Day and Labor Day.

Western New Mexico University Museum   Spread across 80 acres on the west side of Silver City, WNMU celebrated its centennial in 1993. The university boasts a 2,500-student enrollment and 24 major buildings. Among them is historic Fleming Hall, which houses this interesting museum. The WNMU museum has the largest permanent exhibit of prehistoric Mimbres pottery in the United States. Also displayed are Casas Grandes Indian pottery, stone tools, ancient jewelry, historic photographs, and mining and military artifacts. Displays change regularly, so there is always something new to see, such as vanishing Americana, riparian fossils, Nigerian folk art, or a collection of 18th- to 20th-century timepieces. There is a gift shop here.

1000 W. College, Fleming Hall, WNMU. (© **505/538-6386.** www.wnmu.edu/univ/museum.htm. Free admission. Mon–Fri 9am–4:30pm; Sat–Sun 10am–4pm.

SILVER CITY AFTER DARK
Some of southwestern New Mexico's most passionate performances are held at the **Pinos Altos Melodrama Theater** (© **505/388-3848**), 30 Main St., Pinos Altos (in the Pinos Altos Opera House, next to the Buckhorn Saloon). Local actors fight the forces of good and evil in such productions as *The Legend of Billy the Kid or It's Just a Little Gun Play.* Productions are on Friday and Saturday nights from February to November.

EXPLORING THE AREA
NORTH OF SILVER CITY   The virtual ghost town of **Pinos Altos** ⊛, straddling the Continental Divide, is 6 miles north of Silver City on NM 15. Dubbed "Tall Pines" when it was founded in the gold- and silver-rush era, Apache attacks and mine failures have taken their toll.

The adobe **Methodist-Episcopal Church** was built with William Randolph Hearst's money in 1898 and now houses the Grant County Art Guild. The town also has the **Log Cabin Curio Shop and Museum,** located in an 1866 cabin (© **505/388-1882**), and the **Buckhorn Saloon and Opera House** (see "Where to Dine in & Around Silver City," below).

SOUTH OF SILVER CITY   City of Rocks State Park ⊛ (© **505/536-2800**), 25 miles from Silver City via US 180 and NM 61, is an area of fantastically shaped volcanic rock formations, formed in ancient times from thick blankets of ash that hardened into tuff. This soft stone, eroded by wind and rain, was shaped into monolithic blocks reminiscent of Stonehenge. For some, the park resembles a medieval village; for others, it is a collection of misshapen, albeit benign, giants. Complete with a desert garden, the park offers excellent camping and picnic sites. It's also a renowned spot for *bouldering,* a type of rock climbing in which participants don't use ropes. Day use is allowed from 6am to 9pm for

Thar's Copper in Them Thar Hills

Southern New Mexico has carried on its mining legacy into the present, with two fully operating mines. South of Silver City 12 miles on NM 90 is the **Phelps Dodge Tyrone's Open Pit Copper Mine** (© 505/538-5331). Some 80 million tons of rock are taken out every year. Phelps Dodge consolidated its Tyrone holdings in 1909 and hired famous architect Bertram Goodhue to design a "Mediterranean-style" company town. Tyrone, later referred to as the Million Dollar Ghost Town, was constructed between 1914 and 1918. A large bank and shop building, administration office, mercantile store, and passenger depot were grouped around a central plaza. Eighty-three single and multiple-unit dwellings, accommodating 235 families, were built on the nearby hillsides; and a school, chapel, garage, restaurant, justice court, hospital, morgue, and recreation building were added. A drop in copper prices caused it to be abandoned virtually overnight.

After a pre–World War II incarnation as a luxurious dude ranch, Tyrone lay dormant for years until the late 1960s, when the town made way for the present-day open pit mine and mill. A new town site was created 7 miles north. Most of the original homes and major buildings were removed between 1967 and 1969; today, the only remaining structures are Union Chapel, the justice court, and the pump house. The copper mine supplies copper concentrates to the modern Hidalgo Smelter near Playas, southeast of Lordsburg.

The oldest active mine in the Southwest, and among the largest in America, is the **Chino Mines Co. Open Pit Copper Mine** (commonly called the Santa Rita Copper Mine; © 505/537-3381) at Santa Rita, 15 miles east of Silver City via US 180 and NM 152. The multicolored open pit is a mile wide and 1,000 feet deep, and can be viewed from an observation point. Unfortunately, no tours are available at this writing.

Apaches once scratched the surface for metallic copper. By 1800, the Spanish, under Col. Jose Manuel Carrasco, were working "Santa Rita del Cobre." Convict labor from New Spain mined the shafts, with mule trains full of ore sent down the Janos Trail to Chihuahua, Mexico. An impressive adobe fort was built near the mine, along with smelters and numerous buildings, but Apache raids finally forced the mine's abandonment. In the late 19th century, the mine was reopened, and the town of Santa Rita was reborn. The huge open pit, started around 1910, soon consumed Santa Rita. Giant-size machines scoop the ore from the earth and huge 175-ton ore trucks transport it to the reduction mill southwest of the pit.

$5 per vehicle; a campsite costs $8 to $18. The visitor center is typically open from 10am to 4pm, but its hours vary, depending on volunteer staffing.

WEST OF SILVER CITY   US 180, heading northwest from Silver City, is the gateway to Catron County and most of the Gila National Forest, including the villages of Glenwood, Reserve, and Quemado. For details on this area, see "Other Adventures in Gila National Forest," later in this chapter.

WHERE TO STAY IN & AROUND SILVER CITY

Standard motels are strung along US 180 east of NM 90. Some of the more interesting accommodations are listed below. Most lodgings provide free parking.

Holiday Motor Hotel *Kids*   Located about 3 miles east of downtown, near the junction of US 180 and NM 15, this motel is a step above the ordinary, with its landscaped grounds, playground, and all-night security guard. Rooms are medium-size with Southwest decor and basic oak furnishings. The medium-size bathroom has an outer vanity and is very clean. Beds are medium firm. Ask for a west-facing room, and you'll have a view of the lawn.

3420 US 180 E., Silver City, NM 88061. *C* **800/828-8291** or 505/538-3711. Fax 505/538-3711. 80 units. $40–$65 double. AE, DC, DISC, MC, V. Pets allowed. **Amenities:** Restaurant; coin-up laundry; dry cleaning. *In room:* A/C, TV.

The Palace Hotel   If you like the feel of an Old West downtown hotel in the center of the historic district, this is your spot. First established in 1882 as a bank, then opened as a hotel in 1900, it closed for many years but was reopened in 1990 as a small European-style hotel. Each of the rooms on the second floor is shaped and decorated differently. All are eclectic, some with antiques. The beds are medium firm, and the standard-size bathrooms are very clean with old fixtures, some with new toilets. The rooms closest to the upstairs sitting room and breakfast area are the nicest. If you're not accustomed to city noise, you'll want to avoid this place, as traffic can be loud into the night on Main Street, especially Thursday through Saturday nights. Note also that it's not air-conditioned, so open windows and the ceiling fans are a must to cool the rooms during hot summer nights. Breakfast is simple, with canned fruit, baked goods, juice, coffee, and tea, to which guests help themselves in the upstairs sky-lit garden room.

106 W. Broadway (P.O. Box 5093), Silver City, NM 88061. *C* **505/388-1811.** www.zianet.com/palacehotel. 18 units. $38–$49 double; $62 suite. Rates include continental breakfast. AE, DC, DISC, MC, V. **Amenities:** Access to nearby health club and golf course. *In room:* TV.

SMALLER INNS

Bear Mountain Lodge ★★   Set on 160 acres just 3½ miles northwest of downtown Silver City, this lodge, owned and operated by the Nature Conservancy, is ideal for outdoors enthusiasts, from birders to bikers. The lodge was previously the passion of Myra McCormick, a salty outdoorswoman who continued to run the place into her 90s. Her death saddened many of us, but her bequeathing the ranch to the Conservancy ensures its future. The 1920s guesthouse offers large rooms with maple floors and high ceilings. Each is equipped with modern amenities, including country-inn Southwestern decor and comfortable beds. Four rooms have private balconies. This is a nature lover's delight. On-site naturalist Nature Conservancy staff members are on hand to inform visitors about the flora and fauna of the area, and they also conduct guided trips. Dinner is served for guests nightly for an extra fee. It's a buffet-style affair with such offerings as stuffed chicken breasts with vegetable casserole. What's best here is that you can count on complete quiet.

2251 Cottage San Rd., Silver City, NM 88061. (P.O. Box 1163, Silver City, NM 88062). *C* **877/620-BEAR (2327)** or 505/538-2538. www.bearmountainlodge.com. 11 units. $115–$200 double. 2-night minimum stay. Rates include full breakfast. Box lunches available for an extra charge. Horse boarding $15/night. AE, MC, V. Turn north off US 180 on Alabama St. (½ mile west of NM 90 intersection). Proceed 3 miles (Alabama becomes Cottage San Rd.) to dirt road turnoff to left; the lodge is another ½-mile. No children under 10. **Amenities:** Hiking trails; conference and event spaces; mountain bike rental; free naturalist activities and guided hikes. *In room:* A/C, dataport, hair dryer.

Casitas de Gila ★★   If you're looking for a remote and peaceful stay in the quintessential southern New Mexico terrain, this inn is for you. Set on a little bluff above Bear Creek, about a half-hour from Silver City, these five *casitas* (Spanish for "small houses") offer the epitome of Southwestern style. The adobe-style dwellings are decorated with Spanish-style furniture and Mexican rugs. The medium-size bedrooms and baths come well equipped with comfortably firm beds, bath supplies, and bathrobes. Each also has a kiva fireplace and a small porch with a *chiminea* (Mexican ceramic fireplace) and a grill. On hand is a hot tub with a view of the creek, canyon, and sky. The area is great for birding and hiking, and horseback riding can be arranged. Also on the property are 90 acres of hiking trails, an art gallery, and a courtyard.

50 Casita Flats Rd. (P.O. Box 325), Gila, NM 88038. (*C*) **877/923-4827** or 505/535-4455. Fax 505/535-4456. www.casitasdegila.com. 5 casitas. $90–$190 double. Rates include continental breakfast. AE, DISC, MC, V. **Amenities:** Jacuzzi; activities desk; telescopes. *In room:* Dataport, kitchen, hair dryer, iron.

Ciénega Spa & Salon This Queen Anne–style inn dates from 1906, but today it provides a contemporary spa experience in the heart of Silver City. The main floor of the inn/spa/salon has bisque- and azure-colored walls and fine local crafts. The large upper suite, perfect for families, sleeps six and has a lovely private patio. The lower suite could use a little more remodeling, but it's a good buy for more than two guests. A broad range of spa treatments, from facials to massages, are available; and meal service can be arranged.

101 North Cooper St., Silver City, NM 88061. (*C*) **505/534-1600.** www.cienegaspasalon.com. 2 units. $85–$165 double. AE, MC, V. **Amenities:** Spa; salon. *In room:* TV/VCR, kitchen, fridge, coffeemaker, stove.

CAMPING

Silver City KOA ((*C*) **800/562-7623** or 505/388-3351; www.koa.com) has 82 sites and 42 full hookups, and it offers groceries, laundry facilities, and a pool. The campground is 5 miles east of the NM 90/US 180 junction on US 180. **Silver City RV Park** ((*C*) **505/538-2239;** www.silvercityrv.com) has 48 sites (45 with full hookups), showers, laundry facilities, and picnic tables. It's located downtown on Bennett Street, behind Food Basket supermarket. Camping is also available at the Gila Cliff Dwellings (see "Gila Cliff Dwellings National Monument," below).

WHERE TO DINE IN & AROUND SILVER CITY

AIR Coffee Co., Inc. COFFEE AND BAKED GOODS If you're like me, you'll travel a long way to get a good cup of coffee. Here's one of the few places to find one in the entire southwestern part of the state, as far as I can tell. Roasted on-site, the beans are fresh and well brewed. Coffee is served is several styles, including Americano, cappuccino, latte, or mocha. This is where the local artists and shop owners hang in the morning, so you'll be able to pick up on local gossip while sitting within the sunny space filled with some decent and not-so-decent art. Cinnamon rolls and a few other morning treats are offered. Don't let them talk you into one of their smoothies—they're made with some kind of condensed sugar mixture that I found hardly edible. They have a patio and have been featured in *Sunset Magazine* and the *New York Times*.

112 W. Yankee, Silver City. (*C*) **505/388-5952.** Menu items $2–$5. MC, V. Mon–Sat 7am–5:30pm; Sun 7am–3pm.

Buckhorn Saloon and Opera House ✦ SEAFOOD/STEAKS/BURGERS Seven miles north of Silver City in Pinos Altos, the Buckhorn offers fine dining in 1860s decor. It's noted for its Western-style steaks, seafood, homemade desserts, and excellent wine list. If you've got a big appetite, try the New York strip with green chile and cheese. I liked the big fried shrimp. Entrees are served with a salad or soup and choice of potatoes or rice. Live entertainment is offered nightly. The high-personality saloon offers big round tables and a great wooden bar. Many come to this saloon to have excellent burgers and hear live music on selected nights. While waiting for your food, take a moment to peruse the attached opera house, where good melodrama theater is presented seasonally.

32 Main St., Pinos Altos. © 505/538-9911. Reservations highly recommended. Main courses $7–$43. MC, V. Mon–Sat 6–10pm; saloon Mon–Sat 3–10pm.

Diane's Bakery & Cafe ⋆⋆ NEW AMERICAN   This is an amazing find within a relative wasteland of taste in southwestern New Mexico. Diane Barrett, who was once a pastry chef at La Traviata and Eldorado in Santa Fe, has brought refined city food to this small town. At lunch, the atmosphere is bustling, usually with a slight wait for a table. At dinner, the tone is more romantic and low-key, with more nouveau specialties. The service is friendly and adequate. You can't go wrong with any of the baked goods here. At brunch, try the hatch Benedict, a version of eggs Benedict made with home-baked chile cheddar toast. At lunch I suggest the *spano,* a baked spinach pastry, served with a salad; the quiche of the day is also delicious. At dinner, you may want to opt for one of the night's specials, such as grilled lamb with wild mushroom demi-glace or the chef's choice lasagna. Diane's also serves great steaks. There's a small but creative wine and beer menu. Don't leave without sampling one of the desserts, such as blueberry or apple pie.

510 N. Bullard St., Silver City. © 505/538-8722. Reservations recommended for dinner. Main courses $5–$7 lunch, $14–$25 dinner. MC, V. Tues–Sat 11am–2pm and 5:30–9pm. Brunch Sat–Sun 9am–2pm.

Jalisco's (Kids) NEW MEXICAN   Set within an enchanting brick building in the historic district, this festive, nonsmoking restaurant serves big portions of good food. Three dining rooms fill the old structure, which has been Latinized with arched doorways and bold Mexican street-scene calendars on the walls. The combination plates are large and popular, as are the enchiladas. There are also burgers and a children's menu. Whatever you do, be sure to order a sopaipilla for dessert. They're delicious and huge. Beer and wine are served.

103 S. Bullard St., Silver City. © 505/388-2060. Reservations not accepted. Main courses $5–$10 lunch or dinner. DISC, MC, V. Mon–Sat 11am–8:30pm.

Shevek & Mi ⋆ (Finds) ECLECTIC   You can travel to many places at this sweet restaurant in the center of town. Chef Shevek Barnhart has spent much of his life absorbing culinary magic from relatives and friends with backgrounds ranging from Italian to Moroccan. That, combined with training at the Culinary Institute of America, makes for a journey of delicious flavors. The ambiance is clean bistro in the main room, a little more formal in a connecting dining room, and more casual on the patio. Sunday brunch brings bagels made from dough shipped in from New York, an example of the authentic New York deli food that pervades the menu, as is the challa French toast and, at lunch, the kosher pastrami Reuben, made nice and thick. Dinner brings such delights as chicken ashke, a chicken breast rubbed with curry and topped with smoked salmon and béarnaise sauce, served with herb roasted potatoes. Another find is the zarzuela, a Spanish bouillabaisse, made with a medley of seafood, served with home-baked French bread. Entrees come with a choice of soup or salad. Shevek & Mi boasts the largest selection of wines and microbrews in the region.

602 N. Bullard St. © 505/534-9168. Reservations recommended on weekends. Main courses $3–$7.25 brunch, $5–$9.25 lunch, $10–$23 dinner. DISC, MC, V. Mon–Thurs 10:30am–9pm; Fri 10:30am–11pm; Sat 8am–11pm; Sun 8am–9pm (hours may be shorter in winter; call to confirm).

8 Gila Cliff Dwellings National Monument ⋆⋆

It takes 1½ to 2 hours to reach the **Gila Cliff Dwellings** from Silver City, but it's definitely worth the trip. First-time visitors are inevitably awed by the remains of an ancient civilization set in the mouths of caves, abandoned for 7 centuries. You reach the dwellings on a 1-mile moderate hike along which you catch first glimpses of the ruins. This walk is an elaborate journey into the past. It winds its way into a narrow canyon, from which you first spot the poetic ruins perched in six caves 180 feet up on the canyon wall, stone shiny and hard as porcelain. Then the ascent begins up innumerable steps and rocks until you're standing face-to-face with these ancient relics, which offer a glimpse into the lives of Native Americans who lived here from the late 1270s through the early 1300s. Tree-ring dating indicates their residence didn't last longer than 30 to 40 years.

However, the earliest ruin that has been found within the monument is a pit house dated between A.D. 100 to 400. This dwelling below ground level was an earlier type of home occupied by the Mogollon people who grew corn and beans, hunted, and gathered wild plant food.

What's remarkable about the journey through the cliff dwellings is the depth of some of the caves. At one point, you'll climb a ladder and pass from one cave into the next, viewing the intricate little rooms (42 total) and walls that once made up a community dwelling. Probably not more than 10 to 15 families (about 40–50 people) lived in the cliff dwellings at any one time. The inhabitants were excellent weavers and skilled potters.

The cliff dwellings were discovered by Anglo settlers in the early 1870s, near where the three forks of the Gila River rise. Once you leave the last cave, you'll head down again traversing some steep steps to the canyon floor. Pets are not allowed within the monument, but they can be taken on trails within the Gila Wilderness. Be sure to pick up a trail guide at the visitor center.

ESSENTIALS

GETTING THERE   From Silver City, take NM 15 north 44 miles to the Gila Cliff Dwellings. Travel time from Silver City is approximately 2 hours. You won't find any gas stations between Silver City and Gila Cliff Dwellings, so plan accordingly. Also know that at the monument, vehicles are permitted on paved roads only.

VISITOR INFORMATION   For more information, contact **Gila Cliff Dwellings National Monument,** HC 68, Box 100, Silver City, NM 88061 (© **505/536-9461;** www.nps.gov/gicl).

ADMISSION FEES & HOURS   Admission to the monument is $3 per person, with children age 12 and under admitted free. The visitor center, where you can pick up detailed brochures, is open from 8am to 5pm Memorial Day to Labor Day and from 8am to 4:30pm the rest of the year. The cliff dwellings are open from 8am to 6pm in the summer and from 9am to 4pm the rest of the year.

SEEING THE HIGHLIGHTS

Today, the dwellings allow a rare glimpse inside the homes and lives of prehistoric Native Americans. About 75% of what is seen is original, although the walls have been capped and the foundations strengthened to prevent further deterioration. It took a great deal of effort to build these homes: The stones were held in place by mortar, and all the clay and water for the mortar had to be carried by hand up from the stream, as the Mogollon did not have any pack animals. The vigas for the roof were cut and shaped with stone axes or fire.

The people who lived here were farmers, as shown by the remains of beans, squash, and corn in their homes. The fields were along the valley of the west fork of the Gila River and on the mesa across the canyon. No signs of irrigation have been found.

A 1-mile loop trail, rising 175 feet from the canyon floor, provides access to the dwellings.

Near the visitor center, about a mile away, the remains of an earlier pit house (A.D. 100–400), built below ground level, and later pit houses (up to A.D. 1000), above-ground structures of adobe or wattle, have been found.

CAMPING

Camping and picnicking are encouraged in the national monument, with four developed campgrounds. Camping is free and some sites are RV accessible, though there are no hookups. Overnight lodging can be found in Silver City and in the nearby town of Gila Hot Springs, which also has a grocery store, horse rentals, and guided pack trips. For information, contact the visitor center (© 505/536-9461).

9 Other Adventures in Gila National Forest

Gila National Forest, which offers some of the most spectacular mountain scenery in the Southwest, comprises 3.3 million acres in four counties. Nearly one-fourth of that acreage (790,000 acres) comprises the **Gila, Aldo Leopold,** and **Blue Range wildernesses.** Its highest peak is Whitewater Baldy, at 10,892 feet. Within the forest, six out of seven life zones can be found, so the range of plant and wildlife is broad. You may see mule deer, elk, antelope, black bear, mountain lion, and bighorn sheep. Nearly 400 miles of streams and a few small lakes sustain healthy populations of trout as well as bass, bluegill, and catfish. Anglers can head to Lake Roberts, Snow Lake, and Quemado Lake.

JUST THE FACTS For more information on the national forest, contact the **U.S. Forest Service,** Forest Supervisor's Office, 3005 East Camino del Bosque, Silver City, NM 88061 (© **505/388-8201;** www.fs.fed.us).

The national forest has 29 campgrounds, all with toilets and six with drinking water. Car and backpack camping are also permitted throughout the forest.

HIKING & OTHER ACTIVITIES

Within the forest are 1,490 miles of trails for hiking and horseback riding, and in winter, cross-country skiing. Outside the wilderness areas, trail bikes and off-road vehicles are also permitted. Hiking trails in the Gila Wilderness, especially the 41-mile Middle Fork Trail, with its east end near Gila Cliff Dwellings, are among the most popular in the state and can sometimes be crowded. If you are more interested in communing with nature than with fellow hikers, however, you will find plenty of trails to suit you, both in and out of the officially designated wilderness areas.

Most of the trails are maintained and easy to follow. Trails along river bottoms, however, have many stream crossings (so be prepared for hiking with wet feet) and may be washed out by summer flash floods. It's best to inquire about trail conditions before you set out. More than 50 trail heads provide roadside parking.

Some of the best hikes in the area are the Frisco Box, Pueblo Creek, Whitewater Baldy, The Catwalk and Beyond, the Middle Fork/Little Bear Loop, and the Black Range Crest Trail. The Gila National Forest contains several wilderness areas that are off-limits to mountain bikes, including the Gila, Aldo

A Shocking Experience

If you'd like to have an electrifying moment or two, plan a visit to the **Lightning Field**, near Quemado (© **505/773-4560** or 505/898-3335; www.lightningfield.org). An enormous sculpture by American artist Walter De Maria, it consists of 400 stainless-steel poles arranged in a rectangular grid one mile by one kilometer in size. It's purpose? To attract those most picturesque and deadly bolts. Visitors are welcome May through October but must reserve months in advance.

Leopold, and the Blue Range Primitive Area. However, cyclists can access quite a few trails. Some to look for are the Cleveland Mine trail, Silver City Loop, Continental Divide, Signal Peak, Pinos Altos Loop, Fort Bayard Historical Trails, and Forest Trail 100.

The **Catwalk National Recreation Trail** ⚘ (© **505/539-2481**), 68 miles north of Silver City on US 180, then 5 miles east of Glenwood via NM 174, is a great break after a long drive. Kids are especially thrilled with this hike. It follows the route of a pipeline built in 1897 to carry water to the now-defunct town of Graham and its electric generator. About ¼ mile above the parking area is the beginning of a striking 250-foot metal causeway clinging to the sides of the boulder-choked Whitewater Canyon, which in spots is 20 feet wide and 250 feet deep. Along the way, you'll find water pouring through caves and waterfalls spitting off the cliff side. Farther up the canyon, a suspension bridge spans the chasm. Picnic facilities are located near the parking area. There is a $3 fee per car.

OTHER HIGHLIGHTS

The scenic ghost town of **Mogollon** is 3½ miles north of Glenwood on US 180, then 9 miles east on NM 159, a narrow mountain road that takes a good 25 minutes to negotiate. The village bears witness to silver and gold mining booms beginning in the late 19th century, and to the disastrous effects of floods and fire in later years. Remains of its last operating mine, the Little Fanny (which ceased operation in the 1950s), are still visible, along with dozens of other old buildings, miners' shacks, and mining paraphernalia. An art gallery and museum are found along Mogollon's main street. The movie *My Name Is Nobody,* starring Henry Fonda, was filmed here.

Reserve (pop. 300), 100 miles northwest of Silver City, has little to see except a few homes, a store, and a bar. As Catron County's seat, it is noted as the place where, in 1882, Deputy Sheriff Elflego Baca made an epic stand in a 33-hour gun battle with 80 cowboys. Cochise, Geronimo, and other Apache war chiefs held forth in these mountains in the late 19th century.

11

Southeastern New Mexico

I'd been to Carlsbad Caverns and to White Sands National Monument while growing up in New Mexico, but I'd seen them then through the eyes of a child. When I returned to these places as an adult, their immensity overwhelmed me, and their intricate beauty stirred my soul.

Running east of the Rio Grande (the I-25 corridor) and south of I-40, southeastern New Mexico has other sites as well. Along with the natural wonders, this is the home of the fierce Mescalero Apaches and the world's richest quarter-horse race. Billy the Kid lived and died in southeastern New Mexico in the 19th century, and the world's first atomic bomb was exploded here in the 20th. From west to east, barren desert gives way to

high, forested peaks, snow-covered in winter; to the fertile valley of the Pecos River; and to plains beloved by ranchers along the Texas border.

The main population center in this section of the state is **Roswell** (pop. 45,293), famous as the purported landing place of an unidentified flying object (UFO). **Carlsbad** (pop. 27,800), 76 miles south of Roswell, and **Alamogordo** (pop. 35,582), 117 miles west of Roswell, are of more immediate interest to tourists. Other sizable towns are **Clovis** (pop. 32,667) and **Hobbs** (pop. 28,657), both on the Texas border, and **Artesia** (pop. 10,692), between Roswell and Carlsbad. **Ruidoso** (pop. 7,698), in the mountains between Alamogordo and Roswell, is a booming resort town.

1 The Great Outdoors in Southeastern New Mexico

BIKING Several forest roads and single-track trails in this region are favorites with mountain bikers. In the Ruidoso area, near Cloudcroft, the **Rim Trail,** a 17-mile intermediate trail that offers views of the White Sands, is considered one of the top 10 trails in the nation. To reach the trail, take NM 130 from Cloudcroft to NM 6563, turn right, and look for the Rim Trail signs. The Cloudcroft area offers three other good trails: La Luz Canyon, Silver Springs Loop, and Pumphouse Canyon. For directions, contact the Cloudcroft Ranger Station (© 505/682-2551). For beginners, the Bonito Lake Road offers a scenic but easy 20-mile (round-trip) ride through the forest and around the lake. To reach the trail, take NM 48 from Ruidoso and turn off at NM 37. The road from Ski Apache Road up to Monjeau Campground, as well as several other roads in the Bonito Lake area near Ruidoso, are also well-traveled bike routes. The paved road up to **Carlsbad Caverns National Park** is scenic, and the auto traffic drives slowly, but it's very hot in the summer.

BIRD-WATCHING **Bitter Lake National Wildlife Refuge** (© 505/622-6755), northeast of Roswell, is particularly good for watching migratory waterfowl, and **Bluff Springs** (© 505/682-2551), south of Cloudcroft, is popular with turkeys and hummingbirds. If you find turkey vultures particularly fascinating, **Rattlesnake Springs** (© 505/785-2232), located south of Carlsbad, is the place to go.

BOATING   Boating, water-skiing, jet-skiing, and sailing are permitted at **Carlsbad Municipal Park,** which runs through town for just over a mile along the west bank of Lake Carlsbad. The lake also has a beach that's open to swimmers. **Brantley Lake State Park** (© 505/457-2384), 15 miles north of Carlsbad, is popular with windsurfers who favor its consistent desert winds. (To find information on New Mexico state parks, go to **www.nmparks.com.**)

FISHING   **Bonito Lake** and **Rio Ruidoso** are popular destinations for trout fishing, and **Oasis State Park** (© 505/356-5331) just north of Portales, also offers fishing.

GOLF   This region has plenty of golfing opportunities. In Ruidoso, **Cree Meadows Country Club,** Country Club Drive off Sudderth Drive (© 505/257-5815), is an 18-hole public course. Also public in the Ruidoso area are the 18-hole courses at the **Inn of the Mountain Gods Resort & Casino,** 287 Carrizo Canyon Rd. (© 800/545-6040 or 505/464-4100; www.innofthemountain gods.com); and **The Links at Sierra Blanca,** 105 Sierra Blanca Dr. (© 505/258-5330). In Cloudcroft, the nine-hole **Lodge at Cloudcroft Golf Course** (© 800/395-6343 or 505/682-2566; www.thelodgeresort.com) boasts an elevation of 9,200 feet; it's one of the highest courses in the world and one of the oldest in the United States. Alamogordo's **Desert Lakes Golf Course** (© 505/437-0290; www.desertlakesgolf.com) has views of Sierra Blanca and the Sacramento Mountains.

HIKING   More than 225 miles of trails weave a web through the Smokey Bear Ranger District of the **Lincoln National Forest.** From Ruidoso, a favorite destination of hikers is the White Mountain Wilderness, with nine trails, and the Capitan Mountains Wilderness, with 11 trails. **Smokey Bear Ranger District office** (© 505/257-4095), 901 Mechem Dr., Ruidoso, has excellent and inexpensive maps of each wilderness area. Monjeau Lookout is a popular destination off Ski Run Road (NM 532). **Carlsbad Caverns National Park** has an extensive trail system as well (outside the caves, of course).

HORSEBACK RIDING   Horseback riding is easily found in Ruidoso. Try the **Inn of the Mountain Gods Resort & Casino** (© 800/545-6040 or 505/464-4100; www.innofthemountaingods.com) and **Cowboy Stables** (© 505/378-8217).

SKIING   Southern New Mexico's premier ski resort is **Ski Apache** (© 505/257-9001 for snow reports, 505/336-4356 for information), only 20 miles northwest of Ruidoso in the Mescalero Apache Indian Reservation. Situated on an 11,500-foot ridge of the 12,003-foot Sierra Blanca, the resort boasts a gondola, two quad chairs, five triple chairs, one double chair, a day lodge, a sport shop, a rental shop, a ski school, a first-aid center, four snack bars, and a lounge. Ski Apache has 55 trails and slopes (20% beginner, 35% intermediate, and 45% advanced), with a vertical drop of 1,900 feet and a total skier capacity of 16,500 an hour. Though its location seems remote, a lot of skiers fill this mountain during weekends and holidays. Because the mountain is owned and run by the Apaches, you can experience another culture while skiing. All-day lift tickets cost $50 for adults and $33 for children ages 12 and under. The mountain is open Thanksgiving to Easter daily from 8:45am to 4pm. Lift-and-lodging packages can be booked through the **Inn of the Mountain Gods Resort & Casino** (© 800/545-6040 or 505/464-4100; www.innofthemountaingods.com). **Ski Cloudcroft** is a small ski area that is open only some winters. The mountain has 21 runs and a 700-foot vertical drop, served by one double chair and two surface

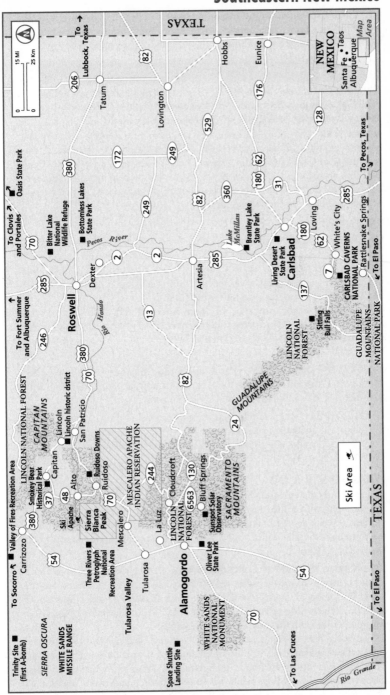

Southeastern New Mexico

TEXAS

NEW MEXICO
Santa Fe • • Taos
Albuquerque •
Map Area

N

0 15 Mi
0 25 Km

To → Lubbock, Texas

82 Hobbs
Eunice
176
128
To Pecos, Texas

206
Tatum

Lovington
529
249
62
180
31
285
To El Paso

172
380
82
360
Lake McMillan
Brantley Lake State Park
Carlsbad
Loving
180
62 White's City
7 CARLSBAD CAVERNS NATIONAL PARK
Rattlesnake Springs

To Clovis and Portales ↗
Oasis State Park
Bitter Lake National Wildlife Refuge
Bottomless Lakes State Park
Pecos River
249
Dexter
2
2
Artesia
285
Living Desert State Park
137
GUADALUPE MOUNTAINS NATIONAL PARK

70
285
Roswell
Rio Hondo
13
Sitting Bull Falls
LINCOLN NATIONAL FOREST

To Fort Sumner and Albuquerque
246
380
70

To Socorro ↗
Valley of Fires Recreation Area
LINCOLN NATIONAL FOREST
CAPITAN MOUNTAINS
Smokey Bear Historical Park
Capitan
Lincoln
Lincoln historic district
San Patricio
82
GUADALUPE MOUNTAINS

Carrizozo
380
54
37
48
Alto
Ruidoso Downs
Ruidoso
70
MESCALERO APACHE INDIAN RESERVATION
244
Cloudcroft
130
24

Ski Apache
Sierra Blanca Peak
Mescalero
La Luz
LINCOLN NATIONAL FOREST 6563
Bluff Springs
Sunspot Solar Observatory
SACRAMENTO MOUNTAINS

Three Rivers Petroglyph National Recreation Area
Tularosa Valley
Tularosa
Oliver Lee State Park
Alamogordo
54

SIERRA OSCURA
WHITE SANDS MISSILE RANGE
Trinity Site (first A-bomb)

Space Shuttle Landing Site
WHITE SANDS NATIONAL MONUMENT

70

To Las Cruces ↙
To El Paso ↙
Rio Grande

TEXAS

Ski Area

343

lifts. It appeals primarily to beginning skiers. When there's snow (usually Dec–Mar), it's open daily from 9am to 4pm. For information, contact the **Cloudcroft Chamber of Commerce** (© **505/682-2733;** www.cloudcroft.net).

2 Alamogordo

Famous for its leading role in America's space research and military technology industries, **Alamogordo** (pop. 35,582) achieved worldwide fame on July 16, 1945, when the first atomic bomb was exploded at nearby Trinity Site. Today, it is home of the New Mexico Museum of Space History, White Sands National Monument, and Holloman Air Force Base. While traveling in this area, I came to jokingly call it "Alamageddin," mostly because the town itself is fairly desolate, without many amenities. Twenty miles east and twice as high, the resort village of **Cloudcroft** (elevation 8,650 ft.) attracts vacationers to the forested heights of the Sacramento Mountains.

ESSENTIALS

GETTING THERE From Albuquerque, take I-25 south 87 miles to San Antonio; turn east on US 380, go 66 miles to Carrizozo; then turn south on US 54 for 58 miles (4 hr.). From Las Cruces, take US 70 northeast (1½ hr.). (Note that US 70 may be closed for up to 2 hr. during tests on White Sands Missile Range.) From El Paso, take US 54 north (1½ hr.).

The nearest major airport is **El Paso International.** The local airport, **Alamogordo–White Sands Regional Airport,** is served by **Rio Grande Air** (**866/880-0464** or 505/439-1275), which has flights from Albuquerque several times daily.

VISITOR INFORMATION The **Alamogordo Chamber of Commerce** and visitor center is at 1301 N. White Sands Blvd., Alamogordo, NM 88311 (© **800/ 826-0294** or 505/437-6120; www.alamogordo.com).

CITY LAYOUT Alamogordo is on the eastern edge of the Tularosa Valley, at the foot of the Sacramento Mountains. US 54 (White Sands Blvd.) is the main street, extending several miles north and south. The downtown district is actually 3 blocks east of White Sands Boulevard, off 10th Street.

WHAT TO SEE & DO

In addition to the attractions in Alamogordo itself, also enjoyable is the small, historic village of **La Luz,** just 3 miles north of Alamogordo. It has attracted a number of resident artists and craftspeople who live, work, and display some of their products for sale. Worth seeing are the old adobe corral and the small Our Lady of Light Church.

New Mexico Museum of Space History ⟨ The New Mexico Museum of Space History comes in two parts: the International Space Hall of Fame and the Clyde W. Tombaugh IMAX Dome Theater. Both are located on the lower slopes of the Sacramento Mountains, 2 miles east of US 54, and just above New Mexico State University's Alamogordo branch campus.

The Space Hall of Fame occupies the "Golden Cube," a five-story building with walls of golden glass. Visitors are encouraged to start on the top floor and work their way down. En route, they recall the accomplishments of the first astronauts and cosmonauts, including America's Mercury, Gemini, and Apollo programs, and the early Soviet orbital flights. Spacecraft and a lunar exploration module are exhibited. Displays tell the history and purposes of rocketry, missiles, and satellites and provide an orientation to astronomy and other planets.

At Tombaugh Theater, IMAX projection and Spitz 512 Planetarium Systems create earthly and cosmic experiences on a 2,700-square-foot dome screen.

Located at the top of NM 2001. ℭ 877/333-6589 outside New Mexico, or 505/437-2840. Fax 505/434-2245. www.spacefame.org. Admission to International Space Hall of Fame $2.50 adults, $2.25 seniors (age 60 and older) and military, $2 children age 4–12, free for children under 4. IMAX Theater $6 adults, $5.50 seniors, $4.50 children; additional charge for double feature; free for children under 4. Prices subject to change without notice. Daily 9am–5pm.

Toy Train Depot   The brainchild of John Koval (whom you're likely to meet at the door), this is an interesting attraction for train fanatics and laypeople. Koval started the nonprofit museum, housed in a genuine 1898 railroad depot, 10 years ago as a means to celebrate the railroad's important presence in the area. The museum meanders back through three rooms, each filled with tracks laid along colorful miniature cityscapes and countryside—1,200 feet of track altogether. The highlight is the last room, a re-creation of Alamogordo, Carrizozo, and Cloudcroft, where six trains swirl over bridges, through tunnels, and along flats, while train whistles blow and switch lights blink. The trains date from the 1800s, and there are also numerous examples from the 1930s to the 1950s. Rides through the grounds on 12-inch and 16-inch gauge trains are offered. There's also a railroad hobby shop.

1991 N. White Sands Blvd. ℭ 888/207-3564 or 505/437-2855. Admission $3. Train rides $4. Wed–Sun noon–4pm.

SOMETHING UNUSUAL
Eagle Ranch Pistachio Groves   This is a tasty and fun step into the nutty world of pistachio farming. New Mexico's first and largest pistachio groves, Eagle Ranch offers free 45-minute tours weekdays at 10am and 1:30pm in summer and at 1:30pm in winter. The tour offers a brief history of the pistachio grove and a tour of the shipping and receiving facility, salting and roasting department, and out through the groves. A visitor center with an art gallery displays the work of local artists, and at the gift shop, you can buy pistachio nuts, custom baskets, and a variety of other items.

7288 US 54/70 (5 miles north of Alamogordo). ℭ 800/432-0999 or 505/434-0035. Fax 505/434-2132. www.eagleranchpistachios.com. Free admission. Gift shop and gallery Mon–Sat 8am–6pm; Sun 9am–6pm.

TRINITY SITE
The world's first atomic bomb was exploded in this desert never-never land on July 16, 1945. It is strictly off-limits to civilians—except twice a year, on the first Saturday of April and October. A small lava monument commemorates the explosion, which left a crater ¼-mile across, 8 feet deep, and transformed the desert sand into a jade green glaze called "Trinitite" that remains today. The McDonald House, where the bomb's plutonium core was assembled 2 miles from Ground Zero, has been restored to its 1945 condition. The site is on the west slope of Sierra Oscura, 90 air miles northwest of Alamogordo. For more information, call the public affairs office of **White Sands Missile Range** (ℭ 505/678-1134).

GETTING OUTSIDE
Fifteen miles southeast of Alamogordo via US 54 and Dog Canyon Road, you'll find **Oliver Lee Memorial State Park.** Nestled at the mouth of Dog Canyon, a stunning break in the steep escarpment of the Sacramento Mountains, the site has drawn human visitors for thousands of years. Springs and seeps support a variety of rare and endangered plant species, as well as a rich animal life. Hiking trails into the foothills are well marked; the park also offers a visitor center with

excellent exhibits on local history, and picnic and camping grounds, with show-ers, electricity, and a dump station.

Dog Canyon was one of the last strongholds of the Mescalero Apache, and it was the site of battles between Native Americans and the U.S. Cavalry in the 19th century. Around the turn of the 20th century, rancher Oliver Lee built a home near here and raised cattle. Guided tours from the visitor center to Lee's restored house give a taste of early ranch life in southern New Mexico.

The park is open 24 hours a day; admission is $5 per car. The visitor center is open daily from 9am to 4pm. Guided tours are offered Saturday and Sunday at 3pm, weather permitting. For more information, call ℂ **505/437-8284.**

EXPLORING THE SURROUNDING AREA

Cloudcroft 🐾 is a picturesque mountain village of 750 people high in the Sacra-mento Mountains, surrounded by Lincoln National Forest. Though only about 20 miles east of Alamogordo via US 82, it is twice as high, overlooking the Tularosa Valley from a dizzying elevation of almost 9,000 feet. It was founded in 1899 when railroad surveyors reached the mountain summit and built a lodge for Southern Pacific Railroad workers. Today, The Lodge is Cloudcroft's biggest attraction and biggest employer (see "Nearby Places to Stay & Dine," below). Other accommodations are also available in town, as are lots of recreational opportunities and community festivals. For information, contact the **Cloud-croft Chamber of Commerce,** P.O. Box 1290, Cloudcroft, NM 88317 (ℂ **505/ 682-2733;** www.cloudcroft.net). It's located in a log cabin in the center of town, on the south side of US 82.

The **Sacramento Mountains Historical Museum and Pioneer Village,** US 82 east of downtown Cloudcroft (ℂ **505/682-2932**), recalls the community's early days, with several pioneer buildings, historic photos, and exhibits of turn-of-the-20th-century railroad memorabilia, clothing, and other artifacts. Call for hours. Nearby, **Lincoln National Forest** (ℂ **505/682-2551**) maintains the unique **La Pasada Encantada Nature Trail,** a short footpath from Sleepygrass Campground, off NM 130 south of town, with signs in Braille inviting walkers to touch the various plants, leaves, and trees. A new trail is a several-mile mod-erate hike to the historic **Mexican Canyon Railroad Trestle.** The trail head is in a U.S. Forest Service picnic area, west of the junction of US 82 and NM 130, where you'll also find a short walk to an observation point offering spectacular views across White Sands Missile Range and the Tularosa Basin. The picnic area also has tables, grills, drinking water, and restrooms.

National Solar Observatory–Sacramento Peak (ℂ **505/434-7000;** http:// nsosp.nso.edu), 18 miles south of Cloudcroft via NM 6563, a National Scenic Byway, attracts astronomers from around the world to study the sun and its effects on our planet. Actually, three observatories are here, with two open to the public for self-guided tours (allow at least 1 hr.), open daily from 8am to 6pm. Free guided tours are offered Saturday at 2pm from May to October. The visi-tor center, which is open daily from 10am to 6pm, has a gift shop and scientific exhibits geared toward children.

For a quick bite in the village, head to **Far Side Food and Health,** 91 Glori-eta Ave. (ℂ **505/682-5000**). It's part health goods store, part little kitchen—and the food is excellent. Diners order at a counter and sit at small tables and com-fortable chairs within the store or on a porch. Sandwiches, such as roast beef or chicken salad, are served on big slices of home-baked bread and grilled if you like. Each day sees a special, such as jambalaya served with corn bread. Best of all are the pastries—cherry or apple tarts, baked fresh daily. It's open daily 11am to 3pm.

If you like outdoor gear and items such as scented candles and tie-dyed clothes, stop next door at **High Altitude,** 310 Burro Ave. (© **505/682-1229**).

WHERE TO STAY IN ALAMOGORDO

All accommodations in Alamogordo are along White Sands Boulevard, the north–south highway through town.

Best Western Desert Aire   This brick-and-stucco hotel (with renovation ongoing) is the place to stay in Alamogordo. The medium-size rooms are cozy and have contemporary furnishings, minifridges, and hair dryers. You'll find firm beds and average-size, functional bathrooms. Also available are kitchenettes, which contain stoves, ovens, and microwaves. The suites are inexpensive and have 3-foot-deep Jacuzzi tubs.

1021 S. White Sands Blvd., Alamogordo, NM 88310. © **800/565-1988** or 505/437-2110. Fax 505/437-1898. www.bestwestern.com. 99 units. $58–$64 double; $65–$79 suite. Rates include continental breakfast. AE, DISC, MC, V. Pets welcome with $50 deposit. **Amenities:** Outdoor pool; Jacuzzi; sauna; game room; coin-op laundry; same-day dry cleaning. *In room:* A/C, TV, dataport, fridge, coffeemaker, hair dryer, iron.

Days Inn Alamogordo   Clean, comfortable rooms with standard furnishings are what you'll find at this two-story motel built in 1987. Remodeling is ongoing, so ask for the most up-to-date room. Each is medium-size, with decent beds and a small bathroom; all have nice amenities.

907 S. White Sands Blvd., Alamogordo, NM 88310. © **800/DAYS-INN** or 505/437-5090. Fax 505/434-5667. www.daysinn.com. 40 units. $49–$55 double. AE, DISC, MC, V. **Amenities:** Outdoor pool; coin-op laundry; laundry service. *In room:* A/C, TV, dataport, fridge, hair dryer, microwave.

CAMPING

I strongly recommend camping at **White Sands National Monument,** especially if you want to see the sunrise over the dunes or catch them under a full moon (see "Camping," under "White Sands National Monument," below). However, it's not an easy prospect; only tents are allowed, you have to walk quite a distance to the campground, and the monument has no formal facilities.

If you'd rather have amenities, try **Alamogordo Roadrunner** (© **877/437-3003** or 505/437-3003; www.roadrunnercampground.com). It has laundry and grocery facilities as well as a recreation room/area, swimming pool, playground, shuffleboard, and planned group activities in winter. The campground is located on 24th Street in Alamogordo, just east of the US 54/70/82 junction. If you're looking for something in between, **Oliver Lee State Park,** 15 miles southeast of Alamogordo via US 54 and Dog Canyon Road (© **505/437-8284**), is a good choice, with 44 sites, 10 full hookups, picnic tables, grills, tenting availability, a playground, and hiking trails.

WHERE TO DINE IN ALAMOGORDO

Margo's 🐾 MEXICAN   For 28 years, the Sandoval family has been feeding New Mexicans and travelers hearty, flavorful food at a decent price. The tradition continues. Set in a windowless building with two main dining rooms, the restaurant isn't much for atmosphere, though colorful Mexican blankets provide a festive touch. Each meal starts with complimentary chips and salsa; with it, you may order from a variety of domestic and imported beers and a few wines. Service is good, though this place can get busy (and noisy), which can slow things down a bit. The Margo's Special is a big seller here, a combo plate with guacamole salad, beef taco, enchilada, chile relleno, Spanish rice, and refried beans. However, the chicken enchilada special is my favorite. Lunch specials provide smaller portions at a great price. For dessert, try sopaipillas or flan.

504 E. 1st St. (1 block east of White Sands Blvd.). © 505/434-0689. Main courses $4.25–$11 lunch and dinner. AE, DISC, MC, V. Daily 10:30am–9pm.

Memories Restaurant ✦ *Finds* AMERICAN   Set in a 1907 Victorian home in a residential neighborhood right on the edge of historic downtown, this restaurant serves excellent food in an old-world setting. Functional tables sit on Brazilian-oak floors within what was once the living room and den, creating a casual, comfortable atmosphere, which is a good thing because the service is overworked and therefore slow. Many of the clients here at lunch are women, who come to sample salads and croissant sandwiches; dinner customers include a more even mix of genders. Basically, the place is packed nonstop while it's open. I recommend the crab salad served over avocado, or the turkey and avocado croissant sandwich. For dinner, a big seller is the prime rib, which comes with salad or soup, bread, a side dish, and vegetable. The grilled shrimp is also good. Beer and wine are available.

1223 New York Ave. (corner of 13th St.). © 505/437-0077. Reservations recommended. Main courses $5–$10 lunch, $11–$17 dinner. AE, DISC, MC, V. Mon–Sat 11am–9pm.

NEARBY PLACES TO STAY & DINE

Casa de Sueños ✦ *Kids* NEW MEXICAN   A fun, south-of-the-border stop, this new restaurant about 15 miles north of Alamogordo, outside Tularosa, serves tasty New Mexican fare, with a good dose of the whimsy of Mexico. Decorated with Mexican folk paintings and a country home mural, it exudes a fiesta atmosphere. Outside, the broad patio is lit with little Christmas lights and has chili peppers on the tablecloths. For breakfast try the huevos rancheros (eggs over tortillas smothered in chile). A lunch buffet provides a good sampling of enchiladas and beans. To start your meal, try the guacamole, made with red onions. For an entree, order anything with the green chile sauce, made with fresh chiles and well seasoned. Otherwise, you might try the chicken *adovado*—marinated chicken breast that's charbroiled—or sample a stuffed sopaipilla. Vegetarian and children's selections round out the menu. You can order from a variety of beers and wines.

35 St. Francis Dr., Tularosa, NM. © 505/585-3494. Reservations recommended on weekends. Main courses $4–$8 breakfast, $7–$13 lunch and dinner. AE, DISC, MC, V. Mon–Fri 11am–9pm; Sat 9am–9pm; Sun 9am–8pm.

The Lodge at Cloudcroft ✦✦   This lodge is an antique jewel, a well-preserved relic of another era. From the grand fireplace in the lobby to the homey Victorian decor in the guest rooms, it exudes gentility and class. Its nine-hole golf course, one of the nation's highest, challenges golfers across rolling hills between 8,600 and 9,200 feet elevation and is the site of numerous regional tournaments. All rooms in The Lodge have views and are filled with antiques, from sideboards and lamps to mirrors and steam radiators. Each room is medium-size, and some suites have jet tubs. Guests are greeted by a stuffed bear sitting on their bed with a sampler of homemade fudge from The Lodge Mercantile. In 1991, more rooms were added in the form of The Pavilion and The Retreat, which were built adjacent to The Lodge. These are most often rented out in blocks and are less desirable than those in the main hotel.

  Rebecca's (© 505/682-2566), the lodge's restaurant, is named for the resident ghost, believed to have been a chambermaid in the 1930s who was killed by her lumberjack lover. Three meals, plus a midday snack menu, are served daily. Service is friendly and very efficient, and the atmosphere is elegant, with bright sunshine during the day and romantic lighting at night. I recommend the marlin with crab béarnaise sauce, served with a twice-baked potato. For dessert, try the chocolate mousse pie with Oreo crust.

1 Corona Place (P.O. Box 497), Cloudcroft, NM 88317. © **800/395-6343** or 505/682-2566. Fax 505/682-2715. www.thelodgeresort.com. 61 units. $109–$159 double; $169–$329 suite. AE, DC, DISC, MC, V. Free parking. Pets welcome, with limitations and fee. **Amenities:** Restaurant; bar; outdoor heated pool; golf course; access to nearby tennis courts; exercise room; spa: Jacuzzi; sauna; bike and snowmobile rentals; fax and photocopying services; babysitting. *In room:* A/C, TV, coffeemaker; hair dryer and iron upon request.

3 White Sands National Monument ⭐⭐⭐

Arguably the most memorable natural area in this part of the Southwest, **White Sands National Monument** preserves the best part of the world's largest gypsum dune field, an area of 275 square miles of pure white gypsum sand reaching out over the floor of the Tularosa Basin in wavelike dunes. Plants and animals have evolved in special ways to adapt to the bright white environment here. Some creatures have a bleached coloration to match the whiteness all around them, and some plants have evolved means for surviving against the smothering pressures of the blowing sands.

The surrounding mountains—the Sacramentos to the east, with their forested slopes, and the serene San Andres to the west—are composed of sandstone, limestone, sedimentary rocks, and pockets of gypsum. Over millions of years, rains and melting snows dissolved the gypsum and carried it down into Lake Lucero. Here the hot sun and dry winds evaporate the water, leaving the pure white gypsum to crystallize. Then the persistent winds blow these crystals, in the form of minuscule bits of sand, in a northeastern direction, adding them to growing dunes. As each dune grows and moves farther from the lake, new ones form, rank after rank, in what seems an endless procession.

The dunes are especially enchanting at sunrise and under the light of a full moon, but you'll have to camp here to experience this extraordinary sight (see "Camping," below). If you're not camping, you'll probably want to spend only a couple of hours here. Refreshments and snacks can be purchased at the visitor center, along with books, maps, posters, and other souvenirs; however, no dining or grocery facilities are available here.

ESSENTIALS

GETTING THERE   The visitor center is 15 miles southwest of Alamogordo on US 70/82. (*Note:* Due to missile testing on the adjacent White Sands Missile Range, this road is sometimes closed for up to 2 hr. at a time.) The nearest major airport is **El Paso International,** 90 miles away. You can drive from there or take a commuter flight from Albuquerque to **Alamogordo–White Sands Regional Airport** (see "Essentials," under "Alamogordo," earlier in this chapter).

VISITOR INFORMATION   For more information, contact **White Sands National Monument,** P.O. Box 1086, Holloman AFB, NM 88330-1086 (© **505/479-6124;** www.nps.gov/whsa). When driving near or in the monument, tune your radio to 1610 AM for information on what's happening.

ADMISSION FEES & HOURS   Admission is $3 for adults 17 and over (free for children 16 and under). Memorial Day to Labor Day, the visitor center is open daily from 8am to 7pm, and Dunes Drive is open daily from 7am to 9pm. Ranger talks and sunset strolls are given nightly at 7 and 8:30pm during summer. During the rest of the year, the visitor center is open daily from 8am to 5pm, and Dunes Drive is open daily from 7am to sunset.

Warning   **Safety Tips**

The National Park Service emphasizes that (1) tunneling in this sand can be dangerous because it collapses easily and could suffocate a person; (2) sand-surfing down the dune slopes, although permitted, can also be hazardous, so it should be undertaken with care, and never near an auto road; and (3) hikers can get lost in a sudden sandstorm if they stray from marked trails or areas.

SEEING THE HIGHLIGHTS

The 16-mile **Dunes Drive** loops through the "heart of sands" from the visitor center. Information available at the center tells you what to look for on your drive. Sometimes the winds blow the dunes over the road, which must then be rerouted. All the dunes are in fact moving slowly to the northeast, pushed by prevailing southwest winds, some at the rate of as much as 20 feet per year.

In the center of the monument, the road itself is made of hard-packed gypsum. (*Note:* It can be especially slick after an afternoon thunderstorm, so drive cautiously!) Visitors are invited to get out of their cars at established parking areas and explore a bit; some like to climb a dune for a better view of the endless sea of sand. If you'd rather experience the park by hiking than on the long drive, try the Big Dune Trail, a good trail right near the entrance. It takes you on a 45-minute loop along the edges of the dunes and then into their whiteness, ending atop a 60-foot-tall one.

In summer, nature walks and evening programs take place in the dunes. Ranger-guided activities include orientation talks and nature walks.

CAMPING

I recommend camping here, especially to see the dunes at sunrise or under a full moon. The park closes at dusk, and you'll have to leave if you're not camping. It doesn't reopen until after dawn, so you'll have no way to see the sunrise unless you camp. White Sands has no campgrounds or facilities, however, so this is strictly a backcountry adventure. Only tent camping is allowed, and you'll hike ¾ mile to the campsite where you can pitch a tent. On a full moon, the campsites go quickly; you may want to arrive early in the morning. At other times, availability shouldn't be a problem. You must register at the visitor center, get clearance, and pay a small fee. Call © **505/479-6124** for information.

If backcountry camping isn't your speed, try one of the other campgrounds in nearby Alamogordo and Las Cruces (see the "Where to Stay" sections under "Alamogordo," earlier in this chapter, and "Las Cruces" in chapter 10).

---

4 Ruidoso ⟨★⟩ & the Mescalero Apache Indian Reservation

Ruidoso (most New Mexicans pronounce it "Ree-uh-*do*-so") is situated at 6,900 feet in the timbered Sacramento Mountains, the southernmost finger of the Rockies. It is a mountain resort town named for its site on a noisy stream and is most famous for the nearby Ruidoso Downs racetrack, where the world's richest quarter-horse race is run for a $2.5 million purse. Outdoor lovers, hikers, horseback riders, fishers, and hunters are drawn to the surrounding Lincoln National Forest. Southern New Mexico's most important ski resort, Ski Apache, is just out of town. The nearby **Mescalero Apache Indian Reservation** includes the Inn of the Mountain Gods Resort & Casino. Not far away, the historic village of

Lincoln recalls the Wild West days of Billy the Kid. Unless you like the bustle of a busy resort town, during summer I suggest staying in Lincoln rather than Ruidoso. During those busiest of months, the town seems to live up to its Spanish name—which translates as "noisy."

ESSENTIALS

GETTING THERE   From Albuquerque, take I-25 south 87 miles to San Antonio; turn east on US 380 and travel 74 miles; then head south on NM 37/48 (4 hr.). From Alamogordo, take US 70 northeast via Tularosa (1 hr.). From Roswell, take US 70 west (1½ hr.). No commercial service is available to **Sierra Blanca Regional Airport** (© 505/336-8111), 17 miles north, near Alto.

VISITOR INFORMATION   The **Ruidoso Valley Chamber of Commerce** and visitor center is at 720 Sudderth Dr. For information, contact P.O. Box 698, Ruidoso, NM 88345 (© 800/253-2255 or 505/257-7395; www.ruidoso.net).

EXPLORING RUIDOSO

GALLERY HOPPING

Many noted artists—among them Peter Hurd, Henriette Wyeth, and Gordon Snidow—have made their homes in Ruidoso and the surrounding Lincoln County. Dozens of other art-world hopefuls have followed them here, resulting in a proliferation of galleries in town. Most are open daily from 10am to 6pm, except where noted. Among my favorites are **De Carol Designs,** 2616 Sudderth Dr. (© 505/257-5024); **Crucis Art Bronze Foundry and Gallery,** 524 Sudderth Dr. (© 505/257-7186); **Fenton's Gallery,** 2629 Sudderth Dr. (© 505/257-9738); **Stampede Leather,** 2331 E. Sudderth Dr. (© 505/258-4029); **McGary Studios,** a bronze foundry at 2002 Sudderth Dr. (© 505/257-1000); and **Hurd–La Rinconada** (© 505/653-4331), in San Patricio, 20 miles east of Ruidoso on US 70 (see "A Scenic Drive Around the Lincoln Loop," later in this chapter), open Monday through Saturday from 9am to 5pm.

RUIDOSO DOWNS

In a stunning setting surrounded by green grass and pine trees, the famous **Ruidoso Downs racetrack** and **Billy the Kid Casino** (© 505/378-4431; www. ruidosodownsracing.com), 2 miles east of Ruidoso on US 70, is home to the world's richest quarter-horse race, the $2.5 million **All American Futurity,** run each year on Labor Day. Many other days of quarter horse and thoroughbred racing lead up to the big one, beginning in May and running to Labor Day. Post time is 1pm Thursday through Sunday. Grandstand admission is free; call about reserved seating prices, which range from $3.50 to $10.

The on-site casino has all the neon, noise, and smoke gamblers love. Though you'll find only slots at this casino (for more variety, head to Inn of the Mountain Gods Resort & Casino), bonuses here include simulcast racing on big-screen

---

Kids Family Fun

Families crave the excitement at **Funtrackers Family Fun Center** (© 505/257-3275), 101 Carrizo Canyon Rd. Spread out below a hill within town are go-cart courses for a variety of ages, bumper boats, bull-riding, and miniature golf. Beware: This place can be crammed with people midsummer. Open Memorial Day to Labor Day from 10am to 10pm; from September to May it's open weekends only, with limited hours.

TVs in the bar and a well-priced buffet with tables overlooking the track. Open Saturday through Thursday from 11am to 11pm; Friday from noon to midnight.

AN INTERESTING MUSEUM

The Hubbard Museum of the American West 🌾 This museum contains a collection of thousands of horse-related items, including saddles from all over the world, a Russian sleigh, a horse-drawn "fire engine," and an 1860 stage-coach. Several great American artists, including Frederic Remington and Charles M. Russell, are represented in the museum's permanent collection. A gift shop has some interesting books and curios.

841 W. US 70, Ruidoso Downs, NM 88346. ℂ **505/378-4142**. Fax 505/378-4166. www.hubbardmuseum.org. Admission $8 adults, $6 seniors and military, $3 children 6–16, free for children under 6. Daily 10am–5pm. Closed Thanksgiving and Christmas.

RUIDOSO AFTER DARK: SPENCER THEATER FOR THE PERFORMING ARTS 🌾🌾

The dream of Alto, New Mexico, residents Dr. A. N. and Jackie Spencer, the 514-seat Spencer Theater, on Sierra Blanca Airport Highway 220, 4½ miles east of NM 48 (ℂ **888/818-7872** or 505/336-4800; www.spencertheater.com), is a model performance space that cost more than $20 million to construct. Opened in 1997, the theater has drawn such talents as the Paul Taylor Dance Company and Marvin Hamlisch. In recent years top billings were the folk revival band the Brothers Four, and the master illusionists the Pendragons. Free tours 10am Tuesday and Thursday. Performances take place weekends and weekdays. The theater runs two seasons year-round, and tickets cost from $25 to $50.

MESCALERO APACHE INDIAN RESERVATION

Immediately south and west of Ruidoso, the Mescalero Apache Indian Reservation covers over 460,000 acres (719 sq. miles) and is home to about 2,800 members of the Mescalero, Chiricahua, and Lipan bands of Apaches. Established by order of Pres. Ulysses S. Grant in 1873, it sustains a profitable cattle-ranching industry and the Apache-run logging firm of Mescalero Forest Products.

SEEING THE HIGHLIGHTS

Even if you're not staying or dining here, don't fail to visit the **Inn of the Mountain Gods Resort & Casino,** a luxury resort owned and operated by the tribe (see "Where to Stay in & Around Ruidoso," below); it's the crowning achievement of Wendell Chino, former president of the Mescalero Apache tribe.

Also on the reservation, on US 70 about 17 miles southwest of Ruidoso, is the **Mescalero Cultural Center** (ℂ **505/671-4494**), open weekdays from 8am to 4:30pm. Photos, artifacts, clothing, crafts, and other exhibits demonstrate the history and culture of the tribe.

St. Joseph's Apache Mission 🌾 (ℂ **505/464-4473**), just off US 70 in Mescalero, on a hill overlooking the reservation, is a grand, stone Romanesque-style structure that stands 103-feet tall and has walls 4 feet thick. Built between 1920 and 1939, the mission church also contains an icon of the Apache Christ, with Christ depicted as a Mescalero holy man, as well as other Apache religious art. Local arts and crafts and religious items are for sale at the parish office. The church is open daily during daylight hours.

DANCES & CEREMONIES

Throughout the year, the Mescalero Cultural Center hosts powwows of colorful dancing and traditional drumming, open to the public and with unrestricted photography. The most accessible to visitors are dances and a rodeo on July 4.

Restrictions do apply, however, to the annual **Coming of Age Ceremony,** held during 4 days in early July. A traditional rite reenacted in the tribal community of Mescalero, it includes an Apache maidens' puberty rites ceremony at dawn and a mountain spirits dance at night. Check ahead to learn what you can and can't see and what you can and can't photograph.

For more information about the reservation before you visit, write to the Tribal Office at P.O. Box 227, Mescalero, NM 88340 or call © **505/671-4494.**

LINCOLN HISTORIC DISTRICT: A WALK IN THE FOOTSTEPS OF BILLY THE KID 🦌🦌

One of the last historic yet uncommercialized 19th-century towns remaining in the American West, the tiny community of Lincoln lies 37 miles northeast of Ruidoso on US 380, in the valley of the Rio Bonito. Only 70 people live here today, but it was once the seat of the largest county in the United States, and the focal point of the notorious Lincoln County War of 1878–1879.

The bloody Lincoln County War was fought between various ranching and merchant factions over the issue of beef contracts for nearby Fort Stanton. A sharpshooting teenager named William Bonney—soon to be known as "Billy the Kid"—took sides in this issue with "the good guys," escaping from the burning McSween House after his employer and colleague were shot and killed. Three years later, after shooting down a sheriff, he was captured in Lincoln and sentenced to be hanged. But he shot his way out of his cell in the **Old Courthouse,** now a state museum that still has a hole made by a bullet from The Kid's gun. Today visitors can hear a talk on this famous jail escape, by request, at the Old Courthouse.

Many of the original structures from that era have been preserved and restored by the Museum of New Mexico, the Lincoln County Historical Society, and an organization called **Historic Lincoln** (© **505/653-4025**), a subsidiary of the Hubbard Museum of the American West.

JUST THE FACTS   At the **Visitor Center,** on NM 380 on the east side of town (© **505/653-4025**), exhibits explain the role in Lincoln's history of Apaches, Hispanics, Anglo cowboys, and the black Buffalo Soldiers, and detail the Lincoln County War. A brief slide show on Lincoln history is presented in an old-fashioned theater. Start your visit here and either join a tour, included in the admission cost, or pick up a brochure describing the trust's self-guided walking tour ($1). Across the courtyard is the **Luna Museum Store.**

An annual **folk pageant,** *The Last Escape of Billy the Kid,* has been presented outdoors since 1949 as a highly romanticized version of the Lincoln County War. It's staged Friday and Saturday night and Sunday afternoon during the first full weekend in August as part of the **Old Lincoln Days** celebration. The festival also includes living-history demonstrations of traditional crafts, musical programs, and food booths throughout the village.

ESSENTIALS   The historic district is open year-round 8:30am to 4:30pm. Admission is $6 for adults (includes entry to seven buildings) or $3.50 per building. It's free for children 16 and under. For more information, write P.O. Box 36, Lincoln, NM 88338, or call © **505/653-4372.**

You can jostle your way back to the 1800s on a ride in the four-horse-drawn **Lincoln County Overland Stage** 🦌, NM 380, mile marker 91–92, west of Lincoln (© **505/653-4954;** www.stagecoach.bz). Morning and afternoon rides from about April to November take 2 hours to cover 5½ miles of an old stagecoach route from near Lincoln to Old Fort Stanton cemetery. The ride costs $25 for adults, $12 for children 3 through 16, and free for children under 3.

WHERE TO STAY IN & AROUND RUIDOSO

If you're looking for a budget stay in Ruidoso, the **Motel 6** on the outskirts of town has clean, reliable rooms. Call ℂ **800/466-8356** for reservations.

IN ALTO

Scarborough House ★★ *Finds*   On a ridgetop 15 minutes northeast of Ruidoso, this new B&B offers rustic elegance and spectacular views. The creation of a couple from Austin, Texas, the inn has a bit of city flair. It is timberframe construction, with high Douglas fir beams above a stacked flagstone fireplace in the great room. Guest rooms offer tasteful, imaginative sojourns, with an eye for detail. My favorite is the East Meets West room, which has Old West rusticness and old East Coast elegance. All rooms have fine touches; one might have a locally made cedar bed or a marble bathroom sink. All have pillow-top mattresses, fine linens, and signature soaps, as well as robes, spa towels, and slippers, handy when you're heading out to the hut tub, which occupies part of the 2,000 square feet of deck space. Those decks offer views of Sierra Blanca Peak and the Capitan Mountains. Breakfast brings such delights as eggs Benedict made with roast duck confit instead of Canadian bacon and home-baked croissants. Smoking is not allowed.

110 Great View Court, Alto NM 88312. ℂ **866/875-2592** or 505/336-4500. www.scarboroughousebandb. com. 4 units. $119–$159 double; ask about discount packages. Rates include full breakfast and afternoon snacks. AE, DISC, MC, V. No children. **Amenities:** Jacuzzi. *In room:* A/C, TV/CD player, hair dryer.

IN TOWN

Best Western at Pine Springs   Nestled within ponderosa pines well above Ruidoso Downs, this inn offers the consistency of a Best Western, with a few extras. Rooms are fairly spacious, set either motel-style so you can park nearby, or in a grassy courtyard, all only minutes from town and a stone's throw from the racetrack and casino. Rooms are decorated in soft colors and have comfortably firm beds and medium-size, clean bathrooms. The inn's two best points: It's located away from the town of Ruidoso, which during busy months is unbearably noisy, and it has a lovely outdoor pool with a view of the mountains.

1420 US 70, Ruidoso Downs, NM 88346. ℂ **800/237-3607** or 505/378-8100. Fax 505/378-8215. www.best western.com. 100 units. $63–$139 double. Rates include continental breakfast. AE, DC, DISC, MC, V. Pets are welcome. **Amenities:** Outdoor pool (summer only); Jacuzzi. *In room:* A/C, TV, fridge, coffeemaker, hair dryer, iron, microwave.

Hawthorn Suites Conference and Golf Resort ★★   Surrounded by a golf course, this most refined hotel in town is a good choice. However, if you find convention traffic daunting, you'll want to ask what's scheduled at the next-door convention center before reserving. When I visited, the hotel was quiet and serene. The grand lobby centers around an Anasazi-style stacked sandstone fireplace, creating an elegance that carries into the rooms. The rooms are medium-size, decorated in a contemporary Southwestern style, with comfortable earth tones and plenty of amenities. The suites, which are large, have sofa beds, fireplaces, and balconies. Many of the rooms have two-person Jacuzzi tubs. The hotel offers golf packages that are worth checking out.

107 Sierra Blanca Dr., Ruidoso, NM 88345. ℂ **866/211-7727** or 505/258-5500. Fax 505/258-2419. www. ruidosohawthorn.com. 120 units. $119–$179 double; $139–$239 suite. Rates include full breakfast, AE, DISC, MC, V. Take Mechem Dr. 5 min. north of Sudderth. Pets allowed. **Amenities:** Indoor pool; golf course; exercise room; Jacuzzi; massage. *In room:* A/C, TV, fridge, coffeemaker, iron, microwave.

Inn of the Mountain Gods Resort & Casino ★★   What's most impressive about this resort is its location, set on a grassy slope above a mountain lake on the Mescalero Apache Indian Reservation, 3½ miles southwest of Ruidoso. It is the successful dream of the former tribal president, Wendell Chino, who wanted to help his people get into the recreation and tourism business. In 2004, the original resort was leveled and a new one built, much in the style of a Lake Tahoe casino, with glossy gaming rooms, restaurants, and spacious guest rooms. The rooms are tasteful, with comfortable beds and balconies with views of Sierra Blanca Peak.

Wendell's, with a mountain view, features steak and seafood, with extensive wine offerings. The resort also has a sports bar, a night club, and a casino with more than 1,000 slot machines and 45 table games.

287 Carrizo Canyon Rd., Mescalero, NM 88340. ⓒ 800/545-6040 or 505/464-4100. www.innofthemountain gods.com. 273 units. $99–$399 double, depending on the season and type of room. Golf, tennis, and ski packages available. AE, DC, DISC, MC, V. Amenities: 2 restaurants; 2 bars; indoor pool; golf course; Jacuzzi; watersports equipment rentals; tour/activities desk; limited room service. In room: A/C, TV, dataport, coffeemaker, hair dryer, iron, safe.

Ruidoso Lodge Cabins ⋆   This 1950s cabin complex ranks as one of the quaintest accommodations in the Ruidoso area. Set on the banks of the Ruidoso River, these cabins have knotty-pine walls and small rooms decorated with quilts and some antiques. All cabins are very clean, with full kitchens, small baths, and porches with gas grills. Newer units adjacent to these, the **Riverside Cottages,** where kids aren't welcome, are more upscale, decorated Santa Fe style, with vaulted ceilings and in-room Jacuzzis. Though the road passing close to the cabins can prove noisy, it quiets down at night. During the day, the river is a nice spot to fish (for trout) or simply watch the minnows swim by. Be aware that the lodge has a strict policy prohibiting nonregistered guests. If you want to socialize at your accommodations while in Ruidoso, choose another inn.

300 Main Rd., Ruidoso, NM 88345. ⓒ 800/950-2510 or 505/257-2510. www.ruidosolodge.com. 10 cabins. Sept–June $99–$129 double; July, August, and major holidays $129–$169 double. Ask about midweek specials. DISC, MC, V. Children not permitted in Riverside Cottages. **Amenities:** Jacuzzi. In room: TV, kitchenette.

Shadow Mountain Lodge ⋆   Advertising "luxury lodging for couples," this is a good spot for a romantic getaway. Although children are permitted, this is not exactly the place for them. Built in 1984, it came under new ownership in 1994, and these owners are constantly updating the decor. Each room has a comfortable king-size bed and a fireplace. I recommend those that open out to the north, with windows facing south, because they get the most sunlight. The pine-covered grounds are attractive and well kept. Inquire about the cabins.

107 Main Rd., Ruidoso, NM 88345. ⓒ 800/441-4331 or 505/257-4886. Fax 505/257-2000. www. smlruidoso.com. 19 lodge units; 4 cabins. Jan 3–Dec 17 $99 double weekdays, $109 double weekends, $105 cabins; Dec 18–Jan 2 $129 double, $155 cabins. AE, DISC, MC, V. **Amenities:** Jacuzzi; coin-up laundry. In room: A/C, TV/VCR, dataport, kitchenette, hair dryer, iron.

IN LINCOLN: TWO HISTORIC B&Bs

Casa de Patrón Bed and Breakfast ⋆   The main building of Casa de Patrón, an adobe, was built around 1860 and housed Juan Patrón's old store (the home is on the National Register of Historic Places). In addition, Billy the Kid used part of the house as a hideout at some point during his time in the Lincoln area. Jeremy and Cleis Jordan have capitalized on the presence of that notorious punk by collecting portraits and photographs and hanging them throughout the cozy sitting and dining areas of the inn.

Rooms in the old part of the house are friendly, with a homey feel created by quilts and a major collection of washboards adorning the walls. More sophisticated are the Old Trail House rooms, one with a Jacuzzi tub, the other for people

with disabilities, both with fireplaces, wet bars, and minifridges. A short walk
from there are two casitas, ideal and reasonably priced places for families to stay.
Both have full kitchens, with stoves, ovens, microwaves, and fridges. If you stay
in a casita, a continental-plus breakfast is delivered to your door. If you stay in
the main house or the recently added Old Trail House, Cleis and Jeremy will
prepare you a full breakfast, such as Dutch babies (a soufflé) served with apple
compote and sausage.

On US 380 (P.O. Box 27), Lincoln, NM 88338. ℂ **505/653-4676.** Fax 505/653-4671. www.casapatron.com.
5 units, 2 casitas. $87–$117 double; casitas $107. Rates include full breakfast, except for casitas, which have
continental breakfast. MC, V. *In room:* No phone.

Ellis Store and Co. Country Inn ✿   With part of this house dating from
1850, this is believed to be the oldest existing residence in Lincoln County, and
as a B&B, it gives visitors a real taste of 19th-century living but with most of
today's luxuries. The house has plenty of history. Billy the Kid spent several
weeks here, although somewhat unwillingly, according to court records that
show payment of $64 for 2 weeks' food and lodging for The Kid and a com-
panion held under house arrest. Today, guests of innkeepers Virginia and David
Vigil can come and go as they please, wandering over the inn's 6 quiet acres, or
using the inn as a base while exploring Lincoln and nearby attractions.

Three rooms in the main house are a step back into the 1800s, with wood-
burning fireplaces or stoves providing heat, antique furnishings, and handmade
quilts. I recommend the Dr. James Room at the end of the house. Often used as
a honeymoon suite, it has a wedding picture of David Vigil's grandfather and
grandmother and access to the front portal. The separate Mill House, built of
adobe and hand-hewn lumber in the 1880s, isn't quite as cozy as the main
house, but it definitely offers an Old West feel. Two suites are good for families
and those seeking solitude. Breakfasts are complete and tasty. Ask about the
gourmet dinners served at Ellis. Service here has become less consistent in recent
years. If you want to avoid surprises, opt for Casa de Patrón (see above).

US 380 (P.O. Box 15), Lincoln, NM 88338. ℂ **800/653-6460** or 505/653-4609. 10 units, 6 with private bathrooms. $79–$139 double. Rates include gourmet breakfast. AE, DISC, MC, V. Pets not allowed inside, but ken-
nels are available. **Amenities:** Restaurant. *In room:* No phone.

IN SAN PATRICIO

Hurd Ranch Guest Homes   Located about 20 miles east of Ruidoso on the
2,500-acre Sentinel Ranch, these attractive casitas are part of the Hurd–La Rinconada Gallery, which displays the work of well-known artists Peter and Michael
Hurd, Henriette Wyeth Hurd, N. C. Wyeth, and Andrew Wyeth. The grounds
also include the San Patricio Polo Fields, where matches take place Memorial
Day to Labor Day.

Units available are two older one-bedroom casitas, built in the early part of
the 20th century, and three new and much larger units. Of the casitas, Orchard
House is my favorite; it sits on the edge of an apple orchard and is furnished in
weathered Southwestern antiques. Both of the larger units are elegant, especially
the newer La Helenita, a pitched-roofed adobe house that's large enough for two
families. All also have fireplaces and comfortable living areas and are decorated
with antiques, primitives, and art by the Hurd-Wyeth family. A stay here wins
you access to fine fly-fishing along Rio Ruidoso.

NM 70 (mile marker 281), San Patricio, NM 88348. ℂ **800/658-6912** or 505/653-4331. Fax 505/653-4218.
www.wyethartists.com. 5 units. $125–$510 per casita (2-night minimum in summer). AE, DISC, MC, V. Pets
welcome, with limitations and $10 per day fee. **Amenities:** Laundry facilities. *In room:* A/C, TV/VCR w/pay
movies, kitchen, iron.

CAMPING

Lincoln National Forest has more than a dozen campgrounds in the region; four of them are within the immediate area. The **Smokey Bear Ranger Station,** 901 Mechem Dr., Ruidoso (© **505/257-4095**), is open Memorial Day to Labor Day from 7:30am to 4:30pm Monday through Saturday, and the same hours Monday through Friday the rest of the year.

WHERE TO DINE IN & AROUND RUIDOSO
IN TOWN
Expensive

La Lorraine 🎄🎄 FRENCH   This piece of Paris is a bit hard to imagine in a New Mexico mountain town, but here it is, in an adobe building on the main street no less. Inside, you'll find French provincial decor, with lace curtains and candlelight. Start with a bisque or salad, and move on to a dish such as canard à l'orange, with apples and almonds in the sauce, and rich mashed potatoes and green beans on the side. The grilled rack of lamb with polenta is another favorite.

2523 Sudderth Dr. © **505/257-2954**. Fax 505/257-0208. Reservations recommended. Main courses $6–$11 lunch, $15–$33 dinner. AE, DISC, MC, V. Wed–Sat 11:30am–2pm; Mon–Thurs 5:30–9pm; Fri–Sat 5:30–9:30pm. Closed Mon May–Oct.

Moderate

Cattle Baron Steak House 🎄 STEAK/SEAFOOD   This is the place to go if you really have an appetite. It's a casually elegant restaurant, part of a chain with six locations around the Southwest, that may not serve the best steaks and seafood you've tasted, but still provides good-quality food. It's a casual restaurant decorated in an opulent Western style with lots of burgundy upholstery and brass. Often the place is busy and festive, so it's not ideal for a romantic getaway. Service is efficient and friendly. For lunch, try the turkey and avocado sandwich or the teriyaki kabob. For dinner, I usually order the filet mignon or the shrimp scampi. A large salad bar dominates the main dining room, and a comfortable lounge sits near the entryway.

657 Sudderth Dr. © **505/257-9355**. Reservations recommended for 6 or more. Main courses $7–$10 lunch, $8–$18 dinner. AE, DC, DISC, MC, V. Mon–Thurs 11am–10pm; Fri–Sat 11am–10:30pm; Sun 11am–9:30pm.

Le Bistro 🎄🎄 FRENCH   In some kind of alchemistic feat, chef Richard Girot has transformed casual into elegant in this downtown cafe set in an oddly round building. Decorated with French posters, the place is laid back enough for folks walking in off the street. But the food is more refined—bistro-style fare like what you might find at a streetside cafe in France. Still, it's usually a quiet place, and it's a good spot for a romantic dinner. The service is friendly, though at times overworked. Try the pork tenderloin with rosemary and whipped potatoes, or one of the daily specials, such as seafood-stuffed sea bass. All dinners come with baguette-style bread and a salad. Finish with a chocolate or strawberry crepe. Wine comes by the glass and beer by the bottle.

2800 Sudderth Dr. © **505/257-0132**. Reservations recommended for dinner. Main courses $5–$9 lunch, $9–$16 dinner. AE, MC, V. Mon–Sat 11:30am–2pm and 5:30–9pm.

Texas Club Grill & Bar 🎄 STEAK/SEAFOOD   Hidden away and somewhat hush-hush, this steakhouse isn't really a club, but because it advertises only by word of mouth, it has an exclusive quality, accented by plenty of Texas twang in the air and longhorns hanging on the walls. The place's secrets are a hometown friendliness and steaks hand-rubbed with signature seasonings. The dining room, which overlooks a small lake, has comfy booths and sturdy chairs. It's a lively place with a broad menu, including many cuts of beef and other dishes, such as chicken, shrimp, pasta, and salads. My favorite dish is the filet, and my mom's is the jumbo charbroiled shrimp, both served with a choice of potato, pasta, or vegetable, and hot rolls. Service is efficient. Also on-site is a lounge with a dance floor, where a DJ spins music every night the place is open.

212 Metz Dr. ⓒ **505/258-3325.** Reservations recommended. Main courses $9–$30. AE, DC, DISC, MC, V. Wed, Thurs, and Sun 5–9pm; Fri–Sat 5–10pm. From Mechem Dr., turn east on Cree Meadows Dr.

Weber's Grill ✶ PUB FARE   This happening place offers tasty food with surprising sophistication. The decor melds pine with Spanish tile to create a comfortable, casual ambience. Though the downstairs maintains a brewpub feel, with a CD jukebox and a big-screen TV, the upstairs is more restaurantlike—a good place for families. Service here is friendly and conscientious. You may want to start with some Roswell Alien Amber Ale or a Way 2 Cool Root Beer. You can select from a variety of appetizers, such as stuffed mushrooms or stuffed shrimp. Pizza, burgers, and salads are big hits here, but in the evenings you'll also find more refined fare, such as sole française (sautéed in wine, lemon, and capers). You can also get a great deal on a rib-eye. During warm months, check out the patio dining.

441 Mechem Dr. (5 min. north of Sudderth). ⓒ **505/257-9559.** Main courses $6–$10 lunch, $7–$19 dinner. AE, DISC, MC, V. Mon and Wed–Thurs 11am–9pm; Sat 11am–10pm; Sun 11am–8pm.

Inexpensive

Cafe Rio *Kids* INTERNATIONAL/PIZZA   This pizzeria-style restaurant is quite out of place in Ruidoso, offering deep-dish pizza like some you'd find in Chicago. My favorite is the Hawaiian combo, with Canadian bacon and pineapple. Some people rave about the calzones, which come with three cheeses and any of four fillings. Greek, Portuguese, and Cajun dishes are also available. You can sample from an extensive selection of domestic and imported beers, including seasonal beers. Finish with the double-layer chocolate cake with chocolate espresso frosting, unless you care about sleeping that night. With its casual atmosphere, it's a great place to bring the kids.

2547 Sudderth Dr. ⓒ **505/257-7746.** Fax 505/630-1612. Reservations not accepted. Main courses $5–$10 lunch and dinner. No credit cards. Daily 11:20am–7:50pm. Closed 3 weeks after Thanksgiving and 1 month after Easter.

Casa Blanca *Kids* NEW MEXICAN   This is a real locals' favorite for the margaritas and fun New Mexican food. You can count on a decent meal here, though it's not at the level of what you can find in Santa Fe or Albuquerque. The decor is casual—four rooms in a sprawling house on a hill within town, each with orange-washed walls. The garden room and patio are my choices. All of them can get a little noisy from the many kids who like the menu selections here. Your efficient and friendly server will start you out with complimentary chips and salsa. The best bet here is the chicken enchiladas with sour cream, or the beef or chicken fajitas. For dessert? What else but sopaipillas smothered in honey.

501 Mechem Dr. ⓒ **505/257-2495.** Main courses $5–$10 lunch and dinner. AE, MC, V. Daily 11am–10pm. Closed Thanksgiving and Christmas.

Cornerstone Bakery and Café ✶ CAFE/BAKERY   In comfortable garden-style decor, diners relish rich, big slabs of chocolate cream pie, while sipping espresso and cappuccino. During breakfast, this place is packed, serving omelets and eggs Benedict to locals and travelers. Lunch is equally bustling, with offerings such as quiche, an almond chicken salad croissant, and excellent French onion soup.

359 Sudderth Dr. (3 miles east of downtown). © 505/257-1842. Most menu items under $7. AE, DISC, MC, V. Daily 7:30am–2pm (cafe); 7am–3pm (bakery).

Hummingbird Tearoom ⋇ AMERICAN   If you're looking for a light, white-bread kind of lunch, go to this little room pinched into a corner of a small strip mall in the center of town. The owners, David and Jerry Sailor, are ever present, seeing to each patron's comfort. Though you won't find anything extravagant on the menu, everything is well prepared and tasty. I had a tuna salad sandwich made with sweet pickles. You can also order roast beef or ham sandwiches. The tomato and cream of broccoli soups are good, too. Jerry does all the baking and usually manages to sell out of her peach cobbler and cheesecake by early afternoon. The Tearoom has outdoor and indoor seating. Now, low-carb options, such as a salad with grilled chicken, are available.

2306 Sudderth Dr., Village Plaza. © 505/257-5100. Main courses $4.25–$7. AE, DISC, MC, V. Mon–Sat 11am–3:30pm; afternoon tea and desserts served until 5pm in summer.

A NEARBY PLACE TO DINE

Flying J Ranch *(Kids* CHUCK WAGON   This ranch is like a Western village, complete with staged gunfights and pony rides for the kids. Gates open at 6pm; a fairly mediocre but fun chuck-wagon dinner of barbecue beef or chicken, baked potato, beans, biscuits, applesauce cake, and coffee or lemonade is served promptly at 7:30. Then, at 8:20pm, the Flying J Wranglers present a fast-paced stage show with Western music and a world-champion yodeler.

NM 48, 1 mile north of Alto. © 888/458-3595 or 505/336-4330. Reservations highly recommended. $19 ages 13 and up, $10 ages 4–12, free for age 3 and under. DISC, MC, V. May–Labor Day Mon–Sat (Labor Day to mid-October Sat only) doors open at 6pm, dinner served at 7:30pm.

NORTH OF TOWN

Greenhouse Café ⋇⋇ *(Moments* NEW AMERICAN   A complete novelty, this little gem in Capitan, about 25 minutes from Ruidoso, serves fresh dishes highlighted by vegetables grown in Tom and Gail Histen's own greenhouse just up the hill. Veggies always vary, ranging from Persian garden cress to arugula to Swiss and gold chards. The setting is eclectic, a gallery displaying lovely jewelry and other art, accented by tile-topped tables and lots of plants, with a patio out back. Food ranges from vegan offerings to meatloaf lasagna. My favorite is the chicken stroganoff, with a light mushroom sauce and served in a puff pastry. The Mediterranean tilapia sits on baby spinach and grilled polenta with fresh dill. Soups, sandwiches, and salads are also delicious, as are desserts such as carrot cake or a float made with local Sierra Blanca Brewery Root Beer. The menu is enhanced by select wines and beers.

103 S. Lincoln, Capitan. © 505/354-0373. Main courses $6–$10 lunch, $13.50–$18 dinner. MC, V. Wed–Sat 11am–2pm and 5–9pm; Sun 9am–1pm.

Rodney's Copa Cabana ⋇⋇ *(Finds* NEW AMERICAN   Imagination flies high at this new spot in the village of Capitan, about 25 minutes north of Ruidoso. Somehow brightly striped walls and funky art create a casual Caribbean feel, and the food is fine-dining quality. You might start with the Club Med, a "carnival" of shellfish topped with tomato and olives. My favorite entree is the seared grouper, served with mashed potatoes and a jungle of veggies, including zucchini, caramelized onions, and baby bok choi. My mother likes the steak and shrimp kabob, with spicy marinade and similar sides. For those on a tighter budget, there's also gourmet pizza in many varieties. Dessert calls for the New York–style cheesecake. Diners can choose from a limited beer and wine menu.

321 Smokey Bear Blvd., Capitan. © 505/354-7637. Main courses $18–$25; pizzas $6–$18. AE, DISC, MC, V. Tues–Sat 5–9pm.

5 A Scenic Drive Around the Lincoln Loop

An enjoyable way to see many of the sights of the area while staying in Ruidoso is on a 1- or 2-day 162-mile loop tour.

Heading east from Ruidoso on US 70, about 18 miles past Ruidoso Downs, is the small community of **San Patricio,** where you'll find (watch for signs) the **Hurd–La Rinconada Gallery** (© 505/653-4331; www.wyethartists.com). Late artist Peter Hurd, a Roswell native, flunked out of West Point before studying with artist N. C. Wyeth and marrying Wyeth's daughter, Henriette, eventually returning with her to New Mexico. This gallery shows and sells works by Peter Hurd, Henriette Wyeth, their son Michael Hurd, Andrew Wyeth, and N. C. Wyeth. Many of the works capture the ambience of the landscape in the San Patricio area. In addition to original works, signed reproductions are available. The gallery is open Monday through Saturday from 9am to 5pm and Sunday from 10am to 4pm. Several rooms and guesthouses are also available by the night or for longer periods (see "Where to Stay in & Around Ruidoso," under "Ruidoso & the Mescalero Apache Indian Reservation," earlier in this chapter).

From San Patricio, continue east on US 70 for 4 miles to the community of Hondo, at the confluence of the Rio Hondo and Rio Bonito, and turn west onto US 380. From here it's about 10 miles to **Lincoln,** a fascinating little town that is also a National Historic Landmark (see "Lincoln Historic District: A Walk in the Footsteps of Billy the Kid," earlier in this chapter). From Lincoln, continue west on US 380 about a dozen miles to **Capitan** and **Smokey Bear Historical Park,** 118 Smokey Bear Blvd. (© 505/354-2748; www.smokeybearpark.com), open daily from 9am to 5pm. Smokey, the national symbol of forest fire prevention, was born near here and found as an orphaned cub by firefighters in the early 1950s. Admission to this park is $2 for adults, $1 for children age 7 to 12, and free for children under 7. The park has exhibits on Smokey's rescue and life at the National Zoo in Washington, DC; fire prevention; and forest health. Visitors can also stop at Smokey's grave and explore a nature path that represents six vegetation zones of the area.

If you hit Capitan around mealtime and like barbecue, head to the **Bar BQ Place** (© 505/354-0046), 316 E. Smokey Bear Blvd. (on the east end of town). As unassuming as its name, the restaurant occupies a plain pine building, and it serves delicious barbecue beef, pork, or chicken, with potato salad, coleslaw, and baked beans, all under $10. Two new restaurants in town serve more upscale fare (p. 359).

Heading west from Capitan about 20 miles takes you to **Carrizozo,** the Lincoln County seat since 1912. One of the best green-chile cheeseburgers in the Southwest can be found at the **Outpost** (© 505/648-9994), 415 Central Ave. They're served in a basket, with fries if you'd like. Inside this dark, cool bar/restaurant, you'll find cowboys and farmers chowing under the gaze of bison and deer heads. Down the street is **Carrizozo Joe's** (© 505/648-5637), 113 Central Ave. The owners, transplants from Minneapolis, Minnesota, have created an eclectic coffeehouse in an adobe home, spread throughout a number of rooms.

You can order espresso, cappuccino, chai, and smoothies, as well as sandwiches made with fresh-baked focaccia.

From there, take 2nd Street east to 12th Street, where a few galleries have opened up. Head south and you'll come to **Sierra Blanca Brewery,** 503 12th St. (© **505/648-6606**), which offers 20-minute brewery tours year-round, Monday through Friday from 9am to 4pm, though be sure to call first. While there, pick up a sixer of their Roswell Alien Amber Ale, a tasty brew with a distinctive little green man on its label.

Continue west on US 380 for 4 miles to **Valley of Fires Recreation Area** (© **505/648-2241**), where you'll find what is considered one of the youngest and best-preserved lava fields in the United States. Among the black lava formations is a ¾-mile self-guided nature trail, which is well worth the walk. Part of it is wheelchair accessible. You'll discover a strange new landscape that at first glance appears inhospitable but really is rich with plant life and wildlife. Be sure to walk far enough to see the 400-year-old juniper wringing itself from the black stone. A small visitor center and bookstore is in the park campground. Admission is $3 per person or $5 per car for day use, and camping costs $5 to $11. The park is open year-round.

To continue the loop tour, return 4 miles to Carrizozo, turn south onto US 54, and go about 28 miles to the turnoff to **Three Rivers Petroglyph National Recreation Area** (© **505/525-4300**), about 5 miles east on a paved road. Some 20,000 individual rock art images are here, carved by Mogollon peoples who lived in the area centuries ago. A trail about ¾ mile long links many of the most interesting petroglyphs; and the view surrounding the area, with mountains to the east and White Sands to the southwest, is outstanding. Be sure to go far enough to see site no. 7, a vividly depicted bighorn sheep pierced with three arrows. The park also includes the partially excavated ruins of an ancient Native American village, including a multiroom adobe building, pit house, and masonry house that have been partially reconstructed. Administered by the U.S. Bureau of Land Management, the park has facilities for picnicking and camping. The day use fee is $2 per vehicle. Overnight camping is $10. The U.S. Forest Service also has a campground in the area, about 5 miles east via a gravel road.

From the recreation area, return 5 miles to US 54 and continue south about 15 miles to **Tularosa Vineyards** (© **505/585-2260**), which offers tours and tastings daily from noon until 5pm. Using all New Mexico grapes, the winery is especially known for its award-winning reds. Wines can be purchased by the bottle, with prices ranging from $7 to $18. (*Note:* A fun pastime while traveling in this area is to read *Tularosa* by Michael McGarrity. Set in the Tularosa Basin, it's a thrilling mystery about the White Sands Missile Range and Spanish gold.)

Continuing south from the winery, drive about 2 miles to Tularosa and turn east onto US 70, which you take for about 16 miles to the village of **Mescalero** on the Mescalero Apache Indian Reservation. From US 70, take the exit for the Bureau of Indian Affairs and follow the signs to the imposing **St. Joseph's Apache Mission** (see "Mescalero Apache Indian Reservation," earlier in this chapter). After you return to US 70, it's about 19 miles back to Ruidoso.

6 Roswell

Best known as a destination for UFO enthusiasts and conspiracy theorists, Roswell has become a household name thanks to old Mulder and Scully. And even if you're not glued to your set for reruns of *The X-Files,* you may remember

⌜ Fun Fact The Incident at Roswell

by Su Hudson

In July 1947, something "happened" in Roswell. What was it? Debate still rages. On July 8, 1947, a local rancher named MacBrazel found unusual debris scattered across his property. The U.S. military released a statement saying the debris was wreckage from a spaceship crash. Four hours later, however, the military retracted the statement, claiming what fell from the sky was "only a weather balloon." Most of the community didn't believe the story, although some did suspect that the military was somehow involved—Robert Goddard had been working on rockets in this area since the 1930s, and the Roswell Air Base was nearby. Eyewitnesses to the account, however, maintain the debris "was not of this world."

Theorists believe that the crash actually involved two spacecraft. One disintegrated, hence the debris across the MacBrazel ranch, and the other crash-landed, hence the four alien bodies that were also claimed to have been discovered. In a 1997 statement, the Air Force said that the most likely explanation for the unverified alien reports was that people were simply remembering and misplacing in time a number of life-size dummies dropped from the sky during a series of experiments in the 1950s.

The main place to go in Roswell to learn more about the incident is the **International UFO Museum and Research Center** (© **505/625-9495**; www.iufomrc.org), located in the old Plains Theater on Main Street. As well as displaying an hour-by-hour timeline of the "incident," the museum has photographs of bizarre and elaborate crop circles, and a videotape in which an alleged witness tells his account. The museum is open daily from 9am to 5pm; admission is free.

If you want to see one of the two possible crash sites, call Bruce Rhodes at © **505/622-0628**. The short tour is 53 miles, takes 3 hours, and costs $75 for one to three people. The long tour covers approximately 123 miles (including the debris site), takes about 5 hours, and costs $125 for one to three people. Call to set up your own private tour.

Roswell hosts a **UFO Festival** every year during the first week in July. Some of the special events include guest speakers, the Crash and Burn Expo Race, concerts, out-of-this-world food, a laser light show, and an alien invasion at the Bottomless Lakes recreation area. For details on the event, call © **505/625-8607**.

Roswell as the setting for major scenes from the 1996 blockbuster *Independence Day*. Government cover-ups, alien autopsies, and cigarette-smoking feds . . . come along as we venture into the UFO capital of the world.

ESSENTIALS

GETTING THERE   From Albuquerque, take I-40 east 59 miles to Clines Corners; turn south on US 285, and travel 140 miles to Roswell (4 hr.). From Las Cruces, take US 70 east (4 hr.). From Carlsbad, take US 285 north (1½ hr.).

Roswell Airport, at Roswell Industrial Air Center on S. Main Street (© 505/ 347-5703), is served commercially by **Mesa Airlines** (© 800/MESA-AIR; www. mesa-air.com), which flies to Albuquerque almost hourly throughout the day and directly to Dallas, Texas, twice daily.

VISITOR INFORMATION The **Roswell Chamber of Commerce** is at 131 W. 2nd St. (P.O. Box 70), Roswell, NM 88202 (© 505/623-5695; www. roswellnm.org). The Roswell Convention and Visitors Bureau is at 912 N. Main (© 888-ROSWELL or 505/624-0889; www.roswellcvb.com).

SEEING THE SIGHTS

Historical Center for Southeast New Mexico

The handsome mansion that houses this historical collection is as much a part of the museum as the collection itself. A three-story, yellow-brick structure, it was built between 1910 and 1912 by rancher J. P. White. Its gently sweeping rooflines and large porches reflect the prairie style of architecture made popular by Frank Lloyd Wright. The White family lived here until 1972; today, this home, on the National Register of Historic Places, is a monument to early-20th-century lifestyles. First- and second-floor rooms, including the parlor, bedrooms, dining room, and kitchen, have been restored and furnished with early-20th-century antiques. The second floor has a gallery of changing historic exhibits, from fashions to children's toys. The third floor, once White's private library, now houses the Pecos Valley Collection and the center's archives. A gift shop sells books and other gift items.

200 N. Lea Ave. (at W. 2nd Street), Roswell, NM 88201. © 505/622-8333. Fax 505/623-8746. http://hssnm. net. Admission by donation. Daily 1–4pm.

New Mexico Military Institute

Considered one of the most distinguished military schools in the United States, the "West Point of the West" celebrated its centennial in 1991. On campus is the **General Douglas L. McBride Military Museum** (101 W. College Blvd.; © 505/624-8220), with a unique collection of artifacts documenting New Mexico's role in America's wars. Among the memorabilia are a machine-gun–equipped Harley Davidson used in 1916 in General Pershing's attack on Pancho Villa and items from the Bataan Death March. Tours of the campus are offered by appointment.

101 W. College Blvd. (at N. Main St.), Roswell, NM 88201. © 505/624-8220. www.nmmi.cc.nm.us. Free admission. Museum hours Mon–Thurs 8:30–11:30am and 1–3pm; weekends by appointment.

Roswell Museum and Art Center

This highly acclaimed small museum is a good place to stop in order to get a sense of this area before heading out to explore. Established in the 1930s through the efforts of city government, local archaeological and historical societies, and the Works Progress Administration (WPA), the museum proclaims this city's role as a center for the arts and a cradle of America's space industry.

The art center contains the world's finest collection of works by Peter Hurd and his wife, Henriette Wyeth, many of which depict the gentry-ranching lifestyle in this area. You'll also find works by Georgia O'Keeffe, Ernest Blumenschein, Joseph Sharp, and others famed from the early-20th-century Taos and Santa Fe art colonies. The museum has an early historical section, but its pride and joy is the **Robert Goddard Collection,** which presents actual engines, rocket assemblies, and specialized parts developed by Goddard in the 1930s, when he lived and worked in Roswell. Goddard's workshop has been re-created for the exhibit. A special display commemorates Apollo 17, which undertook the last manned lunar landing in 1972. The Goddard Planetarium is used as a science classroom for local students and for special programs.

100 W. 11th St., Roswell, NM 88201. © 505/624-6765. Fax 505/624-6765. www.roswellmuseum.org. Free admission. Mon–Sat 9am–5pm; Sun and holidays 1–5pm. Closed Thanksgiving, Christmas Eve, Christmas Day, and New Year's Day.

Spring River Park and Zoo *Kids*   This lovely park, covering 36 acres on either side of a stream a mile east of New Mexico Military Institute, incorporates a miniature train, an antique carousel, a large prairie-dog town, a children's fishing pond, a picnic area, and playgrounds. The zoo features 150 native and exotic animals, as well as some Texas longhorns.

1306 E. College Blvd. (at Atkinson Ave.), Roswell, NM 88203. © 505/624-6760. Fax 505/624-6941. Free admission. Summer daily 10am–8pm; winter daily 10am–5:30pm. Gift shop open summer Wed–Sun 1–5pm.

GETTING OUTSIDE

Fifteen miles northeast of Roswell, on the Pecos River, is **Bitter Lake National Wildlife Refuge** 🐾, where a great variety of waterfowl—including cormorants, herons, and pelicans—find a winter home. The refuge, reached via US 380 and NM 265 from Roswell, comprises 24,000 acres of river bottomland, marsh, stands of salt cedar, and open range. Seven gypsum sinkhole lakes, covering an area of 700 acres, have a peculiar beauty. Once threatened with extinction, the sandhill crane now appears here every winter, along with puddle and diving ducks. Snow geese were unknown here 20 years back, but they now turn up to the tune of some 40,000 every winter. All told, more than 300 species of birds have been sighted here. You can get information at the headquarters building at the entrance, or call © 505/622-6755.

Bottomless Lakes State Park is a chain of seven lakes surrounded by rock bluffs located 16 miles east of Roswell via NM 409, off US 380. It got its name from early cowboys, who tried to fathom the lakes' depth by plumbing them with lariats. No matter how many ropes they tied together and lowered into the limpid water, they never touched bottom. In truth, though, none of the lakes are deeper than 100 feet. The largest, Lea Lake, is so clear that scuba divers frequent it. Another, aptly called Devil's Inkwell, is so shaded by surrounding bluffs that the sun rarely reaches it. Mirror, Cottonwood, Pasture, and Figure 8 lakes got their monikers with similar logic; No Name Lake, which apparently didn't have anything to distinguish it, has been renamed Lazy Lagoon.

This park is a popular recreation site for Roswell residents. The park offers fishing for rainbow trout, swimming and windsurfing, campsites for trailers or tents, shelters, showers, a dump station, and a concession area with vending machines and paddleboat rentals (open 9am–6pm Memorial Day to Labor Day). The park is open year-round from 6am to 9pm daily, and admission is $5 per vehicle. For more information, call © 505/624-6058.

Originally built to raise bass and catfish, the **Dexter National Fish Hatchery,** located 1½ miles east of Dexter on NM 190, about 16 miles southeast of Roswell via NM 2, is now a center for the study and raising of 15 threatened and endangered fish species, such as the razorback sucker, Colorado squawfish, and Chihuahuan chub. Year-round, visitors can take self-guided tours among the hatchery's ponds; from late March to October, the visitor center is open, with exhibits and an aquarium containing endangered fish. The hatchery (© 505/734-5910) is open weekdays from 7am to 4pm, and admission is free.

WHERE TO STAY IN ROSWELL

Best Western Sally Port Inn & Suites ♣   Built in 1976, with remodeling ongoing, this hotel provides bright, spacious rooms with comfortable beds and good amenities, though you have to like to walk. Rooms are built around a huge quadrangle with an indoor pool in a sunny, plant-filled courtyard. Request a room at one of the four corner entrances and you'll avoid trudging down the long hallways. Also request a room facing outside rather than in toward the courtyard, so you won't hear noise from the pool. This is your best bet for full-service lodging. It is at the center of town, adjacent to the New Mexico Military Institute.

2000 N. Main St., Roswell, NM 88201. ✆ 800/WESTERN or 505/622-6430. Fax 505/623-7631. www.best western.com. 124 units. Rates include full breakfast. AE, DC, DISC, MC, V. Pets are welcome in smoking rooms, with $10 fee. **Amenities:** Restaurant; sports bar; indoor pool; nearby golf course; exercise room; Jacuzzi; sauna; room service; coin-op laundry; valet laundry. *In room:* A/C, TV, dataport, coffeemaker, hair dryer, iron.

Days Inn   The clean lines of the outside of this two-story motel are indicative of what you'll find here: good, functional rooms at a reasonable price. Situated at the center of town, it was built in 1962, remodeled in 1999, and receives constant upgrading. The standard rooms are medium-size, with comfortable beds and functional bathrooms with outer vanities. Rooms have dark oak furniture and Southwestern decor. "Business Place" rooms also have microwave/minifridge combinations. Some standard rooms have these "micro/fridges" too, so you may want to request one.

1310 N. Main St., Roswell, NM 88201. ✆ 505/623-4021. Fax 505/623-0079. www.daysinn.com. 62 units. $52–$75 double. Rates include hot breakfast. AE, DC, DISC, MC, V. Pets welcome. **Amenities:** Restaurant; lounge; outdoor pool; Jacuzzi. *In room:* A/C, TV, dataport, coffeemaker, hair dryer, iron.

Fairfield Inn & Suites by Marriott ♣   This inn at the center of town offers bright new rooms with plenty of amenities. The lobby and breakfast area have a living room feel, and the whole place offers the convenience and good prices one can expect from a Fairfield. Elements such as marble and tile in the baths and a nice pool further enhance the place. The suites offer an interesting angled two-room configuration, with a big TV and a CD player, and the standard rooms are medium-size, each with a desk. All rooms have comfortable beds.

1201 N. Main St., Roswell, NM 88201. ✆ 800/228-2800 or 505/ 624-1300. www.marriott.com. 67 units. $84–$94 double. Rates include continental breakfast. AE, DC, DISC, MC, V. **Amenities:** Outdoor pool; exercise room; business center; guest laundry. *In room:* A/C, TV, dataport, coffeemaker, hair dryer, iron, microwave.

CAMPING

Town and Country RV Park (✆ **800/499-4364** or 505/624-1833; www. roswell-USA.com/tandcrv), south of Roswell, is your best bet for camping, with some grass and cottonwood and elm trees for shade. The campground has 75 sites, most with full hookups. Prices range from $21 to $23. Tent campers can set up here as well. Bathrooms are clean and convenient, as is the large pool. The campground is located at 331 W. Brasher Rd. Head south on Main Street for 3 miles. Turn west on W. Brasher Road.

WHERE TO DINE IN ROSWELL

Cattle Baron ♣ STEAK/SEAFOOD   This popular restaurant is always busy during mealtimes. You can usually get a table, however, and they are nicely spaced so that the noise level is minimal. It's an informal place with a wealthy ranch feel—lots of burgundy and brass. Service is fast and friendly. Many come here just to feast at the salad bar, which is one of the best I've seen, and includes many potato and pasta dishes, as well as a choice of two soups. Everything is made fresh here—the bread baked in-house, the beef even hand-cut by the manager. You can't go wrong with the steaks, such as the tender filet mignon wrapped in bacon. You can also get dishes such as shrimp scampi at a price that will make you glad for Roswell's provincialism. The lounge is a comfortable place to come for evening drinks, and there's a full bar here.

1113 N. Main St. (𝒞 505/622-2465. Reservations recommended. Main courses $5–$10 lunch, $10–$20 dinner. AE, DISC, MC, V. Mon–Thurs 11am–9:30pm; Fri–Sat 11am–10pm; Sun 11am–9pm.

El Toro Bravo *Kids* NEW MEXICAN   Close to the International UFO Museum, this spot serves tasty New Mexican fare with a real local small-town ambience—sort of dark but with lots of bright touches, such as piñatas and cheesy bullfighting paintings. Service is friendly, and the food is made with fresh ingredients and good chile. You can't go wrong with the enchiladas or combo plates. Gentler palates can opt for chicken chalupas—*muy sabrosa*. The lunch buffet is quite popular. Kids have plenty of menu options, and adults can enjoy beer and wine.

102 S. Main St. (𝒞 505/622-9280. Main courses $5–$11 lunch and dinner. MC, V. Mon–Sat 11am–8:30pm; Sun 11am–2:30pm.

Farley's *Kids* AMERICAN   This raucous place can really draw crowds. Folks come for the barnlike atmosphere, where they can throw peanut shells on the floor and scream at TVs. Lots of booths inside and a patio outside please kids and their parents, as does the menu variety. Soups and salads, pizza, sandwiches, and burgers are the big sellers. Entrees such as chicken alfredo and baby back ribs will fill you up if you want a real meal. Beware: On weekend nights and holidays, you'll have to wait for a table. A full bar is available.

1315 N. Main St. (𝒞 505/627-1100. Reservations not accepted. Main courses $5–$14 lunch and dinner. AE, DC, DISC, MC, V. Daily 11am–midnight or so, depending on the crowd.

7 Also Worth a Look: Fort Sumner & Environs

The little town of **Fort Sumner,** home to 1,300 people, located 84 miles north of Roswell via US 285 and NM 20, is important in New Mexico history because it's the site of Fort Sumner State Monument and the burial place of the notorious Billy the Kid. Stop by if you're in the vicinity and have some time to spare.

Fort Sumner State Monument 🦌 (𝒞 **505/355-2573**) recalls a tragic U.S. Army experiment (1864–68) to create a self-sustaining agricultural colony for captive Navajos and Mescalero Apaches. Many still recall the "Long March," during which some Navajos walked a distance of more than 400 miles. By fall 1864, some 9,000 people were held captive here, site of the Bosque Redondo Reservation. Disaster followed: disease, blighted crops, alkaline water, Comanche raids, and the Navajos' devastating alienation from their homelands. Some 3,000 Native Americans died here. Part of the fort where the military lived and worked has been reconstructed at the site. A short walking tour takes you to various signposts that explain what was once on the land, illustrated with sad photographs of the dismal conditions. The visitor center (open daily 8:30am–5pm) gives you a good background before you head out to the site. The monument is located 7 miles southeast of the modern town, via US 60/84 and NM 272. Admission is $3 for adults, free for children age 17 and under.

Nearby, the **Old Fort Sumner Museum** (𝒞 **505/355-2942**) displays artifacts, pictures, and documents. It's a private enterprise that may not quite be worth the $3 admission.

Behind the museum (you don't have to go through the museum) is the **Grave of Billy the Kid,** its 6-foot tombstone engraved to "William H. Bonney, alias 'Billy the Kid,' died July 16, 1881," and to two previously slain comrades with whom he was buried. Also in the graveyard is the tomb of Lucien Maxwell, the land czar from the Cimarron area, who purchased Fort Sumner after the military abandoned it.

If you're curious about the notorious Kid, you can learn more at the **Billy the Kid Museum** (℃ 505/355-2380), 1 mile east of downtown Fort Sumner on US 60/84. In operation for over half a century, it contains more than 60,000 relics of the Old West, including some that recall the life of young Bonney himself, such as his rifle. Admission is $4 for adults, $2 for children.

The **Old Fort Days** celebration, the second week of June, is Fort Sumner's big annual event. It includes the World's Richest Tombstone Race (inspired by the actual theft of Billy's tombstone, since recovered), two nights of rodeo, a country music show, a barbecue, and a parade.

Sumner Lake State Park (℃ 505/355-2541), 16 miles northwest of Fort Sumner via US 84 and NM 203, is a 1,000-acre property with a campground (with electric and water hookups). Boating, fishing, swimming, and water-skiing are popular recreations.

For more information on the town, contact the **Fort Sumner County Chamber of Commerce,** P.O. Box 28, Fort Sumner, NM 88119 (℃ 505/355-7705; www.ftsumnerchamber.com).

CLOVIS/PORTALES

Clovis, 110 miles northeast of Roswell via US 70, is a major market center on the Texas border. Founded in 1906 as a railway town, it is now the focus of an active ranching and farming region, with about 38,100 in population. **Cannon Air Force Base,** a part of the Tactical Air Command, is just northwest of the city. The **Lyceum Theatre,** 411 Main St. (℃ 505/763-6085), is a magnificent restoration of a former vaudeville theater; it's now the city's center for performing arts. The **H. A. "Pappy" Thornton Homestead and Museum** in Ned Houk Park (no phone) displays antique farming equipment in a prairie farmhouse. A major rodeo on the national circuit is held the first weekend in June. "Clovis Man," who hunted mammoths in this region about 10,000 B.C., was first discovered at a site near the city. For more information, contact the **Clovis/Curry County Chamber of Commerce** (℃ 505/763-3435; www.clovisnm.org).

Nineteen miles south of Clovis is **Portales,** a town of 12,500 people that is the home of the main campus of **Eastern New Mexico University.** On campus are the **Roosevelt County Historical Museum** (℃ 505/562-2592) of regional ranching history and the **Natural History Museum** (℃ 505/562-2723), with wildlife exhibits, including a bee colony. Anthropology and paleontology exhibits are at the **Blackwater Draw Archaeological Site and Museum** ☆ (℃ 505/562-2202), 7 miles northeast of Portales on US 70 toward Clovis. The museum isn't much, but the archaeological site draws bone buffs from around the world. Especially notable there is the Interpretive Center, where visitors can watch an excavation in progress. The site is located on NM 467, 5 miles north of US 70. For more information, contact the **Portales Chamber of Commerce** at ℃ 505/356-8541.

For lodging in the Clovis/Portales area, try the **Best Western La Vista Inn,** 1516 Mabry Dr. (US 60/70/84), Clovis, NM 88101 (℃ 800/528-1234 or 505/762-3808; www.bestwestern.com), or the **Holiday Inn,** 2700 Mabry Dr., Clovis, NM 88101 (℃ 800/HOLIDAY or 505/762-4491; www.holiday-inn.com).

Clovis is the site of the original restaurant of the **K-Bob's Steakhouse** chain. The restaurant is at 1600 Mabry Dr. (© **505/763-4443**).

In Portales, stay at the **Super 8 Motel,** 1805 W. 2nd St. (© **800/800-8000** or 505/356-8518; www.super8.com); or **Morning Star Bed & Breakfast,** 620 W. 2nd St. (© **505/356-2994**). **The Roosevelt,** 107 W. 2nd St. (© **505/356-4000**), offers good American food in a historic building, and the **Cattle Baron,** 1600 S. Avenue D (© **505/356-5587**), has good steaks and a nice salad bar.

8 Carlsbad & Environs

Carlsbad is a city of 27,800 on the Pecos River. Founded in the late 1800s, its area was controlled by Apaches and Comanches until just a little over a century ago. Besides getting a good tourist business from Carlsbad Caverns, the town thrives on farming, with irrigated crops of cotton, hay, and pecans. The area is the largest producer of potash in the United States. The town was named for the spa in Bohemia of the same name.

The caverns (see "Carlsbad Caverns National Park," later in this chapter) are the big attraction, having drawn more than 33 million visitors since opening in 1923. A satellite community, White's City (www.whitescity.com), was created 20 miles south of Carlsbad at the park entrance junction. The family of Jack White, Jr., owns all its motels, restaurants, gift shops, and other attractions.

ESSENTIALS
GETTING THERE   From Albuquerque, take 1-40 east 59 miles to Clines Corners; turn south on US 285, and travel 216 miles to Carlsbad via Roswell (6 hr.). From El Paso, take US 62/180 east (3 hr.).

Mesa Airlines (© **800/MESA-AIR** or 505/885-0245; www.mesa-air.com) provides commercial service, with four flights daily between Albuquerque and **Cavern City Air Terminal** (© **505/887-3060**), 4 miles south of the city via National Parks Highway (US 62/180). You can rent a car at the airport from **Enterprise** (© **505/887-3039.**

VISITOR INFORMATION   The **Carlsbad Chamber of Commerce** and the **Carlsbad Convention and Visitors Bureau,** both at 302 S. Canal St. (US 285), P.O. Box 910, Carlsbad, NM 88220 (© **800/221-1224** or 505/887-6516; www.carlsbad.org), are open Monday from 9am to 5pm and Tuesday through Friday from 8am to 5pm.

SEEING THE SIGHTS
Carlsbad's pride and joy is the broad Pecos River, with a 3½-mile **riverwalk** along the tree-shaded banks, beginning near the north end of Riverside Drive. This is a lovely place for a picnic, and if you'd like to cool off, a municipal beach at the north end has changing rooms and showers. Annual **Christmas on the Pecos** pontoon boat rides take place each evening from Thanksgiving to New Year's Eve (except Christmas Eve), past a fascinating display of Christmas lights on riverside homes and businesses. Advance reservations, available from the chamber of commerce, are required.

The **Carlsbad Museum and Art Center,** 418 W. Fox St., 1 block west of Canal Street (© **505/887-0276**), contains Apache relics, pioneer artifacts, and an impressive art collection. The museum's store has a small but fine selection of jewelry at reasonable prices. The museum is open Monday through Saturday from 10am to 5pm; admission is free, although donations are welcome.

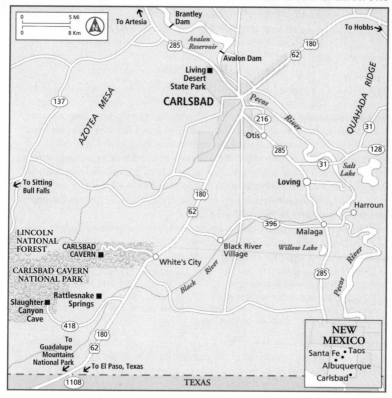

GETTING OUTSIDE

Recreational facilities in the Carlsbad area include some two dozen parks, several golf courses, numerous tennis courts and swimming pools, a municipal beach, and a shooting and archery range. Contact the **City of Carlsbad Recreation Department** (☎ 505/887-1191).

Living Desert Zoo & Gardens State Park *Kids* ☀ Situated within 1,200 acres of authentic Chihuahuan Desert, this park contains more than 50 species of desert mammals, birds, and reptiles, and almost 500 varieties of plants. Even for someone like me, who cringes at the thought of zoos, this is a pleasant 1⅓-mile walk. You pass through displays with plaques pointing out vegetation such as mountain mahogany, and geologic formations such as gypsum sinkholes. In addition to a new nocturnal exhibit, you're likely to see lizards and other wild creatures, as well as captive ones.

Rehabilitation programs provide for the park's animals, which have been sick or injured and are no longer able to survive in the wild. You'll see golden eagles and great horned owls among the birds of prey in the aviary, and large animals such as deer and elk in outdoor pastures. The view from the park, high atop the Ocotillo Hills on the northwest side of Carlsbad, is superb.

1504 Miehls Dr. (P.O. Box 100), Carlsbad, NM 88221-0100. ☎ **505/887-5516**. www.livingdesert.org. Admission $5 adults, $3 children 7–12, free for children 6 and under. Group rates are available. Memorial Dayweekend–Labor Day 8am–8pm, last park entry by 6:30pm. Rest of year 9am–5pm, last park entry by 3:30pm. Gift shop closes 45 min. prior to zoo. Closed Christmas. Take Miehls Dr. off US 285 west of town and proceed just over a mile.

WHERE TO STAY IN & AROUND CARLSBAD

Most properties are located along the highway south toward Carlsbad Caverns National Park (see "Carlsbad Caverns National Park," later in this chapter). Only The Best Western Cavern Inn is located near the National Park. The downside to staying there is that your restaurant and activity options are limited.

Best Western Cavern Inn   If you'd like to be close to the caverns, this is the place to stay. The lobby is within an Old West storefront, and the accommodations are across the street. The staff here seems to be overworked, so you may not get the service you would in Carlsbad. The motel has two main sections. The best is the Guadalupe Inn. This section is built around a courtyard, and rooms have a rich feel, with vigas on the ceilings and nice Southwestern pine furniture. Bathrooms are roomy enough, and the beds are comfortably firm. In back is a big pool surrounded by greenery. Next door, the two-story Cavern Inn provides 1970s rooms that are large and recently remodeled, though the small bathrooms with jetted tubs could use a little sprucing up.

The White's City arcade contains a post office, a grocery store, a gift shop, the Million Dollar Museum of various antiques and paraphernalia, and Granny's Opera House, a theater for weekend melodramas scheduled intermittently.

17 Carlsbad Cavern Hwy. at NM 7 (P.O. Box 128), White's City, NM 88268. ℂ **800/CAVERNS** or 505/785-2291. Fax 505/785-2283. www.bestwestern.com. 63 units. May 15–Sept 15 $65–$115 double; Sept 16–May 14 $50–$80 double. Rates include breakfast. AE, DC, DISC, MC, V. Pets welcome with $10 fee. **Amenities:** 2 restaurants; 2 outdoor pools; tennis court; volleyball; basketball; Jacuzzi; game room; shopping arcade. *In room:* A/C, TV, dataport, coffeemaker, hair dryer, iron.

Best Western Stevens Inn   This is a comfortable and welcoming place after the rigor of traveling in this part of the state, where there are miles between stops. The grounds are carefully landscaped, and the inn offers numerous types of rooms built in different eras. Some need to be upgraded, so be sure to request a remodeled one or, better yet, request one of the brand-new rooms at the south end of the property, which are large and have large bathrooms; each has a fridge and microwave, and some have full kitchens. All the rest of the rooms are medium-size, decorated in a Southwestern print, and have firm beds. Bathrooms are small but have outer double-sink/vanities. The Flume is one of the better restaurants in town.

1829 S. Canal St., Carlsbad, NM 88220. ℂ **800/730-2851**, 800/528-1234, or 505/887-2851. Fax 505/887-6338. www.bestwestern.com. 221 units. $59–$69 double; $69–$99 suite. Rates include breakfast buffet. AE, DISC, MC, V. Small pets allowed, with $25 deposit. **Amenities:** 2 restaurants; bar; large outdoor pool; exercise room; playground; airport shuttle; business center; limited room service; coin-op laundry; laundry service; same-day dry cleaning; executive-level rooms available. *In room:* A/C, TV, dataport, fridge, coffeemaker, hair dryer, iron, microwave.

Days Inn   This pale stucco, two-story motel on the south end of town offers reliable rooms with good amenities. The rooms are medium-size, with firm beds and medium-size bathrooms. To avoid the street noise, request a room at the back of the property.

3910 National Parks Hwy, Carlsbad, NM 88220. ℂ **800/DAYS-INN** or 505/887-7800. Fax 505/885-9433. www.daysinn.com. 50 units. $60–$80 double. Rates include continental breakfast. AE, DC, DISC, MC, V. **Amenities:** Large indoor pool; Jacuzzi. *In room:* A/C, TV, dataport, fridge, hair dryer, iron, microwave.

Holiday Inn 🏵   A handsome Territorial-style building houses this first-rate full-service hotel in downtown Carlsbad. This is my choice of Carlsbad accommodations. It was built in 1960 but continues to receive renovations. Rooms aren't as large as those at the Best Western Stevens Inn (see above), but they're refined, with white wooden furniture and decorated in Southwestern prints. The beds are medium-firm and comfortable; bathrooms are an average size, each with an outer vanity. Large executive rooms have comfortable chairs and ottomans as well as jetted tubs. Amenities in these rooms include robes and nice soaps and shampoo. The Phenix Bar and Grill has sandwiches, burgers, soups, and salads.

601 S. Canal St., Carlsbad, NM 88220. © 800/HOLIDAY or 505/885-8500. Fax 505/887-5999. www.holiday-inn.com. 100 units. $86–$115 double. Rates include full breakfast. AE, DC, DISC, MC, V. Pets allowed, with $25 fee. **Amenities:** Restaurant; outdoor pool; exercise room; Jacuzzi; sauna; playground; airport shuttle; laundry; dry cleaning service. In room: A/C, TV, coffeemaker, hair dryer, iron.

CAMPING

Brantley Lake State Park (© 505/457-2384) in Carlsbad has RV hookups as well as tent campsites. Picnic tables, grills, and recreational facilities are available. Boating and lake fishing are popular here. **Carlsbad RV Park and Campground,** on the south end of town at 4301 National Parks Hwy. (© 888/878-7275 or 505/885-6333; www.carlsbadrvpark.com), is a large, full-service campground with a swimming pool and playground. In Artesia, try **Artesia RV Park** (© 505/746-6184; www.artesiarvpark.com), a more moderately sized campground, located on Hermosa Drive just south of the junction of US 82/285. Laundry facilities and a game room are available.

WHERE TO DINE IN & AROUND CARLSBAD

Bamboo Garden CHINESE   This family-owned spot offers a good alternative to all that New Mexican food. It's a casual place, with comfy booths and elaborate Chinese chandeliers. Service is good. Locals flock to the buffet for lunch and dinner. It offers a huge range of choices, from sweet-and-sour pork to asparagus chicken to egg rolls and even salad, all made with fresh ingredients. The restaurant also serves American food.

1511 S. Canal St. © 505/887-5145. Main courses $5–$11 lunch and dinner. MC, V. Tues–Sun 11am–2pm and 5–9pm.

Blue House 𝕽 *Finds* CAFE/BAKERY   In a quest to find good coffee in even the smallest of New Mexico towns, I now rate Carlsbad high. On a quiet residential street just north of historic downtown is this gem, set in a Queen Anne–style blue house with morning-glory vines adorning the front fence. Inside, Parisian colors warm the walls, contrasting with brightly painted chairs and small round tables. The fare is simple, fresh, and imaginative, with espresso, lattes, and Italian sodas the biggest draws, along with special sandwiches and soups daily. Excellent baked goods top the breakfast menu. For lunch, try the feta spinach croissant, a deli sandwich on French country bread, or, for something sweeter, the cream cheese raspberry coffee cake.

609 N. Canyon Rd. © 505/628-0555. All menu items under $8. No credit cards. Mon–Sat 7:30am–3:30pm. Call to confirm hours. Take Canal Street to Church Street east, then south on Canyon Road.

Lucy's 𝕽 MEXICAN   When you walk in the door of this busy restaurant with festive Mexican decor, Lucy is likely to wave you toward the dining room and tell you to find a seat. Such is the casual nature of the place—and a sign of the good home-style food to come. Since 1974, Lucy and Justo Yanez's restaurant has been dedicated to the words of a Mexican proverb printed on the menu: *El hambre es un fuego, y la comida es fresca* (Hunger is a burning, and eating is a coolness). You'll probably want to start with a margarita or Mexican beer. The food is tasty, with Lucy's personal adaptations of old favorites, often invented by requests from regulars. "Barbara's Favorite Fix" (one beef enchilada and one chile relleno) was named after a local woman who had this meal six times every week.

Everything is made by hand. I recommend the chicken fajita burrito or the combination plate. Finish with a dessert of buñelos, sprinkled with cinnamon sugar. Children's plates are available; diners can choose mild or hot chile. A second Lucy's restaurant is in Hobbs, New Mexico, at 4428 Lovington Hwy.

701 S. Canal St. ⓒ 505/887-7714. Reservations recommended on weekends. Main courses $3.75–$12 lunch and dinner. AE, DC, DISC, MC, V. Mon–Sat 11am–9:30pm.

Pasta Café Italian Bistro ITALIAN   This new restaurant in the center of town works toward an Italian bistro feel but doesn't quite succeed. The main dining room has a hallway feel, and a lot of noise carries. A better bet is the little houselike replica within the dining room, which is cozier. Or, opt for the wraparound porch. The service is good. You might start with seared ahi tuna over baby bok choi, but only if you like your fish done sushi-raw. Move on to the veal picatta, which is tender, with a nice white wine caper sauce. Most, it seems, opt for pasta dishes, a good bet. Try the lasagna or fettuccini alfredo. The pizza is also a good option. A full range of drinks is available—come early and check out the bar, a cozy, inviting place. Live music plays on weekend nights.

710 Canal St. ⓒ 505/887-7211. Reservations recommended in summer. Main courses $6–$15 lunch, $7–$22 dinner. AE, DC, DISC, MC, V. Sun–Thurs 11am–9pm; Fri–Sat 11am–10pm.

Velvet Garter Saloon and Restaurant AMERICAN   This is the only restaurant in the Carlsbad Caverns area, besides the one in the base of the caverns (if possible, plan to eat in Carlsbad instead—this place get crowded). Despite this monopoly, the place does a pretty amazing job of preparing tasty food for a mass of travelers that pass through. The steaks are good quality and come with a trip to the salad bar, baked potato, vegetable, and bread. Your best bet may be one of the pasta dishes. Try the shrimp fettuccini Alfredo or the lasagna. In the same building, Fat Jack's serves breakfast and lunch in a setting heavy with linoleum. The saloon is unmistakable, with longhorns mounted over the door.

26 Carlsbad Cavern Hwy., White's City. ⓒ 505/785-2291. Reservations recommended in summer. Main courses $10–$20 (Velvet Garter); $5.50–$10 breakfast or lunch (Fat Jack's). AE, DC, DISC, MC, V. Velvet Garter daily 4–10pm (last seating at 9:30pm); Fat Jack's winter daily 7am–4pm; summer daily 6:15am–4pm. Saloon daily 4–10pm.

CARLSBAD AFTER DARK

The **Silver Spur,** 1829 S. Canal St. (ⓒ **505/887-2851**), offers live country and Western music most nights and free hors d'oeuvres during happy hour, as well as a big-screen TV. The **Firehouse Fire Escape,** 222 W. Fox St. (ⓒ **505/234-1546**), has DJ-style dancing in the upstairs of an old firehouse. The **Post Time Saloon,** 313 W. Fox St. (ⓒ **505/628-1977**), is a huge place with pool tables, three bars, and a dance floor. The club offers a range of DJ mixes, including country, tejano, and karaoke.

EXPLORING THE ENVIRONS
A SIDE TRIP TO TEXAS: GUADALUPE
MOUNTAINS NATIONAL PARK 🐾🐾

Some 250 million years ago, the Guadalupe Mountains were an immense reef poking up through a tropical ocean. Marine organisms fossilized this 400-mile-long Capitan Reef as limestone; later, as the sea evaporated, a blanket of sediments and mineral salts buried the reef. Then, just 10 to 12 million years ago, a mountain-building uplift exposed a part of the fossil reef. This has given modern scientists a unique opportunity to explore earth's geologic history, and outdoor lovers a playground for wilderness experience.

The steep southern end of the range makes up **Guadalupe Mountains National Park** and includes Guadalupe Peak, at 8,749 feet the highest in Texas, while the northern part lies within Lincoln National Forest and Carlsbad Caverns National Park. Deer, elk, mountain lion, and bear are found in the forests, which contrast strikingly with the desert around them. These isolated basins and protected valleys are home to a proliferation of vegetation rare elsewhere in the Southwest.

JUST THE FACTS   To reach the park, take US 62/180, 55 miles southwest of Carlsbad. Admission to the park is $3, and the visitor center is open June through August daily from 8am to 6pm; September through May from 8am to 4:30pm. For more information, contact **Park Ranger,** HC-60, Box 400, Salt Flat, TX 79847 (℃ **915/828-3251;** www.nps.gov/gumo). The park has more than 80 miles of trails; most are steep, rugged, and rocky. No lodging, restaurants, stores, or gas exist within 35 miles of the park. Leashed pets are permitted only in the campground parking area.

SEEING THE HIGHLIGHTS   The visitor center offers a variety of exhibits and slide programs that tell the story of the Guadalupe Mountains, as well as ranger-guided walks and lectures. Information, maps, and backcountry permits can also be obtained at **McKittrick Canyon Visitor Center** (10 miles northeast via US 62/180 and a side road; ℃ **915/828-3381**) and the **Dog Canyon Ranger Station** (reached through Carlsbad via NM 137 and County Rd. 414, about 70 miles; ℃ **505/981-2418**).

One of the most spectacular hikes in Texas is to the top of **Guadalupe Peak,** an 8½-mile round-trip trek accessed from the Pine Springs Campground. **McKittrick Canyon,** protected by its high sheer walls, with a green swath of trees growing along the banks of its spring-fed stream, is a beautiful location. It is a great spot for hiking, bird-watching, and viewing other wildlife, and it's an especially lovely sight during fall foliage season, from late October to mid-November. The **McKittrick Canyon Trail** travels more than 10 miles into the canyon and up onto a ridge. If you're interested in day-hiking it, be aware that you'll travel a mile before the canyon becomes scenic. Most of the national park's 86,416 acres are reached only by 80 miles of foot or horse trails through desert, canyon, and high forest. The visitor center can provide you with a brief trail guide. A longer guide, titled *Trails of the Guadalupe,* is available for purchase at the visitor center as well. Backcountry hikers must have water and permits; camping must be in designated areas.

CAMPING   Pine Springs and Dog Canyon both have developed camping areas, with restrooms and water, but no hookups or showers. Fires, including charcoal, are not permitted.

ARTESIA

A recent downtown rejuvenation project has brought a sparkle to **Artesia,** a town of 10,692 people, 36 miles north of Carlsbad on US 285. The **Artesia Historical Museum and Art Center,** housed in a Victorian home at 505 W. Richardson Ave. (℃ **505/748-2390**), is worth visiting just to see the Queen Anne–style home with the outside covered with round river stones. Open Tuesday through Friday from 9am to 5pm and Saturday from 1 to 5pm, the museum exhibits Native American and pioneer artifacts, traveling exhibits, and art shows. Admission is free.

Finds Dining on the Oil Fields

In a stroke of brilliance, Artesia oil man Frank Yates, Jr., conceived **The Wellhead** , a brewpub in Artesia designed around the notion of oil wells. It's an open, friendly place, with such touches as a 1924 flowing derrick depicted in tile and stone core samples (from early Artesia wells) embedded into the bar. The friendly and efficient staff serves burgers and pizza, plus more refined dishes like salads, pasta, and fish. My favorite brew is the tasty Rough Neck Red. Check out the patio dining in summer and the TVs for sporting events.

The Wellhead, 332 West Main St. (© 505/746-0640), is open Sunday through Thursday from 11am to 9pm and Friday and Saturday from 11am to 10pm. Reservations are recommended on weekends and holidays. Main courses range from $6 to $20, and most major credit cards are accepted.

If you want to stop over in Artesia, consider the **Best Western Pecos Inn,** 2209 W. Main St. (US 82), Artesia, NM 88211 (© **505/748-3324;** www.best western.com). Further information can be obtained from the **Artesia Chamber of Commerce,** P.O. Box 99, Artesia, NM 88211 (© **505/746-2744;** www. artesiachamber.com).

HOBBS

Located 69 miles east of Carlsbad on US 62/180, on the edge of the Llano Estacado tableland, Hobbs (pop. 28,657) is at the center of New Mexico's richest oil field. Many oil companies base their headquarters here.

Points of interest include the **Lea County Cowboy Hall of Fame and Western Heritage Center** at New Mexico Junior College, on the Lovington Highway (© **505/392-1275**). It honors the area's ranchers (both men and women) and rodeo performers and is open Monday through Friday from 10am to 5pm and Saturday from 1 to 5pm (closed college holidays). The **Confederate Air Force Museum** (© **505/391-2934**) at Lea County Airport, on US 62/180, displays World War II aircraft; and the **Soaring Society of America** (© **505/392-1177;** www.ssa.org) has its national headquarters at the Hobbs Industrial Air Park, north of town on NM 18. Native American artifacts and pioneer mementos are displayed by appointment at the **Linam Ranch Museum** (© **505/393-4784**), located west of town on US 62/180.

Twenty-two miles northwest of Hobbs via NM 18, at the junction with US 82, is the town of **Lovington** (pop. 9,500), another ranching and oil center. The **Lea County Historical Museum,** 103 S. Love St. (© **505/396-4805**), presents memorabilia of the region's unique history in a World War I–era hotel (ca. 1918).

If you plan to stay in Hobbs, try the **Holiday Inn Express,** 3610 N. Lovington Hwy. (© **800/377-8660** or 505/392-8777; www.hiexpress.com). **Harry McAdams Park,** 4 miles north of Hobbs on NM 18 (© **505/392-5845**), has campsites and a visitor center set on acres of lovely grass. You can get a good square meal at the **Cattle Baron Steak and Seafood Restaurant,** 1930 N. Grimes St. (© **505/393-2800**). For more information, contact the **Hobbs Chamber of Commerce,** 400 N. Marland Blvd. (© **800/658-6291** or 505/ 397-3202; www.hobbschamber.org), or the **Lovington Chamber of Commerce,** 201 S. Main St. (© **505/396-5311;** www.lovington.net).

9 Carlsbad Caverns National Park (★(★(★

One of the largest and most spectacular cave systems in the world, **Carlsbad Caverns** comprise some 100 known caves that snake through the porous limestone reef of the Guadalupe Mountains. Although Native Americans had known of the caverns for centuries, they were not discovered by whites until about a century ago, when settlers were attracted by sunset flights of bats from the cave. Jim White, a guano miner, began to explore the main cave in the early 1900s and to share its wonders with tourists. By 1923, the caverns had become a national monument, upgraded to national park status in 1930.

ESSENTIALS

GETTING THERE   Take US 62/180 from either Carlsbad, New Mexico (see "Essentials," under "Carlsbad & Environs," earlier in this chapter), which is 23 miles to the northeast, or El Paso, Texas, which is 150 miles to the west. The scenic entrance road to the park is 7 miles long and originates at the park gate at White's City. Van service to Carlsbad Caverns National Park from White's City, south of Carlsbad, is provided by **Sun Country Tours/White's City Services** (✆ **505/785-2291**).

VISITOR INFORMATION   For more information about the park, contact **Carlsbad Caverns National Park,** 3225 National Parks Hwy., Carlsbad, NM 88220 (✆ **800/967-CAVE** for tour reservations, 505/785-2232 for information about guided tours, and 505/785-3012 for bat flight information; www.nps.gov/cave).

ADMISSION FEES & HOURS   General admission to the park is $6 for adults, $3 for children ages 6 to 15, and free for children under age 6. Admission is good for 3 days and includes entry to the two self-guided walking tours. Guided tours range in price from $7 to $20, depending on the type of tour, and reservations are required. The visitor center and park are open daily from Memorial Day to mid-August from 8am to 7pm; the rest of the year they're open from 8am to 5pm. They're closed Christmas.

TOURING THE CAVES

Two caves, **Carlsbad Cavern** and **Slaughter Canyon Cave,** are open to the public. The National Park Service has provided facilities, including elevators, to make it easy for everyone to visit the cavern, and a kennel for pets is available. Visitors in wheelchairs are common. It's always about 56°F (13°C) in the caves, so bring a jacket or sweater.

In addition to the tours described below, inquire at the visitor center information desk about other ranger-guided tours, including climbing and crawling "wild" cave tours. Be sure to call days in advance because some tours are offered only 1 day per week. Spelunkers who seek access to the park's undeveloped caves require special permission from the park superintendent.

CARLSBAD CAVERN TOURS

You can tour Carlsbad Cavern in one of three ways. The first, and least difficult, option is to take the elevator from the visitor center down 750 feet to the start of the self-guided tour of the Big Room. More difficult, but vastly more rewarding, is the 1-mile self-guided tour along the Natural Entrance route, which follows the traditional explorer's route, entering the cavern through the large historic natural entrance. The paved walkway through the natural entrance winds into the depths of the cavern and leads through a series of underground rooms; this tour takes about an hour. Parts of it are steep. At its lowest point, the trail reaches 750 feet below the surface, ending finally at an underground rest area.

Visitors who take either the elevator or the Natural Entrance route begin the self-guided tour of the spectacular Big Room near the rest area. The floor of this room covers 14 acres; the tour, over a relatively level path, is 1¼ miles long and takes about an hour.

The third option is the 1½-hour ranger-guided Kings Palace tour, which also departs from the underground rest area. This tour descends 830 feet beneath the surface of the desert to the deepest portion of the cavern open to the public. Reservations are required, and an additional fee is charged.

SLAUGHTER CANYON CAVE TOUR

Slaughter Canyon Cave was discovered in 1937 and was mined for bat guano commercially until the 1950s. It consists of a corridor 1,140 feet long, with many side passageways. The lowest point is 250 feet below the surface, and the passage traversed by the ranger-guided tours is 1¾ miles long, but it is more strenuous than hiking through the main cavern. There is also a strenuous 500-foot-rise hike from the parking lot to the cave mouth. The tour lasts about 2½ hours. No more than 25 people may take part in a tour, and then by reservation only. Everyone needs a flashlight (make sure you have fresh batteries), hiking boots or shoes, and a container of drinking water. Slaughter Canyon Cave is reached via US 180, south 5 miles from White's City, to a marked turnoff that leads 11 miles into a parking lot.

OTHER GUIDED TOURS

Be sure to ask about the Left Hand Tunnel, Lower Cave, Hall of the White Giant, and Spider Cave tours. These vary in degree of difficulty and adventure, from Left Hand, which is an easy half-mile lantern tour, to Spider Cave, where you can expect tight crawlways and canyonlike passages, to Hall of the White Giant, a strenuous tour in which you're required to crawl long distances, squeeze through tight crevices, and climb up slippery flow-stone–lined passages. Call in advance for times of each tour. All these tours depart from the visitor center.

BAT FLIGHTS

Every sunset from May to October, a crowd gathers at the natural entrance of the cave to watch a quarter-million Mexican free-tailed bats take flight for a night of insect feasting. (The bats winter in Mexico.) A ranger program is offered around 7:30pm (verify the time at the visitor center) at the outdoor Bat Flight Amphitheater. On the second Thursday in August (usually), the park sponsors a **Bat Flight Breakfast** from 5 to 7am, during which visitors watch the bats return to the cavern. The cost is $6 for adults and $3 for children 12 and under. For information, call © **505/785-2232**, ext. 0.

OTHER PARK ACTIVITIES

Aside from the caves, the park offers a 10-mile one-way scenic loop drive through the Chihuahuan Desert to view Rattlesnake and Upper Walnut canyons. Picnickers can head for Rattlesnake Springs Picnic Area, on County Road 418 near Slaughter Canyon Cave, a primo birding spot. Backcountry hikers must register at the visitor center before going out on any of the trails in the park's 46,766 acres.

Appendix:
New Mexico in Depth

When I was a child in New Mexico, we'd sing a song while driving the dusty roads en route to such ruins as Chaco Canyon or Puye Cliff Dwellings. Sung to the tune of "Oh Christmas Tree," it went like this:

New Mexico, New Mexico
Don't know why we love you so.
It never rains
It never snows
The winds and sand
They always blow.
And how we live
God only knows
New Mexico, we love you so.

Although this song exaggerates the conditions here, the truth remains that in many ways New Mexico has an inhospitable environment. So why are so many people drawn here, and why do so many of us stay?

Ironically, the very extremes that this song presents are the reason. In this 121,666-square-mile state, you are met with wildly varied terrain, temperature, and temperament. On a single day you might experience temperatures from 25°F to 75°F (-4°C–22°C). From the vast heat and dryness of White Sands in the summer to the 13,161-foot subzero, snow-encrusted Wheeler Peak in the winter, New Mexico's beauty is carved by extremes.

Culturally, this is also the case. Pueblo, Navajo, and Apache tribes occupy much of the state's lands, many of them still speaking their native languages and living within the traditions of their people. Some even live without running water and electricity. Meanwhile, the Hispanic culture remains deeply linked to its Spanish roots, practicing a devout Catholicism, and speaking a centuries-old Spanish dialect; some still living by subsistence farming in mountain villages.

New Mexico has its own sense of time and unique social mores. The pace is slower here, the objectives of life less defined. People rarely arrive on time for appointments, and businesses don't always hold to their posted hours. In most cases, people wear whatever they want here. You'll see men dressed for formal occasions wearing a buttoned collar with a bolo tie and women in cowboy boots and skirts.

All this leads to a certain lost-and-not-caring-to-be-found spell the place casts on visitors that's akin to some kind of voodoo magic. We find ourselves standing amid the dust or sparkling light, within the extreme heat or cold, not sure whether to speak Spanish or English. That's when we let go completely of society's common goals, its pace, and social mores. We slip into a kayak and let the river take us, or hike a peak and look at the world from a new perspective. Or we climb into a car and drive past ancient ruins being excavated at that instant, past ghost mining towns, and under hot-air balloons, by chile fields and around hand-smoothed *santuarios,* all on the road to nowhere, New Mexico's best destination.

1 The Natural Environment

THE LAY OF THE LAND

It would be easy, and accurate, to call New Mexico "high and dry" and leave it at that. The lowest point in the state, in the southeastern corner, is still over 2,800 feet in elevation, higher than the highest point in at least a dozen other states. The southern **Rocky Mountains** extend well into New Mexico, rising above 13,000 feet in the **Sangre de Cristo range** and sending a final afterthought above 10,000 feet, just east of Alamogordo. Volcanic activity created the mountain range, and its aftereffects can be seen throughout the state—from Shiprock (the remaining core of a long-eroded volcano) to Capulin Volcano National Monument. Two fault lines, which created the Rio Grande Rift Valley, home to the **Rio Grande,** run through the center of the state, and seismic activity continues to change the face of New Mexico even today.

Although archaeologists have discovered fossils indicating that most of New Mexico was once covered by ancient seas, the surface area of the state is now quite dry. The greater portion of New Mexico receives fewer than 20 inches of precipitation annually. In an area of 121,666 square miles—the fifth-largest U.S. state—there are only 221 square miles of water. The most important source of water is the Rio Grande. It nourishes hundreds of small farms from the **Pueblo country** of the north to the bone-dry **Chihuahuan Desert** of the far south.

However, there is more water than meets the eye in New Mexico. Systems circulating beneath the earth's surface have created all sorts of beautiful and fascinating geologic formations, including **Carlsbad Caverns,** one of the greatest cave systems in the world. Other caves have formed throughout the state, many of which have collapsed over the centuries, creating large sinkholes that have since filled with water and formed beautiful lakes. **Bottomless Lakes State Park,** located near the town of Roswell, is a good example of this type of geological activity.

Other natural wonders you'll encounter during a visit to New Mexico include red-, yellow-, and orange-hued high, flat **mesas,** and the 275-square-mile **White Sands National Monument** that contains more than 8 billion tons of pure white gypsum and is the largest field of sand dunes of this kind in the entire world. Here mountains meet desert, and the sky is arguably bigger, bluer, and more fascinating than any other place in the country. Words can't do justice to the spectacular colors of the landscape, colors that have drawn contemporary artists from around the world for nearly a century, colors that have made Taos and Santa Fe synonymous with artists' communities. This is truly big sky country, where it seems you can see forever.

THE FLORA & FAUNA OF NEW MEXICO

Six of the earth's seven "life zones" are represented in New Mexico, from subtropical desert to alpine tundra. As a result, the state is home to an unusually diverse variety of plant and animal life. You'll see sage-speckled plains and dense stands of pine trees, as well as cactus and tender perennials, typically found in much cooler climates. Living among the trees and out on the desert plains are deer, bears, scorpions, and rattlesnakes.

At the highest elevations (those above 12,000 ft.) is the **alpine zone,** which offers very little in the way of a home for plants and animals. Areas in New Mexico that fall into the alpine zone include Wheeler Peak and several other mountains in the Enchanted Circle area near Taos. These peaks are above the timberline, and conditions are harsh. Only a few animals, such as pikas and marmots, are able to survive at this elevation, and the only trees you'll see are bristlecone pines. In the "summer," only a few hardy wildflowers have the strength to bloom in the alpine zone.

Heading down the mountain, between 9,500 and 12,000 feet, is the **Hudsonian zone.** At this altitude, there is typically a great deal of snowfall in the late fall to late spring. More plants live in this area than in the alpine zone, creating habitats for a greater number of animals. Rodents, birds, bighorn sheep, elk, and mountain goats live in New Mexico's Hudsonian zone, among the bristlecone pine, blue spruce, and sub-alpine firs.

A very small percentage of New Mexico is in the **Canadian zone,** which includes certain areas of the White, Mogollons, Jemez, San Juan, and Sangre de Cristo mountains. Here you will find deer and elk (which migrate to warmer areas during the winter) as well as a variety of spruce, fir, and aspen trees.

With elevations between 6,500 and 8,500 feet, most of north-central New Mexico (primarily Santa Fe, Taos, and portions of Albuquerque) is well within the **transition zone.** This is where you'll find ponderosa pines standing alongside oak trees and juniper bushes. North-central New Mexico gets quite a bit more rain than other areas of the state, and as a result you'll find a large number of wildflowers in bloom here in the spring and summer, as well as a greater variety of wildlife. Keep your eyes open for black bears, mountain lions, deer, elk, quail, and wild turkey, especially if you're hiking in less-populated areas.

The northern portion of the state, from 4,500 to 6,500 feet, is in the **upper Sonoran zone.** Here you'll find a combination of plants and animals found in the lower Sonoran life zone and the transition zone. Cacti are as prevalent as juniper, oak, and piñon; and rattlesnakes, scorpions, centipedes, and tarantulas make their home here, along with mountain lions, javelinas, and pronghorns.

The southern portion of the state, where the heat rises off dusty flatlands and the elevation is below 4,500 feet, falls within the **lower Sonoran zone.** Traveling through Las Cruces, Alamogordo, and Carlsbad, you'll see all sorts of cacti, including prickly pear and cholla. (Don't expect, however, to see the giant saguaro cactus most commonly associated with the desert landscape.) The arid environment in the lower Sonoran zone is home to animals that thrive in the heat and don't need as much water as those found at higher altitudes. It's the perfect climate for rattlesnakes, centipedes, tarantulas, and scorpions.

2 A Look at the Past
IN THE BEGINNING

Archaeologists say that humans first migrated to the Southwest, moving southward from the Bering Land Bridge, around 12000 B.C. Sites such as Sandia Cave and Folsom—where weapon points were discovered that for the first time clearly established that our prehistoric ancestors hunted now-extinct mammals such as woolly mammoths—are internationally known. When these large animals died off during the late Ice Age (about 8000 B.C.), people turned to hunting smaller game and gathering wild food.

Stable farming settlements, as evidenced by the remains of domestically grown maize, date from around 3000 B.C. As the nomadic peoples became more sedentary, they built permanent residences and pit houses and made pottery. Cultural differences began to emerge in their choice of architecture and decoration: The **Mogollon people,** in the southwestern part of modern New Mexico, created brown and red pottery and built large community lodges; the **ancestral Puebloans,** or **Anasazi,** in the north, made gray pottery and smaller lodges for extended families.

The Mogollon, whose pottery dates from around 100 B.C., were the first of the sophisticated village cultures. They lived primarily in modern-day Catron and Grant counties. The most important Mogollon ruins are in the Gila River Valley, including Gila Cliff Dwellings National Monument.

By about A.D. 700, the ancestral Puebloans of the northwest had absorbed village life and expanded through what is now known as the Four Corners region (where New Mexico, Arizona, Utah, and Colorado come together). Around A.D. 1000, their culture eclipsed that of the Mogollon. Chaco Culture National Historic Park, Aztec Ruins National Monument, and Salmon Ruins all exhibit architectural excellence and skill, as well as a scientific sensitivity to nature, that mark this as one of America's classic pre-Columbian civilizations.

Condominium-style communities of stone and mud adobe bricks, three and four stories high, were focused around central plazas. The villages incorporated circular spiritual chambers called *kivas*. The ancestral Puebloans also developed means to irrigate their crops by controlling the flow of water from the San Juan River and its tributaries. From Chaco Canyon, they built a complex system of well-engineered roads leading to other towns or ceremonial centers. Artifacts found during excavation, such as seashells and macaw feathers, indicate that they had a far-reaching trade network.

The diminishing of the Anasazi culture, and the emergence of the **Pueblo culture** in its place, is something of a mystery today. Historians disagree as to why the Anasazi left their villages around the 13th century. Some suggest drought or soil exhaustion; others posit invasion, epidemic, or social unrest. But by the time the first Spanish arrived in the 1500s, the ancestral Puebloans were long gone and the Pueblo culture was well established throughout northern and western New Mexico, from Taos to Zuni, near Gallup. Most of the people lived on the east side of the Continental Divide, in the Rio Grande Valley.

The Pueblos absorbed certain elements of the ancestral Puebloan civilization, including the apartmentlike adobe architecture, the creation of rather elaborate pottery, and the use of irrigation or flood farming in their fields. Agriculture, especially corn, was the economic mainstay.

Each pueblo, as the scattered villages and surrounding farmlands were known, fiercely guarded its independence. When the Spanish arrived, no alliances existed between pueblos. No more than a few hundred people lived in any one pueblo, an indication that the natives had learned to keep their population (which totaled 40,000–50,000) down in order to preserve their soil and other natural resources. But not all was peaceful: They alternately fought and traded with each other, as well as with nomadic Apaches.

THE ARRIVAL OF THE SPANISH

The Spanish controlled New Mexico for 300 years, from the mid-16th to the mid-19th century—twice as long as the United States has. The Hispanic legacy in language and culture is stronger today in New Mexico than anywhere else in the Southwest, no doubt a result of the prominence of the Rio Grande Valley as the oldest and most populous fringe province of the viceroyalty of New Spain.

The spark that sent the first European explorers into what is now New Mexico was a fabulous medieval myth that seven Spanish bishops had fled the Moorish invasion of the 8th century, sailed westward to the legendary isle of Antilia, and built themselves seven cities of gold. Hernán Cortés's 1519 discovery and conquest of the Aztecs' treasure-laden capital of Tenochtitlán, now Mexico City, fueled belief in the myth. When a Franciscan friar 20 years later claimed to have sighted, from a distance, "a very beautiful city" in a region known as Cíbola while on a reconnaissance mission for the viceroyalty, the gates were opened.

Francisco Vásquez de Coronado, the ambitious young governor of New Spain's western province of Nueva Galicia, was commissioned to lead an expedition to the "seven cities." Several hundred soldiers, accompanied by servants and missionaries, marched overland to Cíbola with him in 1540, along with a support fleet of three ships in the Gulf of California. What they discovered, after 6 hard months on the trail, was a bitter disappointment: Instead of a city of gold, they found a rock-and-mud pueblo at Hawikuh, the westernmost of the Zuni towns. The expedition wintered at Tiguex, on the Rio Grande near modern Santa Fe, before proceeding to the Great Plains, seeking more treasure at Quivira, in what is now Kansas. The grass houses of the Wichita Indians were all they found.

Coronado returned to New Spain in 1542, admitting failure. Historically, though, his expedition was a great success, contributing the first widespread knowledge of the Southwest and Great Plains, and encountering the Grand Canyon en route.

By the 1580s, after important silver discoveries in the mountains of Mexico, the Spanish began to wonder if the wealth of the Pueblo country might lie in its land rather than its cities. They were convinced that they had been divinely appointed to convert the natives of the New World to Christianity. And so a northward migration began, orchestrated and directed by the royal government. It was a mere trickle in the late 16th century. Juan de Oñate established a capital in 1598 at San Gabriel, near San Juan Pueblo, but a variety of factors led to its failure. In 1610, under **Don Pedro de Peralta,** the migration began in earnest.

It was not dissimilar to America's schoolbook stereotype. Bands of armored conquistadors did troop through the desert with humble robed friars striding by their sides. But most of the pioneers came up the Rio Grande Valley, with oxcarts and mule trains rather than armor, intent on transplanting their Hispanic traditions of government, religion, and material culture to this new world.

Peralta built his new capital at Santa Fe and named it La Villa Real de la Santa Fe de San Francisco de Asis, the Royal City of the Holy Faith of St. Francis of Assisi. His capitol building, the Palace of the Governors, has been continuously occupied as a public building ever since by Spanish, Mexicans, Americans, and, for 12 years (1680–92), the Pueblo Indians. Today it is a museum.

RELIGION & REVOLT

The 17th century in New Mexico was essentially a missionary era, as Franciscan priests attempted to turn the Indians into model Hispanic peasants. Their churches became the focal point of every pueblo, with Catholic schools a mandatory adjunct. By 1625, the Rio Grande Valley was home to an estimated 50 churches.

But the Native Americans weren't enthused about doing "God's work"— building new adobe missions, tilling fields for the Spanish, and weaving garments for export to Mexico—so soldiers backed the padres in extracting labor, a system known as *repartimiento*. Simultaneously, the *encomienda* system provided that a yearly tribute in corn and blankets be levied upon each Indian. The Pueblos were pleased to take part in Catholic religious ceremonies and proclaim themselves converts. To them, spiritual forces were actively involved in the material world. If establishing harmony with the cosmos meant absorbing Jesus Christ and various saints into their hierarchy of *kachinas* and other spiritual beings, so much the better. But the Spanish friars demanded that they do away with their traditional singing, masked dancing, and other "pagan practices." When the Pueblo religion was violently crushed, resentment toward the Spanish grew and festered. Rebellions at Taos and Jemez in the 1630s left village priests dead, but the Pueblos were savagely repressed.

A long drought in the 1660s and 1670s gave the Apaches reason to scourge the Spanish and Pueblo settlements for food. The Pueblos blamed the friars, and their ban on traditional rain dances, for the drought. The hanging of 4 medicine men as "sorcerers" and the imprisonment of 43 others was the last straw for the Rio Grande natives. In 1680, the Pueblo Revolt erupted.

Popé, a San Juan shaman, catalyzed the revolt. Assisted by other Pueblo leaders, he unified the far-flung Native Americans, who had never before confederated. They pillaged and burned the province's outlying settlements, then turned their attention on Santa Fe, besieging the citizens who had fled to the Palace of the Governors. After 9 days, having reconquered Spain's northernmost American province, they let the refugees retreat south to Mexico.

Popé ordered that the Pueblos should return to the lifestyle they had before the arrival of the Spanish. All Hispanic items, from tools to fruit trees, were to be destroyed, and the blemish of baptism was to be washed away in the river. But the shaman misjudged the influence of the Spanish on the Pueblo people. They were not the people they had been a century earlier, and they *liked* much of the material culture they had absorbed from the Europeans. What's more, they had no intention of remaining confederated; their independent streaks were too strong.

In 1692, led by newly appointed **Gov. Don Diego de Vargas,** the Spanish recaptured Santa Fe without bloodshed. Popé had died, and without a leader to reunify them, the Pueblos were no match for the Spanish. Vargas pledged not to punish them but to pardon and convert. Still, when he returned the following year with 70 families to recolonize the city, he had to use force. And for the next several years, bloody battles persisted throughout the Pueblo country.

By the turn of the 18th century, Nuevo Mexico was firmly in Spanish hands. This time, however, the colonists seemed to have learned from some of their past errors. They were more tolerant in their religion and less ruthless in their demands and punishments.

THE ARRIVAL OF THE ANGLOS

By the 1700s, there were signals that new interlopers were about to arrive in New Mexico. The French had laid plans to begin colonizing the Mississippi River, and hostile Native American tribes were on the warpath. The Spanish viceroyalty fortified its position in Santa Fe as a defensive bastion and established a new villa at Albuquerque in 1706.

In 1739, the first French trade mission entered Santa Fe and was welcomed by the citizenry but not by the government. For 24 years, until 1763, a black-market trade thrived between Louisiana and New Mexico. It ended only when France lost its toehold on its North American claims during the French and Indian War.

The Native Americans were more fearsome foes. Apaches, Comanches, Utes, and Navajos launched raids against each other and the Rio Grande settlements for most of the 18th century, which led the Spanish and Pueblos to pull closer together for mutual protection. Pueblo and Hispanic militias fought side by side in campaigns against the invaders. But by the 1770s, the attacks had become so savage and destructive that the viceroy in Mexico City created a military jurisdiction in the province, and **Gov. Juan Bautista de Anza** led a force north to

Colorado to defeat the most feared of the Comanche chiefs, **Cuerno Verde** ("Green Horn"), in 1779. Seven years later, the Comanches and Utes signed a lasting treaty with the Spanish and thereafter helped keep the Apaches in check.

France sold the Louisiana Territory to the young United States in 1803, and the Spanish suddenly had a new intruder to fear. The Lewis and Clark expedition of 1803 went unchallenged, much as the Spanish would have liked to challenge it; but in 1807, when **Lt. Zebulon Pike** built a stockade on a Rio Grande tributary in Colorado, he and his troops were taken prisoner by troops from Santa Fe. Pike was taken to the New Mexican capital, where he was interrogated extensively, and then to Chihuahua, Mexico. The report he wrote upon his return was the United States' first inside look at Spain's frontier province.

At first, pioneering American merchants—excited by Pike's observations of New Mexico's economy—were summarily expelled from Santa Fe or jailed, and their goods were confiscated. But after Mexico gained independence from Spain in 1821, traders were welcomed. The wagon ruts of the Santa Fe Trail soon extended from Missouri to New Mexico, and from there to Chihuahua. (Later, it became the primary southern highway to California.)

As the merchants hastened to Santa Fe, Anglo-American and French-Canadian fur trappers headed into the wilderness. Their commercial hub became Taos, a tiny village near a large pueblo a few days' ride north of Santa Fe. Many married into native or Hispanic families. Perhaps the best known was **Kit Carson,** a sometime federal agent, sometime scout, whose legend is inextricably interwoven with that of early Taos. He spent 40 years in Taos, until his death in 1868.

In 1846, the **U.S.–Mexican War** broke out, and New Mexico became a territory of the United States. There were several causes of the war, including the U.S. annexation of Texas in 1845, disagreement over the international boundary, and unpaid claims owed to American citizens by the Mexican government. But foremost was the prevailing U.S. sentiment of "manifest destiny," the belief that the Union should extend "from sea to shining sea." **Gen. Stephen Kearny** marched south from Colorado; on the Las Vegas plaza, he announced that he had come to take possession of New Mexico for the United States. His arrival in Santa Fe on August 18, 1846, went unopposed.

An 1847 revolt in Taos resulted in the slaying of the new governor of New Mexico, Charles Bent, but U.S. troops defeated the rebels and executed their leaders. That was the last threat to American sovereignty in the territory. In 1848, the **Treaty of Guadalupe Hidalgo** officially transferred the title of New Mexico, along with Texas, Arizona, and California, to the United States.

Kearney promised New Mexicans that the United States would respect their religion and property rights and would safeguard their homes and possessions from hostile Indians. His troops behaved with a rigid decorum. The United States upheld Spanish policy toward the Pueblos, assuring the survival of their ancestral lands, their traditional culture, and their old religion—which even 3 centuries of Hispanic Catholicism could not do away with.

THE CIVIL WAR

As conflict between the North and South flared east of the Mississippi, New Mexico found itself caught in the debate over **slavery.** Southerners wanted to expand slavery to the western territories, but abolitionists bitterly opposed them. New Mexicans themselves voted against slavery twice, while their delegate to Congress engineered the adoption of a slavery code. In 1861, the Confederacy laid plans to make New Mexico theirs as a first step toward capturing the West.

In fact, southern New Mexicans, including those in Tucson (Arizona was then a part of the New Mexico Territory), were disenchanted with the attention paid them by Santa Fe and were already threatening to form their own state. So when Confederate Lt. Col. John Baylor captured Fort Fillmore, near Mesilla, and on August 1, 1861, proclaimed all of New Mexico south of the 34th parallel to be the new territory of Arizona, few complained.

The following year, **Confederate Gen. Henry Sibley** assembled three regiments of 2,600 Texans and moved up the Rio Grande. They defeated Union loyalists in a bloody battle at Valverde, near Socorro; easily took Albuquerque and Santa Fe; and proceeded toward the federal arsenal at Fort Union, 90 miles east of Santa Fe. Sibley planned to replenish his supplies there before continuing north to Colorado, then west to California.

On March 27 and 28, 1862, the Confederates were met head-on in **Glorieta Pass,** about 16 miles outside Santa Fe, by regular troops from Fort Union, supported by a regiment of Colorado volunteers. By the second day, the rebels were in control, until a detachment of Coloradans circled behind the Confederate troops and destroyed their poorly defended supply train. Sibley was forced into a rapid retreat back down the Rio Grande. A few months later, Mesilla was reclaimed for the Union, and the Confederate presence in New Mexico ended.

THE LAND WARS

The various tribes had not missed the fact that whites were fighting among themselves, and they took advantage of this weakness to step up their raids on border settlements. In 1864, the **Navajos,** in what is known in tribal history as "The Long Walk," were relocated to the new Bosque Redondo Reservation on the Pecos River at Fort Sumner, in east-central New Mexico. Militia Col. Kit Carson led New Mexico troops in this venture, a position to which he acceded as a moderating influence between the Navajos and those who called for their unconditional surrender or extermination.

Moving the Navajos was an ill-advised decision: The land could not support 9,000 people, the government failed to supply adequate provisions, and the Navajos were unable to live peacefully with the **Mescaleros.** By late 1868, the tribes retraced their routes to their homelands, where the Navajos gave up their warlike past. The Mescaleros' raids were squashed in the 1870s, and they were confined to a reservation in the Sacramento Mountains of southern New Mexico.

Corralling the rogue **Apaches** of southwestern New Mexico presented the territory with its biggest challenge. Led by chiefs Victorio, Nana, and Geronimo, these bands wreaked havoc on the mining region around Silver City. Eventually, however, they succumbed, and the capture of Geronimo in 1886 was the final chapter in New Mexico's long history of Indian wars.

As the Native American threat decreased, more and more livestock and sheep **ranchers** established themselves on the vast plains east of the Rio Grande, in the San Juan basin of the northwest, and in other equally inviting parts of the territory. Cattle drives up the Pecos Valley, on the Goodnight–Loving Trail, are the stuff of legend; so, too, was Roswell cattle baron John Chisum, whose 80,000 heads of beef probably represented the largest herd in America in the late 1870s.

Mining grew as well. Albuquerque blossomed in the wake of a series of major gold strikes in the Madrid Valley, close to ancient turquoise mines; other gold and silver discoveries through the 1870s gave birth to boomtowns—now mostly ghost towns—such as Hillsboro, Mogollon, Pinos Altos, and White Oak. The copper mines of Santa Rita del Cobre, near Silver City, are still thriving.

In 1879, the Atchison, Topeka, and Santa Fe Railway sent its main line through Las Vegas, Albuquerque, El Paso, and Deming, where it joined with the Southern Pacific line coming from California. (The Santa Fe station was, and is, at Lamy, 17 miles southeast of the capital.) Now linked by **railroad** to the great markets of America, New Mexico's economic boom period was assured.

But ranching invites cattle rustling and range wars, mining beckons feuds and land fraud, and the construction of railroads often brings political corruption and swindles. New Mexico had all of them, especially during the latter part of the 19th century. Best known of a great many conflicts was the **Lincoln County War** (1878–81), which began as a feud between rival factions of ranchers and merchants. It led to such utter lawlessness that Pres. Rutherford B. Hayes ordered a federal investigation of the territorial government and the installation of Gen. Lew Wallace as governor (whose novel *Ben-Hur* was published in 1880).

One of the central figures of the Lincoln County War was **William "Billy the Kid" Bonney** (1858–81), a headstrong youth who became probably the best-known outlaw of the American West. He blazed a trail of bloodshed from Silver City to Mesilla, Santa Fe to Lincoln, and Artesia to Fort Sumner, where he was finally killed by Sheriff Pat Garrett in July 1881.

By the turn of the 20th century, most of the violence had been checked. The mineral lodes were drying up, and ranching was taking on increased importance. Economic and social stability were coming to New Mexico.

STATEHOOD, ART & ATOMS

Early in the 20th century, its Hispanic citizens having proved their loyalty to the U.S. by serving gallantly with Theodore Roosevelt's Rough Riders during the Spanish–American War, New Mexico's long-awaited dream of becoming an integral part of the Union was finally recognized. On January 6, 1912, President William Howard Taft signed a bill making New Mexico the **47th state.**

Within a few years, Taos began gaining fame as an artists' community. Two painters from the East Coast, **Ernest Blumenschein** and **Bert Phillips,** settled in Taos in 1898, lured others to join them, and in 1914 formed the **Taos Society of Artists,** one of the most influential schools of art in America. Writers and other intellectuals soon followed. Other artists settled in Santa Fe and elsewhere in New Mexico; the best known was **Georgia O'Keeffe,** who lived miles from anywhere in tiny Abiquiu. Today, Santa Fe and Taos are world renowned for their contributions to art and culture.

The construction in 1916 of the Elephant Butte Dam near Hot Springs (now Truth or Consequences) brought irrigated farming back to a drought-ravaged southern New Mexico. Potash mining boomed in the southeast in the 1930s. Native Americans gained full citizenship in 1924, two years after the **All Pueblo Council** was formed to fight passage in Congress of a bill that would have given white squatters rights to Indian lands. And in 1934, tribes were accorded partial self-government. The Hispanics, meanwhile, became the most powerful force in state politics, and remain so today.

The most dramatic development in 20th-century New Mexico was induced by World War II. In 1943, the U.S. government sealed off a tract of land on the Pajarito Plateau, west of Santa Fe, that previously had been an exclusive boys' school. On this site, it built the Los Alamos National Laboratory, otherwise known as Project Y of the Manhattan Engineer District—the **"Manhattan Project."** Its goal: to split the atom and develop the first nuclear weapons.

Under the direction of **J. Robert Oppenheimer,** later succeeded by **Norris E. Bradbury,** a team of 30 to 100 scientists and hundreds of support staff lived and worked in almost complete seclusion for 2 years. Their work resulted in the atomic bomb, tested for the first time at the Trinity Site, north of White Sands, on July 16, 1945. The bombings of Hiroshima and Nagasaki, Japan, 3 weeks later, signaled to the world that the nuclear age had arrived.

Even before that time, New Mexico was gaining stature in America's scientific community. **Robert H. Goddard,** considered the founder of modern rocketry, conducted many of his experiments near Roswell in the 1930s, during which time he became the first person to shoot a liquid-fuel rocket faster than the speed of sound. **Clyde Tombaugh,** who discovered the planet Pluto in 1930, helped establish the department of astronomy at New Mexico State University in Las Cruces. And former **Sen. Harrison (Jack) Schmitt,** an exogeologist and the first civilian to walk on the moon in 1972, is a native of the Silver City area.

Today, the **White Sands Missile Range** is one of America's most important astrophysics sites, and the **International Space Hall of Fame** in nearby Alamogordo honors men and women from around the world who have devoted their lives to space exploration. Aerospace research and defense contracts are economic mainstays in Albuquerque, and **Kirtland Air Force Base** is the home of the Air Force Special Weapons Center. **Los Alamos,** of course, continues to be a national leader in nuclear technology.

Despite the arrival of the 21st century in many parts of the state, other areas are still struggling to be a part of the 20th. Many Native Americans, be they Pueblo, Navajo, or Apache, and Hispanic farmers, who till small plots in isolated rural regions, hearken to a time when life was slower paced.

3 New Mexico Today: From Flamenco to Craps

GROWING PAINS

New Mexico is experiencing a reconquest of sorts, as the Anglo population soars and outside money and values again make their way in. The process continues to transform New Mexico's three distinct cultures and their unique ways of life, albeit in a less violent manner than during the Spanish conquest.

Certainly, the Anglos—many of them from large cities—add a cosmopolitan flavor to life here. The variety of restaurants has greatly improved, as have entertainment options. For their small size, towns such as Taos and Santa Fe offer a broad variety of restaurants and cultural events. Santa Fe has developed a strong dance and drama scene, with treats such as flamenco and opera that you'd expect to find in New York or Los Angeles. And Albuquerque has an exciting nightlife scene downtown; you can walk from club to club and hear a wealth of jazz, rock, country, and alternative music.

Yet many newcomers, attracted by the adobe houses and exotic feel of the place, often bring only a loose appreciation for the area. Some tend to romanticize the lifestyle of the other cultures and trivialize their beliefs. Native American symbology, for example, is employed in ever-popular Southwestern decorative motifs; New Age groups appropriate valued rituals, such as sweats (in which believers sit encamped in a very hot, enclosed space to cleanse their spirits). The effects of cultural and economic change are even apparent throughout the countryside, where land is being developed at an alarming rate.

Transformation of the local way of life and landscape is also apparent in the stores continually springing up in the area. For some, these are a welcome relief from Western clothing stores and provincial dress shops. The downside is that city plazas, which once contained pharmacies and grocery stores frequented by residents, are now crowded with T-shirt shops and galleries appealing to tourists. Many locals now rarely visit their plazas except during special events.

Environmental threats are another regional reality. Nuclear-waste issues form part of an ongoing conflict affecting the entire Southwest, and a section of southern New Mexico has been designated a nuclear-waste site. Because much of the waste must pass through Santa Fe, the U.S. government, along with the New Mexico state government, constructed a bypass that directs some transit traffic around the west side of the city.

New ways of thinking have also brought positive changes to the life here, and many locals have benefited from New Mexico's influx of wealthy newcomers and popularity as a tourist destination. Businesses and industries large and small have come to the area. In Albuquerque, Intel Corporation now employs more than 5,500 workers, and in Santa Fe, the magazine *Outside* publishes monthly. Local artists and artisans also benefit from growth. Many craftspeople have expanded their businesses. The influx of people has broadened the sensibility of a fairly provincial state. The area has become a refuge for many gays and lesbians, as well as for political exiles, such as Tibetans. With them has developed a level of tolerance you would generally find in only large cities.

CULTURAL QUESTIONS

Faced with new challenges to their ways of life, both Native Americans and Hispanics are marshaling forces to protect their cultural identities. A prime concern is language. Through the years, many Pueblo people have begun to speak more and more English, with their children getting little exposure to their native tongue. In a number of the pueblos, elders are working with schoolchildren in language classes. Some of the pueblos have even developed written dictionaries, the first time their languages have been systematized in this form.

Many pueblos have introduced programs to conserve the environment, preserve ancient seed strains, and protect religious rites. Because their religion is tied closely to nature, a loss of natural resources would threaten the entire culture. Certain rituals have been closed to outsiders, the most notable being some of the rituals of Shalako at Zuni, a popular and elaborate series of year-end ceremonies.

Hispanics, through art and observance of cultural traditions, are also embracing their roots. In northern New Mexico, murals depicting important historic events, such as the Treaty of Guadalupe Hidalgo of 1848, adorn many walls. The **Spanish Market** in Santa Fe has expanded into a grand celebration of traditional arts—from tin working to *santo* carving. Public schools in the area have bilingual education programs, enabling students to embrace their Spanish-speaking roots.

Hispanics are also making their voices heard, insisting on more conscientious development of their neighborhoods and rising to positions of power in government. When she was in office, former Santa Fe Mayor Debbie Jaramillo made national news as an advocate of the Hispanic people, and Congressman Bill Richardson, Hispanic despite his Anglo surname, was appointed U.S. Ambassador to the United Nations before becoming Energy Secretary in President Clinton's cabinet. Currently, he is governor of New Mexico.

GAMBLING WINS & LOSSES

Gambling, a source of much-needed revenue for Native American populations across the country, has been a center of controversy in northern New Mexico for a number of years. In 1994, Governor Gary Johnson signed a compact with tribes in New Mexico to allow full-scale gambling. **Tesuque Pueblo** was one of the first to begin a massive expansion, and many other pueblos followed suit.

Though most New Mexico residents appreciate the boost that gambling can ultimately bring to the Native American economies, many critics wonder where gambling profits actually go—and if the casinos can possibly be a good thing for the pueblos and tribes. Some detractors suspect that profits go directly into the pockets of outside backers.

A number of pueblos and tribes, however, are showing signs of prosperity, and they are using newfound revenues to buy firefighting and medical equipment and to invest in local schools. Isleta Pueblo built a $3½-million youth center, and the lieutenant governor says the money for it came from gambling revenues. Sandia Pueblo built a $2-million medical and dental clinic and, most recently, provided a computer for every tribal home. Its governor said these projects were "totally funded by gaming revenues."

4 Art & Architecture
A LAND OF ART

It's all in the light—or at least that's what many artists claim drew them to New Mexico. In truth, the light is only part of the attraction: Nature in this part of the country, with its awe-inspiring thunderheads, endless expanse of blue skies, and rugged desert, is itself a canvas. To record the wonders of earth and sky, the early natives of the area, the ancestral Puebloans, imprinted images (in the form of petroglyphs and pictographs) on the sides of caves and on stones, as well as on the sides of pots they shaped from clay dug in the hills.

Today's Native American tribes carry on that legacy, as do the other cultures that have settled here. Life in New Mexico is shaped by the arts. Everywhere you turn, you see pottery, paintings, jewelry, and weavings.

The area is full of little villages that maintain their own artistic specialties. Each Indian pueblo has a trademark design, such as **Santa Clara's** and **San Ildefonso's** black pottery and **Zuni's** needlepoint silverwork. Bear in mind that the images used often have deep symbolic meaning. When purchasing art or an artifact, you may want to talk to its maker about what the symbols mean.

Hispanic villages are also distinguished by their artistic identities. **Chimayo** has become a center for Hispanic weaving, and the village of **Cordova** is known for its *santo* (icon) carving. *Santos, retablos* (paintings), and *bultos* (sculptures), as well as works in tin, are often sold out of artists' homes in these villages, allowing you to glimpse the lives of the artists and the surroundings that inspire them.

Hispanic and Native American villagers take their goods to the cities, where for centuries people have bought and traded. Under the portals along the plazas of Santa Fe, Taos, and Albuquerque, you'll find a variety of works in silver, stone, and pottery for sale. In the cities, you'll find streets lined with galleries, some very slick, some more modest. At major markets, such as the **Spanish Market** and **Indian Market** in Santa Fe, some of the top artists from the area sell their works. Smaller shows at the pueblos also attract artists and artisans. The **Northern Pueblo Artists and Craftsman Show,** revolving each July to a different pueblo, continues to grow.

Drawn by the beauty of the local landscape and respect for indigenous art, artists from all over have flocked here, particularly during the 20th century. They have established locally important art societies; one of the most notable is the **Taos Society of Artists.** In 1898, the artists Bert Phillips and Ernest L. Blumenschein were traveling through the area from Colorado on a mission to sketch the Southwest when their wagon broke down north of Taos. The scenery so overwhelmed them that they abandoned their journey and stayed. Joseph Sharp joined them, and still later came Oscar Berninghaus, Walter Ufner, Herbert Dunton, and others. You can see a brilliant collection of some of their romantically lit portraits and landscapes at the Taos Art Museum.

A major player in the development of Taos as an artists' community was the arts patron **Mabel Dodge Luhan.** A writer who financed the work of many an artist, in the 1920s Luhan held court for many notables, including Georgia O'Keeffe, Willa Cather, and D. H. Lawrence. This illustrious history goes a long way to explaining how it is that Taos—a town of about 5,000 inhabitants—has more than 100 arts-and-crafts galleries and many resident painters.

Santa Fe has its own art society, begun in the 1920s by a nucleus of five painters who became known as **Los Cinco Pintores.** Jozef Bakos, Fremont Ellis, Walter Mruk, Willard Nash, and Will Shuster lived in the area of Canyon Road (now the arts center of Santa Fe). Despite its small size, Santa Fe is considered one of the top three art markets in the U.S.

Perhaps the most celebrated artist associated with New Mexico was **Georgia O'Keeffe** (1887–1986), a painter who worked and lived most of her later years in the region. O'Keeffe's first sojourn to New Mexico in 1929 inspired her sensuous paintings of the area's desert landscape and bleached animal skulls. The house where she lived in Abiquiu (42 miles northwest of Santa Fe on U.S. 84) is now open for limited public tours (see chapter 9 for details). The **Georgia O'Keeffe Museum** in Santa Fe, the only museum in the United States entirely dedicated to a woman artist, opened in Santa Fe in 1997.

Santa Fe is also home to the **Institute of American Indian Arts,** where many of today's leading Native American artists have studied, including the Apache sculptor Allan Houser (whose works you can see near the state capitol building and in other public areas in Santa Fe). The best-known Native American painter is R. C. Gorman, an Arizona Navajo who has made his home in Taos for more than three decades. Now in his 70s, Gorman is internationally acclaimed for his bright, somewhat surrealistic depictions of Navajo women. Another artist who has achieved national fame is Dan Namingha, a Hopi painter and sculptor who weaves native symbology together with contemporary concerns.

If you look closely, you'll find notable works from a number of local artists. Tammy Garcia is a young Taos potter who year after year continues to sweep the awards at Indian Market with her intricately shaped and carved pots. Cippy Crazyhorse, a Cochiti, has acquired a steady following of patrons for his silver jewelry. All around the area you'll see the frescoes of Frederico Vigil, a noted muralist and Santa Fe native. From Santa Cruz comes a rising star named Andrés Martinez, noted for his Picasso-esque portraits of Hispanic village life.

For the visitor interested in art, however, some caution should be exercised; a lot of schlock out there targets the tourist trade. Yet if you persist, you're likely to find much inspiring work as well.

A RICH ARCHITECTURAL MELTING POT

Nowhere else in the United States are you likely to see such extremes of architectural style as in New Mexico. The state's distinctive architecture reflects the diversity of cultures that have left their imprint on the region. The first people in the area were the ancestral Puebloans, the Anasazi, who built stone and mud homes at the bottom of canyons and inside caves (which look rather like condominiums to the modern urban eye). **Pueblo–style adobe architecture** evolved and became the basis for traditional New Mexican homes: sun-dried clay bricks mixed with grass for strength, mud-mortared, and covered with additional protective layers of mud. Roofs are supported by a network of *vigas*—long beams whose ends protrude through the outer facades—and *latillas,* smaller stripped branches layered between the *vigas.* Other adapted Pueblo architectural elements include plastered adobe-brick kiva fireplaces, *bancos* (adobe benches that protrude from walls), and *nichos* (small indentations within a wall in which religious icons are placed). These adobe homes are characterized by flat roofs and soft, rounded contours.

Spaniards wedded many elements to Pueblo style, such as portals (porches held up with posts) and enclosed patios, as well as the simple, dramatic sculptural shapes of Spanish mission arches and bell towers. They also brought elements from the Moorish architecture found in southern Spain: heavy wooden doors and elaborate *corbels*—carved wooden supports for the vertical posts.

With the opening of the Santa Fe Trail in 1821 and later the 1860s gold boom, both of which brought more Anglo settlers, came the next wave of building. New arrivals contributed architectural elements such as neo-Grecian and Victorian influences popular in the middle part of the U.S. at the time. Distinguishing features of what came to be known as **Territorial-style** architecture can be seen today; they include brick facades and cornices as well as porches, often placed on the second story. You'll also note millwork on doors and wood trim around windows and doorways, double-hung windows, and Victorian bric-a-brac.

Santa Fe Plaza is an excellent example of the convergence of these early architectural styles. On the west side is a Territorial–style balcony, while the Palace of Governors is marked by Pueblo–style vigas and oversized Spanish/Moorish doors. Nearby, you'll see the Romanesque architecture of the **St. Francis Cathedral** and **Loretto chapel,** brought by Archbishop Lamy from France, as well as the railroad station built in the **Spanish Mission style**—popular in the early part of the 20th century.

Since 1957, strict city building codes have required that all new structures within the circumference of the Paseo de Peralta conform to one of two revival styles: Pueblo or Territorial. The regulation also limits the height of the buildings. In 1988, additional citywide standards were established in an effort to impose some degree of architectural taste on new developments.

Albuquerque also has a broad array of styles, most evident in a visit to **Old Town.** There, you'll find the large Italianate brick house known as the **Herman Blueher home,** built in 1898; throughout Old Town you'll find little *placitas,* homes, and *haciendas* built around courtyards which allowed several generations of the same family to live in different wings of a single dwelling. **The Church of San Felipe de Neri** at the center of Old Town is centered between two folk Gothic towers. This building was begun in a cruciform plan in 1793; subsequent architectural changes resulted in an interesting mixture of styles.

Most notable architecturally in Taos is **Taos Pueblo,** the site of two structures emulated in homes and business buildings throughout the Southwest. Built to resemble Taos Mountain, which stands behind it, the two structures are pyramidal in form, with the different levels reached by ladders. Also quite prevalent is architecture echoing colonial hacienda style. What's nice about Taos is that you can see historic homes inside and out such as artist **Ernest Blumenschein's home,** built in 1797 and restored by Blumenschein in 1919. The **Martinez Hacienda** is an example of a hacienda stronghold. Built without windows facing outward, it originally had 20 small rooms, many with doors opening out to the courtyard. It is one of the few refurbished examples of colonial New Mexico architecture.

Today, most new homes are constructed with wood frames and plasterboard, and then stuccoed over. Several local architects are currently incorporating straw bales, pumice-crete, rammed earth, old tires, even aluminum cans in the construction of homes. Most of these elements are used in the same way bricks are used, stacked and layered, and then covered over with plaster and made to look like adobe. Often it's difficult to distinguish homes built with these materials from those built with wood-frame construction. West of Taos, a number of "earthships" have been built. Many of these homes are constructed with alternative materials, most bermed into the sides of hills, utilizing the earth as insulation and the sun as an energy source.

5 New Mexican Cuisine

New Mexicans are serious about eating, and the area's cuisine reflects the amalgam of cultural influences found here. Food here isn't the same as Mexican cuisine or even those American variations of Tex-Mex and Cal-Mex. New Mexican cooking is a product of Southwestern history: Native Americans taught the Spanish conquerors about corn and also chile peppers, a crop indigenous to the New World, having been first harvested in the Andean highlands as early as 4000 B.C. The Spaniards brought the practice of eating beef to the area.

New Southwestern cuisine combines elements from various parts of Mexico, Costa Rica, and other Central American locales. You'll also find Asian elements mixed in.

The basic ingredients of New Mexico cooking are three indispensable, locally grown foods: **chile, beans,** and **corn.** Of these, perhaps the most crucial is the chile, whether brilliant red or green and with various levels of spicy bite. Chile forms the base for the red and green sauces that top most New Mexico dishes such as enchiladas and burritos. One is not necessarily hotter than the other; spiciness depends on the type, and where and during what kind of season (dry or wet) the chiles were grown.

Beans are simmered with garlic, onion, cumin, and red chile powder and served as a side dish. When mashed and fried in oil, they become *frijoles refritos.* **Corn** supplies the dough for tortillas and tamales called *masa.* New Mexican corn comes in six colors, of which yellow, white, and blue are the most common.

Even if you're familiar with Mexican cooking, the dishes you know and love are likely to be prepared differently here. The following is a rundown of some regional dishes, a number of which aren't widely known outside the Southwest:

biscochito A cookie made with anise.

carne adovada Tender pork marinated in red chile sauce, herbs, and spices, and then baked.

chile relleños Peppers stuffed with cheese, deep-fried, and then covered with green chile sauce.

chorizo burrito (also called a "breakfast burrito") Mexican sausage, scrambled eggs, potatoes, and scallions wrapped in a flour tortilla with red or green chile sauce and melted Jack cheese.

empañada A fried pie with nuts and currants.

huevos rancheros Fried eggs on corn tortillas, topped with cheese and red or green chile, served with pinto beans.

pan dulce A sweet Native American bread.

Fun Fact You Say Chili, We Say Chile

You'll never see "chili" on a menu in New Mexico. New Mexicans are adamant that *chile*, the Spanish spelling of the word, is the only way to spell it—no matter what your dictionary may say.

Virtually anything you order in a restaurant is likely to be topped with a chile sauce. If you're not accustomed to spicy foods, certain varieties will make your eyes water, your sinuses drain, and your palate feel as if it's on fire. But don't let these words of caution scare you away from genuine New Mexico chiles. The pleasure of eating them far outweighs the pain.

---

posole   A corn soup or stew (called *hominy* in other parts of the south), sometimes prepared with pork and chile.

sopaipilla   A lightly fried puff pastry served with honey as a dessert or stuffed with meat and vegetables as a main dish. Sopaipillas with honey have a cooling effect on your palate after you've eaten a spicy dish.

tamales   A dish made from cornmeal mush, wrapped in husks and steamed.

vegetables and nuts   Unusual local ingredients, such as piñon nuts, jicama, and prickly pear cactus, will often be a part of your meals.

Index

FROMMER'S® COMPLETE TRAVEL GUIDES

Alaska
Alaska Cruises & Ports of Call
American Southwest
Amsterdam
Argentina & Chile
Arizona
Atlanta
Australia
Austria
Bahamas
Barcelona, Madrid & Seville
Beijing
Belgium, Holland & Luxembourg
Bermuda
Boston
Brazil
British Columbia & the Canadian
  Rockies
Brussels & Bruges
Budapest & the Best of Hungary
Calgary
California
Canada
Cancún, Cozumel & the Yucatán
Cape Cod, Nantucket & Martha's
  Vineyard
Caribbean
Caribbean Ports of Call
Carolinas & Georgia
Chicago
China
Colorado
Costa Rica
Cruises & Ports of Call
Cuba
Denmark
Denver, Boulder & Colorado
  Springs
England
Europe
Europe by Rail
European Cruises & Ports of Call

Florence, Tuscany & Umbria
Florida
France
Germany
Great Britain
Greece
Greek Islands
Halifax
Hawaii
Hong Kong
Honolulu, Waikiki & Oahu
India
Ireland
Italy
Jamaica
Japan
Kauai
Las Vegas
London
Los Angeles
Maryland & Delaware
Maui
Mexico
Montana & Wyoming
Montréal & Québec City
Munich & the Bavarian Alps
Nashville & Memphis
New England
Newfoundland & Labrador
New Mexico
New Orleans
New York City
New York State
New Zealand
Northern Italy
Norway
Nova Scotia, New Brunswick &
  Prince Edward Island
Oregon
Ottawa
Paris
Peru

Philadelphia & the Amish
  Country
Portugal
Prague & the Best of the Czech
  Republic
Provence & the Riviera
Puerto Rico
Rome
San Antonio & Austin
San Diego
San Francisco
Santa Fe, Taos & Albuquerque
Scandinavia
Scotland
Seattle
Shanghai
Sicily
Singapore & Malaysia
South Africa
South America
South Florida
South Pacific
Southeast Asia
Spain
Sweden
Switzerland
Texas
Thailand
Tokyo
Toronto
Turkey
USA
Utah
Vancouver & Victoria
Vermont, New Hampshire &
  Maine
Vienna & the Danube Valley
Virgin Islands
Virginia
Walt Disney World® & Orlando
Washington, D.C.
Washington State

FROMMER'S® DOLLAR-A-DAY GUIDES

Australia from $50 a Day
California from $70 a Day
England from $75 a Day
Europe from $85 a Day
Florida from $70 a Day
Hawaii from $80 a Day

Ireland from $80 a Day
Italy from $70 a Day
London from $90 a Day
New York City from $90 a Day
Paris from $90 a Day
San Francisco from $70 a Day

Washington, D.C. from $80 a
  Day
Portable London from $90 a Day
Portable New York City from $90
  a Day
Portable Paris from $90 a Day

FROMMER'S® PORTABLE GUIDES

Acapulco, Ixtapa & Zihuatanejo
Amsterdam
Aruba
Australia's Great Barrier Reef
Bahamas
Berlin
Big Island of Hawaii
Boston
California Wine Country
Cancún
Cayman Islands
Charleston
Chicago
Disneyland®
Dominican Republic
Dublin

Florence
Frankfurt
Hong Kong
Las Vegas
Las Vegas for Non-Gamblers
London
Los Angeles
Los Cabos & Baja
Maine Coast
Maui
Miami
Nantucket & Martha's Vineyard
New Orleans
New York City
Paris

Phoenix & Scottsdale
Portland
Puerto Rico
Puerto Vallarta, Manzanillo &
  Guadalajara
Rio de Janeiro
San Diego
San Francisco
Savannah
Vancouver
Vancouver Island
Venice
Virgin Islands
Washington, D.C.
Whistler

FROMMER'S® NATIONAL PARK GUIDES

Algonquin Provincial Park
Banff & Jasper
Family Vacations in the National
  Parks

Grand Canyon
National Parks of the American
  West
Rocky Mountain

Yellowstone & Grand Teton
Yosemite & Sequoia/Kings
  Canyon
Zion & Bryce Canyon

FROMMER'S® MEMORABLE WALKS

Chicago
London

New York
Paris

San Francisco

FROMMER'S® WITH KIDS GUIDES

Chicago
Las Vegas
New York City

Ottawa
San Francisco
Toronto

Vancouver
Walt Disney World® & Orlando
Washington, D.C.

SUZY GERSHMAN'S BORN TO SHOP GUIDES

Born to Shop: France
Born to Shop: Hong Kong,
  Shanghai & Beijing

Born to Shop: Italy
Born to Shop: London

Born to Shop: New York
Born to Shop: Paris

FROMMER'S® IRREVERENT GUIDES

Amsterdam
Boston
Chicago
Las Vegas
London

Los Angeles
Manhattan
New Orleans
Paris
Rome

San Francisco
Seattle & Portland
Vancouver
Walt Disney World®
Washington, D.C.

FROMMER'S® BEST-LOVED DRIVING TOURS

Austria
Britain
California
France

Germany
Ireland
Italy
New England

Northern Italy
Scotland
Spain
Tuscany & Umbria

THE UNOFFICIAL GUIDES®

Beyond Disney
California with Kids
Central Italy
Chicago
Cruises
Disneyland®
England
Florida
Florida with Kids
Inside Disney

Hawaii
Las Vegas
London
Maui
Mexico's Best Beach Resorts
Mini Las Vegas
Mini Mickey
New Orleans
New York City
Paris

San Francisco
Skiing & Snowboarding in the
  West
South Florida including Miami &
  the Keys
Walt Disney World®
Walt Disney World® for
  Grown-ups
Walt Disney World® with Kids
Washington, D.C.

SPECIAL-INTEREST TITLES

Athens Past & Present
Cities Ranked & Rated
Frommer's Best Day Trips from London
Frommer's Best RV & Tent Campgrounds
  in the U.S.A.
Frommer's Caribbean Hideaways
Frommer's China: The 50 Most Memorable Trips
Frommer's Exploring America by RV
Frommer's Gay & Lesbian Europe
Frommer's NYC Free & Dirt Cheap

Frommer's Road Atlas Europe
Frommer's Road Atlas France
Frommer's Road Atlas Ireland
Frommer's Wonderful Weekends from
  New York City
The New York Times' Guide to Unforgettable
  Weekends
Retirement Places Rated
Rome Past & Present

Travel Tip: He who finds the best hotel deal has more to spend on facials involving knobbly vegetables.

Hello, the Roaming Gnome here. I've been nabbed from the garden and taken round the world. The people who took me are so terribly clever. They find the best offerings on Travelocity. For very little cha-ching. And that means I get to be pampered and exfoliated till I'm pink as a bunny's doodah.

travelocity®

1-888-TRAVELOCITY / travelocity.com / America Online Keyword: Travel

Travel Tip: Make sure there's customer service for any change of plans — involving friendly natives, for example.

One can plan and plan, but if you don't book with the right people you can't seize le moment and canoodle with the poodle named Pansy. I, for one, am all for fraternizing with the locals. Better yet, if I need to extend my stay and my gnome nappers are willing, it can all be arranged through the 800 number at, oh look, how convenient, the lovely company coat of arms.

travelocity®

1-888-TRAVELOCITY / travelocity.com / America Online Keyword: Travel